EMMA AND CLAUDE DEBUSSY

EMMA AND CLAUDE DEBUSSY

THE BIOGRAPHY OF A RELATIONSHIP

GILLIAN OPSTAD

THE BOYDELL PRESS

© Gillian Opstad 2022

All Rights Reserved. Except as permitted under current legislation no part of this work may be photocopied, stored in a retrieval system, published, performed in public, adapted, broadcast, transmitted, recorded or reproduced in any form or by any means, without the prior permission of the copyright owner

The right of Gillian Opstad to be identified as the author of this work has been asserted in accordance with sections 77 and 78 of the Copyright, Designs and Patents Act 1988

First published 2022
The Boydell Press, Woodbridge

ISBN 978 1 78327 658 5

The Boydell Press is an imprint of Boydell & Brewer Ltd
PO Box 9, Woodbridge, Suffolk IP12 3DF, UK
and of Boydell & Brewer Inc.
668 Mt Hope Avenue, Rochester, NY 14620–2731, USA
website: www.boydellandbrewer.com

A CIP catalogue record for this book is available
from the British Library

The publisher has no responsibility for the continued existence or accuracy of URLs for external or third-party internet websites referred to in this book, and does not guarantee that any content on such websites is, or will remain, accurate or appropriate

This publication is printed on acid-free paper

For Christopher

Contents

List of Illustrations		ix
Acknowledgements		xi
Abbreviations and Note		xiii

Part One. Emma: Wife, Mother, Lover

1	Emma's ancestry and background	1
2	Emma's relationship with Gabriel Fauré	17
3	Debussy's life until 1902	35
4	Emma meets Debussy: 1899 – August 1904	43
5	August 1904 – August 1905: Pourville and Eastbourne	63
6	August 1905 – December 1906: Life in the avenue du Bois de Boulogne	79
7	1907: Stagnation	95
8	1908: Marriage and an ivory tower	105
9	1909: Illness and depression	121
10	1910: Floods and despair	133
11	1911: A marriage and *Le martyre*	151
12	1912: Confined to home	173
13	1913: Troubles and travels	183
14	1914: The approach of war	203
15	1915: Patriotism and love awakened	217
16	1916: Debussy's treatment and mounting concerns	229
17	1917 – April 1918: The last summer	239

Part Two. Emma the Widow

18	April 1918 – December 1918: Emma's mission	259
19	1919: Tragedy and commemoration	271
20	1920–1: Disappointments and disputes	285

21	1922–3: Fiascos and controversies	297
22	1924–7: Friends and enemies	311
23	1928–31: Litigation and invective	325
24	1932–4: The final struggle	339
25	Epilogue	349

Select Bibliography 363
Index 369

Illustrations

All photographs are from the author's collection unless otherwise noted.

1	Daniel Iffla Osiris, c. 1899	4
2	Osiris in his conservatory, rue La Bruyère, Paris, c. 1900. Photograph by Dornac	7
3	Sigismond Bardac near Montmartre cemetery	11
4	Gabriel Fauré as seen on the cover of *Musica*, September 1910. Photograph from Art Femina	19
5	Baby Dolly (Hélène Bardac) of Fauré's *Dolly* suite with her nurse, 1892. Photograph by Eugène Pirou	26
6	Marie Blanche Vasnier, Debussy's first love. Portrait by Paul Baudry, 1885	36
7	Emma Bardac. Portrait by Léon Bonnat, 1903. © Saint-Germain-en-Laye, maison natale Claude-Debussy	47
8	Claude Debussy with Rosalie Texier, his first wife, 1902. World History Archive/Alamy Stock Photo	49
9	Debussy at Pourville, 1904	65
10	Dolly and her grandmother Laure Moyse at Pourville, 1904	66
11	Dolly with flowers at Pourville, 1904	66
12	Debussy in the garden of 64 Square du Bois de Boulogne, 1905	80
13	Debussy and Emma in their garden, 1905	82
14	Chouchou aged about three	113
15	Emma and Chouchou at home	114
16	Dolly aged sixteen with Chouchou aged three, 1908	115
17	Emma and Dolly posing for the camera	116
18	L–R: Sigismond Bardac, Emma, Gaston de Tinan, Dolly wearing engagement ring, 1910	152
19	Dolly (wearing engagement ring) and Emma outside hotel in Dieppe, 1910	153
20	Chouchou on sandcastle, Houlgate, 1911	164
21	Emma with Chouchou at her feet on boat, Houlgate, 1911	165

22	Emma, Houlgate, 1911	165
23	Debussy and André Caplet	167
24	Gabriele d'Annunzio	187
25	Marguerite Long as seen in *Musica*, December 1907	209
26	Raoul Bardac at Melun, 1914	214
27	Gaston de Tinan in uniform	223
28	Chouchou aged nearly twelve between two friends, Saint-Jean-de-Luz, 1917	245
29	Manuel de Falla. Photograph by Studio G. L. Manuel Frères	260
30	Golf Hotel, Saint-Jean-de-Luz, in the 1920s	264
31	Hélène de Tinan (Dolly), 1919	277
32	Emma at her desk	338
33	Emma near Sainte-Maximin-la-Sainte-Baume, 1932	343
34	L–R: Dolly, Françoise, Emma, Madeleine, possibly with Magdeleine Greslé and Greslé's daughter	356
35	Raoul Bardac	360

The author and publisher are grateful to all the institutions and individuals listed for permission to reproduce the materials in which they hold copyright. Every effort has been made to trace the copyright holders; apologies are offered for any omission, and the publisher will be pleased to add any necessary acknowledgement in subsequent editions.

Acknowledgements

Investigating the background and life of Emma Debussy has been a fascinating and fulfilling project. Initially I intended to write a biography of Emma, but I am grateful to an anonymous reader of the first draft of my book who suggested that even after Debussy's death, it was Emma's relationship with him that defined her life, and therefore the book was, in effect, a biography of this relationship. Many people have helped me during years of research. Both M. Philippe Lagourgue, Debussy's current executor, and Maître Henri Thieullent, Debussy's previous executor, who died in 2014, were welcoming and generous with their time, providing illuminating information. I thank M. Lagourgue for copies of official documents concerning Dolly de Tinan, for access to a wonderful collection of family photographs of Emma and Dolly, and a CD of an interview in French with Dolly, unattributed. M. Vincent Laloy was extremely helpful, enabling me to read correspondence from his family archive as well as providing valuable documentation concerning Emma's financial legacy.

I thank staff of the Archives de Bordeaux and the Département de la Musique in the Bibliothèque nationale de France in Paris, in particular Catherine Vallet-Collot. The online resource Gallica is invaluable and it is there that most French newspaper and journal quotations can be accessed. At the Centre de Documentation Claude Debussy, Paris, first Alexandra Laederich then Myriam Chimènes were generous with their time. Staff at the Archivo Manuel de Falla in Granada have been helpful and encouraging. I have also received assistance from the Archives de Rouen, the Bibliothèque Patrimoniale de Pau, the Bentley Historical Library, the University of Michigan and the British Library. Thank you to Elie Balmain for enabling my visit to the Synagogue in the rue Buffault in Paris.

I am indebted to Denis Herlin for patiently answering questions and providing copies of unpublished letters and a supplement to the list of works dedicated to Emma in the tome of *Debussy's Correspondance (1872–1918)*. Manuel Cordejo also kindly sent me copies of unpublished letters which their owner, Michel Pasquier, allowed me to quote. Christopher Collins, Roy Howat, Dominique Jarrassé, Richard Langham Smith, Roger Nichols, Robert Orledge and Étienne Rousseau-Plotto all kindly assisted with enlightening information.

I have included fewer photographs of Debussy than Emma and her children as images of Debussy are better known and can be accessed elsewhere. Most being historical family snapshots over a hundred years old, the quality is variable, but they are certainly of interest.

I am very grateful to Michael Middeke, Elizabeth Howard and Christy Beale at Boydell & Brewer for their patience and advice. I also thank Suzanne Arnold for her skilful editing. I thank my family for their encouragement and Jon for helping me process the photographs. Last but not least I must thank my husband

Christopher for his enthusiastic and passionate support during the many years this research has taken. His perceptive readings of the text and pertinent observations have been invaluable.

Unless otherwise indicated, all translations are my own. The original French has been included in many instances, but not usually of letters or footnotes contained in *Debussy's Correspondance (1872–1918)*, edited by François Lesure and Denis Herlin, published by Gallimard in 2005.

Abbreviations and Note

BnF Musique	Music department of the Bibliothèque nationale de France, Paris.
C.	Claude Debussy, *Correspondance (1872–1918)*, ed. François Lesure and Denis Herlin, annotated by François Lesure, Denis Herlin and Georges Liébert, Paris, Gallimard, 2005.
De Tinan, French interview	CD copy of a recording of an interview in French with Hélène de Tinan and an unnamed female interviewer, untitled, unattributed, kindly given to the author by M. Philippe Lagourgue.
Dolly Bardac, London interview	British Library: *British Institute of Recorded Sound lecture series: Dolly Bardac – Memories of Debussy and his circle.* Recorded 5 December 1972. British Library shelfmark T572.

Note

Since I gathered valuable information from documents held at the Centre de Documentation Claude Debussy, Paris, this organisation has closed and its resources are in the process of being subsumed into the Bibliothèque nationale de France, Département de la Musique. I have been advised by Madame Catherine Vallet-Collot, Cheffe du service Collections patrimoniales, to leave the references as they are. They will be able to be found under a generic reference: VM FONDS 210 CDE. Further information will be made available in 2022 in the *Catalogue Archives et manuscrits* of the BnF.

Emma Bardac family tree

Daniel Iffla *m.* Sarah Fonsèque
1773-1864

Désir Isaac Iffla *m.* Léa Cardozo d'Urbino　　　　　Isaac Jacob Moyse *m.* Charlotte Haïm (Houin)
1799-1869　　　1797-1878

Daniel Iffla *m.* Léonie Carlier　　Rachel (Laure) Iffla *m.* Isaac Jules Moyse　　Aimée Iffla *m.* Auguste François Lejeune
('Osiris')　　1836-1855　　　　　　1830-1915　　　1823-1885　　　　　　1833-1855
1825-1907

Aaron Moyse　　Nelly Moyse *m.* Elie Weil　　　Raoul Moyse　　　　　Auguste Charles Lejeune *m.* Bertha Poitreau
1852-　　　　1854-1884　　　　　　　　　　　　　　　　　　　　　　　　　　　　　　　1851-

Marcelle Weil　Raoul Weil　　　　　　　　　　　　　　　　　　　　　　　　　　　　　Charlotte Lejeune *m.* Sacha Guitry
1880-1965　　1881-1884　　　　　　　　　　　　　　　　　　　　　　　　　　　　　　(Charlotte Lysès)
　　1877-1956
　　　1. Sigismond Bardac *m.* Emma Léa Moyse *m.* 2. Claude Debussy
　　　　1856-1919　　　　　　1862-1934　　　　　　　1862-1918

Raoul Bardac *m.* 1. Yvonne Mabille　　Régina Hélène (Dolly) Bardac *m.* Gaston de Tinan (twice)　　Claude-Emma (Chouchou) Debussy
1881-1950　　　　1881-　　　　　　　　　　　1892-1985　　　　　　　　　1881-1958　　　　　　　　　　1905-1919
　　　　　　2. Joanna Joséphine Manévy
　　　　　　　　1886-

　　　　　　　　　　　　　　　　　　　Madeleine de Tinan *m.* 1. Guy Mortier　　Françoise de Tinan
　　　　　　　　　　　　　　　　　　　1913-1982　　　　2. Jean Bruyère　　　1912-1959

Sigismond Bardac family tree

Lob Bule Heilbronn
|
Léon Bardac *m.* Rachel (Regina) Heilbronn
1823-1872　　1821-1892

Noel Bardac　Joseph Bardac　Sigismond Bardac *m.* Emma Moyse　Édouard Bardac　Julia Bardac *m.* Gaston　Pauline *m.* Guillaume
1849-1915　　1854-1913　　　1856-1919　　　1862-1934　　　1857-1921　　　1852-　　　　van Brock　　(Paule)　　　Kurz
　　　Bardac
　　　1862-

PART ONE

EMMA: WIFE, MOTHER, LOVER

1

Emma's ancestry and background

The Moyse and Iffla families

When Claude Debussy left his first wife Lilly for Emma Bardac, a wealthy married Jewish woman, he found the reaction of his friends and acquaintances painful and his own state of mind bewildering. In view of his family background and his childhood, the relationship with a sparkling hostess of a musical salon initially seems unlikely. Although both he and Emma were the children of shopkeepers, parental circumstances and decisions determined the degree and the rate at which they would be able to climb socially, she escaping a modest background in her teens by way of an aspirational arranged marriage, he an even more modest background by developing his innate talent.

Enlightening facts about Emma's childhood or the truth of her domestic life during her first marriage remain obscure. Apart from official documents and occasional references in newspapers, little has survived in the way of family papers to provide clues about her education or transition from provincial to metropolitan life.

Emma Moyse was born in Bordeaux on 10 July 1862, the same year as Claude Debussy, who was born at St. Germain-en-Laye, to the west of Paris, on 22 August. One of the main shopping streets in Bordeaux is the rue Sainte-Catherine, a long artery which has played an important role commercially in the city since medieval times. At the northern end a smart covered arcade called the Galérie Bordelaise was opened in 1834, linking the rue Sainte-Catherine with the rue de la Maison Daurade near its junction with the rue des Piliers de Tutelle. Nowadays the rue Sainte-Catherine runs south all the way to the Place de la Victoire, but in the days of Emma's ancestors this street from where it crosses the Cours Victor Hugo onwards was called the rue Bouhaut. This area was inhabited by a dense population of Jews; all her grandparents lived either in or near this street.

On her father's side, Emma's grandfather was Isaac Jacob Moyse, a merchant (*marchand*) who had moved from Alsace to Bordeaux, where he married Charlotte Haïm. When Emma's father was born in 1823 their address in Bordeaux was 22 rue des Augustins. On her mother's side her grandparents were Désir Isaac Iffla, a commission merchant (*commis marchand*), one who received a percentage of the sale price when he bought or sold, who married Léa Cardozo d'Urbino. Léa was descended from Italian Jews, two of whom – her grandfather Haïm Athias and her uncle, David Athias – were Chief Rabbis. Désir Isaac and Léa's address at the time of the birth of their daughter, Emma's mother, was 25 rue Bouhaut. Moyse, Cardozo and Iffla are Sephardic names. Many of the large Sephardic Jewish community in Bordeaux were *marchands* and *négociants* who prospered in the city as they established successful businesses and efficient trade networks.

Emma's father, Isaac Jules Moyse, was born on 2 May 1823. One of the witnesses to his birth was Joseph Astruc, 112 rue Bouhaut. The Astrucs were a Jewish bordelais family, the most famous of whom in the artistic world was the impresario and writer Gabriel Astruc, born in 1864, who founded the Théâtre des Champs-Élysées where Stravinsky's *Rite of Spring* received its first performance and who brought Debussy's *Le martyre de Saint Sébastien* to the stage at the Théâtre du Châtelet. Gabriel was the nephew of Adrien Astruc, a banker and cousin of Emma's mother Laure. Adrien was a business associate of Emma's father, and later would be a witness to Emma's marriage.[1]

It is worth noting that another famous bordelais was born in 1838 in the rue Bouhaut, at number 241: Judas Colonna, who would later change his name to Édouard Colonne. He and his second wife would eventually play an important part in Emma's musical life in Paris, where Édouard had become a renowned conductor. In the annual directories for Bordeaux in the 1860s, members of the Colonne family are listed as teachers of music and sellers of music and instruments. Their shop was in the rue Porte-Dijeaux, not far from the Moyse family addresses, but unfortunately it is impossible to know whether Emma as a child received any musical instruction from any members of this family.

Emma's mother, Laure Iffla, one of five siblings, was born on 26 June 1830 at 25 rue Bouhaut, now number 244 rue Sainte-Catherine. In contrast to neighbouring properties, the building itself presents a rather grand façade, with elaborate carvings above the windows. Laure was not her original name, that appearing on her birth certificate being the more Jewish Rachel.

Isaac Jules, known as Jules Moyse, was twenty-seven years old when he married Laure Iffla on 24 March 1851. By this time his parents Isaac and Charlotte had moved to 32 rue Sainte-Eulalie, now 32 rue Paul Louis Lande. On the marriage certificate Jules described himself, like his father, as a *commis marchand*. Laure, aged twenty, had dropped the name Rachel, for it did not appear on her marriage certificate. Her parents, Désir Isaac and Léa Iffla, had moved to 13 Fossés des Tanneurs – now the site of the Musée d'Aquitaine and only a short distance from the rue Bouhaut.

Jules and Laure Moyse's daughter, born on 10 July 1862, was given the names Emma Léa, the latter after her grandmother. By now the family had moved away from the area of the rue Bouhaut to the opposite, more prosperous end of the rue Sainte-Catherine. Whilst her father described himself as a *négociant*, from the trade directory of 1860 we discover that Jules Moyse sold men's and children's clothes at both 63 rue St-Rémi and 17 rue des Piliers de Tutelle, one being just round the corner from the other. This explains why two of the witnesses who signed Emma's birth certificate were tailors.

Emma was born at number 11 rue des Piliers de Tutelle, only a few doors from the shop at number 17. It is clear from its appearance that number 11 was not as prestigious as number 17, but this is also evident from the census of 1861, the year before Emma's birth. That year it housed thirty-six people altogether, ten separate families, one of

---

[1] Information about addresses and businesses is from the relevant volumes of the *Annuaire général du commerce et de l'industrie de la ville de Bordeaux et du département de la Gironde, 1860–1880*.

which was Jules and Laure Moyse with their two children, Emma's older siblings, Aaron Charles, aged nine, and Sarah Nely (known as Nelly), aged seven. This road emerges at its far end opposite the imposing Grand Théâtre, an indication of the more bourgeois character of the neighbourhood compared with the rue Bouhaut.

Significantly, at 71 rue St-Rémi was another business specialising in men's clothes, made to measure (*spécialité de vêtements confectionnés pour hommes et sur mesure*), called W. Iffla, Commerles et Massieu, which also traded in the impressive arcade, 6–8 Galérie Bordelaise. William Iffla, according to Emma's marriage certificate, was a cousin eleven years younger than her father, Jules Moyse. The proximity of these addresses and names of the owners surely indicate that Jules Moyse had come to meet his wife, Laure Iffla, through the trade. As the years went by links between the two businesses became closer and Jules Moyse's tailors' shop expanded to carry out '*commission et exportation*'. By 1878, the year before Emma's marriage, Jules Moyse could be discovered at the opposite end of the Galérie Bordelaise at 4 rue de la Maison Daurade. Both he and William Iffla were respected members of the business community as they were now *électeurs commerciaux* (*élect.com.*), a position created in accordance with the law of 21 December 1871, which enabled them to vote for representatives of their trade in the tribunals of the Chamber of Commerce.[2]

Jules Moyse spent two years at this address, then in 1880 appeared the address given on Emma's civil marriage certificate of 1879: 21 Cours de l'Intendance. This should mark the apogee of his social climb: a prestigious stone-fronted house on this wide boulevard where the bourgeoisie would stroll and shop in an elegant ambience. The census for 1881, two years after Emma's marriage, shows only two families living at the address. This brings with it a puzzle. One family has seven members including servants, the other has four members, but Jules is not mentioned. His wife is listed, not as Moyse, but as Laure Yflar, her maiden name Iffla spelt differently or mistranscribed. Two men were present: a widowed shoemaker (*cordonnier*) aged fifty and a self-employed married man aged forty-nine, neither of whom appear to be related to the Ifflas or Moyses. The fourth person is a maidservant. Perhaps Jules was away at the time of the census, but this does not account for the return to Laure's maiden name. It may be to do with a scandal involving Laure's husband and brother, which will be discussed later.

Daniel Iffla, known as Osiris

Laure's elder brother, Emma's uncle Daniel Iffla, became the most influential and prominent member of this generation of her family.[3] His is an extraordinary tale of wealth and woe which needs to be understood to appreciate the impact of his decisions on Emma's life with Debussy.

---

[2] *Journal officiel de la République Française*, 22 December 1871, reporting on *Assemblée Nationale, séance du jeudi 21 décembre 1871*.

[3] For a comprehensive biography of Emma's uncle see Dominique Jarrassé, *Osiris, Mécène juif, nationaliste français*, Editions Esthétique du Divers, 2008.

1. Daniel Iffla Osiris, c. 1899

When Daniel was born on 23 July 1825 the Iffla family address, as noted, was 25 rue Bouhaut. As a child he attended a Jewish boys' school in the rue des Étuves and was also a choirboy in the synagogue, but whilst still in his teens he left his family for Paris to attend the Lycée Turgot. He was very soon to enter the world of finance, associating with other Sephardic financiers, first working for an *agent de change* called Moreau then entering the bank of Jules Mirès, which had been created by the famous Pereire brothers.

He made an immense fortune on the stock exchange and in investments in railways, but it's unclear exactly how he did this when he had no extended family in the banking business, like the Rothschilds and other Jewish dynasties, and seems to have succeeded entirely due to his own efforts. There was certainly a network of Spanish and Portuguese Jewish financiers from Bordeaux who formed an influential group and who worshipped at the Paris synagogue, which in 1851 was in the rue Lamartine. In 1877 the synagogue moved to a new building nearby in the rue Buffault. Daniel Iffla personally provided the finance for this, his fortune at that time amounting to eight million francs.

On 26 July 1855, at the age of thirty, Daniel married not a Jewish, but a Catholic woman, Léonie Carlier, whom he had met when renting a room in her family's house at 11 rue la Bruyère. She was pregnant at the time of the marriage but, tragically, on 13 October of that year, aged only nineteen, she died, as did the twin girls she had just brought into the world. Devastated, Daniel never remarried. From now on he devoted his efforts wholeheartedly to collecting works of art and philanthropy. He changed his name by legal decree on 24 August 1861,[4] one year before Emma's birth, to Iffla-Osiris and it is the name Osiris by which he is best known.

Why Osiris? There are many hypotheses. Some say that his mother's brother faced many dangers on a ship of that name and his mother vowed to name her son Osiris if he survived them. Osiris kept a model of this ship.[5] Or it may have been the cult of Osiris with which Daniel Iffla became enthused. Osiris was the benign Egyptian ruler and judge of the dead who gave the hope and expectation of rebirth in the next life. Another spur for this insistence on an Egyptian connection could have been Osiris's worship of Napoleon and everything Napoleonic. Following the invasion of Egypt by Napoleon's forces, much research was carried out on the great pyramids and other monuments. Collectors began amassing Egyptian relics. Osiris possessed a collection of little statues of the god after which he had named himself.[6] It is also said that he received advantages from certain friends in government ministries, possibly linked to the fact that Osiris was a symbol of freemasons. For whatever reason, Daniel Iffla now used the name Osiris in all his business transactions.

Despite being one of the richest men in the city, people said Osiris was miserly, for he refused to have electricity installed in his house in the rue La Bruyère, where he acquired several properties through his wife's family, but his defence was that by saving such money he had more to spend on the needy. Philanthropy became the driving force of his life – and of his death for, significantly, writing and rewriting his will to distribute his wealth as charitably and as patriotically as possible became an obsession. Amongst many worthy projects, Osiris funded the equivalent of food banks, *L'Œuvre du Pain pour tous*. For the hungry of Bordeaux a *Bateau soupe* was moored on the quay side, which existed until the Second World War. In 1889 he instituted a triennial prize that is still awarded to this day by the Fondation de l'Institut de France to mark the most important discovery or work in science, literature or the arts benefiting the public interest.[7]

---

4   *Journal Officiel de la République française, décret impérial* no.9504. Cited in J.-P. Ardoin Saint Amand, *Osiris, l'oncle d'Arcachon*, Société historique et archéologique d'Arcachon et du Pays de Buch, Arcachon, 1996, p. 34. Henceforth referred to as 'Ardoin Saint Amand, *Osiris*'.

5   Early biography of Osiris written by Gabrielle Henry, Osiris's secretary: Gab, *Monsieur Osiris*, Paris, 1911, p. 15. Online at https://gallica.bnf.fr/ark:/12148/bpt6k64714068/f13.image.texteImage (last accessed 3 July 2021).

6   Mentioned by Jules Claretie in his preface to Gab, *Monsieur Osiris*, p. 10.

7   https://www.institutdefrance.fr/lesfondations/osiris (last accessed 3 July 2021).

He was extremely patriotic and had statues erected to many famous people. He admired his grandfather, another Daniel Iffla, who had carried out distinguished service under Napoleon. In homage to Napoleon, in 1896 Osiris bought and renovated the Château de Malmaison, home of Napoleon and Josephine, thus saving it from destruction. In 1903 he donated it to the state and later gave his collection of works of art to be exhibited in a special pavilion there.[8] By then he had already received various honours, including the Orden de Isabel la Católica for his promotion of Spanish railways,[9] and he had become a Chevalier de la Légion d'Honneur in 1898, but this gift to the French state ensured that he received the status of Officier de la Légion d'Honneur in 1905. He was nominated for both honours by his friend Jules Claretie, famous writer, drama critic and director of the Théâtre Français. Another gift donated to the state upon his death was the Château de la Tour Blanche with the condition that a Bordeaux Wine School be created there. In 1909 the Ministry of Agriculture created the La Tour Blanche School of Viticulture and Oenology.[10] The words '*Donation Osiris*' still appear on the wine label.

Following his death, a letter written by Osiris on 6 July 1888 was quoted in the newspaper *Le Temps*[11] which showed extraordinary devotion to his deceased wife. He related that whilst he and the Catholic Léonie were still engaged, they were walking through the cemetery of Montmartre when she remarked upon the wall dividing the burial grounds of Jews and Christians. She pointed out to him the exact plot she wished to have reserved, the nearest to the Jewish area. Upon her premature death, this request was refused as a large iron gate was about to be installed between the two parts. Thirty-three years later, the barriers between the Jewish and Christian areas were destroyed, enabling Osiris to satisfy his wife's desire. He had a new coffin made with a pocket for photographs of his mother and sisters, including Laure, Emma's mother, and placed a photograph of himself inside a silk cushion. Wearing his wedding suit, unaided, he transferred her remains, placing her bones tidily in a new grave. Upon his death, Osiris joined his wife in this tomb beneath a vast statue of Moses, a copy of that by Michelangelo,[12] which he had commissioned from Antonin Mercié and which still stands proudly in Montmartre cemetery today.

There were many stages in the process of drawing up Osiris's will. In *Le Monde illustré* on 9 February 1907 it was stated, 'He began this will, which will cause much discussion, in 1890. Quite indecisive by nature, he composed it slowly, page by page, rewording it frequently, very concerned to make judicious, noble and just use of his fortune.'[13] Osiris's first *testament mystique*, a sealed will, was 'made at Arcachon

---

[8] https://musees-nationaux-malmaison.fr/chateau-malmaison/histoire-du-chateau-de-malmaison (last accessed 3 July 2021).

[9] In 1860 he published a book with A. Baudoz, *Histoire de la Guerre de l'Espagne avec le Maroc*, which contained information about the potential for investment in Spanish railways.

[10] L'École de Viticulture et d'Œnologie de La Tour Blanche.

[11] *Le Temps*, 5 March 1907.

[12] The original stands in the church of San Pietro in Vincoli, Rome.

[13] One of several newspaper cuttings at the Archives municipales, Bordeaux. Fonds Evrard de Fayolle: *Coupures de presse relatives à Daniel Iffla Osiris*. 42 S 6366-6367.

2. Osiris in his conservatory, rue La Bruyère, Paris, c. 1900. Photograph by Dornac

where I am at this moment in my Villa Léonie Osiris, where the sky is blue and cloudless, on fifteenth September eighteen hundred and ninety-six.'[14] The original executors were his secretary and a certain Elisa Ferguson, after whose deceased sister he named one of the villas he possessed in Arcachon. In this version he decreed who else should be listed on a plaque and buried in his tomb. This list, still prominent on the immense monument, reflects Osiris's desires rather than the people who actually ended up there. It includes his parents, the mysterious Madame Thomas Ferguson and her daughters Elisabeth and Elisa from Nottingham, his sister Laure and her husband Jules (Emma's parents), his nephews and nieces, including Emma and another niece, a granddaughter of his and Laure's sister Aimée, Charlotte Lysès. Engraved in stone is also the history of his grandfather Daniel Iffla's military service, and yet another plaque commemorates the Chief Rabbi of Bordeaux, David Athias.

During Osiris's lifetime he funded the construction of several synagogues, most notably that in the rue Buffault in Paris, but also at Tours, Vincennes and Bruyères in the Vosges, not to mention Tunis and Lausanne, where he also funded a statue of William Tell, again by Mercié. Despite being refused permission to have the name of his Catholic wife inscribed in the Paris synagogue, he had a large plaque mounted there listing many 'famous children of Israel'. At its base are engraved the names of his parents, their children, including Emma's mother Laure, and 'Madame Léonie Carlier, wife of Daniel Iffla Osiris'. A further list is added of his friends, significantly including the name Bardac. Further plaques bear his name and those of the founders of the synagogue, all of which can be seen to this day.

Emma's marriage

As noted, Osiris's niece, Emma Léa Moyse, was born on 10 July 1862. Of the years between her birth and her marriage at the age of seventeen it appears to be virtually impossible to discover any detail. She had an older brother, Aaron Charles, sister Nelly and a younger brother, Raoul, who died prematurely. As a young lady we know she was musical and that she could speak English. In the trade directories for Bordeaux under the heading *Écoles communales d'enseignement pour les jeunes filles*, there is listed a school for girls run by a certain Dacosta in the rue Sainte-Eulalie, the road in which her Moyse grandparents lived, which she could well have attended, but no list of pupils survives.

Emma had great affection for Arcachon, the resort built amongst pine trees just over thirty miles south of Bordeaux. It was expanding from a small fishing village into a smart destination for the wealthy inhabitants of Bordeaux who enjoyed the newly discovered benefits of healthy fresh air, pine forests and sea bathing. In 1857, on the initiative of another Bordeaux-born banker, Émile Pereire, a new railway line opened to facilitate access from the city and that year Arcachon became an independent town by decree of Napoleon III. It grew from four hundred inhabitants in 1857 to nearly four thousand in 1872. Investment opportunities were recognised by those with means and it is not surprising that Osiris owned at least seven of the many lavish and architecturally distinctive villas there, mainly in the smart district called the Ville d'Hiver.

---

[14] Ardoin Saint Amand, *Osiris*, p. 35.

Later in life, Emma remembered her holidays spent at Arcachon as a child, before Osiris built his properties. In 1910, writing to André Caplet, close friend of both her and Claude Debussy, she told him wistfully how she had stayed in the Villa Riquet when young, the one Caplet was going to visit. 'I expect it has changed a lot since ...'[15] This guest house was originally built by Émile Pereire in the 1860s. It is now called 'Océanique', but outwardly is easily recognisable from contemporary photographs. Emma envied Caplet being near the old pine trees and sandy beaches. One of Osiris's vast villas nearby, built in 1895, was originally called Villa Osiris. He had intended to donate it to the town for use as a library, but this plan never came to fruition. Its name was changed to Alexandre Dumas after Osiris's death in 1907, although that author never actually stayed in it.

One plan that did materialise, however, was the building of a synagogue. The architect Osiris employed was Stanislas Ferrand, designer of the synagogue he had already financed in Paris. This was a private synagogue, a small, simple building on the avenue Gambetta,[16] which Osiris erected and opened, initially, without the knowledge and to the disquiet of the Bordeaux Consistory.[17] In the same road on adjoining plots of land are four of Osiris's villas, three of which were named after members of the Moyse family: Nelly (after Sarah Nely, Emma's older sister), Laure-Raoul (after Emma's mother and her son Raoul, who died young[18]) and Emma. The fourth was named Betsy-Ferguson, who, as noted, was honoured with her name engraved on Osiris's tomb.

On Sunday 21 December 1879, at six o'clock in the evening, this new synagogue was inaugurated unofficially with a special ceremony, a marriage: that of Osiris's niece Emma Moyse to Sigismond Bardac. Rabbi Lodoïs Mendès blessed the couple. It was reported in the local paper that the Rabbi had come especially from Paris, but Emma's father Jules had a correction inserted a week later saying that in fact Mendès was the former choirmaster at the Temple de Bordeaux.[19] Apparently the congregation had to stand because the chairs were not delivered in time.[20] According to the press, the entire population of Arcachon turned out to witness the event which added to the festive atmosphere.[21] True to his principles, Osiris ensured a collection was made during the celebration for distribution to the local poor.

Three days earlier Emma had attended her civil marriage at the town hall in Bordeaux. The certificate signed on that occasion gives her parents' address as 21 Cours de l'Intendance. Three of the witnesses were her cousin William Iffla and two bankers coming from that world of Emma's uncle and her new husband, Adrien Astruc from Bordeaux and Gaston van Brock from Paris. Van Brock was born in Bordeaux on 27 October 1850. He received the Légion d'Honneur in 1884, and was elevated in 1908 to Officier de la Légion d'Honneur, by which time he was *Président du Conseil d'Administration des*

---

[15] *Correspondance (1872–1918)*, ed. François Lesure and Denis Herlin, Paris, 2005, p. 1245: 10 February 1910. Henceforth abbreviated to *C*.
[16] Originally called avenue Euphrosine.
[17] It was not officially inaugurated until 3 October 1891.
[18] Ardoin Saint-Amand, *Osiris*, p. 10.
[19] *L'Avenir d'Arcachon* 28 December 1879 and 4 January 1880.
[20] Gab, *Monsieur Osiris*, p. 74.
[21] *Le XIXe siècle*, 26 December 1879.

Mines de Malines (Gard).[22] His name will recur later as a witness to Emma's marriage to Debussy. In 1874 he had married Julia Bardac, a sister of Emma's husband-to-be.

Mention has been made of a scandal concerning Jules Moyse and Emma's uncle, Osiris, which could have had a bearing on Laure reverting temporarily to her maiden name of Iffla (or Yflar). Needless to say, in an increasingly antisemitic society, a Jew in possession of such wealth as Osiris's gathered much opprobrium, so any whiff of dubious dealings would be seized upon. In a book entitled *Le Testament d'un antisémite* by Edouard Adolphe Drumont[23] there is reference to a case brought before the court in Bordeaux in 1880, only very shortly after Emma's wedding, so the story may well have been spread abroad during preparations for the event. Osiris, in collaboration with Adrien Astruc, who had a limited company Astruc & Cie, had been involved in the bankruptcy of a certain M. Mitraud. Osiris needed to recuperate three hundred thousand francs and managed to persuade his brother-in-law, Emma's father Jules Moyse, to form a new company, Astruc & Moyse, with the purpose of repaying himself at the expense of other creditors. This was judged fraudulent by the court, a verdict confirmed by the Court of Appeal in 1886. Laure Moyse and her daughter Emma must have felt much embarrassment at this unfortunate turn of events around the time of Emma's marriage.

Jules Moyse had great expenditure at this time, for Emma's sister Nelly married Elie Weil on 16 October, only three months before Emma's ceremony, and a dowry would have been required. In Emma's case, on the day of her civil marriage, 18 December 1879, a contract was signed stating that her bridegroom Sigismond would bring with him five thousand francs' worth of furniture and works of art. Emma's dowry consisted of a trousseau valued at six thousand francs and the sum of fifty thousand francs to be paid to her husband.[24]

The Bardac family

Who was Emma's husband, Sigismond Bardac? He was born in Nizhny Novgorod in Russia on 14 October 1856, the son of Léon Bardac born in Odessa in 1823 and Rachel, born in Fulda, Germany, in 1821, daughter of Lob Bule Heilbronn.[25] Rachel was always known as Régina, the name given on Emma's marriage certificate. Sigismond had two older brothers, both born in Odessa, Noël in 1849 and Joseph in 1854. He also had a younger brother Édouard, born in 1857, and two sisters, Julia and Pauline. Pauline was born in the same year as Emma, 1862. We know from Noël's birth certificate, issued originally by the Rabbi of Odessa for the registration of Jews in that city and translated when he was nominated for the Légion d'Honneur, that his father Léon was a *commerçant de la Première Guilde*.[26]

---

[22] http://cths.fr/an/prosopo.php?id=122139 (last accessed 10 June 2020).
[23] Edouard Adolphe Drumont, *Le Testament d'un antisémite*, Paris, 1891, pp. 178–9.
[24] Ardoin Saint Amand, *Osiris*, p. 11.
[25] On her death certificate dated 2 January 1892 her age is given as seventy-one.
[26] https://www.leonore.archives-nationales.culture.gouv.fr/ui/notice/17224 (last accessed 3 July 2021).

3. Sigismond Bardac near Montmartre cemetery

When the Russian-born Bardac family came to Paris they rapidly established themselves as a key force in the world of international banking, being associated in particular with the funding of the fast-expanding Russian railways. The French market was becoming the primary source of loans to finance railway construction and expansion at the time and by the end of the 1880s the French Third Republic was the largest source of credit for the Russian empire. The Bardac bank was a significant investor in this field. When Léon died in 1872, Noel, the oldest son took it over at the age of twenty-three. Sigismond was only sixteen at the time but it was not long before it became the bank N. J. & S. Bardac. The bank also became an ally of the powerful Imperial Ottoman Bank and a regular participant in syndicates it managed, especially in connection with railway concessions.[27]

Osiris and Léon Bardac, Sigismond's father, were of a similar age and it is most probable that their paths crossed both at the synagogue and at the stock exchange in Paris, environments with which none of Debussy's relations would have been remotely familiar. There was also a common interest in financing railways since Osiris was joint author of a book on the subject. It is not possible to determine how or where Léon's son was introduced to Osiris's niece, but in view of the difference in age and the distance between the cities they inhabited, it is clear that this was an arranged marriage, not unusual for orthodox Jewish families. When the marriage banns were published in Paris on 1 December 1879, Sigismond's address was 5 avenue de Messine in the eighth arrondissement. Another Paris address ascribed to Sigismond at the time of his marriage was 3 rue du Colisée, which would recur in official documents on future occasions.

Sigismond quickly followed Osiris's example and began collecting works of art, becoming one of the foremost collectors in France. It was not only for the size and quality of Sigismond's collection but also for its variety that he became a significant figure in that world. Not just beautiful paintings, but ivories, gold statuary, enamels and ancient artefacts can be traced today in many museums internationally which had their provenance in the collection of Sigismond Bardac, including the Louvre and the Victoria and Albert Museum.[28] His reputation whilst he was busy acquiring *objets d'art* became notorious to some. For example, in 1900 there was a rather grudging comment in the *Bulletin de la Commission départmentale des monuments historiques du Pas-de-Calais* that the magnificent reliquary of the Ursulines of Arras, one of the most beautiful pieces of religious works in gold being exhibited at that year's *Exposition Universelle* in Paris was 'lost to the town. It belongs to M. Sigismond Bardac'.[29] This was just one of several items he exhibited.

---

[27] *London and Paris as International Financial Centres in the Twentieth Century*, ed. Youssef Cassis and Eric Bussière, Oxford, 2005, p. 128.

[28] E.g. http://collections.vam.ac.uk/item/O120709/gospel-cover-unknown (last accessed 24 May 2020).

[29] In the *Catalogue Officiel illustré de l'Exposition rétrospective de l'art français* the twelfth century *Reliquaire de la Sainte Épine* is listed on p. 287. There are about twenty other items belonging to S. Bardac: https://archive.org/details/catalogueofficieooexpo (last accessed 3 July 2021).

Someone with a clear memory of Bardac was the art dealer Germain Seligman. 'I do remember Sigismond Bardac quite well,' he wrote.

> Of Russian origin, he was one of three well-known banker and collector brothers, Sigismond, Noel, and Joseph. Sigismond was the most active collector of the three and remarkably well-posted about activities in the art world. To be in the know is of considerable importance if one is to be on hand when a collector is in a mood to buy – more especially when he is in a mood to sell. There was always news to be gleaned from Bardac, and sometimes there was the possibility of acquiring some coveted treasure from him. He was never satiated in his hunt for new possessions and occasionally had to part with one in order to acquire another.[30]

Another well-known art dealer who often mentioned the Bardac brothers in his diary was René Gimpel. When he asked Joseph Bardac what had motivated him to start collecting works of art he received the answer,

> My brother Sigismond gave us a taste for it. Noël followed him first, then me. It was easy after the 1870 war. No one wanted old stuff, it was all gold and red plush … at a sale at the Hôtel Drouot I bought two boxes containing the most beautiful colour engravings, one for eighty francs, the other for seventy. Today that would be a million, a million![31]

In the nineteenth century in France, when a couple married who were of different nationalities the woman automatically lost her nationality and took her husband's. This had been inscribed in the French Civil Code since 1803. Upon marriage to a Russian, Emma therefore automatically lost her French nationality. She would not regain this until a decree of reintegration into French nationality was passed on 18 September 1889.

Birth of Raoul Bardac and Emma's singing lessons

One year and three months after their marriage, in the early hours of 30 March 1881, Sigismond's and Emma's son Raoul was born at 5 avenue de Messine. He, like Emma, would eventually need to be granted full French nationality according to the decree of 1889, when Sigismond was also able to claim this.[32] It is likely that Raoul was named after Emma's young brother who had died prematurely.

When Emma married and moved to Paris, her parents had followed in her footsteps, for it was at a Paris address, 272 rue du Faubourg St. Honoré, that her father, Jules Moyse, died on 20 April 1885. He was described on his death certificate as *rentier*, a person of independent means, as was his wife Laure, *rentière*, now a widow. Emma's sister, Nelly Weil, had died the previous year at the age of

---

[30] G. Seligman, *Merchant of Art 1880–1960. Eighty Years of Professional Collecting*. New York, 1961. Viewed online: https://archive.org/stream/merchantsofart1800seli/merchantsofart1800seli_djvu.txt (last accessed 4 February 2021).

[31] R. Gimpel, *Journal d'un collectionneur*, Paris, 1963, p. 159.

[32] www.généalogie.com lists names of those who successfully applied for *Réintegration de la nationalité française* as printed in the *Bulletin des Lois*.

thirty. Her baby son, another Raoul, had died at the age of two years ten months on 9 March that same year, so there must have been much grieving in the family. Nelly left behind her husband Elie and a daughter Marcelle Henriette Léa Weil, born on 24 August 1880.

For eleven years Raoul Bardac would remain an only child. Clearly, his was a privileged background. He was brought up in a smart area of Paris surrounded by beautiful objects and was given an excellent education. His first school was the Petit Lycée Condorcet in the rue d'Amsterdam, the junior department of the Lycée Condorcet which he later went on to attend, one of the oldest and most prestigious schools in Paris. Evidence of his progress in the lower school by the age of nine is the name Bardac in the list of prizewinners for 1890 published in *Le Figaro*.[33]

He was brought up not just in an artistic environment, but also a musical one for his mother, Emma, was receiving singing lessons from the second wife of the conductor and founder of the Concerts Colonne, Édouard Colonne, who came originally from Bordeaux. Eugénie Élise Vergin was a successful soloist at the Opéra, the Opéra-Comique and the Théâtre Lyrique and much in demand as a singing teacher in Paris.

Emma was a star pupil of Madame Colonne, and it is because of this that we are able to discover her in the press. On 31 May 1889 she performed in a concert given by pupils of Madame Colonne, a 'brilliant' occasion, according to *Le Gaulois*, for some of the participants were already 'véritables artistes' including 'Mme Bardac, a fine dramatic artist, who gave a spirited performance of the *Berceuse* by Guiraud, and *l'éternelle Chanson* by Paladilhe'.[34] At a similar event on 30 May 1890, we learn that she received some of the loudest applause in a concert consisting of both choral and solo works. In *Le Matin*, once again the adjective 'brilliant' was used. Emma was particularly praised as 'the charming Madame Bardac, who applied great artistry to *Le chant de la vigne* by Ch. Lefèvre.'[35] Reviewing the same concert, *Le Gaulois* listed some of the eminent guests among Madame Colonne's audience: 'Mmes la comtesse de Beaumont, Viardot, de Grandval, princesse Davidoff, Comtesse Rostopchine ...'[36] Emma could hardly have had a more aristocratic, if not discerning, audience. Pauline Viardot, (daughter of the tenor Manuel Garcia and sister of the diva Maria Malibran) was the distinguished opera singer, now retired after a vibrant career, who held her own concerts in her salon at 243 boulevard Saint-Germain.

Viardot was to be seen again at a concert of Mme Colonne's the following year, 1891, accompanying some of the performers in her own compositions. In *La Nouvelle Revue* we read of Mme Colonne's universal reputation as a singing teacher. Her pupils were 'virtually artists in their own right rather than pupils', even those selected amongst the *femmes du monde* amongst whom was listed 'Mme Bardac'. The audience comprised aristocracy, musicians and 'many famous authors and composers'.[37]

---

[33] *Le Figaro*, 8 August 1890.
[34] *Le Gaulois*, 4 June 1889.
[35] *Le Matin*, 3 June 1890.
[36] *Le Gaulois*, 31 May 1890.
[37] *La Nouvelle Revue*, 1891/05–1891/06, p. 664.

What confidence Emma must have had to convey, singing in front of such illustrious company. Madame Colonne certainly had faith in her ability to present herself as an extremely talented pupil.

As might be expected for members of society in their position, Emma and Sigismond attended the Opéra. Sigismond's name appeared on the official list of subscribers to this institution from 1893 to 1898. Osiris was also a subscriber.[38] Osiris's secretary, Gabrielle Henry, revealed that despite his care over domestic expenditure, he was not only to be seen at the Opéra every week, but enjoyed the company of singers. He is known to have lent valuable jewels from his collection to certain actresses.[39] In view of later comments, it seems Sigismond Bardac was also well acquainted with ladies of this profession, which at the time was regarded as rife with 'loose' women.

At home, Emma Bardac certainly furthered her son's musical prowess. By the age of twelve (1893) Raoul had already composed several works, and that year his *Romance* for piano and violin was performed by the violinist, Eugène Ysaÿe[40] – the year, incidentally, in which Ysaÿe played in the first performance of Debussy's String Quartet at a concert of the Société nationale de musique given in the Salle Pleyel. Once again Raoul's name appeared in a newspaper for his achievements at school, for he was listed amongst the prizewinners for the *classe de 5ième* of the Petit Lycée Condorcet.[41]

By 1893 great changes had taken place in Emma's life. Her son Raoul's contact with Ysaÿe could have come about through her friendship with Mme Colonne or Pauline Viardot, but it is also possible that it was through someone to whom Emma became very close, the composer Gabriel Fauré, who was to become Raoul's teacher of composition.

---

[38] *Annuaire des artistes et de l'enseignement dramatique et musical* in 1893, 1895 and 1903.
[39] Gab, *Monsieur Osiris*, op.cit., pp. 32, 37; D. Jarrassé, *Osiris*, p. 60.
[40] D. Priest, '"Une causerie sur Claude Debussy" de Raoul Bardac', *Cahiers Debussy*, no.26, 2002, p. 45, n.3.
[41] *Le Temps*, 29 July 1893.

2

Emma's relationship with Gabriel Fauré

Fauré's marriage

Gabriel Fauré was born in 1845 in Pamiers in south-west France, about seventy kilometres south of Toulouse. From the age of nine he was educated in Paris at the École de Musique Classique et Réligieuse founded by Louis Niedermeyer in 1853, a boarding school created specifically for teaching music and the humanities. Upon the death of Niedermeyer in 1861, Fauré became a pupil and close friend of Saint-Saëns, who, although ten years his senior, provided the key which opened the doors to the musical élite of the day. His own first composition pupil was André Messager, also soon to become a close friend. In 1871 Fauré was one of the founding members of the Société nationale de musique (SNM), an organisation which aimed to promote contemporary French music. He became Choirmaster at the church of Saint-Sulpice under Charles-Marie Widor and in the 1870s often took Saint-Saëns' place at the organ of La Madeleine. He was soon assimilated into musical and social society with help from established families, including that of Pauline Viardot. Fauré fell deeply in love with Pauline's daughter Marianne, but her affection could not match his passion. In fear of his ardent nature, it took four years for her to be persuaded to become engaged to Gabriel in July 1877, the year he was appointed to the prestigious but arduous task of *Maître de Chapelle* at La Madeleine under Théodore Dubois. Marianne was twenty-three; he was thirty-two. Unable to reconcile herself to the marriage, three months later she made the inevitable break with her fiancé.

Fauré was by now an attractive, mature bachelor, exerting a magnetic power over the young women who frequented the salons and concerts he attended. A stream of beautiful songs and instrumental works flowed from his pen, performed and admired in the drawing rooms of wealthy patrons of music. A major figure who welcomed him to her salon was Marguerite Baugnies, who in 1892 became Marguerite (or Meg) de Saint-Marceaux after her second marriage to the sculptor René de Saint-Marceaux. Younger than Fauré by five years, she was the dedicatee of his song *Après un rêve* and the first *Nocturne* for piano. In 1875 she moved to 100 boulevard Malesherbes, where she instigated her famous 'Fridays', welcoming such musicians as Messager, Gounod, Hahn, Chausson, Ravel, Dukas and, for a while, Debussy. The salon culture in Paris in this era was so endemic that it became an essential way for composers to meet each other, hear their own works performed, listen to the works of their contemporaries and take advantage of the hospitality and hopefully sponsorship of their hosts and hostesses.

Meg was determined that Gabriel, now aged thirty-seven, should put an end to his carefree bachelor life. According to the composer Georges Migot, she put into a hat the names of three women whose surnames all began with F – Fueillet, Feydeau and Fremiet.[1] The first two were the daughters of writers, and the third was the daughter of a famous sculptor, Emmanuel Fremiet, particularly celebrated for his detailed sculptures of animals. Gabriel pulled out the name Marie Fremiet. On 27 March 1883 he married Marie and nine months later their first son, another Emmanuel, was born.[2]

Marie was reticent and reclusive. She painted quietly, mainly flowers on panels and fans, the opposite of her husband who mingled with the establishment, fulfilled his duties at La Madeleine and was forced to travel constantly to meet his teaching obligations. Her father became a father-figure to the composer, to the extent that some said Fauré had 'married his father-in-law'.[3] Fauré's own father died in 1885, his mother in 1888. There was also a significant link between Emmanuel Fremiet and Emma's wealthy uncle. Osiris, whose patriotism led to his passion for erecting statues of nationally important figures, commissioned Fremiet to create an equestrian statue of La Pucelle (Joan of Arc), which was erected in the Place Lafayette in Nancy in 1890. It was a copy of Fremiet's statue in the Place des Pyramides in Paris, erected there in 1874.

The Fremiets had a second home, a country house in Bas-Prunay near Bougival where, from 1884 onwards, Fauré used to join them in the summer when he was free. Here his second son, Philippe, was born in 1889. Bougival at this time was well established as a desirable destination for Parisians to relax, eat and drink, and dance at open-air cafés, as depicted in paintings such as Renoir's *Danse à Bougival*. The more wealthy, such as Sigismond Bardac, possessed houses there in which they could reside and entertain at will, maintaining their privileged standard of living amongst the society to which they were accustomed.

Emma's 'progressive' salon; Fauré teaches Raoul

At that time the prestigious Paris address of the Bardacs was 30 rue de Berri in the eighth arrondissement, a street running between the Champs-Élysées and the Boulevard Haussmann. There Emma held her own musical salon where she received composers and performers, and sang herself. This has been described as a 'progressive' salon which Fauré attended regularly and to which he eventually brought many of his gifted composition pupils.[4] Emma therefore had the perfect opportunity to provide her son with the best musical tuition and exemplars possible.

---

[1] Migot was named as the source of this story by Jean-Michel Nectoux, *Gabriel Fauré. Les voix du clair-obscur*, Paris, Fayard, 2008, p. 70. Migot (1891–1976) was forty-six years younger than Fauré, so the story must have been relayed to him. He only occurred in footnotes in Meg's diary. Marguerite de Saint-Marceaux, *Journal 1894–1927*, ed. M. Chimènes. Paris, 2007.

[2] Marie insisted on the boys having the double surname Fauré-Fremiet.

[3] Nectoux, *Gabriel Fauré*, p. 73.

[4] Nectoux, *Gabriel Fauré*, p. 248.

4. Gabriel Fauré as seen on the cover of *Musica*, September 1910.
Photograph from Art Femina

When exactly Fauré began teaching Raoul cannot be determined, but in view of Raoul's rapid progress in composition, he must have been encouraging his talent from an early age. Fauré therefore was already familiar with Emma's Parisian home; he was also made welcome in the Bardacs' summer villa in Bougival in the summer of 1892 – a highly significant year in both their lives.

The tranquil, luminous scenes through which Fauré must have wandered from the house of his in-laws to the summer residence of Emma Bardac can be seen in two paintings. Charles Lambinet, who lived in Bougival, painted an idyllic rural image, entitled *Bas Prunay*, of a mother and child walking along a track by the river Seine, towards ancient cottages nestling in a hollow sheltered by trees (1860). In 1874 Alfred Sisley completed a light-infused painting of a track winding through fields and trees entitled *La route de Prunay à Bougival*.

What besides his alluring music did Emma see in Fauré? Photographs and a portrait by John Singer Sargent show a fine, imposing facial structure, silvering hair brushed back in waves, thick eyebrows, a full moustache drooping yet carefully trimmed over both sides of the lips. His looks were a reminder of his southern origins. Charles Koechlin wrote, 'A good appearance, certainly. One recalls, under the white hair, that Mediterranean face, bronzed, with his moustaches and Roman nose, and that aspect as of an Eastern dreamer, the eyes, dark-ringed, lost in strange milky luminosities of the pupil.'[5]

Birth of Hélène (Dolly) Bardac

On 20 June 1892 at six o'clock in the morning, Emma's second child, Régina Hélène Bardac was born. Emma was twenty-nine, one month short of thirty years old, although on Hélène's birth certificate her age is given as twenty-eight. Sigismond was thirty-six. The address where Hélène entered the world is noted as 37 rue des Mathurins, Paris. The witnesses signing the birth certificate were Otto Singer, an *associé de banque* who had also been a witness to Raoul's birth, and Alexandre Michel, a *remisier d'agent de change*, one who introduced clients to stockbrokers, so no names from Emma's world of music. The name Régina was chosen after Sigismond's mother, who had died on 2 January 1892 at the age of 71. This name was rarely used for the baby, however, as the little girl was known as Hélène, but more often as Dolly because of her petite size.

There is no doubt that Fauré was passionately in love with Emma at this time. There is, however, doubt about whether Hélène was the result of this passion or whether she was Sigismond's daughter. Why would Hélène claim in later life to be Fauré's daughter if she were not? Jean-Michel Nectoux wrote that she herself stated in confidence that this was the case.[6] When interviewed in 2010, Debussy's then executor, Maître Henri Thieullent, who remembered meeting Emma as an elderly lady, believed this to be true. He was convinced Hélène was Fauré's daughter because of her resemblance to the composer and because of the length of time

---

[5] Charles Koechlin, *Gabriel Fauré*, trans. Leslie Orry, London, 1945, p. 8.
[6] Nectoux, *Gabriel Fauré*, p. 248.

which passed between the birth of Raoul and Hélène, admittedly both purely subjective conjectures. He also related an anecdote dating from much later on, in which Philippe Fauré-Fremiet, Fauré's younger son, met Dolly at a private concert of Debussy's music being given at the house of friends in 1941 or 1942. When he saw her enter he greeted her with the words, 'Ah, ma petite sœur!' ('Ah, my little sister!'). Apparently she was not amused.[7]

In his biography of Debussy, Marcel Dietschy wrote that Emma 'a donné un fils, puis offert une fille' to Sigismond Bardac, a significant distinction.[8] This difference between two French words for 'to give', *donner* and *offrir*, was not made in the English translation of Dietschy's biography. 'Offert' implied that Dolly was a 'gift', rather than having been conceived by Bardac.[9] Later Dietschy claimed that Dolly controlled very strictly whatever was written about her mother, leading to him having to imply rather than state the truth about her outright. He refused to show Dolly his book before publication, only allowing her to see specific paragraphs. She even wanted him to omit the word 'aimer' with reference to Fauré in his description of the moment Debussy had first set eyes on Emma: 'this Emma Bardac, whom Fauré had admired, *loved* [my italics], and immortalised before him'. Dietschy had not acceded to this demand.[10]

Those who doubt that Hélène was Fauré's daughter argue that the dates when conception would have taken place, during September 1891, do not fit in with Fauré's calendar. He was an admirer of the prestigious salon hostess Winnaretta Singer, later Princesse de Polignac, who, although a lesbian, was married to Prince Louis de Scey-Montbéliard. She provided inspiration and suitable conditions for Fauré to compose, and in the summer of 1891 took him with her husband and two artists and their wives to Venice. From there Fauré corresponded with Marie, who had remained at home painting and obsessively looking after their sons. A wall of silence would eventually rise between husband and wife. Fauré wrote frankly to Marguerite Baugnies during the trip, confessing to feeling something more than mere admiration for Winnaretta. He swore her to secrecy, promising that he did still love his wife.[11] In 1891 Winnaretta was twenty-six years old and Fauré was forty-six.

They returned to Paris on 20 June 1891, upon which Fauré continued to correspond with Winnaretta, desiring her appreciation of the songs he was composing, which were to become the *Cinq Mélodies op.58*, settings of words by Paul Verlaine. She then continued to travel. 'Adieu, chère Princesse, toujours absente', wrote Fauré.[12] He knew that no commitment was called for. Winnaretta was granted an

---

[7] Author's conversation with Maître Henri Thieullent, 26 August 2010.

[8] M. Dietschy, *La Passion de Claude Debussy*, Neuchâtel, 1962, p. 166

[9] M. Dietschy, *A Portrait of Claude Debussy*, ed. and trans. W. Ashbrook and M. G. Cobb, Oxford, 1994, p. 129.

[10] Letter from Marcel Dietschy to André Schaeffner 15 June 1963. N. Southon, 'Une correspondance entre André Schaeffner et Marcel Dietschy', *Cahiers Debussy*, no.34, 2010, p. 102.

[11] 12 June 1891, Gabriel Fauré, *Correspondance présentée et annotée par Jean-Michel Nectoux*, Paris, 1980, p. 174. Referred to henceforth as 'Nectoux. *Gabriel Fauré. Correspondance*'.

[12] Idem. p.188.

annulment on 1 February 1892 and in 1893 she married a gay member of the aristocracy, Prince Edmond de Polignac, a situation agreeable to both as he was a talented amateur composer. There was therefore no reason for Fauré not to pay amorous attention to Emma Bardac, the gifted singer he visited so frequently at Bougival after his return to France in June 1891. It has to be said that Fauré's constant flirtations over the years became a matter of some disapproval to Marguerite de Saint-Marceaux. There are several references in her diaries to his behaviour, which lasted all his life even into old age – his 'little personal interests he cannot control. Love in old age demeans its victims.'[13]

Over the years, other rumours regarding Fauré's possible fatherhood besides that of Dolly were spread abroad. Jean Roger-Ducasse, born in 1873, a musician also eventually to establish very close links to Debussy and his family, entered Fauré's composition class at the Conservatoire in 1896, joining what his biographer described as that 'magic circle' of pupils which included Maurice Ravel, Charles Koechlin, Florent Schmitt, George Enesco and Alfred Cortot. The relationship between master and pupil was so close despite their difference in age and there was such a resemblance between them in appearance that wagging tongues mischievously claimed that Roger-Ducasse was a love-child of Fauré's.[14] There is no foundation for this claim, but it underlines Fauré's reputation for dalliances.

As for Emma's husband Sigismond, he was probably not particularly interested in music. He was passionate about his collection of *objets d'art* and in 1889 was listed officially as a *collectionneur* in the *Agenda de la curiosité, des artistes et des amateurs*, where his address was given as 1 Avenue Montaigne. In 1897 he was elected an official member of the Commission des Beaux-Arts.[15] During the 1890s he also became a member of the cycling club, the Touring Club de France and then the Automobile Club de France, increasingly popular and fashionable activities. He encouraged his son to participate in cycling, for when Raoul was fourteen years old in 1895, he too was listed as a member of the Touring Club de France, his profession being given even at that tender age as *Compositeur de musique* (address: 30 rue de Berri).[16]

Significantly, Sigismond later also followed the Osiris theme so dear to his wife's uncle when he contributed substantial funds to archaeological digs at Abydos in Egypt. In 1895–96 he was one of a committee of only three providing money for the archaeologist Émile Amélineau to excavate the necropolis there, which culminated in 1897 with the discovery of the tomb of a king whom Amélineau identified as the god Osiris.[17]

---

[13] M. de Saint-Marceaux, *Journal 1894–1927*, 26 January 1908, p. 507.

[14] Jacques Depaulis, *Roger-Ducasse (1873–1954)*, Paris, 2001, p. 19.

[15] *Journal Officiel de la République Française*, 15 May 1897.

[16] *Revue mensuelle Touring Club de France*, 1895, p. 439.

[17] Sir E. A. Wallis Budge, A History of Egypt from the end of the Neolithic Period to the death of Cleopatra VII, BC30, 1902, pp. 14–5. Viewed online at https://archive.org/stream/historyofegypto1budg/historyofegypto1budg_djvu.txt (last accessed 28 September 2020); Émile Amélineau. 'Fouilles à Abydos', in: *Comptes-rendus des séances de l'Académie des Inscriptions et Belles-Lettres*, 40e année, no.3, 1896. pp. 197–200.

La bonne chanson

Whether Hélène's father or not, Fauré must have been very aware of Emma's pregnancy. Throughout the summer of 1892 he was possessed by the invigorating spirit of inspiration. Notes flowed from his pen to Paul Verlaine's poetry, whose words he had already found stimulating when composing the *Cinq mélodies*. Every day he visited Emma after his service at the Madeleine. She therefore witnessed the process of creation of his song cycle, *La bonne chanson*. With her natural soprano voice, trained by Madame Colonne, she displayed her considerable gifts as a skilled sight-reader and interpreter. The first, fourth, sixth and seventh songs as they appear in the published cycle were drafted at Bougival in the summer and autumn of 1892; the second, third and eighth in the summer of 1893; the fifth in December 1893; and the ninth in February 1894.[18] Roger-Ducasse knew what was happening: 'Every evening Fauré went to the "château" to show his interpreter his day's work. Often, very often, she would send him back to correct it. I have the first draft of *La Lune blanche* ... she was absolutely right! She used to make him rewrite whole bars.'[19]

Fauré set nine of the twenty-one poems which Verlaine had written for his fiancée Mathilde Mauté in 1870. The music flows ecstatically, in turns excitedly then rapturously calm and reflective. The vocal and piano lines undulate and intertwine, resulting in novel and unexpected harmonic progressions. The rhythmic energy and intensity of the cycle give the feeling of spontaneity, the impression of sheer joy in invention, yet it is so assured in its form that Ravel described it as an 'incomparable symphonie ... un vaste poème lyrique émouvant et parfait'.[20] There can be no doubt that the passion Fauré was experiencing for Emma had unleashed an unprecedented impetuous creative flow in which adherence to the niceties of conventional formal composition or the gentle murmurings of salon songs were abandoned. The first poem Fauré set, 'Donc, ce sera par un clair jour d'été', is the seventh in the printed cycle and culminates in an image of stars smiling down benevolently not just on lovers but on man and wife. The manuscript of this song is dated 9 August 1892, at which time Dolly was not even two months old. This surely bears musical witness to a very intimate relationship with her mother. Charles Koechlin, a pupil of Fauré's, referred specifically to this song in a letter dated 25 September 1945:

> Fauré often took a long time to find exactly the right musical translation of a poetic passage. It was Madame Bardac herself who told me, for the ending of 'Donc ce sera ...', i.e. 'Et quand le soir ...', Fauré had been unable to find [Koechlin's underlining] this admirable ending for months. One summer's evening, on the steps of Madame Bardac's house (on the garden side), Faure told her suddenly, 'That's it! I've found it!'

---

[18] Nectoux, *Gabriel Fauré*, pp. 249–50.
[19] Robert Pitrou, *De Gounod à Debussy*, Paris, 1957, p. 96.
[20] Claude Rostand, *L'Œuvre de Gabriel Fauré*, Paris, 1945, p. 107. Quoted in Graham Johnson, *Gabriel Fauré, The Songs and their Poets*, London, 2009, p. 240.

Koechlin believed Verlaine in his poetry was addressing a young girl, not yet his lover. There was something juvenile, almost naïve, in this love, whereas in Fauré there was maturity. 'Fauré's music seems to transcend the text, giving it an exultancy which makes *La bonne chanson* a "unique work".' Koechlin wrote,

> I am still certain that *La bonne chanson* was *lived* by Fauré. Madame Sigismond Bardac (who later married Debussy), an excellent musician, very intelligent and with very sure musical taste, had drawn his attention to Verlaine's work … it is not impossible that Dolly was Fauré's own daughter … such is life![21]

In his biography of Fauré, Koechlin eulogised the cycle:

> The rhapsodical quality of *La bonne chanson*, its extraordinary vital force, the passion of light and happiness and all the musical treasures it inspires, remains incomparable. Fauré preserved an especial tenderness for this work, unique in its existence for the optimism, the excitement, the kind of happy intoxication that persistently animates it.[22]

The eighth song, 'N'est-ce pas?', contains an image of two lovers, isolated as in a dark wood, 'Our two hearts, breathing gentle peace, Shall be two nightingales singing at evening.' The lovers refuse to consider their Destiny as they walk hand in hand, yet the final line of this poem ends with the words 'Whose love is unalloyed, is that not so?', a question mark, a poignant hint of the unsettling awareness that it cannot last for ever. Thirty years later, Fauré was present when Roger-Ducasse was rehearsing this song cycle with Suzanne Balguerie. He felt moved to tell him,

> I never again wrote anything as spontaneously as *La bonne chanson*. I can, indeed I must add that I was helped by a spontaneity of understanding at least its equal by the woman who remains its most moving interpreter. The pleasure of feeling those little pieces of paper come alive as I brought them to her is something I have never experienced since.[23]

At the age of seventy-eight he could still relive the vibrancy of his love for Emma.

Fauré's son, Philippe, later reflected, 'Apart from some enthusiastic pages of *La bonne chanson* you hardly ever find the sound of true happiness in Fauré's work'.[24] Fauré's affair with Emma marked a crucial stage in his life, eternalised in his composition.

In August 1894 Fauré had to write to Winnaretta from Bas-Prunay to make an excuse for not having dedicated these songs to her. 'You had accepted the five I composed previously [the *Cinq mélodies op.58*],' he wrote. He then promised to dedicate to her his next significant composition. However, she had to wait until 1898 when she

---

[21] Letter to Jacques Longchampt, *Charles Koechlin 1867–1950. Correspondance. La Revue musicale*, 1982, pp. 140–1.

[22] Charles Koechlin, *Gabriel Fauré*, trans. L. Orry, London, 1945, p. 23.

[23] In Nectoux, *Gabriel Fauré, Correspondance*, 17 May 1923.

[24] 'Quelques pages enthousiastes de *La bonne chanson* mises à part, on ne trouve guère, dans l'œuvre de Fauré, l'accent de bonheur.' P. Fauré-Fremiet, 'Réflexions sur la confiance Fauréenne', *Gabriel Fauré*, Paris 1957, p. 136.

received the dedication of his suite *Pelléas et Mélisande*, published eventually in 1901.[25] His passion for her had definitely been overtaken by his love of Emma.

Fauré's *Dolly* suite

But it is not just *La bonne chanson* which reveals more than a simple passing infatuation with an attractive, artistic woman seventeen years younger than himself. Fauré created a musical statement of affection for the little girl she bore, movements of which he presented to her mainly on her birthdays and at New Year for the three years 1893–6. The *Dolly* suite of piano duets remains a perennial favourite with pianists young and old for its charming accessibility, the fresh tenderness of its themes and harmonies and innate allusions to childhood innocence. With its intertwining lines, surely Fauré and Emma must have enjoyed intimate moments as they played it together. It comprises six movements, starting with 'Berceuse', a lullaby Fauré resurrected from an early composition of 1864 originally composed for the daughter of a family friend, but now dated 20 June 1893, Dolly's first birthday. On 20 June 1894 Dolly received 'Mi-a-ou', which does not refer to a cat, but to her older brother Raoul. The original manuscript bears the title 'Messieu Aoul', baby Dolly's pronunciation of his name. Her New Year present for 1 January 1895 was 'Le jardin de Dolly', followed by a birthday present on 20 June 1896, 'Kitty-Valse', originally called 'Ketty Valse', after the Bardac's pet dog. In September–October of the same year she received 'Tendresse', and finally in November 1896 'Le pas espagnol', so named, according to the pianist Marguerite Long, because Dolly loved a bronze statue of a horse, one made by Fauré's father-in-law, Emmanuel Fremiet, which stood on a mantelpiece in the Bardac home,[26] but clearly also a tribute to the colourful Spanish style of Chabrier's writing as displayed in *España*, completed in 1883.

The first public performances of these works so dear to Fauré's heart took place in 1894 and 1898 respectively. *La bonne chanson* was sung by Maurice Bagès, a gifted amateur tenor, accompanied by the composer at the salon of the Comtesse de Saussine on 25 April 1894. The cycle must have surprised his contemporaries. Saint-Saëns, usually so supportive of his pupil, thought Fauré must have gone completely mad.[27] Marcel Proust wrote to a friend that the young musicians present, including Claude Debussy, were almost unanimous in their dislike of it, finding it unnecessarily complicated, inferior to his previous songs, but this was of no matter to him. Proust loved it, even preferring it to Fauré's earlier works.[28] *Le Figaro* reported that the cycle received 'une réception restreinte' (a luke-warm reception) and noted the presence of the Princesse de Polignac. As Graham Johnson surmises, emphasising Emma's heritage, 'The gossip about Fauré's affair with Emma would certainly have reached her omniscient ears, and she might have been jealous of the composer's dedication of a second Verlaine cycle, even more significant than her own, to an

[25] J.-M. Nectoux, *Correspondance de Gabriel Fauré suivie de Lettres à Madame H*, Paris 2015, p. 222.
[26] Marguerite Long, *Au Piano avec Gabriel Fauré*, Paris, 1963, p. 155.
[27] Nectoux, *Gabriel Fauré*, p. 257.
[28] Ibid.

5. Baby Dolly (Hélène Bardac) of Fauré's *Dolly* suite with her nurse, 1892. Photograph by Eugène Pirou

adulterous Jewess.'[29] On 20 April 1895 Jeanne Remacle sang the cycle at the SNM in the Salle Pleyel. The newspaper *Le Temps* reported she had already performed these songs in London a few months earlier in a private recital in the studio of the artist John Singer Sargent.[30]

Three years later, on 1 April 1898, Maurice Bagès sang the work in London in another version – for piano and string quintet. Fauré wrote several letters to his wife, Marie, during this visit to the city. Despite its generous reception, Fauré told her that he preferred the simplicity of the solo piano accompaniment.

Dolly received its first official public performance on 30 April 1898 when it was played by Édouard Risler and Alfred Cortot at a concert of the SNM. This was immediately popular with amateurs and professionals alike, and in 1913 would appear in another incarnation as a ballet score orchestrated by Henri Rabaud, performed at the Théâtre des Arts.

[29] G. Johnson, *Gabriel Fauré. The Songs and their Poets*, p. 246.
[30] *Le Temps*, 21 April 1895.

How many works did Fauré dedicate to his own wife and sons? Upon examining the dedicatees of his catalogue until the publication of the last movement of *Dolly* in 1896, not one. Nor is there any after that. Emma received not only the cycle *La bonne chanson* but also a *Salve Regina* in 1895. His older son, Emmanuel, still recalled with some emotion towards the end of his life the intimate atmosphere, 'les auditions intimes', as his father and Emma played and sang *La bonne chanson* together in the warm summer evenings at Bougival.[31] He would have been only nine years old. His mother's reactions can only be surmised. Her quiet painting of pretty flowers was hardly something which could become a similarly cathartic experience, expressing the inexpressible, baring the soul.

Other works by Fauré inspired by Emma

Fauré's relationship with Emma continued for at least another two years. It is not possible to determine exactly when its power lessened. He had been supplementing his earnings as choirmaster at La Madeleine by giving piano lessons and accompanying choirs, but in 1892 his life was made even more arduous when he was appointed inspector of music teaching in conservatoires in the provinces. On his return from distant institutions he had to keep up with the perpetual round of performances and socialising at the prestigious salons of the bourgeoisie in Paris or its suburbs. He was innately modest and any appreciation of his music helped to spur him on to continue creating. Yet following *La bonne chanson*, his setting of an untitled poem by Verlaine dated 4 December 1894 showed an intensity of a different sort. Fauré called it *Prison*.[32] The poet observes a swaying tree outlined against a blue sky, hears a gently ringing bell and plaintive birdsong. The calm is shattered by the stark realisation that his youth has ended and life has been squandered.[33] Depression, despair – is this the inevitable outcome of a passionate love affair that can never become a permanent bond? Fauré would not be able to divorce Marie, nor would he ever be able to give Emma the sort of lifestyle to which she was accustomed. She was now thirty-two, he was approaching fifty. He obviously appreciated Emma's musicianship, her ability to sight-read and interpret his songs exactly as he wanted. He later wrote, 'The young woman, an excellent musician who was the first to sight-read this manuscript, later became Mme Claude Debussy! She was never put off by successions of sevenths!'[34]

Only a few days after *Prison*, he composed *Soir* to words by Albert Samain, a poet whom he had met in 1891 at the café Weber in the rue Royale.[35] Winnaretta, at that time still Princesse de Scey-Montbéliard, was adamant that the pair should work on

---

[31] Nectoux, *Gabriel Fauré*, p. 249.
[32] In Verlaine's collection *Sagesse*.
[33] Translation by R. Stokes in Gabriel Fauré, *Complete Songs: vol.3: The Complete Verlaine Settings*, ed. R. Howat, E. Kilpatrick, London, 2015.
[34] Letter to René Lenormand, quoted in Nectoux, *Gabriel Fauré*, pp. 259–60.
[35] G. Jean-Aubry, 'Gabriel Fauré, Paul Verlaine et Albert Samain ou les Tribulations de Bouddha', *Le Centenaire de Gabriel Fauré, La Revue musicale*, 1945, p. 40.

a project about the *Tentation de Bouddha*. Samain set to work at once to produce a libretto, but of a score there is no trace. Samain's seven hundred and fifty lines of verse did nothing more for Fauré than bring on dreadful headaches and all inspiration simply evaporated.[36]

Samain gathered together a volume of his verse which resulted in the collection *Au Jardin de l'Infante*, published in 1893, clearly more to Fauré's taste. Emma received a special copy bound in pretty mauve silk from a friend, but more significantly she was presented with a plainer second copy from Fauré himself bearing the inscription: 'I beg you to accept this book and choose the poems you would like to sing. Gabriel Fauré. May 1894'.[37] Emma marked five poems with pencil, *Accompagnement* (blue marks, not set by Fauré until 1902), *Promenade à l'Étang* (page turned down at corner and pencil marks, a tonal plan sketched but no music composed), *Dilection* (begun but never finished), *Arpège* (composed after the relationship ended) and *Élegie*. The last of these has nine verses, of which only the last three have been set to music, and given the title *Soir*. The tenderness conveyed by the gentle accompaniment to the sweet melancholic rapture of the words must have been inspired by deep feelings for the dedicatee of the book. G. Jean-Aubry called this 'one of the most perfect songs by the composer' and quoted a letter written by Samain to his sister in which he told her of a dinner party at Fauré's house on 2 March 1896. There he heard *Soir* performed by Emma, accompanied by the composer.[38] Samain was impressed not only by the performance but by the singer:

> a young woman aged about thirty, ... a pretty, elegant society lady; her husband is a banker. She was very nice to me, and extremely thoughtful, for she showed me a copy of *Au Jardin de l'Infante* which had been beautifully bound in a sort of antique mauve silk with her initials embroidered on it. This was a present from a friend[39] who knew how much she loved the work. After dinner she sang. Fauré told me: 'You will never hear anyone sing it better.' Indeed, she has a real feeling for nuance and above all a purity of expression which are very rare.[40]

The time gap between beginning composition of this song and its publication as a supplement for the journal *L'Illustration* on 18 April 1896 was probably because of the difficulty Fauré had finding just the right ending. Finally he achieved a masterpiece, as Robert Orledge said, 'rounding off *Soir* to perfection and making "art conceal art".'[41]

1894 was also the year two masterpieces for piano were composed at Bas-Prunay. The first was the *6th Nocturne*, inscribed 'Prunay, 3 août 1894'. The gentle rise and fall of its initial melody gives a false sense of peace and security, for as

---

[36] Nectoux, *Gabriel Fauré, Correspondance*, p. 190–1.
[37] BnF Musique, Rés Vmd-131.
[38] Nectoux, *Gabriel Fauré, Correspondance*, p. 53.
[39] The word is '*amie*': a female friend.
[40] Quoted in Nectoux, *Gabriel Fauré*, p. 260.
[41] Robert Orledge, 'The two endings of Fauré's *Soir*', *Music & Letters*, July 1979, pp. 316–22.

the piece develops, an extreme sense of restlessness and emotional agitation is conveyed by syncopated rhythms, changes of tempo and sudden changes of key. Marguerite Long described this Nocturne as 'un vaste poème de passion et de rêve'.[42] His next piano piece, the *5th Barcarolle*, conveys even more extreme passion and excitement, surely stemming directly from the heart before the head. This is an extraordinary, fiery yet tender, achingly discordant yet harmonious piece bearing the inscription 'Bas-Prunay, 18 sept. 1894'. It is no gentle gondolier's song. Long later described it as the song of sailors in a boat under full sail on the crest of a wave.[43] There is a distinct sense of male/female in the way energetic, demanding, rhythmic dynamism contrasts with melodic delicacy. The recurring fierce tritone in the bass is startling yet joyful. A motet, *Tantum ergo*, op.65 no.2, for three part women's chorus, soloist and organ also bears the inscription Bas-Prunay and is dated 14 August 1894. This is a piece of almost childlike simplicity, lullaby-like in its gentle rocking rhythm and sweet harmony.

Not one song was composed in 1895, the year Fauré turned fifty. He can have spent little time in Bas-Prunay for besides his duties at La Madeleine, as inspector of music teaching in conservatoires, and other professional engagements, he stayed in Paris to apply (unsuccessfully) for the post of music critic of *Le Figaro*, following which he spent a fortnight in Dieppe. One work which did receive a dedication to Mme Sigismond Bardac, however, was another religious motet, *Salve Regina* for soprano and organ, dated 25 March 1895. Is it fanciful to link the 'Regina' of the title with Emma's daughter, Régina Hélène (Dolly) for whom Fauré was still composing pieces regularly? The grace and delicacy of the melodic line is charming, but not as strikingly emotive or innovative as the songs dating from this era.

Emma and Dolly were not the only Bardacs to whom Fauré dedicated his works. *La naissance de Vénus* op.29 (*The Birth of Venus*), a 'scène mythologique', which was composed in 1882 for solo singers, choir and piano or orchestra, was originally dedicated to M. Antoine Guillot de Sainbris. However, a later reprint replaced his name with that of Sigismond Bardac.

Whilst 1895 was depressingly sterile for Fauré in terms of composing beautiful *mélodies*, in 1896 he set another poem from Samain's collection *Au Jardin de l'Infante*. He adapted the poem *Larmes* (*Tears*), leaving out one verse and the last three lines to turn it into the song he entitled *Pleurs d'or* or 'Tears of Gold'. It is a duet for soprano and tenor, not written for Emma, but sung by her. Another poem which Emma marked for Fauré's attention was *Arpège*. This is dated 6 September 1897, nearly three years after *Soir*. The following month, on 7 October, Fauré wrote to Samain inviting him to hear a performance of the work.

> Mme Bardac, who sang *Soir* to you at my house, has requested me to ask if you would give her the pleasure of coming to dinner at her house, in informal dress, on Sunday evening (30 rue de Berri). Would you care to? It would be a great pleasure to see you and to introduce the new song to you.

---

[42] 'A huge poem of passion and dreams.' M. Long, *Au Piano avec Gabriel Fauré*, p. 136.
[43] M. Long, *Au Piano avec Gabriel Fauré*, p. 123.

Unfortunately Samain was suffering from a throat infection and was under doctor's orders not to go out. 'Please pass on my sincere apologies. It would have been a rare and delightful pleasure to hear my lines enhanced by such an exquisite female voice and exquisite music.'[44]

Arpège appeared in the supplement of *Le Figaro* on 16 October 1897. Only two months later Samain received a new invitation to Madame Bardac's for 5 December. Unfortunately he gave no indication of his reaction to Fauré's settings. It is quite likely that to his ears they were incomprehensible, for on 25 June 1898 after another soirée at Emma's he wrote, 'Why was the music so modern? I would have liked just three bars of Bellini. Oh, these men from the Société Nationale (d'Indy, Chausson, Fauré etc...) certainly make me pay a penance.'[45]

Albert Samain also met Emma's husband, for he described Sigismond in 1897 as 'quite young still, thirty-five to forty, dark with terribly thick eyebrows. Charming, absolutely charming, to me at least'.[46]

On 11 October Emma wrote a letter of sympathy to Madame Louise Boëllmann on the death at the age of thirty-five of her husband, the composer and organist Léon Boëllmann.[47] This is one of the very rare letters of Emma to survive prior to her relationship with Debussy and demonstrates not only her bold handwriting, but that she signed herself Em S Bardac.

In May 1898 Fauré mentioned in a letter to the mother of one of his pupils that he was going to dine 'chez Madame Bardac' even though he had rejected other invitations due to too much work.[48] On 18 July 1898 Albert Samain dined at the Bardacs' in the company of the renowned aesthete Robert de Montesquiou and composer Pierre de Bréville amongst others to listen to 'several poems from the *Jardin de l'infante* including *Soir* which they repeated, and which Montesquiou is enthusiastic about. As for me [Samain], I have my reservations.'[49] The performers were Emma Bardac and Maurice Bagès, accompanied by Fauré at the piano. Even six years after the birth of Dolly they were still making music together.

Fauré travelled frequently both at home and abroad. His music was greatly appreciated in London, where Mrs Adela Maddison heard Fauré's song cycle *La bonne chanson* and wept at its beauty. She was the wife of Frederick Brunning Maddison, a director of Fauré's publisher, Metzler & Co. Fauré was invited to their country home at Saint-Lunaire in Brittany, where he must have been haunted by memories of Emma and little Hélène, for there in September 1896 he completed the *Dolly* suite.[50] Adela found Fauré irresistible and soon became his pupil. She urged him to visit London to promote his

---

[44] 'Gabriel Fauré, Paul Verlaine et Albert Samain ou les tribulations de Bouddha', ed. G. Jean-Aubry, *Le Centenaire de Gabriel Fauré (1845–1945), La Revue musicale*, 1945, pp. 56–7.

[45] Idem. p. 57.

[46] Nectoux, *Gabriel Fauré*, p. 247.

[47] BnF Musique, La-Debussy Emma-23.

[48] Part of Item no.335 for auction on 27 April 2017 by Ader Norman, Paris: https://www.ader-paris.fr/lot/81952/7191806 (last accessed 16 October 2020).

[49] Nectoux, *Gabriel Fauré*, p. 261.

[50] Nectoux, *Gabriel Fauré*, p. 664.

works, she translated some of his songs into English, as well as the text of *La naissance de Vénus*, which was performed to Fauré's great satisfaction at the Leeds Festival on 8 October 1898. Her teacher's charms were such that Adela abandoned her husband and two children that same year and moved from London to Paris. Fauré took her with him to stay for two days with Marguerite de Saint-Marceaux, who had so keenly found him his wife. She seems to have fully approved of his new love. 'She is charming, a bit childlike, but with heroic courage and determination,' she wrote in her journal on 24 September 1899. 'Fauré brought along a wonderful new *Nocturne*', (Nocturne no.7 in C♯ minor, dedicated to Adela Maddison). Two days later Meg wrote: 'Fauré and Maddison are leaving … Poor Marie [Fauré's wife]. Her life is wrecked without her knowing it, or else she is being totally heroic.'[51]

Dedications to Emma by other composers

Meanwhile, salon society in Paris meant that Emma had plenty of occasions to charm and be charmed by other musicians. Her own salon received attention in the press, such as the occasion on 24 June 1897 when a choir performed *La lyre et la harpe* by Saint-Saëns besides works by her son Raoul Bardac, Hahn, Fauré and others. Emma was one of the soloists. No doubt Raoul conducted his own composition, as it was noted that the composers conducted their own works.[52] Fauré commented on this occasion only a few days later, in a letter to Saint-Saëns dated 28 June 1897: 'We played not too badly at all *La lyre et la harpe* last Wednesday at Mme Bardac's house with Auguez and several lesser lords.'[53]

Besides being hostess in her own home and participating in the salons of other society ladies, Emma regularly attended the opera and concerts and her presence was noted high on lists of illustrious members of the audience. The notorious critic, Willy, (Henri Gauthier-Villars), writing as 'L'Ouvreuse du Cirque d'Été', noted a very select 'sparkling' audience including the Prince de Polignac and Madame Sigismond Bardac and other music lovers 'or people pretending to love music' at a concert of the SNM in May 1896.[54] Emma was first on his list of eminent ladies at a Concert Colonne on 18 January 1898.[55] In 1899 and 1900 her presence was noted at the salon held by the Comtesse de Maupeou, where, with Sigismond at her side, she listened to works by Massenet. What a lavish and glorious occasion this must have been. First the great pianist Louis Diémer played, then the whole of the third act of Massenet's *Werther* was performed in costume in a delightful theatre set specially installed in the drawing room with the hostess singing the role of Charlotte. Massenet himself conducted this and other works at this 'elegant gathering'.[56]

[51] M. de Saint-Marceaux, *Journal 1894–1927*, p. 204.

[52] *Le Figaro*, 25 June 1897, and *Gil Blas*, 26 June 1897.

[53] *The Correspondence of Camille Saint-Saëns and Gabriel Fauré: Sixty Years of Friendship*, trans J. Barrie-Jones, ed. J.-M Nectoux, Aldershot, 2004, p. 59.

[54] 'Lettre de l'Ouvreuse du cirque d'été', *L'Echo de Paris*, 5 May 1896.

[55] Idem., 18 January 1898.

[56] *La Presse*, 2 February 1899; *Le Figaro*, 9 April 1900.

By now the passionate affair between Emma and Gabriel Fauré had subsided into friendship and mutual respect. Fauré was still teaching her son Raoul and they were meeting regularly at musical gatherings. Strong links were maintained between Emma and Fauré's most gifted pupils, who were often invited to perform in her salon. In 1897, aged twenty-four, not long after entering Fauré's class at the Conservatoire, Roger-Ducasse dedicated a song to Emma, 'Les biens dont vous estes la Dame', the first of his *Deux Rondels*, settings of poems by Villon. It is worthy of note that Emma's friendship with Roger-Ducasse dated from much earlier than his friendship with Debussy. Not only did they have their association with Fauré in common but both originated from Bordeaux, Roger-Ducasse having been educated there, then moving to Paris in 1891 to study at the Conservatoire. This composer, who was at Debussy's bedside when he died in 1918, probably first encountered Debussy in person at the time of the first performances of *Pelléas et Mélisande* in 1902.

In 1903 Emma received another dedication 'à Madame Sigismond Bardac', this time from twenty-eight-year-old Maurice Ravel, the third of his songs in the cycle *Shéhérazade*. What can one read into the fact that this is entitled 'L'Indifférent'? The poems are by Tristan Klingsor (Wagnerian pseudonym of Léon Leclère), who that same year had joined the expanding group of young musicians, artists and poets called 'les Apaches' (the undesirables or hooligans), who often met in Klingsor's home, 31 avenue René-Coty near the Parc-Montsouris,[57] sharing a passion for Debussy's unique, poignant opera *Pelléas et Mélisande*.

The atmosphere of 'L'Indifférent' is languorous and evokes the dying heat of the day as the singer watches a young adolescent stranger, a boy, pass by. The sensuous description of his beautiful face 'shadowed with down' (*de duvet ombragé*) is heightened by the lazily rocking, barcarolle-like accompaniment, marked *pp* and *ppp*, played by muted strings. The boy is singing quietly in a foreign tongue. The beguiled watcher longs for him to come into his home so that he can offer him wine – but no. 'You pass. And from my threshold I see you depart with a last graceful gesture to me, your hips gently swaying, your walk feminine, languid.' The ambiguity of the sex of the watcher, the lack of interest of the passer-by, the ambience of a lazy afternoon, none of these suggests a paean of love to Emma Bardac. Yet fascinatingly, when looking back on his compositions over twenty years later, Ravel cited his song cycle *Shéhérazade* as containing 'something in this composition that I have never found again'.[58] How reminiscent of Gabriel Fauré's nostalgia when recalling the composition of *La bonne chanson*, admitting he had never been able to compose so spontaneously since.

Raoul Bardac's progress

Meanwhile, how was Emma's son Raoul progressing? From the Petit Lycée Condorcet he had passed to the senior Lycée Condorcet. From his school friend Roger Martin du Gard we learn that Raoul possessed 'an artist's sensitivity and a

---

[57] *Maurice Ravel, L'Intégrale, Correspondance (1895–1937)*, ed. M. Cornejo, Paris, 2018, p. 93.

[58] R. Nichols, *Ravel*, Yale, 2011, p. 57.

quick intelligence supported by an incredible memory and exceptional intuitions.'[59] He also emphasised his origins: he was 'a typically precocious little Jew'.[60] In 1896 Raoul was fifteen years old. From now on his name appeared regularly in the newspapers as a composer whose songs were performed at the matinées of Emma's teacher and friend Madame Colonne. *Le Figaro* of 5 May 1896 placed his name next to those of Fauré, Saint-Saëns, Bruneau, Widor, Massenet and others. *Le Ménestrel* of 11 April 1897 printed a glowing review of two unpublished works for violin, composed and accompanied by Raoul Bardac with the violinist Weingartner, one of which was encored. Their freshness, ingenious detail and 'piquant harmonisation' are particularly emphasised. The same year, the critic Adolphe Jullien wrote that 'a sixteen-year-old newcomer (Raoul Bardac is his name) could hardly contain his joy' when Mme Colonne herself sang 'deliciously' *mélodies* including Bardac's in a concert in the Salle Pleyel.[61]

The following year Raoul was admitted to the Conservatoire de Musique de Paris to study harmony and composition with Fauré and counterpoint with André Gédalge. In 1899 he was already getting his work published and became a member of the Société des compositeurs de musique. His composition *Fleurs du crépuscule* to words by André Lebey was listed in the *Catalogue des publications du Mercure de France*.[62] His closeness to Fauré is demonstrated by the fact that in 1900 he was determined to go to Béziers in the south of France to be present at the première of Fauré's huge undertaking, the cantata *Prométhée*, a *tragédie lyrique* involving nearly eight hundred performers. Fauré wrote many letters to his wife expressing his anxieties about the organisation of this event, one of which, dated 11 August, told her that out of all his friends who had shown an interest, only Schuster and Bardac had definitely requested accommodation and seats for 27 August.[63] Raoul arrived in Béziers on 26 August – as did Adela Maddison, together with Winnaretta, Princesse de Polignac.[64] Fortunately, after a violent storm on the first night, on the second everything went smoothly, to the delight of the composer and his friends.

Raoul kept himself to himself socially, which is perhaps why Ravel wrote in 1921, 'he is a delicate musician; but also one of the earliest pupils of Fauré who was very fond of him. If he's not very well known that's because of his character, if not over modest, at least very distant.'[65] Yet Raoul was soon to get closer to Debussy than anyone else of his age, having become Debussy's pupil in 1899.

---

[59] François Lesure, *Claude Debussy*, trans and revised ed. Marie Rolf, Rochester and Woodbridge, 2019, p. 171.

[60] Lesure, *Claude Debussy*, pp. 213–4.

[61] *Le Journal des débats politiques et littéraires*, 4 June 1897; *Le Ménestrel*, 6 June 1897.

[62] *Catalogue des publications du Mercure de France*, December 1899, p. 37.

[63] *Gabriel Fauré. Lettres intimes, présentées par Philippe Fauré-Fremiet*, Paris, 1951, p. 40.

[64] Idem. p. 48.

[65] 'C'est un musicien délicat ; mais aussi l'un des plus anciens élèves de Fauré, qui avait une grande affection pour lui. S'il n'est pas très connu, c'est bien grâce à son caractère, sinon trop modeste, du moins très distant.' *Maurice Ravel. L'intégrale. Correspondance (1895–1937), écrits et entretiens*, ed. Manuel Cornejo, Paris, 2018, p. 751.

3

Debussy's life until 1902

Debussy's modest background and social climb

It seems counterintuitive to discuss relations within the Bardacs' and Osiris's world of banking when considering the life of Claude Debussy, a composer from a humble background who lived in garrets far removed from anything the Bardac family would have encountered. He was born on 22 August 1862 to Manuel-Achille and Victorine Debussy, who sold china in the rue au Pain, Saint-Germain-en-Laye. At the time of Emma's first marriage (both she and Debussy were, after all, only seventeen years old in 1879) he was still a student at the Paris Conservatoire living with his parents in the rue Clapeyron in a very modest two-roomed apartment. This year did, however, bring him his first taste of a world of inconceivable luxury and wealth. Upon the recommendation of his piano teacher at the Paris Conservatoire, Antoine Marmontel, he acquired a summer holiday job as resident pianist to Marguerite Wilson-Pelouze, who lived in the château of Chenonceau which spans the river Cher, once the residence of Diane de Poitiers and Catherine de Medici. Her father was Daniel Wilson, a Scottish man responsible for introducing gas-lighting to Paris, and her husband was Eugène Pelouze, an official in her father's company. Madame Pelouze provided Debussy with a certain insight into high society and a brief encounter with the world of politics, for at the time of his residence at her château she was the mistress of Jules Grévy, President of the Republic. Marguerite was known to be a fervent admirer of Wagner and she enjoyed listening to her own chamber group, as a member of which Debussy had been employed to play. For a poverty-stricken seventeen-year-old, the opulent environment must have seemed unimaginably inaccessible, but was no doubt an early trigger of his penchant for acquiring items of luxury which he could ill afford.

Debussy was fortunate to find his next holiday job (and, indeed, for the two following summers) with another prosperous and influential woman who required a resident musician, Nadezhda Filaretovna von Meck, a widow, mother of five boys and six girls, whose husband, like the Bardac family, had made his vast fortune by investing in the Russian railways. She is most famous today for her epistolary relationship with and financial support of Tchaikovsky. Every summer she took her large family around Europe, but she never neglected the musical education of her children. Debussy's role in that summer of 1880 was to give them piano lessons, accompany her daughter Julia, who was a singer, and play duets with Nadezhda herself, including scores arranged for piano by Tchaikovsky. Indeed, she praised her young pianist's prodigious talent for sight-reading to the composer. It was during this employment that Debussy composed his *First Trio in G major*. After joining the

6. Marie Blanche Vasnier, Debussy's first love.
Portrait by Paul Baudry, 1885

family at Interlaken, Debussy travelled with them to Arcachon, where they stayed in the impressive Villa Marguerite. This was not one of Osiris's villas, but coincidentally was situated opposite his Villa Osiris, as it was called at that time.[1]

In 1880 eighteen-year-old Debussy became the accompanist to the singing class of Madame Moreau-Santi, playing twice a week for four years. There he met Marie Blanche Vasnier, a married woman aged thirty-two. Like Emma, Marie, at the age of seventeen, had married an older man, in her case by eleven years. He was a legal expert on property. The Vasniers willingly provided sympathetic and comfortable surroundings for the talented youth to work in, introducing him to works of art and the poetry of Verlaine and Mallarmé. One can well imagine a teenage passion developing for the elegant songstress whom he accompanied so often in the evenings,

[1] Villa Osiris was renamed Villa Alexandre Dumas after Osiris's death.

willing not only to interpret his music with charm, but also to accept the boy as her equal. Her singing was an inspiration to him. In all, Debussy dedicated to her twenty-seven songs written for high soprano voice, thirteen of which he presented to her as a volume of *Chansons* before he left Paris for the Villa Medici in Rome in 1885. There he suffered feelings of loneliness and depression, a sense of exile no doubt exacerbated by his enforced absence from Marie Vasnier. He even managed to take an extended leave from Rome that summer and on 8 July arranged a secret rendez-vous with her in Dieppe, a seaside town to which he would return in years to come with his second wife. His lengthy outpourings in letters to Marie Blanche's husband whilst at the Villa Medici could not betray his passion for her, but one is left wondering what led to the ending of his close relationship with the couple on his return to Paris in 1887. In 1888 Debussy's six *Ariettes* with words by Verlaine were published individually by Veuve Girod. He dedicated a copy 'to Mme Vasnier, in grateful homage',[2] but he no longer consorted with his now middle-aged muse.

Although seventeen years his junior, Debussy must have met Fauré early on in his career, perhaps when he was the accompanist for the amateur choral society La Concordia between 1883 and 1885, a choir founded by Henrietta Fuchs, a singer whose musical salon Fauré attended. When Debussy went to Bayreuth in 1888, subsidised by Étienne Dupin, a friend and wealthy fellow music-lover, Fauré was amongst the musicians with whom he socialised. Fauré and Messager had also been been subsidised for this festival, being the beneficiaries of a tombola organised by Marguerite Baugnies. Debussy joined the SNM in January 1888 and on 2 February 1889 works by both Debussy and Fauré were programmed together when Maurice Bagès gave the first performance of two of Debussy's *Ariettes*, accompanied at the piano by the composer, as well as the first performance of Fauré's *Au Cimetière*.

Evidence that Debussy was not yet at home in the grand world of the salon comes from his publisher and friend Jacques Durand, who told of a performance he and Debussy gave together of the *Petite suite* for piano duet on 1 March 1889. In order to promote this charming work, he arranged to play it with the composer in

> a Parisian salon attended by the elite of those who formed aesthetic opinion … Debussy, very nervous even before sitting down with me at the piano, had told me to be careful not to get faster. I promised him, but hardly had we started the piece when Debussy began to speed up. In spite of all my efforts I could not make him slow down. He wanted this public test to be over as soon as possible.[3]

On 8 April 1893 the first performance of Debussy's cantata *La damoiselle élue* took place at the SNM in the Salle Érard, sung by Julia Robert and Thérèse Roger. On 23 April Debussy was elected a member of the Committee at the general meeting of the Society, then on 29 December his String Quartet was given its first performance by the Ysaÿe string quartet. His artistic credibility was clearly in the ascendant and soon he was introduced to the salon of that lady so significant in Fauré's life, Marguerite de Saint-Marceaux. In July 1893 she had obtained one of the one hundred and sixty copies of the score of *La damoiselle élue*, which had excited her

---

[2] 'À Madame Vasnier, hommage reconnaissant.' C. p. 2227.
[3] J. Durand, *Quelques souvenirs d'un éditeur de musique*, vol.1, Paris, 1924, p. 59.

interest.[4] She encouraged Debussy to accompany her and to play her his works. Whilst Debussy was not in his natural environment in such surroundings, he certainly realised their importance for his professional progress. Soon he was drawn not just into this salon but that of Madame Escudier, mother-in-law of Ernest Chausson, who organised a series of ten musical events on Wagner in her apartment, which Debussy was asked to illustrate musically at the piano.

> I don't recognise myself any more! I am to be seen in salons, smiling sweetly, or I conduct choirs at Countess Zamoïska's! (yes, sir!) ... Then there's Mme de S. Marceaux who has discovered in me a first-rate talent. You could die of laughing. But really you would have to be a pretty feeble character to let yourself get sucked into their world. It's all so ridiculous![5]

Thus wrote Debussy to his friend Chausson on 5 February 1894. Nothing could have been more of a contrast to his current domestic arrangements than the refined surroundings of these drawing rooms. He was always short of money yet managed to borrow or be provided with financial assistance whenever he was desperate. Winnaretta Singer provided a vivid description of the young Debussy, whom she met for the first time at Meg's salon in January 1894: 'Debussy's appearance was most striking; his short nose and deep-set eyes, his faunlike features and rather curly black hair and slight beard gave the impression of an Italian model, especially as his complexion was very dark and he sometimes wore small plain gold hooped earrings.'[6]

Debussy's relationships

In 1890 Debussy met Gabrielle (Gaby) Dupont, the daughter of a dressmaker. René Peter, a friend of Debussy's since the late 1880s, remarked that this may have occurred 'somewhere frivolous', but a 'less frivolous blonde he had never met'.[7] When she first lived with Debussy, she had to accept stoically the miserable conditions of their little flat at 42 rue de Londres, no doubt always hoping for better days. In July 1893 the couple moved to 10 rue Gustave Doré. This was also the year in which Debussy commenced work on *Pelléas et Mélisande*, the first act of which he completed by February 1894. Gaby took on any sort of work to support the composer, but the relationship has been characterised as 'always stormy'.[8]

Marguerite de Saint-Marceaux's recognition of Debussy's talent made her just as ambitious for him as a matchmaker as she allegedly had been for Fauré. Ignorant of his current personal circumstances, she fostered a relationship between Debussy and the young singer who had created *La damoiselle élue*, Thérèse Roger. On 17

---

[4] *Marguerite de Saint-Marceaux, Journal 1894–1927*, p. 77.
[5] C. p. 191 and F. Lesure, *Claude Debussy. Biographie critique*, Paris, 2003, p. 146.
[6] Sylvia Kahn, *Music's Modern Muse. A Life of Winnaretta Singer, Princesse de Polignac.* Rochester N. Y. and Woodbridge U. K., p. 39.
[7] René Peter, *Claude Debussy*, Paris, 1944, p. 32.
[8] 'L'union est toujours traversée d'orages ...' G. et D.-E. Inghelbrecht, *Claude Debussy*, Paris, 1953, p. 119.

February 1894 Debussy accompanied Roger in the first performance of two of his *Proses lyriques*, 'De fleurs' and 'De soir' at the SNM Prior to this concert, Marguerite enthused about Debussy's private rendition to her of *La damoiselle élue*, then the extraordinary revelation of his *Pelléas et Mélisande*, and noted the forthcoming performance of the former by Thérèse Roger, concluding with the remark: 'She has got engaged to the young master.'[9] Later that same month Debussy wrote to Henry Lerolle, 'I must tell you something completely ridiculous! A marriage is planned between Mlle Thérèse Roger and Claude Debussy! It's totally surreal, but that's how it is and it's just like a fairy tale!'[10]

How could this be otherwise to the impecunious composer? By virtue of his prodigious talent and his determination to stick to his own musical path, he had risen from his lowly birth through the ranks of society to become acceptable as a listener and performer, an integral member of the musical salon scene, and now to be regarded as a suitable husband to the daughter of Pauline Roger, a singer and virtuoso pianist who herself conducted a women's choir. Insisting that he had hidden nothing about his financial situation, he begged Lerolle to speak in support of him to Madame Roger, at the same time informing him that Gaby had abruptly left him one morning in February. Both Lerolle and Chausson expressed pleasure at Debussy's joy, underlining the innate difference between him and his companions. 'It is so nice to see someone in love. It's becoming quite a rarity in our circle of intellectual, high-class, sophisticated people,' wrote Chausson.[11] The wedding was arranged for 16 April and an apartment was rented in readiness in rue Vaneau.[12]

Debussy's fairy tale continued when he and Thérèse travelled to Brussels to perform his *Proses lyriques* again on 1 March. She sang 'like a little fairy', he wrote to Chausson. This letter was full of references to light and colour: 'Life is taking on new colours for me ... I feel as if until now I have been walking in the dark and come across many evil passers-by. Now a path full of light is opening up in front of me ...'[13]

How quick was his descent from light to darkness. All Debussy's good intentions to lead a new, respectable life were dashed when someone sent an anonymous letter to Madame de Saint-Marceaux. On 17 March Meg noted in her diary, 'It's all over with Debussy's marriage. There are terrible mysteries surrounding his life ... it is awful to think that such a wonderful artist is living in such sordid circumstances.'[14] The social climber had taken a bad tumble. The day before Meg's musings, Debussy had written to Chausson begging for the loan of fifteen hundred francs to pay off debts and to buy a dress for his mother for his forthcoming wedding. He swore he had been honest with Thérèse, but money was not the worst of his problems. Pauline Roger found out that her daughter's fiancé was still living with Gaby. The engagement came to an abrupt end.

---

[9] M. de Saint-Marceaux, *Journal*, p. 77.
[10] C. pp. 196–7.
[11] Quoted in G. Millan, *Pierre Louÿs ou le culte d'amitié*, Aix-en-Provence, 1979, p. 214.
[12] C. p. 197.
[13] C. p. 200.
[14] M. de Saint-Marceaux, *Journal*, p. 79–80.

Debussy's close friend, Pierre Louÿs, defended him fiercely to Meg:

> ... a young man cannot dismiss as though she were a chambermaid a mistress who has lived with him for two years, who has shared his poverty without complaint, and against whom he has no reproach to make, except that he is weary of her and is getting married. Ordinarily one would extricate oneself by means of some banknotes ... that is the convenient way. You know that Debussy is incapable of making use of it ... If there had been less haste in announcing the engagement, Debussy would have had more time to extricate himself completely.[15]

Chausson was particularly offended by 'this dirty business'.[16] He broke off all relations with the composer. Lerolle maintained his friendship whilst Louÿs actively supported him, but Debussy no longer attended Meg's salon. Ten years later, in 1904, Meg acknowledged in her diary that she was trying to entice him back, but she had no success.[17] Thérèse Roger did not have the courage to return until 4 March 1898.[18]

Summer 1895 brought the first 'completion' of his opera and Debussy entertained the hope that it might be performed if not in Paris then in Brussels or Ghent. But once more he was seeking a permanent relationship. A family supportive of Debussy was that of the Belgian painter Alfred Stevens, who had settled in Paris. In 1892 Debussy had dedicated his song *En sourdine* to Alfred's daughter Catherine: 'In homage and to indicate a little of my joy in being her affectionate and devoted Claude Debussy' and by 1893 he was dining at their house three times a week.[19] When Debussy proposed marriage, assuring Catherine of riches to come when *Pelléas* was performed, he met with her refusal, although she did indicate that she might reconsider when *Pelléas* reached the stage.

Gaby was still sharing his life. One day in January 1897 she discovered in Debussy's pocket a letter which left her in no doubt about another romantic affair, whereupon she took out a revolver. Debussy claimed that this pathetic drama was reported in *Le Petit Journal*, but no such report has been found. Gaby did not hurt herself badly, if at all. René Peter implied that the woman involved was Alice, wife of his older brother Michel Peter, who was now separated from her husband. To her Debussy dedicated the *Chansons de Bilitis*,[20] and he gave her the first draft of the second of these, 'La Chevelure', which was completed in July 1897.

---

[15] Quoted by Vallery-Radot, *Tel était Claude Debussy*, Paris, Julliard, 1958, pp. 41–2, to whom Cortot had shown it. Also C. p. 203 n.4.

[16] Letter to Lerolle, 19 March 1894 (quoted in G. Millan, *Pierre Louÿs ou le culte d'amitié*, p. 215).

[17] M. de Saint-Marceaux, *Journal*, p. 329.

[18] M. de Saint-Marceaux, *Journal*, p. 170.

[19] M. Dietschy, *A Portrait of Claude Debussy*, ed. and trans. by W. Ashbrook and M. G. Cobb, Oxford, 1994, p. 78.

[20] Words by Pierre Louÿs.

Debussy's marriage to Rosalie (Lilly) Texier

By 27 March 1898 Debussy was depressed to the point of tears. Yet only a month or two later René Peter brought about the meeting of Rosalie (Lilly) Texier and Debussy.[21] Lilly came originally from the Department of the Yonne, where her father was Stationmaster at Bichain, in the commune of Villeneuve-la-Guyard. She worked as a model at a fashionable dressmaker's in Paris. She had been living with a man of whom she had been 'physically afraid'. Debussy found her 'quite pretty', but teased her about her mannerisms. Lilly certainly got on well with Gaby and although she did not move in with Debussy immediately,[22] change was in the air. On 15 May 1899 Pierre Louÿs announced his engagement to Mlle Louise de Hérédia. The next day Debussy agreed to write a wedding march, at the same time expressing his fear that 'My long term relationship with Music prevents me from ever marrying!'[23] This sentiment reverberated throughout his life, yet it did not stop him pursuing Lilly. He wrote long, passionate letters to her and eventually persuaded her to move in with him. Once again, the partnership was by no means peaceful and Lilly left Debussy at least once. Debussy, however, claimed he could not live without her. Léon Vallas claimed to have seen a letter Debussy wrote to Lilly threatening to commit suicide if she did not marry him.[24] If true, emotional blackmail must have worked, for on 24 September 1899 he wrote to Georges Hartmann, his publisher and patron, telling him of his forthcoming marriage.

On 19 October 1899 a simple civil ceremony took place with Pierre Louÿs, Erik Satie and Lucien Fontaine as witnesses. A piano pupil, Madame de Romilly, has left a telling account of the composer most unusually turning up late that day to give her a lesson, his excuse being that he had just got married. Money, as ever, was in such short supply that Debussy did not have enough to pay for the wedding or celebration. The priest wanted eighty francs for the ceremony. 'You can see why after that we only went to the town hall!'[25]

Misia Sert,[26] friend and patron of many artists and musicians, wrote in her memoirs that Debussy was 'married to a little fawn-like creature, very dark and slim.'[27] Lilly was neither musical nor cultured. She had had no education, but was kind and sensitive, willing to help Debussy compose in a sympathetic atmosphere. Yet in his eyes she always remained the dressmaker's model, a good wife, but not artistic, unable to climb the social ladder to the same extent as he was eventually to succeed in doing.

Although in 1900 progress was made towards a performance of *Pelléas et Mélisande*, the death of Debussy's publisher Georges Hartmann on 22 April led to

---

[21] Dietschy, *A Portrait of Claude Debussy*, p. 105.
[22] R. Peter, *Claude Debussy*, pp. 41–2.
[23] C. p. 479.
[24] Léon Vallas, 'Death of Mélisande', *The New York Times*, 8 January 1933.
[25] Madame Gérard de Romilly, 'Debussy Professeur par une de ses élèves', *Cahiers Debussy*, no.2, Centre de Documentation Claude Debussy, Paris, 1978, pp. 9–10.
[26] Née Misia Godebska, later Misia Natanson, then Misia Edwards, finally Misia Sert.
[27] M. Sert, *Two or Three Muses, Memoirs of Misia Sert*, trans. M. Budberg, London, 1953, p. 35.

increased anxiety about his finances. A further personal upset was Lilly's pregnancy. How could the couple possibly afford to support a child? It seems Lilly resorted to an abortion. To translate the words of Debussy's biographer, Marcel Dietschy, 'for the most wretched reasons they had not been able to allow what they had so intimately conceived together to reach maturity, and Lilly had to spend ten days in a clinic …'[28] She also showed signs of tuberculosis and it was recommended that she should recuperate in the Pyrenees for three or four months[29] – a vain hope in view of their financial circumstances.

The soprano Mary Garden recognised an inherent trait in Debussy's character when she wrote of Lilly, '*She took care of him like a child* [my italics]. They had worries and debts and disappointments, but nobody ever got into the little apartment of the rue Cardinet to interrupt Debussy at his music. Lily kept the world away, so her beloved Claude could work.'[30] Yet Lilly was not to reap the rewards for her efforts. She had little in common with the highbrow musicians surrounding Debussy, although Debussy often conveyed her regards to correspondents such as Messager and Robert Godet. In a letter written whilst he was in London on 16 July 1902 he was not exactly flattering about the sound of her voice:

> My very dear little wife, Your letter did me immense good – if you knew how lonely I feel in spite of everything, and no longer hearing your imperious voice calling 'Mî-Mî' makes me feel as melancholy as a guitar … did I need the harsh experience of absence in order to understand that I could not get along without you?[31]

Who was he trying to convince? Had he already heard a voice which sounded far more agreeable to his ears? Most people date Debussy's first meeting with Emma Bardac to 1903, but there is a telling PS to a letter Debussy wrote to her son Raoul on 30 March 1902, before this visit to London, asking him to give his best wishes to his mother: 'Mon meilleur souvenir à Madame votre mère'.[32] Why would he do this if he did not already know her?

---

[28] M. Dietschy *La Passion de Claude Debussy*, Neuchâtel, 1962, p.135. Lilly spent 14–23 August in the Maison Dubois. In the English translation it is not implied that Lilly had an abortion, but rather a miscarriage. 'They had lost the child they hoped for …' Dietschy, *A Portrait of Claude Debussy*, p. 109.

[29] C. p. 566.

[30] M. Garden and L. Biancolli, *Mary Garden's Story*, New York, 1951, p. 82.

[31] C. p. 676.

[32] C. p. 641.

4

Emma meets Debussy: 1899 – August 1904

Raoul becomes Debussy's pupil

In 1899 Emma's son Raoul was eighteen years old. This was the year of Debussy's first official contact with the Bardac family, for Raoul dated his first lessons with Debussy to 1899, proud to emphasise his close relationship with the composer despite his youth.[1] It may well be that this course of events came about indirectly via Emma, who had discovered Debussy's *Proses lyriques* and the *Cinq Poèmes de Baudelaire* when she had sung them accompanied by Fauré's pupil, Charles Koechlin. Emma seems always to have had an indelible effect on her accompanists, for writing to her to express his condolences after Debussy's death in 1918, Koechlin recalled the time when he had done what he felt was his inadequate best to accompany her in these songs, saying 'I have never forgotten and will never ever forget those hours of music-making'.[2]

According to Raoul's school friend at the Lycée Condorcet, Roger Martin du Gard, Raoul had first become familiar with the name Debussy and the poetry of Maeterlinck several years before the première of *Pelléas et Mélisande*: 'Young Bardac took inspiration from them to make up rhymes for "legendary" poems for which he composed musical accompaniments which Debussy then corrected.'[3] If so, Debussy and Emma would have been aware of each other during Raoul's schooldays, even if they had not become well acquainted.

Raoul was one of a very small number of Debussy's personal pupils. There was no correspondence between them at this stage, but there must have been a certain compatibility from the start. Raoul claimed that their relationship was not that of teacher–pupil, but of Master and disciple. They would have conversations about music in general and perform pieces both old and contemporary. In particular Raoul remembered his teacher's advice, 'above all, no music which is "not worth the effort",

---

[1] R. Bardac, 'Souvenirs de Raoul Bardac sur Claude Debussy lus à la Radio pour le 30ème anniversaire de sa mort en 1948', Centre de Documentation Claude Debussy, RESE 05.16.

[2] 'Ce sont, constate-t-il avec nostalgie, des heures musicales que je n'ai pas oubliées et que je n'oublierai point …' I am grateful to la Librairie de l'Abbaye-Pinault for providing a copy of the page of the catalogue: Catl. Libr. de l'Abbaye, no.281, 1985, no.153 (letter from Koechlin to Emma, 27 March 1918).

[3] Translated from a letter from Roger Martin du Gard to Pasteur Vallery-Radot, Nice, 18 March 1958: 'Le jeune Bardac s'inspirait pour rimer des poèmes "légendaires" auxquels il composait des accompagnements musicaux que Debussy lui corrigeait.' Available at http://www.auction.fr/_fr/lot/roger-martin-du-gard-l-a-s-1418562#.U4CzztJOXIU (last accessed 1 September 2020).

a maxim he had borrowed from Chabrier'.[4] Raoul was clearly rather detached from the group of young composers who surrounded Fauré. Following the success of Debussy's *Pelléas et Mélisande* he did not join the Apaches, that group of young men who harboured deep admiration for Debussy's work. As noted previously, Ravel was eventually to use the word 'distant' to describe him.

By 1900 the relationship had become close enough for nineteen-year-old Raoul to be invited to Debussy's home along with Maurice Ravel and Lucien Garban to listen to Debussy playing through his opera at the piano.[5] It had just been announced in the press that it would be performed the following season. On 9 December 1900 two of Debussy's orchestral *Nocturnes*, 'Nuages' and 'Fêtes', received their première at the Concerts Lamoureux. The composer now wanted all three, including *Sirènes*, arranged for two pianos and he decided to entrust this task to the same three young musicians, still students at the Conservatoire. Whilst Raoul seems to have been charged with transcribing *Nuages* and Lucien Garban with *Fêtes*, it was Ravel who published the whole work under his name in 1908. This version of the *Nocturnes* did not receive its first performance until 24 April 1911, when Ravel and Louis Aubert played it in the Salle Gaveau in Paris.

How fortunate a pupil Raoul was to have two such original and influential teachers as Debussy and Fauré.[6] The year he was invited to listen to Debussy demonstrating his opera was the same year he attended Fauré's *Prométhée* in Béziers.[7] Raoul certainly provided a fulcrum upon which turned the relationships involving Emma Bardac.

We learn from a letter that Ravel addressed to Lucien Garban on 26 July 1901 that Raoul was in Italy that summer and had taken with him 'some cantata texts with the vague intention of adorning them with outmoded but adequate music',[8] an echo of the words of Roger Martin du Gard quoted above. Just over a month later, Debussy wrote a long, affable letter to Raoul addressed from Bichain, Lilly's parental home. He made a point of emphasising their increasing closeness, calling him '*Cher ami*', and telling him to have no hesitation in doing the same. He even expressed regret that he and Lilly were not able to see Raoul whilst there. He offered sound advice on composing, emphasising the care and time one must take to create the distinct atmosphere of a work of art, never rushing to write things down, giving free rein to the whole range of ideas competing in one's brain, a mysterious process which we disrupt through our lack of patience.[9] Perhaps Debussy's next few sentences summed up the similarity between the two men: 'I don't know how to

---

[4] R. Bardac, 'Souvenirs'.

[5] M. Dietschy, *A Portait of Claude Debussy*, ed. and trans. W. Ashbrook and M. G. Cobb, Oxford, 1994, p. 108.

[6] He also studied counterpoint with André Gédalge.

[7] Chapter 2 p. 33.

[8] *Maurice Ravel. L'Intégrale, Correspondance (1895–1937), écrits et entretiens*, ed. Manuel Cornejo, Paris, 2018, p. 77.

[9] Long after Debussy's death, Raoul wrote respectful and affectionate reminiscences of his teacher and step-father in which he described his methods, which reflected Debussy's own measured process of composition, and which were almost identical to the advice given in this letter. R. Bardac, 'Dans l'intimité de Claude Debussy', *Terres Latines*, March 1936, p. 74.

repay you except to say you can count on me, but I don't think I'll ever be influential. I have taken too far my indifference towards my fellow men, which is probably the only way to make any sort of choice between them.' This point was underlined just before Debussy signed off, 'I'll be back in Paris about 10 September, and I am afraid I'll be fed up with having to cope with more people than usual, so when you come to see me you'll make me forget my tiredness.'[10] The tone of this letter is one of familiarity, almost a conspiracy of two loners uniting against the crowd. Once back in Paris Debussy would be orchestrating *Pelléas et Mélisande* and building up to the first performance on 30 April 1902. Another letter from Debussy to Raoul, written exactly a month before this auspicious première, conveyed the same feeling of collusion. He informed Raoul that subscribers to his opera would soon be able to go to his publishers, Fromont, for the piano reduction of the score, but then asked him not to go into details about his financial difficulties ['de ne pas trop préciser mes embarras!']. He did not reveal here what those were, but the implication must be that Raoul knew. He then complained, 'You know how spiteful our fellow-beings can be and how they can make any excuse for false insinuations.'[11] One wonders what had made Raoul party to this knowledge. Talking in confidence about money worries is surely proof of a very close relationship, despite a difference in age of nearly twenty years. It was the PS to this letter which first revealed in writing Debussy's desire to be remembered to Raoul's mother, 'Mon meilleur souvenir à Madame votre mère'.[12] It is generally thought that he was first introduced to Emma in 1903 at the earliest, but it is strange that this addition to the letter was added so informally in spring 1902. If he were formally asking to be remembered to the mother of a pupil, surely this would be included in the main body of the letter.

A portrait of Emma

To the best of our knowledge, Emma had not yet shown any personal interest in Debussy. His opera was still to reach the stage. She already had a reputation for fostering relationships with successful artists, but Debussy had not yet achieved that status. Hélène de Tinan (Dolly) recorded her memories of Debussy in French[13] and in English,[14] and stated that Raoul had simply asked his mother if she wanted him to introduce her to Debussy at her house: 'Veux-tu que je t'amène Debussy?', an offer

---

[10] C. pp. 615–16.

[11] C. p. 616.

[12] March 1902, C. p. 641.

[13] CD copy of a recording of an interview in French with Hélène de Tinan and an unnamed female interviewer, untitled, unattributed, kindly given to the author by M. Philippe Lagourgue, Debussy's current executor, henceforth referred to as 'de Tinan, French interview'.

[14] British Library: *British Institute of Recorded Sound lecture series: Dolly Bardac – Memories of Debussy and his circle*, recorded 5 December 1972. British Library shelfmark T572. Henceforth referred to as 'Dolly Bardac, London interview'. Edited version published in *Recorded Sound*, 50/51, April–July 1973, pp. 158–61, 163. Also, typewritten notes in French, 'Causerie faite par Madame de Tinan à la Discothèque de Londres, Dec. 1972', Centre de Documentation Claude Debussy, RESE 08.07.(1).

she accepted. With many well-known personalities, it becomes difficult to distinguish between fact and fiction as people magnify their true relationship with them after their death. The respected American pianist and teacher Maurice Dumesnil wrote a biography of Debussy where, both in preparatory notes[15] and in the book itself, he claimed that he heard from Emma's own lips that she first met Debussy at a musical evening. There she said to the composer, 'At the hour of my death, Monsieur, I want to hear the slow movement of your string quartet.'[16]

As a wealthy society lady Emma had money to dispense to charity, and in the second half of 1902 and in 1903 her name appeared several times in *Le Figaro* and other papers as a sponsor of the Mimi Pinson school. This was an organisation set up in the wake of Charpentier's opera *Louise*, which first provided free tickets to the opera then became a free school of music and dance, a *Conservatoire populaire* for working women. It was this year, 1903, when matters began to change both for Emma and for Debussy.

A portrait of Emma painted by Léon Bonnat in 1903 hangs in the Musée Claude Debussy at Saint-Germain-en-Laye. Her head is shown in profile, so she is staring away from the observer, facing to our left. This accentuates her strong, determined impression, her full lips, her skin fair beneath a head of reddish curly hair. Here is no shrinking violet. Being a view only from the shoulders up, it gives us no clue to her height, but from photos taken with Debussy it can be seen that Emma was petite, her head only just reaching above his shoulder. This may be why she had a penchant for large hats. Emma's daughter Dolly was later to say in an interview in English, 'No biographer has ever paid enough attention to my mother's personality and appearance. She was small and pretty with auburn hair and topaz-coloured eyes. What is more, she had an incomparable charm, to which nobody could remain insensible, even during the last years of her life.'[17]

Pasteur Vallery-Radot, who published a volume of letters from Debussy to Emma, did make an attempt to fill this gap in his preface, where he extolled both Emma's character and her looks in poetic language. She had a natural charisma, he said, typical of certain society ladies of the period. All who met her were seduced by her gentle charm. Her pure face with its sweet expression was as if caressed by the shade of her red-blonde hair, her glowing brown eyes conveyed 'every nuance of her tender feelings, as Claude used to say'. Her voice was warm, inviting. Her singing was enchanting. She had an exquisite way of inclining her head and smiling and seemed to be murmuring into your ear, 'How could you not love me?' She dressed simply yet elegantly. She liked to pin a bunch of Parma violets above her heart, their perfume blending discreetly with the stronger one permeating the air around her. Everything about her, her gestures, her words, was harmonious.[18]

---

[15] Bentley Historical Library, University of Michigan, Evangeline Marie Lehman and Maurice Dumesnil papers 1916–1974, box no.1.

[16] M. Dumesnil, *Claude Debussy, Master of Dreams*, New York, 1940, p. 235.

[17] Dolly Bardac, London interview.

[18] Pasteur Vallery-Radot, *Lettres de Claude Debussy à sa femme Emma*, Paris, 1957, pp. 9–10.

7. Emma Bardac. Portrait by Léon Bonnat, 1903. © Saint-Germain-en-Laye, maison natale Claude-Debussy

Marcel Dietschy summed up others' descriptions of Emma, showing her to be quite a *femme fatale*. She was petite, stylish, youthful in her appearance, open to all emotions, simple, forthright, yet persuasive, and exuding charm which won over all types of people. She could not have been more feminine. She turned many heads but was only interested in men who were out of the ordinary. Initially she was reserved because she realised she was impulsive. With one glance she could make clear her sympathy or her antipathy.[19] Interestingly, the following paragraph in French – which listed more qualities, such as 'cultivated, intelligent, a fine musician' – included the word *Sémite*, but the English translation omitted this adjective, saying simply, 'She had her feet on the ground, but she knew how to lose herself in a dream.'[20]

Deterioration of Debussy's relationship with Lilly

Compare these descriptions with a verbal portrait of Debussy left by his first wife Lilly, quoted beneath a telling photograph of her and her husband taken in 1902. Neither is looking at the other. Debussy is looking downwards, bored, his chin cupped in his hand. Lilly is focused more intently on something below the line of view in the photograph, neatly dressed, leaning slightly against Debussy. Following a detailed description of his appearance, Lilly added, 'His character, very generous, spontaneous, frank. His imagination was lively even though he spoke little. Very impenetrable, deep down he was sad by nature. He would have sudden bouts of jollity which lasted only a brief time. More sensual than passionate, quite sentimental, he was literally obsessed by music.'[21] Debussy himself recognised the deleterious effects of this obsession on his relationship with Lilly and later with Emma. He would return to this problem in his writings for the press and in correspondence.

In 1903, as a result of the success of his opera, Debussy was made a Chevalier de la Légion d'Honneur, a decoration he claimed to have accepted only to make his parents happy. Whatever his attitude, he was now famous and sought after, yet this did not bring him riches. He still lived in straitened circumstances with Lilly, who in May went ahead of him to her parental village of Bichain to make ready a small house they were going to rent for three months,[22] so they corresponded with each other frequently until he arrived there in July. Nothing from the news he related to her would indicate anything untoward in their relationship. Paris was unbearable without her, he complained. He was sleeping badly.[23] He grumbled about his work, in particular the effort of composing the *Rapsodie pour saxophone* for Elise Hall. 'It's too desolate

---

[19] M. Dietschy, *La passion de Claude Debussy*, p. 166.

[20] M. Dietschy, *A Portait of Claude Debussy*, p. 130.

[21] 'Au moral, très donnant, spontané, franc. Son imagination était vive bien qu'il parlât peu. Très fermé le fond de son caractère était triste. Il avait soudainement quelques accès de gaieté qui duraient peu. Plus voluptueux que passionné, assez sentimental, il était littéralement obsédé par la musique.' A. Gauthier, *Debussy. Documents iconographiques*, Paris, 1952, Plate 67.

[22] C. p. 733.

[23] C. p. 737.

8. Claude Debussy with Rosalie Texier, his first wife, 1902.
World History Archive/Alamy Stock Photo

here,' he said, quoting from his opera.[24] By the time he arrived in Bichain on 10 July one would expect a letter addressed to André Messager to be full of joy at rejoining his wife. On the contrary.

> Since my last letter I've had an awful time. My poor little Lilly is still suffering. And here we are in the countryside where I don't dare expect too much, but at least some quiet relief. Life is sad, dear old Messager. There are times when I think God is not very nice to us, he puts so many hidden obstacles in our way to trip us up however hard we try to be heroic.[25]

What were these obstacles that were so disruptive to his state of mind? André Messager had shared much of Debussy's anxiety and eventual relief throughout the process of persuading Albert Carré to mount his opera at the Opéra-Comique and had conducted its first season from 30 April 1902 onwards. In May 1903 Debussy dedicated to Messager a copy of his *Ariettes oubliées*. These had been dedicated originally, as noted earlier, to Mme Vasnier, then revised and published in 1903 with a dedication to Mary Garden, his Mélisande, who had been having an affair with Messager, and who also claimed in her autobiography that Debussy had declared his love for her. But in June Emma received a personal dedication of the *Ariettes oubliées*: This read: 'à Madame S. Bardac, dont la sympathie musicale m'est précieuse – infiniment.

---

[24] C. p. 739 (*'Il fait trop triste ici.' Pelléas et Mélisande*, Act II, scene 2).
[25] C. p. 749.

Claude Debussy. Juin 1903.'[26] What had been happening whilst Lilly was in Bichain? Had he and Emma been singing these songs together? What did the word 'infinitely' imply? That the dedication was heartfelt is beyond doubt.

One of the obstacles to Debussy's happiness must have been a large question mark over his feelings for Lilly now that he was becoming closer to someone more in tune, in all senses of the word, with his music and his nature. Another indication of his restless state is in two letters to Pierre Louÿs, written on 17 and 19 June. What was once a close friendship and collaboration had now become strained. Louÿs was keeping his distance despite Debussy's exhortations to meet him.

> My situation as a young married man could not and should not change anything in our relationship. You have been far too close a friend for anyone, even my wife, to think of affecting that. I can even assure you that she feels as close a friendship with you as I do,[27]

wrote Debussy, who consequently removed his dedication to Louÿs of 'La soirée dans Grenade', the second of the *Estampes*, before it was published.

Raoul introduces Debussy to Emma

Meanwhile Raoul kept Debussy in constant touch with his movements, sending him a postcard in July 1903 from an attractive hotel at Martin-Église near Dieppe in Normandy, where he had gone to work and get some fresh air.[28] A month later he was writing from Baden in Switzerland. This was not his choice. He had had only one hour to pack his things in Martin-Église on the orders of his father, Sigismond, and had travelled back to Paris to be told he was going to Greece and Turkey with one of his cousins. He had had to stop off in Baden to say goodbye to his mother, who was staying in the Grand Hotel there, then he would be spending three days in Venice. The Grand Hotel in Baden was in stark contrast to Debussy's tiny country cottage, which Lilly was 'doing up', in Bichain. The question is: had Raoul been invited to Bichain or was he intending to visit Debussy there, for his next sentence read: 'Adieu Bichain! Ou plutôt au revoir, à l'année prochaine –',[29] 'See you next year'. He promised to send further postcards during his travels, which would last until the end of October, sent his best wishes to Debussy and his wife and ended by passing on his mother's 'amitiés attristées' to both Debussy and Lilly – '*regretful* best wishes' (my italics). This was almost a coded message. What was Emma regretting? Surely her absence from the composer.

Debussy's reply to Raoul's news was sympathetic. It was obvious his father did not understand what appealed to his son about Martin-Église, and Debussy could not really see how Raoul was going to adapt to this role of 'Globe-Trotter' in view of his 'charmante indolence', that characteristic laid-back attitude for which Raoul

---

[26] 'To Madame Bardac, whose musical sympathy is precious to me – infinitely.' BnF Musique, Rés.Vma.285.

[27] C. pp. 743–4.

[28] C. p. 755.

[29] C. p. 770.

was well known. He did not omit to tell Raoul to assure his mother of his 'profond dévouement', his deep devotion. 'Your very charming mother must surely be alarmed by so many happenings.'[30]

Postcards from Raoul to Debussy arrived from Venice, then Šibenik and Manastirine in Dalmatia. Debussy, in Bichain, began composing *La mer*, fully aware of the irony of conjuring up the sound of the sea in an environment so far from the coast. He may well have been inspired by reading a short story by Camille Mauclair entitled *Mer belle aux Îles Sanguinaires*, originally published in 1893, thus obviating the need to be by the genuine sea, which years later (in 1914) he said 'paralysed his creative faculties'. 'I have never been able to write a single page of music under the direct and immediate influence of this enormous blue sphinx.'[31] Indeed, originally he gave Mauclair's title to the first piece of the triptych.[32] He was also correcting the orchestral score of *Pelléas et Mélisande* and he completed the three *Estampes* for piano, 'Pagodes', 'La Soirée dans Grenade' and 'Jardins sous la pluie'. Many years later, Vallery-Radot visited Bichain where he saw the little house Debussy rented for two hundred francs a year, and asked a local farmer about him. 'Monsieur Debussy seemed a bit strange to me,' was the reply. 'I used to see him come out of his house, walk along the road then suddenly rush back to sit down at the piano … One day, he told me after playing something or other: It's the rain on the window panes which inspired that.'[33]

Soon after their return to Paris on 1 October 1903, we are told that Raoul invited Debussy and Lilly to dinner with his mother.[34] Some say this was the first meeting of Emma and Debussy and that Raoul felt guilty about it later, but in view of the clues mentioned earlier, sending her regards via her son, dedicating songs to her four months earlier, he must have known her before this. Emma's daughter Hélène (Dolly) told her own daughters that Raoul already knew Debussy through his work with him and used to take him to the Bardac home in the rue de Berri alone. He later introduced Debussy's wife Lilly to Madame Bardac at a concert.[35]

In November, Debussy dedicated to Emma a copy of the piano pieces he had been working on in Bichain, the *Estampes*. This copy bears corrections and reads: 'For Madame S. Bardac and regarding an inkwell … her very devoted Claude Debussy. November 03.'[36] It would appear that Emma had given Debussy a gift which would be close at hand to the composer whilst he was working.

---

[30] C. p. 772.

[31] F. Lesure, 'Une interview romaine de Debussy, février 1914', *Cahiers Debussy*, no.11, 1987.

[32] C. Mauclair, 'Mer belle aux Iles Sanguinaires', *L'Echo de Paris littéraire illustré*, 26 February 1893; M. Rolf, 'Mauclair and Debussy: The decade from "Mer belle aux Iles Sanguinaires" to La Mer', *Cahiers Debussy* no.11, 1987.

[33] Pasteur Vallery-Radot, *Lettres de Claude Debussy à sa femme Emma*, p. 25.

[34] M. Dietschy, *La Passion de Claude Debussy*, p. 166.

[35] 'Raoul travaillait déjà avec lui et l'amena rue de Berri seul. Puis dans un concert présenta la femme de Claude (Lili Texier) à Madame Bardac.' Hélène de Tinan, Carnet rouge, Centre de Documentation Claude Debussy, RESE 08.01.

[36] 'Pour Madame S. Bardac et à propos d'un encrier … son très dévoué Claude Debussy. Novembre 03', BnF Musique, Rés. Vma-290.

The relationship deepens

Emma Bardac and Claude Debussy were both now forty-one years old. This cultivated lady was the antithesis of Lilly, the dressmaker's model, but the two women got on well together, Emma always providing a welcome for Debussy's wife.[37] Yet it is obvious that Debussy could not resist Emma. That is not to say he did not try. It was galling for Lilly that 'Claude stopped loving her in spite of himself and not without remorse'.[38] In the summer of 1902 Debussy had written to Lilly from London mentioning her imperious voice. Robert Godet, who knew both the composer and Lilly well, remarked that 'the voice of his wife (he was singularly sensitive to the sound of a voice) became detestable to the point of chilling the blood in his veins'.[39] Emma's more musical voice must have been the complete antidote.

Although tempted, Debussy did not leave Lilly straight away. Henry Prunières expressed his dilemma in very partisan language:

> When Debussy used to leave Mme Bardac's salon to return to Lilly, who was silent and sulking, mistrustful of him and ready to turn on him in her jealousy and show that passionate and violent side of her nature typical of the common woman she had remained, he realised the huge gulf which separated them. He hesitated for a long time. Many times he left then returned, until the day when he decided to leave once and for all, his marriage in tatters ... there is no doubt that Debussy suffered cruelly himself, even though he was the cause of suffering.[40]

Emma was still pursuing her social life and was recognised by the press amongst various counts and countesses on 23 April 1904 at a concert organised by Adela Maddison at the Salle Hoche in Paris.[41] This concert was also mentioned in an entry in the diary of Marguerite de Saint-Marceaux, who said Adela Maddison 'played and had played by Enesco and Viñes a pot-pourri of works by her, Debussy and Fauré'.[42]

In May 1904 Debussy dedicated to 'Mme S. Bardac' the *Trois Chansons de France*, two songs with texts by Charles d'Orléans, 'Le temps a laissé son manteau' and 'Pour ce que Plaisance est morte', and one by Tristan Lhermite, 'Auprès de cette grotte sombre'. In comparison with Fauré's song cycle *La bonne chanson*, the passion here is far more contained. There is an acute contrast of joy and sadness which mingle both in the words and the music. The first, subtitled 'Rondel', expresses joyful optimism for winter has shed its cloak of wind, cold and rain and donned an embroidered garment of radiant sunshine. Animals and birds sing and cry out. Silver and gold droplets radiate from rivers, fountains and streams. The accompaniment depicts freshly flowing, sparkling water. We move from light to

---

[37] Pasteur Vallery-Radot, *Tel était Claude Debussy*, Paris, 1958, pp. 65–6.
[38] G. and D.-E. Inghelbrecht, *Claude Debussy*, Paris, 1953, p. 182.
[39] Inghelbrecht, *Claude Debussy*, p. 182.
[40] Inghelbrecht, *Claude Debussy*, p. 183.
[41] *La Presse*, 25 April 1904.
[42] M. de Saint-Marceaux, *Journal 1894–1927*, p. 341.

dark in the second song, its title shortened to 'La grotte'. Water disturbs gravel and comes to rest in a dark cave. Light struggles against shade. Narcissus died in this pond. The shadow of a vermilion flower amongst bending reeds brings a suggestion of colour to the ending. The initial mood is sombre and melancholy, intensified by the accompanying piano ostinato motif as the pebbles scrape beneath the water. In fact it is similar to that which Debussy employed five years later in his sixth piano prelude, 'Des pas sur la neige', published in 1910, where footsteps crunch in snow. The song would recur in 1910 as one of three comprising 'Le promenoir des deux amants', also dedicated to Emma. The grave atmosphere and insistent rhythm were etched in his mind. How contrary, however, is the modulation from minor to major at the point where waves rest in the pond where Narcissus died. Here death is no tragedy, but instead there is a sense of release from a burden. Just as puzzling is the third song, another 'Rondel'. What a strange verse to dedicate to Emma at a time when he was supposedly rapturously in love. 'Because Plaisance [Pleasure] is dead I am dressed in black this May. It is a great pity to see my heart so unhappy.' Yet the accompaniment to these words flows gently, ironically changing from minor to major at 'Ce may, suis vestu de noir', 'This May I am clothed in black', a phrase occurring twice. The melody here is charming, chanson-like. It could belong to a captivating song in a nightclub in the sweet melancholic style of Paul Delmet, such as those Debussy would have heard at Le Chat Noir in Montmartre. The darkness of the sentiment, the lightness of the piano part, even as it dies away at the end with a reminder of that melody, bittersweet and nostalgic, are indicative, perhaps, of the emotional confusion he was experiencing.

June 1904: Emma's special date

June 1904 proved to be the decisive month for the doubly adulterous relationship. Emma's unrestrained approach to Debussy confirmed that she was not the reticent type. On 6 June he wrote her a message demonstrating that she was just as capable as he, perhaps even more so, when it came to cementing their liaison, for he acknowledged flowers she had sent him. His thank you, sent by that most Parisian of means, the *télégramme pneumatique*,[43] to her home address, 52 rue Bassano, was ecstatic:

> How kind ... and how good they smell! – But most of all I have been made so happy by your thought. It has gone straight to my heart and settled there, and because of that you are unforgettable and adorable ...
> Pardon me for kissing all these flowers as if they were a living mouth; is it crazy? Whatever happens, you can't begrudge it me – no more than the touch of the breeze, anyway.[44]

---

[43] A network of pneumatic tubes conveying cylinders filled with telegrams and letters.
[44] C. pp. 844–5.

The flowers were received and this note of gratitude sent on 6 June. The fervour expressed in the image of kissing flowers as if they were her mouth surely indicates that they were an acknowledgement of a passionate encounter prior to 6 June. That would be despite the fact that Lilly had not yet parted for Bichain.[45]

Without a specific date in June was another card to Emma, a visiting card with the message:

Oui ... ! Oui! Oui!
        (le chœur)
même pour le mauvais dîner
Votre ... [46]

The three times 'Yes' is a quotation from Act IV scene 4 of *Pelléas et Mélisande*, the passionate climax when the couple meeting clandestinely realise that they are being spied on by Mélisande's husband, Pelléas's step-brother, Golaud. 'Your mouth, your mouth!' cries Pelléas embracing her. 'Yes! Yes! Yes!' cries Mélisande falling into his arms. This card has been dated to June 1904 because Debussy was not yet addressing Emma with the familiar *tu*, but using the formal form of 'your', *votre*. The following year, 1905, and in 1907 Debussy was to dedicate snatches of music to Emma for '*Sa fête*' on 4 June (perhaps that for 1906 did not survive). Since her actual birthday was not until 10 July this cannot mean that they were birthday gifts, but rather in celebration of some other momentous event on 4 June, unnamed, but cementing their relationship.

On 9 June, Debussy sent another missive, a card which began with a play on Verlaine's words 'Il pleure dans mon coeur/Comme il pleut sur la ville', set to music by Debussy in the second of his *Ariettes oubliées*, showing that they were still fresh in his mind, and that he knew Emma would recognise the reference. He wrote, 'Il pleut fortement sur la ville' ('the rain is falling heavily on the town'). He continued, (using the formal '*vous*'):

Would you be kind enough to grant me a few moments this afternoon? – I would like so much to see you for once 'all alone', without counterpoint or development – If you would care to come here I would be overjoyed, but you must do what you please, so we'll meet wherever you would like.
This is written not from a madman, but out of sheer desire mixed with some anxiety![47]

Printemps, 'Spring', was the name of a symphonic suite for orchestra, piano and chorus which Debussy had composed whilst at the Villa Medici in Rome in 1887. The 1904 piano transcription for four hands bears the dedication, 'This copy belongs solely to Madame Bardac. 9 June 1904, a day when it was raining so hard that one

---

[45] On 22 June he wrote to Louis Laloy that 'we' – i.e. he and Lilly – were going there soon. C. p. 849.

[46] 'Yes! Yes! Yes! (Chorus) Even for the bad dinner'. C. p. 850.

[47] C. p. 845.

lost all hope of Spring, and yet … it was there. Claude Debussy.'[48] His request for 'a few moments … all alone' must have been granted.

Even more famous today is the piano composition *L'isle joyeuse*. This was originally inspired by Watteau's painting, *L'embarquement pour Cythère*. How revealing is the dedication of the first known sketch of this work, bars 117–144, over which Debussy wrote, 'These bars belong to Madame Bardac, p.m. – who dictated them to me one Tuesday in June 1904. With the passionate gratitude of her Claude Debussy.'[49] The abbreviation *p.m.* is an early use of the term he sometimes wrote as *a.l.p.m.* It stands for *petite mienne*, or *à la petite Mienne* ('my own little one' or 'to my own little one'). This endearment had its source in a poem by Jules Laforgue, *Ô geraniums diaphanes*: '*Ô ma petite mienne, ô ma quotidienne*' and recurred in Debussy's dedications to Emma.

Spring was mentioned again in one of the last known letters that Debussy wrote to Pierre Louÿs. Debussy was missing his friend, but now the relationship had definitely cooled. The letter of 12 June 1904 began: 'I didn't reply to your two letters straight away because the first hurt me too much and the second made me laugh too much …' They must have been discussing their friendship, which Debussy agreed was:

> absurd, dreamlike (*chimérique*), what's more, incomprehensible. We're not even dead, which would at least be an excuse. But I do have a chronic need to see you, made worse by the little effort we are making to satisfy it. I would never ask you to climb the five floors to my flat. I get too out of breath every day doing that, but in future, when you think you might like to see me, give me a day, a time, and I will arrive, as bright as a spring morning (minus its freshness as I've just found some white hairs).[50]

White hairs or not, he was experiencing a freshness of emotion which led him to leave Paris for a few days with Emma and it becomes clear from Debussy's later recollections that they went to Arcachon, that resort with which both were familiar from their youth. Obviously this must have been Emma's choice of destination and at her expense. It was she who still had significant contact with the town through her uncle. It is likely that the couple stayed in the villa 'Laure-Raoul', the smallest of Osiris's seven villas there, as this would be the one most likely not to have been already let out for the summer.[51] It was next door to the bigger one bearing the name 'Emma' (for the time being). They certainly would not have gone to a hotel or guest house, or paid rent for a villa, as local newspapers such as *L'Avenir d'Arcachon* and *Arcachon-journal* used to print lists each week of the names of significant visitors to the town and the residence they were staying in. Towards the end of his

---

[48] 'Cet exemplaire appartient uniquement à Madame Bardac. 9 Juin 1904, jour où il pleuvait à perdre l'espoir de tout[e] espèce de Printemps, et pourtant … il était là. Claude Debussy.' BnF Musique, Rés. Vma 284.

[49] 'Les mesures ci-jointes appartiennent à Madame Bardac – p.m.- qui me les dicta un mardi de juin 1904. La reconnaissance passionnée de son Claude Debussy.' F. Lesure, *Claude Debussy*, p. 260.

[50] C. p. 846.

[51] Ardoin Saint Amand, *Osiris*, pp. 44–5.

life Debussy would return to Arcachon with Emma and from there he wrote to his friend Robert Godet mentioning the fact that he and Emma had stayed there some twelve years earlier. 'Was I already planning my divorce?' he wondered.[52]

After returning to Paris, Emma surely attended a concert on 16 June organised by her teacher and friend Madame Colonne, for Debussy was accompanying his *Ariettes oubliées* and the first performance of the first set of *Fêtes galantes*, originally composed in 1891–2, in a Debussy–Gustave Charpentier soirée.[53] Between the works of these two composers were inserted two songs by Emma's son, Raoul Bardac.[54]

Very soon after this Debussy was invited to stay with his composer friend Raymond Bonheur at Saint-Rémy-lès-Chevreuse. On 19 June Debussy sent Durand, his publisher, a postcard of the Château de Dampierre with apologies for not having completed his '*Danses*' on time, the *Danse sacrée* and *Danse profane* for chromatic harp and string orchestra, commissioned by the firm Pleyel.[55] Although parted from Emma, she was obviously still uppermost in his mind, for he sent postcards to her on 19 and 20 June, the first consisting simply of a stave with a rush of notes pouring down it, and the second saying cryptically, 'Bonjour Madame Bardac?'[56] That musical quotation was the first one and a half bars of the song 'Le Faune' from the second set of *Fêtes galantes*, the second in the cycle which would soon be submitted to Durand for publication. It is a neat coincidence that these notes bring to mind another descending run, played by the harp in Act II scene 1 of his opera, at the point where Mélisande, playing by the pool with the ring her husband Golaud had given her, throws it into the air and lets it drop into the water, thus symbolically breaking off all former amorous bonds. Verlaine's words in the first verse of '*Le faune*' sinisterly predict 'a bad outcome to these serene moments'[57], so not expressing unalloyed joy.

Only two days after his second postcard, on 22 June, Debussy wrote a dedication in the printed copy of a work to Emma's son Raoul, addressing him with the familiar name Rara, *D'un cahier d'esquisses*: 'à Rara. 22 June/04. (Il fait trop chaud pour en dire plus long). Claude Debussy'.[58] This work was published first in a magazine, *Paris illustré*, at the beginning of 1904, then later the same year by Schott frères in Brussels. Debussy had been envisaging a triptych of works for piano and it is likely that *D'un cahier d'esquisses* would have been the middle piece of three. Another was *L'isle joyeuse*, two works so closely associated with Emma and her son. The links are not simply in the dedications, but there are many marked similarities between them in key, structure, rhythm and melody. Because *D'un cahier d'esquisses* was published separately and not by Durand, the triptych did not materialise, but the third piece would have been another that Debussy was working on, the in turn energetic and lyrical *Masques*. Again there are similarities between this and *L'isle joyeuse* in

---

[52] C. p. 2033.
[53] Review in *Le Ménestrel*, 26 June 1904.
[54] Lesure, *Claude Debussy*, p. 261.
[55] C. p. 847.
[56] C. p. 848.
[57] 'Présageant sans doute une suite/Mauvaise à ces instants sereins'.
[58] 'It's too hot to say more', Pierpont Morgan Library, New York, accession no.PMC949.

rhythm and structure.[59] One would assume, given the association of masks with the Commedia dell'arte and Debussy's amorous state of mind, that all would be light-hearted and full of joy, but there are certainly dark undertones to *Masques*. Marguerite Long, who worked on Debussy's piano works with the composer himself in his later years, described this piece as giving a special insight, 'une sorte de transparent', into him. He was masking deep feelings with irony, just as in that 'Rondel' in the *Trois Chansons de France* and 'Le faune' discussed above. When Emma discovered a note in Debussy's hand after his death she shared it immediately with Long. 'It's not *Comédie Italienne*! But the tragic expression of existence'.[60] Another source of inspiration for the title *Masques* could have been the second line of Verlaine's poem 'Clair de lune', third of Debussy's first series of *Fêtes galantes*, published in 1903, 'Que vont charmant masques et bergamasques'. One is struck by the irony that Verlaine was also the poet of the cycle *La bonne chanson*, so inspirational to the impassioned Fauré twelve years earlier.

Before the end of the month Raoul received a dedication on a copy of the piano duet reduction of *Printemps*, just published by Durand, 'à Rara ... , son vieux dévoué. Claude Debussy, juin 04'.[61] His 'old faithful friend' – this relationship was certainly close. Now both Emma and her son possessed personal copies of this work. June 1904 was a month full of emotion stirring in Debussy, but it is unsurprising that he was aware of disturbing, tragic undercurrents, for life was becoming very complicated.

Besides dedicating *D'un cahier d'esquisses* to Raoul on 22 June, Debussy wrote to Louis Laloy, whom he had known since 1902, wondering why he had not heard from him and saying he would like him to visit him and Lilly very soon as they were about to leave for Bichain.[62] This wish would be fulfilled on 2 July when Laloy dined with the Debussys, their sole guest, and made light-hearted comments in his memoirs on their jokes about their dinner plates: cheap pottery heated up in the oven to make the surface crackle to resemble genuine artistic stoneware (a trick passed on from his father's china shop?). This surely is another symbolic indication of the difference in financial position between Debussy and Emma Bardac, whose house was full of beautiful, original artistic creations. Emma would never have had to resort to such a ploy.

On 23 June 1904 the second set of *Fêtes galantes* was performed for the first time exactly a week after the first set at another 'jeudi musical' (musical Thursday) organised by Madame Colonne. Grouping his works in sets of three was becoming significant. Like the *Trois Chansons de France*, these songs would soon be dedicated to Emma and comprised three settings of Verlaine, 'Les ingénus', 'Le faune' and 'Colloque sentimental'. Debussy had already quoted the descending opening bar of 'Le faune' to Emma on his postcard from Saint-Rémy-lès-Chevreuse. Once again, it cannot be said that either the words or the music convey unalloyed happiness.

---

[59] For detail on the relationship of these three pieces see R. Howat, *The Art of French Piano Music*, New Haven and London, 2009, pp. 200–2 and 'En route for L'isle joyeuse: the restoration of a tryptich,' *Cahiers Debussy*, no.19, Centre de Documentation Claude Debussy, 1995, pp. 37–52.

[60] M. Long, *Au Piano avec Debussy*, Paris, 1960, p. 148.

[61] Pierpont Morgan Library, New York, accession no.PMC 1042.

[62] C. p. 849.

The ingenuous, naïve girls and foolish young men of the first song are not flirting in springtime but on 'an equivocal autumn evening'. Witnesses to the taunting faun of the second song, that mythical half-human, half-goat figure, are 'melancholy pilgrims'. The sentimental conversation of the third song is between two spectres walking in a park at night evoking the past. Contrary to Debussy's burgeoning relationship with Emma, the 'extase ancienne' of these ghosts is over. 'Do you still see my soul in your dreams?' 'No'. Depressingly hope has fled, vanquished, into the black sky. Irony, introspection, the music conveys both of these.

July 1904: double adultery; *L'isle joyeuse*

By July Debussy was addressing Emma with the familiar '*tu*', rather than '*vous*'. Now she received an even larger package from him, the corrected proofs of *Pelléas*, which bore the message, 'To Mme Bardac, these 409 pages of varying timbres which hardly deserve the shadow cast by your little hand over this large book.'[63] Lilly had stood by his side as he worked on this masterpiece, protectively maintaining the conditions necessary for concentration. Now another woman was receiving the reward.

Was Emma's husband away or at another address for Debussy to be able to send post so frequently and so openly to 52 rue de Bassano? This address was one of several which occur in lists of societies to which Sigismond Bardac belonged. The address of the Bardac bank was 43 rue de Provence, but residential addresses shown in various documents were 3 rue du Colisée, 1 avenue Montaigne, 37 rue des Mathurins and 30 rue de Berri. In 1904 it was the rue de Bassano address which was given in the *Annuaire des grands cercles* and for his membership of the *Société des amis du Louvre*. This was some contrast to Debussy's single home up all those stairs on the fifth floor of 58 rue Cardinet. Emma does not seem to have had any qualms about this evident difference in financial and material circumstances.

Emma's forty-second birthday was on 10 July; Debussy's was still to come on 22 August. On 16 July, Debussy wrote to Lilly – in Bichain. He had sent her there alone the day before. As Laloy wrote, 'There was nothing to foretell the storm to come'.[64] Knowing what we do now, to read this letter to Lilly in response to her letting him know that she had arrived safely is to wonder at the duplicity of the man, the cruel deception of his wife, but at the same time, the conscience that must have been pricking him. 'Don't think I felt any pleasure in putting you onto the train so unemotionally. It was hard for me! But for reasons I will tell you later, it was necessary.' He went on to make feeble excuses about needing to work on new ideas for composition, essential in order to make money to keep her.

> If I have not always been nice to you, at least I need to be of use. In any case, you would not be able to bear an even lower standard of living than our present one, so I had to choose between two evils … God willing I have chosen the lesser of the two. In life we reach dangerous turning points, which for me are even more

---

[63] 'À Mme Bardac, ces 409 pages de timbres variés qui valent à peine l'ombre que fait ta petite main sur ce gros livre.' Lesure, *Claude Debussy*, p. 260.

[64] L. Laloy, *La Musique retrouvée*, Paris, 1928, p. 140.

complicated as I am both a man who makes Art (what sort of a job is that?) and your husband. Try to understand and above all, don't miss any opportunity for the laughter you enjoy so much.[65]

Three days later he responded to another letter from Lilly in which he referred to her 'long letter written in red ink'. 'You are a very spoilt little girl who doesn't want anyone to argue with her whims and fancies.' She must have quibbled with his definition of himself as both a 'man who makes Art and a husband'. He admitted that he found it difficult to explain exactly what he meant. This was obviously a topic which had occupied his mind for a long time. Here was the crux of his problems with long-term relationships. 'Don't you see, my poor love, an artist is altogether a detestable introvert and probably also a deplorable husband. So, turning the question round, a perfect husband often makes a pitiful artist. It's a vicious circle. Will you tell me then that in that case one shouldn't marry?'[66]

He had already understood this dichotomy in 1899 when he had suggested to Pierre Louÿs that his enduring relationship with music prevented him from marrying.[67] In 1903, when he was first becoming better acquainted with Emma Bardac, Debussy had written an article in the journal *Gil Blas* which showed that he was deliberating on the awful dilemma of the artist whose involvement with his art is so intense that it is impossible for him to be objective about it. As a critic, however hard one aims for objectivity, this is very difficult to achieve. He ended the paragraph,

> I love music too much to speak about it in any way other than with passion … those passionate about art are hopelessly in love with it, and besides, you simply don't know to what extent music is a woman. This probably explains the frequent chastity of men of genius.[68]

Lilly's comment that he was obsessed with music was confirmed here. No wonder Debussy was suffering mental anguish over his relationships with both women – Lilly with her grating voice, Emma who epitomised pure music when she sang so beguilingly and who was now behaving like a true siren, enticing the wavering soul towards her, rewarding him with flowers, admiration, true love. Irresistible as she was, he still needed time and space to lose himself in that mysterious process of composition to earn the money to live. This, of course, also included having to meet deadlines, to appear in public, to perform. This more mundane aspect of the musical life was a burden. Could there ever be a way out of it?

Debussy insisted to Lilly that he had sincerely thought he could bring her happiness by asking her to entrust her life to him, but so much anger had arisen between them that now he was suffering grave doubts. He passed on to small talk about the house in Bichain, still giving the impression he would join her there in patronising

---

[65] C. pp. 852–3.

[66] C. pp. 853–4.

[67] Chapter 3 p. 41.

[68] 'J'aime trop la musique pour en parler autrement qu'avec passion … les passionnés d'art étant d'irréductibles amoureux, et d'autre part, on ne saura jamais combien la musique est femme, ce qui explique peut-être la chasteté fréquente des hommes de génie.' *Gil Blas*, 28 June 1903.

terms: 'Try not to get bored waiting for me. You must be happy there. Hopefully your proud and independent little character will help you with that.' He promised to send her money at the end of the month and hoped *La mer* would 'let go of him' by 15 August. To top it all, shockingly, he signed the letter simply 'Debussy'! Not even Claude. No words could express his true feelings.[69]

A third letter, written on Sunday 24 July, again tried to justify his position:

> I still think my character rubbed yours up the wrong way, and you on your side did not respond to what I wanted from you out of a sort of pride which I don't blame you for, but which perhaps you shouldn't have shown in those circumstances? ... This current separation of our two lives will teach us more than any reasoning about what we mean to each other. Words cause pain because we always say more than we mean to ...[70]

As Debussy explained to Lilly, his friends Lucien Fontaine and Abel Desjardins had turned up on Saturday to see him and they had gone out together for the day. We learn from his next letter that on Sunday they had returned to drive Debussy to Bichain and take Lilly by surprise. From his letter of 28 July it seems she gave the two men a warmer reception than her husband: 'Abel and Lucien were thrilled at your welcome! I could have been jealous of the joy you showed on seeing them!'

They had an awful drive back that night in stormy weather, arriving home at one in the morning. There had clearly been no question of Debussy staying on. But Lilly took his comments on her attitude to Abel and Lucien the wrong way, thinking he was mocking her. She accused him of trying to hurt her on purpose. Once again he had to explain and excuse himself. He claimed he would try to visit her towards the end of the following week. On the back of his envelope Lilly wrote in red ink, 'Mauvais' ('Bad'). Something must have angered her further the next day, for on the envelope of the letter dated 24 July she wrote in red ink: '29 Juillet méchant' ('29 July horrid'). Debussy, on the same day as writing to Lilly, 28 July, also began a letter to Emma in a very different tone, a letter which he did not complete: 'Je t'écris ceci, petite Mienne adorée, la tête ...' ('I am writing to you my own adorable Little One, my head ...')[71]

Sometime in July Lilly found another missive obviously intended for Emma. It read:

> Prière pour dire avant d'aller se coucher.
> =
> Petite mienne qui êtes plus jolie que tout
> Petite mienne qui êtes meilleure que les fleurs.
>
> [Prayer to be said before going to bed,
> =
> My own Little One who is prettier than all things
> My own Little One who is better than flowers.][72]

---

[69] C. p. 854.
[70] C. p. 854.
[71] C. p. 855.
[72] C. p. 858.

Debussy did not go to see Lilly. Instead, without informing her, he departed with Emma to Jersey. Their destination was the Grand Hotel in Saint Helier, where they stayed from 31 July until 4 August. There the couple could relax to their hearts' content. There could have been no question of Debussy being able to afford such an escapade, especially to such lavish accommodation. He also had the benefit of having nearly finished *La mer* and now being able to enjoy the real thing in all its glory. Only one person was asked to connive in their secret and that was Jacques Durand, Debussy's publisher, for Debussy posted to him the corrected proofs of the piano piece *Masques* and of *Fêtes galantes* (second set). He had a special request regarding the latter: it had to contain the dedication 'Pour remercier le mois de Juin 1904', ('To thank the month of June 1904'), followed by the letters A.l.p.M, the coded message he was so determined to include as a term of endearment.[73] He implored Durand to keep his address a secret even from his family. Any post should be sent *poste restante* to Dieppe, where he would eventually pick it up.

However bad things might have been for Lilly, however severely Debussy's friends and acquaintances might have judged him, Durand must have been looking forward to the presumed advantages life with Emma would bring for Debussy, a 'respectable' bourgeois status so different to the casual life of a bohemian artist. On 4 July Debussy signed a contract giving him his first increase in earnings for the second series of *Fêtes galantes*. Instead of one hundred francs he now received two hundred francs per song. On 29 July a contract was signed for *Masques* and *L'isle joyeuse* for one thousand francs.[74]

Only a few days of bliss in Jersey, but they were productive musically for Debussy, who was finishing *L'isle joyeuse*. The energetic mood of the piece reflects the elation in his spirit, although in view of the fact that he had already written some bars to Emma's 'dictation' earlier in the year, this element of joy was already present. On 5 August they were briefly back in Paris, for Debussy told Durand he had called into the publisher's office that day, to find that he was still in his family house Bel Ébat (Avon, near Fontainebleau). He assured him that he was still finishing the copy of *L'isle joyeuse* and the piano transcription of his *Quartet* 'but it is not very fresh (the *island*) and I am making slow progress'.[75] The lack of freshness probably referred to the weather in Jersey, which was extremely hot, culminating in a violent thunderstorm on 4 August.[76]

---

[73] BnF Musique, Ms 17734.

[74] D. Herlin and V. Giroud, 'An Artist High and Low, or, Debussy and Money', in E. Antokoletz and M. Wheeldon, *Rethinking Debussy*, Oxford, 2011, p. 153.

[75] C. p. 860.

[76] D. E. Moore, *Debussy in Jersey*, http://www.litart.co.uk/jersey.htm (last accessed 2 August 2020).

5

August 1904 – August 1905: Pourville and Eastbourne

Pourville and Osiris's will

After the brief return to Paris the couple continued their 'elopement' to Pourville, two miles west of Dieppe where Debussy would be able to pick up his post. They arrived a few days before 11 August, the date of letters to Durand and to Lilly.

Why did they choose Pourville? Debussy did not want to reveal their address there to anyone. They may have stayed initially at the Grand Hôtel du Casino but then they moved on to the villa Mon Coin. Here, just as with Arcachon, there was a link with Emma's uncle, Osiris. On 17 September 1897, nineteen years after Emma's marriage to Sigismond and whilst 'residing at Arcachon in my Villa Alexandre Dumas',[1] Osiris had made a codicil to his will with additional executors, who remained the same in the next version in 1898. One of these was Sigismond Bardac, Emma's husband.

Sigismond was not only an executor. It is evident from the terms of the will that he had collaborated with Osiris in speculating in land in Pourville prior to 1896, which probably meant travelling there, perhaps with his wife Emma. At that time Osiris intended to bequeath to the town part of the land he owned together with 'MM Berger (of the Ottoman Bank), Naville and Bardac', under certain specific conditions. He wanted a church or Catholic chapel built there, which was to be given the name 'Léonie' or 'Léonie Osiris' in memory of his wife. The town could dispose of any leftover land as it pleased.[2]

Emma in 1904, with her husband being party to the terms of the will, might have had reason to believe that she would inherit some money, but the sum specified is not nearly as great as one might surmise. Her inheritance had already been affected, presumably because Osiris knew of her affair with Fremiet's son-in-law, Gabriel Fauré, through his dealings and friendship with Emmanuel Fremiet.

Osiris's initial 1896 and 1897 wills stipulated that his sister Laure and his niece Emma were to be buried in his tomb in Montmartre. They were each to choose ten items from his various residences. Emma's financial inheritance depended on whether her mother was still alive. When Laure died, a sum of eight hundred thousand francs was to be shared between Emma's children. Emma was to receive the interest on this, approximately twenty-four thousand francs a year. Whilst Laure was still alive, all Emma would receive was half the interest from a separate sum of

---

[1] Ardoin Saint Amand, *Osiris*, p. 55.
[2] Idem. p. 45.

one hundred thousand francs left to Raoul, about fifteen hundred francs a year at a typical rate of three per cent (the other half went to Sigismond). Raoul would keep the whole amount when he was twenty-five or married. Dolly was also to receive one hundred thousand francs when she reached majority (twenty-one) or married, but in her case she was to keep all the interest for herself.[3] Thus, after Osiris died, Emma's children would benefit considerably once they were of age or married, but Emma herself would receive only fifteen hundred francs annually until her mother's death. Laure did not die until 1915.

It should also be mentioned that Emma had a younger cousin who led a colourful life, Charlotte Lejeune, born in 1877, the granddaughter of her mother's and Osiris's younger sister Aimée. In 1896 Osiris believed she would be taking the veil, for he mentioned this in his first will. However, her career took her in an entirely different direction. Adopting the name Charlotte Lysès she became a well-known actress, was the lover of Lucien Guitry, then in 1907 became the wife of his famous actor son, Sacha Guitry, taking the lead in many of his plays. In 1896 Osiris's will specified that she was to receive one hundred thousand francs immediately, giving her an annual income of three thousand francs.

Dieppe in the latter part of the nineteenth century and beginning of the twentieth was a very fashionable resort for artists and musicians from France, England and beyond. Debussy was already familiar with Pourville, as there is evidence of his visits to the town since 1888 to visit the studio of Armand-Constant Mélicourt-Lefèbvre at the Bas-Fort-Blanc, an artist who exhibited at the Paris Salon between 1844 and 1876, and to see his friend Jacques-Émile Blanche who painted his portrait in 1902 and 1903.[4] Blanche related an anecdote concerning twenty-three-year-old Debussy when he was in love with Marie Vasnier. She and her husband were spending a holiday at Mélicourt's home. 'One night coming back late to Bas-Fort-Blanc ... we could distinguish in the shadows a rope ladder, Mme V. at the window and Debussy clambering up.'[5] Clearly Pourville already had romantic associations for Debussy. By the time he returned there in 1904, Blanche had moved to Offranville, about seven kilometres from Pourville.

The villa Mon Coin, a house to which they would return in later years, belonged at that time to Paul Milliet Monchicourt, a playwright and librettist.[6] Photographs show Debussy and Emma individually, each gazing with half smiles at the gently rolling coastal countryside, leaning on a corner of a wooden balcony. Emma stares

[3] Idem. p. 59.

[4] I am grateful to the Archives départementales in Rouen for providing me with a copy of C. Feron, 'Claude Debussy et Pourville-sur-Mer', *Connaissance de Dieppe et de sa région, no.69* (Archives départementales, Rouen cote ADSM RH 267/6). Blanche also painted a portrait of Marie Vasnier.

[5] J.-E. Blanche, *La Pêche aux souvenirs*, Paris, 1949, p. 224 and see Chapter 3 p. 41.

[6] He wrote the librettos for operas by Massenet, Bruneau and many others. Subsequently the villa was owned by Alexandre Hugot, followed by the family of Gaston Letourneur, a Rouen industrialist. The villa today is a reconstruction as it was so badly damaged during the Canadian landings at Pourville on 19 August 1942 that it had to be demolished. It was rebuilt in 1952. C. Feron, 'Claude Debussy et Pourville-sur-Mer', op.cit.

9. Debussy at Pourville, 1904

to the left, her face sheltered by a large-brimmed hat in the shepherdess style, with a wide ribbon around it tied in an elaborate bow beneath her chin. A pastoral idyll. Debussy shelters his eyes as he looks to the right, relaxed despite the smart bow tie and suit he is wearing. In another he looks to the left standing on the same spot, studying the horizon, cigarette in his left hand, more serious, contemplative.

However, from photographic evidence it can be seen that Debussy and Emma had not travelled alone to the seaside. Standing in the same corner of the same balcony we find young Dolly leaning on her grandmother Laure's shoulder. Other photographs show Dolly with a dog, or posing with flowers, sitting on a wall overlooking the sea or standing on a wooden terrace. On the back of the pictures is pencilled the date '1904'. In June of that year Dolly turned twelve years old. They stayed in Pourville until mid-October, so it is logical that Emma would have wanted her daughter there, too. Evidently that brief return to Paris after Jersey enabled her to fetch Dolly and her mother (and the dog!).

In Pourville Debussy continued to work despite amorous and other family distractions. On 11 August he wrote again to Durand to repeat his assurance that he was working on *L'isle joyeuse* and the *Quartet* and again swore him to silence about his precise whereabouts. If Durand needed to get in touch he was to do it '*poste restante*'. On the same day, 11 August 1904, he forced himself to write to Lilly in Bichain. Although he had made up his mind to tell her he was leaving her, nowhere did he give the true reason. In fact, he told a downright lie. Whilst admitting that he was in Dieppe for a few days, he said he was with, not Emma, but J.-E. Blanche,

10. Dolly and her grandmother Laure Moyse at Pourville, 1904

11. Dolly with flowers at Pourville, 1904

who, he said, was paying for him to go with him from there to London. He then explained that upon thinking objectively about their life together, he realised he had never made her happy. When angry she used to beg him to give her back her freedom. For some reason he had decided he should agree to this today. She was still young and pretty (words that would be interpreted by others as having an offensive significance) and should not be prevented from finding the true happiness that his presence was denying her. 'Nous ne sommes plus des enfants,' ('We are no longer children'), he wrote, knowing Lilly would recognise the reference to Golaud's rebukes in *Pelléas et Mélisande*. He expressed the invincible desire to be alone. His lies were almost as numerous as those of Mélisande. Their incompatibility made it impossible for him to work in Lilly's presence, he complained. He promised to try to provide for her material needs and exhorted her to think of the happy times in their relationship and take no notice of the opinions of others.[7]

Lilly returned to Paris at the beginning of September. Debussy remained with Emma in Pourville until October, apart from what seems to have been a flying visit home on 22 August to send some money to Lilly in Bichain, and again on 13 September when he actually saw her face to face. Writing the next day, he declared he had returned to Dieppe, 'tired, exhausted, at a loss for what to think or do'. At the same time, he was under pressure of work, being hassled for the completion of *Le Roi Lear*, incidental music for the play being produced by André Antoine upon which he had been collaborating with René Peter. He desperately needed peace and quiet. He even wished he could die. Emotional blackmail or truth? Whatever he did would cause pain to someone. 'Tu es jeune,' ('You are young') he reminded her, again paraphrasing Golaud.[8]

No wonder he wrote to André Messager on 19 September, 'My life the last few months has been peculiar and bizarre, more than anyone could ever have wished. I can't give you any details at the moment, it's too difficult. Much better would be to meet face to face over that excellent whisky we used to enjoy.' He complained about his inability to work as well as he would have wished and expressed nostalgia for the good old days when 'Claude Debussy worked so happily on *Pelléas*, for, between ourselves, I have not found him since – and this is just one of the things making me so sad, amongst many others.'[9]

Lilly's suicide attempt; vilification of Debussy and Emma

It is clear that Debussy's elopement with Emma had not brought unalloyed joy. So many questions were tormenting him. Not only was his marriage to Lilly clearly over in his mind, but now he was distracted and experiencing severe difficulties with composing. Debussy and Emma did not leave Pourville until mid-October and, when they did return to Paris, Debussy did not go back to Lilly, but moved alone to a new address, 10 avenue Alphand, furnishing it on credit. Work on *Le Roi Lear* was inter-

[7] C. p. 861.
[8] C. p. 864.
[9] C. p. 866.

rupted. André Antoine needed the music by 1 October and eventually used music by Edmond Missa for the delayed opening on 5 December 1904.[10] Nor did Debussy finish orchestrating the *Proses lyriques* for Édouard Colonne, and he had to excuse himself again to Durand for his tardiness correcting the piano transcription of his *Quartet*.

Echoing Debussy's thoughts on the conundrum of how to combine the necessarily solitary and self-seeking life of composer with the role of faithful husband, the conductor D.-E. Inghelbrecht commented in his biography of Debussy,

> By their very nature, artists, more than anyone else, demand from their wives that they devote their lives to them, participate in their difficulties, their success, share the darkness and the light, that they provide instinctive, subconscious support, so when they discover that they have been abandoned they feel more forsaken and more deeply distraught than others.[11]

Lilly's abandonment hurt her so cruelly that she threatened four times in letters to Debussy to commit suicide. On 13 October 1904 she shot herself in the stomach, but not fatally. Presumably in preparation for his divorce, Debussy scribbled notes in a little black notebook in which he stated, 'suicide attempt 13 Oct. after four letters announcing her intent. Nothing in the papers until 3 November.'[12] The press inevitably dwelt on the beauty of the jilted wife, whose despair, prior to shooting herself, had led her to try to starve herself to death.[13] Debussy recorded bitterly, 'Mme D. claimed she wanted to die of starvation. The maid, who did not leave her side, claims she devoured 4 egg yolks a day in tea.'[14] Lilly was taken to a clinic in the rue Blomet, where she was operated on by Doctor Abel Desjardins. This must have been at her request, for Debussy wrote another entry: 'When someone really wants to die they do not demand to be cared for in a home like the RB [rue Blomet].'[15] Rather pathetically, amongst all these comments was a very brief summary of some intentions for *Le Roi Lear*: 'Prélude', '3 Interludes', 'Le Sommeil de Lear', 'Le Roi Lear dans la lande', followed by some hastily sketched musical notes. Small wonder he made little progress on this project during his emotional distress.

Meanwhile, the scandal became the talk of musical and artistic circles. As Debussy's friend, the music critic Louis Laloy wrote, 'It gives such pleasure to cast judgement on one's neighbour, that many people could not resist doing so.' Needless to say, the main accusation was that Debussy was leaving Lilly for Emma simply for financial reasons, to free himself from his perpetual money worries.

> People took great pleasure in pitying the victim, blaming the unfaithful one, exaggerating the grievances of one, the wrong-doings of the other, pouring fat onto the fire. As it seemed Debussy would be freed from his financial woes through this event, people accused him cruelly of doing it in a calculated way, of selling himself.

---

[10] R. Orledge, *Debussy and the Theatre*, Cambridge, 1982, p. 249.
[11] G. and D.-E. Inghelbrecht, *Claude Debussy*, Paris, 1953, p. 182.
[12] BnF Musique, Rés. Vmf MS-53.
[13] *Le Temps*, 4 November 1904.
[14] BnF Musique, Rés. Vmf MS-53.
[15] Ibid.

Laloy insisted that Debussy did not stop caring about Lilly. 'He suffered cruelly when he left her, seeing her in despair.'[16]

Another biographer, Heinrich Strobel, emphasised the fact that Debussy seemed to have decided to leave Lilly long before actually doing so and suggested that it was Madame Bardac who was forcing him into this situation. Strobel claimed Lilly said that Emma had 'seized him by the throat' by offering him a luxurious lifestyle and that when Debussy visited Lilly in hospital he told her that she was still young and pretty, thus implying she should resort to prostitution.[17] He must have been aware of similar words in Debussy's letter to her of 11 August 1904. Dolly, in defence of her mother, made comments on the draft of Strobel's biography and one of her corrections read sternly, 'Debussy married Lilly in 1899 and did not know Madame Bardac until between 1903–1904. Debussy was not motivated to enter into this second marriage for financial reasons, but for true love which was proved constantly until the day he died.'[18]

In unpublished notes, Strobel also described Emma unflatteringly as being chubby (*potelée*), and being of very marked Jewish appearance (*en type sémite très accentué*). He remarked that Debussy's friends called her *la Mère Claude* or *la Vénus juive* and that, in fact, Debussy did not actually want to marry her, despite truly loving her.[19] Emma's Jewish background certainly contributed to negative comments from many about the relationship.

Debussy actually realised early on in his relationship with Emma the accusations others would be able to throw at him, saying Madame Bardac had 'the disadvantage', one dare say, of being rich – '… you can see what that makes me look like …'[20] Rumours abounded painting Debussy as a money-grubbing chancer. His first Mélisande, Mary Garden, had become a close friend of both him and Lilly and was a welcome visitor to their flat in the rue Cardinet. The drama of his desertion and Lilly's suicide attempt took up nearly ten pages of her autobiography. She was one of the first to visit Lilly in her hospital bed. Lilly told her that it was Debussy's father who had revealed that his son was in Dieppe living with Madame Bardac. Before shooting herself Lilly had written to Debussy, sending the letter by messenger in the care of his father. Debussy was therefore the first to arrive and call for an ambulance, Garden claimed. He waited at the hospital whilst the surgeon operated, but when told that his wife would live, he muttered '"*Merci*". And he walked out of the hospital and out of the lives of all of us'.[21]

It may not have been quite 'all of us', but Debussy certainly lost a number of former friends through his actions. Not least amongst these was his old confidant, Pierre Louÿs, who wrote to his brother Georges, a diplomat, that he had been to see Lilly, who would now be penniless and without anywhere to live. His antisemitic attitude was manifest:

---

[16] Louis Laloy, *La Musique retrouvée*, Paris, 1928, pp. 141–2.
[17] H. Strobel, *Claude Debussy*, Paris, 1940, pp. 164–5.
[18] Heinrich Strobel, Hélène de Tinan, Corrections, Centre de Documentation Claude Debussy, RESE 06.03.
[19] Centre de Documentation Claude Debussy, DOSS-01.017.
[20] E. Lockspeiser, *Debussy. His Life and Mind.* vol.2, London, 1965, p. 6, n.2. Louis Laloy reported these words in conversation with Lockspeiser in 1935.
[21] M. Garden and L. Biancolli, *Mary Garden's Story*, New York, 1951, pp. 82–3.

> Her husband has left with a forty-something year-old Jewess, Mme S. Bardac. I think you know Bardac, or at least he has been to your office. Quite accustomed to his wife going off with other men, he replies with a smile to those who enquire after her, 'She has just bought herself the latest fashionable musician, but it is I who have the money. She will be back.' What a nice breed ... I wrote to Louise [Pierre's wife] to ask if she would like to welcome the poor woman to our house, at least for a few weeks.[22]

André Messager no longer corresponded with Debussy. Debussy also lost touch for several years with Paul Dukas and René Peter, amongst others, although the latter wrote in his biography of Debussy, 'There were, of course, people who commented ... she was rich. No one can argue against the fact that Claude loved her sincerely.'[23] Looking back on Debussy's life, he reflected on the effect of Debussy's decision:

> Where had he gone, the Debussy of my youth ... ? He had the courage, supported by a beloved woman, to exile himself, and not being able any longer to belong to his friends, from then on he belonged only to his work. But without intending to, he had created a formula and this formula enveloped him! He began to produce works more slowly ... [24]

A fund was set up for Lilly, to which Debussy's former pupil Nicolas Coronio contributed, as well as Pierre Louÿs and Maurice Ravel and many others including Misia Natanson,[25] an influential member of Ravel's circle, and Lucienne Bréval, the singer. As René Peter commented ironically, Lilly never knew she had so many friends. He suspected the motive of some was to gain publicity.[26] Accommodation was paid for for Lilly in the Hôtel Américain before she moved to the avenue de Villiers. None of this was contributed to by her husband, who remained as invisible as possible. Misia wrote, 'When he left his wife she was reduced to dire poverty. Ravel, Bréval and I settled a small income on her, and Debussy never forgave me for this.'[27] These circumstances probably contributed to the cooling of the friendship between Ravel and Debussy.[28]

The vilification of Debussy by some knew no bounds. 'His first wife was young and poor. His second was old and rich,' wrote Mary Garden, despite the fact that Emma and Debussy were the same age.[29] Mary's sister Helen later told an interviewer that Debussy took money that Lilly had been given by friends.[30] This accusation was the result of rumours that a two hundred franc note had been stolen by

---

[22] Quoted in G. Millan, *Pierre Louÿs ou le culte de l'amitié*, Aix-en-Provence, 1979, p. 252.
[23] R. Peter, *Claude Debussy*, Paris, 1944, p. 44.
[24] R. Peter, 'Du temps d'Achille', *La Revue musicale*, 2, 1 December 1920, p. 163.
[25] See Chapter 3 p. 41.
[26] R. Peter, *Claude Debussy*, pp. 42–4.
[27] M. Sert, *Two or Three Muses. Memoirs of Misia Sert*, trans. M. Budberg, London, 1953, p. 37.
[28] R. Nichols, *Ravel*, London, 2011, pp. 58–9.
[29] G. Opstad, *Debussy's Mélisande. The Lives of Georgette Leblanc, Mary Garden and Maggie Teyte*, Woodbridge, 2009, p. 121.
[30] Ibid.

Debussy, or even his father, from Lilly's bedside table.[31] Debussy expressed his pain at this allegation in a letter to the artist Paul Robert, in which he traced its origins to the salon of Madame Charles Dettelbach, where a doctor at Lilly's clinic had initiated it. It had then been passed on via Reynaldo Hahn at a concert in the presence of Fauré, Pierné and Astruc. His misery at being cast aside by his 'friends' in favour of his wife was unspeakable. He couldn't care less, he wrote, if his music was never played again as he possessed the 'terrible fault of loving music for its own sake', not for any fame it might bring him. As for his financial circumstances, his poverty was extreme and 'Madame Bardac has no more intention of giving me money than I have of accepting it'.[32] How reliable this resolve was on Debussy's side is debatable, as he requested and received money from friends and other sources constantly throughout his life before and after his liaison with Emma.

There are further scribbled entries in Debussy's black notebook where he was gathering arguments in his own defence; he placed a large cross at the side of his words: 'Anger, even in front of her family. Violence with the servants.' Other marked entries complained about their quarrels about money, Lilly's lies, her constant pretence that he had never loved her and her insistence that he was now only trying to improve his financial situation. She had tried to control his thoughts, his relationships and his material needs for the last four years.[33]

Pasteur Vallery-Radot emphasised Debussy's essential incompatibility with Lilly by telling of a trip he made to Bichain when he was doing research for his book on Debussy. He spoke to the daughter of the woman who owned the little house Debussy wanted Lilly to renovate. There he learnt that three months before the divorce, Debussy's mother had gone to Bichain to pay her the outstanding rent of one hundred francs and told her directly, '"Rosalie Texier was a woman incapable of understanding my son." With these few words she summed up the whole reason for the drama.'[34] Just as his father was delighted that Debussy was awarded the Légion d'Honneur, clearly his parents did not object to his rise up the social ladder into the world of the *bourgeoisie*.

Antisemitism

There were many witnesses to Debussy's behaviour, many comments on his infidelity, many expressions of sympathy for Lilly amongst the accounts of this period of their lives, but there were no references to Emma's reactions, or those of her husband – just snide comments about Emma's wealth and, of course, emphasis on the fact that she was Jewish.

Antisemitism was rife at the time of Debussy's liaison with Emma, both casual and more direct. One only has to read the diaries of a society lady like Marguerite de Saint-Marceaux to realise how ingrained it was in otherwise respected individuals.

---

[31] C. p. 876.
[32] C. p. 877.
[33] BnF Musique, Rés. Vmf MS-53.
[34] P. Vallery-Radot, *Lettres de Debussy à sa femme Emma*, p. 29.

The Dreyfus Affair had been causing controversy since 1894, when Captain Alfred Dreyfus, a young Alsatian Jew, was convicted of treason and sentenced to life imprisonment for allegedly communicating French military secrets to the German Embassy in Paris. Not until 1906, two years after the vilification of Debussy and Emma, was he completely exonerated of all charges. As noted previously when introducing Emma's uncle, Osiris, it was a mystery how the latter had made such a fortune without family connections to other rich Jewish dynasties at a time when there were so many personal connections through marriage or business between the Rothschilds, Ephrussis and other big Jewish families who became an integral part of Parisian high society. It seems that Emma and her husband did not participate actively in that scene. Strobel noted that they did not mix with other Jews.[35] When Sigismond died in 1919, the French historian Gustave Schlumberger wrote in his *Souvenirs*,

> Of all the Bardacs, Jewish financiers who were all over Paris, I only knew one quite well: Sigismond, who has just died. He was a very great and very intelligent collector, and better still, a very kind man, very generous. He was one of those rare Jews who I used to have the pleasure of meeting even after the [Dreyfus] 'Affair', which we never ever discussed.[36]

To what extent Emma had to deceive her husband we do not know. Doubtless Sigismond dallied with actresses and other well-known performers. He showed his admiration of the famous dancer Cléo de Mérode when in 1901 he commissioned a portrait of her from Giovanni Boldini.[37] His interests were different to Emma's. However, his belief recounted by Pierre Louÿs that 'she will be back' showed a lack of insight into the true nature of his wife's feelings for Debussy, for now both parties instigated divorce proceedings.

Financial arrangements with Durand; Emma's pregnancy

Debussy still had to cope with his other, first love – composition. Whilst undergoing huge emotional tumult he was in the process of completing 'Jeux de vagues', the third movement of *La mer*. The manuscript bears the precise date and time of completion: Sunday 5 March 1905 at six o'clock in the evening. He once again wrote a special dedication on it, 'Pour la p.m. dont les yeux rient dans l'ombre.' ('For my own little one whose eyes laugh in the shade'). For some reason this inscription was erased and the work only bears a simple dedication to his publisher, but it has since been deciphered.[38] *La mer* was eventually published on 15 November 1905.

---

[35] DOSS-01.017, Centre de Documentation Claude Debussy.
[36] Gustave Schlumberger, *Mes Souvenirs 1844–1928*, vol.1, Paris, Plon, 1934, pp. 323–4.
[37] http://www.19thc-artworldwide.org/index.php/spring12/portraits-of-the-belle-epoque (last accessed 14 June 2020).
[38] Manuscript in the Sibley Music Library, University of Rochester. See https://www.rochester.edu/pr/Review/V67N1/feature2.html (last accessed 14 June 2020).

Meanwhile, to his stress was added the problem of illness. In letters to Durand in January 1905 he tried to keep him up to date with his progress on the symphonic sketches whilst having to stay in bed with influenza and dose himself with quinine and other remedies. Lilly had still not given up her efforts to keep Debussy, for she too corresponded with him, desperate to meet and come to some arrangement without involving lawyers. Someone kept the scandal-mongering going, for a false report appeared in *Le Figaro* on 3 January 1905 that Lilly had tried to commit suicide a second time.[39] Others tried to help bring about a reconciliation,[40] but to no avail. In his last extant letter to Lilly on 22 March, Debussy refused to meet her again and set out conditions for financial support which depended on the rights to his opera *Pelléas et Mélisande*. Although it was also in his own interests, Jacques Durand showed support by buying these rights from the composer and the author, Maeterlinck, for a sum of twenty-five thousand francs. Debussy would receive two-thirds of this amount, Maeterlinck one-third. On the same day, 31 March 1905, Debussy signed a second contract assigning to Durand all physical materials and copies still in his possession concerning *Pelléas et Mélisande*, but this was not all. Since October 1903 Debussy had been receiving five hundred francs a month from Durand for his opera on Edgar Allan Poe's tale, *Le diable dans le beffroi (The Devil in the Belfry)*. He had originally been due to deliver this work by 15 May 1905, which clearly now would not happen. Therefore in this second contract Debussy agreed to provide the first act of *Le diable* by 15 April 1906 and the rest of the work by 15 April 1907 – another vain hope. Whilst he gladly accepted the resumption of monthly payments for *Le diable* from 15 April 1905, it was for an opera that Durand was never to receive.[41]

On the very day Debussy received the first instalment of his share of the twenty-five thousand francs for *Pelléas*, 31 March 1905, Emma received a special letter and a gift from him.

> Petite mienne aimée,
> For ages I have been wanting something from me to be on your dear little hand. Please accept this ring – among so many others. It won't be jealous of them because for me life only began on the day I met you and I hope you feel the same?
> All my love,
> Claude[42]

By now Emma was two months' pregnant. Only a couple of weeks later, on 13 April, it was reported in the press that she was amongst the 'extrêmement aristocratique' audience at a gala evening of the Société des grandes auditions musicales organised by

---

[39] *Le Figaro*, 3 January 1905, p. 5.

[40] Edouard Rist was named by M. Dietschy, *La Passion de Claude Debussy*, p. 174. He also said an impartial friend of Debussy, Lucien Monod, who defended and helped Lilly, said that the composer never tried to see her again and never did see her again; p. 179, n. 14.

[41] Debussy's finances are discussed in detail in D. Herlin, V. Giroud, 'An Artist High and Low, or, Debussy and Money', *Rethinking Debussy*, E. Antokoletz and M. Wheeldon, (ed.), New York and Oxford, 2011, pp. 149–202.

[42] C. p. 896.

Comtesse Greffulhe in the ballroom of the Automobile Club.[43] Sigismond's name did not appear, although he was a member of this association. Her position in her social milieu appears not to have been affected by the affair. In somewhat caustic vein Marguerite de Saint-Marceaux wrote in her diary on 25 April, 'Mme Bardac is pregnant, Debussy very happy!'[44] Debussy had not graced her salon in person since the scandal of his engagement to Thérèse Roger.

Emma's divorce

On 14 April 1905 Debussy had the opportunity to pour out his heart to his friend, Louis Laloy, who had decided not to be judgemental and to renew contact with him, even to invite him to write an article for Le Mercure musical, a review he had founded that year with Jules Écorcheville. Overcome with relief that he had not been abandoned, Debussy found it impossible to express the depths of mental suffering he had reached. So many friends had deserted him that he felt revulsion at anything that could be called human.[45] But surely his heart must have leapt with joy when Emma and Sigismond were finally granted their divorce on 4 May 1905.

Pasteur Vallery-Radot claimed that 'Emma's split with her husband was a very straightforward affair.'[46] Sigismond took just as much of the blame as Emma, officially acknowledging relationships with several actresses which had come to the attention of his wife. She, it was noted, had formed a relationship with a 'Monsieur D ...' during Sigismond's long absences abroad. The latter had been particularly affected by the public nature of the scandal when 'sieur D's wife had tried unsuccessfully to commit suicide and failed to bring her husband back to her'.[47] As a result of the proceedings, Emma was given custody of Dolly, then aged thirteen. She was also granted alimony of one hundred thousand francs, which would give her an annual income of ten thousand francs payable in instalments three times a year. This would eventually pay the rent for the house they moved into, but must have also been intended to contribute to the costs of bringing up her daughter.[48]

Debussy's financial affairs were far more complicated. On 17 July 1905 he received a court order to pay Lilly a pension of four hundred francs per month. On the same day, his publisher, Durand, signed a contract with Debussy confirming ownership of all Debussy's works and agreeing to pay this sum to Lilly on the fifteenth of each month for the rest of Debussy's life. In return Debussy was to deliver a minimum of four scores a year. If Debussy failed to meet the conditions, as a guarantee for this sum, Durand could claim all royalties due in future from the two professional organisations, the Société des Auteurs Dramatiques and the Société des Auteurs, Compositeurs et

---

[43] Gil Blas, 14 April 1905.
[44] Marguerite de Saint-Marceaux, Journal 1894–1927, p. 391.
[45] C. pp. 900–1.
[46] Pasteur Vallery-Radot, Lettres de Claude Debussy à sa femme Emma, p. 28.
[47] Ardoin Saint Amand, Osiris, p. 46.
[48] C. p. 1259, n.1 and D. Herlin and V. Giroud, 'An Artist High and Low, or, Debussy and Money'.

Éditeurs de Musique. This money therefore went to Lilly directly, without Debussy having to find the means to pay it from August 1905 onwards. Thus, in effect, Debussy was being paid for compositions in progress. On 2 August 1905 when his divorce was officially finalised, the Civil Tribunal of the Seine decreed that in case Debussy predeceased Lilly he also had to take out a life annuity of three thousand six-hundred francs a year with the insurance company La Nationale.[49] The announcement of Debussy's divorce appeared in the newspapers on 3 and 4 August.[50]

Jacques Durand never gave up his support of Debussy through all his crises. In his autobiography he said Debussy used to meet him almost every day, either in his office or at home. They exchanged ideas constantly and if they could not meet they would write to each other. Upon arrival at his office, Debussy would light his cigarette, they would chat about art in general, music in particular, then Debussy would go over to the piano and play either from the manuscript he had brought along or give him an idea of a work he was sketching out in his mind.[51] Durand realised the difficulty he had relaxing in company:

> In his private life, Debussy was charming, impulsive, easy-going. He loved reading, held strong opinions on all sorts of things, possessed sound judgement of people's characters. As soon as he was in society he turned in on himself, fearing he might reveal too much of himself, preferring to day-dream than to follow a general conversation. At heart, a gentle man, at the same time passionate. He chose his friends carefully. I am still very proud of the fact that he counted me amongst those few rare privileged people.[52]

On Sunday 4 June 1905, that significant date,[53] Debussy sent Emma the gift of a composition, a short fragment for piano, nine bars, in celebration of her special day.[54] Again, one wonders what this *Fête* can be. It must have been something very personal for him to want to express his heartfelt feelings in purely musical terms, something he would never have been able to do with Lilly. He knew she would understand his meaning when he wrote: 'The seventh chords apologise!!! But look how happily the 9th chords armed with all their harmonics send packing the regrettable 7ths and borrow from the colours of the sky the radiance of apotheosis to celebrate your dear fête, dear petite mienne.'[55]

---

[49] Lesure, *Claude Debussy*, p. 270.

[50] *Le Figaro*, 3 August 1905; *Le Temps*, 4 August 1905.

[51] J. Durand, *Quelques souvenirs d'un éditeur de musique*, vol.1, p. 122.

[52] Idem. p. 125.

[53] Chapter 4 p. 54.

[54] Robert Orledge discussed each of these in his paper entitled 'Debussy's Musical Gifts to Emma Bardac' in *The Musical Quarterly*, October 1974, pp. 544–56. I am grateful to him for correspondence on this subject.

[55] 'Les accords de septième regrettent!!! Mais voici que heureusement les accords de 9e armés de tous leurs harmoniques, vous envoie [sic] promener les regrettables 7e et emprunte [sic] à la couleur du ciel des lueurs d'apothéose pour célébrer ta chère fête de chère petite Mienne. Et ces accords sont tellement beaux que j'aime mieux te laisser les imaginer ou regarder tes yeux'. C. p. 911; BnF musique, MS-14517.

There are several details here typical of the composer. First, the deep awareness of the feelings aroused by combinations of notes, the harmonics produced by the ninths creating a mystical effect. Second, worship of nature in all its glory. Debussy adored no god, but felt closest to something approaching the spiritual when in the open air. He wrote articles promoting the performance of music away from the confines of the concert hall, where music would be 'a mysterious collaboration between the air, the movement of leaves and the scent of flowers',[56] he described music as being allied to the movement of waters, to the play of curves described by the changing breezes. 'Nothing is more musical than a sunset!'[57] Here, the 'radiance of apotheosis', that ascent to a glorious heavenly state by appropriating the colours of the sky, was achieved through his sequence of ninths. Emma had inspired in him emotions requiring ecstatic expression. But this was not all. Beneath the fragment of manuscript he wrote, 'And the chords are so beautiful that I prefer to let you imagine them or to look into your eyes.' 'Regarder tes yeux …' How those words echo those of all the men in *Pelléas et Mélisande* who long to gaze into Mélisande's eyes.

Eastbourne

Debussy and Emma did not wait for the pronouncement of his divorce to escape Paris and wagging tongues. In July 1905 they arrived in Eastbourne as a family trio, for once again they brought Dolly with them, who had turned thirteen the month before.[58] Emma was by now about six months' pregnant. The Grand Hotel was obviously in the style to which she was accustomed, providing every comfort and convenience and many servants, so Dolly's presence would probably not have been too tiresome. The circumstances in which Debussy now found himself brought a huge sense of relief and relaxation, which he conveyed to Jacques Durand in letters full of contrast to the anxiety and depression that had plagued him in the preceding months. On 26 July he extolled the peace and charm of the resort.

> The sea unfurls with British correctness. In the foreground an immaculately mown lawn over which wander the small figures of important-looking, imperialist English men. But what a spot for working! No noise, no pianos except delightful mechanical ones, no musicians pontificating about art, no artists pontificating about music – altogether a charming place for cultivating the ego … I think I will be able to post you some music next week.[59]

Whilst he probably avoided it, there was in fact a hotel orchestra led by Dutch-born Jacques Van Lier, known professionally as Herr Von Leer. Van Lier's daughter, Mrs. Sachs, remembered her father saying that Debussy was very shy and was hardly

---

[56] *La Revue blanche*, 1 June 1901.
[57] *Musica*, May 1903.
[58] Debussy sent best wishes to Édouard Colonne from '*Dolly et sa maman*', C. p. 916.
[59] C. p. 912.

ever seen in the public rooms, although he had been to the top gallery in the hall and listened to a transcription of one of his piano arabesques.[60] There were certainly many options in the hotel for comfortable surroundings away from the sound of music.

Following the finalisation of his divorce, on 7 August Debussy wrote again to Durand:

> Here I am, free at last from the nightmare I have been living for a year ... Now, even though I think I have fulfilled my duty as an honest man, it is most likely people will find reasons for judging me severely ... But I intend to live as I please without taking any notice of all the tales people will invent. My story is really childishly simple.[61]

Already he was promising to send him proofs of a piano transcription for four hands of *La mer* and the first set of *Images* for piano. On 18 August he was able to say, 'I am beginning to see things clearly again in my mind and my thinking machine is gradually recovering. I am actually forgetting the man I am in order to become the man I ought to be, the Gods permitting!'[62]

His 'thinking machine' now enabled him to revise 'Reflets dans l'eau', the first of the three *Images*, the original version of which did not satisfy him. It was to be 'based on new ideas and the most recent discoveries of harmonic chemistry'. His newfound peace of mind, his love of Emma and his proximity to the sea enabled him to access those stored impressions and develop this 'harmonic chemistry' which has had an infinite influence on composers since. It is fascinating how Emma possessed this ability to free up a composer to access his deepest wells of inspiration. Just as Fauré had written *La bonne chanson* so unrestrainedly, now Debussy was once again able to compose in a way satisfying and pleasurable to himself, an indelible need,[63] and at the same time bring pleasure to performer and listener. Even though ostensibly on holiday with Emma and Dolly, it is clear that he was spending the majority of his time composing. Music was still the 'other woman', but one with whom Emma was evidently willing to share him.

Her recognition of this fact led to the acquisition of something most dear to Debussy's heart – a grand piano. It was in Eastbourne that Debussy purchased a Blüthner baby grand from S. Hermitage & Sons, a *quart-de-queue*, which undeniably the composer could never have afforded himself. In a notebook in which Dolly later made detailed lists and notes for her two daughters, she wrote that he bought it second-hand [*d'occasion*] in England or in Jersey and that it had the number 72.5 53.[64]

---

[60] P. Pugh, *Grand Hotel (Eastbourne)*, Eastbourne, 1987, p. 36.

[61] C. p. 913.

[62] C. p. 914.

[63] 'What is your guiding principle?' – 'My pleasure!' said the student Debussy in 1883. M. Emmanuel, 'Les ambitions de Claude-Achille', *La Revue musicale*, May 1926, p. 46.

[64] Centre de Documentation Claude Debussy, Hélène de Tinan, Carnet rouge, RESE 08.01. D. Enget Moore confirms that it was purchased in Eastbourne: http://www.litart.co.uk/bluthner.htm (last accessed 21 September 2020).

This piano had a particular timbre, for it was constructed with the 'aliquot musical system' – it possessed a supplementary rank of strings tuned at the upper octave and strung above the traditional strings so as to vibrate in sympathy with those strings without being struck by hammers. The piano was duly brought to Paris and used by Debussy for the rest of his life.

6

August 1905 – December 1906: Life in the avenue du Bois de Boulogne

Debussy's initial delight with the eccentricities of the English and the fresh air of the English Channel faded somewhat as time progressed. By 28 August 1905 he was complaining to Durand and to Louis Laloy about the 'murderous' draughts and extraneous music disturbing the peace and his grumbles continued until his return to Paris. On the way back, he and Emma spent a few days in London 'without much joy except for the music of the grenadiers who pass by every morning with their joyous *'bug-pipes* [bag-pipes] and wild little fifes ...'[1] By 11 September they were staying not in a grand hotel, but in a *pension de famille*, La Feuilleraie, in Bellevue (Meudon), Seine et Oise. Debussy's awareness of the consequences of his relationship with Emma is highlighted by the fact that he had no one to whom he wished to dedicate his first series of *Images* for piano;[2] after all, he had been deserted by those he might have previously wished so to honour.

Finally, in October, Debussy and Emma moved into a grand address: 64 avenue du Bois de Boulogne, sometimes called Square du Bois de Boulogne and which in January 1908 became 80 avenue du Bois de Boulogne (now Avenue Foch). This must have been tiring for Emma, who was approaching term with her pregnancy. Thirteen-year-old Dolly lived there with Debussy and Emma for nearly six years, until shortly before her marriage in 1911 and was permitted to call Debussy by his first name.[3] Debussy's parents moved nearer, perhaps with financial help, from Levallois-Perret to 35 bis, rue La Fontaine in Auteuil.[4] From then onwards they would come to lunch with Claude, Emma and Dolly twice a week.[5]

How could this new élite lifestyle be supported by Debussy's inadequate pocket? The property was rented in the name of Madame Emma Moyse from an Englishman, an alcoholic, according to Debussy, called Mr. Fairbin.[6] Their neighbours included various aristocrats, counts and wealthy foreigners, English, American and Russian,[7]

---

[1] C. p. 920.
[2] Ibid.
[3] Dolly Bardac, London interview.
[4] M. Dietschy, *La Passion de Claude Debussy*, Neuchâtel, 1962, p. 176.
[5] 'Ils venaient régulièrement déjeuner à la maison deux fois par semaine.' De Tinan, French interview.
[6] Letters to J. Durand and L. Lalande, C. p. 1536 and p. 1546.
[7] C. Charle, 'Debussy in fin-de siècle Paris' in Jane F. Fulcher (ed.), *Debussy and his world*, Princeton, 2001, pp. 286–7.

12. Debussy in the garden of 64 Square
du Bois de Boulogne, 1905

a world completely alien to the composer dedicated to his art, who denigrated the superficiality of these monied social circles.

Significantly, Raoul Bardac insisted that it was not his mother, but Debussy who chose this house and that their home life there was built around his desires.[8] Emma was able to pay the huge rent of eight thousand five hundred francs from her annual allowance of ten thousand francs which she received from Sigismond Bardac.[9] This rent was in the highest bracket for the Parisian élite of the day. It has been calculated that the total income the family would have needed to maintain such a residence would have been at least twenty thousand francs per year, the equivalent of the salary

---

[8] R. Bardac, 'Souvenirs sur Claude Debussy', 1948, Centre de Documentation Claude Debussy, RESE-05.16.

[9] C. p. 1259, n.1.

of a very senior functionary.[10] What was left over of Emma's allowance would not be enough to cover the significant cost of servants and living expenses for a family of three, soon to become four. It was imperative that Debussy should earn enough to contribute to day-to-day necessities, not to mention his frequent indulgence in little luxuries. They employed a cook and, no doubt, a housemaid for Emma. At the end of the garden was a car, not purchased but hired, and a chauffeur, Jules, always ready to take Debussy out at his pleasure.[11] The couple would invite their few close friends to the house (there were never more than a total of eight people), giving them dinners on regular days of the week.[12] There are several references in his correspondence to the noise of the trains of the *ceinture*, a circular railway which ran behind the house, but he rarely seemed to be troubled by this.

There is no hint that Emma was unwilling to exchange the certainty and security of living with a wealthy banker for the precarious prospects of a striving composer. Perhaps she had a blind faith in his ability to command large sums for his compositions, which necessarily would depend on his continuous output. They must have assumed that providing a perfect aesthetic environment for inspiration and peace for committing his compositions to paper should make that possible. But it was unlikely that the earnings of a composer, however successful, would ever be enough to cover their huge expenditure. As noted earlier, Emma could not depend on a large inheritance from Osiris.

Photographs show a bourgeois man-about-town outside his smart abode. He is wearing a suit, leaning on a stick, holding a wide-brimmed felt trilby hat and gloves, accoutrements of a gentleman. There is a series of these formal photographs. In some he adds a coat, supposedly casually hung over his left arm. The background of wrought iron work in front of tall windows reveals the grandeur of the house. Others show Debussy and Emma together, sitting on a garden bench, looking at a book. She looks at him, he, cigarette in mouth, is not looking back at her. In another, she reaches out an arm protectively while he looks downwards, frowning. In the same setting Debussy sits by himself, staring into the distance, one hand supporting his head, the other grasping the arm of the bench. The photographs remind one of the impressions his friend Raymond Bonheur recounted when looking back to Debussy's return from Rome in 1887 in the very early days of his musical career. When sitting in the Brasserie Pousset in the evenings,

> he seemed to me then withdrawn and a bit distant ... his forehead, that powerful forehead like a faun's, such a strange profile, jutting out at the front like the prow of a ship; his eyes brown, covered by bushy eyebrows gathered in a frown, staring fixedly into the far distance towards some imaginary point, whilst with that habitual movement of his index finger he tapped the ash from his cigarette.[13]

[10] Charle, 'Debussy in fin-de siècle Paris', p. 287.
[11] De Tinan, French interview.
[12] R. Bardac, 'Dans l'intimité de Claude Debussy', p. 73, and de Tinan, French interview.
[13] R. Bonheur, 'Souvenirs et impressions d'un compagnon de jeunesse', *La Revue musicale*, May 1926, p. 4.

13. Debussy and Emma in their garden, 1905

To reach the house one entered a tree-lined cul-de sac through a grand iron gate. Debussy had a pleasant study on the ground floor, filled with light from large bay windows opening onto the garden. He appreciated comfort and beauty rather than luxury for its own sake, and possessed a large armchair made of wood and leather in the Morris style, the last word in 'English comfort'. As Dolly later explained, Debussy was extremely sensitive to atmosphere and to interior decoration. He had great taste and a certain instinct for beautiful things despite having been born into a family of very modest means.[14] He loved to work surrounded by flowers. 'His study overflowed with them, summer and winter,' wrote Durand,[15] who with Louis Laloy remained one of the few true friends faithful to Debussy. According to Dolly, Laloy, a writer, linguist and sinologist, was in Debussy's opinion the most intelligent person he had ever known.[16]

As both Raoul and Dolly recalled, Debussy hardly ever went out. He would relax by walking up and down the garden, noting down musical ideas in a small red notebook, and by doing small gardening tasks himself. Suddenly he would rush inside to try out his thoughts on the upright Bechstein or the Blüthner grand piano.[17] Dolly added that once he played a work through on the piano this meant it was finished. Everything was worked out in his head.[18] This was echoed by Robert Godet. 'No composer ever wasted less paper. Debussy did not start writing down a work until he had completed it in his head, without any recourse to an instrument.'[19]

He possessed many books and magazines in English, which he would get Emma or Dolly to translate for him. When he did go out it was usually to a bookshop, or to see Jacques Durand, his publisher. Sometimes he would visit his favourite antiques shop, where he admired, and occasionally purchased, Chinese objects. He enjoyed playing bridge, but badly.[20] Raoul was later to write, 'his everyday happiness derived from the satisfaction of little habits within an atmosphere of love and devotion',[21] devotion surely provided with great sensitivity by Emma. Emma's and Debussy's mutual friend and admirer Pasteur Vallery-Radot commented that she created an atmosphere of tenderness, gentleness and charm around this man 'who had remained a big child',[22] a comment that brings to mind pointed references to

---

[14] 'Debussy était excessivement sensible aux ambiances, bien entendu sans ça il n'aurait pas été Debussy, et également au décor, si l'on peut le dire, parce que lui-même avait beaucoup de goût, et c'était un garçon qui était né dans une famille excessivement simple et qui malgré ça, tout petit, a eu l'instinct des belles choses', de Tinan, French interview.

[15] J. Durand, *Quelques souvenirs d'un éditeur de musique*, vol.2, Paris, 1924/25, p. 91.

[16] De Tinan, French interview.

[17] R. Bardac, 'Dans l'intimité de Claude Debussy', *Terres Latines*, March 1936, p. 72.

[18] De Tinan, French interview.

[19] 'Jamais compositeur ne gâcha moins de papier. Debussy ne se mettait à écrire un ouvrage qu'alors qu'il l'avait achevé dans sa tête, et sans aucun secours instrumental.' Quoted in F. Lesure, *Catalogue de l'œuvre de Claude Debussy*, Geneva, 1977, p. 13.

[20] R. Bardac, 'Dans l'intimité de Claude Debussy', p. 73, and de Tinan, French interview.

[21] Bardac, 'Dans l'intimité de Claude Debussy', p. 72.

[22] '… celui qui était resté un grand enfant.' Pasteur Vallery-Radot, *Lettres de Claude Debussy à sa femme Emma*, p. 29.

Emma mentioned earlier as 'la Mère Claude',[23] as well as Mary Garden's statement that Lilly looked after Debussy 'like a child'.[24]

Emma and Dolly had to submit to Debussy's regular domestic routine. He loved certain items of English silverware and used them every morning at breakfast, which, as Dolly says, they took in the 'English' style, in the dining room. It was Debussy himself who prepared this meal with extreme attention to detail, and, much to young Dolly's frustration, as with all things he did, very slowly. In fact she used the word 'childish' (*puéril*) to describe this behaviour and even expressed her frustration out loud.[25] Raoul commented that Debussy's whisky was served from his own special decanter and his tea in his own special glass. Dolly described him as being acutely sensitive, youthful in character with a childlike propensity and a great sense of humour. He could, however, have sudden bursts of violent anger, which frightened her.[26]

Dolly had to suffer piano lessons – suffer, because her teacher, Roger-Ducasse, was terribly strict with her to the extent that she was 'paralysed', with the result that she claimed modestly never to have become a proficient pianist. It was Raoul who had brought about this arrangement.[27] She did, however, enjoy sight-reading the scores of operas she had seen at the Opéra-Comique with Emma's mother, Laure, who, Dolly said, loved music too.[28]

Birth of Chouchou

October 1905 proved an eventful month for Emma and Debussy, both professionally and domestically. Durand published the first set of piano *Images* (with no dedication), the first of which, 'Reflets dans l'eau', Debussy had rewritten when inspiration had struck him in Eastbourne. In November he showed his continuing affection for Raoul by dedicating a copy 'à mon vieux Rara. Son jeune ami Claude Debussy. Nov.05', thus not trying to assume the position of step-father to this young man he had known and advised for several years, but rather addressing him as an equal by describing himself (at forty-three) as 'his young friend'. 'My old Rara' was now

---

[23] See Chapter 5 p. 69.

[24] See Chapter 3 p. 42.

[25] 'Oui, il aimait, c'est un peu puéril si vous voulez, mais il aimait beaucoup les jolis objets d'argent pour la table, surtout pour le breakfast, alors nous prenions le breakfast à l'anglaise, c'est à dire dans la salle à manger. C'est lui qui préparait le thé lui-même, avec un soin extrême, très lentement, parce qu'il était très lent dans tout ce qu'il faisait, et moi qui étais toujours d'un caractère très vif, j'étais un peu exaspérée et j'ai dit "tu fais trop longtemps".' De Tinan, French interview.

[26] Dolly Bardac, London interview.

[27] 'J'avais comme professeur un camarade de mon frère qui s'appelait Roger-Ducasse, qui était un des meilleurs élèves de Fauré ... et qui était d'une sévérité épouvantable avec moi ... il m'a paralysée', de Tinan, French interview.

[28] 'Au lieu de faire des exercices en dehors de mes leçons je me faisais un peu de déchiffrage des opéras-comiques que j'avais été voir avec ma grand-mère maternelle qui adorait la musique aussi.' De Tinan, French interview.

aged twenty-four. Raoul was still composing songs, for on 23 December in *La Revue hebdomadaire* there was a review of *Mélodies* by Bardac immediately following a review of Debussy's *Images*. Neither criticism was very positive, Debussy's creations being described as superficial, and Raoul's as demonstrating an incessant desire for originality and a very intermittent promise of talent.[29]

On 15 October *La mer* received its first performance at the Concerts Lamoureux, conducted by Camille Chevillard. It seems almost incomprehensible to us today that these three symphonic sketches for orchestra should have been received with such scepticism by critics who had previously spoken so favourably of his opera. 'They seem particularly mistaken …', Debussy wrote to Laloy. 'Mr G. Carraud accuses me of working for America. Another, whose name I can't remember, declares I am a composer of the "impalpable"'.[30] Pierre Lalo wrote in *Le Temps* that Debussy *wanted* to feel, but 'I do not hear, I do not see, I do not smell the sea'.[31] Debussy's pain at the lack of understanding of his music was deeply felt, despite his assertion to Lalo that it really didn't matter at all that he disliked *La mer*. What he regretted was that the critic used this as a pretext for suddenly claiming that all his works lacked logic and were only the results of a search for the 'picturesque'. He accused Lalo of defending traditions which no longer existed. 'I love the sea and I have listened to it with the passionate respect it deserves … The dust of the past is not always respectable.'[32]

That letter was written on 25 October. On 30 October 1905, at two o'clock in the morning, a daughter was born to Emma and Claude Debussy, both of whom were now aged forty-three. The only intimation of this in Debussy's extant correspondence is a letter to Louis Laloy which combines extreme gratitude for a positive and understanding review of *La mer* with an urgent request to see him soon, for 'I have so many things to tell you! Amongst other things, some days ago I became the father of a little girl. The joy this brings has overwhelmed me and I still find it a bit frightening.'[33]

Registering the birth of the child was not without issues, as Debussy and Emma were unmarried. She was given the first names of both parents, Claude Emma, and officially described as the daughter of 'parents non dénommés' (parents not named), a designation permitted in France until 1922 in the case of illegitimate children. A witness who had signed previous certificates concerning Emma, Gaston Van Brock, recurred here, now aged 55 and living at 30 avenue Kléber. He had not abandoned her after her divorce. The other witnesses were Claude Debussy and the doctor, Pierre Budin. Dolly loved her new half-sister, always known as Chouchou, and in fact was very helpful, for the baby eventually slept in

---

[29] *La Revue hebdomadaire*, no.12, 1905, pp. 502–3.
[30] C. p. 926, quoting L. Schneider in *Gil Blas*, 16 October 1905.
[31] P. Lalo, *Le Temps*, 24 October 1905.
[32] C. pp. 927–8.
[33] C. p. 929.

her room and Dolly recalled affectionately that she looked after her as if she were her mother.[34]

On 3 February 1906 Emma was asked to come into the room when Ricardo Viñes came to their house at Debussy's request to play the piano *Images* which had been published the previous October. Viñes wrote in his diary that Debussy made him play them several times and was 'very pleased, for afterwards he asked his current wife (Madame Bardac) to come. Then they asked me to introduce them to Ravel's *Miroirs* which I played to them. I left at 6 o'clock.' Dolly had fond memories of Viñes coming to the house and playing Debussy's music. Physically, she said, he was not impressive, but he was extremely intelligent, funny and witty. It was always a delight to be in his company.[35]

Emma's and Raoul's susceptibility to illness; Debussy's problems with composing begin

From that February onwards, Emma had much to contend with. Debussy admitted to Raoul that he was indeed writing very little music, partly because he simply did not like the results, ('tout en écrivant très peu de musique, elle me déplaît beaucoup'), but most likely also because he was occupied with personal concerns for Emma. In a long, thoughtful letter he told him that Emma was suffering from influenza, the first of many references to her susceptibility to illness. She was not just suffering, but was '*merveilleusement grippée*', implying rather sardonically that she was in the throes of a serious attack. As Raoul knew, he said, she reacted against all kinds of medicine. Adding to this, a new nanny had to be found for *la petite Claude*, owing to marital problems of the original one.[36]

Most of this letter was taken up with sound advice on composing, as it is clear that the Société nationale de musique had rejected a submission by Raoul who, Debussy pointed out, had no support and did not belong to any of the groups 'who are permitted to dip their toes into music' – in other words, Raoul was still an outsider. As before, he encouraged him to take his time, not to give the impression that he wanted to rush to the end of a piece at all costs. 'Have patience!' he exclaimed, and revealingly added, 'This is a major virtue – even a domestic one – which solves many a problem.'

That little word 'domestic' revealed something of Debussy's realisation of the necessity for himself to be patient and to adapt to home life with a sick wife and nanny problems. These unavoidable distractions were keeping him from musical inspiration. Clearly Raoul had not lost his propensity for laziness, but Debussy

---

[34] 'Chouchou, qui était un bébé adorable, vivait dans, en fait couchait dans ma chambre, et je m'en occupais absolument comme si j'étais moi-même sa maman.' De Tinan, French interview.

[35] 'C'était un homme qui avait une physique pas du tout avantageux pour lui, mais il était tellement intelligent, tellement drôle et tellement spirituel, quand on oubliait complètement son physique on était ravi d'être avec lui.' De Tinan, French interview.

[36] *C.* pp. 940–1.

agreed he could turn this to good use: 'Your description of your daily routine is delightful; the hours spent doing nothing seem carefully scheduled. You are right! It is better to let your brain marinate under a hot sun – to look at flowers and snapshots – whilst your nervous system is still capable of responding.' Signing off, once again he revealed his affection for the young man: 'Au revoir mon cher Rara. Ma sincère amitié.'[37]

This affection must also have been tinged with sympathy. Emma's son had long been suffering with poor health, as is shown by his military service record.[38] Raoul belonged to the class of 1901 – that is to say, at the age of twenty his name was drawn by ballot to carry out compulsory military service. Since 1904 he had been a member of the 26th Infantry Regiment based in Nancy. However, on 6 January 1905 he was declared unfit because of chronic dyspepsia and a problem with the upper right lung. From then until 1917 he passed in and out of the regiment depending on the state of his health.

Satie's visits; Sigismond Bardac's legal statement

A musician who shared Debussy's and Raoul's propensity for remaining on the fringes of society was Erik Satie. Debussy had known him well since the early 1890s, when Satie was a cabaret pianist at the Auberge du Clou and the Chat Noir. Debussy was a staunch advocate of Satie's music, defending him to others and orchestrating two of Satie's *Gymnopédies*, the only time he orchestrated the work of another composer. Their friendship was such that he had asked Satie to be a witness at his marriage to Lilly Texier, after which they continued to meet at least once a week. Satie would come every Saturday to his apartment in the rue Cardinet, where Debussy cooked for him. Apparently, Debussy knew 'the most absolute secret' of how to cook perfect eggs and lamb cutlets, which they washed down with 'a delicious white Bordeaux wine'.[39] Satie did not desert his friend and following Debussy's move into the avenue du Bois de Boulogne, these weekly rendezvous continued but, according to Dolly, Emma banned Satie from the kitchen. Dolly looked forward to his visits, loving Satie's 'comical way of expressing himself and his repartee in conversation'.[40] To Debussy he spoke respectfully, but in retrospect Dolly was unsure whether this was intentional or rather artificial. 'He never seemed completely at ease,' she commented,[41] significant in view of his later behaviour towards Debussy. Debussy's biographer Lockspeiser informed

---

[37] C. pp. 940–1. The advice given in this letter was similar to that given in 1901. See Chapter 4 pp. 43–4.

[38] Paris Archives, *Registres matricules du recrutement*, Cote D4R1 1186.

[39] O. Volta (ed.), *Erik Satie: Écrits*, Paris, 1977, p. 51. See also R. Orledge, 'Debussy and Satie' in *Debussy Studies*, ed. R. Langham Smith, Cambridge, 1997, for details of their relationship.

[40] Dolly Bardac, London interview.

[41] 'Il n'avait jamais l'air d'être tout à fait à son aise. Il parlait avec Debussy avec une sorte de respect voulu, ou artificiel, je n'en sais rien.' De Tinan, French interview.

us that Satie was accustomed to accepting an inferior brand of wine, set aside for him, whilst Debussy enjoyed a finer bottle. Lockspeiser ascribed this to Satie's hankering after self-humiliation.[42] Since being 'astounded' by *Pelléas et Mélisande* in 1902, he had told Jean Cocteau that he 'had to search for something else or I am lost'.[43] This year, 1905, was the year Satie decided to enrol at the Schola Cantorum in the counterpoint class, which was necessary in order to progress to the composition class. Debussy feared this move might damage Satie's individuality.[44] Little wonder, therefore, if Satie's attitude to Debussy was somewhat equivocal. He was, though, a welcome guest, particularly after the birth of Claude Emma, for he adored children. 'He acted as unpaid child-minder and general ray of sunshine for the Debussy household, in addition to exchanging ideas and discussing works in hand with Claude in his study', wrote Robert Orledge.[45]

On 14 March 1906, Debussy signed another contract with his publisher, Durand, reinforcing the stipulations in that of 17 August 1905 ceding him the rights to his royalties and giving Durand the power to pay Lilly four hundred francs a month. Two days later, on 16 March 1906, a significant judgement was made by the Civic Tribunal of the Seine in favour of Sigismond Bardac, which was recorded in a note added to Claude Emma's birth certificate on 24 August 1906. It stated that 'the person named opposite will not be able to bear the name Bardac who is not her father and to whose family she cannot belong.'[46] By instituting civil proceedings to deny paternity, Sigismond had made absolutely sure that he would have nothing to do with the child and certainly run no risk of financial commitment. He clearly had knowledge of his wife's impecunious state now that she was living with Debussy and feared the possibility of her making a claim of some sort as she was not married to Debussy and therefore did not officially bear his surname. The stress of dealing with this turn of events in addition to domestic problems could well have contributed to Emma's susceptibility to illness at that time.

It is hardly surprising that Debussy did not manage to publish as many works as usual in 1906. His little girl was a constant source of wonder to him, and the only new composition was 'Sérénade à la poupée', the 'Serenade to the Doll', which would become the third piece in *Children's Corner*. He appears to have dedicated only two works to others in 1906 and both of these are dated January of that year: one to Eric Satie in a copy of the *Images (1ère série)*, 'janvier 1906, à mon vieux Satie, le célèbre contrapuntiste, Claude Debussy', and one in a copy of *Prélude à l'après-midi d'un faune* to the violinist Eugène Ysaÿe, 'À Eugène Ysaÿe, avec l'hommage de

---

[42] E. Lockspeiser, *Debussy. His Life and Mind*, vol.1, London, 1962, p. 148.

[43] R. Orledge, *Satie the Composer*, Cambridge, 1990, p. 55.

[44] Idem. p. 57.

[45] R. Orledge, 'Debussy, Satie and the Summer of 1913', *Cahiers Debussy*, no.26, 2002, Centre de Documentation Claude Debussy, Paris.

[46] 'L'acte ci-contre a été rectifié en ce que la dénommée ci contre ne pourra porter le nom de Bardac qui n'est pas son père et à la famille duquel elle ne peut appartenir.' Birth certificate of Claude Emma Debussy.

ma constante admiration, Claude Debussy, Janvier 1906'.[47] The latter was probably prompted by a performance of this piece at the Conservatoire conducted by Georges Marty, the first time Debussy's music had been performed there. Since 15 June 1905 Gabriel Fauré had been the Director of the Conservatoire and on 28 June Debussy wrote to Fauré, probably prompted by Emma, congratulating him on his appointment and exclaiming about the number of old cobwebs that he would need to blow away from that institution.[48]

Factories of Nothingness

By March 1906 it was not only Emma's health that was worrying Debussy but, more painfully, that of 'ma petite Claude'. He expressed his anxiety to Louis Laloy, worried that 'it is so difficult to know what is going on inside these little beings'.[49] Socially there must have been some concerns about Debussy's position, for he claimed that 'Madame de Greffulhe' [sic] had done the right thing in dropping him from her musical salon and inviting Laloy instead, he being so much more sociable. Not only did Debussy take little interest in writing music at this time, but he did not even want to write about music, for he vehemently rejected Laloy's invitation to contribute to the journal he had just co-founded, Le Mercure musicale. He did not want to join the company of musicians who, when they no longer know what to compose or say, become critics and talk rubbish. Better to remain aloof and conserve a little mystery.[50]

Besides not being invited to the Countess Greffulhe, it seems that the customary round of salons was now eschewed by Emma as well as Claude. If Emma had imagined that having ensnared one of the most celebrated composers of the age she would have played a more central part in the social round, she must have been bitterly disappointed, but it is also likely that since alienating so many previous friends and acquaintances, she no longer sought such exposure. There is no evidence that she sang in public or even privately any more. Since dedicating the second set of Fêtes galantes and the Trois Chansons de France to Emma in 1904, Debussy was no longer composing songs for her to sing. In fact, the next set of mélodies did not appear until 1910 when 'Auprès de cette grotte sombre', the second of the Trois Chansons de France, was resurrected as one of the three songs, Le promenoir des deux amants and Emma received a dedication. Family life, illness on her part, reluctance or lack of inspiration on her husband's, whatever the reason, song was no longer an integral part of Emma's existence.

Her husband certainly did not want to play his own music to audiences. In March 1906 he wrote, 'I have to admit, I am no longer used to performing my own music in public. On various occasions recently I have had to turn down invitations

---

[47] C. p. 2227.

[48] C. p. 912.

[49] 'On sait si mal ce qui se passe dans ces petits êtres ...' Language reminiscent of Pelléas et Mélisande. C. p. 944.

[50] Ibid.

to do so as I felt so embarrassed. It would have been a disservice to well-meaning people.'[51] His lack of inspiration to compose was worrying. 'I am still stagnating in factories of Nothingness', he wrote to Durand in April, a reference to a poem by Jules Laforgue,[52] the poet who had inspired his designation of Emma as *ma petite mienne*. He had already referred to 'usines' (factories) in an article in the first issue of the journal *Musica* in 1902, where he expressed the hope that art would never become 'something utilitarian, sad as a factory',[53] thus demonstrating the negative connotations he felt for this word. 'Can you imagine a blind brain?' he continued in his letter.[54] He would often repeat this phrase, *les usines du Néant*, over the years to come, as he struggled to meet the requirements of his publisher and endeavour to fulfil his ever-growing financial commitments.

'For two years my life has been like a penny dreadful ...', wrote Debussy to Paul-Jean Toulet on 9 May 1906.[55] How telling that he viewed the years since his relationship with Emma negatively, with no emphasis on any joy she had brought to his life. He had just renewed his friendship with this poet and novelist, whom he had first met in his younger days at the Café Weber or some other venue where he enjoyed the company of writers and artists, and with whom he had once been planning to collaborate on a setting of *As you like it*, a plan which was later revived but never came to fruition. This was not entirely Debussy's fault. Toulet had visited Hanoi in 1902, just when Debussy was discussing his ideas enthusiastically, and returned in 1903 heavily addicted to opium. Debussy had then turned his attention towards another theatrical work, Edgar Allan Poe's *Le diable dans le beffroi*. Only four days before this letter, Debussy had written to Toulet expressing astonishment that he had seemingly ignored him at the auction house Durand-Ruel on 5 May,[56] and subsequently received an apology from Toulet, who had only caught sight of him as he was leaving. He had felt equally hurt that Debussy had not acknowledged him. Debussy replied with his declaration of misery, and an invitation to visit him 'at my home – because of the lovely garden', any time. Clearly Debussy was still extremely sensitive regarding the loss of friends whose company he had appreciated before his liaison with Emma. Toulet became one of their regular visitors whom Dolly remembered, commenting that he used to sleep all day and work at night.[57]

Musical inspiration was certainly in short supply. There is no evidence of any gift to Emma this June of 1906 to celebrate her *fête*. Instead, on 9 June Debussy wrote to Durand apologising for not going to see him in his office and insisting that he was working hard to make up for a bad period. In July he still sought to

---

[51] *C*. p. 950.
[52] 'Je croupis dans les Usines du Négatif', Jules Laforgue, *Dragées grises*. F. Lesure, *Claude Debussy. A Critical Biography*, trans. and revised ed. Marie Rolf, Rochester N. Y. and Woodbridge, 2019, p. 498, n.1.
[53] 'Une chose utilitaire, triste comme une usine.' *Musica*, October 1902, p. 5.
[54] 'Je continue à croupir dans les usines du Néant ... imaginez un cerveau aveugle?' *C*. p. 951.
[55] *C*. p. 955.
[56] *C*. p. 954.
[57] Dolly Bardac, London interview.

convince Durand that he was working on his orchestral *Images* despite having to have a tooth extracted, in particular the second piece, 'Ibéria', as well as *Le diable dans le beffroi*. 'I am making use of my life as fully as possible and if Music will not smile upon me, she is truly hard-hearted,' he told him.[58]

Dieppe

Emma and Chouchou would certainly profit from some fresh air after their various illnesses, so on 8 August the family went to the Grand Hôtel Château de Puys near Dieppe, only a short distance from familiar Pourville. Debussy was relieved and delighted to be back with his 'old friend, the Sea', but disliked seeing so many 'bodies deformed by everyday life' flailing around in it when really only *Sirènes* should be allowed. Whilst there he had to attend to various matters concerning the imminent performance of *Pelléas et Mélisande* in Brussels, pacify Édouard Colonne about *Le Roi Lear*, the score of which he had still not completed (and never would), and reassure Durand that he would soon be providing him with the three *Images*. The environment did not prove conducive to inspiration, however, Debussy soon finding fault with the sea which resembled a leaking bathtub, the ugly, noisy English guests, the hotel's mendacious proprietor and his inadequate table for working on.[59] Soon after their return home on 1 September he wrote to Laloy envying him for returning to 'an old house which has been a friend to you since childhood',[60] his family home in Rahon in the Jura. How sad that Debussy felt the house Emma was making so comfortable for him was not yet a familiar environment with family associations. The strain of its upkeep was beginning to show. He pointed out that he had just celebrated another birthday. He and Emma were now forty-four.

Back home, Debussy still had to worry about the cast of *Pelléas et Mélisande* for its first performance in Brussels in January 1907. At the same time, rehearsals were taking place for its revival in Paris, the fiftieth performance, at the Opéra-Comique on 23 December 1906. He was uncomfortable with the attitude of the performers, who now seemed to be taking his opera for granted. In the event, all went well and he was able to congratulate his soloists on their insightful performances.

Only two days later it was Christmas Day. An affectionate message to Emma survives:

To my *petite Mienne*,
Mère de Chouchou C. Debussy
Et directrice de mon amour le plus cher
From Claude Debussy

Xmas/06[61]

---

[58] *C.* p. 960.
[59] *C.* pp. 962, 965, 968.
[60] *C.* p. 969.
[61] 'To my own little one. Mother of Chouchou C. Debussy And director of my fondest love'. *C.* p. 981.

This was written on an English card with a message printed in English: 'With Kind Remembrances and all good wishes for a Merry Christmas and a Happy New Year', a reminder that Emma spoke English and that Chouchou had an English governess. Debussy showed his appreciation of Emma's role as mother of Chouchou at the same time as giving Chouchou her full name – including the surname that Emma was not yet entitled to.

Chouchik Laloy; *Pelléas* in Brussels

The same day, Debussy wrote a letter of congratulation to Louis Laloy.[62] Laloy was just about to get married to Susanik Babaïan, known as Chouchik, an Armenian who would soon become a very close friend of Emma. Chouchik was the sister of Marguerite Babaïan, a soprano who became an admired interpreter not just of Armenian and Greek music, but of songs by Ravel and Debussy. Debussy and Emma were unable to attend the wedding on 27 December as they would be leaving for Brussels, but looked forward to playing bridge again and meeting Madame Laloy. It was in Brussels that Debussy wrote what one assumes was a New Year's greeting to Emma, even though she was by his side, having travelled with him, assuring her of his undying love, 'mon amour infini', and his 'passionate gratitude' for everything she did, so 'graciously constant'.[63] They were staying at the Hôtel Métropole and had brought Chouchou with them.

No doubt Emma had much to contend with during this stay in Brussels, including Debussy's black moods. Perhaps influenced by his dealings with Maurice Maeterlinck over *Pelléas et Mélisande* in 1902, Debussy disliked Belgium and the Belgians. He complained of the rain, he disliked this small nation, which 'resembles a lot of little men with a bombastic pretentiousness which is usually merely silly, but which becomes dangerous when it's a question of the fate of a work of art.'[64]

Another guest at the hotel was Debussy's first Mélisande, Mary Garden, Lilly's faithful supporter, who claimed that Debussy never came on stage.

> He sat there, silent and detached, and when he had anything to communicate to one of us on the stage, he would write it down on a slip of paper and send it up by a boy ... Debussy lived in a world of his own, where no one, not even his first wife, Lily [*sic*], with all her care and attention, could reach him.[65]

On top of everything, Chouchou, once again, was unwell. This was the last straw for Debussy, who wrote to Durand that he was going to leave Brussels before the first night. On 9 January, the very day of the first performance, the family left for Paris.

---

[62] C. p. 982.

[63] It is undated. 'Ma gratitude passionnée de ce que tu fais de si gracieusement constant.' C. p. 985.

[64] C. p. 985.

[65] M. Garden, *Mary Garden's Story*, p. 73.

Despite the success of the opera, it was not until 23 January that Debussy wrote to Laloy that he had had to spend a fortnight re-educating the orchestra amongst a whole list of other complaints: 'a constant battle – how exhausting – to achieve something passable.' Yet, it was a triumph.[66]

---

[66] C. p. 993.

7

1907: Stagnation

Attacks on Debussy

The New Year 1907 did not bring inspiration. Contrary to when bursting with emotion upon first eloping with Emma, Debussy was now suffering from an inability to compose new material in a style which would please both him and his critics. Colonne was anxious to programme *Le Roi Lear*, to which Debussy replied, 'it might be necessary to replace this with another piece, which I would like to surprise you with.'[1] Eventually he provided not a brand new composition, but an orchestrated version of a song, 'Jet d'eau', the third of the *Cinq Poèmes de Baudelaire*, originally composed in 1889. When it was performed on 24 February 1907 at the Concerts Colonne, sung by Hélène Demellier, it met with a luke-warm reception. Now Debussy certainly needed the support of his faithful friend Louis Laloy, for Émile Vuillermoz, sixteen years younger than Debussy and a former pupil of Fauré, wrote a stinging attack on Debussy accusing him of providing his followers with material dredged up from the bottom drawer, which is precisely what Debussy had feared people would say when he had written to his publisher a year earlier.[2] This was a foretaste of similar criticism Emma would receive after Debussy's death. Vuillermoz asserted that Debussy was only trying to make sure his name did not miss a year appearing on Colonne's posters. The crowning insult was to insist that the young composers following on from Debussy were composing 'Debussy … better than him!'[3]

Laloy, however, managed to upset Debussy about another matter. On 12 January 1907 the controversial first performance of *Histoires naturelles* by Maurice Ravel took place. Laloy, to Debussy's astonishment, expressed great admiration for Ravel's iconoclastic song cycle which ingeniously and to many, shockingly, managed to combine rather frivolous-sounding settings of colloquial speech with contemporary harmonies and rhythms. Debussy wrote to Laloy disputing the whole idea of 'humorous music'.[4] Debates had already arisen as to who had influenced whom of the two composers. Now this rift was heightened by the migration of some 'Debussystes' to the support of Ravel, of whom people were saying, 'you'll see he will go further than Debussy.'[5] Laloy reported that he tried to prevent any misunderstanding between

---

[1] C. p. 993.
[2] C. p. 948.
[3] *La Nouvelle Presse*, 3 March 1907.
[4] C. p. 999.
[5] L. Laloy, *La musique retrouvée*, Paris, 1928, p. 165.

them. Despite Ravel's admiration for Debussy, to their mutual regret their friendship cooled.[6] This episode took place at what must have been a very sensitive time for both Debussy and Emma, for in February they received a blow which would affect their lives together.

Death of Osiris and consequences of his will

On 4 February 1907 Emma's uncle Osiris died. Such was his importance that this news was reported in many newspapers, local, national and international.[7] A column and a half was devoted to him in *Le Figaro* the following day. And what was the headline? 'Twenty-five million left to the Institut Pasteur'.[8] 'Almost his whole fortune, fifty million', it continued, 'has been left to good causes.' In the first paragraph were listed his executors: no longer Sigismond Bardac, but more influential and important figures in French society, Émile Loubet, former President of the Republic, Maître Jacques Bétolaud, former *bâtonnier*, head of the Bar (*Ordre des avocats*) at the Court of Appeal of Paris, and Osiris's own lawyer, Monsieur Philipott. In obituaries his modest life style was emphasised, his self-imposed separation from fellow Jewish financiers, his gifts to the nation, his amassing of a fortune quietly and without ostentation. The Château La Tour Blanche was left to the Ministry of Agriculture to become a School of Viticulture and Œnology, which continues to this day, his villas at Arcachon were left to that town, his Paris houses to the state.

The front page of *Le Grand Illustré de la petite Gironde* was covered with exclamations about the huge sum of money Osiris had left. The Insitut Pasteur today acknowledges that it received the sum of thirty-six million gold francs, the largest legacy in its history.[9] Most of the remainder was divided between many other charitable causes. By now Osiris's will had gone far beyond being a family matter and was an affair, not just of the Institut Pasteur but of the state. There is a certain irony in the fact that one of Debussy's closest friends and admirers ever since he had been present at the première of *Pelléas* and who remained faithful to both Debussy and Emma all his life was Pasteur Vallery-Radot, Louis Pasteur's grandson.

The last version of Osiris's will, after many revisions, was made on 15 March 1906, but even this was modified up to 29 December of that year. As in his previous will, Emma's inheritance depended upon her mother's death. Finally, Osiris left a life annuity of forty thousand francs to his sister Laure. When she died this was to be divided into sums including five thousand francs' annuity each to Emma, Raoul, Dolly and Emma's cousin Charlotte. However, with Laure still alive, an immediate annuity of three thousand francs went to Raoul, and Dolly would receive one hundred thousand

---

[6] Idem. pp. 166–7.

[7] Several cuttings have been preserved at the city archives of Bordeaux, 42 S 6366-6367. Fonds Evrard de Fayolle.

[8] *Le Figaro*, 5 February 1907.

[9] https://www.pasteur.fr/en/research-journal/news/daniel-iffla-osiris-great-19th-century-philanthropist-and-institut-pasteur-s-most-generous-donor (last accessed 27 May 2020).

francs' capital when she reached her majority or married. Emma was to receive *nothing* until the death of her mother, upon which an annuity of five thousand francs would become available to her – considerably less than the twenty-four thousand francs in the previous will.[10] Laure Moyse did not die until 1915. Obviously, Emma's life as first Fauré's, then Debussy's mistress and its consequent implications for her involvement in Lilly's suicide attempt had had an indelible effect on Osiris, whose fidelity to his dead wife was renowned. In any event, the amount of money left to family was extremely insignificant compared to that left to charities and institutions.

Osiris's disapproval of Emma's behaviour had also been manifested in another way before his death. One of his villas in Arcachon was already called 'Betsy-Ferguson'. Now the house next door to this, originally named 'Emma', was dedicated instead to the second sister, Elisa, and renamed 'Ferguson'.

The funeral took place on 6 February. The coffin was laid out in the conservatory of Osiris's house in the rue La Bruyère. Emma's mother, Laure, and Raoul Bardac were amongst the relatives present, but not Emma herself. The gentleman named in the newspapers as M. Van Bogh 'his cousin' was in fact Gaston Van Brock, witness to so many personal family events. Rabbi Weill led the prayers. Demonstrating Osiris's love of economy, the coffin was placed on a '3rd class hearse', one simple wreath of violets was laid on it, then Raoul led the procession to the cemetery of Montmartre, where the enormous statue of Moses towered over the tomb Osiris had so fastidiously provided for himself and those he deemed worthy of a place in it. Amongst members of the procession besides his esteemed executors were the Under-secretary of State for the Beaux-Arts, M. Dujardin-Beaumetz, the Chief Rabbi of Paris, J. H. Dreyfus, Doctors Roux and Metchnikoff of the Institut Pasteur and 'other representatives of the world of politics, science and the arts'. Military honours were provided by a company of the 24th Infantry Regiment.[11]

It is no wonder that Emma was so often unwell at this time. Tension over her own affairs and the involvement of her mother and brother in the personal and financial brouhaha must have been worrying. Besides his lack of inspiration and output, Debussy was having to minister to her needs during this time of stress. There is no mention of anything to do with Osiris, his death or his will, in his correspondence, but in mid-February he wrote to Durand apologising for not being able to attend an event, saying, 'You are so kind, but given *Ibéria*, my daughter and my wife whom I can not leave alone, please excuse me ...'[12]

A further reminder of Emma's Jewish origins came in April 1907 in the form of a suggestion that the Swiss Jewish composer Ernest Bloch might introduce himself to Debussy. Robert Godet, a friend of Debussy since 1889, who had not corresponded with him since Lilly's suicide attempt and would not do so until November 1910, suggested to Bloch on 23 April 1907 that he should visit Debussy and ask him for advice, taking with him his opera *Macbeth*, which he was in the process of composing. He believed that since Emma was also Jewish, this might facilitate contact. 'Are you

---

[10] Ardoin Saint Amand, *Osiris*, p. 60.
[11] *Le Figaro*, 7 February 1907.
[12] C. p. 994.

loath to take advantage of your racial connections? This is one of the biggest facets of your personality', he wrote to Bloch.[13] It is unlikely that the meeting between Debussy and Bloch had anything to do with Emma's Jewish background as she did not actively seek to consort with other Jews, but Debussy certainly wrote to Bloch suggesting a date for his visit to their house. Godet's perceived attitude to her influenced Emma's opinion of him after Debussy's death.

Unfinished projects; a gift for Emma

Musical revelations continued to impress themselves upon Debussy. In May, he and Emma were given two seats by his 'cher ami', Paul Dukas, to attend the open dress rehearsal of his opera, *Ariane et Barbe-Bleue*. Dukas had renewed his friendship, strained since the Lilly scandal, and wanted Debussy's opinion on his opera. Then there was a series of five 'historical' Russian concerts at the Opéra organised by Gabriel Astruc and Sergei Diaghilev, followed by Debussy's first experience of Richard Strauss's *Salomé*, an opera which he called immediately 'a masterpiece ... a phenomenon almost as rare as the appearance of a comet'.[14] Perhaps Debussy himself could turn to a new project for the theatre? In July an old friend, whom he had known since 1889, the poet and playwright Gabriel Mourey, offered him a libretto based on *Le roman de Tristan* by Joseph Bédier, which Debussy approached initially with considerable enthusiasm. He had wanted to make an opera out of the book when it first appeared in 1900, but had then forgotten about it. Now, he told Victor Segalen, a doctor, orientalist and writer who had introduced himself to Debussy in 1906, that his enthusiasm had been rekindled.[15] This, however, was yet another project that would never come to fruition, just like a collaboration with Segalen on the subject of Buddha, *Siddartha*. Nor would *Orphée-roi*, another work by Segalen.

One miniature composition did see the light of day prior to this exchange of correspondence – a very private work, the score and vocal parts of which were written out ironically in the style of an entry for the Prix de Rome. This brief parody, only twenty-two bars long, was entitled *Petite cantate sur grand papier pour le jour de Sa fête* ... ('Little cantata on large paper for the day of Her celebration ...') The manuscript is dated 4 June 1907, following the pattern of June celebrations for Emma. Surely it is 4 June itself which is of mutual significance, for Debussy had noted at the end, 'Tuesday 4 June 07. (Half-past midnight), with the apologies of the author who loves you, Claude Debussy.' Presumably the apologies were for the half hour's lack of punctuality. The two soloists indicated are Chouchou (now 17 months old) and the first '*Récitant*', a bass-baritone part to be sung by the composer himself.

---

[13] C. p. 1004, n.2, quoting J. Lewinsky, E. Dijon, *Ernest Bloch (1880–1959). Sa vie et sa pensée, suivi de l'analyse de son œuvre*, Geneva, 1998.

[14] C. p. 1009.

[15] C. p. 1020. Victor Segalen had already spent a long period in Polynesia and would leave for China in 1909.

Chouchou: *Ah! Maman ah! Papa ah! dédé!*
1st 'Récitant' [narrator]: Madame, permit us on this beautiful day, the most beautiful day in the world, since it is the blessed day of your *fête*.
Voices (behind the walls): Permit us to sing for you crazy things composed for you alone.
1st 'Récitant': Permit us to tell you tenderly of the infinite love which Claude Debussy has for you.
Chouchou (*her voice rising above the noise of the crowd and the bells*): It is true! It is true!
Voices (behind the walls): Glory! Glory! Glory be to Chouchou's mother, glory be to Chouchou's mother.
Chouchou: I am going to bed! Bâââ------jour!

As is evident, this does not translate well as it is in grandiose (typical of Prix de Rome set texts) yet childish language. Chouchou's words at the end are a mixture of a yawn and a '*Bonjour*'. From double forte the dynamics drop to pianissimo for this exhausted final sigh. Besides the two soloists there is a four-part chorus ('behind the walls') and it is scored for bells ('behind the foliage'), presumably glockenspiel or carillon, and an imposing accompaniment, generally chordal in nature, which has the appearance of the piano reduction of a score.[16] There is an echo of the very first dedication to Emma of the *Ariettes oubliées* of 4 June 1903 in the dedication of this 'cantata', which surely gives a clue to the reason for celebration. The earlier: 'à Madame S. Bardac, dont la sympathie musicale m'est précieuse – infiniment. Claude Debussy. Juin 1903' had now become 'Permettez-nous de vous dire tendrement l'amour infini qu'a pour vous Claude Debussy.' The infinity of the initial precious mutual love of music had lasted and mutated into tender infinite pure love of both Emma and Chouchou, indicated by the plural form of you, 'vous'. Just as in the piano fragment of 1905, those mystical ninths were present in the part of the first 'récitant', Debussy himself. Chouchou may not yet have been old enough to perform her own part, but clearly Emma's role as the mother of this little miracle was as important to the composer as her role as his wife. It was already June, yet this brief piece of music was the only work Debussy had 'completed' in 1907 thus far. Life was still not conducive to the solitary state of inspiration required by this other 'woman', music.

A small circle of friends; return to Pourville

Socially he and Emma still entertained regularly, if informally. Paul-Jean Toulet invited himself to dinner on Friday 28 June, promising to bring a bottle of good Jurançon wine from the region of his birth, Pau, and from remarks in other letters it is clear that Friday (later, Thursday) visits became regular. It has already been noted that Dolly recalled that he was one of the Debussys' small circle of welcome guests. But yet again, there is clear evidence of Emma's poor health. On 13 July Debussy thanked Toulet for sending over a prescription for her so promptly. Just as before,

---

[16] BnF Musique, MS-14519. The composition is described in detail in R. Orledge, 'Debussy's Musical Gifts to Emma Bardac', *The Musical Quarterly*, October 1974, pp. 544–6.

when he had grumbled to Raoul that Emma reacted against all kinds of medicine,[17] he informed Toulet sardonically that 'It didn't do her any good, but that doesn't mean to say that it won't cure the rest of the world.'[18] Emma, in fact, came to rely entirely on homeopathic remedies and to favour them for her family.

Emma proved her usefulness as an interpreter in the same month when Sir Henry Wood came to visit Debussy. Sir Edgar Speyer was determined that Debussy should come to Queen's Hall in London to conduct his own works, and sent Sir Henry on a mission to persuade him. 'Tell Debussy what you like,' he said, 'but make him come over.' They agreed to offer Debussy the sum of a hundred pounds. 'I made up my mind to tackle him through Madame Debussy who, as it happened, spoke perfect English,' wrote Sir Henry. ' … I tactfully approached Madame Debussy and revealed my mission. When she told her husband and mentioned the fee he jumped up, furious.

"What? A hundred guineas … for *me*? And yet you pay Caruso four hundred guineas?"' Sir Henry assured him that they never engaged any singer for such a fee, and after calming down, Debussy agreed to come to London the following year for a fee of two hundred guineas.[19]

Another English contact who wanted to 'make Debussy's art-product in any way better known in England'[20] was Louise Liebich, who visited Debussy in 1907 to interview him for the biography which, when published the following year, would become the first in English of the composer. In her catalogue of his works at the end of the book she listed three in preparation, *King Lear*, *Willowwood* and *Histoire de Tristan* (opera).[21] None of these came to fruition. Instead of commencing a new composition, Debussy now worked on the re-orchestration of the cantata *L'enfant prodigue*, his competition piece for the Prix de Rome, first performed in 1884, in order for it to be performed by Sir Henry Wood at the Sheffield Festival of 1908. Wood said that this was at Debussy's own suggestion during his visit to him in Paris. 'Incidentally,' Wood wrote, 'we rather startled Yorkshire by singing it in French.'[22]

Jacques Durand remained Debussy's outlet for expressing frustration with life. They corresponded about the London trip, but clearly Durand also had Debussy's well-being in mind, for the latter exclaimed that he could never take Durand's advice to smoke less. 'If I did not smoke so keenly, I would be thinking about contradictory things infinitely worse than this dear grey substance.' Now, in addition to his wife's health and other distractions, there was the domestic problem of a malfunctioning boiler as well as half a dozen other faults in the house which the architect claimed would collapse on top of them if they delayed repairs. This meant the family was 'forced out' and had to escape to familiar Pourville for the summer, not a destination he relished. 'An absurd

---

[17] Chapter 6 p. 86.

[18] C. pp. 1013–4.

[19] Henry J. Wood, *My Life of Music*, London, 1938, p. 238.

[20] L. Liebich, *Claude-Achille Debussy*, London, 1908, 'Author's note'.

[21] Idem. p. 92.

[22] Henry J. Wood, *My Life of Music*, p. 280.

little beach,' he told the composer and conductor Francisco de Lacerda. 'No doubt we will be most uncomfortable there and I am counting on being able to work without fearing the pervasive charm of the countryside!' Grumbling to Louis Laloy about the prospect of staying in an awful hotel, he expressed the sincere hope that without distractions he would be able to end the conflict going on inside him between music and himself. His depression is obvious. 'I am working and – I am afraid of tomorrow. – It's unpleasant, but not of any interest.'[23]

Thus on 2 August Debussy, Emma, Chouchou and Dolly[24] left for the Grand Hotel, Pourville. Whilst there he spent time reading and reconsidering his collaboration on *Siddhartha* with Victor Segalen, but eventually rejected this. He was unable to find 'music capable of penetrating these depths!' He did not fail to grumble to him and to Toulet about the 'horrible place' (*endroit odieux*) he was staying in. He was also hoping to finish work on the *Images*.

Now it was not just Emma who was ill. Debussy told Durand he was suffering terrible stomach cramps made worse by the sea air. The only positive comment was that he was glad to see the Channel again, smaller than the Atlantic but such a delicate sea, with such diverse harmonies. 'She is also delightfully hypocritical and tells lies to you with a woman's smiles.' A fortnight later he was still suffering. His pains were making him terribly tired. The work on the boiler had been held up so they could not yet return home. By 27 August his frustration was boiling over. He grumbled to Toulet about the ridiculous people around him, the lack of hot water, tasteless food, the English, the ugly women. 'Music', he told Durand, was 'not something that can flow within a rigorous, traditional form. It consists of colours and rhythmic time …' Colour and rhythm are certainly essential characteristics of the 'Rondes de printemps', the third of the *Images* for orchestra that he was working on. However, on his return to Paris he wrote to Gabriel Mourey, saying that he had spent more than a month doing nothing of any use.[25]

André Caplet joins the select few

During October and November 1907 Debussy was occupied with plans for a concert to be entirely dedicated to his works in Le Havre the following year. Georges Jean-Aubry introduced him to André Caplet, a composer and conductor whose 'sureness of taste' he appreciated and to whom he was willing to delegate the task of organising such an event. This was the beginning of Caplet's long and fruitful friendship and collaboration with both Debussy and Emma. Debussy had to attend rehearsals for the first orchestral performance of his *Petite suite*, orchestrated by Henri Busser, which took place on 3 November, conducted by Camille Chevillard at the Concerts Lamoureux. He also wrote a memorable article for the journal *Musica* in praise of his Mélisande, Mary Garden, to be published in January 1908, for which he received the welcome sum of one hundred francs.

---

[23] C. pp. 1016–9.
[24] All were mentioned in a letter of 27 August, C. p. 1029.
[25] C. pp. 1027–31.

On 26 November Debussy and Emma entertained to dinner Louis Laloy, his wife Chouchik and the pianist Ricardo Viñes, to whom he played the now-completed second book of piano *Images*. The second of these, 'Et la lune descend sur le temple qui fut', was dedicated to the orientalist, Laloy. Viñes was delighted to receive the dedication of 'Poissons d'or', the first time Debussy had paid him such an honour. He also commented in his diary that 'Debussy's wife (the former Mme Bardac) is very likeable and has a daughter of about fifteen, quite sweet'.[26] Viñes's admirable interpretation of 'Poissons d'or' and Debussy's own approval of it remained etched in Dolly's memory. The 'rippling quality' of his playing was particularly suited to it. She was at pains to point out that the piece was inspired by a Chinese lacquered wood panel that Debussy had bought in his favourite shop on one of his rare outings from the house and which hung in his study.[27]

The move with Emma to their smart home, her claims on his time and domestic matters weighed heavily on Debussy's mind, still disrupting that all-important instinctive process of inspiration. Constant rain mirrored his mood.

> I am working on important things alternating between feelings of joy and sadness … all in all, there is no peace in my soul. Is it because of the restless landscape in this corner of Paris …? Is it that I am definitely not made for domestic life? So many questions for which I don't have the strength to find an answer.[28]

It is increasingly evident that the circle of friends and acquaintances invited to dine at the Debussy household was restricted only to those whose company both Debussy and Emma enjoyed, the closest being Laloy and Toulet. On 14 November 1907 Victor Segalen assumed that Emma still entertained formally in the socially accepted fashion, for he asked Debussy if Madame Debussy was receiving 'at home' that winter. 'Est-ce que Mme Debussy recevra cet hiver?' 'My wife never holds "at homes"', Debussy replied. 'Nor do I. She will see you whenever you like, with the greatest pleasure.' He made another revealing confidence: 'I don't even talk about music to my wife. Or if I do, it is purely anecdotal.' Besides giving up holding events in her home to maintain her position socially, Emma had certainly reigned in any desire to mingle at soirées or salon concerts. One wonders how much self-sacrifice this involved. She must have spent much time upstairs in her room whilst her husband worked in his study below. It is evident that those scurrilous rumours from the time of their elopement that Debussy was marrying Emma to gain access to the high society of Paris were total fabrication. During the same conversation, Segalen asked Debussy to play him *L'isle joyeuse* and wondered where the inspiration for this joyous piece had come from. In his reply Debussy made no reference to Emma. 'Purely from my imagination,' was the response.[29]

There is a note from Debussy to Emma without a precise date in 1907, but perhaps written about this time, the first of several in which he asked her to come downstairs to say hello to him. It was playfully written, for it was contained in a little basket, for

---

[26] F. Lesure, *Claude Debussy*, p. 240.
[27] De Tinan, French interview; Dolly Bardac, London interview.
[28] C. p. 1036.
[29] C. pp. 2204–5.

which he gave instructions on how to open the lock, and implied an urgent need to see her. 'Once open, you must read the letter and come down straight away to say good day to Claude'.[30] Had she shut herself away feeling neglected or upset, or was he lonely in his study, feeling the pangs of love and had an urgent need to see his wife? Considering the mood of his letters, either scenario is quite possible.

There is no extant Christmas message to Emma this year. On 18 December Debussy wrote to Durand with dates for a prospective journey to Italy in April 1908, the month Toscanini was to conduct *Pelléas et Mélisande* in Milan, which would, in fact, never take place. On this same day he dedicated to Emma a copy bearing his handwritten corrections of the second series of *Images* for piano, with the words, 'This copy belongs to *Chouchou mère*. 18 déc. 07. Son ClD'.[31] Her role as mother had superseded that of wife and lover. These *Images* had been completed in October 1907 and were published by Durand in January 1908.

---

[30] C. p. 1047.
[31] 'Cet exemplaire appartient à Chouchou mère. 18 déc.07. Son ClD.' C. p. 2219; BnF Musique, Rés.Vma. 296.

8

1908: Marriage and an ivory tower

Besides the concerts in England being organised by Speyer, Debussy now also had to prepare the score of *La mer* for a performance which Édouard Colonne was planning for 12 January 1908. Colonne's familiarity with Emma, dating from her early days in Paris when she had lessons with his wife, was evident in a letter he addressed to her on 31 December 1907, which began 'Bien chère amie'. He was planning to conduct the work himself, and asked Emma to arrange a long session for him with Debussy. By the time he finished this note, it was quarter past midnight – the New Year – and he ended it with the warm greeting to the whole family, 'je vous embrasse tous de tout mon cœur'.[1] He would not be the only one to find it easier to write to Emma to arrange meetings with her husband than to contact him directly. However, things did not go as planned. We learn from a letter Debussy wrote to Victor Segalen that the rehearsals were '*lamentable*' leading to Colonne replacing this work with *L'après-midi d'un faune* on 12 January and asking Debussy to take up the baton himself for *La mer* on 19 and 26 January.[2] His debut as a conductor at the first rehearsal on Tuesday 14 January was undertaken with a 'pounding heart', but the experience was a revelation. He felt he had entered the heart of his own music and turned into an instrument unleashing all its sonorities simply by waving a little stick.

The performance on Sunday 19 January 1908 was also a revelation to the audience. The sharp-tongued critic, Willy (Henry Gauthier-Villars), writing as *l'Ouvreuse* in *Comœdia*, commented that the final note unleashed an ovation which proved victoriously the solid construction of the theatre. Never before had he heard such a din as caused by this enthusiasm.[3]

Marriage of Emma and Debussy

The timing of both the rehearsal and the performance must have been particularly stressful for Debussy, for that Sunday 19 January 1908 was the evening before his official marriage to Emma. Whether Debussy believed he was made for domestic life or not, Emma soon had sure grounds to persuade him to confirm their status together, something about which they must have had much discussion in private. On 7 November 1907 a law was passed modifying article 331 of the Civil Code. Children born outside wedlock could now be made legitimate if the parents married. A note had to be added to the child's birth certificate acknowledging this legitimisation.

---

[1] C. p. 1046.
[2] C. pp. 1054–5.
[3] *Comœdia*, 20 January 1908.

On 15 January 1908, the day after the rehearsal, Debussy and Emma signed a contract for the *séparation des biens* which ensured that each party kept their own property and possessions,[4] and on Monday 20 January, at four o'clock in the afternoon, only two months after the law came into effect, Achille-Claude Debussy, Composer of music, Chevalier de la Légion d'honneur, married Emma Léa Moyse at the town hall of the 16th arrondissement of Paris. It was specifically stated on the marriage certificate that as a result, their daughter Claude Emma would be made legitimate according to the new law. The address of Debussy's parents was that to which they had moved upon his father's retirement in the rue Lafontaine, whilst Emma's mother's address was given as that which appeared on other official Bardac documents, 3 rue du Colisée. Once again, Emma's cousin Gaston van Brock was a witness. The others were lawyers. On Chouchou's birth certificate, there is a note added on the side, beneath that in which Sigismond Bardac repudiated all responsibility for her, which confirmed that she was now the legitimate daughter of Claude Debussy and Emma Moyse. This is dated 19 April 1908.

It is striking that fifty-four years later, in his biography of Debussy, Marcel Dietschy should promote the myth that Emma's only desire in officially marrying Debussy was to ensnare the composer, 'l'attacher définitivement',[5] and that he subconsciously acceded to this because of his innate need for 'an atmosphere of considerate ease, of discretion, of discriminating intimacy, and of passionate tenderness'.[6] There was no hint of the legal reason for the marriage. He continued, 'There he spent the last ten years of his life, and they were irradiated with happiness.' This statement was misleading. Happiness would not be the most characteristic feature of the ten years of Debussy's married life. Dietschy's translators ascribed the author's attitude to the wishes of Dolly, who only permitted positive descriptions of her mother.[7] It is sad that so long after Emma's death opinion should still be inconsiderately stacked against her. She did indeed do her best to accede to Debussy's desires for comfort and ease, but not without encountering considerable obstacles. By 1908 she had already lived with him for three years, so could have been under no illusions about the problems of life with an irascible composer. She may initially not have understood how difficult it would be to provide the right conditions and allow him to work at his own pace with no guaranteed regular income, a problem encountered by most composers and artists, but she had wanted to share her life with a musician far removed from the material world of banking, which had been her world for some twenty-five years before she eloped with Debussy. She had not needed the security of a marriage contract to convince her to stay with him. Clearly, after agreeing to live with the woman he had fallen in love with, Debussy enjoyed the comfort and ostensible security this relationship brought, despite reservations about the restrictions it inevitably brought to his freedom to compose. The legitimisation of the birth of Chouchou was the prime motivation for the marriage.

---

4   Ardoin Saint Amand, *Osiris,* p. 70.
5   M. Dietschy, *La passion de Claude Debussy*, p. 193.
6   M. Dietschy, *A Portrait of Claude Debussy*, p. 151.
7   Ibid.

At some stage during Chouchou's short life, whether at birth or now when officially married, Emma invested in French government bonds for her daughter. This is evident from two sources, the official probate statement of Chouchou dated 16 January 1920 and Emma's own probate statement of 27 June 1935, both of which show that Chouchou possessed twenty-six thousand five hundred francs of *Rente Française*, or government bonds, the '*nue propriété*' (ownership) being hers, but being under the 'legal administration' of Claude Debussy.[8] This is significant in view of the ever-worsening financial situation of Emma and Claude Debussy. Claude certainly could not have afforded the bonds. The money must originally have been Emma's own, deriving from her previous marriage, although obviously not directly from Sigismond. He had completely rejected all links to her third child.

One wonders how last-minute the arrangements for the marriage were, for on 17 January Debussy had written to Gabriel Mourey inviting him to his house on that afternoon of Monday 20 January 1908. Obviously this meeting had to be postponed and two days after the visit to the town hall he wrote to Mourey again, apologising for not having seen him, not mentioning the reason, and expressing pleasure that he had enjoyed *La mer*.[9] Mourey actually wanted to mount *La damoiselle élue* at the Théâtre des Arts, but the composer was unenthusiastic, lacking trust in the way it would be done.

The marriage was quite a clandestine affair. Nowhere in the extant correspondence of January 1908 is there any reference to the official change in the couple's personal circumstances. Paul-Jean Toulet had written a pleasant letter to Debussy on 14 January asking after his family, hoping in particular that 'Mademoiselle Claude' was well and growing nicely, and commenting on the 'person you brought over from the other side of the sea who speaks such a strange idiom', Chouchou's English governess, known as 'Miss'. In his reply Debussy exclaimed that since last seeing him he had launched his career as a conductor, and would be conducting again in England, then Italy. 'Life is full of surprises.' 'Mademoiselle Claude,' he informed Toulet, 'tells strange stories in English–French patois, which leaves her two grandmothers rather stupefied'.[10]

On 24 January, in the first of many extant letters to Chouchik Laloy, wife of Louis Laloy, Emma thanked her for a soirée which Dolly had attended and sent her Chouchou's greetings but, again, there was no talk of her marriage, something you would imagine close friends would discuss. She did, however, sign herself Emma C Debussy.[11] In almost every letter to any correspondent from now on, the C or even the full Claude was included in her signature. Emma Léa Bardac née Moyse had become Emma C Debussy, Emma Claude Debussy, Emma Cl Debussy or, to close friends, occasionally Emma, but more often Emma CD, not, of course to be confused with her daughter, Claude Emma Debussy.

---

[8] *Formule de Déclaration de Mutation par Décès, Succession de Mlle Debussy*, 16 January 1920 and *Formule de Déclaration de Mutation par Décès, Succession de Madame Veuve Debussy*, 27 June 1935. Copies kindly provided by M. Vincent Laloy.

[9] C. pp. 1056, 1059.

[10] C. pp. 1053, 1061.

[11] C. p. 1062 and Laloy archives B, Dossier 81, A1.

To London to conduct

By 30 January 1908 Debussy and his family were in London, staying at the Grosvenor Hotel. A witness to the rehearsal of *La mer* and the *Prélude à l'après-midi d'un faune* was Victor Segalen. He spent the rehearsal time sitting next to Emma, who remarked to him that they were listening to 'the sea in bits' whilst Debussy tried to make each orchestral section conform to his wishes. They also discussed the version Debussy had made for four hands, which Emma said was unplayable and had indeed never been played except by the composer, who played it with two hands. André Caplet was working on a transcription for two pianos, which would be far more approachable.[12] Henry Wood saw that Debussy was delighted with his reception, believing that Londoners appreciated his music more than his own countrymen. Not even Richard Strauss had received a warmer welcome.[13] On his return to Paris Debussy told Mourey that all had gone well but the Grosvenor Hotel was 'hard on our purse strings'.[14] Finances were clearly an issue, despite having persuaded Speyer to pay him double what he originally intended.

We are reminded once again of Emma's English skills in a letter from Paul-Jean Toulet to Debussy in March. Toulet had received a letter from Singapore written on paper from the Raffles Hotel, and he joked that in spite of tuition from Madame Debussy he had made no progress in the pronunciation of this extraordinary word, 'Raffles'. Debussy in his reply informed him that he would not be going to Italy to hear the performance, in Italian, of *Pelléas et Mélisande* at La Scala, Milan, conducted by Toscanini. Nor had he been to New York to hear *Pelléas* at the Manhattan Opera, sung by Mary Garden on 19 February.

Comments on the Debussys' lifestyle

Gossip about the Debussys had spread far beyond the shores of France, for even on the other side of the Atlantic there were malicious tongues. In preparation for this performance, a full-page spread was published in the *New York Times* on 16 February 1908, which began with some personal comments about the composer. Richard Aldrich wrote regarding his lack of musical output: 'Latterly he has put forth little. A somewhat cynical brother musician of distinction remarked … that he had married a rich wife and that his only concern now was stocking his wine cellar.'[15]

The *bordelais* composer Jean Roger-Ducasse knew Debussy well. As noted earlier, he taught Dolly the piano, and he and Debussy often played their compositions to each other and discussed the current musical scene. Both men had in common a reserve towards their fellow men, familiarity being kept for only a select few, but he became a regular visitor to Debussy's house and often played bridge with him and

---

[12] C. p. 1063. Caplet's version for two pianos, six hands was performed on 6 March 1908. It did not receive much attention in the press.
[13] H. Wood, *My Life of Music*, p. 297.
[14] C. p. 1067.
[15] *New York Times*, 16 February 1908.

Emma. To Roger-Ducasse Debussy expressed the opinion that an artist should not have to depend on the fruit of his labours for financial reward, but that a patron or even a rich aristocrat, a 'prince of the State', should provide for him.[16] If this was true, it illustrated a sense of entitlement which would explain why Debussy never wanted to earn money by teaching. On 8 February 1908 Roger-Ducasse commented to his friend André Lambinet on the second series of *Images* for piano, recently published, 'Look at the titles!' Of the third he wrote, 'Ouch! "Poisson [sic] d'or" [Goldfish] … Where did the title of the third piece spring from, causing tongues to wag?'[17] The allusion was, of course, to Debussy's relationship with Emma, the assumption being that he was fishing for her money, this despite the fact that eleven years earlier Roger-Ducasse had dedicated the first of his *Deux Rondels* to her. Clearly there had been no let-up in the spiteful comments so readily made by contemporaries. On 21 February Ricardo Viñes performed this set of *Images* at the *Cercle musical*, but it did not meet with success. Indeed, the pianist described it as *'un véritable fiasco'*.[18]

Following her visit in 1907, Louise Liebich's biography of Debussy was published in London in March 1908.[19] She was clearly very struck by Debussy's reserve, noting his

> insistent claim to reticence and even silence regarding the intimate details of his career and existence. He has elected to shelter himself from publicity and advertisement … He is sometimes supposed to have enclosed himself within a self-constructed mental tower of ivory whence the visible world is no longer perceptible, and where the passions and emotions of ordinary men reach him only as echoes or shadowy dreams …[20]

Dolly herself later used the term 'ivory tower' when reminiscing on Debussy's life with Emma. 'Usually life was excessively calm. It was life in an ivory tower.'[21]

Liebich made no mention of Debussy's wife. Debussy's realisation that the image perceived of him by those outside his close circle was not a happy one was expressed in a dedication of a somewhat serious photograph of himself to Emma made on 6 April 1908. 'Only my own dear little one, my wife, knows this sad official Claude Debussy in happier moods.'[22] He also wrote a personal dedication in a pocket score of *Pelléas et Mélisande*, 'To my dear little wife, this music which would be waiting

---

[16] 'Debussy me disait (et dans sa bouche, cela est cruel) qu'un artiste ne devrait pas attendre son pain de son travail, mais au contraire, d'un mécène, d'un prince d'État, qui lui fournirait tout ce qu'il faudrait.' J. Roger-Ducasse, 1 November 1907, *Lettres à son ami André Lambinet*, Sprimont, 2001, p. 44.

[17] 'Aië! Poisson d'or … D'où est né involontairement le 3e titre qui fait parler quelque peu!' Ibid. The title is 'Poissons d'or'.

[18] C. p. 1065, n.1.

[19] L. Liebich, *Claude-Achille Debussy*, p. 13.

[20] Idem. pp. 1–2.

[21] 'Normalement la vie était excessivement calme. C'était plutôt une tour d'ivoire.' De Tinan, French interview.

[22] 'Á ma chère petite Mienne femme, ce triste et officiel Claude Debussy, dont elle connaît – seule – des attitudes plus heureuses.' Photograph by Otto with dedication, Bnf Musique, Est. Debussy Cl. 014.

for her. Claude Debussy, April 1908.'[23] As Dolly would later tell Heinrich Strobel, Mélisande was not inspired by any specific woman in Debussy's life.[24] Now, at least, he could give Emma the assurance of his love by implying that his masterpiece belonged to her.

On 15 April Debussy and Emma must have been relieved when a contract was signed with Durand for his second series of orchestral *Images* for four thousand eight hundred francs, the first for some time. However, it is no doubt significant that this sum matched exactly the alimony which Durand paid to Lilly each year, so it was not going to provide any great security for the future. Debussy would still have go outside his comfort zone and consider engagements beyond Paris and encourage performances of his works, particularly his opera, to receive more fees and royalties.

By now André Caplet had become one of the select few close friends of the family, addressed in familiar terms and receiving greetings from Emma, Chouchou, whom Debussy described as '*votre amie*', and Dolly in a letter of 18 May. He was invited to dinner to meet Jean Roger-Ducasse, and to go with Debussy to a performance of Mussorgsky's opera *Boris Godunov*.[25] Debussy teased Caplet with words adapted from the third of the *Chansons de Charles d'Orléans* on which he was working, 'Caplet, vous n'êtes qu'un vilain', chiding him for not having been in touch. Louis Laloy and his wife were also welcome in May, Debussy hoping that his roses would be in full bloom for the arrival of Madame Laloy, Emma's friend Chouchik.[26]

Debussy was much happier at home, dining and playing bridge with his small circle, working in his study and enjoying his garden than travelling, but needs must. In June he accepted Henry Wood's invitation to return to the Queen's Hall in London the following February and to go to Edinburgh on 1 March 1909.

Maggie Teyte; contract for two Poe operas

On 12 June 1908 a new Mélisande was heard, the first at the Opéra-Comique since Mary Garden, when Maggie Teyte took over the role. Teyte spent nine months studying her part with Debussy, who, she said, was a man of few words – except for one day when André Caplet joined them. Debussy 'suddenly let forth on the subject of Wagner and Mozart – they had spoiled a lot of paper!'[27] In her autobiography, *Star on the Door*, Maggie Teyte included a photograph Debussy allowed her to take, very similar to the ones previously seen of him, standing in the garden, typically gazing into the distance away from the camera, hands in pockets, for once not holding a cigarette. She did not become a close member of the family circle. There was no

---

[23] 'À ma chère petite femme, cette musique qui l'attendrait. Claude Debussy, avril 1908.' F-Pn, Mus., Rés.2729. I am grateful to Denis Herlin for informing me of this dedication.

[24] Heinrich Strobel, 'Tinan, Hélène de, corrections', Centre de Documentation Claude Debussy, RESE-06.03.

[25] C. p. 1090.

[26] C. p. 1092.

[27] M. Teyte, *Star on the Door*, London, 1958, pp. 66–7. See also G. Opstad, *Debussy's Mélisande. The Lives of Georgette Leblanc, Mary Garden and Maggie Teyte*, pp. 177–80.

mention of Emma, or any sort of informal hospitality. Emma mentioned the opera in a fond letter to Chouchik, undated, thanking her for her affectionate concerns, for a delicious cake and for her kind message on the occasion of *Pelléas*, which enabled her to feel Chouchik close to her.[28]

On 23 June a contract was signed with Durand for the *Trois Chansons de Charles d'Orléans*, for fifteen hundred francs.[29] These songs are for unaccompanied four-part choir, a vocal work indeed, but no solo vocal work inspired by Emma. Debussy had begun the first and third songs ten years earlier for an amateur choir and had now completed the second song, 'Quand j'ai ouy le tabourin'. A couple of weeks later, on 5 July, he signed a contract with Gatti-Casazza, Director of the Metropolitan Opera, New York, for the exclusive rights to perform two stage works based on Edgar Allan Poe: *La chute de la Maison Usher* (*The Fall of the House of Usher*) and *Le diable dans le beffroi*, to be performed in succession on the same evening. Upon signing he received two thousand francs. A further eight thousand francs was to be paid to him upon receipt of the completed operas. Not only this, he agreed to give the Metropolitan Opera the first option on other works to come, in particular *La légende de Tristan*, that work he had been eager to collaborate on with Gabriel Mourey. Debussy seems to have been under no illusions as to the true state of affairs. All three of these stage works had been in his mind for some time, but were nowhere near any state of completion – hardly even begun, in fact. They would all remain unfinished. He himself said to Gatti-Casazza, 'This is a bad deal for you. I even feel some remorse at taking these few dollars off you, as I don't think I will ever manage to finish any of these works. I write for myself alone, and do not care how impatient others get.'[30] This was not the first nor the last time Debussy would obtain money by any means within his power.

With finances permitting no prospect of a summer holiday this year, the family had to make do with days out. How jealous Debussy was of Jacques Durand when he called to see him in his office only to find he had just left for his country house, Bel-Ébat at Avon, near Fontainebleau. To add insult to injury, 'it was raining cats and dogs and my nice grey hat is probably ruined!'[31] On 18 July he told Durand of a planned outing to Bois-le-Roi, not far from Durand's house, and asked if he and his family might visit him and his wife – 'apologies in advance for this invasion of urban barbarians!' At the same time money was still uppermost in his mind as he had to ask Durand to remind his agent to collect his royalties from the relevant organisations.[32] On 31 July another three thousand francs were forthcoming from a contract for *Children's Corner*, one thousand francs for the orchestral version of *L'enfant prodigue* and eight hundred francs for *Printemps*, the latter two, of course, having originally been composed many years earlier.

---

[28] Laloy archives, Dossier 81, A13.
[29] C. p. 1099.
[30] Quoted from A. Schaeffner, *Debussy et Edgar Poe*, Monaco, 1962, in C. p. 1101 n.1.
[31] C. p. 1096.
[32] C. p. 1102.

In her fond reminiscences of Debussy, his former piano pupil Madame Gérard de Romilly recalled the poverty-stricken young man who used to come to her house before and after his marriage to Lilly. She had clearly admired Lilly for the care she took of her husband and ability to manage the household on a 'budget which was more often than not next to zero'. When she reminisced about Debussy since 1908, the tone changed. She had almost lost sight of him despite the fact that now he lived in the Square du Bois de Boulogne, 'not far from my district', implying far more prosperous surroundings than previously. When she did come across him at a concert or in the avenue du Bois, 'he walked with difficulty, absorbed, sad, and in spite of always greeting me affectionately, I already felt he was very distant ...'[33]

Chouchou's upbringing

It is well known that Debussy adored his daughter Chouchou, this 'miracle' as Dolly described her. They were very close, but there is evidence of Debussy's preoccupation with her upbringing in the transcription of a conversation with Victor Segalen, dated 6 May 1908. Chouchou was now two and a half years old. Segalen provided a quotation from Debussy regarding 'the education of girls in general and of Miss Chouchou in particular': 'People are turning the young girl into an equivocal creature, half angel, half monster. It's worrying. I will try to instil in my daughter a degree of loyalty and also of kindness. But in order to do so I will even have to fight against her mother.'[34] These are strong, puzzling words, presumably a remembered excerpt of a conversation. The word *rosse*, translated here as 'monster', is a pejorative term inferring nastiness. One wonders how this subject arose, and why there was implied adverse comment on Emma. The implication was that Emma's intentions for her daughter were different to Debussy's, also that he did not want Chouchou to develop negative qualities. Debussy clearly felt a level of personal responsibility for Chouchou's moral development despite his commitment to music, but it is difficult to understand what Emma could have been opposed to. The language and sentiments were extreme. Segalen may simply have been quoting remarks which underlined his dislike of Emma. In 'Du côté de Debussy' in *Segalen et Debussy*, André Schaeffner pointed out that transcripts of two of Segalen's letters had been curtailed because of his adverse comments on Madame Debussy.[35]

---

[33] 'Il marchait péniblement, absorbé, triste, et malgré son accueil toujours affectueux, je le sentais déjà très loin.' Madame Gérard de Romilly, 'Debussy professeur par une de ses élèves (1898–1908)', *Cahiers Debussy*, no.2, 1978, p. 10.

[34] 'Sur l'éducation des filles en général et de Miss Chouchou en particulier. "On fait de la jeune fille un être équivoque, qui joue moitié l'ange et moitié la rosse. C'est inquiétant. J'essaierai de donner à ma fille un peu de loyauté et aussi de bonté. Mais pour cela, j'aurai même à lutter contre sa mère." C. p. 2206. I am grateful to Roger Nichols for advice in translating this passage.

[35] *Segalen et Debussy*, ed. A. Joly-Segalen, A. Schaeffner, Monaco, 1961, p. 44.

14. Chouchou aged about three

When one sees photographs of Debussy with Chouchou, and reads comments to his friends, it is obvious that he adored her with an unexpected intensity. This little girl looked more like Debussy than her mother. There are many photographs of her, including a series of twelve taken when she was about three, in one single mount, which must have originally hung in a frame in the Debussy's house, her hair in ringlets, first confidently striking poses in a pretty dress, then in winter coat, hat and muff. Stravinsky was to comment in 1911 that 'her teeth were exactly like her father's i.e. like tusks'.[36] The piano suite *Children's Corner* was published by Durand on 30 September 1908 and bore the dedication, 'To my beloved little Chouchou, with her father's tender apologies for what follows'.[37] This set of pieces is a sure sign of the lightness of heart and the sense of humour Chouchou invoked in her father. Bringing her toys to life, witnessing her wide eyes as the snow danced outside her window, even making a joke of the serious piano technique which she might have to master in the future was clearly a labour of love.

---

[36] R. Nichols, *The Life of Debussy*, Cambridge, 1998, p. 127.
[37] 'À ma très chère Chouchou ... avec les tendres excuses de son père pour ce qui va suivre', BnF Musique, Ms 983.

15. Emma and Chouchou at home

Not only did Debussy compose the music. He was fastidious about the design of the finished piano score, lovingly creating the cover illustration of a toy elephant (Jimbo) holding a golliwog's head on a string. Just as he was meticulous about physical objects around him, he was explicit about the precise colour of red-orange to be used on light grey paper covered with snowflakes.[38] As Louis Laloy pointed out in his updated version of his original biography of Debussy, published in 1944, Debussy observed the child without any of the anxiety and pity which pulls at our heart strings in the music of Schumann, Mussorgsky or Ravel as they, unlike him, had not experienced the true joys of paternity when they wrote *Scenes from Childhood*, *The Nursery* and *Mother Goose*. Laloy sensed the essential Englishness of this nursery, its warmth and comfort, due no doubt to Chouchou's English nanny.[39] He had seen it for himself.

Emma's friendship with Chouchik

In July Emma wrote to Chouchik wishing her all the best for the imminent birth of her first child, urging her to be patient, just as she herself had been, 'contrary to my nature', in her last days of pregnancy, and offering any help she could give. Yet all was not sweetness and light. Once again Emma's health was troubling her. She wanted to make Chouchik smile, but felt unable to do so as she had been suffering the whole week from intolerable headaches. Everyone in the family, even

[38] C. p. 1107.
[39] L. Laloy, *Debussy*, Paris, 1944, pp. 96–7.

16. Dolly aged sixteen with Chouchou aged three, 1908

17. Emma and Dolly posing for the camera

Chouchou, was thinking of Chouchik in Meudon[40] – including her old mother, possibly an indication that Laure was staying in the Square du Bois de Boulogne with her daughter, no doubt another distraction for Debussy.[41]

One Friday, Chouchik sent Emma a beautiful bouquet of flowers, for which Emma could not thank her enough. Chouchou's health had been a concern, but she was now better so Chouchik was invited to visit the Debussys, something which would delight Chouchou as she too regarded Chouchik as her '*grande amie*'. Pregnant Chouchik would be able to rest in the garden, where Chouchou would take great care of her![42] Nicole, known as Nicolette, Laloy was born on 2 August and on 5 August Emma wrote to express her joy, refraining this time from complaining about herself, longing to see mother and baby. They could not go to the seaside, but Debussy and Emma had made up for this by creating a little 'beach' for Chouchou at the bottom of their garden with some sand. They called it '*Chouchou-Plage*' (Chouchou Beach), 'where the little tyrant you know will definitely be spending the month of August with her family', Emma told Chouchik. Both Dolly and Chouchou were working in their different ways, and Debussy rewarded them all with secret 'first performances'![43] These may have been of 'Ibéria', still in the process of composition. Although he must have known the precarious state of Debussy's finances,

---

[40] The Laloys had a residence in rue des Capucins, Bellevue-Meudon.
[41] C. p. 1105.
[42] Laloy archives B, Dossier 81, A12.
[43] C. p. 1105.

Jacques Durand sent him information about the Savoy hotel in Avon, near his house in Bel-Ébat, but Debussy gave him two reasons for being unable to stay there: mainly the depleted state of his current budget but also the fact that he was working hard, his head filled with the street noises of Catalonia and music in Granada.[44]

Raoul Bardac's illness

In October and November of 1908 Debussy was preoccupied with concerns about the performances of *Pelléas et Mélisande* due to begin at the Opéra-Comique in December, the rehearsals for which were '*déplorable*', he told Albert Carré. 'Just think!' he remarked to Victor Segalen, 'No one at the Opéra-Comique knows *Pelléas* any more!'[45] He was also occupied with auditions for singers for the presentation of the opera in London the following year. A combination of no change of scene during the summer and illness affected his mood and inevitably his irritation was exacerbated by money problems. A telling letter to an unnamed person informed him desperately that he had only received his letter at 9.35 a.m. Since he had to go to the bank to withdraw the money, he would certainly not be able to pay this person until at least 10.45 a.m. Someone was clearly demanding immediate repayment. Debussy's debts were accruing.

There was little reference to family matters this season, except that Debussy did have a specially bound edition made of the *Trois Chansons de Charles d'Orléans* in which he wrote, 'pour Emma X 08'. She herself added her name in black ink and later her daughter Dolly added a signature in green.[46]

Suddenly in November we learn from a letter Emma wrote to Chouchik Laloy that to her great consternation she had received a telegram from Toul at 10.30 p.m. informing her that her son Raoul was seriously ill.[47] It has already been noted that Raoul had been diagnosed in 1905 with chronic dyspepsia and trouble with the upper right lung.[48] Since 1907 he had been serving with the 26th Infantry Regiment in Toul and from his military records we now learn that he was suffering with enteritis and chronic weight loss.[49] Emma and Dolly left home immediately, leaving Debussy in charge of Chouchou. Fortunately Raoul was out of danger when they arrived. Emma managed to ensure he did not have to stay in hospital. Instead his former tutor (*précepteur*)[50] would bring him back to Paris, where a doctor would visit him every day. Emma also said her sister would look after him, as she could not do so herself. Perhaps she meant her sister-in-law as her own sister, Nelly, had died on 30 December 1884. Emma was clearly not good at coping with stressful situations. She

---

[44] C. p. 1108.
[45] C. pp. 1124, 1130.
[46] Listed in C. Genovesi, 'Ventes aux enchères et dans librairies spécialisées (2012–2014)', *Cahiers Debussy*, no.37–8, 2015, p.181. (Hôtel Drouot, 27 March 2014, no.10).
[47] C. p. 1136.
[48] See Chapter 6 p. 87.
[49] Paris Archives, *Registres matricules du recrutement*. Cote D4R1 1186.
[50] Presumably M. Freuder, who, it is said, often visited Debussy. C. p. 1337 n.3.

felt a sense of relief at being able to confide her difficulties in a friend. 'I'm reassured, but terribly on edge and I wasn't sure I should "let myself go" with you,' she told Chouchik.[51] One can imagine Debussy's state of mind having to calm Emma down, look after Chouchou and deal with the revival of *Pelléas* at the Opéra-Comique, plans for concerts and the auditions for the London *Pelléas*. He also agreed to participate in a series of concerts of French music in Manchester the following year.

On 18 December *Children's Corner* was performed for the first time in public by Harold Bauer at the Cercle musical. The programme also included the *Estampes* and Maggie Teyte performing two of Debussy's *Proses lyriques*, 'De grève' and 'De soir'. Just as he rarely attended performances of his opera, Debussy did not go into the hall, but waited outside, to find out from the pianist how it went down with the audience.[52] He feared experiencing their immediate reactions, knowing how split they could be between supporters and detractors of his music. Louis Laloy found Bauer's interpretation of both works too heavy and romantic with inappropriate emphases. He also criticised Maggie Teyte for the superficiality of her interpretation.[53]

The next day was Christmas Eve. At last 'Ibéria' was finished. 'Attached is the real ending of Ibéria!', wrote Debussy on a sketch of the work he gave to Emma. 'To wish you a happy Christmas I have only my songs and my love ... like little birds.'[54] 'Que mes chants et mon amour'. How true! Also from around this time dates a letter to Jacques Durand referring to 'the Hugo affair', nothing to do with Victor Hugo, but a tailor in the rue Vivienne who out of the kindness of his heart had provided Debussy with a whole wardrobe of smart clothes after his return from Italy and the Prix de Rome. 'You can pay me back when you are famous', he told him. Vain hope! Twenty years later the tailor was to claim his money from the Société des auteurs.[55]

Not only was 'Ibéria', the second of the *Images*, finished but the short score of 'Rondes de printemps', the third piece, bears the date 30 December 1908. This has an epigraph that Debussy would later use in a personal context to his wife: 'Vive le Mai! Bienvenu soit le Mai, avec son gonfalon sauvage' ('Long live May, welcome May, with its streaming banner'). The short score of 'Gigues', the first in the set, is dated 4 January 1909, but this work would not be completed until 1912.

La mer was the subject of a letter addressed to Emma by Édouard Colonne written on 31 December 1908. Once again, Colonne's familiarity with his fellow *bordelaise* and former pupil of his wife is striking. Through her he was trying to arrange a long meeting with Debussy on the evening of either 3 or 4 January. He ended his letter, 'As it is quarter past midnight, I send you all my love', an affectionate signing off proving their longstanding friendship.[56]

---

[51] C. p. 1136.

[52] Lesure, *Claude Debussy*, p. 305.

[53] *Bulletin français de la SIM* 1909.01–1909.06, p. 72.

[54] 'Ci-joint la fin réelle d'Ibéria ... Moi je n'ai pour te souhaiter un joyeux Noël que mes chants et mon amour ... – comme les petits oiseaux.' C. p. 1139 and BnF MS-14518.

[55] C. n.2, pp. 1142–3.

[56] 'Et comme il est minuit ¼, je vous embrasse de tout mon cœur.' BnF Musique, Nla-32(79).

Arthur Hartmann

Another fruitful friendship, perhaps a rather unexpected one, was formed with the American violinist Arthur Hartmann. The first letter from Debussy to Hartmann is dated 6 September 1908. Having been overcome with enthusiasm for Debussy's music since hearing *Pelléas et Mélisande*, Hartmann had written to him twice previously asking if he had written anything for violin. Debussy answered in the negative but agreed to meet him if he ever came to Paris. The violinist, overjoyed, immediately started searching through Debussy's songs for suitable works for transcription. Upon visiting the composer in his house, he received Debussy's permission to transcribe 'Il pleure dans mon cœur', the second of the *Ariettes oubliées*. The same evening Debussy returned a visit to Hartmann, who was staying at the Grand Hotel, taking him a signed photograph of himself. When Hartmann told Durand of this, the publisher was 'dumbfounded'. It was exceptional for Debussy to receive a stranger, entertain him for hours and endorse an arrangement of one of his works.[57] The reason this friendship is significant is that Hartmann kept not just the correspondence, but also notes of all his meetings with Debussy, often with Emma present, who was to form a close friendship with his wife, thus furnishing us with a warm and unusually familiar insight into their lives.

---

[57] A. Hartmann, *Claude Debussy as I knew him and other writings*, ed. Samuel Hsu, Sidney Grolnic, Mark Peters. Rochester N. Y. and Woodbridge, 2003, p. 16.

9

1909: Illness and depression

Concerts curtailed

As the years passed, Debussy's inability to find a way to ease the financial burden through purposeful composition contributed to the emotional and practical difficulties faced by Emma, in turn affecting her ability to cope with her increasingly depressed husband. Now 'la maladie du retard', the disease of lateness, 'this curious need never to finish anything, which does not fit in at all with the opposite needs of my publisher' was a growing problem acknowledged by Debussy to Gabriel Mourey on 6 January 1909. He told Édouard Colonne he had not finished the *Images*. He sent New Year's greetings to Jacques Durand as well as to his father, adding those of Chouchou, who greeted Durand's father 'in a strange anglo-french dialect complicated by the "petit nègre"!', a reference to the piano piece Debussy was composing, *The little nigar*, which bears the note, 'Cakewalk = Danse nègre dite Danse du gateau', language so unacceptable today, but at that time reflecting the popularity of cheerful American ragtime. Durand only had to wait a fortnight into the New Year before Debussy's driver, Jules, arrived at his office bearing a note from the composer asking urgently for the loan of a thousand francs until April. A debt had to be settled by the very next day. Just as with Lilly's alimony, this sum was lent on the basis of money to be earned through work in progress, and eventually had to be deducted when the contract was signed for the first book of *Préludes* the following year.[1]

Now the debilitating first signs of the illness, cancer of the rectum, which would eventually lead to Debussy's death, aggravated an already depressing situation. In retrospect Raoul Bardac dated the initial stages of Debussy's cancer to January 1909, when the symptoms were deceptively benign. The doctor advised him to exercise, keep active, not sit for too long, but Debussy, determinedly sedentary, virtually ignored this. By February things had worsened to the extent that he had to take drugs constantly, which dulled his mind and only served to fuel his bad moods.[2] Raoul's is one of the few honest accounts of Debussy's behaviour from now onwards. He says that the illness recurred in various forms between 1910 and 1913, forcing him to suspend work for weeks at a time. On 26 January 1909 Debussy wrote again to Durand, who had left for a holiday in the south of France, beginning

---

[1] C. pp. 1144–6.
[2] R. Bardac, *Causerie sur les dernières années de Claude Debussy*, Centre de Documentation Claude Debussy, RESE 05.15.

the letter with the complaint that he was not seriously ill, but had the miserable symptoms of those who spent too much time sitting down.[3]

Only ten days later Debussy told Durand the weather was gloomy, he was suffering miserably and taking various medications, morphine, cocaine, which were completely wearing him out. Little wonder his wife succumbed to depression and illness. It was clearly a struggle for Debussy to cope with orchestrating the *Images* and corresponding with Henry Wood about the forthcoming visit to London, where he would conduct the *Prélude à l'après-midi d'un faune* and the *Nocturnes*. He also had to ask Édouard Colonne to return his copy of the score of the *Nocturnes*, which bore corrections he needed to see. How strange that the envelope with the letter bearing this request should be addressed to Monsieur Judas Colonne, the conductor's original name, now so rarely used,[4] evidence, perhaps, that his mind really was befuddled by the pain-killing drugs he was taking. Colonne sent the music straight away and Debussy's acknowledgement and invitation to lunch was duly addressed to Monsieur Ed. Colonne.

This was a big tour to undertake with Emma at his side. From London he was due to go to Manchester for a concert of his works on 2 March, then travel on immediately to Edinburgh. It was evident to Henry Wood that Debussy disliked appearing in public. He understood that he was retiring and sensitive, but also commented that Debussy was 'not a good conductor, even of his own works'. Whilst the rehearsals at the Queen's Hall went smoothly, in the actual performance of the *Nocturnes* on 27 February suddenly Debussy lost the beat and attempted to make the orchestra stop in order to start again. To Wood's amazement, and no doubt Debussy's as well, the orchestra simply carried on playing. The audience reacted in a truly English fashion and through their applause compelled Debussy to repeat the movement, 'Fêtes'.[5] He was pleased, but how difficult an experience it must have been for him. He was constantly ill, even 'marinating' in blood and having great difficulty standing. It is unlikely that Emma was able to give her husband much support, for, as so often, she too was unwell. The next day, Sunday 28 February, Debussy wrote to both André Caplet and Alexandre Charpentier to tell them of the regrettable state they were both in, and that they would be returning to Paris without going on to Manchester and Edinburgh. 'London could not be more like London – it is snowing, the fog smells of smoked herring …'[6]

Regular routine and friendships

It is clear that neither Emma nor Debussy could take the stress of travel. Their indisposition abroad did not stop either of them being anxious to see their close friends on their return, however. Normal routine was crucial to both of them. Having arrived home on Monday night, Emma wrote to Chouchik Laloy in the morning saying she had often thought of her whilst away 'for all sorts of reasons', desperate

[3] C. p. 1148.
[4] C. pp. 1149–51.
[5] H. Wood, My *Life of Music*, pp. 298–9.
[6] C. pp. 1158–60.

for her to come round as soon as possible if she could manage the snow. They would send the car. Two days later we learn that the couple would visit them on Friday, but Alexandre Charpentier, to whom Debussy had only just written whilst in London, had died on 3 March.[7] Their distress at this news cannot have helped their state of mind. P.-J. Toulet was also invited to resume his regular Thursday visits. The first of these on 11 March coincided with the first performance of *Trois Chansons de Charles d'Orléans* and other Debussy songs and piano works in a recital given by Jane Bathori and Pierre-Émile Engel. As usual, the composer had no desire to be present. Toulet's visit of Thursday 24 March had to be postponed to the next day, however, as Debussy was conducting *L'après-midi d'un faune* at the Concert Séchiari on 25 March. On 9 April he did hear the *Trois Chansons* at the Concerts Colonne, more from necessity than choice, for he was also conducting Maggie Teyte in *La damoiselle élue*. The audience was enthusiastic, the critics less so. Louis Laloy met Emma at the dress rehearsal of this concert and accompanied her back home afterwards.[8]

Debussy had had some contact with Gabriel Fauré in February before his trip to London for, to his delight, the older man had put him forward as a member of the *Conseil supérieur du Conservatoire* to replace Ernest Reyer. In return, in March Debussy congratulated Fauré on his election to the *Institut de France*. This letter he ended by including Emma's best wishes,[9] evidence, if it were needed, that there was no hard feeling between the two composers as claimed by some. Indeed, Dolly Bardac emphasised the fact that there was no rift between them in two talks, saying in one, 'There was no question of coolness and even less a musical rivalry between them'[10] and in another, 'Professionally Debussy and Fauré remained permanently in contact',[11] although she was rather contradictory about how often they saw each other. In the first she claimed that 'Fauré was a frequent visitor at my parents' home', whilst in the second she said 'He was not a regular visitor to the house.'[12]

Now Louis Laloy was reaching the end of his biography of Debussy.[13] 'You are the only person who knows the real Claude Debussy,' Debussy told him, 'without a big bass drum roll or embroidery.'[14] The lack of 'embroidery' was due to the fact that there was virtually no mention in the book of Debussy's private life – noteworthy, considering the closeness of Laloy to Debussy and Emma. Laloy remedied this omission when he revised the book shortly before his death in 1944, for here not only did he comment on works composed after 1909, but added a brief passage emphasising the sparseness of Debussy's accommodation at 58 rue Cardinet during the *Pelléas* years. Without naming him, he contrasted this with the background of one of his pupils (Raoul Bardac), who came from 'une famille financière'. It was this pupil,

---

7   C. pp. 1160–1.
8   C. p. 1167.
9   C. p. 1163.
10 Dolly Bardac, London interview.
11 De Tinan, French interview.
12 'Ce n'était pas un familier qui venait à la maison.' De Tinan, French interview.
13 L. Laloy, *Claude Debussy*, Paris, 1909.
14 C. p. 1173.

he explained, who introduced Debussy to the woman who would 'illuminate his life and turn it completely upside down'.[15] He also stressed Debussy's pain at leaving a woman (Lilly) who still loved him and having to suffer the intrusion into his private life this caused, so agonising for a man who refused to tell lies. There was nothing as inexcusable as sincerity in the hypocritical bourgeois society of the times, Laloy remarked with irony. This revision was published ten years after Emma's death, yet there were no personal insights into her character. Laloy still avoided any 'embroidery', despite the close friendship of his wife with Emma.

Debussy and Emma were delighted that Laloy's sister-in-law Marguerite Babaïan had been to see them in April 1909, each writing separate letters, Debussy to Louis and Emma to Chouchik.[16] They had been pleased to hear her news of the Laloys and little Nicolette, who were in their country home at Rahon in the Jura. Emma expressed relief that 'Victor le Terrible', (Victor Segalen) had just left. Clearly she disliked him as much as he disliked her.[17] Segalen was about to leave for China, which led Emma to sympathise with his wife, exclaiming how good she was to resign herself to her situation because of her love for him. 'Elle est bonne, profondément.' She must have seen a parallel in the position of this woman sacrificing her own wishes in the interest of her husband's. She quoted *Pelléas et Mélisande*, telling Chouchik how she loved her family's habit of arriving 'les mains pleines de fleurs'. She was, however, very preoccupied with the forthcoming visit to London for *Pelléas et Mélisande*. This combined with domestic problems with servants meant she had very little time for anything else. They would be away from 9 until 20 May. 'So much trouble for so little time!' she complained. She ended the letter abruptly because 'Chouchou is stopping me writing'.[18] Again, Emma was succumbing to stress, an inability to cope with domestic pressures. Debussy's letter to Laloy had a distinctly more ironic and humorous tone. He joked about Segalen's wife's strange hat – the only excuse for its colour could be that you would be able to spot it a long way away from the bridge of the ship carrying them off so far away![19]

The dates Emma had envisaged for the London trip were changed. The first performance of the Covent Garden *Pelléas* was scheduled for 18 May, so there was still time for Chouchik and her daughter to visit before they left. Emma had arranged for Rara (Raoul) to meet Chouchik, but their reunion had to be postponed by a day for some reason to do with the baby. She endeavoured to rearrange what she called this '*délicieuse children-party*' and expressed frustration at having to wait so long.[20] How mundane a social life she was leading now, organising domestic tea parties rather than elegant soirées.

---

[15] 'La femme qui devait illuminer et bouleverser son existence.' L. Laloy, *Claude Debussy*, Paris, 1944, p. 86.

[16] Ravel admired Babaïan's interpretations of his *Cinq Mélodies populaires grecques* and had dedicated the Greek song *Tripartos* to her earlier in 1909.

[17] See Chapter 8 p. 124.

[18] C. p. 1174.

[19] This separation would cause the end of their collaborative project to compose *Orphée-roi*. Debussy had not even begun to write the music.

[20] C. p. 1176.

To London for *Pelléas*

Once in London, Emma, Chouchou and Debussy (there was no mention of Dolly) stayed at the Royal Palace Hotel,[21] a luxury hotel overlooking Kensington Palace, from where Debussy wrote to Durand on 13 May grumbling that the beds were hard. His uncomfortable symptoms were recurring. He was, however, able to revel in the innocent delight of Chouchou, who had already 'taken possession' of Kensington Gardens. He was very dubious about the prospect of only four orchestral rehearsals. On 18 May he informed both Durand and Laloy that the first performance had been postponed until 21 May at his request. His frustration with problems concerning the production was reaching boiling point. On top of all this, all he wanted was to get back home. Only Chouchou brought light relief and provided rare pleasure in life. In a PS he wrote light-heartedly as if from her, begging permission to replace macaroni, which she did not like, with jam.[22]

Emma had been constantly ill ever since their arrival, unable even to write to Chouchik. On the day of the première, Debussy grumbled to P.-J. Toulet that his wife had been ill the whole time. He and Emma simply could not wait to get back home.[23] His problems, professional and personal, were not helped by Emma's incapacity to support him because of her own precarious health.

What could be more typical after all this anxious preparation than Debussy failing to attend the first night? He wrote to his parents on 23 May saying he had stayed in his hotel, far away from the noise of applause. He had therefore not witnessed the wild appreciation of the audience, who called for a whole quarter of an hour for the composer. Yet again, however, a sombre note was introduced when he emphasised their anxiety to get back home as Emma was so unwell. Not only that – he asked for their help. 'It would be very kind if you could come and see Emma. She will probably be exhausted when she gets back.' Whilst there is no further correspondence between Debussy and his parents to show how often such help was requested or offered, this is an indication that they were willing to support the couple when they were in difficulties. Emma, despite having a nanny for Chouchou and Dolly still living at home, required even more help.

Writing to Durand the same day, Debussy commented that he himself had no desire for any personal glory, but was far more concerned for his wife. Emma's illness made him fear for her and long for the journey to be over. He did not even say a proper goodbye to the conductor, Percy Pitt, instead leaving him a letter of appreciation, saying his wife was so ill he had not been able to leave her side to shake him by the hand.

Back home on 25 May they waited in vain all morning for Doctor Vannier, a specialist in homeopathic medicine, to visit. Debussy's message asking him to come as soon as possible had crossed with a telegram from the doctor, who was away.

---

[21] This stood at 6 Kensington High Street on the corner with Palace Avenue. It was demolished in the 1960s and has been replaced by the Royal Garden Hotel.

[22] C. pp. 1177, 1179.

[23] C. pp. 1181–2.

Debussy beseeched him to visit his wife urgently if he got back that night. 'I beg you personally as she really needs a better night'.[24] Yet once again routine worked its magic and Emma's health soon improved. Only two days later they were hoping to resume the Monday visits of the Laloys as soon as possible.

Obsession with *The Fall of the House of Usher*

A highlight for Debussy in June was a performance by the Ballets Russes on 11 June of Rimsky-Korsakov's *Ivan the Terrible* and the ballet *Le Festin*, which had a scenario by Diaghilev and music by various Russian composers. He was impressed with Chaliapin as Ivan, but bored by the ballet, and mystified by the costumes, designed by Léon Bakst and Alexandre Benois. Surely Emma accompanied him to this event. It was certainly a day on which he thought of her, for his traditional June offering to her did not arrive on the fourth of that month, but on this 11 June. He had turned his attention once again to his stage work for *La chute de la Maison Usher* – not just the libretto, but now the music, for Emma received a manuscript sketch bearing the dedication, 'What will perhaps be the prelude to The Fall of the House of Usher' ('Ce qui sera peut-être le prélude à La Chute de la maison Uscher [sic]'), signed *Claude*, and dated '11 juin 1909'. This has a double significance as it is the first known dated music for this work,[25] one which haunted him whenever he felt low.

On 26 June he mentioned this opera again in a letter to Durand, who was in Switzerland. Feeling depressed by both appalling weather and a series of strikes in Paris, he was at least able to say that Emma's health had improved and that Chouchou was well. He had been working hard on a monologue of 'poor Roderick' (Roderick Usher), which was 'sad enough to make the stones weep', quoting Golaud's heart-breaking words from the last scene of *Pelléas et Mélisande*.[26] Whilst Poe's story struck a sombre chord matching his current state of mind, its oppressive atmosphere would impinge on him increasingly as the years passed. He could identify with Roderick Usher both physically and mentally, with his 'intolerable agitation of the soul', this man whose family possessed 'a passionate devotion to the intricacies, perhaps even more than to the orthodox and easily recognisable beauties, of musical science'. Amongst the dirges Roderick played on his guitar was 'the wild air of the last waltz of von Weber',[27] a composer Debussy had long admired. He worked on *The House of Usher* to the detriment of the *Images*, for he was supposed to be completing the first, 'Gigues', a far happier-spirited piece of music, which clearly did not reflect his mood. When Durand returned from Switzerland, Debussy had to admit to him on 13 July that instead he had been working on *La chute de la Maison Usher*.

---

[24] C. pp. 1184–7.
[25] BnF Musique, Ms-14520.
[26] C. p. 1192.
[27] E. A. Poe, *The Fall of the House of Usher and Other Writings*, ed. David Galloway, Penguin Classics, London, 2003, pp. 90–109.

Louis Laloy was present on 17 July when Diaghilev asked Debussy to compose a ballet for his company. Debussy thought he could manage the piano score by January 1910 and the orchestral score by May and asked Durand to negotiate payment on these terms, in particular hoping for a first instalment of the payment on delivery of the piano score.[28] This was intended to be *Masques et bergamasques*, for which it was planned that Laloy would write the scenario and Debussy the music. Debussy, however, immediately decided to write the scenario himself. Laloy was in the Jura when Debussy wrote to him on 27 July not only to insist on this, but concealing the fact he had already done so. To compensate, he conveyed to Laloy the desire to work with him on Aeschylus's *Oresteia*.[29] Obviously Laloy was hurt. Three days later Debussy wrote again to his friend to lay out emphatically the course of events which had led up to his writing the scenario, insisting that this did not imply he no longer needed his collaboration. In the end, as so often the case, apart possibly from one sketched bar, Debussy never did compose the score for this work.[30]

Caplet as confidant; Emma's frustration; Debussy's apathy

Meanwhile, Emma may have felt better, but now Chouchou was suffering with tonsillitis.[31] She had an operation and fortunately recuperated quickly and on 30 July Debussy was relieved to tell Caplet that she was beginning to sing her famous repertoire of operetta and opera again. Yet he still had little peace of mind. After explaining to Caplet that he had taken two days to write a ballet scenario for the next season of the Ballets Russes, the message took a sombre turn. He confided in this man, sixteen years his junior, his innermost feelings. He had had bad days since Caplet had left, he felt low, the rain drowned his will to be a genius when he got up in the morning. Yet again, the family was not going away in the summer. He did not mention finances as a reason, but the undesirable likelihood of rain, poor working conditions and 'meeting people who do not always want to stay anonymous'.

> As you can tell, I am in that state of mind where I would rather be a sponge at the bottom of the sea, a vase on the mantelpiece, anything but a man of intellect, such a fragile kind of machine which only works when it wants to and against which the will of man is nothing … you give an order to someone who does not obey you, and that someone is yourself![32]

It is curious that Debussy tended to open up his innermost thoughts to younger friends, such as Raoul Bardac before his close relationship with Emma, and now Caplet. This is something that Emma also felt able to do, eventually continuing this friendship with Caplet and being criticised for her closeness to other younger (male) musicians.

---

[28] C. p. 1196.
[29] C. p. 1198.
[30] R. Orledge, *Debussy and the Theatre*, Cambridge, 1982, pp. 321–2.
[31] C. p. 1196.
[32] C. pp. 1197–8.

Debussy's frustration with life was echoed in Emma's state of mind, which was no calmer. On 3 August she managed to send an illuminating letter to Chouchik Laloy describing her fury the previous morning when she had torn up her attempts to write to her in anger because she had had so many interruptions and had been pestered to do so many things. In the afternoon she had fared no better. One by one, everyone came into her room to talk to her, they all got on her nerves and again she tore up – not the letter she was writing, but the letter Chouchik had written to her. Now she could not even remember what it had said. And yet, she said, nothing had changed. Their life was as quiet as ever, indeed ever fewer boring people were coming to see them. They had refused an invitation to the *Société des grandes auditions musicales de France*, presided over by the Comtesse Greffulhe, Debussy giving the excuse that he had too much work. Emma was certainly missing Chouchik's company ('if only we still had our Mondays!') and was envious of her enjoying sunshine in beautiful surroundings. In order to get some peace and quiet to write this letter she had had to send her two daughters off for a walk in the Bois de Boulogne. Her boredom and anger were revealing. Domestic life with little respite from chaotic family pressures was resulting in frustration and loneliness.[33] Debussy also expressed loneliness and a feeling of pressure in a note to Emma written on an unspecified date in 1909, complaining of having to go off all alone, 'a poor little boat [pauvre petite barque] on the hateful Parisian ocean, amongst the pretentious women[34] and the false artists. How delightful! … and I love you. Your Claude.'[35] 'Une barque sur l'océan' was the third of Ravel's *Miroirs*. No doubt Debussy was just leaving for an appointment amongst artists and society ladies, but it is interesting that this was a handwritten note rather than something said face to face. Emma must have been ensconced alone in her room.

Debussy succumbed to apathy. To Edgard Varèse he excused himself on 10 August for not responding to his letter as he had been away so had only just read it. This was a lie. On 23 August he asked Reynaldo Hahn to excuse his 'natural nonchalance', having delayed replying to a request from him. However, Debussy's closeness to Caplet continued to grow as the latter helped him check the proofs of 'Rondes de printemps' and transcribe all the *Images* for two pianos. He found himself able to write long letters to him, criticising others such as the critic Pierre Lalo and the composer Arrigo Boito with a barbed tongue. The grim atmosphere of the *House of Usher* was wreaking its harrowing effect on him:

> not exactly a house to calm the nerves, just the opposite. You become obsessed with listening to the dialogue of the stones, expecting houses to fall down as if that were a natural, even necessary, phenomenon. What's more, if pushed, I will admit to liking those people better than – many others, who can't be named![36]

It is clear that black moments, the darker side of life, professional and family, contributed not only to his ability to enter the world of Roderick Usher, whose house

---

[33] C. p. 1202.
[34] *Les dindes:* lit. 'turkeys'.
[35] C. p. 1235 and Pasteur Vallery-Radot, *Lettres de Claude Debussy à sa femme Emma*, p. 38.
[36] C. p. 1206.

was about to collapse around him, but to identify with its inhabitants. He was hurt when Caplet contacted him via Durand rather than directly, saying he would have loved to have seen him. He and Emma talked about him every day.

In September Debussy received Louis Laloy's biography, published on 10 July 1909, and expressed to him his delight at being so well understood. The following month he willingly agreed to support Laloy in his bid to become Professor of Music History at the Conservatoire, but added that he was unwell and his activity could only be compared to that of a broom without a handle.[37]

Manuel de Falla meets the Debussys

Debussy had been corresponding with Manuel de Falla since the beginning of 1907, when the Spanish composer had sought advice on his *Deux danses pour harpe*. They had met in person soon after Debussy's return from Pourville in September of that year. Falla was a cripplingly shy personality, fourteen years younger than Debussy and Emma, and it took a while to get into the stride of the relationship, but by the end of June 1908 Falla was addressing the older man as '*cher Maître*', grateful for his help and encouragement. Debussy had introduced him to Durand's publishing house, where his *Four Spanish Pieces* (*Pièces espagnoles*) were published in 1909. This was the year of the death of Falla's compatriot Albeniz, whose widow suggested that Falla should ask Debussy, Ravel and Stravinsky to orchestrate some of Albeniz's works. When Falla went to Debussy's house without forewarning him of his visit, he was told by a servant the composer was out for a walk. He had to wait in a room which was quite dark and full of Japanese and Chinese masks. One of the doors opened into the dining room. Eventually Falla heard people entering the dining room and recognised the voices of Debussy, Emma and Erik Satie. Whilst no one came to see him, he overheard talk of clarinets. 'Debussy's wife began to say something, but Debussy interrupted her: "You know nothing about it," he said.' Falla did not reveal his presence and became overcome with nerves, the masks with their gaping mouths inducing hallucinations. When it seemed dinner was over, he peeped through the door into the passage, but still no one came to see him. 'Finally he heard footsteps. It was Debussy's wife, who, alarmed at meeting an unexpected man, screamed.' Apparently the servant had forgotten to tell anyone that a gentleman was waiting. Emma invited him to have some belated lunch, but all Falla wanted was to leave. He did, however, manage to explain to Debussy why he had come and Debussy agreed to orchestrate *El Abaicin* by Albeniz, a task he never did carry out.[38]

In October Falla returned to play Debussy his *Trois mélodies* to texts by Théophile Gautier. It was on Debussy's recommendation that they were published by Rouart, Lerolle et Cie in 1910 after Durand rejected them. These were particularly significant in a personal context to the Debussy household, for the third, 'Séguidille', was dedicated to Emma Debussy. This marked the beginning of a friendship between Falla and Emma which would blossom after Debussy's death. The songs were eventually given their

---

[37] *C.* p. 1220.
[38] J. Pahissa, *Manuel de Falla. His Life and Works*, trans. J. Wagstaff, London, 1954, pp. 47–8.

first performance on 4 May 1910 at the Société musicale indépendante (SMI) by Ada Adiny-Milliet, accompanied by Falla himself. Debussy was to remain his much admired and venerated 'cher Maître' throughout Falla's later correspondence with Emma.

Caplet could not visit the Debussys in November for he had fallen seriously ill with pleurisy, whilst Debussy himself was busy auditioning pianists for admission to the Conservatoire. P.-J. Toulet was in Dinard. 'I'll keep my descriptions of society's splendours for Madame Debussy', he commented, knowing Debussy himself was indifferent to such spectacles. He had visited Mont Saint-Michel, to which Debussy replied that Chouchou knew a song about *la Mère Michel* and complained of the usual rain and wind in Paris.[39] Thus the year 1909 was drawing to an end, with Debussy still preparing the orchestral *Images*, 'Ibéria' and 'Rondes de printemps' for engraving prior to their performance the following year.

Préludes at Christmas

Debussy's Christmas message to Emma on 25 December 1909 was far more perfunctory than any of the previous ones.

> Happy Xmas
> From Claude Debussy et toutes
> Ses dépendances
> To: P.M.[40]

There was no evidence of a musical offering or dedication. It was written on a formal visiting card. How things had changed. Where was the message of love? The previous year there had been the words '*mon amour*' and '*ton Claude*'. 'Claude Debussy and all his dependencies' feels distant compared with former effusiveness. However, it may be that he was simply too busy to pay her much attention, for he seems suddenly to have been inspired to compose for the piano. Perhaps his disgust at the choice of music performed at the Conservatoire auditions could have had a role in this, or even the sight and sound of a talented young Brazilian girl applicant. In December alone he managed to complete 'Danseuses de Delphes', 'Le vent dans la plaine', 'Voiles', 'Les collines d'Anacapri' and 'Des pas sur la neige'. The last two of these *Préludes* are dated 26 and 27 December, so little wonder Emma did not receive a special message.

As Marcel Dietschy commented, 'Des pas sur la neige' 'seems to express the searing sadness of the artist alone with his thoughts and haunted by the fleeting footprints that symbolise the unhappy path of man across the immensity of the world'. In a footnote he added that this prelude is 'like a tender, mournful nostalgia' for an impossible longing. The 'emotional disturbances of middle age' showed themselves harshly in Debussy.[41] As pointed out earlier, the ostinato motif of this piece has its precursor in 'La Grotte', the second of *Trois Chansons de France*, dedicated to Emma

---

[39] C. p. 1226.
[40] C. p. 1230.
[41] M. Dietschy, *A Portrait of Claude Debussy*, p. 160.

in 1904[42] and soon to be resurrected in another set of songs. The instructions to the pianist accompanying that song read *'très lent et très doux'*, very slow and very gentle. The word *doux* also has overtones of sweetness. How times had changed since Emma first stole his heart. The sadness was now unrelieved. This piano prelude bears the instruction *triste et lent* (sad and slow), sadness preceding slowness. The rhythm of the motif must sound bleak, like a 'sad icy landscape' ('ce rythme doit avoir la valeur sonore d'un fond de paysage triste et glacé'). A melodic phrase expresses 'a tender, sad regret' ('comme un tendre et triste regret').

No doubt Debussy was disturbed to have to cope with yet another indisposition of Emma on the same day this prelude was completed, 27 December. He wrote to Jacques Durand to postpone his wife's visit to Emma, who had been taken ill at the dentist's, probably because she had been given too strong an injection of cocaine. The doctor had prescribed 'rest, tea and a boiled egg'.[43]

In December Debussy also began work on a commission for the conservatoire competitions, the *Rapsodie* for clarinet and orchestra, which he completed in January. He managed to find the time to write to André Caplet, worried about his ill health. Caplet had written a sad letter to Emma (not to Debussy) saying he was planning to go to Beaulieu, on the Mediterranean to recuperate.[44] On the last day of the year, Debussy signed a contract with Durand for the piano piece, *Hommage à Haydn*, for a welcome five hundred francs.

---

[42] Chapter 4 p. 53.
[43] C. p. 1231.
[44] C. p. 1232.

10

1910: Floods and despair

The year 1910 became pivotal for the relationship of Debussy and Emma. January was marked by exceptional floods in Paris during which the River Seine rose some six metres above its normal level, which cannot have lightened the mood in their household. On 12 January, Debussy signed a contract with Durand for the sum of fifteen hundred francs for the *Rapsodie* for clarinet with both an orchestral accompaniment and a piano reduction. Intestinal troubles meant that he was unable to attend a rehearsal of two of his *Nocturnes*, 'Nuages' and 'Fêtes' on 30 January conducted by Gabriel Pierné, but when he did eventually hear them he told Pierné 'You could feel the floods in "Nuages"'. On 9 February a contract was signed with Durand for the sum of seven thousand francs for the first book of piano *Préludes*.[1]

He was also receiving help from André Caplet with corrections of the proofs of 'Ibéria', and was able to pass on the score to Pierné in preparation for its première on 20 February. Caplet needed to recuperate from pleurisy, and left for Arcachon where he stayed in the Villa Riquet, the guest house Emma had stayed in as a child.[2] It was she rather than Debussy who wrote to Caplet on 10 February. Memories of Arcachon had struck a chord. Her first sentence did not express sympathy for him, but rather asked him to sympathise with her and her husband in view of the distress caused by the floods, 'this misery and the sobbing surrounding us'. The 'sobs' (*sanglots*) were perhaps not merely a metaphor. She longed to revisit the pines and the sand and felt envious, for their own health was woeful.[3]

Debussy was certainly solicitous for his wife. Only three days later he wrote to the homeopathic specialist Dr. Vannier requesting a remedy for Emma, mentioning two other doctors who had prescribed pills for her which she had been unable to tolerate.[4] Despite this, he and Emma were still able to maintain the regular Monday visits of the Laloys, apart from Monday 14 February, which had to be postponed a day as Pierné needed Debussy's presence at a rehearsal of 'Ibéria'. This letter was signed with three names, Claude and Emma Debussy and Dolly Bardac, showing the fondness of all three for the Laloys and also demonstrating that Dolly maintained her original surname and, significantly, was still living with them. Twice in the same week Debussy made excuses on grounds of ill health, first to evade conducting at the Princesse de Polignac's and, second, a writing commitment. In a long letter to Caplet, besides making pointed comments about Pierné's 'intelligent conducting' of

---

[1] C. pp. 1240, 1244.
[2] See Chapter 1 p. 9.
[3] C. p. 1245.
[4] C. p. 1246.

'Ibéria', he apologised for not writing earlier, using as an excuse 'illness, rehearsals, nerves on edge, the whole horrible scenario of life in Paris.'[5]

In January 1910 Arthur Hartmann, the American violinist whom the Debussys had met in 1908, moved temporarily into the Square du Bois de Boulogne with his wife. He could not wait to renew his acquaintance with Debussy and his entertaining recollections give a rare insight into the life of the couple and their children. On his first visit he presented his card to 'the butler' and had to wait in an antechamber to see the composer. Hartmann's lack of formality and cheerful banter soon helped Debussy to relax and express opinions on many topics from doctors and preachers to German composers. They both smoked continually and Debussy even confided in him his problem with haemorrhoids. His next visit was not so pleasant, for when Debussy demanded his opinion of 'Ibéria', he was clearly annoyed when Hartmann described the first part as 'more photography than painting'.[6] On 2 March Debussy himself conducted 'Rondes de printemps', third of the *Images*, in the Salle Gaveau, after which he declared himself well satisfied.[7]

A turning point

There was a mounting sense of despair in Debussy's letters in 1910. On 23 March he wrote a note to bookseller and publisher Louis Dorbon asking him to come to his house to value books he wanted to sell. Finances were truly desperate. On the same day he expressed bewilderment at his situation to Caplet, unable to explain why he had not written to him earlier, declaring, 'My life at the moment is being frittered away in a whole pile of annoying, demoralising little things'. His state of mind recalled that at the time of his dilemma when he wanted to leave Lilly for Emma and confided in friends such as André Messager. 'As happens to me so often, I am at a dangerous turning point in my life. Don't let's talk about it,' he insisted to Caplet.[8] In fact, Debussy was reminded of Messager only a few days later. On 3 and 10 April Messager was conducting *La damoiselle élue* at the Société des concerts du Conservatoire, but Debussy wrote to him on 2 April, first pretending he did not know when the rehearsals were and then making excuses for not attending. 'I would rather not promise to come to the concert tomorrow because of a stirring of old emotions – a bit ridiculous, perhaps …'[9] Here was a reflection of his current relationship with Emma, so often ill and stressed, perhaps excusably, at the behaviour of her husband and their financial difficulties. He was aware that looking back, nostalgia for times prior to his marriage, maybe even to his engagement to Thérèse Roger who had been the first to sing this work,[10] would exacerbate his discontent.

---

[5] C. pp. 1252–3.
[6] A. Hartmann, *Claude Debussy as I knew him*, p. 61.
[7] J. Durand, *Quelques souvenirs d'un éditeur de musique*, vol.2, p. 5.
[8] C. p. 1259.
[9] C. p. 1265.
[10] See Chapter 3.

On 30 March Debussy complained to Durand, 'My life is sadly still in disarray, but I don't want to cast a shadow on yours at the moment'.[11] He managed to attend a rehearsal on 9 April and congratulated the soloist Rose Féart afterwards. Nowhere did he mention the funeral that both he and Emma attended of Édouard Colonne. Emma's fellow *bordelais* had died on 28 March and she and Debussy were at the top of the list in *Le Figaro* of friends and associates attending the ceremony at Père-Lachaise cemetery on 31 March.[12]

On 14 April Debussy and Emma had attended a noteworthy dinner party given by Gabriel Pierné. Their fellow guests were Paul Dukas, Gustav Mahler and his wife Alma, Paul and Sophie Clemenceau, Gabriel Fauré and Alfred Bruneau. On the afternoon of 17 April they all met again at the Théâtre du Châtelet to see Pierné conducting Lalo's overture *Le roi d'Ys*, Handel's Organ Concerto in D, followed by Mahler conducting his second symphony the *Resurrection*. Whilst neither Debussy nor Emma left an account of this, Alma Mahler wrote that Pierné, Debussy and Dukas got up and left the hall during the second movement of the symphony. Apparently they found it 'too Schubertian'.[13] However, this may be purely apocryphal. The critic Willy in his *Lettre de l'ouvreuse* specifically mentioned Debussy amongst others who applauded at the end of the concert 'with ironic smiles'.[14]

Close friendship with the Hartmanns

Reading between the lines in Arthur Hartmann's recollections, it is possible to glean some inkling of the situation in the Debussy household. Hartmann wanted to make everything sound jolly, larger than life, painting a picture of an eccentric, intense, opinionated maestro whom he revered, yet Debussy's nervous manner also emerged, and the sense of a 'great sorrow'.[15] On about his sixth visit Madame Debussy came into the room and invited Arthur and his wife to dinner. This marked the start of a friendship between Emma and Marie Hartmann, whom Emma greeted in subsequent letters as *Ma chère Grande Petite*, an affectionate reference to Marie's height. The Hartmanns invited the Debussys to tea one day and were surprised when Emma arrived with Chouchou but without her husband. Debussy had had to return home because of one of his haemorrhages. A revealing sentence occurred when Hartmann was discussing the terms of endearment Debussy used for his wife and child. 'The French have peculiar terms of endearment, for *when Debussy was not angry with his wife* [my italics], he called her "Mon chat" ("my cat", and masculine at that) and she addressed him as "Mon chou".'[16] That almost casual aside made it

---

[11] C. p. 1263.

[12] *Le Figaro*, 1 April 1910.

[13] A. Mahler, *Gustav Mahler. Memories and Letters*, trans. B. Creighton, ed. D. Mitchell and K. Martner, 4th ed., London, 1990, p. 170; see also S.-P. Perret and M.-L. Ragot, *Paul Dukas*, Paris, 2007, pp. 266–7.

[14] *Comœdia*, 18 April 1910.

[15] A. Hartmann, *Claude Debussy as I knew him*, p. 61.

[16] Idem. p. 62.

sound as if it was normal for Debussy to be angry with Emma. His friends must have been used to his outbursts. Hartmann had heard Emma comment that after two friends had dined with them at home and afterwards played bridge, '*as always* [my italics] the evening ended by Claude's being in a high temper'.[17]

When Debussy did eventually join the tea party, Chouchou's strong personality was revealed. She was very precocious both socially and musically for a not-quite-five-year-old, for after initially refusing to sing to 'Uncle Arthur', she eventually consented and sang what would normally be regarded as adult repertoire – songs by Fauré including *Les roses d'Ispahan*, and others by Chausson and Duparc. 'Chouchou was a perfect miniature copy of her father, with the peculiarities of appearance, the odd forehead, the black hair, warm eyes and mouth, the sturdy little body, and also the amazing independence of spirit', wrote Hartmann. Evidently all Debussy's staff, except his faithful chauffeur Jules, were subject to instant dismissal – whilst sitting in the garden with Hartmann one day, Debussy was disturbed by the whistling of 'the butler' in a room nearby. 'Debussy's anger struck with unrestrained force, and the servant was dismissed on the spot!' When they went inside, Debussy proceeded to play and sing *Le promenoir des deux amants*, and give him a signed copy of the music. Hartmann was touched, particularly as this bore the dedication 'à Emma-Claude Debussy ... p.m. ... de son mari, Claude Debussy.' He also received a copy of the first book of *Préludes*.[18] The cook was no less vulnerable than Debussy's other servants; on 23 July Hartmann received a letter saying the Debussys would have liked to invite him to dinner, but the cook, who was a master of poisoning, had been dismissed and would be recommended to one of Debussy's colleagues![19]

Hartmann's transcriptions for violin and piano of *Il pleure dans mon coeur* and *La fille aux cheveux de lin*, the eighth prelude, were both appreciated by Debussy. On 2 June he obviously felt duty-bound to attend a recital by Hartmann at the Salle Érard, having written to him on 30 May to say that, in spite of his instinctive horror for this type of occasion, he would drag along Madame Debussy.[20] Hartmann's colourful account of the occasion described the disruption caused amongst the audience, agog at the late entry of Debussy and Emma into the hall after the first movement of Bach's E major violin concerto. His awareness of the composer's presence also caused him to make a mistake. Debussy, however, wrote to him the next day to express his appreciation of the violinist's great talent.[21] In March Hartmann began endeavours to organise an American tour for Debussy. This would never materialise, mainly because Debussy demanded a far higher fee than that originally offered.

---

[17] Idem. p. 64.

[18] Idem. pp. 67–8. In fact, these two gifts were made on separate occasions, and in reverse order. The dedications to the violinist show that he received the *Préludes* on 21 May 1910 and *Le Promenoir des deux amants* on 27 July of that year, when he was also given a copy of *La plus que lente*.

[19] C. p. 1305; A. Hartmann, *Claude Debussy as I knew him*, p. 117.

[20] C. p. 1284.

[21] A. Hartmann, *Claude Debussy as I knew him*, pp. 73–4.

The 'stirring of old emotions' Debussy had been so afraid of when corresponding with Messager in April did not cease, for on 5 May he wrote to Gabriel Mourey using a memorable phrase he had first written in 1906 when struggling to come to terms with the constraints of family life and lack of musical inspiration, 'I am stagnating in factories of Nothingness ... '.[22] His desperation for money was once more visible in a letter to the financier Léon Bertault dated 23 May, when he demanded an immediate loan of six thousand francs.[23] On 1 June he did, however, sign a contract with Durand for three thousand francs for *Trois Ballades de François Villon*. Four of the *Préludes* received their first performance with Debussy himself at the piano on 25 May, and in the same concert Theodore Szanto, a Hungarian pianist and composer, played his own compositions. Szanto was invited to Debussy's house in June together with Jenö Hubay to discuss an invitation to Debussy to give concerts in Budapest and in Vienna. Knowing Debussy's hatred of being away from home and disruption to a quiet life, one can imagine the dire straits he and Emma must have been in for him even to consider taking on this commitment, which would eventually have to be fulfilled before the end of the year.

Le promenoir des deux amants 'in the midst of drama'

In April two contracts had been signed with Durand, one for *La plus que lente, valse pour piano*, and the second for *Deux poèmes de Tristan Lhermite*, 'Crois mon conseil, chère Climène' and 'Je tremble en voyant ton visage'. To these two poems Debussy suddenly added another, 'Auprès de cette grotte sombre', which had already appeared as the second of the *Trois Chansons de France* in 1904. This new set of three was published as *Le promenoir des deux amants* and, like the *Trois Chansons*, was dedicated to Emma, 'À Emma Claude Debussy ... p.m. son mari C.D. 1910', the first such dedication to her of songs since 1904, before the birth of Chouchou. This cycle made a special mark on Durand's memory, for he particularly cited it in his autobiography. The composer sang it to him at the piano with warmth and expression, yet, Durand wrote, 'Debussy had many worries at this time and when I expressed my astonishment that he could have composed this delightful work in the midst of all his troubles, he replied, '*In the midst of drama* [my italics], I feel able to compose.'[24]

It must have been useful for Debussy that he could re-use a song by Tristan Lhermite when he was short of new inspiration, but what an apposite one to include when he was so plagued with doubt. The ambiguity of 'La Grotte' was discussed earlier.[25] There must have been a reason for making *Deux poèmes* into three. One could well have been that Debussy's inclination when creating sets of pieces was often for the number three. However, the fact that now of all times he dedicated this triptych to Emma would seem to indicate that he had something

---

[22] See Chapter 6 p. 53. 'Je croupis présentement dans les usines du Néant.' C. p. 1273.

[23] C. p. 1281.

[24] 'Dans le drame, je me sens à l'aise pour composer'. J. Durand, *Quelques souvenirs d'un éditeur de musique*, vol.1, p. 124.

[25] See Chapter 4 pp. 52–3.

personal to say to her. When 'Auprès de cette grotte sombre' had received its dedication to Emma as part of the original set of *Trois Chansons de France* six years earlier, he had been making the decision to give up one lifestyle (with Lilly) for another. Now shadow was once again struggling with light. 'Crois mon conseil, chère Climène' with its Mélisande-like references to a fountain, the art-nouveau images of roses and lilies, their scent carried by the sweet west wind, heighten the lover's pleading for the other to sit beside him, but the third song, 'Je tremble en voyant ton visage' conveys fear that the lover's sighs will cause the expression on the face of the other mirrored in the water to be distorted and wrecked. Flowing water, that 'faithless element', is a metaphor for the ephemeral nature of desire. The lover begs to be placed above all humans. It is in the other's hands whether this wish will be granted.

As noted above, on 1 June Debussy signed a contract with Durand for the *Trois Ballades de François Villon*. According to a questionnaire published in the journal *Musica* in March the following year, he had been waiting to set these ballads for a long time.[26] Now had become the right moment. These were composed in May and published in September 1910, when they were dedicated to Emma, turning words from the last song, 'Il n'est bon beq que de Paris' ('The best talkers are from Paris') into 'Il n'est bon bec que ton cher bec' ('The best talker is you'). Yet, just as with the ambivalent message in the *Trois Chansons de France*, the first of these songs in particular, 'Ballade de Villon à s'amye' ('Ballad of Villon to his Lady') is no pretty love song. Instead, there is anger aimed at the 'false beauty who costs me dear ... hypocritical sweetness ... sister of my undoing'. The second verse reads: 'I had been better off had I cried out for help elsewhere, help that would have brought me happiness: nothing could stop me from acting as I did, and now I can only escape in dishonour. Shame, shame, great and small!'[27] Moreover, the piano accompaniment once again echoes that monotonously rhythmic, sad, crunching footstep motif, first heard in 'La Grotte,' then in 'Des pas sur la neige'. This time the motif falls like tears, 'triste et lent' ('sadly and slowly'), the instruction to the singer reading 'avec une expression où il y a autant d'angoisse que de regret' ('with an expression just as much of anguish as regret'). Durand had expressed surprised that Debussy could compose when he had so many worries at this time. To what 'drama' – a strong word – in his life was Debussy referring in his reply to Durand?

Dolly's letters

Emma was still close to Chouchik Laloy and on 2 June visited her at the Laloys' house in Bellevue, Meudon, taking Chouchou with her. Chouchik described this visit in some detail to her husband in a letter of 3 June. At first the words she chose to

---

[26] 'What Should One Set to Music: Good Poetry or Bad Poetry, Free Verse or Prose? Inquiry led by Fernand Divoire', *Musica*, March 1911. F. Lesure, *Debussy on Music*, ed. and trans. R. Langham Smith, London, 1977, p. 251

[27] Trans. R. Miller in *The Poetic Debussy. A Collection of his Song Texts and Selected Letters*, ed. M. Cobb. Rochester, N. Y. and Woodbridge, second edition, 1994, p. 181.

describe Emma seem somewhat strange: 'good Madame Debussy with Chouchou and her poor anxious nature, simultaneously clear-sighted and blind …'[28] Anxious, yes, this one can understand, but blind? To what? Emma brought sweets and a present for two-year-old Nicolette. Five-year-old Chouchou obviously had fun playing with Nicolette, who fell into a little stream, swollen since a storm that afternoon. Chouchou got her dress dirty making mud pies. Meanwhile, Chouchik enjoyed strawberries and white wine with Emma, whom she described to Laloy as a 'peony' (*pivoine*). Mysteriously Chouchik mentioned something Dolly had told Emma: that the letters she (Dolly) had written to Claude and his to her had been deposited with the Durands.[29] On 5 June Chouchik wrote again to her husband, mentioning that Emma had written to her (typically in pencil) to say she had been in bed since her visit. Was this because of the 'petit faune' she wondered or the strawberries? Once again she referred to Emma as a charming peony, but this time a faded one, 'la charmante Pivoine épanouie'. Despite everything, Emma was being kind enough to send samples of material for new curtains.[30] Although Emma regarded Chouchik as her best friend, it seems that Chouchik had a rather more objective view of Emma. The words 'petit faune' evidently applied not to Chouchou but to Dolly. This became clear in an exchange of correspondence carried out in the 1970s between two writers on Debussy, Marcel Dietschy and André Schaeffner, where Dietschy referred to the 'Faune Debussy Dolly Bardac'.[31]

Emma considers divorce

On 25 June 1910 the première took place of Stravinsky's ballet *The Firebird*. Debussy was not only present – he was taken backstage after the last curtain and introduced to the younger composer by Diaghilev. Louis Laloy initiated another meeting when he invited both composers to his house soon afterwards. Debussy took the opportunity of inviting Stravinsky to dinner and presented him with a signed photograph of himself. It was with this photograph in front of him that Stravinsky began composing *Petrouchka*. This was the beginning of an enduring friendship which included Emma.

Writing on 8 July, Debussy described *The Firebird* to Durand as 'not perfect, but in certain respects very fine because the music is not the docile slave of the dance'. He particularly remarked on the unusual combinations of rhythms. But prior to these opinions, he opened the letter by literally pouring out his own anguished state of mind. In the first sentence Debussy talked about his 'curious existence which will be my life henceforth'. He then castigated all those around him

---

[28] Laloy archives B13, Dossier 9, no.90.
[29] 'Dolly lui a dit les lettres qu'elle a écrit [sic] à Cl [aude] et réciproquement avaient comme dépôt et siège "les Durands …"' Ibid.
[30] Laloy archives B13, Dossier 9, no.92.
[31] N. Southon, 'Une correspondence entre André Schaeffner et Marcel Dietschy', *Cahiers Debussy*, no.34, 2010, p. 109.

who obstinately refuse to understand that I have never been able to live in the real world of things and people. That's why I have this insurmountable need to escape from myself and go off on *adventures which seem inexplicable* [my italics] because I reveal a man no one knows and that is probably what is best about me. Besides, an artist is by definition a man accustomed to dreaming who lives amongst phantoms … How can anyone expect this same man to behave in his daily life according to the strict observance of its traditions, laws and other barriers erected by the hypocritical and cowardly world.
So you see I am living surrounded by memories and regrets … These are my two sad companions. They are constant, more so than joy and happiness.[32]

The only thing he could work on was his opera, *La chute de la Maison Usher*. He found it therapeutic and useful for 'satisfying my taste for the inexpressible'.

Things had clearly reached crisis point with Emma. Debussy's inability to adapt completely to domestic responsibilities weighed on him; the initial joy of his love of Emma had given way to regret at a feeling of confinement. Who else can it be but she who refused to understand his inability 'to live in the real world'? 'Refuse' implied not even wanting to understand. This lady who had been so accustomed to leading a social life with all its niceties was disappointed to find he regarded such behaviour as hypocritical. He dreamt and lived in the world of his imagination. Yet there was also the question of 'adventures which seem inexplicable'. These surely are related to the 'drama' and Emma's 'blindness' referred to earlier. 'Memories', as he revealed in the comment quoted earlier to Messager, were also an ever-present danger to his peace of mind.

A letter Emma wrote to her solicitor in 1910, but which bears no specific date, proves that she was seriously considering divorce. Hardly surprisingly, yet again she was ill, for she began, 'Please accept my sincere apologies, but the terrible state I am in both mentally and physically means I could not have attended the appointment you so kindly arranged …' She then explained that she had still not made up her mind. 'It would cause me so much anguish to separate from the man who causes me so much suffering. Alas, there will never be a shortage of reasons to do so.'[33] One possible reason, which also throws light on Chouchik's earlier comments, which became clear at the beginning of 1911, will be explained in the following chapter.

In addition to this depressing state of affairs, Debussy's father fell ill in July and had to undergo an operation. As Debussy told Durand, he himself was alternating between one good day and two bad, or vice versa.[34] On 24 August he admitted to Laloy that he was in a detestable mood, harbouring an ever-growing desire to destroy himself. His misery was not solely his fault. He likened his family to the Usher family – the best he had.[35] The grim atmosphere of Poe's story was mirrored in Debussy's mental state. Just as the childlike characters of *Pelléas et Mélisande* had obsessed him when composing that opera, now he was fully entering this dark gothic world of tormented spirits.

[32] C. p. 1299.
[33] C. p. 1366.
[34] C. p. 1306.
[35] C. p. 1308.

A disastrous dinner party

From Debussy's correspondence with Arthur Hartmann one would never guess there was anything wrong with his family life. The Hartmanns had dined twice at the Debussys' but, being nervous about entertaining them for dinner and an entire evening at their own house in return, Marie Hartmann insisted on booking a table at the elegant – and expensive – Hotel Majestic. Emma would surely have regarded this as something to look forward to, but she wrote to Marie on 2 August, 'my husband asks why the "Majestic?" He dreads the obligatory evening dress in places called "Majestical".'[36] Debussy's own response was to write to Arthur, 'It would seem that we are dining together tomorrow evening at the "Majestic". I will go at once to get my beard trimmed to look more American.'[37]

The whole occasion was a disaster. According to Hartmann, Emma was 'well-dressed' but Debussy wore his blue suit, blue shirt and blue collar, regarded as a 'faux-pas'. A fashionable American-style dinner of grapefruit topped by a cherry, a dish the composer had never seen before, followed by thin consommé, initially served without bread, then rather dry roast chicken with stuffing, was clearly anathema to Debussy, who commented frankly and rudely on this strange fare. Emma constantly tried unsuccessfully to control her husband, who annoyed Hartmann to such a point that he turned to him saying, 'Would you perhaps prefer to order your own dinner?' At this point Debussy ordered himself a complete dinner of soup, lamb, red wine, salad, soufflé and a bottle of champagne. By the end of the evening, he was mollified, but back home Hartmann took his anger out on his wife. In return the Hartmanns were invited once more to the Debussys' for dinner, at which Hartmann could not help teasing Debussy, saying he could not eat the delicious food provided. Despite financial difficulties, Emma had certainly organised a lavish meal: two meat courses with wonderful sauces, a soufflé, a *bombe glacée* with choice of dessert wines, coffee and two bottles of champagne. Hartmann referred to such occasions as 'these intimate little dinners ... when champagne was served in this atmosphere of exquisite perfection of tastes ... the luxury was of the kind that one almost suffocates.' When he sat back and observed Emma, he described her as 'rather petite, vaporously gowned, and always affecting a little 'moue' [pout] and who had one, just one, short exotic white curl in a head of short, curly, golden hair.' He found bizarre this

> small white curl, so closely resembling the fancifully cut little papers one sees wrapped around the bone of a broiled lamb chop. Like Debussy, the Madame had a keen gift for cryptic comments, a love for subtle, sly, and not entirely unmalicious humour, and thus I placed her on a par with her husband.[38]

At the end of August the Hartmanns left for Norway, and in a letter dated 15 September Debussy assured Arthur he would write him the *Poème* for violin, already promised in July. Needless to say, nothing would come of this, but his excuse for

---

[36] A. Hartmann, *Claude Debussy as I knew him*, p. 83.
[37] C. p. 1307.
[38] A. Hartmann, *Claude Debussy as I knew him*, pp. 84–9.

not getting on with it at once was his full concentration on *The Fall of the House of Usher*. He had to finish this or he would go mad.[39] Hartmann would never forget this promise of a violin piece.

Debussy ceases payments guaranteeing Lilly's alimony; death of his father

Debussy was clearly incapable of finding peace of mind. Since his divorce in 1905, he had had to pay insurance premiums guaranteeing the alimony of four hundred francs a month paid to Lilly Texier by Durand.[40] In 1910 he stopped paying these, a decision which would eventually come back to bite him in 1916.[41] In September he signed a contract with the Canadian-born dancer Maud Allan for a ballet *Isis* (soon to be renamed *Khamma*), but significantly this was kept from Durand, nor was it mentioned in letters to him until over a year later, for it certainly breached the contract he had made with his publisher on 17 July 1905 giving Durand exclusive rights to all his future compositions. No doubt Debussy was eager to receive the ten thousand francs which were paid to him on signature, and looked forward to the other large sums of money he would earn from delivering the score (stipulated date, end of February 1911) and from future performances. However, the whole process of collaborating with Maud Allan and the difficulties so habitual with Debussy of delivering his work on time would lead to many complications which eventually required Durand's involvement. Despite Durand's faithful support over the years, it seems Debussy resorted to deviousness when he saw an opportunity to obtain money in the short term.

By 25 September he was once again admitting to his publisher that he was depressed and worried. Emma was unwell, Chouchou was obviously being a typically energetic five-year-old, full of 'charm and tyranny' and 'joyously scandalising her grandmother!' This seems to imply that Emma's mother, Laure, was in the house, perhaps supporting her daughter. But Debussy was feeling a desperate desire to escape, yet knew he could not do so. 'I am going through a period of anxiety – a bit like someone waiting for a train in a sunless waiting-room. I want to go somewhere, anywhere, but at the same time am afraid to leave. I need a lot of patience to be able to tolerate myself!'[42]

Chouchou was the one person who always brought Debussy deep comfort and a sweet postcard exists postmarked 4 October, saying simply, in English, 'Good Morning. My Chouchou beloved.' It pictured a bear on the telephone, saying 'What! Come Home? Not likely, when I'm in *Paris!*'[43] This actually bears a postmark. Could it be that Debussy was spending time away from home? Was he keeping out of Emma's and Laure's way for a few days? Was he staying with his parents, helping to care for

---

[39] C. p. 1313.
[40] See Chapter 5 p. 75.
[41] See Chapter 16 p. 232.
[42] C. p. 1316.
[43] C. p. 1320; BnF Musique, La-Debussy Claude-78.

his sick father? These questions cannot be answered. Apart from a contract ceding to Durand ten per cent of the rights to Le diable dans le beffroi, signed 'à Paris' on 19 October, there are no extant letters from Debussy between 1 and 23 October. On that date, writing to Varèse, he complained of all sorts of troubles, his seriously ill father, sick wife and too much work.[44] However, home life did have its benefits, and Debussy was not about to have to renounce these. No separation or divorce took place. On the contrary, on Debussy's part there seems to have been a growing recognition that he needed Emma's support, for as the year progressed and he had to travel abroad, he sent her letters full of loving appreciation and regret at being parted from her.

Debussy's father died on 28 October at the age of 74. Debussy needed to be by his mother's side and inform Durand and other friends, sending out invitations to the funeral, at which his siblings and their families were present. It took place at the Church of Notre-Dame in Auteuil on 31 October. He later wrote to Caplet, now in America as conductor of the orchestra of the Boston Opera, that although he had hardly anything in common with his father, he felt the loss more deeply with every day that passed. He was particularly touched that P.-J. Toulet managed to attend the funeral, regarding this as proof of true affection.[45]

Pasteur Vallery-Radot's admiration of the family

On Wednesday 2 November a huge admirer of Pelléas et Mélisande, Pasteur Vallery-Radot, grandson and namesake of the great Louis Pasteur, visited the Debussys for the first time. Ever since the first performance of the opera in 1902, on 30 April he had sent a bouquet of flowers anonymously to Debussy to mark this auspicious anniversary. In 1910 he included with the bouquet his visiting card and now, his identity revealed, he was invited to dinner. As a twenty-four-year-old, half Debussy's age, he was flattered and enchanted to become a friend of the composer, realising that he was one of a select few. 'Debussy was always careful to protect his independence. He feared intruders who might disturb the charm of his home where he enjoyed a pleasurable life.'[46] Or again,

> He had very few friends, as he feared anything which might upset the rhythm of his existence and he had maintained the wild character of his youth: for him, there were two types of people, those he liked and those he could not bear. The former were the exceptions.[47]

Vallery-Radot's account of Debussy's relationship with Emma was coloured by sincere admiration and devotion. He was determined to present both as an idyllically happy couple, secure in each other's love, leading an existence in which Debussy's 'life and work from henceforth were in complete harmony'. Emma loved her husband to the point of feeling jealous of his music, he believed. Debussy's reply to her

---

[44] C. p. 1321.
[45] C. pp. 1331, 1325.
[46] P. Vallery-Radot, Lettres de Claude Debussy à sa femme Emma, p. 6.
[47] Idem. p. 40.

was that if there was anyone who should be jealous, it was music and if he continued to compose it and to love it, that was because he owed to it, to this music she was maligning, the fact that he had met her, loved her and everything that followed. He added, 'You may be sure that if for some reason I could not write it any more, it would probably be you who stopped loving me, for it is certainly not the rather inhibited charm of my conversation, nor my physical attributes which would help me keep hold of you.'[48]

On his very first visit, Vallery-Radot claimed, he witnessed the love uniting these two beings, expressed through the glances and the words they exchanged with each other. He was deeply moved to find them in such perfect agreement.[49] Did he never witness any of Debussy's cross words, impatience or frustration that others told of? If he noticed Emma's jealousy of her husband's music, surely there must have been reason for this remark. He was silent on this, but emphasised Emma's femininity. When she entered the room her perfume ensured that no man could remain insensitive to her feminine charm. Immediately the atmosphere was filled with love and tenderness. She spoke in a quiet voice evoking the words of Pelléas to Mélisande, 'It is as if your voice had come over the sea in the spring'.[50]

Like others, Vallery-Radot found Chouchou adorable, and noted Debussy's deep love of this intelligent, sensitive child. Not only did she sing, she danced minuets. When she rebelled against the strict discipline of her English governess, Debussy would side with her: 'She is so little,' he said. 'She must have a bit of freedom.' Vallery-Radot appears to have had no idea of the marital troubles Emma and Debussy were experiencing. 'His affection for his wife was such that he could not live even for a few hours away from her', he observed.[51] This would indeed be proved in a month's time.

Travels to Vienna and Budapest

Following some administrative confusion, Debussy was now definitely committed to a week away conducting his *Petite suite* (orchestrated by Henri Busser), *La mer*, *Prélude à l'après-midi d'un faune* and *Ibéria* at the Vienna Musikverein on 2 December, and taking part in a chamber concert in Budapest on 5 December. There he was to play the *Estampes* and *Children's Corner* in a programme which also included the String Quartet and the *Proses lyriques*, sung by Rose Féart. To Caplet Debussy expressed his anguish at having to present himself in public. It caused him 'almost physical suffering' when his own music was involved. However, reading the telegrams and letters he sent to Emma during his journey and sojourn abroad, it was not physical, but mental suffering that he was experiencing, anguish not just at being away from home, but at being separated from her. What misery their financial problems were bringing. Only his side of the exchange of correspondence is available to read.

[48] Idem. p. 30
[49] Idem. p. 36.
[50] 'On croirait que ta voix a passé sur la mer au printemps.' Act IV, scene 4.
[51] Vallery-Radot, *Lettres de Claude Debussy à sa femme Emma*, p. 37.

Two telegrams dated 29 November reported on his progress, first to Salzburg ('dismal journey and fellow travellers. Am missing you horribly'), then from Vienna on his safe arrival at the Hotel Krantz.[52] The same evening he wrote a long letter to Emma which he signed, then continued the next day and signed again. Quoting a phrase from the poem 'Le Balcon', the first of the Cinq poèmes de Charles Baudelaire, he emphasised how much he was missing 'la douceur du foyer', the sweetness of home. Thinking of Emma in their double bed and of Chouchou in her little bed made him want to cry. This experience was convincing him with the force of a nail being hammered into his head that he loved them both infinitely. Having to unpack his bags by himself was a grim task which persuaded him of Emma's 'domestic virtues', and not having his belongings arranged in the neat way she would have done was very troubling to him. 'To think that just yesterday you were lying on my chest and our bodies were entwined – as Mademoiselle Bilitis says[53] – and now I am going to bed with nothing, desiring everything.'

He continued in the morning with the news that he had received two telegrams from Emma. She must stop worrying. He reminded her that he was only undertaking this journey for both their sakes. Its sole purpose was to overcome the financial hard times dogging them, but for which he would never travel so far from her and her caresses. After a bad night he had found the first rehearsal stressful, all the more so as he had to communicate through an interpreter who, he feared, was probably not passing on his comments accurately. He wanted to tell the players 'what Chouchou says: "Look me in the eyes."' Not being able to shout and swear at Emma on the spot was obviously a lesson to him in how much she had to put up with, but certainly did not make him want to give up this habit – rather, to show her how much he appreciated being able to do so. He had only been in Vienna for a day and had already bought a doll for Chouchou.[54]

On 2 December he replied to a letter from Emma. The pain of his loneliness was tangible. She was living amongst familiar things. 'Your bed is full of history, whilst I am in a random, anonymous room, whose history I will try not to think about!' He now appreciated what she had to put up with when he complained to her at home: 'Often when I talk to you it's not you I am addressing directly, but it's another me whom I can question and who replies as if it is my own thoughts speaking. Perhaps this is a very subtle way of missing someone.' Even at this distance their debts were a concern. He tried to assure Emma that everything would be all right as long as the 'vultures' accepted the dates being spread out, a reference to repayments of money borrowed. The final rehearsal did not go too badly despite the fact that 'the pretentions of the Viennese seem to me to go beyond all limits'. Only by thinking of Emma and Chouchou would he be able to hide signs of endless boredom, even distaste. He denigrated the audience, composed for the most part of idiots, whose approval he was trying to gain, which in itself was ridiculous. But he could stay sane as long as Chouchou stayed satisfied with Teddy and Weagle Top (her soft toys).[55]

---

[52] C. p. 1336.
[53] 'Tant nos membres étaient confondus' in 'La chevelure', second of the Chansons de Bilitis.
[54] C. pp. 1337–9.
[55] C. pp. 1341–2.

There followed a series of six postcards sent to Chouchou all on the same day, 2 December, depicting pompous Austrian soldiers in various ridiculous poses, not exactly children's fare, but amusing to Debussy. On each of these he wrote part of what became a tiny short story beginning, 'Once upon a time there was a father living in exile …' and ending with the signature, 'Lepapadechouchou'.[56]

The Vienna concert was a great success, although Ferdinand Löwe, conductor of the Konzertverein orchestra, was reported as having congratulated Debussy on having abolished melody. Debussy's reply was, 'But Monsieur, all my music aspires to be nothing but melody!'[57]

The first telegram to Emma from Budapest the next day, 3 December, was to say he couldn't understand why she had not received his letters. Later that day he wrote a long letter describing the atmosphere at the previous night's concert and the 'stunning' (*fulgurante*) performance of 'Ibéria'. Considerate of her nervous disposition, he had not sent her a telegram immediately afterwards. 'You are too easily alarmed, you invent troubles which make you ill and upset your poor little liver.' Negotiations for a tour to Amsterdam were clearly in the offing, even though he complained about the bad pay. He did not want to be away from his 'chouchous' again.[58] The most delightful experience on the journey was stopping at the train station of Eusellujvar (Ersekujvar) and cheering in excitement at hearing a gypsy band playing the Ràkóczy march.

On 4 December he returned to despondency. In Budapest the Danube was no longer blue. He had managed to get his dismal room overlooking houses upgraded, telling the manager that he had not come to Budapest simply for pleasure, and he must not aggravate the situation by inciting him to suicide. Yet again he was solicitous for Emma's health. He implored her not to ignore the cold she mentioned in her last letter. If she had not called Dr Crespel yet, she must do so at once. Chouchou was obviously being troublesome with her father away and Emma was finding it difficult to cope with her. 'What has Chouchou done to deserve your anger?' he asked. He knew she could invent terrible things, but she was so little, he pleaded, you mustn't take it out on her. He wished Emma could have heard the amazing gypsy violinist, Radics, who played like Hartmann but with more imagination and more genuine melancholy. 'You are made to understand the art of such people and its special quality'.[59] Here was a positive compliment to his wife, appreciating her innate understanding of good musicianship. Also, for the first time he had heard a cimbalom, an instrument he would later introduce into his orchestration of his piano piece, *La plus que lente*.

Debussy's last letter to Emma from Budapest on 5 December described a dinner following the concert, given by a confectioner with a worldwide reputation from whom he had acquired a chocolate St Nicholas, which he would be giving to Chouchou. Thoughtfully, he advised Emma not to come to the station to meet him

---

[56] C. p. 1343. BnF musique, La-Debussy Claude-77.
[57] E. Lockspeiser, *Debussy: His life and mind*, vol.2, London, 1965, p. 129 n.
[58] This tour would eventually take place four years later.
[59] C. pp. 1346–8.

on his return if she was not feeling well.[60] He sent two telegrams on the way home, the first quoting *Pelléas et Mélisande*, 'C'est le dernier soir', the second expressing impatience to embrace his *chouchous*. His relief was intense. He had spent only a week away from Emma, but surely the tide had turned in their relationship.

Le martyre de Saint Sébastien

Whilst in Vienna Debussy received a letter forwarded to him from Gabriele d'Annunzio, written on 25 November 1910. How did Debussy and Emma become familiar with this flamboyant, often outrageous poet and playwright who became an inspiration to Mussolini?

In 1910 d'Annunzio had moved to Paris from Settignano near Florence because of the huge financial debts he had accumulated. Small, bald, unimpressive in appearance, he possessed a seemingly magical power over women, proving irresistible to many. His letter to Debussy was written in Arcachon, where he had spent that summer with the artist Romaine Brooks, whose only male lover he was. For eight years previously he had had an affair with the actress Eleonore Duse, who was rumoured to be bisexual. Now he was trying to find a composer who would set to music his work, *Le martyre de Saint Sébastien*, the first he had written in French, intended as a vehicle expressly for Ida Rubinstein, whom he had seen performing in Diaghilev's Ballets Russes and with whom he had become infatuated. It was a perfect match, the androgynous saint and the equally androgynous, tall, exotic Ida Rubinstein. What was more, Rubinstein was to fund the whole project. D'Annunzio had first asked Roger-Ducasse to collaborate with him. He was horrified at the idea, ridiculing both the poet and the dancer to his friend André Lambinet, sure that d'Annunzio would die of astonishment to discover that a young, unknown composer would 'refuse to collaborate with HIM'.[61] The poet also considered Henry Février, and friends suggested Paul Dukas, but eventually, on the advice of the celebrated aesthete, Robert de Montesquiou, he wrote a florid letter to Debussy. 'Do you like my poetry?' he asked. Debussy's reply was surprisingly enthusiastic, but typically hypocritical. 'How could it be possible that I would not love your poetry? I already feel slightly feverish with excitement at the idea of working with you.'[62] D'Annunzio was so pleased with this last phrase that he underlined it on receipt of the letter. Debussy did not know that he was not d'Annunzio's first choice of composer.

To Emma in his letter of 3 December from Budapest, Debussy was more honest and dismissive. Saying he had replied to d'Annunzio, he added, 'This whole business has nothing of any worth. And I seem to command a special attraction for female dancers! Think of Miss Maud Allan ... *Khamma* (soutra)!'[63] Emma, however, had already corresponded with Ida Rubinstein, who was anxious to know the reason for Debussy's delay in writing to d'Annunzio. Right from the start of this project

---

[60] C. pp. 1349–50.
[61] Roger-Ducasse, ed. J. Depaulis, *Lettres à son ami André Lambinet*, Sprimont, 2001, p. 75.
[62] C. p. 1339.
[63] C. p. 1344.

d'Annunzio wrapped Emma round his little finger. He wrote a cringingly sycophantic letter to her on 7 December, thanking her for his first visit to her house. 'I will never forget your welcome, so simple and so noble, in the house tucked away, where silence is music.' He sent with the letter a copy of his latest book,[64] and an invitation on behalf of Robert de Montesquiou, 'one of the most passionate admirers of the works of Claude Debussy, and – after me – the one who bears in his heart the most ardent wishes for the realisation of the great dream.'[65] Emma's reply of the same day was brief but accommodating, appreciative of the book, which she already knew, telling him her husband had returned and that he should come to their house the next day without even telephoning first.

Debussy can have had no let-up on his arrival home. He wrote a long letter of appreciation to Gusztav Bárczy, organiser of his stay in Hungary, in which he also thanked him on behalf of Chouchou for some dolls given to her by Madame Bárczy. Emma had noticed that he had left his glasses case behind. More importantly, he had left his copy of the *Estampes* and *Hommage à Rameau* on the piano and asked him to return these with the popular Hungarian music Bárczy had promised him. He also wanted him to pass on his compliments to the violinist Radicz, whose music was still ringing in his ears.[66] Despite tiredness, he then wrote a note to P.-J. Toulet asking him to come round the next day, again proving that routine visits of chosen friends were therapeutic to Debussy and Emma.

Presumably d'Annunzio did visit the Debussys as Emma had arranged on 8 December, for on that same date Debussy was in contact with Gabriel Astruc, the impresario who was organising the presentation of *Le martyre* at the Théâtre du Châtelet, already indicating the orchestral resources he would require. Let us not forget that not only had Emma already been courted by d'Annunzio and Rubinstein regarding Debussy's involvement, but Astruc was also a distant relation of hers. Debussy addressed his letter to him, 'Cher ami'. There was an ironic quotation cited by d'Annunzio's biographer Tom Antongini, his secretary and manager, from Astruc who was initially anxious

> 'because there is a group of ladies of the French aristocracy who have written to me to express their concern that Saint Sébastien could give the impression from a religious point of view of profanation. I would not like to be accused of having crucified the Lord for the second time.' (Astruc is a Jew).

D'Annunzio's response was that the work was essentially mystical, unassailable from a religious point of view. 'And what is more, dear Astruc, when Ida Rubinstein shows herself almost naked at the moment of supplication, it will be too late to protest. The audience will already have been won over.'[67]

D'Annunzio was clearly sympathetic towards Emma. Speaking of the Debussy household, he told Antongini,

---

[64] *Forse che si, forse che no*, translated into French as *Peut-être oui, peut-être non*, Paris, 1910.
[65] C. p. 1351.
[66] C. p. 1353.
[67] T. Antongini, *D'Annunzio inconnu*, Paris, 1938, p. 511.

The egoism of certain artists is incredible. Madame Debussy is an ideal woman and one could never deny the love her husband feels for her … they live near the Bois du Boulogne in a small villa. The railway passes below their house. For months and months Madame Debussy has found it impossible to sleep. She can't bear noise. It makes her ill. Debussy knows that perfectly well, but he won't hear of changing accommodation because of the effort of moving. He told me this himself![68]

This assertion is significant, for it reveals that it was Debussy rather than Emma who was insisting on staying in the financial millstone around their necks. Often it is she who is blamed for being unable to give up her elegant and expensive lifestyle. It also supports Raoul Bardac's claim that it was Debussy who chose this house and that their home life was built around his desires.[69]

On 9 December, only two days after Debussy's return, the formal contract was signed with Astruc, the music to be delivered in time for rehearsals envisaging the performance around 20 May. Considering how long the composer had taken to write *Pelléas* and his customary dilatoriness in producing finished compositions, there was a remarkable amount of detail in requirements specified in this contract. Rubinstein's dances in each act were to be ready by the end of February. Debussy was to receive eight thousand francs on signing, six thousand when he delivered the dances in February and a further six thousand when the orchestral material was ready in April. It was agreed that the work could not be performed without Debussy's music.[70] D'Annunzio's delight at the signing of the contract was expressed in a telegram sent the same day. 'Gloire ô Claude roi.' ('Glory to Claude the king!') Emma's persuasive intervention so soon in the commissioning process meant that Debussy had taken on the work without having read one word of the text he was about to set.

The press were informed, and Roger-Ducasse soon learnt of Debussy's acceptance of the commission. On 11 December he commented to Lambinet, 'You must have seen our great Achille-Claude has succeeded me in the collaboration with the great Gabriele … Our musician must have been offered and received a large sum, or he would not have gone along with it.'[71]

Gabriel Astruc did not hesitate to write directly to Emma to express his 'infinite gratitude' for her intervention. 'You have been at the very start of great things to come.' Now he wanted to invite both Emma and Claude Debussy to meet Saint Sébastien himself in the form of Ida Rubinstein at the Café de Paris on Sunday evening. He also invited d'Annunzio. Emma accepted, 'although unwell'.[72]

Thus d'Annunzio became a regular visitor to the avenue du Bois de Boulogne and was not only welcomed by Debussy and his 'admirable compagne', but became attached to Chouchou, 'cette enfant qui est la plus fraîche mélodie de votre cœur' ('This child who is the freshest melody in your heart').[73]

---

[68] Idem. p. 411.
[69] Chapter 6 p. 80.
[70] C. pp. 1355–7.
[71] Roger-Ducasse, *Lettres à son ami André Lambinet*, p. 76.
[72] C. pp. 1357–8 and n.1.
[73] C. p. 1360.

That Christmas Emma received a musical greeting from Debussy, only four bars long of vocal line, to be sung 'as often as desired and loudly'. 'Noël pour la petite mienne – Noël! Noël pour qui la j'aime.' It bore the message 'Noël, made by the little owl, apologising for not yet knowing the harmony, but from the whole of his black little devoted heart.' It was signed, 'the publisher responsible, Claude Debussy'.[74] What with that and Chouchou's chocolate Saint Nicholas, there must, thankfully, have been some laughter in the household.

---

[74] 'Noel, que fit le petit hibou, en s'excusant de ne pas savoir encore l'harmonie, mais avec tout son noir petit cœur dévoué.' C. p. 1362.

11

1911: A marriage and *Le martyre*

Dolly's marriage

Debussy's arrival home from Budapest on 7 December was marked not only by the requirement to collaborate with Gabriele d'Annunzio, but also the announcement that very day in *Le Figaro* of the engagement of 'M. Gaston de Tinan to Mlle Bardac, daughter of M. Sigismond Bardac, the great collector. The fiancé is the brother and brother-in-law of Commandant de Tinan and of Mme de Tinan, née Comtesse de Caraman-Chimay.'[1] It was clearly Sigismond who had this published, for no mention was made of Emma. Nor had there been any comment on this impending event whilst Debussy was abroad – certainly not in his side of the correspondence. Surely Emma must have been pleased that her daughter was to marry into a distinguished and wealthy family.

Nowhere in the tome of collected *Correspondance* of Debussy is there a letter concerning the engagement or marriage of his step-daughter, Dolly, and any mention by Emma has yet to be discovered. There does exist, however, a photograph of Emma standing next to Sigismond Bardac, her arm through his, he looking sternly away as if wanting nothing to do with Emma, who is looking somewhat downcast, and Dolly standing next to Gaston, her engagement ring visible on her left hand. Leaves on the ground indicate that the photograph was taken in the autumn. Another photograph shows Dolly and Emma standing alone outside a hotel. On the back Dolly has written 'Dieppe' and the date 1910. Again, one can just see the ring on Dolly's left hand. This indicates that she and her mother had travelled to a hotel there at some stage of the engagement. There had been no family holiday in 1910.

Significantly, prior to the marriage Dolly had to renounce officially her Jewish heritage and convert to Catholicism. A copy of her Baptismal certificate shows that on 23 December 1910 Hélène Regine Bardac[2] was baptised in the Catholic church. Her address was given not as the avenue du Bois de Boulogne, but 6 rue de la Baume, one of Sigismond's addresses since at least 1908.[3] Her godparents were her uncle Georges Noël d'Arnoux and aunt Paule (Pauline) Bardac. On the same certificate is a note that the marriage took place on 25 January 1911 at the Roman Catholic church, Saint-Pierre-de-Chaillot, in the Avenue Marceau.

---

[1] *Le Figaro*, 7 December 1910.
[2] A reversal of her given names at birth. The copy is dated 1940. It was kindly provided by M. Philippe Lagourgue.
[3] This address was listed in *Annuaire des grands cercles* and *Paris Mondain* 1908.

18. L–R: Sigismond Bardac, Emma, Gaston de Tinan,
Dolly wearing engagement ring, 1910

The civil marriage certificate dated 24 January 1911 states that Dolly married Gaston Pochet Le Barbier de Tinan, born in Le Havre, son of Georges Alphonse Pochet and Marie Caroline Louise Nathalie Berthe Lebarbier de Tinan, both deceased. This was an aristocratic family. Gaston's brother was Charles Pochet Le Barbier de Tinan, at that time Commander of the Cavalry of the Amalat of Oujda (a French military base in Morocco), whose wife was Geneviève de Riquet de Caraman-Chimay. Her sister was Countess Elisabeth Greffulhe, the main inspiration for the Duchess of Guermantes in Proust's *In Search of Lost Time*. Gaston was also a cousin of Jean de Tinan, a writer and friend of Debussy whom he had known through Pierre Louÿs since 1895. The family home of the de Tinans was in Le Havre.

Gaston, born on 1 January 1881, the same year as Dolly's brother Raoul, was thirty at the time of the marriage. Dolly was eighteen and a half years old, an eleven-year difference, greater than that between Emma and Sigismond. The marriage certificate shows that Dolly was residing with her father at 1 avenue Marceau, yet another of the Bardac addresses. The couple had four witnesses, Maurice Taconnet, *courtier maritime* (Shipping Broker) at Saint Adresse (near Le Havre), Gaston's brother-in-law Paul Aubry, *Colonel d'Artillerie*, Sigismond's brother Noël Bardac, banker and Chevalier de la Légion d'Honneur, and the husband of Sigismond's sister Julia, Georges Comte d'Arnoux, *directeur de la dette publique Ottomane*, also Chevalier de la Légion d'Honneur.

19. Dolly (wearing engagement ring) and Emma outside hotel in Dieppe, 1910

Newspapers provided the information that Dolly's bridesmaids were Bardac cousins, Germaine and Madeleine, and Paule, her aunt and godmother. Raoul Bardac was a member of the entourage, so had clearly not been tainted by his association with Debussy. The bride's and bridesmaids' dresses and the fashionable clothes worn by the groom's mother and the Comtesse d'Arnoux were described in detail. The reception was hosted by Sigismond Bardac and the Comtesse d'Arnoux at 1 avenue Marceau.[4] There was no mention of Emma having been present. The Comtesse de Caraman-Chimay appeared constantly in the press in society lists of important guests at gatherings which often included her sister, the Comtesse Henry Greffuhle. The Comtesse d'Arnoux was another aristocrat well known to Marcel Proust.[5] These connections seem a world away from Emma's social and domestic life. Osiris's will stipulated that Dolly would receive one hundred thousand francs when she married or upon her majority, whichever was the soonest. Obviously she would now be considerably better off financially with this and her well-to-do husband than at home with Emma and Debussy.

[4] *Le Figaro* 26 January 1911.
[5] Mentioned by him in a letter to Reynaldo Hahn in 1906, in which he told Hahn that the adoring countess wanted to give him a delightful rug: M. Proust, *Lettres à Reynaldo Hahn* VI-155: https://reynaldo-hahn.net/lettres/06_155.htm. (last accessed 16 November 2019).

Debussy and Dolly

Why did Dolly marry so suddenly? Why is there no extant comment from Emma or Debussy? It is necessary to mention here that rumours exist that she had to leave the Debussy household because of Debussy's inappropriate behaviour towards her. Marcel Dietschy hinted in his biography of the composer that there was a secret liaison in 1910. 'There was a final attachment, secret and very tender, but it led to no rupture.'[6] Surely, no one reading his book would have associated these words with Dolly. However, when he was researching his biography, Dietschy made notes claiming that Louis Laloy's son, Jean Laloy, informed him on 7 April 1954 that Madame de Tinan had been assaulted by Debussy. No one apart from Dietschy went as far as mentioning assault, and this was merely hearsay. Assault does not imply tenderness. Jean's son Vincent Laloy later told him that Debussy had written passionate letters to Dolly which had eventually been passed on to the Laloys, who in turn had later returned them to her.[7] Because of this unwelcome and improper attention, Emma had ensured that her daughter moved out to Sigismond's home and married Gaston de Tinan swiftly. Therefore, as in Emma's case, this was an arranged marriage, but for quite a different reason.

Strong evidence for the existence of such letters between Debussy and Dolly is provided within the archives of the Laloy family. In the previous chapter, a long letter from Emma's close friend Chouchik Laloy to her husband Louis written on 3 June 1910 was quoted in which Chouchik described Emma as 'blind'.[8] Chouchik also included the information that 'Dolly had told her the letters she had written to Cl. [Debussy] and his reciprocal letters ... were deposited "chez Durand"'.[9] So here is evidence in writing that Chouchik knew of correspondence between Dolly and Debussy. Was Emma's 'blindness' to do with not having immediately realised what was happening between her husband and her daughter? Vincent Laloy's aunt Ninette told him that his grandfather, Louis Laloy, had been an intermediary between Debussy and Dolly, delivering their letters to each other, thus contributing to the clandestine relationship, and implying that Dolly reciprocated Debussy's advances. In the nineteen-sixties, Ninette had returned to Dolly the bundle of letters, which had until then been carefully tied with string then hidden in a secret drawer in a desk in the Laloys' country house. Since being returned, Vincent Laloy wrote, they had no doubt been burnt. Vincent himself had often asked Dolly to write her memoirs, even suggesting she should dictate them to him.

---

[6] M. Dietschy, *A Portrait of Claude Debussy*, ed. and trans. William Ashbrook and Margaret G. Cobb. Oxford, 1994, p. 160. This is Ashbrook's and Cobb's translation of the words: 'Dernier éblouissement, secret, très doux, qui ne porte pas de conséquence.' *La Passion de Claude Debussy*, Neuchâtel, 1962, p. 204.

[7] Centre de Documentation Claude Debussy DOSS-08.04(10)-1-7 and 8. Discussed and reproduced in N. Southon, 'Une correspondence entre André Schaeffner et Marcel Dietschy. Dialogue et controverses debussyistes (1963–1971)', *Cahiers Debussy*, 34, 2010, p. 110.

[8] Chapter 10 p. 139.

[9] 'Dolly lui a dit des lettres qu'elle a écrites à Cl. [Debussy] et réciproquement, avaient comme dépôt et siège "chez Durand"', Laloy archives, B13, Dossier 9, no.90.

Eventually Dolly asked Ninette to explain to him that her unwillingness stemmed from the fact that she did not want to reveal that her step-father had felt attracted towards her.[10]

Nowhere can these accusations be validated, nor can they be denied, and there is certainly no evidence of assault. Even if there were letters, one must ask oneself first what were the letters between her and Debussy that Dolly deposited with Durand, referred to in June 1910 and, second, why would Dolly have originally passed on the letters to this outsider, if they existed, rather than get rid of them? The implication must be that Durand was party to this deceit. In 1910 Debussy himself had made remarks to Durand about the *'drame'* affecting his life, which implied that Durand already knew of it.[11] Chouchik certainly had knowledge of a matter upsetting for Emma involving her *'petit faune'*, Dolly.[12] After Debussy's death Dolly was always careful to present Debussy and Emma in a positive light, proud to relate the circumstances of her six years in their household and of the care she took of the baby Chouchou. In any event, she kept strict control of material published about her mother and herself. This is corroborated by the fact that there are so few letters from Emma in existence prior to Debussy's death. If the hypothesis is true, it is little wonder that Emma had considered divorcing Debussy in 1910, although his character and behaviour since their marriage had not been easy to adapt to even without this extra, unsubstantiated, possibility. In Dolly's writings and talks about Debussy and Emma after their deaths, there was never any hint of criticism which could lead one to suspect any sort of unsuitable relationship.

Le martyre de Saint Sébastien

Dolly moved out of the Debussy household before her marriage. The stress of these circumstances must have taken a toll on both Emma and her husband. Despite this, on his return from Budapest Debussy started work on *Khamma* at the same time as being asked by d'Annunzio to compose *Le martyre*. 'I don't need to tell you that in it the cult of Adonis meets that of Jesus', he exclaimed to Robert Godet.[13] New Year's greetings to and from d'Annunzio revolved around Chouchou.[14] To d'Annunzio, who was in Arcachon, Debussy put his daughter's greeting first. 'Chouchou sends you her fondest wishes and her respectful homage to St Sébastien. Her mother and I join her in sincere greetings.' D'Annunzio wrote to Emma rather than Debussy, 'To you and Claude all the happiness with which Chouchou's eyes overflow'. Debussy invited the poet to dinner on the evening of his arrival in Paris, 11 January. On 23 January Debussy received one of d'Annunzio's flowery missives, offering various alternative treatments of his words, even to replace some of his text with a traditional *Te Deum*, and express-

---

[10] V. Laloy, *Souvenirs épars, (Dolly de Tinan, née Bardac)*, unpublished paper, copy kindly given to the author by M. Vincent Laloy.
[11] Chapter 10 p. 137.
[12] Idem. p. 139.
[13] C. p. 1384.
[14] C. pp. 1368–9.

ing deep emotion as he looked forward to the blessed hour when he would finish the work. D'Annunzio's affection for little Chouchou was genuine. She remained an inspiration to him, but the idea she created in his mind was typically obscurely classical: 'The thought of Chouchou's eyes makes me smile. She has the eyes of *Panisque*, because she is indeed the daughter of your *paniscus* soul.' *Panisque* is d'Annunzio's translation of the Latin name *Paniscus*, little god Pan.[15]

D'Annunzio's poetic words were overpowering. Debussy found even his letter 'charming and terrifying; you can hear the triumphant fanfares of a march to glory.' His language almost rivalled the poet's as he tried to express his feeling of inadequacy beside the ceaselessly innovative splendour of d'Annunzio's imagination. He was experiencing a feeling of terror, he said, as he approached the moment when he would have to write something down. Perhaps it was because he was so absorbed in his composition that he completely forgot to send Jules the chauffeur to collect Emma from somewhere. 'I do have an excuse', he claimed.[16]

Family troubles; anxiety concerning *Le martyre*

From a long letter from Debussy to Robert Godet dated 6 February we learn once again that Emma was ill with liver trouble. Not only that, Chouchou had flu, so domestic life was troublesome. After all, Emma no longer had the company of her older daughter in the house to help her. She had to send a fountain pen back to d'Annunzio when he returned to Arcachon, one he had left behind in Paris, for in his letter of thanks he described it as a 'stylograph decorated with a crystallised drop of Sébastien's blood'.[17] Debussy had clearly 'borrowed' the pen, for he exclaimed 'The man who wrongfully took possession of your pen must have been touched by grace after several nights of remorse!'[18] Knowing the composer's love of luxurious objects this is not surprising.

On 12 February Debussy wrote several letters despite the pressure to get on with composing *Le martyre*. To d'Annunzio he regretted time passing so fast and asked for specific advice on where the dance music should enter. He was appreciative of the words which were inspiring the rhythm and form of the music. Whilst Emma's health was improving, her mother was 'un phénomène de vie suspendue', indicating that she was weak and hovering between life and death. This may also indicate that Laure Moyse, a widow since 1885, was now living with them. 'Chouchou is more chouchou than ever' indicated that his daughter was well over her flu.[19] To Durand he repeated the description of his mother-in-law's precarious state of health, as well as telling him Emma was ill in bed, whilst he was toiling away. 'This is no life … !'[20] There were other mundane worries: Albert Carré was preparing the new run of *Pelléas et Mélisande* at the Opéra-Comique to begin on 18 February, for which Debussy had expected four orchestral rehearsals, but frustratingly only one was scheduled.

[15] C. p. 1378, n.4.
[16] C. pp. 1380, 1382.
[17] C. p. 1386.
[18] C. p. 1387.
[19] Ibid.
[20] C. p. 1388.

He found time on 14 February to write a long letter to André Caplet, who had just conducted his orchestration of Debussy's *Children's Corner* in Boston, informing him he had given up Poe for the time being in favour of Ida Rubinstein and the 'irresistible whirlwind', d'Annunzio. Again emphasising the pressure he was under, he thought Caplet may be interested in the project – an indication that he might want to involve him in it. Chouchou, as so often, featured in the letter. She had just completed the composition of her first symphonic tone poem, for voice, two paper knives and piano *ad libitum*. Its title was *L'éléphant sur la branche*. 'It is very dramatic!'[21] Little wonder that amidst all his stress Debussy found great solace in his precocious daughter.

Owing to the exigencies of *Pelléas* preparations, Debussy was not able to write to d'Annunzio until 20 February, when he declared it impossible to fulfil Rubinstein's demand to separate the dances from the rest of the score of *Le martyre*. By 2 March the text was finished. Poet and composer met at last on 22 March for lunch at the Grill Room of the Mercedes Hotel, as there was no cook at home, a recurring domestic problem. D'Annunzio's thoughts still turned to Chouchou, despite having to cope with problems of casting. He imagined he suddenly heard music wafting over him emanating from Debussy's room every time Chouchou opened the door a little.[22] Pressure was mounting. An exchange of letters with Gabriel Astruc showed that Debussy had no time to meet him, Emma having had to write on Debussy's behalf, to which Debussy added a message congratulating him on the choice of Inghelbrecht as chorus master.[23] At least Emma was now well enough to be a helpful intermediary.

Satie's success

Time was also needed to rehearse and present a concert devoted entirely to works by Debussy which he himself conducted in the Salle Gaveau on 25 March. One of the items was Debussy's orchestration of the first and third *Gymnopédies* by Erik Satie. This concert had some considerable effect on the relationship between the two men. It has already been noted that Satie was a welcome guest at the Debussys' and loved playing with Chouchou, whose pet name for him was Kiki, a corruption of Erik.[24] They would play 'bows and arrows' in the garden, getting told off by a fatherly Debussy if they strayed onto the beautiful lawn.[25] However, a letter from Satie to his brother Conrad dated 11 April 1911 proved that all was no longer sweetness and light. He reminded Conrad that Debussy had married a very wealthy woman, lived in a splendid house on the avenue du Bois de Boulogne with a magnificent garden and liked to invite him to lunch there every Friday. But after the concert of 25 March a distinct bitterness was evident in Satie's attitude to the older man. 'The success achieved by the *Gymnopédies* at the concert conducted by him at the Cercle Musical – a success which he [Debussy] did everything to turn

---

[21] C. pp. 1391–3.
[22] C. p. 1404.
[23] C. p. 1406.
[24] See Chapter 6 p. 88.
[25] R. Orledge, 'Debussy, Satie, and the Summer of 1913', *Cahiers Debussy*, no.26, 2002, p. 32.

into a failure – gave him an unpleasant surprise,' he wrote. 'I'm not angry with him about it. He's the victim of his social climbing. Why won't he allow me a very small place in his shadow? I have no use for the sun.'[26]

The problem was Debussy's surprise at the success of Satie's music. Whilst Ravel had acknowledged openly the influence Satie had had on him and had even organised a whole concert of Satie's music in January (which Debussy did not attend), Debussy was reluctant to do so. Yet despite this, Satie still dined at Debussy's house and in September Satie asked Debussy to help him correct the proofs of his *Morceaux en forme de poire*.[27]

Completion of *Le martyre*

In order to get the score of *Le martyre* finished on time, Debussy did indeed enlist Caplet's help. He orchestrated most of Acts 2–4 and assisted at rehearsals. In April Rubinstein was getting anxious. 'Le Saint demande sa musique!' wrote d'Annunzio, to which Debussy replied 'The Saint must give me a few more days! … I am a bit like a factory manager fearing a strike!' He sent off the completed sections to Durand, eventually exclaiming, 'I am pleased to send you the last cry of St Sébastien … as I have already told you several times, I can't go on any more!'[28] His publisher was impressed with the music. In his *Souvenirs*, Durand described the intense satisfaction he felt when Debussy sat down at the piano and played the 'Passion' section. They were both moved to tears.[29]

The fact that Debussy wrote a note to Emma (undated) around this time must mean she was upstairs, probably incapacitated. It was 4.30p.m., d'Annunzio had left and Debussy was going to visit his sick mother. A lady had been to call on Emma, a masseuse, whose address he had noted, another pointer implying Emma was ill since she could not meet her herself.[30]

On 1 May she received a May Day message written on a printed visiting card from her husband.

> Vive le Mai!
> Bienvenu soit le Mai
> Avec son gonfalon sauvage et
> l'amour de Claude Debussy.[31]

The words of the first three lines were not new. He had already used them as an epigraph to his *Rondes de printemps*, the third of his orchestral *Images*.

---

[26] O. Volta, *Satie seen through his letters*, London, New York, 1989, p. 147.
[27] Lesure, *Claude Debussy*, p. 345.
[28] C. pp. 1411, 1413.
[29] J. Durand, *Quelques souvenirs d'un éditeur de musique*, vol.1, p. 124.
[30] C. p. 1414.
[31] 'Long live May!/Welcome May!/with its streaming banner and/the love of Claude Debussy.' C. p.1415. BnF Musique, La-Debussy Claude-94.

Emile Vuillermoz, who was one of three chorus masters for *Le martyre*, wrote that Debussy stayed shut away at home writing and revising the score up to the last minute, sending the music to the theatre page by page with corrections in pencil. When the composer did hear the first full run-through of *Le martyre* he 'quite simply, wept'. The piano reduction had given little idea of the orchestral timbres which conjured up this 'stained glass window of sound' (*vitrail sonore*).[32]

D'Annunzio sent Debussy flowers, but multiple problems soon arose, with disagreements over Bakst's scenery for 'Paradise', lack of co-ordination between action and music, the static production, lighting. Even worse, on 8 May the Archbishop of Paris judged the work offensive to the memory of 'one of our most glorious martyrs' and forbade Catholics to attend performances. All d'Annunzio's works were put on the Papal Index, in response to which composer and poet wrote a joint letter to the press on 17 May defending their approach as 'profoundly religious'. Debussy was obviously upset. He wrote a rushed note to P.-J. Toulet during a rehearsal the next day and it is clear that yet again, Emma's health was allowing him no respite from worry. They were now awaiting X-ray results. She was also controlling his movements, for he could not meet Toulet that evening as he was not allowed to stay out late: 'first, I am condemned to be home every night by 9 p.m., then the house is rather disorganised',[33] clearly a distraction for one who loved order. Toulet was concerned enough to write to Emma himself on 20 May, for she responded to him saying the X-rays were fine. 'Bravo! But what if I am still ill?' He was to meet her in her box at the theatre the next day for the open dress rehearsal. In a PS she added, 'Your friend Ida [Rubinstein] is beautiful(!)' She sent a similar invitation to Pasteur Vallery-Radot. However, yet another disaster occurred before then: the Minister of War, Maurice Berteaux, was killed in a flying accident on 21 May and the rehearsal was cancelled. Debussy then had to organise seats at the first performance for his friends by writing personally to Astruc.

Première of *Le martyre*; gifts for Emma and Chouchou

At the première of *Le martyre* on 22 May at the Théâtre du Châtelet Emma was present in her box with Paul-Jean Toulet and Pasteur Vallery-Radot. Despite his aversion to being present at his own first nights, Debussy was there too, for Vallery-Radot mentioned that both he and Emma accompanied him to the performance.[34] D'Annunzio shared this phobia, for he did stay away and was found later in the small hours fast asleep in a nearby café.[35] In a performance lasting more than four hours, there were only fifty-five minutes of music. In common with others, Madame de Saint-Marceaux, despite the charm of the music, found

---

[32] E. Vuillermoz, 'Autour du martyre de Saint Sébastien', *La Revue musicale*, Paris, December 1920, pp. 156–7.
[33] C. pp. 1418, 1419.
[34] P. Vallery-Radot, *Lettres de Claude Debussy à sa femme Emma*, p. 47.
[35] L. Hughes-Hallett, *The Pike. Gabriele d'Annunzio, Poet, Seducer and Preacher of War*, London, 2013, p. 332.

it 'long and incomprehensible',[36] Louis Laloy became impatient waiting for the music between long periods of dialogue and, when it did at last arrive, his relief was so tempered by exhaustion that he did not have enough strength left to cope with the emotions it aroused.[37]

Because this work was composed far more quickly than usual for Debussy, it displays a variety of musical styles. The Wagnerian richness of the scoring in certain parts brings to mind the interludes in *Pelleas et Mélisande* which were also composed in haste, but nonetheless convey deep emotional commitment. The reviews were very mixed, some regretting that Debussy had deserted his *Pelléas* style, others preferring it. The staging was criticised, particularly the lighting, and of course Ida Rubinstein was eulogised by oglers transfixed by the sight of her bare legs and her entrancing androgynous portrayal of Saint Sebastian.[38] D'Annunzio's text certainly divided the public. Its sheer length was bewildering, so cuts were made to the second act before the second performance and subsequently, so the work was never again performed in its original version. In 1911 Caplet, who conducted the first performance, made a piano transcription of the work and in 1912 he arranged an orchestral suite of symphonic fragments.

This year Debussy remembered to send Emma his greeting commemorating her special day on 4 June. It was a bouquet of flowers with a card from the shop Lachaume, to the name of which he had added the words, 'and Claude Debussy with all his love for his p.m. [petite mienne].' The date has been added by Emma in red ink.[39] This was an extravagant present from the most prestigious florist in Paris. Since his travels, Debussy was more inclined to show his love and appreciation to his wife – and perhaps had been inspired a little by the flamboyant d'Annunzio. On 13 June the score for piano and voice of *Le martyre* was published by Durand and Emma received a copy with the dedication, 'for my little one in memory of three months of Martyrdom which only she knew how to sooth with these pretty words: "what is it to you!" Her loving grateful Claude Debussy, June 1911'.[40]

The relief at having reached the end of the project was felt all round, for d'Annunzio also sent a present with a double dedication of the libretto of *Le martyre*, to Emma and to Chouchou.[41] First Debussy told him how moved both his 'adorable companions' (as d'Annunzio called them) were, Chouchou leaping round the garden proclaiming his name in a mode which was 'not quite dorian', then Emma wrote to him herself expressing her gratitude for the double gift, which brought affectionate and anxious memories. 'When Chouchou is old enough to understand, what joy it will bring ... ' She signed off with evidence of the closeness of the poet and the child: 'Chouchou's little hands in

---

[36] M. de Saint-Marceaux, *Journal 1894–1927*, p. 651.

[37] L. Laloy, *La musique retrouvée, 1902–1927*, Paris, 1928, p. 207.

[38] See R. Orledge, *Debussy and the Theatre*, pp. 227–8, for a summary of reviews.

[39] C. p. 1427. BnF Musique, La-Debussy Claude-19.

[40] 'Pour ma petite Mienne en souvenir de trois mois de Martyre qu'elle seule sût apaiser par cette jolie formule: "qu'est-ce que c'est que cela pour toi!" son tendrement reconnaissant Claude Debussy juin 1911.' Centre de documentation Claude Debussy, RESE-1.6.

[41] I am grateful to Denis Herlin for correspondence on this subject.

your unique yellow goatee, and all my devoted admiration, Emma Claude Debussy.'[42] What a striking image of a child stroking the beard of this famous (and infamous) man! They all met the next day, 13 June, for lunch at the Trianon Palace, the luxurious hotel in Versailles where d'Annunzio and Ida Rubinstein were staying – a taste of luxury Emma must have relished despite the cost. Here was something else Debussy and d'Annunzio had in common – debt problems and a penchant for the finer things in life.

Friendship with Stravinsky; the family travels to Turin

On 13 June 1911 the first performance took place of Stravinsky's *Petrouchka* at the Théâtre du Châtelet, the masterpiece he had composed with Debussy's signed photograph in front of him.[43] On 16 June Stravinsky dedicated to Debussy a copy of the *Firebird* and Debussy invited Stravinsky and Satie to dine at his house once again, an occasion commemorated by photographs taken in turn of Debussy with Satie, then Debussy with Stravinsky.[44] Stravinsky also took a photograph of Debussy. In view of references in future correspondence it is clear that he, like so many of Debussy's friends, was captivated by Chouchou.

The family hardly had time to breathe after this excitement, for on 19 June Debussy, Emma, Chouchou and her nanny left for Turin, where Debussy was to conduct a concert of French music on 25 June which included *Children's Corner* (Caplet's orchestration), the *Prélude à l'après-midi d'un faune* and 'Ibéria'. Obviously the motive for this uprooting was financial. The young conductor Vittorio Gui was a member of the party at the station who met

> a group composed of a little woman (very chic), a little girl of seven or eight, a nurse, and finally a tall man with dark eyes and beard, gentle of demeanour and laboured in his movements, sparing of gesture, with the resigned good-humoured expression of the father of a family on holiday ... And so he had come for a week's stay, bringing with him all his dear ones because he could not bear to be parted from them even for such a short time.[45]

Debussy expressed his inner feelings about the trip in his letters to Caplet and Durand. Emma, as ever when away from home, was ill every day right from the start of their stay in Turin. Inevitably, the journey had turned into a horrible nightmare, Debussy told them. 'This is the way fate usually works when it is determined to remain hostile.' Despite staying in the Grand Hôtel and Hôtel d'Europe, he found Turin ugly and was disturbed by the noisy trams. The only consolation was that Chouchou was as cheerful as ever, making up stories about her friends Caplet, Kiki (Satie) and Teddy.

---

[42] C. pp. 1438–9.
[43] See Chapter 10 p. 139.
[44] F. Lesure, *Debussy. Iconographie musicale*, Paris, 1980, pp. 134–5.
[45] V. Gui, 'Debussy in Italy', *Musical Opinion*, January 1939, pp. 305–6; February 1939, pp. 404–5. Quoted in R. Nichols, *Debussy Remembered*, London 1992, pp. 224–31. See also A. S. Malvano, 'Claude Debussy à l'exposition internationale de Turin en 1911', *Cahiers Debussy*, 36, 2012, pp. 25–46.

Gui, the youngest member of Debussy's welcoming committee, felt particularly aware of his kind focus on him, commenting on Debussy's lack of deference to those who would have most expected it. The day before the concert Debussy complained bitterly to Caplet and Durand about six hours' rehearsal a day, which left him in a state of exhaustion.[46] This was not a complete description of the state of affairs. Gui reported on the confusion caused to the orchestra when Debussy showed his lack of skill on the rostrum, his head buried in the score, even turning over pages with the hand holding the baton. Consequently Debussy accepted the proposal that Gui should do all the preparation himself and let Debussy conduct the final performance sure that everything would go 'like clockwork'. Unfortunately Debussy was unable to provide a convincing interpretation when the moment came, and the atmosphere was further spoilt by the noise of pelting rain on the glass roof, but Gui was profoundly moved by the intellect and spirit of the man and overjoyed to receive a personal dedication on his score of 'Ibéria'.

Debussy's dissatisfaction; Durand's assistance

Debussy's grumbles about the city did not cease on his return to Paris, when he wrote to Fauré agreeing to be a member of the jury for trials at the Opéra-Comique on 3 July and to an anonymous recipient commenting that he and his wife were overjoyed to be back to their local railway (the *ceinture*) after the abominable noise of the Turin trams. Emma was still ill and unable to attend a reading (unspecified), which if possible should be postponed until the end of the week for her sake. On 2 July he remembered to go out to buy flowers for Emma's real birthday on 10 July – rather early if they were to stay fresh for that date. Perhaps this was simply an excuse for not meeting Gabriel Mourey, to whom this letter was addressed.

By 13 July Emma was at last feeling better, although now she was worried about Dolly, who was expecting her first child. Debussy, however, was ill. 'Heat, overwork, nervous exhaustion'. Saint Sébastien had taken it out of him and the journey to Turin had finished him off, he told Durand. Under doctor's orders, he was to take a month off so he and Emma and Chouchou were going to go to the seaside. This was another of those letters which displayed Debussy's true state of mind, something he only revealed to his closest confidants.

> How right you are, my dear friend, to love your house [Bel Ebat, Avon] ... everything in life is so transitory. There must be something quite unique about a charming house where you played as a child, dreamt as a young man. At my age I feel sad not to have had that.[47]

How revealing this was, considering Debussy's smart address, his entourage of wife, child and servants. His own dreams as a young man were upwardly mobile, enabled in the end by Emma. Yet he felt out of place. Despite his gifts as a composer, he had

---

[46] C. pp. 1431–3.
[47] C. pp. 1434–6.

refused to compromise in order to earn money, preferring to borrow rather than teach or compose hack works, and to receive advances from Durand and others for works uncompleted. He was permanently dissatisfied with life. Whilst he loved Emma and could not do without her and Chouchou, her constant illness was wearing. They were hermetically sealed in their villa near the Bois de Boulogne, only admitting a small, close circle of friends. His constant source of joy was his daughter, who, he told Durand, was 'like a peony' (that flower attributed by Chouchik Laloy to Emma).

He had an anxious wait for a response from Durand, to whom he replied on 19 July. If anything, this letter was even more depressing as he admitted to the parlous state of financial affairs which was preventing him and Emma from being able to go away. Who else could he write to and hint heavily about the lack of three thousand francs to pay bills, the landlord, domestic staff? They couldn't afford to go to Arcachon so were considering Houlgate on the Normandy coast, some considerable distance to the west of Pourville. 'Life is not funny and is full of complications. You have no idea how exhausting it is to fight against Nothingness.'[48] This expression, 'de lutter contre le Néant' recalled the 'factories of Nothingness' ('les usines de Néant') he had written about to Durand as long ago as April 1906. Prior to his next letter to Durand we learn from a letter to P.-J. Toulet that yet again the cook had left.

Durand was as generous as ever, providing him with exactly three thousand francs, one thousand for the orchestration of his *Rapsodie pour clarinette* and two thousand for foreign rights. Now they could go to Houlgate and Chouchou would build lots of sandcastles for Durand. Not only would he take the *Rapsodie* with him, but also *Usher* and *Le diable dans le beffroi*.[49] The night before leaving, Debussy wrote to André Caplet not so enthusiastically about his destination, telling him that the mere idea of going away on holiday meant stress and aggravation. What he really wanted was 'a little house in large grounds where you felt afraid when you were little'.[50] Again he was harbouring a longing for a space nostalgically familiar from childhood, something he would never experience.

Houlgate

A whole month in the Grand Hotel in Houlgate was never going to be conducive to Debussy's peace of mind or inspiration. Although she was not mentioned, photographic evidence shows that Emma's mother Laure also travelled with the family.[51] At first Debussy appreciated the fresh air and sea. He admitted straight away to Durand that he had forgotten to bring the *Rapsodie* and asked him to send a copy.

---

[48] C. p. 1437.
[49] C. p. 1439.
[50] 'Une petite maison dans un grand parc où l'on a eu peur étant petit'. C. p. 1440.
[51] For a detailed description and the social background of Houlgate, including photographs of Debussy, Emma and family in 1911, see R. Campos, *Debussy à la plage*, Paris, 2018.

20. Chouchou on sandcastle, Houlgate, 1911

At the hotel a Monsieur Paul Vizentini conducted awful music and there was a lady who sang a Massenet opera every day, but for the moment these were the only black marks against the place. Chouchou's legs were already brown and she loved *la Mer* (the sea) as much as her own *mère* (mother).[52] But by 11 August he was disillusioned. 'I still think hotel life is not for a man of my age.' He couldn't wait to return to the familiarity of home, where life was peaceful and tumultuous at the same time. He hated having to dress up four times a day, a habit he blamed on the Americans whom the French loved to imitate. Photographs of Debussy on the beach show him dressed in a suit. He was disparaging about the clientele. Quoting Pelléas 'et les enfants descendent vers la plage pour se baigner' ('and the children come down to the sea to bathe'), he commented that whilst some of the children were fine, their parents were ugly. He wished Caplet could visit. The arrival of proofs of the orchestral score of *Le martyre* made him feel nostalgic for those precious moments of early rehearsals of the work when they had still felt in control.[53]

[52] C. p. 1442.
[53] C. p. 1445.

21. Emma with Chouchou at her feet on boat, Houlgate, 1911

22. Emma, Houlgate, 1911

On 22 August there is the sole evidence of Emma commemorating Debussy's birthday. She used one of her visiting cards. Above her name she wrote 'Ta fête!', and below it added, 'Tout mon amour. Tout moi.' ('Your birthday! All my love. All of me'.)[54] Despite her effort, this did not lighten Debussy's – or Emma's – state of mind. On 26 August he wrote to Durand, 'The truth is, that at the end of this holiday we'll have to admit we don't know why we came. Have we lost the faculty to enjoy things together? I don't know."[55] Even his pen was weeping, he exclaimed when he made a blot on the page.

Emma prevents Debussy from travelling to Boston

Upon their return home, almost immediately Emma was to be seen in the company of her first husband's family once again, which can't have helped Debussy's state of mind. On 13 September 1911 she attended the funeral of M. Gaston Auboyneau, managing director of the Imperial Ottoman Bank.[56] This took place at the church of Saint Augustin and was attended by many figures from the world of banking and finance, including Sigismond and all the Bardacs associated with that milieu. The Count and Countess d'Arnoux were also present, so closely linked to Dolly at her baptism and marriage. Unsurprisingly, Debussy did not attend.

The Debussys' precious routine social life soon resumed with visits from friends including Vallery-Radot, Gabriel Mourey and P.-J. Toulet. Toulet wrote an apologetic postcard to Emma, probably in September, ashamed not to have thanked her earlier for the magnificent catalogue she had sent him 'which I will bequeath to the *Arts Décoratifs*', he quipped.[57] He adored these lavish catalogues provided at certain times of the year by firms providing luxury goods and fashion items, appreciating their colours and quality artistic design. Emma made a point of regularly fulfilling his passion for collecting them, skilfully wrapping them up attractively. In the same message Toulet also mentioned that she and he had chatted about the nannies who accompanied young ladies to and from their schools. He wondered if she could help a friend of his who would like to apply for such a *'gentlewomanlike'* job.

Manuel de Falla came to the house to play through *La Vida breve*. Stravinsky wrote in gratitude for a signed score of *Le martyre*, sending his sincere regards to Emma and 'charming little Chouchou'.[58] Meanwhile, a difficult situation was growing into another crisis between Emma and Debussy. *Pelléas et Mélisande* was to be performed in Boston.

Henry Russell had been the director of the Boston Opera Company since its opening in 1909. He invited Georgette Leblanc, the mistress of Maurice Maeterlinck, to sing the role of Mélisande,[59] and wanted Debussy himself to conduct the opera,

---

[54] C. p. 1448. BnF Musique, La-Debussy Claude-97.
[55] C. p. 1448.
[56] *Le Figaro*, 14 September 1911.
[57] C. p. 1455.
[58] C. p. 1462.
[59] G. Opstad, *Debussy's Mélisande, the Lives of Georgette Leblanc, Mary Garden and Maggie Teyte*, pp. 152–4.

23. Debussy and André Caplet

four performances of which were to be given in January 1912. On 22 October 1911 Debussy began a letter to Russell which opened with the words, 'I must definitely renounce going to Boston ... '[60] He truly regretted this decision, which was for 'family reasons' too serious to ignore. There was no further explanation. He expressed pain at having to forgo such an experience and suggested to Russell the obvious replacement for him: his friend and collaborator André Caplet, conductor of the Boston Symphony Orchestra since 1910. Caplet had already assured the public of Debussy's arrival, claiming in a magazine interview that Debussy could not bear to be apart from him. 'We are very closely related; always together in Paris,' he is alleged to have boasted.[61] Debussy insisted that Caplet had a deep love of the opera and he had every confidence in him.

[60] C. p. 1464.
[61] Q. Eaton, *The Boston Opera Company*, New York, 1965, p. 132.

He felt so bad about withdrawing from the Boston trip that he did not post this letter to Russell until 17 November, nearly four weeks later. 'I did not have the courage to send you this letter,' he wrote in a PS. 'It's a bit childish, but I was hoping for a chance intervention or some other miracle! It's over …'

On the same day Debussy wrote to Caplet making it clear that Emma was at the root of the problem. Since he and Caplet had last met, he had been leading an absurd, empty life, not to be wished on anyone. He had given up all hope of travelling to Boston, such obstacles stood in his way. Everything was contradictory and upsetting. The rows, the daily battles were so painful that he had put off writing to him for as long as possible. He felt completely lost and demoralised. Debussy then added a PS to say that if he made an effort, he could possibly come to Boston *on his own* (underlined), but this he did not dare to do.[62] Clearly, in view of his comments made to Durand on his and Emma's inability to enjoy life together and this admission to Caplet of quarrels they were still having nearly a year after Dolly's sudden marriage, wounds had not healed and Emma was keeping a close watch on her husband.

He received no reply. Adding to Debussy's despair was the usual need for money, as evidenced by a third letter written on 17 November, this time to Durand asking for another three thousand francs by the next morning. The long-suffering publisher duly gave him the money in exchange for seeing the contract Debussy had signed with Maud Allan for *Khamma*.[63] More letters to an unspecified correspondent, probably the financier Léon Bertault, show a continual need for loans. His debt was mounting.

A note to Emma, thought to have been written in 1911 but date unspecified, was set out in the form of an invoice:

With affectionate wishes
From your young lover   Claude
And your old husband   *Debussy*

Total   Claude Debussy[64]

Perhaps this was a symbolic expression of the permanence of his love at a time of continuous financial pressure. Or was it a bill for the sacrifice he was having to make?

Still having heard nothing from Caplet, Debussy wrote to him at great length on 22 December, addressing his letter to the Boston Opera House. He was obviously hurt. 'Not to reply to Saint Sébastien, that's not kind! Even if he was used to arrows, he did not expect to receive them from you'. There is a distinct sense of loneliness expressed in this letter:

> Of course I have not told anyone what it has cost me to give up the journey to America … I am like a child who is shown a cake which is then eaten by others. That may be character-forming, but at my age it's a bit late for that type of experience. All in all, it has hurt me.

---

[62] C. p. 1463.
[63] See Chapter 10 p. 168. C. p. 1465.
[64] C. p. 1480.

He was not making good progress with his two Poe operas, which led to a depressing train of thought he had uttered in the past – the difficulty of combining composing with family life.

> All in all, you should suppress everything consuming the best of your thoughts and reach the position of loving nothing but yourself with fierce attention to detail! But in fact exactly the opposite happens. First there's the family which gets in the way, either by being too sweet or with blind severity. Then there's the Mistresses or the Mistress, which don't even count because you are all too happy to forget yourself in passion. I do without them and other temptations. You can't actually do anything about it. You are passed on a soul by a whole load of people completely unknown to you, who have an effect on you handed down through the generations, more often than not without your being able to do much about it.

There was no mention of Emma by name in this letter until a PS passing on her regards. The arguments they had about going to America were taking their toll. Chouchou was ever present, however. She 'continues to be a good little girl who doesn't forget her friend Caplet and talks about him to people who have never heard of this illustrious kapellmeister, which makes them in her eyes some sort of savage Iroquois.' He also mentioned Erik Satie, who agreed with him that Caplet should return soon to France.[65]

It is striking that Debussy wrote in such deeply personal tones to his best friends. He clearly found it therapeutic to be able to express his frustrations, anxieties and emotions to someone outside the immediate family circle in a way he could not do with Emma. From Arthur Hartmann we learnt that he was often cross and bad tempered with Emma and his domestic staff. On paper he was more measured, but sad and regretful and, quite clearly, lonely. Caplet was sixteen years younger than Debussy, yet he confided in him as if he were his own age, as Emma would later do. Shortly before the letter to Caplet, on 18 December Debussy had written an even longer one to his old friend Robert Godet, the Swiss journalist and composer, a man nearer in age to Debussy, being only four years younger. This letter first gave a vivid and appreciative account of his visit to the Salon d'Automne, where he had seen an exhibition by the artist and sculptor Henry de Groux, who had made two portraits and a bust of Debussy in 1909. He had just sent Godet a score of *Saint Sébastien*. He suggested Godet should visit Stravinsky in Clarens. But then the tone changed. Just as to Caplet, he grumbled that he had not been able to make progress with the two Poe dramas. 'How much you have first to find, then suppress, to arrive at the naked flesh of emotion. Pure instinct ought to warn us that textures, colours are no more than illusory fancy dress!' How he wished Godet were near.

> Sometimes I feel so miserable and lonely. There is no way round this and it's not the first time. Chouchou's smile helps me to get through some dark times, but I can't worry her with stories which to her would only be an irritating variation on the theme of the ogre's wicked deeds. So I remain all alone with my discomfort![66]

---

[65] C. pp. 1472–4.
[66] C. pp. 1469–72.

The ogre's unhappy wife, Emma, was relegated to second place in his emotions below smiling, innocent Chouchou.

However frustrated with Emma over the trip to America, Debussy did send her a Christmas greeting on 25 December. He did not exactly let the matter rest, for it contained an ironic reference to that country. It took the form of a Christmas card with an illustration of a boat sailing into the sunset with English text quoting a poem by Robert Southey.[67] Knowing his love of the sea, these words alone might have been enough to attract the composer:

> She comes majestic with her swelling sails,
> The gallant ship; along her watery way
> Homeward she drives before the favouring gales;
> Now flirting at their length the streamers play,
> And now they ripple with the ruffling breeze.

Debussy's personal greeting consisted of three bars of handwritten score. He wrote for bass voices divided into three, singing the words 'Hisse hoé', a pastiche of the sailors' chorus in Act 1 scene 3 of *Pelléas et Mélisande*, when Mélisande sees the ship which brought her to Allemonde departing over the horizon. Above them is a line of music in the treble clef sung by 'Un petit mousse', a ship's apprentice, 'irreverently but with conviction: "Zut! rezut! Et zut! Pour l'Amérique!"', which can roughly be translated as 'Damn! Damn again! And damn it! To America!'[68]

Beneath this is his own handwritten poem based on the first lines of the Southey poem:

> Il s'avance, toutes voiles gonflées,
> Par le souffle tendre et passionnée,
> De tout mon amour
> De tous mes vœux
> Pour l'Impérieuse petite Mienne
> Subtile Magicienne![69]

How ironic that the adjective applied to Emma was *impérieuse*, the word he had used to describe Lilly's chilling voice in 1902 when he was tiring of her.[70] The ship was certainly departing without him aboard.

Charmingly, that Christmas Chouchou wrote a letter in English to her mother. Surely this early honing of her language skills must have given Emma pleasure.

> Dear Mummie,
> Many good wishes for a happy Christmas and many kisses from your little Chou chou.[71]

---

[67] C. pp. 1475–7; BnF, La-Debussy Claude-20.

[68] This tiny composition has been realised and is performed on a CD included with the book by R. Campos, *Debussy à la plage*, Paris, 2018.

[69] 'It moves onwards, with swelling sails/Blown by the soft passionate breath/Of all my love/Of all my wishes/For my own Imperious little one/Subtle Magician!'

[70] C. p. 676 and Chapter 3 p. 42.

[71] BnF Musique, La-Debussy Claude Emma-4.

Since his divorce from Lilly, Debussy had had very little contact with René Peter, yet the latter invited both Debussy and Emma to his forthcoming marriage on 30 December. On 26 December Debussy wrote to him to decline the invitation, saying that whilst Emma had been touched by it, he was to blame for their not attending. He put this down to 'my naturally unsociable nature, as well as my white hair – a phenomenon caused by the sure but melancholy march of the years.' A second letter emphasised his affection for his younger friend. 'Perhaps such distant friendships are the dearest, for they are protected from the frequent pain of life which often has toothache.'[72]

These were the final letters from the composer that René Peter quoted in his biography of Debussy, which ended with his comments that they sum up the 'impassive serenity' which life had imparted to the composer. 'He has become somewhat distant, almost unreal'. It was as if he had already passed over to the other side and from there was sending a sign of friendship.[73] He avoided the conclusion that Debussy was simply anti-social.

Meanwhile, Emma corresponded with her erstwhile neighbour, Marie Hartmann, who had written to her from America. On 28 November she expressed her pleasure at hearing from her, then complained that they had only been away for a month in the summer, but were only too glad to return home. Dolly's pregnancy was a cause of much worry to her. On 31 December she penned New Year's greetings to Marie, and yet again she was in bed suffering from inflammation of the liver. However, on 19 January she discovered that she had never sent this letter and added another paragraph. She had been ill ever since her initial words. This was her third inflammation of the liver since 1 January.[74] What a start to the New Year!

---

[72] C. pp. 1477–8.
[73] R. Peter, Claude Debussy, pp. 225–6.
[74] A. Hartmann, *Claude Debussy as I knew him*, pp. 133–5.

12

1912: Confined to home

New Year's Greetings

Erik Satie's New Year's greeting to Emma for 1912 was a picture of a hand holding a bouquet of flowers.[1] In his message Satie asked her to shake hands with him. By mistake he had left behind the macaroons last time he had visited them, he added, and promised that on Saturday he would keep them on his knees all the time, even at the table. Satie's fondness for Emma is demonstrated by the fact that it was she, not her husband, who received this personal New Year's greeting. It may well be that Satie acted as an intermediary between her and her husband when their relationship was strained,[2] despite feeling overshadowed by Debussy.

Whilst Emma began the year 1912 suffering from a recurrence of liver trouble, Chouchou was delighted to receive New Year's gifts of two fragile miniature table settings from Gabriel Mourey, which to her frustration were placed behind glass in a cabinet,[3] a Hungarian doll from Madame Bárczy[4] and a book with illustrations by Arthur Rackham from Robert Godet. The latter delighted Debussy as much as his daughter, for he loved Rackham's watercolours. He was also proud of the grown-up way in which Chouchou had asked him to pass on her wishes for a Happy New Year to Godet.[5] The singular maturity of this child never failed to impress.

The first contract of the new year signed with Durand on 31 January 1912 was for the second book of piano *Préludes*, the fourth of which was entitled *Les fées sont d'exquises danseuses*, one of Rackham's illustrations for J. M. Barrie's *Peter Pan in Kensington Gardens*, the very book given by Godet to Chouchou. For this collection Debussy received twelve thousand francs – two-thirds now, the other third constituting performing rights – a considerable and no doubt welcome advance on the sum of seven thousand francs for the first book of *Préludes*.[6] The new contract stipulated that the composition would be delivered by 1 April 1912. In fact, he did not complete the *Préludes* until January 1913.

---

[1] C. p. 1478.
[2] R. Orledge, 'Debussy, Satie, and the Summer of 1913', *Cahiers Debussy*, no.26, 2002, p. 32.
[3] C. p. 1483.
[4] C. p. 1492.
[5] C. p. 1483.
[6] C. p. 1486.

Emma to guarantee loan; her first granddaughter

On 23 January Louis and Chouchik Laloy were invited to dinner with the Debussys, as well as Ricardo Viñes and Madame Charpentier. 'Naturally there was no music-making and we hardly talked about it, as happens amongst *real* artists,' wrote Viñes in his diary. 'Debussy and his wife grumbled that I rarely go to see them'.[7]

Possibly that same month (no specific date was indicated) Debussy wrote a letter to Louis Laloy desperate to borrow the large sum of twenty thousand francs 'without delay'. He was doing this in collaboration with Emma, for his guarantee for the loan would be the annual pension paid by Sigismond Bardac to Emma following their divorce, despite the fact that this money in fact paid the rent for their house. Debussy was adamant that the Bardac bank could only be approached in the case of non-payment of the loan. Any hint of it otherwise would be too embarrassing. They intended to pay back the money from July onwards, with interest.[8]

No wonder Emma was still ill. On 20 February Debussy told Paul-Jean Toulet that she had had a bad attack of liver trouble,[9] but there could have been another reason for this. On 21 February it was announced that a daughter had been born to Mme Gaston de Tinan,[10] Emma's daughter Dolly. Just as with Dolly's marriage, there is no mention of this in any of Debussy's correspondence, no comment from either of them on Emma's reaction to being a grandmother for the first time. The child's full names were Françoise Geneviève Emma. The family address on the birth certificate was 40 rue Boissière in the sixteenth arrondissement.

Debussy's unwillingness to have early works resurrected

Khamma, which should have been finished a year ago, was still demanding attention, Debussy feeling mentally stifled by the scenario of this ballet. By 1 February 1912 he had managed to complete a short score and create a 'new version' with which he sounded quite pleased, and asked Durand if he could dedicate it to Madame Durand, perhaps to smooth over some of the problems he had had initially with his publisher when he had signed the contract with Maud Allan.[11] This proposition was firmly vetoed by Allan later in the year, when she insisted that the work had been composed especially for her and she should therefore be the only dedicatee. At the beginning of March, Debussy was to enter into another collaboration, this time with Charles Morice for a 'poème chanté et dansé' in three acts based on poetry by Verlaine, called *Crimen amoris*. This would turn out to be yet another of those troublesome ideas which would go through various transformations, leading to working instead with Laloy on a version entitled *Fêtes galantes*, which in turn was

---

[7] R. Nichols, *Debussy Remembered*, London, 1992, p. 193.
[8] C. p. 1491.
[9] C. p. 1493.
[10] *Gil Blas*, 21 February 1912.
[11] C. p. 1491; R. Orledge, *Debussy and the Theatre*, p. 134.

eventually abandoned, despite being advertised as appearing at the Opéra in the 1912–3 season. In March, in correspondence with Morice and with Gabriel Astruc, Debussy lamented his influenza, which seems to have affected the whole family. Perhaps Henri Busser's orchestration of his early work, *Printemps*, which had taken three years to complete, might have cheered him up? It would seem not, for when Busser took his score to Debussy, the composer declared that he disliked the music of this composition, his second *envoi* from Rome dating from 1887.[12] As noted earlier, Debussy was wary of having his early works brought to light, significant in view of events after his death.[13]

Easter 1912 was commemorated by a brief note from Debussy to Emma written on a piece of manuscript paper – just the message 'Pour les Pâques de ma petite Mienne. Son Claude Debussy.' ('For my own little one's Easter.')[14] Brief and to the point. Not even the word 'love'. That was on 7 April. On 10 April he was complaining to Durand yet again of illness in the family. Emma was not getting any better. Her homeopathic remedies were of no avail, so they were considering reverting to normal medical advice. His mother was also unwell, so it was only Chouchou who was on good form. This news took precedence over the impending arrival of Maud Allan in France, which meant he was hastening the printing of the piano reduction of *Khamma*.[15]

One day André Caplet received a charming note from Chouchou, having returned from Boston where he had been conducting the orchestra of the Boston Opera. This is undated, but reveals her affection for him and a talent for expressing herself even in English with maturity:

> Dear mr Capley
> I thank you for your letter. Did you have a good voyage. and did you like America.
> I give you many kisses.
> Good bye from Chouchou[16]

Emma's illnesses certainly took their toll on Debussy and he made no secret of this. Even to his younger friend Stravinsky he gave the reason for his delay in writing to him to thank him for his dedication of the score of *Petrouchka* as being surrounded by illness. 'Above all my wife who has been ill for some time … I have even had to be the "househusband" ["l'homme de ménage"] and I have to say I have absolutely no talent for that sort of job.'[17] One can hardly imagine how stultifying for Debussy the combination of *Khamma* and household duties must have been. He had, however, been enjoying playing *Petrouchka* during the Easter holidays, revelling in its 'sonorous magic' and its 'orchestral certainties' such as he had previously only encountered in *Parsifal*.

---

[12] C. p. 1499 n.1.
[13] See also Chapter 7 p. 95.
[14] C. p. 1501.
[15] C. p. 1502.
[16] Original orthography. *Lettres inédites à André Caplet (1908–1914)*, ed. Edward Lockspeiser, Paris, 1957, p. 83.
[17] C. p. 1503.

Khamma and *L'après-midi d'un faune*

On 29 April Debussy signed a contract with Durand handing over to him all rights for *Khamma*.[18] Relations with Maud Allan continued to deteriorate as she objected to various terms in the contract and insisted that no music should be published before the ballet was performed. She wanted more music and threatened to have it lengthened or revised by 'another'.[19] Debussy expressed in no uncertain terms his refusal to change anything.[20]

Ballet was the talk of the town in Paris, for Diaghilev's Ballets Russes were once more in residence at the Théâtre du Châtelet. At Emma's request, Debussy invited Paul-Jean Toulet to share her box to see Balakirev's *Thamar* on 22 May. Only six days later the public dress rehearsal took place of the ballet *L'après-midi d'un faune*, choreographed by Nijinsky, which Debussy attended, having been invited into the box of Misia Edwards.[21] Perhaps reluctant to compromise his relations with Diaghilev in view of the prospect of further commissions, Debussy did not comment publicly at the time on the production, which caused a scandal and divided opinion owing to Nijinsky's angular movements, based on images from Greek antiquity and, in particular, his final overtly suggestive love-making to a scarf left behind by a fleeing nymph. Debussy expressed his shock to Misia, but not until February 1914 did he make his disapproval public in an interview to an Italian paper. Pasteur Vallery-Radot remembered Debussy's exasperation with the 'ugly, dalcrozian' choreography.[22] On 18 June 1912 he signed a contract with Diaghilev for the ballet *Jeux*, promising to deliver the score by March 1913, for which he was to receive ten thousand francs.

Despite such distractions, Debussy did not forget his commemoration of Emma's special day on 4 June. Once again, he sent flowers from Lachaume with the message: 'The Roses are Chouchou. The Hydrangeas are me and forgive my head in favour of my heart which is all yours, your Cld.'[23] Although he emphasised his heart over his head with regard to Emma, it is surely, even if subconsciously, significant that it was Chouchou who was associated with the flower which is a symbol of love, and it was he who was associated with the hydrangea, a symbol of gratitude towards Emma.

Duet with Stravinsky; confinement in the city

Debussy's friendship with Stravinsky and his admiration of his music were furthered when he and Emma, Stravinsky and his wife were invited to the house of Louis Laloy on 2 June. There the two composers sight-read a piano duet reduction of the *Rite of Spring*, Debussy playing the bass, Stravinsky the treble part – a feat in itself impres-

---

[18] See Chapter 10 p. 142.

[19] C. p. 1524.

[20] C. p. 1529.

[21] A. Gold and R. Fizdale, *Misia. The Life of Misia Sert*, London, 1980, p. 143.

[22] P. Vallery-Radot, *Lettres de Claude Debussy à sa femme Emma*, p. 48.

[23] 'Les roses c'est Chouchou. Les Hortensias c'est moi et pardonne à ma tête en faveur de mon cœur qui est tout à toi. Ton Cld.' C. p. 1517.

sive. When they finished, there was no congratulatory embrace, not even mutual compliments. 'We were all struck dumb, overwhelmed by this hurricane which had come from the depths of ages to grab our lives by the roots,' wrote Laloy.[24]

Interspersed with Debussy's correspondence concerning music and musicians are notes to Léon Bertault concerning the arrangement of his debts. Little wonder that this year there were no plans for leaving Paris for the seaside. Even an invitation from P.-J. Toulet,[25] who was becoming increasingly ill, to spend some time with him in Guéthary near Saint-Jean-de-Luz was refused. The long journey would no doubt have been too expensive, as well as tiring for Emma. Sadly they regretted their confinement in the city, for on 23 July Debussy complained to Durand about the excessive heat, which, combined with the noise of trains, was stifling his brain. He needed to complete the orchestration of 'Gigues', the first of the *Images* for orchestra, and was desperate not to allow the familiar demon to take over, which played tricks on him every time he had to work to a deadline. Chouchou had a cold which was preventing them from visiting Durand at his country house. It sounds as if she was taking after her mother, making a fuss about her state of ill health ('c'est toute une histoire!'), something Debussy found amusing, calling it her 'si comique préoccupation'.[26] Perhaps it was to relieve the oppressive atmosphere at home that Debussy would have liked to have taken Emma to the recently established travelling theatre of Firmin Gémier, but on investigation he found the price of a box, which contained nine seats, exorbitant. He does not seem to have considered a cheaper alternative. 'I am all alone and will do some meditation (on a Bach prelude),' he concluded.[27]

The 'all alone' indicates a recurrence of the habit of sending notes to each other even though in the same house. They were not even sharing a bedroom, as another note seems to indicate. He commented sardonically: 'When hair is not in "existence" one never has enough of it ...', and ended his message: 'I won't wait much longer to send you my morning kisses. You will find them in Mercury-Chouchou's hair'.[28] Clearly, he would be saying good morning first to his daughter, who would then greet Emma before he did, bearing in her person the message of his love.

Completion of *Jeux* despite surfeit of negativity; return to Poe

On 11 July Emma received a note for her birthday, a day late, as Debussy admitted. 'Always late ... But always the best as sardines and lovers say. Your old pianist, Claude.'[29] The reference to sardines was to the name on the tin of a famous brand:

---

[24] L. Laloy, *La musique retrouvée*, p. 213. Date from letter from Laloy to Stravinsky quoted in C. p. 1554 n.2.
[25] C. p. 1527.
[26] C. p. 1531.
[27] C. p. 1568.
[28] C. p. 1569.
[29] 'Toujours en retard ... Mais toujours à mieux comme disent les sardines et les amoureux. Ton vieux pianiste. Claude.' C. p. 1528.

Amieux, on which he was implying the pun, '*à mieux*', always the best, not a very romantic association. But by 29 July Debussy was yet again expressing worry over the state of Emma's health and sliding into deep depression. That word 'néant', (nothingness), which he had used before in the phrase 'les usines de néant' ('factories of nothingness') was now combined with 'stupidité'. He had fallen into 'un néant de stupidité', wasting his energy fighting himself, destroying himself. There was a surfeit of negative concepts in this letter to Godet. This ridiculous, dangerous 'game' was like waking up with a hangover. It made him feel diminished, confused, as if he had been wasting time battling something non-existent. He could prove himself as neither idiot nor genius. Perhaps it all came to the same thing and he should simply admit to being weak.[30] Godet was so upset by this letter that he confided in Ernest Bloch, 'Received a very short note from Debussy which was intensely sad ["d'une noire tristesse"], almost a cry of distress ["une angoisse"], almost an appeal for help, to which, alas, I have no answer.'[31]

Between that date and 9 August Debussy had some respite, for he and his family did manage to visit Durand at his country house, Bel-Ébat near Fontainebleau. Being in an old family house like Durand's always caused him frustration with his own surroundings. The sense of history, a continuous past exuded by such an established building, the feeling that Durand had a natural connection to the place through the ages made Debussy aware that he did not fit innately into his more pretentious, nouveau environment. 'Oh, this avenue du Bois de Boulogne which smells of Brazilians, Americans, completely lacking in any sense of the Past. I am also seeing my landlord again, an English alcoholic who would not hesitate to throw me out if he ever found a flashy millionaire.'[32]

The brief change of surroundings had certainly not banished his depression. Chouchou, precocious as ever, was not helping matters, having composed a little song in English, saying 'the Sea is annoyed at not having had a visit from M. and Mme Debussy and their charming little daughter.' He tried to convince her that this year the Sea had gone out so far that people were despairing of ever finding it again, a proposition that did not go down too well. There were times, he complained, when it was very difficult being a father. Meanwhile, Nijinsky had visited him with his 'nanny' (Diaghilev) in the hope of speeding up the composition of *Jeux*. Debussy refused to play them any of the music already composed, but knew he had to get down to it by the end of the month.

On 25 August he told Caplet it was finished. 'How did I manage to forget the troubles of this world and write music which is almost joyful … ?'[33] The contract for *Jeux* was to be worth six thousand francs to Debussy. Stravinsky wrote from Venice expressing his joy on hearing it was finished, suggesting it should be called '*Le parc*' since that is where the ballet takes place. Apart from wanting some modifications to the ending, which Debussy complied with, Diaghilev was satisfied. Debussy was less

---

[30] C. pp. 1533–4.

[31] C. p. 1534 n.1.

[32] C. p. 1536.

[33] C. p. 1540.

willing to comply with the continuing demands of '*la détestable Maud Allan*' to alter *Khamma*, decrying her 'appalling behaviour' to Durand.[34]

After all these modifications and negotiations Debussy was relieved to return to his 'old projects', by which he meant the Poe works, *La chute de la Maison Usher*, in which he seemed to wallow in the depressing atmosphere, and *Le diable dans le beffroi*. Little wonder. The letter to Durand was written on 12 September, the same day as he had to negotiate new terms of his rent for the house. He agreed to accept the increase proposed by Mr. Fairbin. As usual the lease was to be renewed in Emma's name.[35] It is a mystery how he thought he and Emma would be able to keep up this extravagant lifestyle. There is no hint of his considering leaving the environment which ensured he could compose in peaceful, comfortable surroundings. Three days after this he was dealing with the financier Bertault with respect to repaying a creditor a thousand francs. Once again Durand advanced him money. When thanking his publisher, Debussy mentioned that his brother (Alfred Debussy) had been helping him arrange matters.[36] We are also reminded in a letter Debussy wrote to Caplet on 11 October that in 1910 he had been lent five thousand francs by Henry Russell, a sum which he would never be able to repay. He had not written earlier to Caplet because he had so many problems – 'I only have to bend down to pick them up'.[37] Besides his worries and grumbles, Debussy gave Caplet permission to orchestrate any of the *Ariettes oubliées* he wanted, commenting that he never orchestrated his own songs. He had previously, in fact, orchestrated *Le jet d'eau* in 1907 and the *Trois ballades de François Villon* in 1910. Caplet was a trusted orchestrator to whom not only Debussy, but in later years also Emma turned.

By the end of October Debussy's despair knew no bounds. The 'money-men' had described his financial condition as 'ridiculous'. He was desperate to borrow more and it would have to come personally from Durand, not from further advances on his music. If Durand would let him have twelve thousand francs he promised to pay back three thousand francs a year starting the following year.[38] For this Debussy would somehow have to find another source of income, which is surely why he started contributing articles to the bulletin of the SIM (Société internationale de musique), edited by Émile Vuillermoz. On 6 November he submitted the first of these on the Concerts Colonne.

Chouchou's piano lessons

Raoul Bardac commented that Debussy suffered mentally more than physically in consequence of his illness. How revealing is a memory he recounted after spending several months in 1912 on the coast. When he returned to Paris he visited his mother and Debussy, only for Emma to grumble that she did not like his tanned,

[34] C. p. 1545.
[35] C. p. 1546.
[36] C. p. 1547.
[37] C. p. 1549.
[38] C. p. 1553.

sunburnt look. Debussy, however, responded: 'Compare his complexion and mine: beneath his dark skin blood is circulating, there is life. Beneath mine nothing lives, everything is fading.'[39]

More cheerfully, Debussy wrote to Stravinsky on 7 November to express his continuing appreciation of *Petrouchka* and *Le sacre du printemps*. Chouchou had composed her own fantasy on *Petrouchka* – 'which is enough to make a tiger roar'! Even though the noise made Debussy threaten her with punishment, she simply carried on, insisting that Stravinsky 'would find it wonderful'. He remembered fondly playing *Le sacre du printemps* with Stravinsky. He would send him a copy of *Jeux* as soon as possible and looked forward to hearing his opinion of it. He included Emma's and Chouchou's greetings with his own.[40]

Chouchou, now aged seven, started receiving piano lessons 'from a lady whose name is more difficult to learn than the piano', Debussy told Caplet on 19 November.[41] He was obviously fascinated by this teacher and her effect on his daughter, for a few weeks later he told P.-J. Toulet that Chouchou's imagination was being fed by this 'lady dressed in black who looks like a cross between a drawing by Odilon Redon and a nihilist who has run out of bombs'![42] Toulet himself wrote to Debussy on 19 December to exclaim once again about the beautiful catalogues Emma had sent him.[43]

Debussy's 1912 Christmas card to Emma portrayed his recurring theme: a ship sailing in the wind, this time with a poem by Sir Walter Scott:

> Upon the gale she stoop'd her side.
> And bounded o'er the swelling tide.
> As she were dancing home;
> The merry seamen laugh'd to see
> Their gallant ship so lustily
> Furrow the green sea-foam.

His message told Emma that the ship was bearing her not just his love, but the first piece of a series of twelve, 'if Buddha, Krishna, Jehova, Ambroise Thomas and the Maharaja of Kapoutala permit it.' They would be in the purest Debussy style.[44] He was referring to the second book of piano *Préludes*. Debussy's first communication to Durand in the New Year would be not only to thank him for his New Year's gift to Chouchou, but also to ask if he had safely received two new preludes.

Chouchou was growing fast and no doubt proving a demanding piano pupil, for when Debussy told Robert Godet about her teacher, 'a lady dressed strictly in black – right to the tips of her finger nails ... who has the sad look of someone

---

[39] R. Bardac, *Causerie sur les dernières années de Claude Debussy*, Centre de Documentation Claude Debussy, RESE 05.05.

[40] C. p. 1555.

[41] C. p. 1557.

[42] C. p. 1581.

[43] C. p. 1562.

[44] C. p. 1566.

who has escaped a terrible catastrophe', he added that she 'possesses patience which Chouchou soon realised she would never exhaust'. From the tone of the letter it is clear that he needed the welcome distraction Chouchou always brought him from negative thoughts. Having returned to critical writing for the SIM review, he was ever more aware of what he considered the lowering of standards endemic in this age. 'Honestly, living the life of an artist and creating Art in Paris is becoming ever more incompatible with the spirit that reigns here … I'm haunted by the Mediocre and frightened.' He put the blame for his not being able to escape the city squarely on Emma and her demands.

> If for family reasons my wife did not cling so firmly to Paris, I assure you I would be asking you to find me a little spot in Savoy … I could then shake off this atmosphere of false grandeur which creeps in under our door whatever we do to avoid it.[45]

It is difficult to be convinced by this argument. He might not have liked 'false grandeur', but he did enjoy comfort and space to house his special possessions. It was noted earlier that both Raoul and d'Annunzio believed Debussy clung to the money-devouring house. It was harsh to blame Emma when she did her best to ensure optimal working conditions. One can see, though, that Emma would not want to move away from Dolly and her family and had to be near her ageing mother as well.

[45] C. p. 1580.

13

1913: Troubles and travels

Pelléas centenary and *Préludes*

On 25 January 1913 *Pelléas et Mélisande* received its one hundredth performance at the Opéra-Comique. A celebratory dinner was held on 28 January at the Café Riche which both Debussy and Emma attended.[1] Marcel Proust wrote to his close friend and lover Reynaldo Hahn à propos of this centenary performance that he had read an article in the paper *L'Intransigeant* which noted that Fauré and Debussy had chosen the same heroine, Mélisande. 'Perhaps Sigismond Bardac thinks they ought to have left it at that,' he remarked.[2] Even nine years after Debussy had abandoned Lilly for Emma, Proust still felt that scandal and that of Emma's prior relationship with Fauré worthy of scurrilous comment. It is hardly surprising that neither Proust nor Hahn were ever part of Debussy's and Emma's circle of friends.

At the beginning of 1913 Durand commissioned Charles Koechlin to orchestrate *Khamma*. On 5 March he presented the third of his concert series in the Salle Érard, at which Debussy himself performed the first three of his second book of piano *Préludes*. No one would ever forget his luminous interpretations, Durand wrote. Typically, when he had to take numerous bows to acknowledge the enthusiastic applause, Debussy came onto the stage wearing his overcoat, hat in hand, indicating to the audience that he was going home.[3] But it was a copy not of the second, but of the first book of piano *Préludes* that Debussy dedicated to his wife in March 1913, with the affectionate wording, 'In these 12 preludes there is not one harmony which is as engaging or tender as the name "petite Mienne". Her Claude, her husband, Claude Debussy, March 1913.'[4] This was his first dedication to her since June 1911. At the end of the month Ricardo Viñes came to Debussy's house to play him his interpretation of three more preludes, which he performed in public on 5 April. The whole second book was published on 19 April.

---

[1] *Gil Blas*, 29 January 1913.
[2] Reynaldo Hahn, *Lettres* 236–7: http://Reynaldo-hahn.net/lettres/12_011.htm (last accessed 8 July 2020).
[3] J. Durand, *Quelques souvenirs d'un éditeur de musique*, vol.2, Paris, 1925, p. 20.
[4] 'Dans ces douze préludes, il n'y a pas une harmonie qui soit aussi charmeuse et tendre que le nom de "petite Mienne" … son Claude, son mari Claude Debussy, Mars 1913.' C. p. 2219; Centre de Documentation Claude Debussy, RESE-1.1.

Birth of Emma's second grandchild; dedications to Emma

On Easter Day 1913 Debussy gave a gift to Emma and Chouchou of a bowl of chocolates saying the dish was for 'Chouchou-mère' and the accompanying chocolates were for Chouchou.[5] It was the role of Emma as mother of his beloved daughter, rather than wife or lover, that was foremost. On 28 March Emma's second granddaughter Hélène Madeleine Julie Marie was born. She would be known as Madeleine. Emma was known to her grandchildren as *Nounouthe*.[6]

Meanwhile, whilst Debussy penned articles for the SIM review and worked on the orchestration of *Jeux*, Durand continued to assist with financial problems, advancing money which would become due from Diaghilev for the performance of this work, even though the impresario had not even arrived in Paris. At the same time, Emma continued to cause worries over her health.[7] Debussy must have been hermetically sealed in his study for Chouchou to have to write politely to him (probably mid-April) to request that she might accompany him and Emma to a concert of his music in the Salle Gaveau. 'I have written to mama and said to mama that I would like to go with you and mama to the Salle Gaveau to hear your music', said her note in a formally addressed envelope to 'C. Debussy, Compositeur de musique, 80 Avenue du Bois de Boulogne, Paris.'[8]

At least Debussy found the time this month to dedicate three pocket scores to his *petite Mienne*, though not with any particular sign of affection, saying no more than that each was for her own personal collection, La mer, 'Gigues' and 'Ronde de Printemps', (first and third of the *Images*).[9] He was certainly feeling overworked, for he told Gabriel Astruc that he did not even have time to go out and buy a newspaper. The impresario was putting on a performance of Debussy's *Nocturnes* at his new Théâtre des Champs-Élysées on 5 May. This splendid addition to Paris's theatres had opened on 2 April with several composers conducting their own works, including Debussy conducting *Prélude à l'après-midi d'un faune*. Now Loïe Fuller was to present her school of dance there in the first and third of the *Nocturnes*, 'Nuages' and 'Sirènes', whilst the second was played with the curtain down and no choreography. Fernand Ochsé used lighting effects to add atmosphere to the ballet and the orchestra was conducted by Inghelbrecht. The event was described as 'un spectacle exquis!'[10]

Hot on the heels of this stage work came rehearsals, then the first performance at the Théâtre des Champs-Élysées on 15 May 1913 of the ballet *Jeux*. Nijinsky's Dalcroze-based choreography for the seemingly inconsequential tale of three tennis players losing their ball, the contemporary costumes by Léon Bakst based on early twentieth-century tennis outfits and Debussy's rhythmic, atmospheric score

---

[5] C. p. 1591.
[6] Hélène de Tinan, Carnet rouge, Centre de Documentation Claude Debussy, RESE 08.01.
[7] C. p. 1596.
[8] C. p. 1598 (undated).
[9] Each had the same wording: 'Collection particulière de ma petite Mienne. Son Claude Debussy, Avril 1913'. Information kindly provided by Denis Herlin.
[10] *Comœdia*, 15 May 1913.

should have made a striking impression, but left the audience bemused. A month later Debussy gave his honest opinion of Nijinsky's interpretation to Robert Godet. 'Nijinsky's perverse genius was applied to special mathematical skills, counting up demisemiquavers with his feet, checking them with his arms, then, suddenly paralysed on one side, staring with an evil eye at the music as it went past.' He hated it.[11]

However, *Jeux* was quickly overtaken as a talking point in that spectacular month, for only a fortnight later on 29 May Stravinsky's *Le sacre du printemps* burst onto the scene in the same theatre. On the day of the performance of *Jeux*, Debussy dedicated a score to Emma, not of this work, but the second book of piano *Préludes*. It is notable that his wording was somewhat less affectionate than that of the dedication of the first book, for it simply read, 'for my *petite Mienne*'s special collection, Claude Debussy, 15 May 1913'.[12]

More secret correspondence and cancellation of London visit

It seems harsh that only one day after the première of *Jeux* Debussy had to write to Henry Russell to explain yet again that he could not pay him back the generous loan of five thousand francs made to him some three years earlier. 'Unfortunately I am still in the same situation. Whenever I think I am going to emerge from it some unexpected crisis sets me back again.'[13] What becomes clear is that Debussy had to hide the disgrace of this state of affairs from Emma. 'Please be kind enough to send your reply to Caplet for reasons you will easily guess!' From this it must be deduced that Emma opened Debussy's post, so Caplet had to act as intermediary if matters were to be kept secret. For how long had Emma been opening her husband's letters? Perhaps since discovering that there had been secret correspondence between Dolly and Debussy? Now it was Caplet indulging Debussy's secrecy, whilst previously it was Laloy who had been persuaded to be an intermediary.[14] It could have been simply that now Emma wanted to keep an eye on her husband's financial commitments. The fact that Henry Russell was supposed to guess an obvious reason for using Caplet as a go-between means that Debussy did not hide this ignominy from others.

Coincidentally, he was hoping to receive the sum of five thousand francs in July for a concert in London organised by Sir Edgar and Lady Speyer. He could combine this with the return of *Pelléas et Mélisande* to Covent Garden in June, which was to be conducted by Caplet, whom Debussy himself had recommended. This hope was short-lived, however. The letter to Edgar Speyer is dated 25 May. On 29 May, the day of the première of *Le sacre du printemps*, Debussy told Caplet that the five thousand francs had fallen into the English Channel. Once again Emma was ill and he was required to stay at home. 'Of course I'm very annoyed and have lost all hope of hearing *Pelléas* as it was

---

[11] C. p. 1618.
[12] 'Pour la collection particulière de ma petite Mienne. Claude Debussy. 15 mai 1913.' Corr. p. 2219; Centre de Documentation Claude Debussy, RESE-1.2.
[13] C. pp. 1605–6 and p. 1606 n.1.
[14] See Chapter 11 p. 154.

written!' He repeated the message to Caplet on 3 June, fearing he had sent the original to the wrong address.[15] Caplet even offered to make arrangements with the management for the Debussy family to come to the opera, but in reply Debussy emphasised his concern for Emma. She was suffering from insomnia and a high temperature, which worried him more than he could say. In the unlikely event that she accepted Caplet's invitation, he would not dare to let her undertake the journey, which she found difficult even when well. There was no question of him travelling to London alone, although he was desperate to escape Paris, where there were too many Russians. He hated their snobbery and their lack of artistic discrimination, so detrimental to music.[16]

D'Annunzio's affection for the family

Russian participation was once again to the fore when Ida Rubinstein financed and took the lead in d'Annunzio's stage work *La pisanelle ou la mort perfumée* at the Théâtre du Châtelet on 11 June. This provided an opportunity for d'Annunzio to be in touch with the Debussys, offering the composer a seat in the stalls for the dress rehearsal. He also invited Debussy to his *Phèdre* the next afternoon. His lasting affection for Emma and in particular for Chouchou is evident from his messages to them. In typically pictorial language, d'Annunzio made the delightful suggestion that Chouchou should change her name to 'Brugnon' ('Nectarine') as she was so round, rosy-skinned and smooth.[17] Given that he hoped that 'a new dream and new work' would bring them together once more, it would appear that he and Debussy were considering collaborating on a new project. On sending his *chère amie* Emma tickets for two seats, d'Annunzio claimed that his previous collaboration with Debussy provided the fondest memories of his life. Emma was not long in replying. D'Annunzio was exerting his fascination on her once again. Just as it was she who spurred Debussy on to work with d'Annunzio on *Le martyre* in the first place, now she was encouraging the two to work together anew. For her, she claimed, this would be 'a new enchantment'.[18] What the new project was remains unclear – perhaps a 'drame indien' mentioned by Léon Vallas in his 1932 biography of the composer. Years after Debussy's death, on 31 March 1928 d'Annunzio wrote to the committee organising the erection of a monument to the composer mentioning this collaboration, saying the two had spent 'hours and hours' working on it during the war years, 'the greatest reward for my relentless four years of war'.[19] Typical hyperbole. There is nothing to corroborate this statement. After seeing *La pisanelle*, Debussy expressed his and Emma's appreciation of this work, so different to *Le martyre*, although he found the production overcomplicated.[20]

---

[15] C. p. 1612.

[16] C. p. 1614.

[17] C. p. 1615.

[18] C. p. 1620.

[19] L. Vallas, *Debussy et son temps*, 1932, p. 332. Robert Orledge confirmed this in *Debussy et le Théâtre*, p. 277.

[20] C. p. 1621–2.

24. Gabriele d'Annunzio

Preparations for Debussy's journey to Russia

On 28 May Debussy attended the public dress rehearsal of *The Rite of Spring*. It is strange that when he wrote to Stravinsky only two days later to invite him and his wife Catherine to dinner, he made no mention of the masterpiece. However, Stravinsky fell ill with typhoid a few days after the première due to eating bad oysters at the subsequent celebratory dinner, which explains why he received no reply. Emma took this opportunity of writing to Catherine, asking for news. Despite her own ailments she was generous in her desire to help, offering to arrange to have anything she needed sent over by car.[21]

---

[21] C. pp. 1620–1 and E. W. White, *Stravinsky. The Composer and his Works*, London, 1966, p. 551.

Debussy hated being in Paris in 'La Grande Saison', which increased the number of 'idiots' one met, he declared to Robert Godet.[22] Yet on 19 June Émile Vuillermoz organised a Debussy Gala at the Comédie des Champs-Élysées at which Ibéria (Caplet's two-piano version, played by Debussy and Ricardo Viñes), the Proses lyriques, Le promenoir des deux amants, Cinq poèmes de Charles Baudelaire, three Preludes from the second book and the Trois Chansons de Charles d'Orléans were performed. Ninon Vallin was the soprano soloist. Once again it was with Emma that d'Annunzio corresponded asking for a seat, expressing a 'desperate thirst' for Debussy's music. She was happy to invite him to join her in her box, where he would also find his little 'Chouchou Nectarine', who could not wait to see her 'Magician with the golden goatee'.[23] A month previously, d'Annunzio had sent a book of the collected verse of Charles d'Orléans to Debussy, with the dedication, 'To the divine Claude Debussy, these old songs which he is renewing. May MCMXIII. Gabriele d'Annunzio.'[24] Writing about this concert to Caplet, Debussy once again longed for pastures new. 'How I would love to forget all those galas and escape to a little farm in your Normandy.'[25]

The orchestral version of 'Ibéria' was performed on 22 June at the Théâtre du Châtelet which, even though he felt ill, entranced d'Annunzio, who claimed to Emma the next day that its wonderful 'essence of life' had cured him. At her request, he sent her two seats for another performance of La pisanelle on 23 June and invited himself to dinner on 24 June, but by return of post Debussy sent back the tickets, saying Emma was ill. D'Annunzio could, however, still come to dinner.

It is quite likely that Emma's illness was yet again exacerbated by the stressful thought of Debussy having to participate in another tour abroad. Negotiations had been under way since earlier in the year for Debussy to conduct concerts in Russia in December 1913, led, independently of each other, by Alexandre Ziloti, conductor and organiser of concerts in Saint Petersburg, and Sergei Koussevitzky, whose orchestra was in Moscow. It was the latter's proposal that Debussy finally accepted as he would be paid more, but in June he was still trying to fit in rehearsals as well as a concert with Ziloti.[26] Emma was not going to travel with him. One can only imagine her fear of such a journey and the freezing cold conditions of Moscow in December. In view of the fact that he had not been allowed to go to America without her, and journeys to London had been rejected, the financial situation must have been dire for her to submit to Debussy's acceptance of this project. There was an additional complication which could also have led to her not accompanying him: in the 1913 Bradshaw's Continental Railway Guide, it is stated that 'Visitors to Russia must be provided with Passports bearing the visa of a Russian Diplomatic or Consular officer. Without such visa they will not be allowed to enter the country. To persons of Jewish faith the visa is only granted in special circumstances.'[27]

---

[22] C. p. 1619.

[23] 'Sorcier à la barbiche dorée.' C. p. 1625.

[24] 'Éléments de la bibliothèque de Debussy dans la vente de 1933', Cahiers Debussy, no.1, 1977, p. 38.

[25] C. p. 1630.

[26] C. p. 1632.

[27] Bradshaw's Continental Railway Guide and General Handbook 1913, p. lxvii.

More loans; more tensions

Letters to the financier Léon Bertault in June and July show Debussy begging for rescue from yet another difficult situation. Henry Russell still wanted his five thousand francs back.[28] Durand acceded to another urgent request for a loan of six thousand francs to pay off a bill, for which Debussy thanked him, but he did not stop there. He clearly felt the need to share his problems. The huge pressure weighing on him from the burden of his domestic life was almost unbearable. Emma, he explained, had been advised by her doctor that it was essential for her to take the waters at Vichy. This was causing great tension between them, and their unspoken thoughts were making the atmosphere intolerable. This implies that they were hardly talking to each other. Struggling on alone was nothing, but to struggle 'en famille' was appalling, he continued. It was hard to believe that the comfort they were accustomed to from days gone by had now become impossible to afford. This emphasis on 'un ancien luxe' shows it was not just Emma but he too who felt a sense of entitlement to a high standard of living. The question of whether they would be able to support their élite lifestyle indefinitely was raised earlier, when the exorbitant rent for the house in a fashionable area of Paris was discussed.[29] Debussy does not seem to have been able to understand why it was impossible to sustain it. He was clearly also disturbed by the stifling clutter of family responsibilities. He was desperate to avoid the insinuation from others that he had accepted his domestic situation simply for his own advantage. Those piercing comments made by many accusing him of abandoning Lilly for Emma for financial security had obviously left their mark. Pride was a dominant factor, 'a point of honour' driving him on. He indulged in self-pity, regretting his lack of practical expertise, saying that perhaps he was to blame for the situation. His only energy was intellectual. 'In everyday life I stumble over the smallest pebble which anyone else would easily send flying with a little kick.' Yet self-pity or not, Debussy's deep concern for Emma was expressed in a letter addressed to her doctor, Victor Crépel, that very day, asking him to come and visit her as soon as possible. She needed his visit if only for the reassurance it brought her.[30]

Chouchou and *La boîte à joujoux*

Durand must have been moved by Debussy's letter, for on the same day, 15 July 1913, Debussy signed a new contract with him for two works, *La boîte à joujoux* and *Trois poèmes de Stéphane Mallarmé*, no doubt looking forward to an advance. A new collaborator was André Hellé, who had been in touch with Debussy in February about a ballet based on a children's book he had written and illustrated himself called *La boîte à joujoux* (*The Toybox*). Hellé was already known to Emma and Chouchou for his beautifully designed letter paper. Debussy passed on to him Emma's request

---

[28] C. p. 1637.
[29] See Chapter 6 pp. 79–81.
[30] C. pp. 1641–2.

for 'Noah's Ark' paper, which she was no longer able to find in the Printemps store. Chouchou already used paper decorated with a little frog. 'Chouchou says she can only write on your paper,' Debussy told Hellé.[31] A delightful example of her use of paper illustrated with a cow can be found with an unspecified date in 1913 expressing her pleasure at dining with her parents. It is very formal for an eight-year-old, full of mistakes in her efforts to sound grown-up.[32]

Chouchou, or rather her toys, certainly inspired Debussy's *La boîte à joujoux* for, as he told Durand, he was listening to the secrets kept by Chouchou's old dolls and learning to play the drum. To Hellé he expressed his delight with the illustrations and was very specific about where they should appear on the page, in particular a rose, around which the whole little tragedy revolved when it was cast aside – 'the eternal story of women and roses'. There was no humorous exclamation mark after this comment. He had to write this letter again a few days later, thinking it had got lost in the post, being even more specific about the position of the rose. It had to be in a central position on the cover of the album under the *à* in the title. It had assumed even greater significance now than when he had first mentioned it: 'This rose is just as important as any of the characters.'[33] Robert Orledge, in a discussion of Debussy's occult activities, pointed out that the rose is 'the symbol of beauty, regeneration and pure love favoured by alchemists', linking this to Maeterlinck's use of the rose as the symbol of the innocent love between Pelléas and Mélisande.[34] Debussy's comment emphasising the rose being cast aside was perhaps also indicative of his interpretation of Emma's feelings towards him. Disparaged by her for not being able to meet her needs, he was turning for comfort to the scenario of the triangular love affair of the toys, finding solace in Chouchou's miniature environment. On the other hand, the significant central position of the rose could simply have indicated his love of Chouchou. His message accompanying flowers sent to Emma on 4 June 1912 had said that 'les roses sont Chouchou ...'[35] Given that the whole work is centred on his beloved daughter and her box of toys, this is quite feasible. Even so, he felt a dearth of inspiration, for in August he told Hellé that 'I have just been passing through days of drought feeling like a field devastated by locusts.' Chouchou herself did not help matters by having suspected whooping cough. This turned out to be bronchitis, from which she was recovering 'slowly, because of the benefits this condition brings her'.[36] She obviously knew how to wrap everyone around her little finger.

The *Trois poèmes de Stéphane Mallarmé* did not have an easy gestation, for after setting the poems 'Soupir', 'Placet futile' and 'Autre éventail de Mademoiselle Mallarmé' (to be known as 'Éventail') to music, Debussy discovered not only that he needed the permission of Mallarmé's son-in-law, Dr. Edmond Bonniot,

---

[31] C. p. 1628.
[32] BnF Musique, La-Debussy Claude Emma-5.
[33] C. pp. 1646–8.
[34] R. Orledge, *Debussy and the Theatre*, pp. 125–6.
[35] See Chapter 12 p. 176.
[36] C. pp. 1651–2.

but that by coincidence Ravel was also setting three of Mallarmé's poems, including 'Soupir' and 'Placet futile'. Ravel had already received Dr. Bonniot's permission. It required the intervention of Roland-Manuel to persuade the latter to allow Durand to proceed with the publication of Debussy's composition.[37]

Debussy's despair; his mother ailing

Besides these tribulations, Debussy was also berated severely by Alexandre Ziloti for choosing to accept Koussevitzky's invitation rather than his rival one to conduct his works in Russia. His bitterness at what he perceived as a great injustice was expressed in very strong terms.[38] The summer, which once again brought no change of scene, proceeded from bad to worse. Letters to Pasteur Vallery-Radot, which begin on 13 August asking him urgently for some unspecified information, ended on 18 August with the desperate cry 'What is happening? I waited all day and night for you yesterday!' Was his concern a medical one, appealing to his friend as a doctor, or a financial one?

On 25 August we learn he had the additional worry of his 76-year-old mother now ailing. 'She will probably die,' he told Durand.[39] This state of affairs prevented him from making progress with *La boîte à joujoux*, for which he apologised to Hellé, saying he was tormented with worry.

Depression led to suicidal thoughts. At the end of August Durand was, as ever, his confidant. 'You can't imagine the hours of anguish I am going through at the moment. I can tell you, if it weren't for my little Chouchou I would blow my brains out, despite the cowardly ridiculous nature of such an act.'[40] It is impossible to overstate Debussy's love of his daughter. Only for her was it worth continuing his struggles. Whilst expressing his concern over the state of Emma's health, never did he write about her with similar passion.

Following lunch with the Debussys on 5 September, Victor Segalen told his wife that Debussy was thinking of moving to a less ridiculously expensive house in the suburbs of Paris. He was having to accept commissions for irritating 'little things' and couldn't finish the Poe operas, which was what he really wanted to do.[41] It is characteristic of Segalen's comments on Debussy and his family that he stressed negative implications when describing his situation. As seen previously,[42] he seems to have disliked Emma and her influence on her husband. Moving to cheaper premises would have been logical considering the couple's financial circumstances, but it never happened. Whilst Segalen implicitly blamed Emma, it has been shown that others such as d'Annunzio ascribed their failure to move to Debussy.[43]

[37] C. p. 1651 and n.1.
[38] C. pp. 1643–4.
[39] C. pp. 1656–7.
[40] C. p. 1659.
[41] C. p. 1660, n.1.
[42] Chapter 8 p. 112.
[43] Chapter 10 p. 149.

Satie's ironic dedication to Emma

As noted earlier, Satie loved playing with Chouchou, having an instinctive affinity with children. Now in 1913 he found himself engaged like Debussy in composing several sets of pieces of piano music centred around children. In view of the similarities of their approaches, they must surely have discussed their projects. Satie completed his *Croquis et agaceries d'un gros bonhomme en bois* (*Sketches and Provocations of a Portly Wooden Mannequin*) on 25 August and *Enfantillages pittoresques* in October. Debussy worked on *La boîte à joujoux* between July and October. He took extracts from popular classics, quoting popular songs and extracts from Gounod's *Faust*. He quoted himself several times, as well as including folksongs he had used in previous works, such as *The Keel Row* (also in 'Gigues', the first movement of *Ibéria*, on which he had been working quite recently) and *Nous n'irons plus au bois*, a song he had used in *La Belle au bois dormant*, the third of his piano *Images* of 1894, then in 'Jardins sous la pluie', the third of the piano *Estampes*, and in 'Rondes de printemps' in the orchestral *Images* (1905–9).[44]

In September Satie dedicated the last of his set of three piano pieces *Chapitres tournés en tous sens*, 'Regrets des enfermés (Jonas et Latude)', ('Regrets of the confined (Jonas and Latude))' to Madame Claude Debussy. On reading the titles and Satie's own words, which appear between the staves (not to be sung), all three could be ironic or joking references to Debussy and Emma. The first piece, 'Celle qui parle trop' ('She who talks too much') has the instruction above the first stave 'Marques d'impatience du pauvre mari' ('Signs of impatience from the poor husband'). This nonsense poem about a loquacious wife wanting a hat made of mahogany (Emma with her expensive taste and love of large hats?) ends with the poor husband dying of exhaustion. The second piece is entitled 'Le porteur de grosses pierres' ('The carrier of big stones'), which brings to mind the passage in Act 4 scene iii of *Pelléas et Mélisande* where Yniold tries unsuccessfully to move an enormous boulder. In Satie's composition the character is almost crushed by his burden and the piece ends with it rolling off his back. The joke here is that the boulder is only light pumice stone. The title of the third piece, dedicated to Emma, 'Regrets des enfermés (Jonas et Latude)', surely referred to Debussy and Emma's confinement to their house, their inability to leave the city for a holiday. Jonas is a reference to Jonah enclosed in the stomach of the whale. Jean-Henri Masers de Latude was imprisoned in the Bastille for his plan to make advances on Madame de Pompadour, mistress of Louis XV. Satie's words on the score, to be read by the performer, not heard, translate as follows:

> They are sitting in the dark.
> They are thinking.
> Several centuries separate them.
> Jonas says: I am Latude at sea.
> Latude says: I am the French Jonah.

---

[44] For detailed discussion see R. Orledge, *Satie the Composer*, Cambridge 1990, pp. 61–4, 'Debussy, Satie and the summer of 1913', *Cahiers Debussy*, no.26, 2002, pp. 31–44 and 'Debussy and Satie', *Debussy Studies*, ed. R. Langham Smith, Cambridge, 1997 pp. 172–3.

They feel shut in.
They think they can see the good old sun.
They can only think of going out.

It is based around the intervals and tune of the folksong so beloved of Debussy, *Nous n'irons plus au bois*, rubbing in the message of this song, 'We'll go to the woods no more'. There are nods to *Pelléas et Mélisande* – for example, the initial sequence of fourths in the piano right hand recalling the fourths introducing the damp claustrophobia of the vaults in the castle of Allemonde. Both words and music show how well Satie knew his dedicatee and her husband. He was certainly pleased with his achievement, for he wrote to Roland-Manuel on 6 September, 'I've just finished the *Chapitres tournés en tous sens*. It's a great victory.'[45]

Debussy wrote to Astruc at the end of August assuming he had no work for him. The impresario was in extreme financial difficulty himself, owing to the demands of Diaghilev and his Ballets Russes, which had made his tenure at the Théâtre des Champs-Élysées unsustainable. Debussy's situation was descending into a black hole, 'I mean: towards the bailiffs'.[46] Yet again Durand received a request for the loan of 'one or two thousand francs'. Amongst other things, Debussy needed this to support his sick mother, whose needs he could not meet. He suggested making a two-piano arrangement of *Jeux*, but on 5 September he received an advance of one thousand francs for the orchestral arrangement of *La boîte à joujoux*, followed by two further payments of five hundred francs a few days later.

Raoul Bardac's collaboration with Louis Laloy

In September 1913 Emma's son Raoul was having problems of his own. He was living in the Normandy fishing village of St Valéry-en-Caux endeavouring to compose the music to a scenario with words by Louis Laloy. This was '*Le Songeur*', a *drame lyrique*. However, echoing his mother's allergies, Raoul suffered from hay fever. His running eyes and general lethargy were preventing him from making progress. Like her, he was resorting to homeopathic remedies, having been recommended an 'English' medication by a doctor comprising injections of ducks' blood which had been injected with flower pollen.[47] Just under a fortnight later he acknowledged an encouraging letter from Laloy, but insisted the work would not be finished before the following summer.[48] Following his step-father's example, Raoul never completed it. Act I was finished, dated first at St Valéry-en-Caux then at Saint-Germain-en-Laye. Only sketches of the second act exist.[49] Yet despite his own problems, Debussy tried to help Raoul, who had sent a manuscript (unspecified) to the conductor Inghelbrecht, by asking the music critic Robert Brussel to

---

[45] *Erik Satie. Correspondance presque complète*, ed. O. Volta, Paris, 2000, p. 188.
[46] 'Je veux dire: vers les hommes noirs,' C. p. 1659.
[47] September 1913, Laloy archives, B12, Dossier 35, no.1.
[48] September 1913, Laloy archives, B12, Dossier 35, no.2.
[49] BnF Musique, MS-18480.

help him to have this work performed. He wrote to Inghelbrecht saying the work would merit performance even if Raoul were not a dear friend. Inghelbrecht was now also involved in the history of *Khamma* since he was asking for this score, presumably in order to conduct it. Nothing could be done about this, however, until Maud Allan returned from travels abroad.[50]

Debussy reclaims ownership of rights to his works

Even though *La boîte à joujoux* was making progress, Debussy could never write to Durand without conveying misery at his situation, Emma unable to cope with the damp, cold autumnal days and feeling very ill, his mother in poor condition, leaving only Chouchou to raise his spirits. On 3 October 1913 Durand made a financial concession to Debussy when he revoked Clause seven of the contract signed originally on 17 July 1905. This had stated that Durand could claim any royalties owed to Debussy by the *Société des Auteurs Dramatiques* and the *Société des Compositeurs et Editeurs de Musique*, its purpose being to guarantee regular monthly payments to Lilly. Now, significantly, Debussy regained his complete ownership of these royalties, so he would be entitled to some extra income.[51]

Only two days later, on 5 October Henry Russell threatened to make his financial debt to him public knowledge but, as Debussy pointed out, this was hardly going to help him get hold of the necessary money. He suggested being allowed to pay it back in instalments, but in fact this debt was never paid during Debussy's lifetime.[52] It is telling that after his death, listed in the postmortem inventory was a debt of twenty-four thousand four hundred francs that Debussy had borrowed on 27 October 1913 from *L'Avenir du proletariat*,[53] the first of several sums from this organisation. This is not mentioned in any correspondence.

Louis Laloy bumped into Debussy by the '*Théâtre d'Astruc*' (Théâtre des Champs-Élysées) at the beginning of October and had lunch with him. He did not mention any revelation from Debussy about his misery or his financial affairs,[54] but he cannot have exuded happiness for the next day Laloy told Chouchik he had just spent an evening at the Debussys, who were 'sombre and kind' (*dolents et gentils*).[55]

---

[50] C. p. 1666.
[51] Copy of contract kindly provided to the author by the owner of Raoul Bardac's house in Meyssac in 2010.
[52] C. pp. 1669, 1670.
[53] D. Herlin, 'An Artist High and Low, or, Debussy and Money,' in *Rethinking Debussy*, ed. E. Antokoletz, M. Wheeldon, p. 197.
[54] Laloy archives, B12, Dossier 19, 1913, 243.20.
[55] Laloy archives, B12, Dossier 19, 1913, 243.21.

Work on *La boîte à joujoux*;
Satie's dedication to Chouchou

Further stress was caused in October with travel arrangements for Moscow under way, then Debussy himself succumbing to influenza.[56] He had bad toothache yet had to provide articles for Vuillermoz's SIM review. He was also having problems with *La boîte à joujoux*, having reached the opinion that the work must be performed by puppets rather than humans. Debussy's familiarity with the use of puppets derived from his close encounters with the works of Maurice Maeterlinck, whose early plays were described by their author as *'petits drames pour marionnettes'*. No doubt Debussy, imprisoned with Emma in a lifestyle he could neither afford nor escape from, could sympathise even more now than in his younger years with Maeterlinck's philosophy of lack of control over one's own destiny. Chouchou's toys were assuming human characteristics in Debussy's imagination and he was discovering that the souls of dolls were even more mysterious than Maeterlinck could have imagined. 'In my opinion only puppets will convey the true meaning of the work ['l'intelligence du texte'] and the expression of the music,' he told Durand.[57] Appropriately, the manuscript of the piano version was finished on Chouchou's eighth birthday, 30 October, the last work Debussy completed before the war. The contract between Durand, Debussy and Hellé was signed on 31 October 1913.

For a work that is not often performed and which is referred to only in passing in many accounts of Debussy's life and compositions,[58] it seems invidious to ignore Debussy's state of mind when composing *La boîte à joujoux*. His insistence on familiarising himself with Chouchou's toys, the central position of the rose on the title page and the evidence from the actual themes of the pieces that he was entering her world of nursery rhymes and folk tunes seem to indicate a therapeutic process for one so depressed. There is a reminder that Chouchou had an English governess in the quotations from the nursery rhymes 'If all the world were paper and all the sea were ink', 'Pop goes the weasel' and 'One two, three four five, once I caught a fish alive' – just the sort of songs that would come naturally to a nanny bringing up an active child. The work contains so many quotations, near quotations or parodies of earlier works that it is as if Debussy was looking back over his composing life: there are reminders of *Chansons de Bilitis* (1897–8), *La soirée dans Grenade* (1903), several references to *Children's Corner* (1906–8), *The little nigar* (1909), preludes from both the first and second book (1909–12) and several opportunities for him to include fanfares, a recurring feature of his compositions. Debussy himself would not complete the orchestration of *La boîte à joujoux*. This was eventually done by Caplet and it was not performed until after Debussy's death.

Once again Satie demonstrated his closeness to the family, for he too gave a birthday present to Chouchou by dedicating a piece to her: the third of his *Croquis et agaceries pour un gros bonhomme en bois*, 'Españaña', originally completed on 25

---

[56] C. p. 1674.
[57] C. pp. 1667–8.
[58] Exceptions being R. Orledge, 'Another look inside Debussy's 'Toybox'', *The Musical Times*, December 1976, pp. 987–9; *Debussy and the Theatre*, pp. 177–85.

August that year. This piece contains many playful references to Chabrier's *España*. Here is an ironic turn of events, for it was on the Spanish style of Chabrier's *España* that Fauré based the final movement of the *Dolly* suite, 'Le Pas espagnol,' dedicated to Emma's first daughter, Hélène. Was Satie aware of this?

Plans were already afoot for Debussy to conduct his works in Holland and in Rome the following February. The urgency to reduce his growing mountain of debt meant desperate measures. He was troubled to hear from Chouchou that a Monsieur Crevel had telephoned when he was out one day, no doubt about money owed. How telling that this eight-year-old, not her nanny or her mother, answered the phone. He was also worried that it would be difficult to arrange travel insurance, for the doctor who came to examine him had left him no information on his findings. He asked the financier Léon Bertault if he could help with both these problems.[59]

Emma's anxiety prior to Debussy's departure

It must have been depressing to witness the end of Astruc's brief tenure of the Théâtre des Champs-Élysées. Debussy faithfully supported Inghelbrecht in his preparations and performance of *Boris Godunov* on 6 November, which went ahead despite theatre staff receiving no pay. Emma was with her husband at this event. They both bemoaned the closure to the Stravinskys, Debussy expressing his frustration that the only place in Paris where music was made with complete sincerity had failed,[60] and Emma calling it 'un vrai chagrin et un vrai désastre'. Catherine Stravinsky was left in no state of uncertainty as to the difficulties being experienced by the Debussy household. Emma told her that if she had to list all their troubles since the Stravinskys had left the city, she would need a whole book. 'My mother-in-law, very ill – My mother, ill – My husband, ill – Chouchou, ill – and your devoted friend, ill as well, worried and in despair.'[61]

On 13 November Emma wrote to Fauré in his role as Director of the Conservatoire on behalf of a young girl wishing to join the music theory (*solfège*) classes. She received a reply from him addressed to his 'chère amie'. Despite his own influenza and overwork, he agreed to meet the girl's parents to discuss the matter. Tongue in cheek, he commented that these classes were like fortified bunkers guarded by ladies of a certain age who invented all sorts of means to get rid of unsatisfactory pupils! He sent big kisses to Chouchou, the tone of the letter being one of fond affection towards the whole family.[62]

Their life in Paris never changed, they never got away – except that Debussy was about to leave for Russia. Emma claimed she had more reason to feel depressed about

---

[59] C. p. 1685.

[60] C. p. 1687.

[61] C. pp. 1689–90.

[62] 'Maintenant il faut que je vous confie que les classes de solfège sont des réduits fortifiés et gardés par des dames pas jeunes et qui ont eu le temps d'inventer mille moyens d'écarter qui ne leur plaît pas!' Gabriel Fauré to Madame Debussy, 13 November 1913. Copy kindly provided by Manuel Cornejo of original belonging to Michel Pasquier.

the situation than he. She was obviously suffering anxiety at the thought of his departure alone. This was inevitable but unreasonable, considering it was he who would have the hardships of travel and she who was always ill when they went abroad.

Koussevitzky did his best to make Debussy's journey to Moscow and Saint Petersburg as smooth as possible. Debussy had to go to various offices in Paris one day to collect his visa and other documents, which necessitated the use of the car. Clearly he was anxious not to upset Emma by depriving her of it, for he sent a note to her on headed paper explaining that it was 4.20 and he knew she required it at 4.35. He also wrote to his financier, Bertault, insisting that nothing must be done which might upset his wife during his absence.[63] He sent a humorous postcard to Stravinsky hoping that he might come to Moscow. 'There you will meet Claude Debussy, *musicien français*, …'[64] This appears to have been the first time Debussy used this term to describe himself, no doubt spurred on by the thought of being in a foreign country, but it was something he would cling onto as the First World War spread its tentacles across Europe.

November also brought reminders of two projects never completed. Since 1909 Debussy was supposed to have been composing incidental music for Gabriel Mourey's *Psyché*. Only the solo flute piece, *La flûte de Pan*, intended to begin the third act, was ready, and received a performance (offstage) on 1 December. This eventually became known as *Syrinx*. On 21 November a contract was signed with Durand for *Le palais du silence*, a ballet whose first performance was envisaged at London's Alhambra Theatre, which would never see the light of day.

Debussy's departure for Russia; his urgent correspondence with Emma

On the day of departure for Moscow, 1 December 1913, there is evidence of a certain feeling of panic as Debussy used his wife's notepaper to send an urgent message to Gaston Choisnel, Durand's colleague, requesting copies of the orchestral score of *Rondes de printemps* and a copy of the *Trois poèmes de Stéphane Mallarmé*, only recently published.[65] The train was due to leave at 13.45 so there can have been little time to complete the task.

Now Debussy embarked on the journey, taking him further than he had ever been from Emma and Chouchou and for his longest absence. Tearfully, Emma blew kisses to him as the train left the Gare du Nord.[66] No fewer than twenty-four communications from Debussy to Emma and Chouchou exist, written every day except one between 1 and 16 December, ranging from a few lines on a telegram or postcard to several pages.

---

[63] C. pp. 1693–4.
[64] Ibid.
[65] C. p. 1706.
[66] C. p. 1711.

Matching this correspondence to the timetable of the Nord Express, which travelled on Tuesdays only, it becomes clear how anxious he was to communicate. The train left the Gare du Nord at 13.45. His distress and loneliness were such that he had only been away for a couple of hours, arriving at Erquelinnes just over the Belgian border at 16.24 local time, when he sent a telegram at 16.36 to Emma reading 'Trains travel fast. Regrets remain. All Claude's poor love. Kiss Chouchou.' The next day he sent a telegram from Alexandrowo (now Poland) at 15.20. 'Sad night. Sleeper even sadder. Love = Bousniky. Your Claude.' This was just before the train departed to Warsaw at 15.33, where it was scheduled to arrive at 19.14. At 21.36 he sent a telegram reading 'Don't forget your Claude.' After travelling through the night he arrived in Moscow on 3 December at 20.18. A telegram was already under way at 21.41: 'Have arrived, alas. All my love your Claude.'[67] He also sent a postcard to Chouchou revealing his sadness at not being with her: 'Travelling from Warsaw to Moscow there was a little girl taking tea with her father. She did not look at all like you, my little Chouchou, but her father looked too happy.' She was to kiss Emma for him.

Just as with previous journeys, none of Emma's communications to Debussy whilst he was away for nearly a fortnight survive, so we only ever read one side of the correspondence. It is clear from his responses that there was a constant stream from her, which occasionally comforted but more often upset him. On 4 December he thanked her for her telegrams and the next day his telegram to her read, 'Received nice letter. Happy but sad. Your Claude.' She cannot have been sending positive messages, for on 6 December he wrote, 'Beg you to be brave. All my loving thoughts Claude.'[68] Emma was not to know that on Thursday 4 December he had copied out a letter he had already started writing earlier on the train, adding to it each day until he sent it on Sunday 7 December.

Debussy had been dreading leaving his home environment, having his domestic routine completely overturned, and it was clear from the beginning that his worst fears were being realised. He missed Emma more than words could express, his own dear *petite Mienne*. He felt completely shattered, as if his soul were being trampled on, 'que l'on marche sur mon âme'.[69] His little vignettes of their home life reveal Emma's rather grudging attitude to domesticity and her unreceptive response to his desire to make love. Whilst still on the train he imagined himself leaning over her as she looked at her 'damn books' (*ces damnés livres*), peering through her large glasses, trying to decide what sauce to have with chicken, a moment which could have been delightful if she were not so agitated by domestic affairs. He wanted to bend down and kiss the back of her neck, an image interrupted by his realisation he was imprisoned on the train. At this moment he was brought her first telegram, which had been delayed by the conductor first asking all the women passengers if they were called Claude – not a man's name in Russia. Imagining Emma writing at the table in her room made him even more acutely aware of the ever-growing distance between them. Continuing the next day he again referred to physical contact.

---

[67] 'Toute la tendresse de ton Claude'.
[68] C. pp. 1707–9.
[69] C. p. 1709.

Longing for the moment of reunion he added a series of dots, saying, 'Allow me to let these dots represent the most disturbing caresses – you know! – the ones you stop me from without me knowing precisely why!'[70] Debussy's insistent physical passion was evidently not reciprocated, yet he could not do without the hermetic domestic environment and familiar routine which Emma helped to organise.

Koussevitzky tried to make Debussy's stay as comfortable as possible. Following the formal greeting on the platform by a reception committee, he took him to his house for a meal. Merely seeing two bottles of Evian water on the table made Debussy want to cry. He was given his own apartment with three rooms, but found it impossible to sleep, so obsessed was he with envisaging his tender loving life with Emma and her tearful farewell, the kisses she blew as the train left the station. He paced up and down, fell asleep in a chair, only to be woken by the intense cold.

On his return from rehearsals the next morning a letter from Emma was awaiting him. Here was the first indication of what was to become the theme of this absence from his wife. Emma was clearly incapable of maintaining a positive attitude, of encouraging him to do his best, wishing him luck, being stoical herself or encouraging her husband to be stoical in the face of adversity. His joy on opening the letter was short-lived. It is obvious from his reaction that she regarded his tour as a selfish act. Her agitation and suffering at being left behind were making her ill. Debussy tried to assure her that this was a natural reaction, for he too was suffering. Whilst he did not want her to get used to being without him ('to no longer feel me within you'[71]), this journey was being undertaken for *both* their sakes. It must not be regarded as a punishment and held against him. They must regard it as a test of their love, which would emerge not more beautiful, for that would imply it was not beautiful enough already, but with a new freshness, brought about by having suffered for the thing one loved most in all the world. 'If we suffer, it is in relation to what our love is worth'.

Debussy described his hard work at rehearsals, his growing exhaustion, but did not yet post the ever-lengthening letter. Her second letter, meanwhile, upset him even more than the first. She was obviously pouring out her worries and couldn't stop herself from upbraiding him. He was desperate to give her courage and comfort, but knew this was in vain. Even in the tiny gaps during rehearsal he had tried to cheer himself up by envisaging himself shut in a tiny room alone with her, telling her all about what he had been doing, leaning over her little curly blond head, leading to 'a result which no doubt bears no resemblance to reality' (again that physical sensuality), and for just a moment he had felt less lonely. That was Friday 5 December. The continuation of the letter on Saturday began with the words, 'What is to become of us? Your letters are more and more despairing.' He realised nothing would calm Emma down. She must try to grant them both some good will. Surely two such unhappy beings would be rewarded for their suffering. No doubt Emma would have been jealous to read that rehearsals were cancelled that afternoon and that Debussy

---

[70] C. p. 1712. P. Vallery-Radot in *Lettres de Claude Debussy à sa femme Emma* omitted this sentence, p. 105.

[71] C. p. 1712.

was dining with Diaghilev, who happened to be in Moscow. The letter was posted at last on Sunday morning, 7 December, and a fresh one started the same evening.

He tried to convince Emma that suffering was necessary. You could not possess a being who embodied all the happiness in the world without having to suffer for it. Yet even as he tried to recall all the qualities that make her so dear to him he could hear her voice 'which is able to utter the harshest as well as the sweetest words'.[72] He was determined to accept suffering. 'Suffer, old chap, (I say). If someone breaks little fragments off your heart, be thankful for your suffering. It is more beautiful than that vague void [*néant*] felt by those who have nothing more to regret than an even deeper void.' Debussy was returning to the 'usines de néant', factories of nothingness. This obsession recurred whenever he was deeply depressed. Better to have a true cause of suffering than to suffer that. The only positive comment in this section of his letter was that it must have been Emma who suggested that Chouchou should write to him. He could not bear to have been forgotten by his daughter.

Yet again he broke off then continued after further rehearsals. Another letter from Emma had arrived, which upset him so much he had had to postpone answering it. Whatever had she been writing? 'What unjust, nasty words ... How can you think such things? Does your suffering have to make you forget how much your poor Claude loves you? ... You know perfectly well why I am undertaking this journey.'[73] He could not understand her anger. However justified, its effect was more wounding than she could imagine. He pleaded exhaustion from his uncomfortable journey and paraphrased Golaud in *Pelléas et Mélisande*: if she could see him as he was now, 'you would feel sorry for me as I feel sorry for you'.[74]

In his letter of Monday 8 December we discover one of the accusations Emma had been making. 'I don't know how to stop feeling jealous of your music'.[75] Debussy had to counter this by insisting that between Emma and music it was the latter that should be jealous. 'If I continue to make music and to love it, that is because I owe to it, to this music you treat so badly, the fact that I met you, fell in love with you and everything else!' He assured her that if he ever stopped writing music it would be she who stopped loving him, for it was certainly not his conversational ability nor his physical attributes which contributed to his ability to keep her. It was music which acted as a diplomat between them when they were ill-tempered, when he was so bad at dealing with things. Once again he tried to tell her of his duties in Moscow. Surely she must have had a little sympathy for his state of mind when he added that his train for St. Petersburg was to leave at 12.30 that night? His next rehearsal would begin there at 11.30a.m., hardly an hour after his arrival in the city.

Knowing the letter would not reach her before this departure, Debussy also sent a telegram saying he was going to St. Petersburg, and the next day managed to find time in between rehearsals to send another with his love. He must have been thinking of Emma constantly to be so assiduous in contacting her when time was at a premium.

---

[72] 'Cette voix qui sait dire les pires comme les plus doux mots ...' C. p. 1715.
[73] C. p. 1716.
[74] Act V.
[75] 'Que de mots injustes, méchants ...' C. p. 1717.

At 9 p.m. he managed to snatch a few minutes to write a letter following rehearsals and 're-rehearsals', hardly having had time to have a proper meal. 'I hope you have managed to find better reasons than mine for not carrying on cursing me ...', he wrote.[76] On 10 December he wrote a series of three postcards to Chouchou with little (almost) rhyming couplets, followed by a long letter just for her the next day. He missed her pretty face, her songs and laughter, all the noise which could make her unbearable, but more often was utterly charming. He asked after her Czerny piano studies, which he described as a 'ballet for fleas', and after their dog, Xantho. How she would love the Koussevitzkys' bulldogs and a bird which sang almost as well as Miss (Maggie) Teyte. In a PS he stressed she should look after Emma. 'Be very nice to your poor little mama. Do all you can to stop her getting too upset!'[77]

At 1.30 p.m. that same day, he found time to begin a letter telling Emma he was setting off for Moscow again that evening.[78] The concert had gone well, but it is moving to read that he had actually shed tears in the interval. He did not know if she would understand that usually when he conducted she was present so he could tell her on the spot all the things he could say only to her. However kind the Koussevitzkys were, they could not fill this void. Only some instinctive sense of propriety had stopped him from crying in front of two thousand five hundred people. 'You should accept these tears as a mark of my love for you.' Debussy was clearly overtired, yet still there was no let-up. He caught his train and arrived in Moscow at 8.15 the next morning. That afternoon he thanked Emma for her telegram, desperate for news of her health. He was conducting a concert on Saturday and would be back home on Tuesday.

On Sunday 14 December, he telegraphed Emma complaining of dreadful toothache. The concert had gone well. 'Do not be ill', he commanded. His train left Moscow at 2.00 p.m. and arrived in Warsaw at 2.48 p.m. the next day. A message two hours later saying he would be arriving back at 11.30 the next day was not his last missive of the journey. Arriving in Berlin at 5.51 a.m., twelve hours after leaving Warsaw, he sent her another telegram and posted four postcards, one to Chouchou simply saying 'Bonjour Chouchou!', others to Jacques Durand, Inghelbrecht and P.-J. Toulet. From Liège he sent a final telegram to Emma, 'for the joy of saying one last time, see you tonight *petite Mienne*'.[79] There is no record of their reunion to indicate how they eventually greeted each other in person.

Debussy's return home; Hartmanns' return to Paris

None of the letters from Emma, so full of complaints and self-pity, are extant. Whether they were eventually destroyed by her or Debussy, or even by Dolly, we will never know. There was no further correspondence between Debussy and Emma for the remaining few days of 1913, no Christmas greetings, no special little composition. Debussy did, however, dedicate a score of *La boîte à joujoux* to his wife

---

[76] C. p. 1719.
[77] C. p. 1722.
[78] The train left at 9.30 p.m.
[79] C. pp. 1724–6.

that December, 'for my *petite Mienne*'s special collection, and also to mark my joy at returning from that far too distant Russia. Claude Debussy, Dec. 1913.'[80]

There can have been little lasting joy, however, for only a week after his return Debussy wrote to the financier Bertault saying things were going from bad to worse. He had had a new loan of twenty-five thousand francs refused.[81] The situation had not been resolved three days later, for on 26 December he wrote again complaining that the year 1913 was playing tricks on him right up until its end. He was being harassed by Émile Vuillermoz for an article for the SIM review despite his extreme tiredness after his travels, but of course he needed to earn what little fee he could, so wrote a short article, which appeared on 1 January 1914.[82]

Emma was presumably ill in bed over Christmas, for that is where she was on 26 December when Debussy wrote to the pianist Walter Rummel. Meanwhile she was able to renew her friendship with Arthur Hartmann's wife Marie, for the couple had returned to Paris that autumn. Hartmann was not overjoyed at the reunion, for he claimed that once again 'began that chain of never-ending visits, exchange of dinners and squabbles, fits of ill nature as of clowning or bantering and of practically no allusions to matters musical, not to speak of musical discussion.'[83] Certainly Emma was pleased to invite the Hartmanns to tea on 2 January 1914, even though she admitted to having been confined to bed prior to this.[84] She also sent New Year's greetings to Stravinsky.[85]

Chouchou rather than Emma was honoured with a personal message from P.-J. Toulet on 29 December. He sent all best wishes possible to her and her parents, signing off, 'Your old invalid friend, Toulet'.[86] Thus the year 1913 came to its sombre end. Debussy wrote to Robert Godet on 1 January, 'I'm not expecting great things in this year 1914. It would have to be pretty bad to be even worse … '[87]

---

[80] 'Pour la collection particulière de ma petite Mienne, et aussi pour marquer la joie d'être revenu de la trop lointaine Russie. Claude Debussy, Dec. 1913.' C. p. 2219.

[81] C. p. 1727.

[82] C. p. 1728.

[83] A. Hartmann, *Claude Debussy as I knew him*, p. 90.

[84] Idem. p. 136.

[85] C. p. 1731.

[86] Ibid.

[87] C. p. 1735.

14

1914: The approach of war

Financial dilemmas

Early in the New Year Debussy was working on a ballet entitled *Le palais du silence*, commissioned for performance at London's Alhambra Theatre. As with so many projects, despite a change of title to *No-ja-li*, this would never be completed. Yet there is also a sign of work on the project that Debussy regularly turned to when in the depths of despair. In the sketch book for *No-ja-li* he wrote 'Le Scorpion oblique et le Sagittaire retrograde ont paru sur le ciel nocturne.' Robert Orledge has shown that this applied not to the ballet but to a scene in *La chute de la Maison Usher*.[1] The inscription shows Debussy's familiarity with Tarot cards dating back to his interest in the esoteric and the occult during his youth. The relevance here is to the struggle between life and death in *The Fall of the House of Usher*. It echoed his own depressing, doom-laden situation and his obsession with this dark work. This state of mind can have done nothing to lift Emma's mood.

Now it was Chouchou rather than her mother who became ill with influenza, but naturally this caused Emma much anxiety.[2] More worrying for Debussy, however, were his constant financial problems. Letters to his financier Bertault show his mounting despair, even his fear of a ring of the doorbell,[3] all of which led to an inability to concentrate. 'I still can't work as I should … sometimes I envy those people who are dying of cold.'[4] Hence the essential undertaking of more foreign tours, all of which needed planning and preparation.

The year also brought further contact with the Hartmanns. On 5 February, in a recital at the Salle des Agriculteurs, Debussy accompanied transcriptions by Hartmann of his song *Il pleure dans mon coeur* and two piano preludes, *La fille aux cheveux de lin* and *Minstrels*, as well as Grieg's violin sonata.

Hartmann gave a vivid account of Debussy's attitude towards him. One day, prior to the concert, he entered to find the composer at his table 'bare as always of any manuscript paper'. From Debussy's restless behaviour it was clear 'he was suffering in silent, but not subdued agony'. He eventually explained to Hartmann that he was desperate to escape his situation of financial embarrassment. It transpired that it was not a loan Debussy wanted, but to have the *Minstrels* transcription published under

---

[1] R. Orledge, *Debussy and the Theatre*, Cambridge, 1982, pp. 124, 126.
[2] C. p. 1749.
[3] Ibid.
[4] C. p. 1750.

his name in order that he might claim the royalties. 'Published under my name, as my first violin piece, I could sell it outright and it pulls me out of a hole!' Hartmann consented, and also agreed to keep this from his wife.[5] This would imply that Emma knew nothing either, since she was so close to Marie. Debussy duly received five hundred francs from the publisher on 17 February.[6]

To Rome and Amsterdam alone

On 18 February Debussy left Paris alone on the Rome Express. He sent his first telegram to Emma from Dijon after having travelled for under four hours, already exhausted. The next day he posted a letter from Pisa expressing acute anxiety, which, he claimed, would only disappear upon receiving news of her. She had, however, managed a thoughtful gesture by enclosing two photographs, one of her, one of Chouchou, in Debussy's medicine box. He was touched and delighted by this surprise. He had time in Pisa to notice violets 'which you love, but you are not here! Why are there violets?' The next day he announced his safe arrival in Rome, adding 'You are not ill.' Yet he had no news of her, no letter awaited him.

That evening he felt like a condemned man being punished for a serious crime, such was his loneliness and depression in the Grand Hôtel de Russie. At every station he had been conscious of the distance growing between him and Emma. 'I felt such anguish at the thought that it is over, I might never see you again!'[7] *'C'était fini.'* Had Emma been threatening once again to leave him? Added to this was his worry at the situation he had left her in with regard to creditors. Cancelling the trip would only have left them worse off. In the morning he had still received no news from her. 'What does this mean? Whatever state are your poor nerves in? They are always so sensitive.'

A telephone call from the Count of San-Martino[8] explained that communications had been held up in both directions. Eventually a telegram from Emma reached Debussy, to which he replied as soon as he had a moment. His letter was full of extreme emotion. It is amazing that he was able to conduct a concert at all with his mind in such a state of panic and distraction. 'In the night I really thought I was going to die,' he exclaimed.

> I hardly dare write this, but I have to admit to my excruciating fear of losing your love. Every journey takes me a bit further away from it and finally I will end up by being no more to you than a passing stranger you no longer need to be attached to … For me it is the opposite. Your smallest gestures, your words, angry as well as affectionate, become so precious that my anxiety is doubled.[9]

---

[5] A. Hartmann, *Claude Debussy as I knew him*, pp. 97–9.
[6] C. p. 1738 n.2.
[7] C. p. 1762–4.
[8] President of the Accademia Nazionale di Santa Cecilia in Rome and concert promoter.
[9] C. p. 1767.

During a rehearsal on 21 February for the programme, which comprised *La mer, Rondes de printemps, Prélude à l'après-midi d'un faune* and the *Marche écossaise*, Debussy gave an interview to a journalist, Alberto Gasco. This was full of admissions. He could be considered neither a good conductor nor a good pianist, not possessing the necessary qualities for either. His work on the two Poe operas was progressing well despite gaps in both scores. But the most surprising aspect of the interview was the unusual amount of personal information he revealed. For a start, he was totally satisfied with his working conditions in his room at home, despite it being in a city, and had no need for peaceful countryside for inspiration. There he would lack the requisite home comforts satisfying his 'penchants délicats', (another indication that Debussy clung onto the expensive house just as much as Emma). The sea fascinated him to the extent of paralysing his creativity. Until that day he had been in despair at having received no news of his loved ones. He would leave immediately after the concert on Monday morning.

> I cannot hide the fact that my family exerts an excessive, all-encompassing power over me. This extremely strong spiritual link has led me more than once to reach a very difficult conclusion: that an artist should not marry. The immense adoration I feel for my wife and my little daughter means that I have never regretted for one second the step I took, but I am totally convinced of this truth: an artist must aspire to being as free as possible in life. As to family, his father and mother suffice. Even a sister is already one too many.[10]

Once again Debussy was expressing a sense of entitlement, that of a composer driven by the need for isolation, the instinctive desire to shut himself away to respond to inspiration undisturbed. Gasco responded in amazement that in that case a dog would be ideal company, to which Debussy replied that he did indeed have a dog which kept him and, to an even greater extent, his daughter happy.

That same day Debussy found time to write a sad postcard to Chouchou with a picture showing the garden of the Grand Hôtel de Russie seen through a window, telling her he was not able to enjoy this beautiful garden without her there.[11] To Durand he complained that he was no longer the twenty-year-old he had been when he first came to the city and now, completely at a loss, he could not wait to return home.[12] The concert at the Augusteo left him exhausted as the audience reacted with varying degrees of warmth towards the pieces. Immediately he sent a telegram to Emma, followed on 22 and 23 February by two more as the train transported him all too slowly back to Paris. How could he acknowledge publicly he felt so stifled by marriage when he was so anxious to return to his wife? He clearly felt a need to be looked after, to have his needs met. One can't help but be reminded of the epithet ascribed to Emma by some: '*la mère Claude*'.

How cruel to have to depart almost immediately for Amsterdam. On 26 February he would be on his way again. He had left his batons in Rome and had to ask

---

[10] F. Lesure, 'Une interview romaine de Debussy (février 1914)', *Cahiers Debussy*, 11, 1987, pp. 3–8.

[11] BnF Musique, La-Debussy Claude-86.

[12] C. p. 1768. He was twenty-two when he first went to the Villa Médicis.

Inghelbrecht to lend him one. He asked Gabriel Pierné for a ticket for Emma for the open rehearsal of the concert version of *Jeux* on 28 February, which he himself would be unable to attend.

We do not know what words passed between Debussy and Emma in their short reunion, nor how the situation with the creditors proceeded, but clues emerge from Debussy's constant correspondence with his wife. His first telegram on this new journey, sent from Antwerp, implies that they had not argued. 'Not too much to complain about. We had a lovely time. Thanks for telegram. Kisses.' But from his next stop, Roosendaal, anxiety crept in as there was nothing awaiting him there. Upon arrival in Amsterdam he was already experiencing 'heures noires' ('dark times').

The truth of the situation was revealed in his next long letter of 27 February. He felt the cruelty of separation even more keenly than on his last journey, as their reunion had been so brief but so full of pleasure. 'I saw you, I had you, then suddenly nothing!' On receiving a telegram from her in Brussels he had felt her lips on his. After a disturbed night he awoke with consternation to find himself in an anonymous bed on a dismal, foggy morning. Rehearsal, then lunch, after which he received a letter. Here Emma must have expressed more tender emotion than usual. Debussy agreed it was difficult for her to be logical in this state of separation, but 'don't forget that one word too laden with meaning only adds to my pain'. The sensual time they had spent together had left its mark. Some of her sentences were as good as a kiss, he wrote; others made him feel as if he were embracing her body ('when you want to!') which melted between his arms in those moments when they could no longer tell the difference 'between yours and mine'.[13] He thought of her constantly.[14]

The concert in Amsterdam on 28 February was a great success, but a revealing description by the president of the Concertgebouw, Richard Van Rees, told of the contradiction between the spontaneous welcome Debussy received and the rather awkward impression of lack of self-confidence he gave on the podium. Debussy was clearly not good at hiding his emotions.

> Not because of his external appearance ... but there was over his whole personality a faint cloud of lethargy and boredom such as you find with people suffering from home-sickness – a disease which, according to him, never left him when he was far from Paris.[15]

Debussy conducted the first two *Nocturnes*, *Prélude à l'après-midi d'un faune* and the *Marche écossaise*, then played three piano *Préludes*. The same performance was repeated at the Hague in front of the Queen Mother who, as he told Emma, 'left me indifferent'. Following another concert in Amsterdam he was invited to dinner with Van Rees in the company of some members of the orchestra. His host was left in no doubt about Debussy's home-sickness. 'At table, Debussy's attention was immediately attracted by a small Empire clock which he admired very much. "You'll see me looking at it frequently," he said to his hostess, "because every minute that passes brings me closer to Paris".'

---

[13] When Pasteur Vallery-Radot quoted this letter he omitted this last suggestive phrase. P. Vallery-Radot, *Lettres de Claude Debussy à sa femme Emma*, p. 138.

[14] C. pp. 1774–5.

[15] R. Nichols, *Debussy Remembered*, London, 1992 p. 232.

Despite this lack of manners, he relaxed in the company of his hosts to the extent that he remained later than the other guests and was complimentary about the food ('I did not know one could dine so well outside Paris') and wine. He then talked freely about his wife and his daughter, explaining that 'because of his very sensitive stomach, he regularly used to go the market himself to choose the food he liked; in short he spent an hour talking with us about the most ordinary, everyday things.'[16]

Although appreciative of his host's hospitality, Debussy told Emma his impatience to get home was exceeding all limits. 'I have to find my happiness, my life again, for living amongst people who are doubly foreign to me is a kind of latent suicide!' He could not wait to return to the familiar scent of the perfume so unique to her.

Debussy's return; Emma's constructive help

On 2 March Debussy was reunited with his wife. During his absence Emma had not only attended the dress rehearsal of *Jeux* on Debussy's behalf, but had had to deal with a solicitor, Maurice Martin, who was helping to arrange a further loan. Nothing went smoothly. She demanded that Martin return to her the papers he had been sent as her husband needed them urgently, but received no response. Debussy had to write to him himself twice on 3 March demanding their immediate return. As for *Jeux*, Debussy eventually managed to attend a rehearsal on 5 March, for which he thanked Pierné, remarking that he had the impression that the orchestra liked the work less than Pierné did.[17]

On 18 January P.-J. Toulet, who was becoming increasingly ill, had asked Debussy if Emma could send him a couple of the beautiful catalogues he so loved,[18] and on 9 March he wrote to her personally, overwhelmed with the beauty of the package he had received. She had wrapped it up as prettily as a work of art. He exclaimed about the beauty of items in the catalogues, enquired in florid terms about Emma's health and asked lovingly after Chouchou who, last time he had seen her, believed firmly in fairies. How he hoped she had not yet lost this innocence.[19] A little clue to other games with which the nearly nine-year-old Chouchou amused herself is revealed in a letter she wrote to a friend thanking her for a box of shells she had been sent: 'I play shops with them'.[20]

On 21 March Debussy participated in a significant concert of the Société Philharmonique, accompanying Ninon Vallin in the first performance of his *Trois poèmes de Stéphane Mallarmé* as well as *Le promenoir des deux amants*. He also played several of his piano pieces, including *Children's Corner*, and garnered praise for the sensitivity of his playing despite having injured his left thumb in a train door on the way back from Amsterdam.[21] He was also sickening, for towards the end of March

[16] Idem. pp. 232–4.
[17] C. p. 1783.
[18] C. p. 1748.
[19] C. p. 1786.
[20] C. p. 1790.
[21] C. p. 1787; F. Lesure, *Claude Debussy. Biographie critique*, Paris, 2003, p. 381.

Emma was having to be the stronger of the couple, explaining to various correspondents that Debussy was ill in bed with a severe case of influenza but, what is more telling, he was also suffering from shingles, one of the causes of which can be physical and emotional stress.[22]

The dancer Loïe Fuller now wanted to stage *La boîte à joujoux* at the Opéra-Comique. However, Debussy had not yet orchestrated this, another project he would never complete. It was left to Emma to answer Fuller's request for permission and to postpone his refusal as long as possible: 'My poor husband is very ill. He has flu, a fever, and what is more, shingles, which is terribly painful and takes a long time to get over.' She took a while to acknowledge Fuller's next letters, eventually explaining that because of her husband's illness, there had been no progress in the matter.[23] Fuller also choreographed *Children's Corner* and performed it at the Théâtre du Châtelet on 7 May. Debussy passed André Caplet the task of orchestrating this as well as *La boîte à joujoux*.

By 17 April Debussy had recovered. No sooner was he up and about than he agreed to accompany Ninon Vallin and play seven of his piano pieces at the Brussels home of Monsieur and Madame Wittouck on 28 April. Once again it was Emma who had to correspond with a businessman about financial matters before he left. She was proving resilient, not succumbing to weak health as an excuse for not carrying out these essential tasks. Three affectionate telegrams were sent by Debussy during this two-day absence from his wife.

D'Annunzio's 'illness'; Marguerite Long

Debussy's return to Paris coincided with renewed contact with Gabriele d'Annunzio. One thing the two men had in common was difficulty with creditors, but there is something slightly incongruous about this friendship, d'Annunzio being such an extrovert hedonist. According to the American writer Natalie Barney, that winter of 1913–4 d'Annunzio 'was all the rage. The women who had not slept with him became a laughing-stock'.[24] In March 1914 d'Annunzio announced in the social columns of newspapers that he would not be accepting invitations owing to an injury from playing hockey in the Italian ambassador's garden. He kept to his bed from March to May. In fact, the problem was more personal. He had been incapacitated by a sexually transmitted disease. Emma and Chouchou must have sympathised with his ostensible plight, for he wrote a charming letter to Chouchou thanking her profusely for the flowers she had sent him.[25] He had, he said, bought her some beautiful dolls, but on seeing them in their boxes at home had not sent them as they brought him such pleasure. They were therefore to be considered as being for both of them. One might say he gave her too much detail: he informed the little girl that he was already experiencing the first shivers of a raging fever he was expecting that afternoon. She should pray to

[22] C. pp. 1790–2.
[23] BnF Musique, La Debussy Emma 3 and 4.
[24] L. Hughes-Hallett, *The Pike*, London, 2013, p. 345.
[25] C. p. 805.

25. Marguerite Long as seen in *Musica*, December 1907

Music to cure him! He signed himself off to her, 'Le Sorcier à la barbiche jaune' ('the Wizard with the little yellow goatee'). Only a couple of days later Emma expressed her joy that he was better. 'No doubt in sympathy with you, Claude has also been ill, but now he has recovered.' Little did she know the truth about d'Annunzio's disease. He seemed to exert a power of attraction over her as over other women. She invited him to accompany them to a performance of Verdi's *Otello* on 5 May at the Théâtre des Champs-Élysées, which had recently re-opened for a season of productions imported from London and Boston. His reply to her rendered a poetic image of a convalescent walking somewhat unsteadily in the shade of trees: '… someone said that all illness is a musical problem. Actually only Music and Love can cure me.'[26] They met again at the opera on 24 May but could not sit next to each other as Debussy and Emma were being hosted by Misia Edwards.

The pianist Marguerite Long first encountered the Debussys in person in spring 1914. She organised a concert at the Conservatoire in aid of the charity *L'Entr'aide*

[26] C. p. 1808.

artistique in which Chevillard conducted the Orchestre Lamoureux in three works with her as soloist: Saint-Saëns' third piano concerto, *Symphonie sur un thème montagnard* by d'Indy and Fauré's *Ballade*. There was also the prelude to the fourth act of *Messidor* by Bruneau and Debussy's *Chansons de Bilitis* and *Le promenoir des deux amants* sung by Rose Féart – altogether a huge concert. Debussy himself accompanied his vocal works. According to Long's husband, Joseph de Marliave, it was Emma who persuaded Debussy to participate. When she phoned Long to tell her he had agreed, Emma said, 'Now, you know, you will have to play his piano music', adding Long was the only pianist they had heard who could play Debussy's music to the composer's liking. Emma invited her to come and study with him.[27] Long spent two Sundays in July working with Debussy on *L'isle joyeuse*, then the war intervened with devastating consequences. Her husband was killed on 24 August 1914, but his body was not identified until October. Long later remembered that 'it was that final Sunday, sitting next to Madame Debussy, my husband heard me play for the last time'.[28]

Spring progressed with constant financial problems, administrative matters concerning the prospective performance of *La boîte à joujoux* at the Opéra-Comique and forthcoming performances in June of *Pelléas et Mélisande*. D'Annunzio again corresponded warmly with Emma to express his emotions after hearing the opera, the charm of this 'ineffable music' now running through his veins. He even sent her a personal present, a whole demi-john of *Zagarella*, an orange flower water, which he said came from the estate of which he was *Seigneur* in Sardinia. He was suffering from a red eye, for which Emma thoughtfully provided some drops. He was also trying to organise a film of *Le martyre* in collaboration with a certain M. Péquin who was in Venice, and continued to correspond with her over negotiations for this project.[29] This would never come to fruition due to the financial demands of Ida Rubinstein and Monsieur Péquin. On Debussy's behalf Emma invited d'Annunzio to a performance of Wagner's *Tristan* on 11 June, but he declined due to illness.

There is no evidence in 1914 of any commemorative note or present from Debussy for Emma's special day on 4 June. He was having to argue his corner with the solicitor Maurice Martin, whose fee he was unable to pay in full, and he had to write to his sick mother's landlady to say she would moving out of her flat at 35 bis rue La Fontaine in Auteuil in October,[30] yet this remained Victorine Debussy's home address, as shown on her death certificate the following year.

Inspiration for composition was scarce. Grim events were taking place abroad. On 28 June Archduke Franz Ferdinand and his wife were assassinated in Sarajevo. On 11 July came the first evidence of recent compositional activity, even if not completely new, when Debussy wrote to Durand with the titles and sub-titles of six *Épigraphes antiques*, which he had expanded from incidental music for the *Chansons de Bilitis*, originally composed in 1901. He had wanted to make them into an orchestral suite,

---

[27] C. Dunoyer, *Marguerite Long. A Life in French Music*, Bloomington and Indianapolis, 1993, p. 59.
[28] M. Long, *Au piano avec Debussy*, Paris, 1960, p. 21.
[29] C. p. 1820.
[30] C. p. 1827.

but needing money so urgently he now asked Durand for three thousand francs for a four-hand piano version.[31] Accordingly he signed a contract for this amount on 15 July.

Debussy and Emma visit London

Soon Robert Godet, Debussy's Swiss friend, experienced the full force of Debussy's depression. The accident to his thumb, flu, shingles, his tension aggravated particularly by the latter, had all led to worry and troubles at home

> and times when one could really think of no other solution than suicide to escape it all … for a long time now, I have to confess, I have felt lost, terribly diminished. Where has the 'magician' gone that you so loved in me. He is no more than a performer of morose tricks who will soon collapse in a final clumsy pirouette.

He was soon to depart for London for a few days 'for reasons of domestic economy'.[32] He had been invited by Sir Edgar and Lady Speyer to conduct a private concert in London on 17 July. Emma was willing to travel with her husband on this brief visit, perhaps because the company and surroundings would be agreeable enough for her. They were accommodated at the Grosvenor Hotel from 16 to 19 July. There was a magnificent reception, which Debussy might have detested were it not for the great admiration and courtesy of all the guests, Emma later told Jean-Aubry.[33]

Home life in Paris was even more detestable to him on his return. On 29 July, the day Austria-Hungary declared war on Serbia, Debussy told Durand, 'Paris is becoming ever more repugnant to me and I would love to be able to leave for a short while. Literally, I can't go on! I'm tormented with problems in this house.'[34] Only Chouchou can have been spared some of this melancholy, being cheered up once again by her 'Wizard with the little yellow goatee'. D'Annunzio sent her a gift of a tiny bracelet weighing 'less than a flower', asking her to think of him when she wore it.[35] Another moment when Chouchou should have had reason to be happy was a visit with both her parents to the Bellevue home of Chouchik and Louis Laloy. She was disappointed, however. Chouchik wrote a card to her now six-year-old daughter Nicolette telling her that Chouchou had searched everywhere in the house for her and was very sad to discover that she was at their home in Rahon in the Jura. She had spent her time instead making sand pies alone, in the garden.[36]

---

[31] C. p. 1834.
[32] C. p. 1836.
[33] C. p. 1836 n.3.
[34] C. p. 1840.
[35] C. p. 1839.
[36] Laloy archives, B13, Dossier 17, 436.1.

Outbreak of war

On 1 August Debussy invoked as a reason for not having paid his tailor for bespoke clothing: 'illness which has prevented me from any work for three months'. The situation as the country mobilised was also aggravating matters.[37] Two days later Germany declared war on France. On 8 August Debussy expressed to Durand his frustration at possessing no inclination for anything concerned with the military. Never had he handled a gun, he exclaimed, and something else inhibited his enthusiasm for any warlike state of mind – the memories of 1870, when his father had been given a four-year prison sentence for fighting in support of the Paris Commune.[38] He was disturbed. 'My life is both intense and troubled. I am nothing more than a miserable atom being tossed around by this terrible cataclysm. Everything I do seems so terribly petty. It makes me envy Satie who is taking on defending Paris as a corporal.'[39] Amongst all the catastrophes he was dreading was a total lack of money. He revealed that Emma had only received half of her alimony from Sigismond Bardac. This was because 'she had to give money to her daughter [Dolly] to go to her sister-in-law's in Normandy'. Presumably this arrangement only applied to one instalment of Emma's allowance. It seems extraordinary, however, that the wealthy Bardacs and de Tinans could not cover this expenditure. That she had only received half the money implies it had been taken at source. Sigismond Bardac was obviously unwilling to fund these costs incurred by his and Emma's daughter. Considering Sigismond's alimony covered the rent for the house, this was a serious depletion of the Debussys' budget.[40]

Ten days later Debussy expressed a xenophobic gratitude that foreign workers (he used the disparaging word 'métèques') had either been shot or expelled from Paris, leading to it immediately becoming a charming place.[41] The best he himself could do would be to man a barricade, which he would do without hesitation if necessary. In fact he had joined a committee formed by Albert Dalimier to look after the wives and children of orchestral musicians who had gone off to war.[42]

Emma and Debussy go to Angers; Raoul Bardac in hospital

There is a gap in Debussy's correspondence between 18 and 31 August, a time of huge anxiety for all French citizens, for the French army was in retreat and fear was growing of the imminent arrival of German forces in Paris. For the sake of Emma's nerves, on

---

[37] C. p. 1841.

[38] Only after his wife's pleadings had he been freed after a year and had his civil rights suspended for a further four years. Debussy had hidden this fact about his background from his friends, yet it must surely have had an irrevocable effect on him as he was only eight years old at the time.

[39] Satie served in the Home Guard in his local area, Arceuil.

[40] C. p. 1842.

[41] An exaggeration. Some foreigners were evacuated to other departments prior to being moved into internment camps.

[42] C. p. 1843–4.

31 August Debussy wrote to Arthur Fontaine, whom he had known prior to his marriage to Emma, asking for advice on what to do in view of the grave circumstances. He must have heeded Fontaine's reply, for the next letter addressed to Durand on 21 September was from Angers in the department of Maine-et-Loire. The official pass permitting Debussy and four other people to travel there by train was dated 5 September,[43] two days after the government had moved its headquarters from Paris to Bordeaux. Debussy emphasised that it was his wife's fear that had driven them out of the city. He would rather have stayed put. To make matters worse, he suffered a bout of enteritis which kept him in bed for six days, 'in addition to my usual little troubles'. For two months he had written not one note of music nor touched a piano. Although not significant in the grand scale of things, 'at my age time lost is lost for ever'. In particular it was the Durands' departure for Bel-Ebat without saying goodbye which had made Emma force Debussy to leave the city, 'a departure which for me was like committing suicide'. Now he was hoping to persuade Emma to return to Paris in a few days' time. Anything was better than hanging around in Angers.[44]

Emma had the double worry of both her son Raoul and son-in-law, Gaston de Tinan, being in the army. On 4 August, only one day after mobilisation, Raoul wrote to Louis Laloy to tell him he was in the 19th Squadron of the *Train des Équipages*, (École Militaire de Paris). 'Give a thought from time to time to *Le songeur*,' (that *drame lyrique* he and Laloy were working on together[45]), he begged him.[46] The *Train* organised logistics, transport and movements of the army. On 16 August he told Laloy he had been sent to Versailles to await departure for an unspecified destination. 'I am thinking of you, of you all, of *Le songeur* … of projects, so many projects … '[47]

Debussy told Durand that Emma was receiving regular news of both her son and son-in-law. Yet this was not as straightforward as it would seem. On 6 September 1914 Erik Satie wrote to Raoul at the military hospital in Melun, asking him to write to his mother to reassure her that he was well. It was noted earlier that Raoul's military career was interrupted by bouts of illness, including trouble with his lungs.[48] Now Satie told him that there were rumours that he had been seriously injured. 'I hope, dear friend, that this is not true'.[49] It is significant that it was Emma who had asked Satie to write to Raoul on her behalf, believing Raoul would more readily give the details to him rather than to her. Whether this was because Raoul's relationship with his mother had cooled, or it was simply that he would not want to worry her, is a moot point. Raoul's music had been performed from time to time prior to the outbreak of war, for the music critic Émile Vuillermoz had written two reviews in *Comœdia*, one on 23 March 1914, the audience having given a warm reception to *Les heures*, performed at the Concerts Monteux, and another on 18 May, when he

---

[43] BnF Musique, Nla-32 (Bis).
[44] C. p. 1846.
[45] See Chapter 13 p. 193.
[46] Laloy archives, B12, Dossier 35, no.3.
[47] Laloy archives, B12, Dossier 35, no.4.
[48] See Chapter 8 p. 117.
[49] *Erik Satie. Correspondance Presque complete*, ed. O. Volta, Paris, 2000, p. 205.

26. Raoul Bardac at Melun, 1914

commented on the first performance of Bardac's *Horizons*. Vuillermoz appreciated these compositions and regretted Bardac's reticence, which he ascribed to refined taste and modesty. Louis Schneider commented on a performance of a song, *Simone*, at the SMI, saying that it revealed a likeable, elegant musician of a gentle nature.[50]

Raoul wrote to Louis Laloy on 1 October to inform him of his condition, listing all the places he had had to drive to in his military role, his total exhaustion and his transfer to the *Hôpital mixte* in Melun, where English and German soldiers were also arriving. Once he had recovered sufficiently he worked as nurse, interpreter and cyclist, even applying dressings, but, he added, this was nothing compared to the sufferings of others.[51] Debussy and Emma did indeed travel to the hospital to visit him, where they found he was certainly in no state to fight.[52] His military record

---

[50] *Le Gaulois*, 10 March 1914.
[51] Laloy archives, B12, Dossier 35, no.5.
[52] C. p. 1852.

shows that he was suffering from tuberculosis in the upper right lung.[53] Raoul in turn was struck by Debussy's appearance. To him it was obvious that his illness had progressed. He looked worn out and clearly experienced pain when walking.[54]

Return to Paris

By 30 September the Debussys had returned to Paris. In letters to Durand, Nicolas Coronio and Paul Dukas, Debussy explained that one of the main factors leading to their self-imposed evacuation had been the bombs dropped by German Taube ('Dove') aircraft, beginning on 30 August 1914. This had contributed to Emma's terror, but in the end the expense of the journey and primitive, flea-ridden accommodation besides their discomfort in the provincial town had not been worth the effort. He was overwhelmed by the barbarity of the Germans and the senseless damage to Leuven, Mechelen and, in particular, Rheims Cathedral. He revealed a fast-growing sense of patriotism in comments about Richard Strauss, Arnold Schoenberg and Richard Wagner, the latter having merely summarised centuries of music in a formula which was something 'only a German could have attempted'. Now it was time for the French to act: 'French art must take revenge just as seriously as the French army does!'[55] A germ of his own version of French art was already expressed on the very pass used for travelling from Paris to Angers and back. Both sides are covered with sketched musical staves and notes, which eventually became one of the piano *Études*, the 'Étude pour les notes répétées'.[56]

Durand meanwhile gave Debussy the task of editing Chopin's piano works for his new all-French editions of the classics. Debussy wanted to express his patriotic support of the French nation by writing 'une marche héroïque', but was instinctively aware of the hypocritical nature of sounding heroic whilst sitting impotently at home. However, on 19 November 1914 he signed a contract for a *Berceuse héroïque* for piano, as a tribute to King Albert 1 of the Belgians and his soldiers. This was part of a project conceived by Hall Caine of the *Daily Telegraph*, eventually published on 4 January 1915. Describing it to Godet on 1 January as a contribution to *King Alfred's Book*, Debussy found it a challenge, for he felt restricted by the proximity of the German army. The Belgian national anthem did not stir patriotic thoughts in his breast and he had a sense of inferiority at his inability to use a gun.[57] This frustration was expressed repeatedly. He wrote on 22 December, '... this war, which I can't get personally involved in for miserable reasons, troubles my life more than I can politely say. Being prevented from taking action has

---

[53] 'Baccillose pulmonaire sommet droit', Paris Archives, *Registres matricules du recrutement*, Cote D4R1 1186.

[54] R. Bardac, *Causerie sur les dernières années de Claude Debussy*, Centre de Documentation Claude Debussy, RESE 05.15.

[55] C. pp. 1848–51.

[56] BnF Musique Nla-32 (bis).

[57] C. p. 1862.

repercussions on my thoughts making me incapable of concentrating, and anyway they seem superficial and useless.'[58]

His own national anthem, the *Marseillaise*, did rouse his emotions. He had already used a passage from this in 'Feux d'artifice', the last of the second book of *Préludes*, published in 1913, and now he quoted the same passage, 'Aux armes citoyens, Formez vos …' in his Christmas message to Emma dated 25 December 1914. No pretty yuletide card this year, but a musical manuscript prefaced with a note saying, 'For Christmas 1914. With no pretentions. To replace the "Christmas-Card".' It comprised twenty-seven bars for a chorus of voices in the street singing that snippet of the *Marseillaise*, then solo baritone with piano accompaniment. The text asked Emma's permission to sing to her words which were

> sweeter than honey! Christmas for *ma petite Mienne*. In this year of war may she enclose my love in her arms which gently bind us together more strongly than chains. (Trumpet calls on the ramparts). What does war matter, what do trumpet calls matter, when you are there! That it is my war and all its victories.[59]

Meanwhile, the nearest member of the family in active service, Raoul Bardac, was still at the hospital in Melun, from where he wrote to Louis Laloy complaining of an eye infection and exhaustion. He believed he would be working there for the duration of the war.[60]

---

[58] C. p. 1857.
[59] C. pp. 1858–61.
[60] Laloy archives, B12, Dossier 35, no.6.

15

1915: Patriotism and love awakened

Anxiety, patriotism and frustration at not being able to participate meaningfully in the war had an effect on Debussy similar to that of his journeys abroad and contributed to a reawakening of fervour for his wife. Now in his enforced confinement at home he was moved to express intense emotions to her and also the desire to compose. On 1 January 1915 Emma received a New Year's greeting in the form of an English greetings card which he admitted was banal, but contained all his love which existed for her alone, 'mon amour – qui n'existe que pour toi'.[1]

Stirrings of patriotism fuelled a longing to return to 'la clarté française'. Raoul Bardac believed it was Debussy's determination not to let his illness beat him that led to his desire to contribute in his own way to the war effort by re-creating truly French music.[2] On 6 January Debussy told Vallery-Radot he had begun to write in what he called the 'true' eighteenth-century style of Rameau. He echoed this ambition to the conductor Bernadino Molinari a few days later, saying it was necessary to guide French music back to its 'true path' from which, since Rameau, outside influences had led it astray.[3]

Domestic concerns since the outbreak of war were confined to caring for his close family, following Emma's wishes, visiting Raoul and going to the Cinéma des Champs-Élysées in January to please Chouchou, where they saw *Calvaire d'une reine*, starring the popular actor and comedian Max Linder. However, financial matters came to the fore once again with a reprise of correspondence between Debussy and the lawyer dealing with his loans. His debts were spiralling, and he was being pursued by a Monsieur Lelarge, whom he wished would 'take into account the situation we are in at the moment, one which affects artists just as severely as others'.[4] The current agreement needed the cooperation of the Bardac Bank, since the money Emma received from Sigismond was being used as a guarantee for the loan. In fact, things got so serious that Lelarge threatened Debussy with producing evidence that he could claim a whole year of the Bardac allowance, which, he maintained, was a seizable asset. On 20 February Lelarge acknowledged receipt of seven hundred francs but at the same time notified Debussy of a further five thousand five hundred francs of outstanding debt.[5]

---

[1] C. p. 1862.
[2] R. Bardac, *Causerie sur les dernières années de Claude Debussy*, Centre de Documentation Claude Debussy, RESE-05.15.
[3] C. pp. 1865–6.
[4] C. p. 1869.
[5] C. pp. 1875–6.

The five hundred francs Debussy had received from Durand on 11 February for his work on the Chopin edition was but a small contribution to this.

Chouchou's piano lessons and Raoul's dedication to her

Erik Satie continued to lunch with Emma and Claude. He confirmed to Emma on 31 January in his typically elaborately embellished hand that he was coming the next day, but perhaps she had not received the message since she had been in the company of some 'douces demoiselles' (sweet young ladies), probably her granddaughters. He commented that Chouchou was playing the piano very well now – 'Better than me'.[6] This was despite the fact that she found conditions for practice less than ideal. Chouchou once complained to Marguerite Long that 'Papa wants me to practise but he wants complete silence in the house for his work. So how can I?'[7] In fact Chouchou attended piano lessons with Long. In a conversation between Madeleine Milhaud and Roger Nichols, Madame Milhaud explained, 'His daughter was following the same piano lessons as myself with Marguerite Long. Debussy sometimes came to pick her up …'[8] Long did not mention these lessons in her book *Au piano avec Claude Debussy*, but commented simply that she had heard Chouchou playing 'Le petit berger' from *Children's Corner* and found it a very moving experience as she played so like her father. A few years later Chouchou was sitting next to Long when she was playing 'Hommage à Rameau'. The young girl's impressive attention to detail was evident when she commented on a missing G sharp. 'Already meticulous, just like her father!'[9]

Raoul Bardac was still working as a nurse in the hospital in Melun,[10] and from there sent a copy of his composition *Une semaine musicale* to his little step-sister. This collection of seven pieces for piano bore the dedication 'pour Chouchou'. Debussy wrote to his 'cher Rara' on 10 March to acknowledge this gift, of which Chouchou was very proud and which had touched him deeply, praising the pleasant, spiritual quality of Raoul's music.

Deaths of two mothers; ramifications with Laloys

When Debussy developed influenza in February, he described his condition as being like 'a little village after it has been visited by the Boches'.[11] At the same time, he was concerned for his mother's health. On 22 March 1915 he told d'Annunzio

---

[6] C. p. 1872.

[7] C. Dunoyer, *Marguerite Long. A Life in French Music 1874–1966*, p. 61.

[8] R. Nichols, *Conversations with Madeleine Milhaud*, London, 1996, p. 12. I am grateful to Roger Nichols for correspondence on this matter.

[9] M. Long, *Au piano avec Claude Debussy*, Paris, 1960, pp. 95–6.

[10] 5ᵉ Sect. d'Infirmiers, Paris Archives, *Registres matricules du recrutement*, Côte D4R1 1186.

[11] C. pp. 1872, 1874.

he could not leave her bedside. The following day she passed away.[12] He informed many friends and acquaintances, but one of the most personal comments was to Gabriel Pierné. 'You are', he wrote, 'the only one of my old friends whom she cared to remember'.[13] The funeral took place at Notre-Dame d'Auteuil on Monday 29 March. Only about thirty people attended, which accorded with Debussy's wishes. Debussy was 'très démoli' (completely shattered), wrote Dukas.[14]

Even though unwell, Emma made a contribution to the war effort by being a member of the committee of the charity 'Le vêtement du blessé' ('Clothes for the wounded'). To raise funds, she organised a concert on 24 April 1915, for which Debussy composed a piano piece *Pour le vêtement du blessé*, the manuscript of which was auctioned immediately afterwards. He also accompanied Claire Croiza in several of his songs. He did not sound too happy about having to participate in this event in a letter to Pierné where he 'curses' this concert: 'je maudis le concert'.[15]

On 1 May Debussy sent Emma greetings. This year he needed to show sympathy with his wife, for on 29 April her mother Laure had died aged eighty-five. In less than two months they had both lost their mothers. His greeting read: 'In spite of so much gloom! Fresh, pretty May for you, even so. Claude Debussy's *Petite Mienne!*'[16] Laure Moyse's home address was given on the death certificate as 3 rue du Colisée, that Bardac address attributed to her at the time of both of Emma's marriages.

On Saturday 1 May and Sunday 2 May 1915 the announcement appeared in the newspapers that Laure's funeral would take place on 2 May at the cemetery of Montmartre, where Osiris was buried.[17] It was to be an intimate family affair. Monsieur and Madame Debussy and their daughter (Chouchou), Raoul Bardac and Monsieur and Madame Gaston de Tinan (Dolly and her husband) placed the notice as well as Marcelle Weil, Laure's granddaughter, Emma's niece. What can Emma's emotions have been as she returned to the great tomb, the monumental statue of Moses, where her mother's name was already engraved on a plaque? Thus Laure fulfilled her brother's wish that in death he should be surrounded by close family members, something Emma would not do, despite her name being indelibly carved in stone.

On 12 May Emma wrote to Chouchik Laloy, whom she described as 'like a young sister I love'. We learn that her mother's breathing, which had been so troublesome from pneumonia, had calmed down near the end and she had died peacefully in Emma's arms.[18] In fact Chouchik, in Rahon in the Jura, had already heard of Laure's death from her husband on 3 May. Louis Laloy sounded grudging when he told her of Madame Moyse's burial, saying that since no one had thought to inform him of

---

[12] C. p. 1882.

[13] C. p. 1884.

[14] C. p. 1889 n.1.

[15] C. p. 1893.

[16] 'Malgré tant de noir! Tendre et joli Mai pour toi quand même. Petite Mienne à Claude Debussy! 1 Mai 1915'. C. p. 1893.

[17] *Le Matin*, 1 May 1915; *Le Temps*, 2 May 1915.

[18] C. p. 1894.

the event he had not attended it.[19] Chouchik made some very pointed comments in her reply. She told Louis to send his sympathies and say he had received the date of the funeral too late to be able to attend. How telling that she then referred to Emma as 'la pauvre *mère Claude*' ('poor mother Claude') as if this were her normal nomenclature. 'Poor *mère Claude* must be sick with grief, for she was very attached to her mother, as a true little Jewish woman can be attached to her birth mother, physically painful ties,'[20] wrote Chouchik. She added that she hoped that good *mère Moyse* would leave the Debussys a million francs if she had not already made arrangements for everything to go to her grandchildren and charities, since she mistrusted her son-in-law, even hated him. She was very devout.[21] The startling implication here is that Laure Moyse disapproved of, even disliked her daughter's second husband. Was it Louis Laloy or Emma herself who had made Chouchik aware of this antipathy? It is not mentioned elsewhere. If Laure knew of allegations of Debussy's attraction towards his step-daughter Dolly, she might have had reason. There is also the false assumption that being Jewish, Laure Moyse possessed great wealth.

By 5 May Louis Laloy had still heard nothing from either Emma or her husband. 'So much for them,' he commented, clearly offended by the lack of communication from the Debussys.[22] He told his wife to write to *la mère Claude* without mentioning him. Rara (Raoul) had asked to meet him on Saturday (8 May). 'It's he who will tell me the news'.[23] By 10 May Rara had passed on Laloy's apologies to Claude and Emma. Emma's mother had not been ill when the Debussys had neglected to reply to his offer to have lunch with them. This, Laloy told Chouchik, was 'a customary lack of manners on their part, but one which I do not accept.'[24] Surely Emma would have been mortified had she known of Laloy's disgust at their perceived attitude and his attribution of bad manners as a normal state of affairs to both of them.

Chouchik tried to pacify Louis, saying that when she had seen 'poor Mother Moyse' on the Thursday before her death she was already ill, so all could be explained. 'Pauvre Claude' ('Poor Claude') must have been completely overcome by all the illness and stress around him. She was sure he was not being intentionally rude. 'But you haven't told me what Raoul said to you'.[25] Raoul, however, had not asked to meet Laloy in order to inform him of Laure's death. Laloy wrote, 'Rara told me nothing, except that his father had reduced his allowance to 1/3rd, therefore

---

[19] Laloy archives, B12, Dossier 19, 1915, 254.31.

[20] 'La pauvre mère Claude doit être malade de chagrin, car elle a été attachée à sa mère comme une vraie petite juive peut être attaché a sa génératrice, les liens physiquement douloureux.' Laloy archives, B, Dossier 10, 1915–27, 115.

[21] 'Mais j'espère au moins, qu'elle les dotera d'un million, si toute fois, se méfiant de son gendre, tant détesté, l'aïeule israélite s'est arrangée de façon à ce que tout passe à ses petits-enfants et aux œuvres de charité, car elle était très pieuse …' Ibid.

[22] Laloy archives, B12, Dossier 19, 1915, 254.33.

[23] Laloy archives, B12, Dossier 19, 257.34.

[24] 'C'est une grossièreté bien naturelle de leur part, mais que je n'accepte pas.' Laloy archives, B12, Dossier 19, 1915. 261.38.

[25] Laloy archives, B13, Dossier 10, no.123.

theirs [Emma's] as well.'[26] Laloy was implying that Raoul received regular money from his father which had been reduced in view of his inheritance from Osiris, which would now come into force. He also believed Emma's payments had been reduced, although no reason was given. Osiris's will had stipulated that upon the death of her mother Emma should receive an annuity of five thousand francs per annum. Perhaps Sigismond had reduced his alimony payments in the knowledge that Emma would now benefit from this inheritance.

On 5 May, when Debussy acknowledged his customary gift of flowers from Vallery-Radot commemorating the première of *Pelléas*, he told him he missed both his mother and mother-in-law almost to the same degree. Both were 'aimables et bonnes' (kind and good). He clearly did not reciprocate Laure Moyse's antipathy towards him. His feeling of uselessness was growing. He described the expressions of sympathy expressed by those around him as 'rather ridiculous'.[27]

This year he remembered Emma's special day on 4 June on time. The message was heartfelt and romantic. 'I cannot find any new ways of expressing my love because it is "*un*", unique, in the sense that nothing can compare with it and in it is contained the beauty and hope of my whole life.'[28] He was, he said, writing intentionally on blue paper, implying that was to give his words the weight of a mock legal document.[29] Emma also received a copy of the manuscript he had composed for the charity auction, saying 'Here are some flowers of war …' with a dedication 'Pour le "vêtement" de ma petite Mienne, son Claude' ('For clothing my own Little One'). This was eventually published in 1933 as *Page d'album*.

Pourville

Desperate for a break from Paris, on 19 May Debussy managed to obtain an official pass (*sauf conduit*) for the family to travel to Dieppe and back,[30] their first holiday since 1913. He was working on the French edition of Bach Sonatas for Durand, but hoped there was no rush for this as he had some ideas for a composition of his own. After the prolonged drought which the war had imposed on his brain, he needed to get away as soon as possible. 'The house has been weighing me down for a long time'.[31] He was thinking of pieces for two pianos and a projected *Fêtes galantes*, a collaboration with Charles Morice which would not materialise. Another factor was that Chouchou had chickenpox and could do with fresh air. Typically, she was 'dramatising' her illness! How typical of Debussy that he should end a letter to Durand with the reminder not to forget 'poor Claude's poverty',[32] which resulted in an advance of two thousand francs

---

[26] 'Rara ne m'a rien dit, sinon que son père avait réduit sa pension au 1/3, donc la leur aussi.' Laloy archives, B12, Dossier 19, 1915. 265.42.

[27] C. p. 1894.

[28] C. p. 1900.

[29] Blue paper was used by the *huissier de justice*, the legal officer who served court orders.

[30] BnF Musique, Nla32bis.

[31] C. p. 1904.

[32] C. p. 1906.

from his publisher. On 9 July he signed a contract for *Caprices en blanc et noir*, which would appear on 31 December 1915 as *En blanc et noir*.

Emma and Debussy were relieved to return to the villa 'Mon Coin' in Pourville near Dieppe from 12 July until 12 October 1915, now without Laure or Dolly. Here they felt at home, having stayed in Pourville in 1904 and 1907. Needing the consolation of familiarity, Debussy placed Arkel, the large wooden toad named after the character in his opera, on his desk, a talisman which he believed brought him good luck. He loved being by the sea again despite constant rain, and the sound of church bells reminded him of the scene in *Pelléas* where Pelléas sees children running down to the beach to play.[33] He lightened the tone of the second of his *Caprices*, perhaps owing to the lightening of his own mood. On 22 July he sent Durand that piece, which symbolically quotes both Luther's hymn *Ein feste Burg* and *La Marseillaise*, the latter, at first barely audible, coming to dominate the former. He also sent what he described as a 'prospectus' for six sonatas for various instruments, to be composed by Claude Debussy, *musicien français*. Emma was suffering from rheumatism, but Chouchou was her usual energetic self, 'like a young animal'.[34]

There was little to distract Debussy from composition and he was now in full flow. On 1 August, he told Durand he would soon be sending him the proofs of the Cello Sonata. He was becoming more and more obsessed by the horrors of war, the wider involvement of other countries and, in particular, the waste of young lives being senselessly mown down by '*Kultur* merchants'. Patriotically, he was paying 'secret homage' to the young men who had given their lives. He was much concerned with the proportions of the music in both the *Caprices* (*En blanc et noir*) and the Cello Sonata and in particular with clearing the atmosphere of poisonous vapours induced by Luther's chorale (what it represented, not the tune itself). He was also working on the piano *Études*,[35] which he finished by 12 August. Chouchou was enjoying messing around in rock pools. Debussy ascribed Emma's illness to the fact that she was a 'town' lady used to breathing cosmopolitan air. Whilst she did not dislike the sea, it was too unrefined for her,[36] a hint of his awareness of her previous role in 'society'. This did not prevent him from dedicating to her the manuscript of his study 'Pour les sixtes', not for her birthday on 10 July, but for his own on 22 August, 'For you, petite Mienne, this "Study" whilst waiting for the others and to wish myself Happy Birthday. Are you not my only earthly possession and the beauty of my inner life?'[37]

Debussy's many letters to Durand during this stay in Pourville attest to his horror of war, and to the 'love and faith' he put into the *Studies*.[38] He was also grateful for the return of his faculty to think and work in the peaceful atmosphere of Mon Coin. He

---

[33] Act III scene 3.

[34] C. pp. 1910–1.

[35] C. p. 1915–7.

[36] C. p. 1921.

[37] 'Pour toi, petite Mienne, cette "étude", en attendant les autres et pour me souhaiter mon anniversaire … N'est-tu pas, mon seul bien terrestre et la beauté de ma vie morale? Ton ClDebussy' C. p. 1923.

[38] C. p. 1925.

27. Gaston de Tinan in uniform

would have loved to buy the property. The 'factories of nothingness' had become a distant memory. 'When I think of the Nothingness of last year I get a shiver down my spine. I am frightened of going back to Paris and returning to the factory of nothingness my study had become!' The contract for the Cello Sonata was signed on 9 August 1915 and that for the *Études* on 3 September.

Despite his peaceful surroundings, Debussy still bore Raoul Bardac in his thoughts and wanted his Chopin edition dedicated to his step-son. Raoul now held the post of *Secrétaire infirmier* to the Chief Medical Officer at the Military Hospital in Melun.[39] At some point in 1915 Debussy sent a certain Lucien (unspecified) the address of Dolly's husband: 'Monsieur Gaston de Tinan, interprète, 10th Hussars, 3rd Cavalry Division, British Expeditionary Force.'[40] This implies that de Tinan, an interpreter, accompanied the British Expeditionary Force to the front line where the 10th Hussars joined the third Cavalry Division fighting on the Western Front in some of the hardest-fought battles, including Antwerp and Ypres.

On 19 September Debussy wrote to Dr. Crépel simply to keep in touch. He was delighted to tell him of his own new-found energy and desire to compose, wondering if it was due to the peace and fresh air or perhaps to the homeopathic remedy Pareira-Brava (for urinary and prostate problems). Emma, however, did not know how to cope with her terrible headaches and intolerable pains behind the eyes, no longer relieved by the adrenaline he had prescribed.

---

[39] C. p. 1932.
[40] C. p. 1963.

Debussy was dreading his return to Paris planned for 12 October. Having 'rediscovered' music he could not bear the thought of bidding the sea or the beautiful silence in Pourville farewell.[41] Paris was like an open-air prison.[42] He told the Italian conductor Molinari that he had completed not only the *Études* and Cello Sonata but also the Sonata for Flute, Viola and Harp in his rush of inspiration, just two of the six sonatas he intended to compose. However, Arkel soon had to go back into his box whilst Debussy hurried to write down all he could, right up until the moment of departure. Before they left, a letter arrived from Stravinsky bearing good wishes to Debussy, Chouchou and Emma.

Chouchou's Birthday Book; Debussy's operation

On returning to Paris, Debussy assured Robert Godet he had not forgotten the war whilst in that nondescript little place where he had rediscovered the ability to compose, endeavouring to recreate some of the beauty being destroyed with meticulous brutality by the Germans. Again he advocated a return to the style of Rameau and the old French harpsichordists who made 'real music', containing the secret of profound grace, 'emotion without epilepsy'.[43] He reiterated similar thoughts in his reply to Stravinsky, at the same time urging him to remain a 'great Russian artist'. He himself had been writing nothing but 'pure' music whilst by the sea, twelve studies, two sonatas for various instruments 'in our old style'. Emma was still suffering from dreadful pains in the eyes and chronic rheumatism. Chouchou had a cold which, he insisted, she was exaggerating in order to attract attention.[44]

A week later, on 19 October Debussy signed a contract with Durand for the Sonata for Flute, Viola and Harp. On 25 October his *Berceuse héroïque* was performed by the combined orchestras of the Concerts Colonne and Lamoureux, conducted by Camille Chevillard, but sadly the interpretation lacked expression, Debussy complained.[45] Perhaps no one could have performed it with the depth of feeling he had experienced whilst composing it.

When Debussy had needed a loan of a large sum of money two years earlier, he had turned to *L'Avenir du Proletariat*. Circumstances must have dictated his return to this organisation, for the inventory of his liabilities after his death indicated that he contracted a loan for thirty thousand francs on 29 October 1915.[46] At a rate of twenty-five French francs to the pound, this converts to approximately £124,170 today,[47] a staggering amount. There is no mention of this in his correspondence.

---

[41] C. pp. 1937, 1939.

[42] C. p. 1941.

[43] C. pp. 1947–8.

[44] C. pp. 1952–3.

[45] C. p. 1954.

[46] D. Herlin, 'An Artist High and Low, or, Debussy and Money,' in *Rethinking Debussy*, ed. E. Antokoletz and M. Wheeldon, Oxford, 2011, p. 197.

[47] https://www.in2013dollars.com (last accessed 3 November 2020).

A charming reminder of Chouchou's tenth birthday on 30 October survives in the form of the *'Little Folks' Birthday Book*. This small volume bound in red leather with gold lettering bears a handwritten inscription in English,

To dear Chouchou
From
Maman
October 1915

Nursery rhymes and poems are printed on every page for each day and Chouchou has carefully filled in her relations' and friends' birthdays, including her cousins Françoise and Madeleine de Tinan, Rara, her parents and her cousin Marcelle. But most intriguing are her entries for 4 and 6 June. The first reads *'Sainte Emma'* and the second *'Saint Claude'*. The significance of that date, 4 June, has already been questioned, and now we find that Chouchou has been led to believe it is a Saint's Day to be celebrated for her mother. No such day exists in official calendars so the conclusion must be drawn that it was simply a date given that appellation by her parents. On the other hand, conveniently, Debussy's day, Saint Claude, was celebrated officially on 6 June.

Emma was still suffering on 23 November when Debussy commented to Durand that, whilst not feeling better, he could be a lot worse. A few days later, however, he was brutally honest to Fauré when he excused himself from supervising entrance examinations to the Conservatoire. The one day he had managed to attend had completely exhausted him and left him 'suffering like a dog'.[48] That day was 26 November, which hardly surprisingly had left its mark on Debussy, for he had also had an official diagnosis from two doctors of cancer of the rectum. Four days later he wrote to Gheusi, director of the Opéra-Comique, regretting not having been able to meet him, explaining that he was to undergo an operation to relieve 'some annoying little things which cause me abominable suffering'.[49] Yet he still went to the home of Jacques Durand, where he played *En blanc et noir* with Louis Aubert at the second piano. He was so intent on achieving the interpretation he desired that he practised with Aubert for three hours.[50] On 4 December he signed the contract for two versions of the song for which he had written both words and music, *Noël des enfants qui n'ont plus de maison*, one for solo voice and piano, the second for children's choir and piano. On 6 December he informed Durand his operation was to take place the next day. His wry sense of humour had not deserted him. 'I did not have time to send out invitations. Next time I will try to remember to do so'.[51]

It is difficult to imagine how Emma coped with this dreadful turn of events, to what extent she could be a moral support to her husband when she herself succumbed so easily to stress. At eleven o'clock the night before his operation Debussy wrote her a moving letter telling her,

[48] C. p. 1957.
[49] C. p. 1958.
[50] J. Durand, *Quelques souvenirs d'un éditeur de musique*, vol.1, pp. 124–5.
[51] C. p. 1959.

> As one never knows what the outcome might be of the simplest event, I want to tell you one last time how much I love you, and how awful it would be if any sort of accident prevented me from achieving all I wanted to do to ensure your happiness, now and in the future.
> And you, who will always be my *petite Mienne*, love me in our little Chouchou ... you are the only two beings for whose sake I do not want to leave this life altogether.[52]

His sense of fatality led him to spend hours before the operation tearing up bits of paper with musical ideas and sketches, 'such precious bits of paper', wrote Emma many years later to Arthur Hartmann.[53] He obviously wanted to leave nothing he deemed unworthy of future attention or, as Roy Howat suggested, 'it could be conjectured that the few sketches that remain are those that divulge no secrets', no clues as to his methods of composition.[54]

The cancer had progressed too far for a cure, but despite exhaustion and discomfort, Debussy had the strength to write by hand a dedication to Emma of the *Noël des enfants qui n'ont plus de maison*. Dated 23 December, the inscription on the cover reads,

> The little Belgians, the little Serbs, the little Poles, as well as Claude Debussy wish you the most beautiful Christmas. I would have liked to have done better, but wickedly illness has blown its breath over my plans! Pardon my sorrow at being so incapable, except for my love and grateful affection. Your Claude.[55]

On 27 December Emma received a second dedication, this time of *En blanc et noir*, reading, 'For the private collection of *ma petite Mienne*, with all Claude's heart, the rest of him being under repair at the moment'.[56] He had not lost the ability to cloak his pain with a sardonic comment, despite the fact that he had the added discomfort of rectitis. He told Durand of this latest complication,[57] and mentioned it again in his last published letter of 1915 to Paul Dukas, sending his condolences for the death of Dukas' father. The sad end to the year was not enlivened by any extant note or greeting to Emma.

Marriage of Raoul Bardac

An event happened on 23 December 1915 of which neither Emma nor Debussy seem to have had any inkling. Raoul Bardac married Yvonne Marie Albertine Mabille at the community centre of the tenth arrondissement in Paris at 3.30p.m. Both he and his wife-to-be registered the same address, 14 rue de Dieu, so perhaps were living

---

[52] C. p. 1960.
[53] A. Hartmann, *Claude Debussy as I knew him*, letter from Emma to Hartmann, pp. 165–9.
[54] R. Howat, *Debussy in Proportion. A musical analysis*, Cambridge, 1983, p. 6.
[55] BnF Musique, Rés Vma-291.
[56] 'Pour la Collection particulière de ma petite Mienne ... avec tout le cœur de Claude, le reste étant momentanément en réparation. Claude Debussy. 27 Dec. 1915.' BnF, Musique, RES Vma-294.
[57] C. p. 1961.

together prior to the marriage. She had no profession, was born in Neufchâtel-en-Bray (Seine-Inférieure) on 12 September 1881, so was just six months younger than Raoul. The marriage certificate states his father Sigismond's address as 55 avenue Hoche. His mother is declared as Emma Léa Moyse, no profession, of 80 avenue du Bois de Boulogne. Raoul had no family members as witnesses, his own being Charles Leforestier, 41, *négociant*, 25 rue de Poissy, Saint-Germain (Seine et Oise) and Constant Dupré, 39, *commis des postes* (post office clerk). Yvonne's were Alfred Jacques Germain, 59, *industriel*, and Marie Bernard aged 61, who was an *artiste-peintre* and who lived at the same address as the couple. Perhaps even his father did not know of this event. There was certainly no grand ceremony. Ravel's description of Raoul as 'distant' was still appropriate. In his occasional letters to him Ravel always addressed him formally as 'vous' rather than 'tu'. From Ravel's letters it becomes clear that he had known Raoul's wife for some years, as from 1908 onwards he always asked to be remembered to 'Yvonne'.[58] The couple had therefore known each other for at least seven years.

---

[58] *Maurice Ravel. L'Intégrale*, ed. M. Cornejo, Paris, 2018, pp. 182, 257, 311.

16

1916: Debussy's treatment and mounting concerns

Given his state of health, it is hardly surprising there was no message from Debussy to Emma at the beginning of 1916. He did find the strength to write a long letter to Robert Godet on 4 January. It is significant that the *House of Usher* was once again at the front of Debussy's mind, as so often when he was in a black mood. He regretted not just the unpleasant effects of his illness and operation, but the interruption to the flow of this work, which he had been hoping to complete. We also learn that Stravinsky had visited him whilst in Paris to conduct his *Firebird*, and had expressed gratitude to Debussy for helping him to 'climb a ladder from which he can hurl grenades which don't all explode'.[1]

Four days later, Debussy had good reason to write to Emma, even though in the same house. Little wonder he identified himself with Roderick in *The House of Usher*. 'Why am I being punished for a crime I have not committed?' he exclaimed. His 'punishment' was not simply having to recover from his serious operation, but Emma had now retired to bed. He had not seen her in person for a while, surely a waste of whatever time was left to him. This letter is heart-rending.

> To go so long without seeing you is not funny, not even bearable. To eat without you is a bit like dining in a hotel in an occupied country. So? Don't you think it's possible to carry dinner up to you? It may be unpleasant because of the smell of festive fare, but so what?

Then there was a reminder of an earlier song, the *Rondel* 'Pour ce que Plaisance est morte', the third of the *Trois Chansons de France* which Debussy had dedicated to Emma in 1904, that song with words which seemed so ambivalent at a time of supposed bliss, 'Because Plaisance [Pleasure] is dead I am dressed in black this May. It is a great pity to see my heart so unhappy.'[2]

> Needless to say, my brain is dressed in black,[3] because days go by, medication has no lasting effect. I wonder where I am going? And I can find no answer, alas. And now you are ill … it is simply too much! … Have you thought (you must have done!) about the number of days of happiness lost to us? I know you will be able to make up for it (horrible expression) with your affection … but I am suffering from missing *too many celebrations*!

---

[1] C. pp. 1963–5.
[2] See Chapter 4 p. 53.
[3] 'J'ai le cerveau vêtu de noir'.

Stravinsky had visited him, as had Satie, who played backgammon with him, yet his own wife had now absented herself at a critical time. 'I love you,' he ended the letter.[4]

Debussy certainly needed support, for he was about to undergo radium treatment. On 15 January he ordered books from E. Lemercier's bookshop, including two by Jules Verne for Chouchou. But his loneliness and despair were intense. At some unspecified date in 1916 he wrote a note to his wife saying merely, 'Will you come … I really am too lonely.'[5] In the same house, so near to each other, yet so far.

One assumes that they would not have heard the première of *En blanc et noir*, which took place on 22 January 1916 in a charity concert at the *atelier* of Winnaretta, Princesse de Polignac, performed by Walter Rummel and his wife Thérèse Chaigneau,[6] but by 31 January Emma had recovered enough to invite Vallery-Radot to the house. She begged him to hide his feelings and disguise any anxiety when he heard what Debussy had to tell him, hoping her husband did not realise the severity of his condition. However, there was no doubt as to her state of mind. Apologising for the incoherence of her letter, she exclaimed over the two months of anxiety she had had to endure. She then postponed the invitation to the following afternoon, when there would be more time to talk without worrying her husband. Debussy managed to write to Inghelbrecht inviting him to visit the 'poor invalid'.[7] In a letter to Godet on 4 February, he was stagnating once again in the 'factories of nothingness' as he underwent risky radium treatment, sitting in his rubber ring (about which he complained constantly) and expressing disgust at the nonchalant way in which the war was continuing.

Debussy signed a contract with Durand for the *Sonate pour violon et piano. No 3 des Six Sonates* on 5 February and four days later expressed exasperation that a servant, having been told not to let in certain visitors, had prevented his publisher from entering the house. He kept a constant count of the days of his incapacity and gave an illuminating picture of his room: Buddha keeping an eye on him from his mantelpiece and his wooden toad Arkel contemplating his 'useless suffering'. Between sessions of radium treatment Emma complained to Vallery-Radot of her husband's 'disobedience',[8] her despair at not being able to do more to relieve his suffering and his dislike of his vegetarian diet. Debussy's doctor was ill, which meant he had to wait for another – 'always waiting!! That depresses him more than anything.' What a state Emma was in, writing in haste on a wobbly table.

She also kept d'Annunzio informed of Debussy's condition. This passionate hedonist had had the opportunity in the war to exercise the extreme militaristic side of his personality. He had been carrying out daredevil missions as a fighter pilot and on 16 January 1916 permanently lost the sight of one eye when the plane in which he was flying was hit by anti-aircraft fire. Now he told Emma that Claude's music had

---

[4] C. pp. 1965–6.
[5] C. p. 2069.
[6] S. Kahn, *Music's Modern Muse. A Life of Winnaretta Singer, Princesse de Polignac*, p. 195.
[7] C. p. 1971.
[8] C. p. 1976; 1978.

been his only consolation for weeks. Her card had been brought to him whilst he was listening to Debussy's *Préludes*. They must both get better quickly, he insisted, so that they could collaborate again. He did not forget to send his love to Chouchou.[9] D'Annunzio was only one year younger than Debussy. Their experiences of the First World War could not have been more contrasting.

On 3 May, Debussy received a visit from Victor Segalen, the doctor poet with whom he had once considered collaborating on *Siddhartha*, then *Orphée-Roi*. Not only was Segalen moved by Debussy's fragile condition, but he commented to his wife upon Emma's behaviour. Once again his dislike of her was evident. 'His wife remains faithful to her principles of society life [*ses principes mondains*]. This woman is a living illness; she too is incurable.'[10]

Hardly surprisingly, the thought of death was preoccupying Debussy in several letters written in April and May. 'Illness, that old servant of death[11] lives at 24 Square du Bois de Boulogne', he told Jean-Aubry. 'If I described just one of my nights to you it would give you vertigo,' he told Dukas. He was amazed to see his own face again in the morning, not a death mask.[12]

Medical bills and Lilly's demand for money

To make matters worse and literally give him nightmares, Debussy's medical treatment meant that he was running up huge bills for both doctors' visits and medication. He implored Durand to help him and obligingly his publisher advanced him some money.[13] 'Alors! Oh! Alors!' exclaimed Debussy, quoting Golaud's groans of anguish in Act IV scene 4 of *Pelléas*.[14] He had not, however, lost the knack of inventing excuses to his creditors – even extremely far-fetched –for the advancement of funds. 'Please note that my royalties will increase when I return to health and that next year I have an engagement in Buenos Aires which will allow me plenty of room for manoeuvre.'[15]

On 24 June 1916 Debussy wrote a long letter to Arthur Hartmann explaining his condition and recalling their many good times together. He had been preparing the sonata for violin and piano, but now did not know when he would regain the energy to complete it. 'There are times when I feel as if I never knew music'. There followed a hint that Hartmann might lend him some money when he told him, 'You will never be able to understand the meaning of what it is to have to earn money. Publishers here have become hard as stone and unfortunately I have used up all my credit with Durand.' He did not admit that Durand continued to advance him sums of money.

---

[9] C. pp. 1983–4.
[10] C. p. 1999 n.4.
[11] *Pelléas et Mélisande*, Act IV scene 1.
[12] C. pp. 1985; 1995.
[13] C. p. 1990.
[14] C. p. 2000.
[15] C. p. 2002.

He sent Emma's love to the couple, who were expecting their second child.[16] Not until the end of the year do we learn that Emma sent a little jacket for the new baby in September 1916, which was not acknowledged.[17] She too had happy memories of her friend, whom she used to call 'ma grande petite'.

July brought further calamities. Chouchou suffered from tracheitis, followed by whooping cough, disturbing her parents' nights.[18] Then, as if this was not enough, on 15 July Debussy received a court order to make a payment of thirty thousand francs into the Caisse des Dépôts et Consignations (Deposits and Consignments Fund), which would guarantee his first wife, Lilly Texier, alimony of up to three hundred francs a month. In 1910 Debussy had suddenly stopped making these payments. Lilly had actually demanded an indemnity of fifty thousand francs. She had been receiving four hundred francs on the fifteenth of every month, agreed to at the time of the divorce in 1905 and paid to her regularly by Durand.[19] A note in one of Debussy's notebooks expressed disbelief that she should be entitled to any extra sum. The four hundred francs a month she was already receiving was far more than she had ever had when living with him, she was not working and as far as he was concerned she had no right to make such demands. He was also disgusted that his wife's supposed personal fortune had been brought up, something which was non-existent.[20] Now all Paris was informed of his sins of omission, as his name was once again associated with Rosalie Texier in the newspapers.[21] He had no means to pay, so all he could do was provide a guarantee based on royalties after his death.[22]

Lilly was the equivalent of another illness added to Debussy's misery. All that was keeping him from committing suicide was the desire as well as the 'duty' to complete the two Poe operas.[23] He descended again to the darkness of Poe's world. To André Caplet he included in a letter three lines which he entitled *Échos*, showing that Chouchou had passed on her illness to her mother:

> My wife has violent tracheitis.
> Chouchou has vile whooping cough.
> As for me, I continue to cultivate the flora of rectitis ... [24]

Fuel was added to the flame when Maud Allan resumed her mission to perform *Khamma* and in collaboration with Ernest Bloch, who was to conduct it, made impossible demands on Debussy to revise the score to suit a smaller orchestra. She never would perform this work.

---

[16] C. pp. 2004–6.
[17] A. Hartmann, *Claude Debussy as I knew him*, pp. 143–4.
[18] C. pp. 2007, 2019.
[19] See Chapter 6 p. 88.
[20] C. p. 2007 n.1.
[21] *Le Figaro*, 16 July 1916; *Le Petit Parisien*, 16 July 1916.
[22] C. p. 2010.
[23] C. p. 2008.
[24] 'Ma femme a une violente trachéite,/Chouchou une vilaine coqueluche./Pour moi je continue la culture des fleurs de rectite,...': C. p. 2009.

The heat of August in Paris augmented Debussy's eczema, bringing further misery. Desperate for a good masseur to relieve his pain, he asked Durand to advance him more money, which was duly provided 'for work in progress'. He was not allowed any more morphine so requested further reading matter from E. Lemercier to help divert his mind, books by Mark Twain or Paul Féval. Towards the end of July Dukas found Debussy slightly improved physically but suffering intensely mentally. With both his wife and child ill with whooping cough, he was worried Debussy too might catch it. 'He has had enough and even expressed the desire to die on the front!' To Dukas Debussy complained of wrought nerves. He was battling not just the illness but himself. When he tried to work, his brain resonated like dead wood. 'Is it possible that the *Fall of the House of Usher* could also be the *Fall of Claude Debussy*?'[25]

Emma's correspondence with Vallery-Radot and Caplet

On 18 August Emma wrote a letter of sympathy to Vallery-Radot, who had just lost a close friend in the Battle of Verdun. She wanted him to regard her as a sister or mother to spare his own mother the grief of listening to his woes. This is typical of the maternal concern she would show for younger friends after Debussy's death. Also involved in the battles in that area was André Caplet, in the same company as the violinist Lucien Durosoir. Durosoir wrote to his mother with vivid clarity, describing the terrible pounding of the canon as the Germans deployed vast quantities of men and artillery. 'Yesterday,' he wrote,

> Caplet received twelve studies for piano by Debussy. Just as we were reading through them, with me seated right beside him, seven shells fell less than fifty metres from our farm, which injured no one and caused no damage. There was a moment of stupefaction for there is nothing here at all. Just a little incident.[26]

Emma's domestic news can have done nothing to cheer up either Caplet or Vallery-Radot. Since both she and Chouchou were ill, the family were trapped in their house, for no hotel would accept them in such a state. They were hoping to go to Le Moulleau in Arcachon in September, a place Debussy loved. Her one positive comment was that Debussy was actually getting better, working, even singing, something she believed was due to her care, for 'without a nurse, or a valet even, often without a doctor, I admit to some secret pride …'[27] 'Without a valet' would imply that the household was saving the expenditure of at least one servant.

The work she referred to was the Sonata for Flute, Viola and Harp, for which Durand sent Debussy the published score at the beginning of September. Also, still obsessed by *La chute de la Maison Usher*, he was completely rewriting the libretto. In a long lugubrious letter to Robert Godet, he yet again drew parallels with his own surroundings and the eponymous house. 'This house bears curious similarities to the House of Usher … We have a certain hypersensitivity in common.' No wonder he believed 'It would be for the best if we could leave this house'. With the 'stupid

---

[25] C. pp. 2015, 2016.
[26] M. Maréchal, L. Durosoir, *Deux musiciens dans la Grande Guerre*, Paris, 2005.
[27] C. p. 2019.

illness' in the family, his own disease, 'that old servant of death' (*Pelléas* Act I scene 4), his life was a nightmare. He even wished he could take Caplet's place in the trenches at Verdun, despite the hail of gunfire he had to withstand, although with his luck he would already have been killed several times over. He promised to send Godet a copy of the sonata.[28] Emma received her copy in September, 'For the private collection of P.M. [Petite Mienne], her faithful wounded ClD.'[29]

To Arcachon

On 11 September Debussy, Emma and Chouchou left for Arcachon, where they stayed in the Grand Hôtel, Le Moulleau. Surely there must have been some benefactor subsidising this escape from Paris? Arcachon must have brought back many nostalgic memories to Debussy. He had stayed there first with Nadezhda von Meck and her family in 1880, then with Emma briefly in the early days of their relationship. Significantly, the day before their departure Debussy wrote to two friends, Dukas and Inghelbrecht, emphasising that it was not for his sake they were leaving Paris. It was above all for his wife, who would 'never get better staying in this house where illness and worries have spun an atmosphere of sorrow.'[30]

Once there, his first words to Durand quoted the poet Edmond Haraucourt, 'To depart is to die a little …'[31] The train journey had been slow and painful, there were too many pianos in the hotel. He had even heard someone making a poor attempt at 'Danseuses de Delphes' that morning. As for Emma, 'If this change of air could make my wife feel better I would regret nothing. But I am not confident of this either. Whilst I am writing to you I can hear her coughing miserably.'[32] Emma's susceptibility to illness was not something she could help. It was always aggravated by a change of atmosphere and the stress of an unfamiliar environment. In the hotel there was no gas or electricity, not ideal for a convalescent. Roger-Ducasse, whose family home was in Le Taillan near Bordeaux, invited the Debussys over, but the journey would have been too difficult. Debussy also thought it best not to expose him to Emma's cough.

Writing to Godet on 6 October, Debussy explained that he had visited Arcachon some twelve years ago. 'Was I already thinking of divorce [from Lilly]? Life has extraordinary "encores".'[33] The fact that Lilly was now pursuing him for money he had ceased paying must have contributed to this feeling of déjà vu. He would rather have been in Pourville than this mediocre hotel. Once again he returned to the *Usines de Néant*, the Factories of Nothingness, and instinctively Roderick Usher sprang to mind: 'You are my sole friend (alias, Roderick Usher) of course', a quotation from

---

[28] He received a dedicated copy with Debussy's handwritten corrections in December 1916. C. pp. 2021–3.

[29] 'Pour la Collection particulière de P.M. son fidèle éclopé ClD.': C. p. 2220.

[30] C. pp. 2024–5.

[31] E. Haraucourt, *Rondel de l'adieu*: 'Partir c'est mourir un peu'.

[32] C. p. 2026.

[33] C. pp. 2032–4.

his libretto.[34] He complained of living in a numbered box in a hotel and hated hearing his cello sonata played by a Mr Roos,[35] which proved to him that there were bad musicians everywhere, which probably contributed to people not understanding his music. One rare satisfaction was to have found the germ, the '*idée cellulaire*' for the finale of his violin sonata.[36]

Whilst in Le Moulleau Emma received a letter from Gabriel Fauré forwarded from Paris. Affectionally, Fauré expressed regret that Debussy was not able to attend the latest meeting of the *Conseil Supérieur* of the Conservatoire and worried about the state of his health. He exclaimed warmly, 'Neither in time nor space do I forget you, your husband, your children and grandchildren, oh very young grandmother!' He also asked after Raoul, and told her that his own son Philippe was serving in Salonica.[37]

On 23 October the Debussys returned to Paris. Besides discussing Henri Busser's request to orchestrate some of his piano works and the accompaniment to the *Noël des enfants qui n'ont plus de maison* (Debussy refused the latter), he managed to see Caplet who had been wounded twice and received the Croix de Guerre and two mentions in despatches.

Ode à la France; Raoul Bardac's career

Towards the end of 1916 Debussy began another project with patriotic intent, the subject of which was the execution of Joan of Arc. This involved the collaboration of Louis Laloy, who wrote a libretto for a cantata for soprano, chorus and orchestra entitled *Ode à la France*. Debussy continued sketching an orchestral score for this the following year, but he had not completed it by the time of his death in 1918. There would, however, be ramifications concerning the work when Emma was involved in its resurrection in years to come.

Whilst in Arcachon, and even more urgently on his return home, Debussy endeavoured once again to help Raoul Bardac forge a career. At the beginning of the year he had enlisted the help of an acquaintance, Louis Barthou, a politician who had been Prime Minister in 1913, and who in 1917 would become Minister for Foreign Affairs. This led to Raoul joining the South-American Propaganda Service. Now Debussy asked Gabriel Astruc for support to ensure Raoul was kept on as an attaché in the *Maison de la Presse*.[38] French foreign cultural and media policy in neutral Latin America had already been significant before 1914 and with the outbreak of war, propaganda became intensive in that francophile part of the world. Raoul now not only had an important liaison role but he was also given the responsibility

---

[34] 'Vous êtes mon ami, mon seul ami …'

[35] C. p. 2036; Louis Rosoor.

[36] C. p. 2037.

[37] 'Ni dans le temps, ni dans l'espace je ne vous oublie, vous, votre mari, vos enfants et vos petits enfants, ô très jeune grand-mère!': Gabriel Fauré to Madame Debussy, 10 October 1916. Copy kindly provided by Manuel Cardejo. Original in possession of Michel Pasquier.

[38] C. p. 2047.

for organising the first Latin American Congress at Lyons in April 1916.[39] For such a reclusive and sensitive personality this must have been a daunting task. He surely understood the effort his step-father had made for him, for he later summarised Debussy's life in 1916 as 'belonging completely to doctors and surgeons, to operations, to radium and to morphine'.[40]

Meanwhile Emma received a letter from Toulet, who announced in a somewhat sardonic manner that his family, tired of looking after him (he had been ill for two years), had married him off and he was now living in Guéthary near Saint-Jean-de-Luz. He had heard nothing of 'Rara', hardly surprising as news had not even reached him about Debussy's operation. He sympathised with Emma over the loss of her mother, which had happened nineteen months previously. Just as in previous correspondence, he was eager to receive more of the beautiful catalogues and books on art such as she had sent him previously, and it seems that his opening courteous comments were but a preamble to this desire.[41] He had still not received these by 24 December, when he repeated his condolences and sent affectionate wishes to Chouchou and Claude.[42]

Emma writes to Satie; Debussy performs his own music

Illness continued to predominate in the Debussy household. Emma was so worried about her husband that she wrote to Erik Satie in November. He in turn wrote to Jean Cocteau, with whom he was collaborating on the ballet *Parade*, saying, 'Madame Debussy has sent me a long letter upon which I would like you to give me some advice. Her letter troubles me deeply.'[43] Satie was very fond of Emma and appreciated her sense of humour, as a letter sent to Walter Rummel earlier in the year proves. 'Madame Debussy gently "pulled my leg" about my virtuosity. I adore Mad. [*sic*] Debussy, most of all when she makes fun of me. I could die of laughing.'[44] Things were not so amusing now.

Debussy received 'more than a thousand francs' worth of radium,[45] but on 26 November he informed Rummel that Emma was still ill and confined to bed.[46] However, on 7 December they were both able to go to Rummel's house in Passy, where surely he played the *Études* to them, which he was due to perform in a charity concert on 14 December, and on 10 December at Durand's publishing house they heard in person the *Sonata for Flute, Viola and Harp* performed by Albert Manouvrier

---

[39] Raoul Bardac, *Curriculum Vitae*, Centre de Documentation Claude Debussy, RESE-08.04(1)-(3).

[40] R. Bardac, *Causerie sur les dernières années de Claude Debussy*, Idem, RESE-05.15.

[41] C. p. 2048.

[42] C. p. 2062.

[43] O. Volta, *Satie/Cocteau. Les malentendus d'une entente*, Le Castor Astral, Paris, 1993, p. 100.

[44] *Erik Satie. Correspondance presque complète*, ed. O. Volta, Paris, 2000, p. 236.

[45] C. p. 2048.

[46] C. p. 2050.

on flute, Darius Milhaud on viola and Jeanne Dalliès, chromatic harp. Milhaud visited Debussy at home before this to mark up his part, the only time he met him in person, and was taken aback by his appearance. 'He had a very sallow complexion and his hands were trembling slightly. He sat down at the piano and played me the sonata twice. I was so shy and respectful that even though I had already written *Les Choéphores* I did not tell him about my own compositions.' To Godet the next day, Debussy commented that this sonata was by a Debussy he no longer knew. He did not know whether to laugh or cry. He was terrified of taking on any project now, 'that is enough for it to end up in the waste-paper basket – the cemetery of bad dreams. What a life! What days! Tired of vain pursuits, but not tired enough to sleep.'[47]

Writing in pencil to Vallery-Radot, Emma began with the dire news of her own bad health. She was in bed with painful liver congestion, for which there were no remedies that she could tolerate. Her husband was much better and would improve further if only he would go to bed earlier and get more sleep.[48] But Debussy told Durand Emma had to go out in the damp air to see Dolly, who was now ill as well.[49] It is not difficult to imagine her reluctance to do so.

On 21 December a charity concert was held at the salon of Mme Georges Guiard in aid of the *Vêtement du prisonnier de guerre*. Debussy accompanied Jane Bathori in the *Noël des enfants qui n'ont plus de maison*, *Le promenoir des deux amants* and the *Chansons de Bilitis*. He had to play the *Noël* three times.[50] He also played *En blanc et noir* with Roger-Ducasse at the second piano. Completely exhausted, Debussy excused himself from a further engagement with Bathori, but at least he felt he was making a contribution to the war effort. He also dedicated a score of *Pelléas et Mélisande* to the same charity.[51]

At the end of 1916 Debussy sent two Christmas cards to Emma, one on Christmas Eve, the other on New Year's Eve. In spite of her constant indisposition, the words he composed were passionate and tender. The first bore a picture of a ballet dancer and a poodle with the English text 'Many Happy Days'. Debussy began with a complaint that Father Christmas was at the front this year, where communications were so difficult he had not been able to fulfil requests. He therefore had no flowers or music to give her, just his poor anxious heart. How he longed not to have to mark time, waiting for better days. It feels like a premature burial. But for her – he described her as 'so agreeably courageous' (si joliment courageuse) – he would have been on another planet reading her 'communiqués'.

> Never has your love been more precious or dear to me. I am almost afraid when you go away. Please don't lose your patience, I beg you. Let me pay you back … may the time return when we can count our kisses. That is the only thing that matters. Believe me.

---

47 *C.* p. 2056 and n.5, which quotes D. Milhaud, *Notes sans musique*, Paris, 1949, p. 77.
48 *C.* p. 2058.
49 *C.* pp. 2059–60.
50 *C.* p. 2064.
51 *C.* p. 2060 and n.2.

If I did not know that your spirit was so strong I would be afraid for you living this life with an invalid. However it is you who will calm the many worries devouring me.

Forgive me for loving you … Wait for me!

The letter ended with a chorus:

> Noël, Noël,
> The bells are cracked.
> Noël, Noël,
> They have wept too long![52]

The second card showed a snow-covered village with the text 'Christmas Greetings'. Here Debussy composed five bars of music entitled *La neige sur le village*, a *Poème symphonique en 5 mesures*. Repeated tremolando chords and a rising motif represent bells which continue 'etc. ... into the New Year!' 'I would not advise anyone to walk in the little village opposite tonight,' Debussy adds. 'Just imagine that the piles of snowflakes are my wishes for your happiness. And still there are not enough! (My heart is bursting with postponed desire).'[53]

The only extant New Year's greeting from Emma is addressed to Vallery-Radot,[54] to whom she reiterated that her husband was not getting enough sleep. During these sleepless nights Debussy mulled over the state of French music and its relation to international events. He found the energy to write a long letter to Paul Huvelin, who wanted a preface to a collection of twelve papers presented in Lyons in 1915 by the Friends of French Music. Debussy urged the protection of a pure French tradition. French composers did not need to write heavy symphonies in the German style. He bemoaned the adulation of 'fake' great masters and the notorious 'imbecility' of opinions expressed daily on music. His thoughts were with the soldiers plodding heroically through mud to marching songs. One of the means of achieving victory was through music.[55] Debussy was certainly living up to his self-imposed title of *Musicien français*.

---

[52] 'Noël! Noël!/Les cloches son fêlées./Noël! Noël!/Elles ont trop pleuré!': C. p. 2061.
[53] C. p. 2066.
[54] C. p. 2168.
[55] C. pp. 2067–8.

17

1917 – April 1918: The last summer

A harsh winter

In January 1917 Emma received a telegram from the swashbuckling Gabriele d'Annunzio who, although blind in one eye, had returned to battle against medical advice as an aviator, then spent time on the ground constantly in danger in the eastern sector of the Italian Front. Now he was back in Venice with a fever. Always the aesthete, d'Annunzio lived on the Grand Canal in the Casetta Rossa, a miniature palace rented from an Austrian prince. There, musicians turned soldiers who were stationed at gun batteries on the Lido formed his 'Wartime Quintet'.[1] He hastened to tell Emma that virtuosi in uniform had been performing Debussy's String Quartet at his home on beautiful Stradivarius, Guarneri, Amati and Guadagnini instruments. Emma was to pass on to 'Mon grand et cher frère' his gratitude and to give Chouchou his love.

The winter of 1916–7 was particularly harsh. Fuel for domestic purposes was in short supply. Debussy quoted Mélisande's 'fear of the bitter cold'[2] in a letter to Dukas, where he brought up the subject twice. 'My God, I'm cold!'[3] No wonder he asked Durand when he sent him the first movement of his Violin Sonata, 'Would it be possible to let me have a bit of wood or coal?' How grateful he was to receive the promise of a delivery from the coal merchant Monsieur Tronquin. 'My little daughter jumped for joy when she read your letter. These days little girls prefer sacks of coal to dolls!'[4] Emma must have been just as grateful in view of her constant aches and pains. As payment, Debussy gave Tronquin the manuscript of a piano piece, thirty-one bars with the epigraph 'Les soirs illuminés par l'ardeur du charbon', a line from *Balcon*, the first of the *Cinq Poèmes de Charles Baudelaire*.

Satie's break with Debussy; charity concerts and the Cello Sonata

Since 1911 Satie's bitterness about Debussy's patronising attitude to his success had not diminished. Just as Emma was the pathway when d'Annunzio wanted to communicate with Debussy, it was through her that Satie delivered to Debussy

---

[1] L. Hughes-Hallett, *The Pike*, p. 408.
[2] *Pelléas et Mélisande*, Act V.
[3] C. pp. 2074–5.
[4] C. p. 2076.

the news of his estrangement. Satie had been completing his ballet *Parade*, which would receive its first performance by Diaghilev's Ballets Russes on 18 May 1917.

Brief, shocking in its finality, his letter to Emma, dated 8 March, read,

> Dear Madam, decidedly it is preferable that the Precursor* stays at home henceforth, far away.
> *Amicalement*
> ES
>
> *Painful teasing. And at a rehearsal – again. Yes. Quite unbearable in any case.
>
> PS What snow! I hope you are all well. Will write often. Love you all – dearly.[5]

The conclusion must be that Debussy had attended at least one rehearsal and had teased him in front of others over the unconventional score. How very sad that after years of weekly visits to the Debussys', meals at their house, playing with Chouchou, Satie wrote to Henry Prunières on 14 September 1917: 'You speak to me of Debussy? I no longer see him. *Parade* separated me from a great many friends. This work is the cause of many misfortunes.'[6]

Meanwhile, Debussy and Emma were contributing to the war charity, *Aide affectueuse aux musiciens*. Debussy participated in a concert on 9 March and helped to organise another on 17 March, to which Emma's nieces Maude and Yvonne Weil were invited. The cold winter was still taking its toll. Debussy was forced to beg Tronquin for another delivery of coal as soon as possible, so little wonder that Emma blamed the freezing weather in recent months for Chouchou's tonsillitis, her own kidney troubles and Debussy's enteritis. She hoped Vallery-Radot would be able to come to their next charity concert in aid of Le Vêtement du Blessé on 24 March.[7] This was devoted entirely to works by Debussy, and included the first public performance of his Cello Sonata played by Joseph Salmon, which the composer himself accompanied. Turning the pages was a young pianist, Daniel Ericourt, whom, years later, Emma would recommend to Arthur Hartmann in America. This was also the concert at which the piano piece later known as *Page d'album* was performed, which Debussy had dedicated to Emma in June 1915. It was exhausting for Debussy to help organise such events and he admitted to Durand that he was not cut out for such duties. Fortunately, his brother Alfred, who was attached to the British Expeditionary Force as an interpreter, arrived back in Paris and was able to help him.[8]

The Violin Sonata

Whilst the cold was causing Debussy to suffer 'like Saint Sebastien' he was encountering problems with completing the last movement of the Violin Sonata. He

---

[5] BnF Musique, Nla-32 (84-85); Erik Satie, *Correspondance presque complète*, p. 282.
[6] Satie, *Correspondance presque complète*, p. 308.
[7] C. p. 2087.
[8] C. p. 2091.

braved deep snow one day to reach Durand's office in the Place de la Madeleine to play the sonata to his publisher but, still dissatisfied with the finale, took it back home with him. Eight days later he played the new version to Durand, which definitely 'eclipsed' the first. Durand found it quite remarkable and invited Debussy and the violinist Gaston Poulet to play it at his house.[9] Poulet was no less moved by the work than he was. 'He's trembling!' Debussy exclaimed and, of himself, 'Poulet gives me gooseflesh!'[10]

On Easter Sunday, 8 April 1917, Debussy presented Emma with a notebook with a red leather cover. Inside were the sketches for his Violin Sonata. His dedication to her read:

> Very humbly, this little red notebook will be my Easter present to you this year. There's a bit of everything, but mainly: the whole history of the finale of the sonata for Violin and Piano which did not want to … end! Will you alone, my *petite mienne*, be able to understand its melancholy?
> There are other 'agonies' which we don't need to mention here (…)
> Happy Easter! All the same
> Claude Debussy.[11]

On 25 April Debussy received a letter from Fauré inviting him to play some of his *Études* at the first concert in three years of the Société nationale de musique. In this warm-hearted letter Fauré also begged Emma and Chouchou to help persuade him to agree to this request and sent 'mille amitiés' to all three,[12] but Debussy declined. He could no longer play the piano accurately enough and joked he could not even remember where the pedals were.[13] Yet this did not stop him from accompanying Poulet in the first public performance of his Violin Sonata on 5 May at the Salle Gaveau in a concert in aid of blind soldiers. Rose Féart sang the *Chansons de Bilitis*, the three *Ballades de Villon* and the *Noël des enfants*. In the 1958 edition of his biography of Debussy, Léon Vallas reported on this concert, adding the detail of the presence of Madame Debussy, describing her as being 'on guard' near the stage, and of Chouchou with her English governess.[14]

Debussy's life was still moving on like 'a tired machine'. He pointed out to Godet that his sonata sounded deceptively happy. Joyful works often arose from the shadows of a gloomy brain.[15] Yet Emma was pleased to announce to Vallery-Radot on 2 May that he was better at the moment and being more 'obedient'. He had even admitted that her strictness (*sévérité*) was indeed necessary. In July they were going to travel to Saint-Jean-de-Luz, where they would stay for three months. Debussy did not mention these plans to anyone. Even in May he was still affected by the cold and could not

---

[9] J. Durand, *Quelques souvenirs d'un éditeur de musique*, vol.2, pp. 78–9.
[10] C. pp. 2099–100.
[11] C. p. 2097.
[12] C. p. 2102.
[13] C. pp. 2103–4.
[14] L. Vallas, *Debussy et son temps*, p. 422.
[15] C. p. 2106.

believe that Tronquin had run out of coal. Unable to provide any more signed manuscripts as payment, he was having to rely on the coal merchant's generosity.[16]

He found the energy to attend the Ballets Russes at the Châtelet on 16 May, surely with Emma, where Stravinsky's *Firebird*, a ballet entitled *Les femmes de bonne humeur* with music arranged from works by Domenico Scarlatti and Vincenzo Tommasini, and Borodin's *Polovtsian Dances* were performed, conducted by Ansermet. Afterwards he reminded Diaghilev of their meeting in Russia in 1913.[17] He managed a second visit to the theatre on 25 May, when Massine's ballet *Las Meninas* (choreographed to Fauré's *Pavane*), Stravinsky's *Petrouchka*, *Les femmes de bonne humeur* and Satie's *Parade* were performed. Congratulating Diaghilev afterwards, significantly, he made no mention of *Parade*.[18]

The same month, a concert linked the names of Roger-Ducasse and the pianist Marguerite Long, two musicians who would become closer to both Emma and Claude Debussy in months to come. Long's husband, Capitaine Joseph de Marliave, had been killed on 24 August 1914. Roger-Ducasse was supportive in her devastation, and it was he who encouraged her to return to the stage in 1917. He composed two *Études* for her, which she performed in a concert at the Société nationale de musique in May 1917 which also included Debussy's *En blanc et noir*. According to Long, after the concert Debussy told her, 'I would like to feel these arms and find out what they are made of to play and master all this difficult music.' Emma added, 'And we will expect you for lunch tomorrow'.[19] Perhaps it was at this event that it was agreed that Long should join the Debussys in Saint-Jean-de-Luz and work with him on his piano music, even if his attitude to the pianist was not as welcoming as that of his wife.

As you like it; summer in Saint-Jean-de-Luz

In the middle of May Debussy repeated the dirge to both Dukas and Vallery-Radot, 'I am stagnating in factories of Nothingness'.[20] Responding emotionally to a humorous letter from Toulet, who was grateful for a parcel of catalogues from Emma,[21] he exuded depression, melancholy nostalgia for the days when they used to meet in bars in Paris at the turn of the century, the demoralising effects of his long illness and the war. However, a visit to the theatre gave him the impetus to write with renewed energy to Toulet. He had seen the actor and manager of the Théâtre Antoine, Firmin Gémier, playing Shylock in *The Merchant of Venice* and spoken to him about his 'old passion' for *As you like it*. Gémier had agreed that Debussy could write incidental music for the play and that Toulet, with whom Debussy had initially planned to collaborate on this many years earlier, should be the translator.

---

[16] C. p. 2107.
[17] C. p. 2113.
[18] C. p. 2116.
[19] M. Long, *Au piano avec Claude Debussy*, p. 24.
[20] C. pp. 2114–5.
[21] C. p. 2100.

Following this up, the sick and nervous Toulet wrote not to the composer, but to Emma. He did not want to make a literal translation of *As you like it* and distrusted Gémier. Hardly any time later he wrote to her again, consumed with anxiety about the project. He wondered if Emma might come to Biarritz or Saint-Jean-de-Luz with Chouchou. It was Debussy who answered two days later to reassure him that he would be able to resurrect his previous work and write a lyrical text, for he envisaged the vocal element, '*chansons*', playing a large part in the work.[22]

The *sauf conduit* or official pass for travel to Saint-Jean-de-Luz was valid for a stay of just over three months, from 2 July until 14 October 1917.[23] Prior to their departure Debussy received a welcome gift from Dukas, some manuscript paper, the shortage of which he had been bemoaning for some time.[24] Debussy made it clear to Durand that neither he nor Emma were looking forward to the upheaval – only Chouchou was excited. They did not know what to expect from the house they were to rent, the Chalet Habas, except that it was owned by an Englishman, Colonel Nicoll, who was now fighting on the front, and that it had mountain views and a pergola. Marguerite Long would be staying nearby. 'God be with her, and please not let her be "semi-detached"!'[25] He needed peace and tranquillity to work on all the projects he was so behind with, one of these being the collaboration with Toulet to whom he wrote, looking forward to meeting him soon.[26]

At least the house proved better than they had expected. Debussy described it as charming and characterful to the extent that you almost expected to meet Mr. Pickwick on the stairs! It was full of pictures and guns, relics of the Boer War, and had a lovely garden facing gentle mountains, providing biblical calm, 'Un silence extraordinaire', wrote Debussy, as so often quoting his opera.[27] He was still affected by enteritis, completely exhausted, running a constant battle with both illness and himself.[28] Emma was relieved to find her surroundings quiet, warm and pretty, the only disadvantages being the small garden and the distance of the house from the sea. However, she later told Arthur Hartmann that it would have been too draining for Debussy to be close to the sea, and impossible for him to stay in a hotel in his state.[29]

The house is indeed at least fifteen minutes' walk from the beach, downhill on the way there, consequently uphill on the way back. It has three stories and is in the typical basque style with a sloping roof and wooden balconies. Some years later Emma was to remember with affection and nostalgia the garden full of roses, the view of mountains and its pretty stream. Twice a day, she told Hartmann, she would take Debussy to the beach in the morning and to the cliffs in the evening, which he adored. In order to do this they hired a horse-drawn carriage, which in those days

---

[22] C. pp. 2117–22.
[23] BnF Musique, Nla-32 (Bis).
[24] C. p. 2125.
[25] C. p. 2128.
[26] C. p. 2129.
[27] Act II scene 1.
[28] C. pp. 2131–2, 2133.
[29] A. Hartmann, *Claude Debussy as I knew him*, p. 158.

was a cheap means of transport.[30] The cliffs would have been those of the nearby Sainte-Barbe at the northern end of the bay, just the spot beneath which Maurice Ravel, born in neighbouring Ciboure, had had his photograph taken in 1902.

The tenth of July was Emma's fifty-fifth birthday, and on that day she received a letter from Debussy expressing deep love and admiration. Whilst poets such as Ronsard complained of the passing years and approaching old age, his own *petite Mienne* was upright and pretty, like a flower untouched by the years, indeed possessing a wonderful aura which no flower could ever match. All he wanted was to tell her of his love and infinite gratitude for everything she had been to him these last years. There should be a medal for epidemics of love or an Order of the Blue Cross, of which she would be the Commander. 'Please accept once again, this year, my unadorned love ["*mon amour tout nu*"], stronger than these wretched circumstances.'[31]

They often saw Toulet, Emma told Vallery-Radot, but he was so ill himself that it was as if he were dead and alive at the same time. His nervous tension left Debussy feeling exhausted. Chouchou loved bathing in the sea, something Emma would also have loved to do, but her neuralgia prohibited it.[32] She wished Caplet could come and visit them at the Chalet Habas, where he would enjoy the peace and quiet just as much as they did.[33] This was an understatement, when one considers his soldier's life fighting in Northern France.

Both Debussy and Toulet were so ill that no progress was made on *As you like it* despite correspondence on the subject. Once when he and Emma ventured as far as his house they did not even call in, not wanting to disturb him.[34] Writing to Inghelbrecht, Debussy commented that in the delightful Basque country they had everything they needed to be happy, if only he did not have to drag his old carcass around. He was glad their house was outside the town so he could not hear all the pianists staying there, Ricardo Viñes, Joaquin Nin and Marguerite Long, although to read Long's version of events one would imagine that she had been constantly practising with the composer. She worked with him 'relentlessly'. She was virtually 'tied down to the piano. He would not let me go.'[35] However, according to Debussy, the piano in the Chalet Habas was temperamental to the extent of notes not sounding. Chouchou 'punished' it, practising a little prelude by J. S. Bach in E Major, giving it a bad quarter of an hour every morning. 'I can't hold it against her,' he wrote affectionately.[36]

According to their official pass, Debussy and his family had permission for an excursion to Hendaye on 29 August, a resort adjoining Spain. He could also go to

---

[30] Letter from Emma to Arthur Hartmann 21 September 1924, A. Hartmann, *Claude Debussy as I knew him*, p. 159. Emma did not drive a car. I am grateful to Étienne Rousseau-Plotto for information regarding this matter.

[31] C. p. 2130.

[32] C. p. 2132.

[33] C. p. 2134.

[34] C. p. 2136.

[35] Long, *Au piano avec Claude Debussy*, p. 25.

[36] C. pp. 2141–2.

28. Chouchou aged nearly twelve between two friends, Saint-Jean-de-Luz, 1917

Biarritz on 6 September, but in fact needed to go there more often. He was delighted to hear Gaston Poulet was going to give a concert in Saint-Jean-de-Luz and agreed to accompany him himself in his Violin Sonata if he could make his rusty old fingers work.[37] This he succeeded in doing on 11 September and even repeated the whole work as an encore. They performed it again on 14 September in Biarritz. These proved to be the last concerts Debussy was ever to play in in person. Emma later told Hartmann of her distress as she listened. 'It seemed to me each time that it would never end!'[38] In frustration, however, Debussy told Durand in September that he had intended to write a series of little *Concertos*, but was now unable to achieve the level of inspiration to match that of 1915.[39]

Emma gave Debussy another challenge that summer. We learn from a letter she wrote to Gabriel Fauré after Debussy's death in 1918 that 'he was so happy last summer to study *La bonne chanson* …'[40] Despite her husband's illness (and the temperamental piano) the two of them worked together on the great song cycle that Fauré had composed for her. Was she nostalgic? This is a very rare reference to Emma ever singing again after marrying Debussy. He had not been unwilling to play these songs. 'People were unaware of his kindness, his sincerity, and his loyal affection for "the music",' she told Fauré, in this very personal note.

Despite Emma's recollections to Hartmann of taking Debussy to the sea twice a day, this cannot have happened as frequently as she recalled, for only three days after the Biarritz performance of the Violin Sonata she had to arrange for a local doctor to

[37] C. p. 2145.
[38] Letter from Emma to Arthur Hartmann, 21 September 1924, *Claude Debussy as I knew him*, p. 159.
[39] C. pp. 2148–9.
[40] J. Barrie-Jones, *Gabriel Fauré. A Life in Letters*, London 1989, p. 172.

give injections to Debussy, who was depressed and needed rest. She complained to Marie Toulet about the difficulties of arranging transport of any sort, so they were now only going out when they had to. They had visitors, for Dolly and her daughters Françoise and Madeleine were staying at Salies-de-Béarn, a spa about seventy kilometres from Saint-Jean-de-Luz, no doubt rather more luxurious than the Chalet Habas. They all visited the Toulets in Guéthary on 21 September.[41]

Emma and Debussy attended two concerts given by the pianist Francis Planté, who gave admirable performances of the 'Toccata' from Debussy's *Pour le piano*, amongst other works.[42] It was raining so hard in Saint-Jean-de-Luz that Emma told Caplet it was diluting her ink. Thoughtfully, she had sent him some paper and envelopes in acknowledgement of his complaint that he had nothing more to write on. She would have liked to send him some *eau de Sologne* but worried this might annoy his *Marraine de guerre*.[43] She warned Caplet that when he saw Debussy again, he must not introduce the subject of composition he had been unable to undertake. It would be too upsetting.[44] Caplet must also have been frustrated by his own lack of time and opportunity to compose whilst serving in his regiment, his efforts being mainly confined to military marches.[45]

Raoul Bardac in London

Emma was terribly worried about the bombardment of London, where Raoul was based, and was having to wait two or three days for replies to her telegrams to him (none of which survive). By July 1917 Raoul had changed jobs again and was working in London for the French High Commission in charge of '*organisation matérielle*'. He described himself as '*chef du Service Intérieur*' in a letter to Louis Laloy, feeling exhausted and troubled by the sheer amount of work. He asked for Laloy's support in an application to become '*Officier d'administration de 1ère classe du service des bureaux de l'Intendance*' (Supplies Office) for which he had been recommended, believing Laloy might have useful contacts. The letter is written on official notepaper, but he informed Laloy of his home address, 15 Trevor Square, Knightsbridge, London SW7. Just as Emma feared, he was affected by bombing raids, but in a strange way. 'Every day brings raids,' he wrote. A literal translation of his next words reads: 'Every now and again they are aborted, but when they do reach London something really pretty and pleasant happens – but no warning. You feel afraid

---

[41] C. p. 2150.

[42] C. p. 2151.

[43] The *marraines de guerre* were ladies who corresponded with soldiers during the war as if they were their godmothers.

[44] C. pp. 2152–3.

[45] From the violinist Durosoir's letters one gains a vivid impression of life on the front lines in Northern France. He often expressed frustration at his mother's lack of understanding and that of her friends and relations, of the hardships and deprivations of the soldiers. M. Maréchal and L. Durosoir, *Deux Musiciens dans la Grande Guerre*, Paris, 2005.

when the bombs come crashing down or when shrapnel falls.'[46] Raoul succeeded in his desire for promotion, for he became assistant to the Secretary General and Head of the Service intérieur, and Expenditure Manager of the Office of the High Commissioner, appointed by the Ministry of Finance.[47]

Chouchou's piano lessons; Debussy's concern for Emma

On 14 October the family returned home. Caplet was one of the first people they saw, for on 18 October Debussy told Gaston Poulet he had come to stay with them during his leave. He wanted Poulet to come over that evening and play Caplet the Violin Sonata. Debussy had to forgo a performance by Alfred Bruneau of *L'après-midi d'un faune* on 21 October owing to recurring enteritis.[48]

Three days later he wrote a stern letter to Chouchou's piano teacher, nineteen-year-old Ada Killick. For two years, he complained, Chouchou had made little discernible progress. However, he conceded 'it is no one's fault'. She simply must have someone stricter. There was also the problem of the times of her lessons changing constantly. Now he and Emma were going to 'orientate her musical studies in a different direction'. He assured her that it was not her character that was in question and was grateful for her help.[49] It seems that in fact Chouchou did continue her lessons with Killick as Debussy was too ill to arrange a successor.[50] Emma appears to have played no part in this and we do not hear of the matter again until after Debussy's death, when Chouchou corresponded with her teacher on her mother's behalf about payment for lessons.

One can sense Debussy's relief to have returned home with its familiar and beloved garden, its two trees in their autumn colours and the sound of bugle calls from the nearby barracks, yet also his deep sadness at the blankness of the manuscript paper he had brought back. 'Music has completely abandoned me,' he told Godet. 'Even if it's nothing to cry about, it is somewhat ridiculous, but I can do nothing about it and I've never forced anyone to like me.'[51]

It is difficult to come to terms with the visible decrease in Debussy's powers of concentration. He could not go out because of his enteritis. He tried to sound encouraging about plans for the orchestration of *La boîte à joujoux* and an operatic version of *Le martyre de Saint Sébastien* on which he was collaborating with Laloy.

---

[46] 'Ici chaque jour amène son raid. De temps en temps il avorte. Mais quand il parvient jusqu'à Londres, il se fait quelque chose de vraiment joli et agréable – avec cela, pas d'avertissement. On est peureux lorsque les bombes dégringolent ou que les shrapnells retombent.' Laloy archives, Dossier 35, no.7.

[47] 'Régisseur des dépenses du Haut-Commissariat nommé par le Ministère des Finances.' Raoul Bardac, *Curriculum Vitae*, Centre de Documentation Claude Debussy, RESE-05.18.

[48] C. pp. 2155–6.

[49] C. p. 2156.

[50] J. E. Martins, 'Les trois dernières lettres connues de Chouchou Debussy', *Cahiers Debussy*, 2007, no.31, p. 78.

[51] C. pp. 2157–9.

D'Annunzio's celebrity following his wartime exploits had encouraged Jacques Rouché, director of the Opéra, to consider this idea. Debussy and Laloy's version did not proceed very far. It must have been dispiriting for the composer to realise that 'in 3,995 lines there is little substance. Words, words …' He also told Durand of his plans for music for *As you like it*, 'yet for so many beautiful ideas I only have ill health which reacts to the slightest shock, to the slightest change in the weather.'[52] Godet wrote to him at length, inspired and moved by the act of sorting all Debussy's compositions in his possession.[53]

Marguerite Long told of the night before her recital of 10 November at the Société nationale de musique where she performed some of the *Études*. She went to the Debussys' house to rehearse with the composer, with Emma listening. When Long finished playing, Debussy got up without saying a word. 'Are you going upstairs, Claude?' asked Emma. 'I don't feel well,' he replied. 'He did not get up again,' wrote Long.[54] According to Emma, he took to his bed permanently from 6 November.[55] Toulet asked Emma for news of Debussy, at the same time complaining of his own failing health, and hoping she would send him a family photograph.[56]

Debussy managed to mark the end of his final full year with a note written in pencil to Emma on New Year's Eve expressing his love:

> Following a tradition which was dear to us both, it used to be last night that I sent you my good wishes for the New Year.
> This time sadly I am bound hand and foot and have only these sadly restricted means of expressing my love for you.
> But if it is true that love is stronger than death …
> How could that not be

He then felt the need to write on New Year's Day itself, again in pencil with an unsteady hand:

> Dear *Petite Mienne*
> Excuse this ever more restricted means of writing to you!
> And here is the revolution! (I mean Albertine[57])
> Obviously I do not claim to be able to make this little piece of paper contain all my love – it would not even want to do so!
> Not even the slightest one of my wishes is excluded.
> Your
> Claude

---

[52] C. pp. 2159–60.
[53] C. pp. 2163–5.
[54] Long, *Au piano avec Claude Debussy*, p. 78.
[55] Emma to Madame Molinari, C. p. 2169.
[56] C. p. 2166.
[57] The housemaid.

Even this was not enough. Another note followed on the same day: 'Dear *Petite Mienne*, Years pass and are all the same – this is not new and it is the age of restrictions ...'[58]

In response to New Year's greetings from Vallery-Radot, Emma gave him the news that Debussy had managed to give her a handwritten message for the first time for at least two months. Her apprehension about the year ahead is evident. To the wife of the conductor Molinari, she expressed her fears that 'This New Year is full of mysterious uncertainty, yet how many wishes one whispers under one's breath!' She repeated the words 'mystérieuse année' to the pianist Francis Planté, and again to Marie Toulet, 'Cette nouvelle année est pleine de mystère ...' Toulet himself told Debussy he would love to see more of those magazines from Paris that Emma had promised him. He complained that Marie had managed to break a little bowl from Saint-Jean-de-Luz, presumably a gift from the Debussys. 'Grounds for divorce?'[59]

On 8 January 1918 Debussy once again managed to write a few words but, as so often, it seems that it was Emma's health he was concerned for rather than his own.

> Dear *petite Mienne*,
> I do so want to have some news of your health. If ... you are not any worse ... nothing will be any worse and we can look forward to more flamboyant new years.
> Your
> Cl[60]

But why was he writing this question and not speaking it? Was Emma once again ensconced in her own room? The worry was overwhelming her.

Emma was surrounded by illness. She sympathised with Vallery-Radot on 9 January, who had been taken ill, and offered to supply him with books. Later in the month, late at night, she wrote to Marie Toulet, who was also having to cope with a seriously ailing husband, expressing misery at the freezing winter weather. The house was unbearably cold except in Debussy's room, where their meagre coal rations were being burnt. Debussy's nights were better without morphine and he was even managing to get up every now and then in the mornings. Of their daughter she wrote,

> Chouchou is well and is sleeping peacefully. She is quite badly brought up – but where can we find time to try to prevent this? Her parents aren't exactly fun these days ... but we get on well together and I try not to let her get too annoyed with her mother – but it's tiring nevertheless.[61]

In February Vallery-Radot informed Toulet that he had seen the composer in his bed, emaciated, but not too depressed. He had known when Debussy had his initial operation eighteen months earlier that it must be cancer, but thought it important to deny the rumours. He did not know if Emma had realised this and was bravely

[58] C. p. 2168.
[59] C. p. 2170.
[60] C. p. 2172.
[61] C. p. 2173.

pretending to know nothing. They had mutually feigned ignorance when they met, but now the truth was inescapable. Emma had not uttered the word 'cancer'. He obviously admired her strength of mind.[62]

Emma's efforts to get Debussy admitted to Beaux-Arts; Ode à la France

Amidst her troubles, Emma still sent Caplet tobacco and cigarettes when she could, promising to provide anything else he needed. Once she was forced by the Post Office to remove a tin of pâté to reduce the weight of a parcel. She was hoping to go to a recital of Caplet's songs given by Rose Féart, who had been performing Debussy's songs recently.[63] She also kept him informed of her own exhaustion. It was unbearable to witness Debussy's suffering yet be unable to do anything about it. On 26 February, she told him Debussy had a fever and the doctor appeared anxious. Dolly was writing to him (Caplet) about 'necessary documents'.[64] By 20 March Emma could see Debussy's strength ebbing away and feel her own courage dissipating. Despite knowing her husband could die that night, she was still thoughtful enough to ask Caplet to give her an address so that she could send food parcels by rail.[65]

Emma made one more important move on Debussy's behalf: to remind Charles-Marie Widor, now the Permanent Secretary of the Académie des Beaux-Arts, that in 1914, before the outbreak of war, he had nominated Debussy to succeed him to his chair as a member of that institution. The initial candidature had been prevented by Saint-Saëns, who was shocked by Debussy's composition *En blanc et noir* (which he had called *Noir et blanc*). Was this important to Debussy, or was it Emma who was willing him on, for on 17 March 1918 she wrote another letter to Widor, which she managed to get Debussy himself to sign: 'Since you are being kind enough to help me cross the threshold of the Institute, I should be very pleased to apply now for the chair which you held.' On 24 March, the day before Debussy's death, Emma even wrote in her own hand, pretending to be Debussy, to Alfred Croiset, President of the Institut de France, expressing the desire to be Widor's successor.[66] That same day *Le Figaro* reported that the election would take place on 20 April and that Debussy was a candidate.[67] It was never to be, however, and eventually Henri Rabaud was elected.

Paris was under constant attack from the Germans. There were not just aerial bombardments from the heavy Gotha bombers, which had started in January, but now the city was being shelled by the long-range Paris Gun, similar to Big Bertha.

---

[62] C. p. 2183, n.3.
[63] C. pp. 2182–3 and n.1.
[64] C. p. 2184.
[65] C. pp. 2187–8.
[66] C. pp. 2187, 2189.
[67] *Le Figaro*, 24 March 1918.

The first shell landed early in the morning of 21 March 1918 on the Quai de la Seine, the explosion being heard across the city, after which shells continued to land at the rate of about twenty per day. Emma's despair over Debussy's condition was therefore augmented by fear of bombardment. 'What will happen tonight? Then tomorrow?' Emma wrote to Caplet. 'Will there be Gothas? I can only wait for them at the side of my *Maître* in our papier mâché shell. It is impossible to go anywhere else as I can't leave him and he can't be moved.'[68]

Knowing how much Debussy loved Rameau, Louis Laloy expressed his regret that he had been unable to attend the dress rehearsal of Rameau's *Castor et Pollux*, which was being revived at the Opéra.[69] The rehearsal had been moved to the afternoon of 21 March because of the fear of night-time aerial attacks. He expressed pride in having been the author of the words to the cantata, *Ode à la France*, which Debussy had requested in 1916 when affected by news of the battles of Verdun and the Somme.[70] Debussy had drafted fifteen pages of short score during 1917 for soprano, choir and orchestra, but it was unfinished at his death. For Raoul Bardac, summarising Debussy's final years, this was one of the few significant events of that year. It was conceived by Debussy, he wrote, but only rough outlines remained.[71]

Death of Debussy; Chouchou's strength of mind

On 23 March 1918 Emma sent a telegram to Caplet. 'Am in despair. Still fever'.[72] The next day Jacques Durand visited Debussy. This last meeting was etched deeply in his memory.

> Paris was under attack from the enemy. There were constant air raids. One of them, exceptionally violent, had struck the immediate neighbourhood of Debussy's house. I went to visit my poor friend one evening ... I knew his days were numbered. The ravages of suffering were written on his highly expressive face. Debussy ... wanted to talk to me alone. First he described to me the horror of the preceding night when, realising the danger of the bombs, he had not had enough strength to get up and shelter in the cellar with his family who had not left his side. He was tormented by this physical incapacity added to the agony of war ... staring me straight in the eyes with a look that already saw beyond this life, he said everything was over, that he knew it was only a matter of a few hours now. Alas! That was true. When I tried to deny it he signalled that he wanted to embrace me. Then he asked me for a cigarette, his final consolation.[73]

---

[68] C. p. 2188.

[69] C. p. 2187 n.4.

[70] L. Laloy, *La musique retrouvée*, Paris, 1928, p. 228 .

[71] 'Et 1917 le voit préparant l'*Ode à la France*, œuvre conçue par lui mais dont il ne reste que des brouillons sommaires.' R. Bardac, *Causerie sur les dernières années de Claude Debussy*, 1940; Centre de Documentation Claude Debussy, RESE-05.15.

[72] C. p. 2188.

[73] J. Durand, *Quelques souvenirs d'un éditeur de musique*, vol.2, pp. 90–1.

Vallery-Radot, on leave, came to see Debussy lying in bed, emaciated, his eyes staring into the distance, his hands trembling. He managed to say a few words, then his voice faded away. One important task had to be completed before he died. Debussy's brother Alfred, who was fighting in the trenches, was appointed guardian to Chouchou.[74] His civilian job was as a representative for a coal firm.

On the evening of 25 March Vallery-Radot and Emma held Debussy's hands. He no longer recognised them. He passed away at about six o'clock. 'Emma, overcome with grief, went out whilst I shut his eyes,' wrote Vallery-Radot. Dolly later confirmed that this task fell to him.[75] Then André Caplet arrived from the front, knelt down, and together they stayed beside Debussy.[76] The first person to think of informing Raoul was Chouchou. Vallery-Radot told us that in tears she wrote to him in her little bedroom. Two weeks later, on 8 April, she wrote Raoul a long, detailed letter, which began by asking if he had received her telegram. 'I was the first to think of sending it to you.' She must have reminded her mother to carry out this task, as Raoul remembered receiving first a telegram from Emma then a letter from Chouchou.[77]

One cannot fail to be astounded at the maturity of this twelve-year-old girl. She wrote at great length describing the course of events. Having seen her mother's distraught face prior to Debussy's death, she thought of Raoul, got her mother to write the telegram informing him that Debussy was dying, then realised that she would probably need to show identification to be able to send it, so asked Dolly to come to the house and take it to the post office. As soon as Dolly had left with it, Emma was called to Debussy's bedside by the nurse and two doctors were sent for. They gave Debussy an injection to ease the pain. Roger-Ducasse was also present by then and it was he who told Chouchou to kiss her father for the last time. Chouchou must have then been sent to her room, for she told Raoul that Debussy had slept peacefully until 10.15 p.m.[78] Vallery-Radot explained that Emma had not wanted to tell Chouchou immediately that her father had died, which was why Chouchou gave a later time than six o'clock.[79]

'I can't describe what happened afterwards,' she continued.

> A flood of tears built up in my eyes but I held them back because of *Maman*. All night, all alone in *Maman*'s big bed, I could not sleep for one minute. I had a fever and I stared with dry eyes at the walls, questioning, unable to believe what had happened.
> The next day far too many people came to see *Maman* who could not hold out any more by the end of the day. That came as a relief for her and for me.[80]

---

[74] C. p. 737 n.2.
[75] 'Quand Debussy est mort il était auprès de lui et c'est lui qui a fermé les yeux.' De Tinan, French interview.
[76] P. Vallery-Radot, *Lettres de Claude Debussy à sa femme Emma*, p. 66.
[77] R. Bardac, 'Dans l'intimité de Claude Debussy', *Terres Latines*, March 1936.
[78] C. p. 2195.
[79] P. Vallery-Radot, *Lettres de Claude Debussy*, p. 67.
[80] C. p. 2195.

'Claude is dead', wrote Emma to P.-J. Toulet that day.[81]

It was faithful Caplet who carried out the duties of arranging the funeral and organised the death mask, photographs and sketches made of Debussy. The death mask was to be made by Elisa Beetz-Charpentier, second wife of Alexandre Charpentier. One of the artists Caplet invited to the house was Othon Friesz, from whose sketch a woodcut was made by Lucien Dumser which would eventually appear in *La Revue musicale*. Caplet stayed in the house for two days.[82] When Emma pencilled a letter of gratitude to Vallery-Radot, who had already sent flowers, she complained of painful rheumatism in her right hand.

News spread fast, for Emma received several letters on 26 March and of course many thereafter. The messages were sincere, the grief, the respect for the man and the significance of the loss for French music were expressed by many great contemporary musicians in appreciative terms. Debussy died whilst enemy shots were being fired into Paris, and even though he had not fought in the war it is often Debussy's patriotism which is stressed. He had signed his final works composed in the war years 'Claude Debussy, musicien français'. D'Annunzio had called him 'Claude de France'.

The funeral took place on Thursday 28 March. Louis Laloy wrote, 'I see as in a bad dream the coffin near the piano and the musicians in their soldiers' uniforms … The door kept on opening and closing and there was no more room for the flowers."[83]

'On 29 March,' Vallery-Radot wrote,

> on a dull afternoon in a Paris alarmed by the news arriving from the front and frightened by the bombardment from Bertha, the coffin left the Square du Bois de Boulogne. There were about twenty of us following it in the drizzle. None of the passers-by had any doubt when they saw the very simple hearse decorated with a few flowers, that France had lost one of its greatest artists of all time.[84]

Within earshot of the canon, the coffin was carried to the Père-Lachaise cemetery to a temporary resting place. The distance was considerable, nearly nine kilometres, almost two hours on foot. Emma, Chouchou and 'Miss', Chouchou's governess, followed in a funeral coach.[85] Laloy tells us that about fifty people gathered in the Debussys' garden, but most left the procession en route, so only about twenty were left by the end. Laloy was wearing his military uniform. Camille Chevillard and Gabriel Pierné completed the whole journey;[86] others who accompanied them were Alfred Debussy, who had come straight from the trenches, arriving just as the procession was setting off,[87] André Caplet, Paul Dukas, Jacques

---

[81] C. p. 2189.

[82] G. Durosoir, *Le sergent André Caplet, 1916–1918*, http://www.megep.net/IMG/pdf/le_sergent_caplet.pdf (last accessed 13 July 2020).

[83] E. Lockspeiser, *Debussy: His Life and Mind*, vol.2, p. 224.

[84] P. Vallery-Radot, *Lettres de Claude Debussy*, p. 67.

[85] M. Dumesnil, *Claude Debussy, Master of Dreams*, New York, 1940, p. 318.

[86] L. Laloy, *La musique retrouvée*, p. 229.

[87] E. Lockspeiser, *Debussy: His Life and Mind*, vol.2, p. 224.

Durand, Roger-Ducasse, Henri de Régnier and Gustave Samazeuilh. None of them mentioned the presence of Misia Sert, but she was at the graveyard for in her memoirs she wrote,

> When Debussy died in 1918 … there were only about a dozen of us at his burial. Recently I chanced to find a postcard from Madame Debussy, thanking me for the flowers I sent. Under the printed name 'Mme Claude Debussy' she had written, 'You will weep for him often. What a disaster!'[88]

Also present initially was the Minister of Education, M. Lafferre, an acknowledgement of the significance of Debussy for French music. He did not, however, complete the whole route.[89]

Chouchou's behaviour at the funeral was impeccable. Her letter to Raoul continued:

> Thursday arrived, Thursday when he was to be taken away from us for ever! I saw him for one last time in that horrible box – on the floor – He looked happy, so happy, and then I did not have the strength to keep back my tears. Almost collapsing, I could not hug him – At the cemetery Maman could not have behaved better and as for me, not thinking of anything except that 'I must not cry for Maman's sake,' I summoned up all my courage, which came from where? I don't know – I didn't shed one single tear – tears held back are worth just as much as tears shed, and now it is night for ever. Papa is dead! These three words, I don't understand them, or rather, I understand them all too well – And being all alone to struggle with Maman's indescribable grief is truly horrific – for a few days that has made me forget mine, but now I feel it more deeply than ever – oh – you, who are so far away, spare a little thought for your little sister who longs to give you a hug and tell you how much she loves you – Do you understand everything I am feeling and can't put into words?
> A thousand kisses and all my love
> Your little sister,
> Chouchou
>
> It's unbelievable. I do not know how I am staying alive and I can't believe the horrible truth.[90]

Thus it is clear that Emma managed to remain dignified and composed during the funeral, but went to pieces immediately after. Twelve-year-old Chouchou was having to deal with this alone, for Raoul stayed working in London and Dolly stayed at home with her own family.

Erik Satie did not attend Debussy's funeral, but just over a month before he died he had renewed contact with him. He wrote to Henry Prunières on 3 April 1918, 'You know about Debussy's death of course. I wrote to him – luckily for me – a few days

---

[88] M. Sert, *Two or Three Muses. The Memoirs of Misia Sert*, p. 37.
[89] E. Lockspeiser, *His Life and Mind*, vol.2, pp. 224–5.
[90] C. pp. 2195–6.

before he died. Knowing that he was finished, alas, I did not want to stay angry with him.'[91] On receiving Satie's apology, Debussy simply muttered 'Sorry!'[92]

Now Chouchou had to cope with living with her suffering mother. Both their lives were unbearably sad.

[91] Satie. Correspondance Presque complete, p. 324.
[92] R. Orledge, Satie the Composer, p. 66.

PART TWO

EMMA THE WIDOW

18

April 1918 – December 1918: Emma's mission

Friendships furthered with Falla and Caplet

The war was not yet over. Yet more devastating for Emma, Debussy was dead. She was inconsolable. The news spread abroad rapidly, and on 29 March Manuel de Falla sent a telegram from Madrid, mourning 'the glorious creator of the new music'.[1] Emma responded by asking Magdeleine Greslé, a singer who became an ever closer and very helpful friend, to send him a photograph and autograph of Debussy. In his reply Falla not only thanked her for these mementoes of the 'unforgettable and adored Maître', but also sent her a copy of a talk he gave at the Ateneo in Madrid on 27 April 1918 entitled *El arte profundo de Claude Debussy*.[2]

This correspondence marked the start of a close friendship between Emma and the composer. Falla had spent seven fruitful years in Paris between 1907 and 1914 and established friendships with Debussy, Dukas, Viñes, Ravel, Satie and Stravinsky, despite acute innate shyness. He was in good health during these years, but as time went on became increasingly hypochondriac, relying on a vast array of medications, filtering his water and wearing gloves when shaking hands with people. Emma no doubt felt a kindred spirit, being so concerned for her own health, and would take a close interest in his welfare.

Gabriel Fauré was in Nice at the time of Debussy's death and on 6 April wrote a very touching letter to Emma, wishing he had been nearer at hand. How revealing is the sentence reading, 'I can't tell you how sorry I am to have got to know Debussy so late, for I was not attracted to him immediately!'[3] As in previous correspondence, his warm affection for Emma and Chouchou is evident.

P.-J. Toulet knew that time would not heal Emma's pain, but must surely bring her some calm. He warned her against taking notice of letters and articles which would exasperate Debussy in the world beyond if that were possible. He even offered to help her write her own biography of the composer 'professionally'. He hoped she and Chouchou would soon visit his part of the world, a wish which would soon be fulfilled.[4]

---

[1] C. p. 2193.
[2] Archivo Manuel de Falla, Centro Cultural Manuel de Falla, Granada, 6898-2-061.
[3] 'Je ne pourrai assez vous dire combien je suis peiné d'avoir connu si tardivement Debussy, car je n'étais tout de suite attaché à lui!' Gabriel Fauré to Madame Debussy, 6 April 1918. Copy kindly provided by Manuel Cardejo. Original in possession of Michel Pasquier.
[4] *Correspondance de Claude Debussy et P.-J. Toulet*, Paris, 1929, p. 126.

29. Manuel de Falla.
Photograph by Studio G. L. Manuel Frères

André Caplet told Emma, 'Claude Debussy lives on in my deepest heart and soul, as he lives and will live for ever in the soul and heart of all those who loved him.' He addressed Emma as 'Madame Amie et bien chère', empathising with her suffering, sad that he could offer no more than his humble affection.[5] He had resumed military duties as a '*sergent colombophile*', meaning he had been responsible since April 1917 for the care and use of pigeons for carrying military messages. Upon his return he had had the great pleasure of finding a present from Emma, presumably the customary supply of tobacco upon which he depended. Gradually, he told her, the awful vision of Debussy's tortured face during his final hours was giving way to a memory of his lively expression in better days.

In her reply, Emma responded to his warm mode of address by calling him 'Mon pauvre André Caplet' ('my poor André Caplet'). 'By what secret magic do you manage to picture him alive?'[6] Despite the existence of Chouchou, she was having to cope within a labyrinth of sadness, without the beauty Debussy brought to their

[5] C. p. 2194.
[6] April 1918, BnF Musique, Nla-269 (170).

tender, intimate existence together. Clearly, any memories of cross words between her and her husband were erased from now onwards. She realised she should have been wishing Caplet the courage to face life 'in the midst of the furnace', and apologised for her lack of organisation when he had left her. Significantly, she was sure he would be asked to complete Debussy's 'work in progress', but had been unable to find the relevant papers. Plans were already forming in her mind to ensure her husband's work was kept alive and Caplet was at the centre of these. Emma wrote to him with Elisa Beetz-Charpentier's address, which she had forgotten to send previously. She had tried to visit the sculptress to see the plaster cast of the death mask which Caplet had helped to arrange, but Madame Charpentier had not been able to receive her. Transport was a problem. 'Impossible to get a taxi this morning to drive me to and from Père-Lachaise – you can guess my exasperation and sadness thinking that his more than sacred remains are now in that dangerous grave … how can we remove them?'[7] Debussy's faithful driver, Jules, as well as the car, were no longer available, hardly surprising when one understands the parlous state of finances in which Emma and Chouchou had been left.

Battle to get Debussy's body transferred to Passy commences; dire financial situation

Emma was desperate to get Debussy's body transferred from his 'dangerous grave' in Père-Lachaise to the cemetery at Passy, as her husband had desired. Pasteur Vallery-Radot confirmed that Debussy had wanted to be laid to rest in Passy as this was 'less gloomy than other Paris cemeteries and he would be able to lie there amongst the trees and birds. But the Debussys had no family vault there.'[8] She was finding it impossible to get the relevant permission. War conditions had taken their toll. The art dealer René Gimpel described this cemetery in his diary on 6 November 1918:

> I had never seen the old cemetery at Passy, on the place du Trocadéro. I went up there, it's in the rue des Réservoirs. On the gateway, a blue plaque. It is at number 2. I go in and read the sign: turn right for curator's office. I carry on and growing in the empty plots I see lettuces, cabbages and vegetables. That's war![9]

Upon Debussy's death, the *notaire* made an inventory of the amounts Debussy owed to various people. The formal inventory was begun a year later, on 7 March 1919, and not completed until 24 December 1923. The two most outstanding liabilities related to huge loans provided by the organisation *L'Avenir du Prolétariat*,[10] which with interest amounted to 44,843.40 francs, and to Debussy's publisher Durand et Cie, 66,235.10 francs. There were twenty-three further outstanding payments total-

---

7   BnF Musique, Nla-269 (169).
8   P. Vallery-Radot, *Héros de l'esprit francais*, Paris, 1952, p. 108n.
9   R. Gimpel, *Journal d'un collectionneur*, Paris, 1963, p. 81.
10 See Chapter 13 p. 194 and Chapter 15 p. 224.

ling over seventy-three thousand francs.[11] At an exchange rate of twenty-six French francs to one British pound in 1918,[12] Debussy's total debt of 189,452 francs would have been the equivalent of approximately £7,280 in 1918, which according to one website today converts to over £416,000.[13] Such sums vary according to the rate of inflation calculated but, whatever the amount, it was left to Emma, Raoul and Dolly to sort out the financial mess.

Because royalties from Debussy's works now went primarily to *L'Avenir du Prolétariat*, Emma had no income from Debussy's estate. She must have tried to raise money immediately, for on 11 May 1918 René Gimpel made a note in his diary: '"*L'invocation à l'amour*". Sepia drawing by Fragonard. It is too pale, lacking detail, but what passion! Bought for fifteen thousand francs from Mme Widow Debussy, former wife of Sigismond Bardac.'[14] In descriptions of Debussy's own collection of works of art there is no mention of Fragonard, so this must have belonged to Emma alone, dating from the years of her first marriage.

On 17 May, Emma wrote to Arthur Hartmann in America expressing deep regret for 'the beauty and joy' she had lost. Whilst she could not 'abandon' the future for Chouchou's sake, Chouchou couldn't actually replace her loss. Then there was another clue to something Emma would be blamed by many for doing in the wake of Debussy's death: distributing his manuscripts, in part or whole, to people outside the family. Hartmann asked if she could find a specific piece, the *Poème* for violin and orchestra, which he claimed Debussy had begun in 1910 for performance on the American tour which never took place. Emma, however, was unable to locate it. She promised to let him know should she find it.[15] Besides the photograph of Debussy and his autograph that she had already sent to Falla, she must have sent him sketches for *La chute de la maison Usher* and *Ode à la France*, for he was later found to possess two pages of each.[16] Starting only weeks after her tragic loss, Emma was asked directly or through intermediaries for permissions to publish or for copies of Debussy's music, an aspect of his legacy that she would have to learn to deal with quickly despite her distraught state of mind and frail health.

The presence of Chouchou must surely have been some consolation to Emma. Such a level-headed twelve-year-old daughter was a rare gift. The remarkable letter Chouchou had written to her half-brother on the death of her father was evidence enough of her maturity, but now Emma tasked her with writing to her piano teacher, Ada Killick, who clearly had not been dismissed as Debussy had intended. In clear, bold handwriting Chouchou explained that her mother was too tired to write herself

---

[11] D. Herlin, V. Giroud, 'An Artist high and low, or, Debussy and Money' in E. Antokoletz and M. Wheeldon, *Rethinking Debussy*, Oxford, 2011, pp. 149–202.

[12] A conversion table for 1918 is presented in R. Gimpel, *Journal d'un collectionneur*, Paris, 1963, p. 473.

[13] https://www.in2013dollars.com/uk. £1 in 1918 = £33.76 in 2020 (last accessed 4 June 2020).

[14] R. Gimpel, *Journal d'un collectionneur*, p. 36.

[15] A. Hartmann, *Claude Debussy as I knew him*, pp. 144–6.

[16] C. G. Collins, *Manuel de Falla and his European Contemporaries: Encounters, Relationships and Influences*, D.Phil thesis, University of Bangor, 19 July 2002, pp. 141, 148.

to say that she would be unable to have her piano lessons on Monday or Tuesday. She was to send the bill for the lessons on receipt of this letter.[17] It is touching to witness the common sense of the young girl taking over responsibilities for a mother who was in dreadful pain with rheumatism and now in such distress that she could not cope with all she had to do. Chouchou had to write a second letter, for Emma lost Ada Killick's bill so needed another copy. Once received, the bill was paid with Chouchou including yet another note pointing out that she had left off the cost of some music. She began this letter by explaining that her mother's ailments had meant that they had not departed for Annecy as planned.[18]

Chaotic packing of Debussy's works; to Saint-Jean-de-Luz

By 20 June the family had managed to get away from Paris not to Annecy, but to more familiar surroundings. In Chouchou's last known letter to Ada Killick, written some time after 30 May 1918, we learn that Dolly and her daughters, Françoise and Madeleine, intended to accompany Emma and Chouchou to Arcachon.[19] These plans were thwarted, for on 20 June Emma wrote a detailed letter to André Caplet from the Golf Hotel in Saint-Jean-de-Luz, explaining that she and Chouchou had been driven out of Paris by the nightly bombardments, which were making Chouchou very nervous. She herself could not take the dampness of the night shelters, which aggravated her neuralgia. They had indeed wanted to go to Arcachon, but Miss (Miss Gibbs, Chouchou's governess), had not possessed the necessary papers. She blamed Dolly for 'dragging' them to Saint-Jean-de Luz, where they had been unable to find a small house to rent as everything was already taken. They had therefore had to move into the Golf Hotel which, although pleasant enough, was let down by its bad food and poor service. This brought little peace for Emma for now it was not she, but Dolly who was ill in bed. Emma complained that she was having great difficulty providing for her needs. Fortunately, four ladies staying nearby had taken it upon themselves to help Emma, one of whom was Magdeleine Greslé who was also a close friend of Roger-Ducasse.

Her feeling of guilt at leaving her *Maître* behind in Paris was haunting her. 'Have I committed a sort of moral desertion … ?' She used a word often used by her husband in times of despair: 'Wherever I go there is nothing [*le néant*]. Just the pain of every minute lived without him.' She had got nowhere in her efforts to get Debussy's body transferred to Passy. Meanwhile she had entrusted Debussy's belongings to their faithful friend, Roger-Ducasse.

> Fearing the bombing he had to undo countless little parcels and put everything he could get into a safe of the *Société Générale* and the big *Pelléas* score and large photos did not fit so he entrusted those to Durand who accepted them with no guarantee, but ensured that I wrote one.

---

[17] April 1918. J. E. Martins, 'Les trois dernières lettres connues de Chouchou Debussy', *Cahiers Debussy*, no.31, 2007, p. 79.

[18] May 1918. Idem. p. 81. Copies of letters at Centre de Documentation Claude Debussy.

[19] Ibid.

30. Golf Hotel, Saint-Jean-de-Luz, in the 1920s

She was now hoping the few things left which were 'without security' would reach her as soon as possible. Emma did express her realisation that Caplet had great problems to contend with. 'All this must be grotesque and seem trifling to a soldier (*poilu*). How can one fail to think of all those heroes fighting for years on end, often without complaint.'[20]

Louis Laloy was also later to remind his readers of the chaos surrounding the packing up of the composer's work. Because of the dangers posed by constant bombardment, Debussy's manuscripts had been hastily gathered together and placed in a safe deposit box of a financial institution, which was not opened, according to him, until a few months prior to March 1928.[21] This would lead to future problems recovering and preserving precious pages.

The Golf Hotel in Saint-Jean-de-Luz was a large establishment close to the beach at the northern end of the promenade, near the cliffs Debussy had so loved to see when staying at the Chalet Habas. It still stands today, a prominent curved building now converted into flats. The change of scenery brought no comfort to Emma. Her nights were terrible, her neuralgia plagued her. She had wanted to escape ever since her arrival, but had no idea where to go. Madame Charpentier's plaster cast of Debussy was causing trouble, for she had received only a distressing negative response from her. She referred to her 'ignoble lettre', which would seem to indicate a rift between Emma and

---

[20] Emma to André Caplet, 20 June 1918, BnF Musique, Nla-269 (171).

[21] *Le Gaulois*, 26 March 1928. In his biography of Debussy, Laloy said the box was not opened for several years. L. Laloy, *Debussy*, pp. 123–4.

the sculptress. Emma also complained to Caplet that everything she had been reading about Debussy was generally unsatisfactory and inaccurate.[22]

Godet requests access to Debussy's writings; Emma's plea to Laloy

Emma was probably thinking of Robert Godet amongst others when she wrote those words. In April she received the first of several long letters from Debussy's Swiss friend. He told her of commemorative concerts being performed in Geneva, particularly by Rose Féart and Ernest Ansermet, and sent her the text of a speech given by Jean Bartholoni, Director of the Geneva Conservatoire. He also mentioned a talk of his own and his articles on the composer, hoping she would read them.[23] In his next letter Godet claimed he was being asked to provide a more complete work on the composer.[24] He particularly wanted to use material from Debussy's critical writings. 'Am I being indiscrete in asking if you have plans for something like this?' he asked.[25] He remembered Debussy telling him Louis Laloy would be an excellent person to select articles and write the preface and introduction to such a volume. He also thanked Emma for already having given permission to a young conductor, Roger Jenoc[26] to form a 'Cercle Debussy'.

On 5 July Emma received a formal typewritten letter from Gaston Gallimard, one of the founders in 1909 of *La nouvelle revue française*, which would eventually become *Librairie Gallimard*. He was asking on behalf of Godet for permission to publish a book of Debussy's writings. He insisted Debussy admired his publishing house. Gallimard also wanted Emma to agree to the publication of a biography of Debussy by Godet.[27] A long letter to Louis Laloy written on 9 July gives an insight into Emma's multiple worries. She urgently needed advice, but did not know to which writings Gallimard was referring. She was cross with Laloy's wife Chouchik for not having replied to an earlier letter and was therefore having to resort to corresponding with her husband.[28]

In the past, Debussy had sold books to Louis F. Dorbon, a bookseller and publisher, to raise money.[29] In 1913 he had deposited the manuscript of *Monsieur Croche antidilettante* with Dorbon with the intention of his company publishing this collection of his criticisms and thoughts on music. Debussy had mentioned the idea

---

[22] Emma to André Caplet, 20 June 1918, BnF Musique, Nla-269 (171).
[23] Robert Godet to Madame Debussy, 27 April 1918. Copy kindly provided by Manuel Cardejo. Original in possession of Michel Pasquier.
[24] Robert Godet to Madame Debussy, 31 May 1918. Ibid.
[25] 'Serais-je indiscret en vous demandant si vous formez quelque projet à cet égard?' Ibid.
[26] Roger Jenoc (1891–1976), violinist, composer, conductor.
[27] Laloy archives, Dossier 81, C32. Godet published articles on the composer but no biography.
[28] Laloy archives, Dossier 81, C27.
[29] See Chapter 10 p. 134.

to Laloy as long ago as December 1906.[30] Laloy had indeed advised Debussy on the choice of articles to appear in *Monsieur Croche* and on 11 February 1914 he and Debussy had met to discuss the matter.[31] Correspondence had also taken place between the printer in Liège and Debussy when the proofs needed correcting.[32] Now, as Emma told Laloy, Debussy's writings from before 1905 were with Dorbon and there was talk of a biography by Robert Godet. Godet had already asked Emma to arrange for Laloy to write a preface, but she did not want this to prevent Laloy from writing his own 'volume'. She would far rather pass all relevant information to him than to Godet, to whom it would appear she felt some antipathy.

The letter continued with a liturgy of woes. The family were 'camping' in their hotel as holiday villas were too expensive, Dolly was still ill and Emma herself had broken her left arm so had had to travel to Bayonne for a plaster cast. She had heard nothing about getting Debussy's body transferred to Passy. Even more exasperating, 'La Ville de Paris' was demanding a contribution to the social security services (*l'assistance publique*) and the Registration Department (*l'enregistrement*) as compensation for her not making proper use of the plot she had bought at Père-Lachaise cemetery and planning to move Debussy's remains to Passy. Emma also mentioned Charles-Marie Widor. Widor was a member of the *Jury de Musique*, one of the *Jurys des Concours d'Art*. These *Jurys* were elected by the Conseil Municipal de Paris, the body ultimately responsible for overseeing cemeteries, so perhaps she wanted to enlist his support for moving Debussy to Passy. After having made Debussy sign the letter to him immediately prior to his death, asking to be considered for his chair at the Institut de France, she now felt she dare not write to him again. The letter ended with love to the Laloy children, 'but not to Chouchik' until she wrote to Emma again.

Included with this letter was an unattributed newspaper cutting entitled *La jeunesse de Pierre Louÿs. Gide et Louÿs à l'École alsacienne. Louÿs et Claude Debussy*, written by Debussy's friend and painter of his portrait, Jacques-Émile Blanche.[33] Emma was clearly disgusted by the passage on Debussy. Blanche described Louÿs' generosity to his poorer friends, buying them precious objects, which was how Debussy came to acquire some prized pottery by Delaherche. He emphasised Debussy's lack of education, saying he was virtually illiterate before Louÿs guided his reading, and described Louÿs' 'secret museum' with its model of a naked woman draped in Algerian cloth. Louÿs and his friends were privileged to hear the first drafts of *Pelléas*, but this was qualified by the assertion that Debussy was trying to pull in (*attraper*) publishers. The article ended with the image of Debussy leaving Louÿs' flat to choose a pastry from the Pâtisserie Favart, but not without first fingering several, which disgusted the lady behind the counter. Debussy hated the theatre, Blanche claimed.

---

[30] C. p. 982.

[31] C. p. 1762. When *Monsieur Croche* was eventually published in 1921, Debussy's corrections had not been observed. F. Lesure stated that the evidence is preserved in some pages of corrected proofs belonging to G. Jean Aubry. *Claude Debussy, the special centenary edition of Debussy's birth* published in 1962 by *La Revue Musicale*, numéro special 258, F. Lesure, 'Les expositions consacrées à Debussy en 1962', p. 140.

[32] C. p. 1814.

[33] Laloy archives, Dossier 81, C27.

The fashion was already for circuses and acrobats. Six words appear in Emma's hand beneath the article: 'La boue du Castrate! Quelle honte!' (literally: 'The filth of the Castrato. What a disgrace!') She clearly despised the antisemitic Louÿs and was sickened by this article by Blanche.

By 18 July Emma was in touch once again with her dear friend Chouchik Laloy, wanting to 'let herself go' to her, longing to see her. Her misery was indescribable. It felt like years since she had left her 'poor dear home'. Her daughters were behaving 'more or less', but her arm was still in plaster and very painful.[34]

Soon she was recounting further troubles to André Caplet. She was proud to have refused any morphine in spite of terrible pain in her arm. Her surgeon had forgotten about her in the midst of the many sick people he had to deal with, but she had managed to keep moving her swollen fingers to prevent them atrophying. She was now waiting for the doctor to remove her 'little arm' from its plaster prison ('mon petit bras', Yniold's words when hurt by Golaud in *Pelléas et Mélisande*[35]). Although feeling unsettled for the last two months, 'they', Dolly and her family, were keeping her there at all costs. 'They are spoiling me', said Emma, an indication that it was Dolly paying the bills. The letter was rambling, written on two pages with writing continued down the margins and at the top of the first page. Clearly Emma's distress was growing. Without Debussy, rain and darkness would be more in tune with her pain than the beautiful light around her, but at least she still had both daughters there, Chouchou being as helpful as ever.[36]

Laloy's help with Godet's proposal

Not until August did Emma receive a third letter from Robert Godet referring to the matter of Debussy's writings.[37] Because of postal delays he had only recently found out that she had already been approached by Gallimard himself. He insisted that it was the latter who had suggested to him the idea of a small volume in which he would expand on articles he had already sent to Emma and upon which she had made kind comments. He thought it essential to print the collection of articles in which Debussy expressed his own thoughts. The modest study of the composer which he was envisaging would also be good publicity for this book. As well as informing Emma about Debussy recitals and concerts taking place in his memory in Geneva, Godet referred again to the conductor Jenoc. His *Cercle Debussy* would give concerts of Debussy's works in the South of France as well as Grenoble and Lyon. Jenoc had asked Emma to become Honorary President of this society. Godet took it upon himself to advise Emma that before accepting such a position she should first see this group at work. Perhaps it is unsurprising that Emma's attitude to Godet was somewhat reserved. He certainly seemed to be pressurising her very soon after her husband's death to further his own ambitions.

[34] Laloy archives, Dossier 81, B15.
[35] Act III scene 5.
[36] Emma to Caplet 3 or 4 August 1918, BnF Musique, Nla-269 (172).
[37] Robert Godet to Madame Debussy, 4 August 1918. Copy kindly provided by Manuel Cardejo. Original in possession of Michel Pasquier.

From a letter to Chouchik dated 10 September, written late at night whilst she was suffering from a migraine, we learn that Louis Laloy had responded to her previous plea regarding Debussy's writings by sending her details and a receipt from the publisher Dorbon. She could not yet return to Paris as there were no seats available on the train, but she dreaded her inevitable distress on doing so, when she would have to try to arrange the burial plot at Passy.[38]

On the six-month anniversary of Debussy's death Emma wrote another long rambling missive to Laloy.[39] She always referred to her beloved and revered husband as *le Maître*, or *Il* or *Lui* with a capital letter, never *Claude*. Her grief was growing rather than diminishing as the days passed. Gallimard was now in contact with her about *Monsieur Croche* and she referred to Godet dismissively, having informed him that Laloy was publishing a revised edition of his own biography of Debussy.[40] She was anxious about the forthcoming revival of *Pelléas* at the Opéra-Comique, not knowing who would be performing or conducting, and wrote a note down the side of the page that Gheusi (Director of the Opéra-Comique) should appoint Messager or Caplet to conduct. Another reason for fearing her return to Paris was Dolly's insistence that she should go to a hotel rather than back home now that the Gothas were bombing again and there were no servants there.

Chouchou's essay published

Chouchou, meanwhile, managed to fill the time with some astonishingly mature creative writing. On Thursday 11 September 1918 a poetic essay was published in the *Journal de Saint-Jean-de-Luz*.[41] Its title is '*Le petit poilu*' ('The little soldier'), its subtitle 'La Lande en plein midi' ('The landscape at midday'). It is in the first person, an atmospheric description of a solitary foot soldier following a dusty track through a deserted landscape in the heat of the midday sun. There is not another soul in sight, not even a poor cow whose rusty old bell would sound harsh in this half-silence, nor even a miserable lost dog with its tail between its skinny legs. It is remarkable for its vivid strokes of colour. The rays of the sun are not yellow as a child might describe them, but white. Poppies beyond waving ears of corn are like a great sea of blood. Blue mountains in the distance seem to be watching the soldier. Muffled sounds fill the air, the song of the cricket blending with the rustling of the 'deaf, sad grass'. We become the soldier wandering along the dusty lane, head bowed before the immensity of the fields, a shudder going through him as branches sway as if all these soulless, yet immortal things were quietly saluting him. How reminiscent of her father is the last sentence: 'How can I ever thank you enough, nature, as you open up your heart to us, pouring on us all your bounty. My humble gratitude will never suffice.'

---

[38] Laloy archives, Dossier 81, B16.
[39] Laloy archives, Dossier 81, C28.
[40] Laloy's original biography appeared in 1909. The revised edition was not published until 1944.
[41] BnF Musique, La-Debussy Claude Emma-6.

Dolly and her children returned to Paris on 5 September. Emma remarked to Caplet that they were probably regretting this after the latest devastating bombings. She was unable to leave until between 5 and 10 October. Despite Dolly's and others' advice, Emma could not bear the thought of abandoning her beloved house in Paris. They kept reminding her it had only two miserable floors and no cellars, there was a garden and a square to get across beneath the shrapnel from 75s (a field gun) and it would be freezing cold in the winter. She was clearly putting much faith in Caplet's fidelity to Debussy and his interpretation of his works, for she was longing to talk to him about *Pelléas* and the *Fantaisie* amongst other matters. The pressure of the responsibility she bore for publications and performances of Debussy's music was mounting and she wished fervently that people would 'have the intelligence' to discuss their plans with Caplet first. Her efforts to purchase a plot of land in Passy for her husband's grave were still making no progress. 'For 5 months (soon 6 alas!) they have not even granted him the little piece of earth he wanted and which I have begged them to grant me.'[42]

Calamitous return to Paris; hotel life

An undated letter to Chouchik shows that upon her return to Paris Emma did Dolly's bidding and moved into the Princess Hotel, 10 rue de Presbourg, close to the Arc de Triomphe.[43] This residence was only temporary, for on Saturday 9 November 1918 Emma informed Chouchik of yet another disaster which had befallen her. She was becoming so immune to calamity that she claimed she remained calmer than she would have expected in the circumstances. She had been due to return to her house the previous Thursday. A valet, seemingly a very pleasant character, had been hired by the caretakers, M. and Mme Auger. Whilst the Augers were out one evening, he had emptied every drawer, cupboard and jewellery box and left with three hundred and fifty items of silver and jewellery. The police were taking fingerprints, but there was no hope of getting her precious property back as it would no doubt have been melted down. Devastated, she feared she could never return to her house, which felt violated. There was nothing for Chouchou to eat so now they had to go to the Hôtel Majestic. The only accommodation available there was on the fifth floor, but at least it felt safer than her house. She would have to go down to the restaurant twice a day. 'C'est une torture!' Most important of all was to find a flat to move into permanently.[44]

Unsurprisingly Emma was becoming confused, for less than a week later she wrote again to Chouchik unsure whether she had already informed her that she had moved out of the Princess Hotel.[45] She hinted that Chouchik should visit her at the Majestic, but not without prior warning, as she might be out looking for an apartment. 'Quelle horreur!'

---

[42] Emma to Caplet March, September or October 1918, BnF Musique, Nla-269 (173).
[43] Laloy archives, Dossier 81, B14.
[44] Laloy archives, Dossier 81, B17.
[45] Laloy archives, Dossier 81, B18.

Emma's eventual residence was the Hôtel Plaza Athénée at 25 Avenue Montaigne, where she would stay until she solved her housing problems. From here she wrote again to her friend on New Year's Eve. She was upset because the day Chouchik had at last fixed to come to visit her was the one day Emma had to go back to the 'poor house' in the avenue du Bois de Boulogne. 'Campbell', presumably the current tenant to whom it was sublet, had been conscripted, and had had to move out. Now she had to show the house to another prospective tenant. She longed for Chouchik to come as soon as possible to her hotel situated by Astruc's theatre (des Champs-Élysées), which brought such fond, sad memories. Touchingly, down the side of this card she wrote, 'feast days are for ever dead for me.'[46] Chouchou's festive season must have been very muted.

[46] Laloy archives, Dossier 81, B19.

19

1919: Tragedy and commemoration

Reliance on Laloy

On 11 January 1919 Emma continued to urge Louis Laloy to help her.[1] Gallimard wanted to add more writings of Debussy to those originally included in *Monsieur Croche antidilettante*, but she was determined to keep to the plans as Debussy had conceived them. She echoed her request for Laloy to write a preface to this edition and to speed up his own revised biography of Debussy, expressing her instinctive dislike of Godet, 'le Suisse', with whom she was only corresponding with feigned affection for the sake of her husband.[2] Although fearful of pestering Laloy, she then sent a telegram addressed to the Opéra, where he worked as Secretary General.[3] When he did not reply to this she turned to Chouchik in her anxiety. She was suffering mentally and physically and a week later both she and Chouchou were ill with tracheitis.

Transfer of Debussy's body to Passy

In January 1919 there was no apparent progress in Emma's battle for a plot in the cemetery at Passy even though she told Laloy that she had shown the concession she had been given to the head of the *Bureau des Inhumations*. Again she referred to Widor as if he could bring influence to her case, upset at his 'incomprehensible' response.[4]

Maurice Dumesnil wrote that it was Magdeleine Greslé who volunteered to attend to obtaining the plot at Passy on Emma's behalf and managed to persuade officials, who originally insisted that the cemetery was unused and no plots could be sold.[5] At long last, towards the end of February, Emma told Caplet that she had received permission to purchase a plot and that she would shortly be meeting the surveyor there.[6] On 10 March Emma informed him that on Wednesday 12 March she was going to Père-Lachaise at nine o'clock in the morning to take her 'poor, good Maître' to the Passy cemetery, saying she had only told him and Pasteur

---

[1] Laloy archives, B12, Dossier 81, C29.
[2] Robert Godet remained friendly with Lilly until her death. G. and D.-E. Inghelbrecht, *Claude Debussy*, p. 182.
[3] Laloy archives, B12, Dossier 81, B20.
[4] Laloy archives, B12, Dossier 81, C29.
[5] M. Dumesnil, *Claude Debussy, Master of Dreams*, p. 319.
[6] Emma to Caplet, undated. Between March 1918 and March 1919. BnF Musique, Nla-269.

Vallery-Radot.[7] However, Jean Roger-Ducasse was also present. Despite his familiarity with the family, his comments were ambivalent:

> We took Debussy's body from Père-Lachaise to Passy and yesterday, some friends, only very few, came to the cemetery to see a tomb without a cross, without any sort of religious symbol, just flowers, and at neither of these two ceremonies, even though they were sad, did I feel any sort of emotion! All that remains of him is his music. Is that enough, even when one has been a great musician? He had no friends and never knew how to make himself liked.[8]

On 23 March it was announced that friends of Debussy would meet at the tomb on the first anniversary of his death, 25 March. Emma asked Laloy to say a few words 'to our poor Maître who will at last be resting at Passy as he desired ... at least He will no longer be tormented.' She had chosen Laloy for this sad task as a mark of deep affection and the fond memories she had of him with Debussy. She hoped Chouchik would also attend.[9] Debussy's friends gathered round the tomb, which was covered with blue hydrangeas, black irises and violets. Amongst those present were Alfred Bruneau, Théodore Dubois, Jacques Durand, Marguerite Carré, Claire Croiza, Paul Dukas, Roger-Ducasse and Gustave Samazeuilh.[10] Laloy's speech was brief, expressing gratitude to the present company for their loyalty. Whilst there was as yet no headstone, the simplicity of the flowers would have pleased the composer.[11]

That afternoon Emma put pen to paper to thank Laloy for his respectful words, referring to her husband in almost religious terms. 'You must be close to Him at this moment, dear friend', she writes. Every day He was not there was an anniversary of the day He left her. She can't bear the thought of going back to the graveside and standing next to 'les indifférents'.[12] She wrote again the next day feeling she had not expressed sufficient gratitude and invited him and Chouchik to lunch two days later. So depressed, so tired of the misery brought by each new day, it is obvious she was in need of support. There is no extant correspondence with Chouchik between mid-January and the latter part of May 1919. It was Louis Laloy rather than his wife who bore the brunt of Emma's desolation.

The stone eventually placed on the simple tomb is inscribed with the words, 'Claude Debussy. Musicien français.' Funeral expenses and the monument would amount to ten thousand five hundred francs, as noted in the list of liabilities of Debussy's estate.[13] Emma and her family could not pay outright for this memorial. It was in this month of March 1919 that the formal inventory of Debussy's liabilities began.[14]

---

[7] Emma to Caplet, 10 March 1919, BnF Musique, Nla-269 (178).

[8] J. Roger-Ducasse, *Lettres à son ami André Lambinet, présentées et annotées par Jacques Depaulis*, Sprimont, 2001, p. 126.

[9] Laloy archives, B12, Dossier 81, C26.

[10] *Le Gaulois*, 23 March and 26 March 1919.

[11] *Excelsior*, 26 March 1919.

[12] Laloy archives, B12, Dossier 81, C30.

[13] D. Herlin and V. Giroud, 'An Artist high and low, or, Debussy and Money', in E. Antokoletz and M. Wheeldon, *Rethinking Debussy*, p. 197, n.7.

[14] Ibid. and Chapter 18 p. 261.

Formation of monument committee and a bust by Calvet

Since Debussy's death there had been talk of a permanent monument to the composer and now his friends and advocates formed a committee to this end. Its members included musicians Fauré, d'Indy, Ravel, Albert Roussel, Florent Schmitt, Gabriel Pierné, Camille Chevillard and Rhené-Baton, the writer Camille Mauclair and critic Robert Brussel.[15] The Belgian artist and sculptor Henry de Groux was the first to be commissioned. He founded a society with writer Carlos Larronde and composer Louis Carol-Berard with the intention of giving subscription concerts to raise the considerable amount of money necessary. He particularly wanted the monument placed at the entrance to the Bois de Boulogne. Both Madame and Mademoiselle Debussy were enthusiastic about the idea, he wrote.[16] Having attended a Debussy Festival, he was inspired to sculpt a bronze which is held today at the Bibliothèque-musée de l'Opéra, but his plan for a monument would never come to fruition. A photograph of the original plaster maquette shows a wild, godlike figure astride a Pan with his pipe amidst breaking waves.[17] Carol-Berard disliked it and it was never even shown to the committee.

A more sober depiction is a marble bust by Grégoire Calvet. Listed in the catalogue *Le Salon 1920* is item 2905: 'Claude Debussy compositeur. Commandé par l'État pour le foyer de l'Opéra-Comique'.[18] Presumably commissioned in 1919, this is evidence that the state did provide money for a commemoration soon after Debussy's death. Three undated letters from Emma to Albert Carré, director of the Opéra-Comique, refer to this bust and show that it must have been Carré who proposed the idea. First she told him that as far as she knew, her 'cher Maître' had never had a bust made of him. The Minister (des Beaux-Arts) had told her that Carré had already received official consent. Later she informed Carré that she had met Calvet and provided him with her best photos of Debussy. In the third letter she remarked that the presence of what must be the bust of her husband was incomprehensible and could not be tolerated out of respect for the 'Grand Maître disparu', but did not specify the location to which she was referring. Little wonder that she also refuted the accusation that she had given information to the paper *Le Cri de Paris*.[19] This must refer to an article claiming that the director of L'Opéra-Comique wanted a bust of Debussy, but the composer had never agreed to pose for one. Scurrilously it also reported that Debussy was very bad-tempered when rehearsing with his soloists, but also got angry with himself for singing out of tune when correcting them. Before the

---

[15] M. Wheeldon, *Debussy's Legacy and the Construction of Reputation*, Oxford, 2017, p. 137.

[16] https://www.bibliorare.com/lot/33856/ and https://www.bibliorare.com/lot/33853 (last accessed 22 September 2020).

[17] J.-M. Nectoux, *Harmonie en bleu et or. Debussy la musique et les arts*, Paris, 2005, p. 180.

[18] 'Claude Debussy, composer. Commissioned by the state for the foyer of the Opéra-Comique.' *Le Salon, 133e Exposition universelle 1920*, p. 161, https://gallica.bnf.fr/ark:/12148/bpt6k98116220/f341.image.r=buste%20Debussy%20Calvet (last accessed 22 September 2020).

[19] Three letters from Emma to Albert Carré. I am grateful to Denis Herlin for copies.

war, the journalist claimed, Marguerite Carré used to practise the role of Mélisande with Debussy every morning. He used to greet her in his pyjamas.[20]

Death of Sigismond Bardac

On 6 May 1919 it was announced that Sigismond Bardac, father of Raoul Bardac and Mme Gaston de Tinan, had died on 4 May. He had been suffering from a long illness at his home, 20 Avenue Victor-Emmanuel-III (now Avenue Franklin-D.-Roosevelt). The funeral took place in strict privacy, in accordance with Bardac's own wishes, on 7 May.[21] On 23 May an acknowledgement was published by M. et Mme de Tinan and Raoul Bardac in appreciation of the many messages of sympathy they had received.[22] By law, his children Raoul and Dolly would inherit a substantial portion of his estate. Those parts of Sigismond's will which were published listed his many legacies to charities, including those founded by Osiris.[23] No longer would Emma receive ten thousand francs a year alimony.

Rapsodie pour orchestre et saxophone; scepticism regarding the resurrection of Debussy's works

Emma was determined that her husband's compositions should be performed, wanted a say in who should perform them and, above all, wanted unfinished compositions to be completed. Clearly, not only would this be done out of love and reverence, but since Debussy's publisher Durand owned the rights to the compositions for which he had drawn up contracts in the past, these unpublished, randomly preserved manuscripts might bring her some much-needed financial benefits if published by a different firm.

In the boxes she had saved was the manuscript of the *Rapsodie pour orchestre et saxophone*, originally commissioned by the American Elise Hall, 'la dame au saxophone', as Debussy called her. He had signed a contract with Durand on 17 August 1903, but had completed no more than the short score. At that point it was entitled '*Esquisse d'une "Rapsodie mauresque" pour orchestre et saxophone principal*'. It still needed full orchestration. Emma turned to André Caplet for help. In the New Year he had been demobilised. Consequently the letter she wrote to him was addressed to him in his new capacity as Director of the American Expeditionary Force Bandmaster and Musicians School at Chaumont, founded by the American conductor Walter Damrosch. She wanted to meet him towards the end of January

---

[20] *Le Cri de Paris*, 13 April 1919.

[21] *Le Gaulois*, 8 May 1919. His death certificate gives his address as 39 Avenue Victor Emmanuel III.

[22] *Le Gaulois*, 23 May 1919.

[23] *Receuil des actes administratifs de la Préfecture du Département de la Seine 1920/03*, BnF, département Droit, économie, politique, F-27043.

to discuss a 'rhapsodie' [sic][24] and on 1 March she needed to see him urgently again to talk about the music (unspecified) of her Maître.[25]

Despite this, by 24 April 1919 it was not Caplet but Jean Roger-Ducasse whom Emma commissioned to work on this composition. He informed his friend Lambinet that 'As it contains two or three really tasty passages, I am transforming the saxophone into a cello. I have to do all the orchestration as it has only been sketched out on four staves. It's not boring although it's a lot of work – but I will take my time.'[26] In fact it remained a saxophone rather than a cello rhapsody. This was not the only item Roger-Ducasse would receive from Emma. Later she passed on an incomplete version of one of the *Proses lyriques*, 'De grève', as well as scores of *La mer* and *Nocturnes* with the composer's own corrections.

On 14 May 1919 his completed orchestration of Debussy's *Rapsodie pour orchestre et saxophone* was given its first performance by Pierre Mayeur at the Société nationale de musique in the Salle Gaveau, conducted by Caplet. The programme was announced as comprising only previously unpublished works.[27] Few newspapers published reviews of the concert, *Le courrier musical* regarding the *Rapsodie* as 'worthy of the *Nocturnes* and *Images*' but in contrast *Le monde musical* saying it was a work in which 'Debussy sounds least like himself.'[28] However, it has been pointed out that Roger-Ducasse remained true to Debussy's intentions, being intimately acquainted with Debussy's mathematical methods of composition, and having a deep understanding of Debussy's techniques of orchestration from around 1903–5, the years of *La mer*.[29] In 1944, Léon Vallas, scathing about any of the works resurrected by Emma, was to comment that the performance of this *Rapsodie* was virtually never repeated, even though the instrument became fashionable. 'It hardly counts in Debussy's œuvre.'[30] Another sceptic where the revival of Debussy's early works was concerned was Georges Jean-Aubry. Not long after Debussy's death he had already published an article in English expressing deep concern about the 'legacy of unpublished MS'.

> I trust that the brutal game which consists in publishing the very 'bottom of the drawer' of a great artist may not be played at his expense. I hope that the careful artistic consideration which often impelled Claude Debussy to keep a work a goodly length of time in his portfolio, until he was well content with it, as a man without petty vanity could expect to be with his creation, may be respected.[31]

---

[24] Emma to Caplet, 18 January 1919, BnF Musique, Nla-269 (174).

[25] Emma to Caplet, 1 March 1919, BnF Musique, Nla-269 (176).

[26] Roger-Ducasse, *Lettres à son ami André Lambinet*, p. 120.

[27] E.g. *La Lanterne*, 6 May 1919; *Journal des débats politiques et littéraires*, 15 May 1919.

[28] J. R. Noyes, 'Debussy's Rapsodie pour orchestra et saxophone revisited', *The Musical Quarterly*, 2007, vol.90, issue 3–4, p. 417.

[29] Idem. pp. 429, 431.

[30] L. Vallas, *Achille Claude Debussy*, Paris, 1944, p. 183.

[31] G. Jean-Aubry and F. H. Martens, 'Claude Debussy', *Musical Quarterly*, vol.4, no.4, 1918, p. 533.

Emma attended another concert of Debussy's orchestral works on 30 May with Chouchik and Louis Laloy, having invited them to meet her at her box in the Salle Gaveau. They heard Inghelbrecht conducting the Orchestre des Champs-Élysées with her friend Magdeleine Greslé amongst other soloists.[32]

Pelléas et Mélisande

Caplet's fidelity to Emma is touching after the demands of his wartime experiences, his illness, conducting work and now his marriage on 4 June 1919 to Geneviève Perruchon. The couple moved to Saint-Eustache-la-Forêt in Normandy, but Emma gave him little peace for, not long after this, Caplet received a letter asking if he had recovered not only from 'toutes vos récentes émotions', but also from influenza. She was worried by all the requests she was receiving for permissions: 'People ask my opinion, want my permission, neither probably will be respected. One never knows, or rather, I know only too well.' Above all she was disturbed by the thought of *Pelléas et Mélisande* being directed by anyone other than him. She needed his views on the matter, and was sad that he was now so far away.[33] As early as March she had expressed horror at the thought of Marguerite Carré singing the role of Mélisande again – 'effroyable!'[34]

On 26 April the announcement appeared in *Le Figaro* that the opera was to be revived at the Opéra-Comique for the first time since the war on 5 May 1919 with Messager, its original conductor. Emma thanked Carré for inviting her to rehearsals, but did not accept. 'I keep trying in vain,' she explains, 'but I never have the courage.'[35] She used the same excuse to Caplet on 26 April. Even if she went with Chouchou and Miss she still wanted Caplet's support.[36] The production was postponed until 9 May, upon which she was invited to attend a rehearsal by Messager. More excuses followed when she did manage to attend and felt unable to approach Carré or his wife. All her 'young friends' had had 'une délicieuse soirée.'[37] Gabriel Fauré wrote to Emma saying he would be in Carré's box on 16 May.[38] The date Emma attended is not known.

Chouchou's diary

An insight into Emma's and Chouchou's hotel life can be gained from Chouchou's diary, which she kept from 31 January to 5 February 1919, followed by some random

---

[32] Laloy archives, Dossier 81, B22; *Le Figaro*, 11 May 1919, p. 6.
[33] Emma to Caplet, June 1919 – November 1920, BnF Musique, Nla-269 (184).
[34] Emma to Caplet, 1 March 1919, BnF Musique, Nla-269 (176).
[35] Three letters to Albert Carré; see note 19.
[36] BnF Musique, Nla-269 (175), undated 1919.
[37] Three letters to Albert Carré.
[38] Gabriel Fauré to Madame Debussy, 15 May 1919. Copy of letter kindly provided by Manuel Cordejo. Original in possession of Michel Pasquier.

31. Hélène de Tinan (Dolly), 1919

notes.[39] Raoul was still working in London at the time, for an entry for February gave his address as Logan Studios, Logan Place, Earls Court. It is evident that Magdeleine Greslé was a constant visitor and sometimes brought her daughter with her. Her name appeared almost daily sometime between 3.30 and 6.30 p.m. Chouchou's cousin Madeleine visited, either with or without Dolly, but one tantalising entry for 31 January read '5.30: argument and Dolly stays for dinner.' The last formal entry on 5 February read 'Chopin', followed by the name Christiane then Madame Greslé and her daughter.

Following this, the music Chouchou must have been practising was listed. She named two pieces, *Fantaisie en ut mineur* by Mozart and *La Dauphine* by Rameau. Under the heading 'For Thursday 20 February' were works which perhaps she was going to play to others.

1st Arabesque (finie [finished])
Prélude Chopin (par coeur [by heart])
Presto Beethoven
Bach Invention
Étude Cramer

She was beginning to think about a similar list for Thursday 28 June, but sadly got no further. However, she and her mother were not short of music. Whilst at the Hôtel Plaza Athénée Emma invited the pianist Alfred Cortot to play to her. He said that he played Debussy's *Préludes* on Debussy's own piano. This was the first time that Emma had listened to her husband's music since his death. Weeping, she expressed her appreciation of his performance. She was not the only member of the family present. Chouchou sat in silence until Cortot asked her, 'And you, Chouchou, do you think I played the *Préludes* like your father did?' In reply, he recounted, he received a most eloquent lesson. 'Father listened more'.[40] Another pianist who played Debussy's works after his death in the presence of Emma was Walter Gieseking. Dolly told us that her mother was affected by his playing as it was so similar to Debussy's. Full of emotion she congratulated him personally.[41]

Death of Chouchou

Emma's sense of loss of her husband, then of ownership and responsibility for his music was overwhelming, but far more so was an appalling event on Wednesday 16 July 1919. Chouchou died unexpectedly of diphtheria. She was only thirteen years old. Her death certificate states that she died at 'her mother's residence, Avenue Montaigne 25'. This was the address of the Hôtel Plaza Athénée. An undated letter from Caplet to Emma expressed his incredulity at the awful news.

---

[39] Debussy, Claude-Emma, Agenda de Chouchou, 191 RESE-06.02 (6), Centre de Documentation Claude Debussy.

[40] 'Claude Debussy. Conférence de M. Alfred Cortot', given on 23 February 1933, *Conferencia*, no.18, 1 September 1933, p. 314.

[41] Dolly Bardac, London Interview.

> Madame Debussy! Madame Debussy! What can I say? What can I say? Any words would be so empty, so feeble, that I prefer to remain silent – the same appalled silence with which I met the terrifying news that Dolly had the kind thoughtfulness to tell me ...
> Poor, poor Madame Debussy! Your heart is bleeding. How can it bleed even more? How sorry I am for you and how near I am to you.[42]

Indeed, Chouchou died in the arms of her step-sister. Her death was the result of diphtheria having been wrongly treated. In addition, Emma had been treating Chouchou with homeopathy.[43] During an interview in 1952, Dolly called Dr. Crépel *'un médecin imbécile'* who had mistakenly been treating Chouchou for *'un embarras gastrique'*. A throat specialist had been called to carry out a tracheotomy, but it was too late. Chouchou died the next day.[44]

How could Emma cope with two such bereavements, so close together? Acknowledging a letter of sympathy from Marguerite Long, she wrote,

> But the horrible nightmare in which I live is so deep in me that I do not quite know where I am – it does not matter – nothing matters anymore. She does not live, my only reason to live. So why do I have to stay? She, gone! All her dear projects, all her future, all is dead! How in the world can my damned health endure such suffering? To have lost her, my pretty little girl, whose only wish was to blossom like a beautiful little flower![45]

Roger-Ducasse, who had been at Debussy's bedside when he died, had been close to Chouchou on Monday night before her death on Wednesday morning. He wrote to Jacques Durand on 19 July, realising that the publisher had not heard the awful news. 'Such a beautiful child. Poor Debussy seems to have brought bad luck with him. I fear that when she [Emma] realises the truth of this death, her solitude, and the sadness of her life from now on, our friend will just be marking time until the end of her days.' He then expressed sympathy in a very personal way. He blessed his own parents for having given him strong religious faith which enabled him to resist despair and look forward to the day when he was sure he would meet again those he had lost. In the Debussy household, however, 'Nothing of the sort. No religion, no hope of eternal life and nothing to sooth the anguish of mourning. I can't write any more as I am more upset than I can express, for her who has passed away and for the one who is left behind.'[46]

Chouchou was buried at Passy in the same grave as her father. Broken-hearted, Emma moved from one hotel to another, from the Hôtel Plaza Athénée to the Hôtel d'Albe, 55 avenue Georges V. A letter from André Caplet written on 3 October

---

[42] Letters from André Caplet to Emma Debussy 1918–1921, BnF Musique, Nla-32 (74–7).
[43] Information kindly provided by Roger Nichols, who was told this by Dolly.
[44] Notes in folder 'Tinan, Dolly de', Centre de Documentation Claude Debussy, RESE 04.68.
[45] C. Dunoyer, *Marguerite Long, A Life in French Music 1874–1966*, p. 75.
[46] Jacques Depaulis, 'Lettres de Roger-Ducasse à son éditeur Jacques Durand', *Revue de la Société liégeoise de Musicologie*, 8, 1997, pp. 5–126.

reached her there, expressing great regret for not having contacted her earlier. He had good reason. He had been suffering severely from the complications of having been gassed twice during the war – making it still more laudable that he had managed to be amongst the first to attend to the necessary arrangements after Debussy's death and to continue to support Emma.[47] Not until early October did Emma bring herself to inform Arthur and Marie Hartmann that 'in four days' Chouchou was gone. The doctors knew nothing, she said, not even whether it was diphtheria or meningitis.[48] It was Miss, still faithfully at Emma's side, who answered the Hartmanns' letter of sympathy. How she too missed her 'poor beautiful girlie'.[49]

Emma sent her new address to Chouchik on 16 October. Her normally strong writing was getting more uneven and illegible. Wherever she was, she was 'searching in vain' for her love, suffering constant torture. She had little time for the sympathy expressed by Gheusi, Chevillard and Pierné[50] who, she implied, could have little understanding of her situation. Chouchik, being a mother, would have far more empathy.[51] On 30 October Chouchik wrote to her own daughters Nicolette and Ninette, now aged eleven and nine, about the flowers she and they would lay on family graves on 1 November, 'La Toussaint', All Saints' Day. Touchingly, hers would be laid in memory of Debussy and his little daughter. It was, she wrote, as if he had carried her off with him into the other world.[52] She, like so many others, recognised the closeness of father and daughter.

Fantaisie pour piano et orchestra; further revivals

Since Debussy's death, Emma had kept in touch with Marguerite Long, who gave several recitals in 1918, sometimes advising her as to which works of Debussy she should perform. In June Emma attended a recital in which Long played three of her suggestions, *L'isle joyeuse*, 'Hommage à Rameau' and 'Mouvement'. She wrote to her afterwards expressing her deep emotion at hearing her perform the music 'which you knew how to penetrate'.[53] At the end of 1919 an early work of Debussy was resurrected, the *Fantaisie pour piano et orchestre*, composed in Rome in 1889. It should have been his fourth and final official submission (*envoi*), but was never performed or published in his lifetime, although Choudens engraved an edition but never released it for publication. It was dedicated to René Chansarel, who was to

---

[47] Letters from André Caplet to Emma Debussy 1918–1921, BnF Musique, Nla-32 (74–7).
[48] A. Hartmann, *Claude Debussy as I knew him*, p. 146.
[49] Idem. p. 147.
[50] Pierre-Barthélemy Gheusi (1865–1943), a director of Opéra-Comique, then of Théâtre Lyrique du Vaudeville, then editor of *Le Figaro*. Camille Chevillard (1859–1923), conductor of Orchestre Lamoureux. Conducted premières of *Nocturnes* and *La Mer*. Gabriel Pierné (1863–1937), fellow student of Debussy. Composer and conductor.
[51] Laloy archives, B12, Dossier 81, B22.
[52] 'Je porterai des fleurs à la mémoire de Debussy et sa petite fille, qu'il a comme emportée avec lui dans l'autre monde.' Laloy archives, B13, Dossier 16, no. 416.5.
[53] C. Dunoyer, *Marguerite Long*, p. 76.

have been its first performer in 1890. In 1909 Debussy had told Edgard Varèse that he intended to revise the combination of piano and orchestra and modify the scoring.[54] It was eventually published by Fromont and received its first performance in London at the Royal Philharmonic Society on 20 November 1919 with Alfred Cortot as soloist. However, when it was performed in Paris only a couple of weeks later on 7 December, Emma's wishes were granted when her conductor of choice, André Messager, directed the Orchestre des Concerts Lamoureux in the Salle Gaveau with her pianist of choice, Marguerite Long. She was too distressed to stay behind afterwards to speak to the performers, but wrote to Long to assure her that Debussy himself would have approved of her interpretation, and praised her virtuosity, saying she was admired not only by Debussy, but also by Chouchou. 'Where is the manuscript? I would like to give it to you,' she wondered.[55] Emma found this, for soon afterwards she presented Long with the original manuscript of sketches on three staves of the 'première partie' bearing Debussy's indications and alterations, dated October 1889 – April 1890. Inside Emma wrote, 'To Marguerite Long de Marliave in grateful memory Emma Claude Debussy 7 December 1919'.[56] Reminiscing on playing the piano with Debussy, Long remarked that the composer himself had not wanted the work published. She claimed that it was the publisher Jobert who possessed the manuscript and wanted it performed.[57] When Emma agreed, it was she who named the performers her husband would have desired.[58] It is most likely that it was Emma who initially instigated this revival, not just to keep her husband's music alive, but for financial reasons. The royalties would not disappear into Durand's coffers.

On 10 December 1919 three works were performed in one concert at the Théâtre Lyrique du Vaudeville, *L'enfant prodigue*, *La boîte à joujoux* and *La damoiselle élue*. *L'enfant prodigue* was given in the full orchestrated version first performed in Sheffield in 1908. In October 1919 André Caplet had signed a contract with Durand to complete the orchestration of Debussy's ballet *La boîte à joujoux*, not at Emma's request, but that of Gheusi, director of the Théâtre Lyrique du Vaudeville. The scenery and costumes were those originally conceived by Hellé, but the dancers were adults, not puppets as Debussy had wished. Claire Croiza sang the eponymous Damoiselle in *La damoiselle élue*, Inghelbrecht conducted. Emma took a personal interest in the production, for in a letter to Gheusi mainly concerned with *Khamma*, she requested that he corrected the lighting for *La damoiselle élue*.[59]

Not everyone was convinced that the resurrection of Debussy's early works was a good idea. Of *L'enfant prodigue* Léon Vallas commented, 'What possesses the publisher to think that this retrospective "creation" would be of any value? Scarcely has

---

54 *C.* p. 1204.
55 C. Dunoyer, *Marguerite Long*, p. 78.
56 'À Marguerite Long de Marliave reconnaissant souvenir Emma Claude Debussy 7 décembre 1919', *Cahiers Debussy*, no.34, 2010, p. 141. M. Long, *Au piano avec Claude Debussy*, p. 50.
57 Jobert did not purchase the publishing business of Eugène Fromont until 1922.
58 M. Long, *Au piano avec Claude Debussy*, pp. 49–50.
59 Letter in the possession of R. Orledge, reproduced in *Debussy and the Theatre*, p. 44.

a musician died than we exploit him like a forest: he is cut to pieces.'[60] One reviewer remarked that the very least one could say about this concert was that it was original compared with the *Tarass-Boulba* of Samuel Rousseau, performed the previous week. Each of the three works was characteristic of a 'moment' in the composer's artistic life, but none marked a decisive turning point. In *L'enfant prodigue* Debussy had written the music necessary to satisfy the requirements of the Prix de Rome. *La damoiselle élue*, although from almost the same period, was more characteristic of the 'true' Debussy, whilst *La boîte à joujoux* dating from 1913 was the most successful piece of the evening.[61]

Gheusi also wanted to mount a performance of *Khamma* at the Vaudeville, but was not able to trace Maud Allan. Emma promised to write to Jacques Durand, who was more familiar with 'the very nomadic Miss Maud Allan'. She was, in fact, in America.

Toulet's final requests to Emma

It becomes clear from P.-J. Toulet's letters that Emma had spent a brief time in the summer months of 1919 in Saint-Jean-de-Luz. An undated letter, written before Chouchou's death, expressed his pleasure that she was trying to find a villa there and hoping he would see her and Chouchou again.[62] Emma had had the thoughtfulness to send him some more of his beloved catalogues which, he remarked, he found less tasteful than five years previously. Now he requested some personal mementoes of Claude Debussy: two volumes of Baudelaire, *Curiosités esthétiques* and *l'Art romantique*, which he had given to Claude. In addition she should enclose any other small ordinary book he had read and a photograph of the composer, one of him gazing into the distance that evidently she had promised him before. It would be best if she brought the latter personally rather than entrust it to the post. It is clear from his next letter that she did indeed go to Saint-Jean-de-Luz, but it must have had too many associations, for she left abruptly, having only seen Toulet's wife.

On 19 December Toulet explained he had been meaning to write to her for three months, but had been even more ill than before. Emma had only been able to find one of the Baudelaire books he had asked for, so he reminded her to send him the other if she should discover it and also the ordinary cheap book he wanted, something Debussy had turned to often, such as his paperbacks of Stendhal. She must have sent photographs of Chouchou with her friends, for he would have preferred Chouchou to have been with Claude, or Emma or Dolly, rather than strangers who meant nothing to him. He had a recurring image in his mind of Chouchou popping into her father's study before bedtime, before the adults set about one of those 'dangerous card games' in which Dolly usually got caught out.[63]

---

[60] B. L. Kelly, *Music and Ultramodernism in France. A fragile consensus 1913–1939*, Woodbridge, U.K., The Boydell Press, 2013, p. 32.

[61] *L'Intransigeant*, 11 December 1919.

[62] *Correspondance de Claude Debussy et P.-J. Toulet*, p. 128.

[63] Idem. p. 129.

Toulet's final letter to Emma was sent in February 1920 thanking her for a small red notebook which had brought back memories of their games of whist. He had won more often than Claude even though he did not play any better, which infuriated Debussy. 'He seemed to think Heaven lacked any respect'. Emma should not worry if she could not find the missing Baudelaire, but he still wanted a book, such as Stendhal, which had no value, but which Debussy loved. He was sending Emma one of his own novels, *La jeune fille verte*, which had just been published. This letter was to serve as his dedication to her.[64]

[64] Idem. p. 131.

20

1920–1: Disappointments and disputes

Indifference to anniversary of Debussy's death

On 17 March 1920 Emma wrote to Chouchik Laloy, having had no success reaching her on the telephone. She was enquiring after Louis Laloy's plans for a gathering of Debussy's friends round his grave on the second anniversary of his death, leaving him to determine the time at which people should meet. Writing to her friend gave her the excuse she needed to 'let herself go' and express her perpetual acute misery. It was eight months since the death of Chouchou. She knew Chouchik's husband would have been just as sensitive to the presence of 'la lumineuse petite créature' whom he had watched growing up. She reminded Chouchik that Debussy used to call her 'mon plus beau chef d'oeuvre', his greatest masterpiece.[1]

On 15 April 1920 Émile Vuillermoz, music critic and ardent defender of Debussy's music, gave a lecture at the *Concerts historiques Pasdeloup*, which began with his expression of disappointment at the sparse number of musicians who had turned up at Debussy's graveside three weeks earlier. He decried the indifference of the powers-that-be towards a musician of such calibre, the silence of his contemporaries, the fact that there was no demand for a blue plaque whilst far less-deserving people had avenues and boulevards named after them. In some ways, given Debussy's personality, this was hardly surprising. 'He lived in a sort of proud misanthropy, hiding behind a wall of irony, zealously avoiding fools and bores'. He never encouraged words of gratitude or appreciation. 'Debussy was adored. He was not liked. He inspired love, discouraged affection.' He summarised his development since student days, the influence of poets and artists on his style, illustrated with practical examples sung by Blanche Marot and Ninon Vallin. Marcel Chadeigne played examples of piano works. He praised Debussy's liberating influence on orchestration and harmony, finishing with a demonstration of Debussy's genius for writing orchestral music with a performance of the *Nocturnes* played by the orchestra of the Concerts Pasdeloup.[2] This paean of praise by Vuillermoz is cited here in the light of future appeals for a monument to Debussy and the public disputes which would involve him and others decrying Emma's attempts to promote Debussy's previously unpublished compositions. Vuillermoz certainly did not support Debussy's widow in her choice of works or performers.

---

[1] Laloy archives, B12, Dossier 81, B23.
[2] E. Vuillermoz, *Claude Debussy, Conférence prononcée le 15 Avril 1920 aux Concerts historiques Pasdeloup*, au Ménestrel, Paris, Heugel, 1920. Also *Le Ménestrel*, 11 and 18 June 1920.

Summer in Saint-Jean-de-Luz

A brief message from Emma to Caplet on 20 June 1920 merely told him that if he thought of getting in touch with her, she was leaving the next day for Saint-Jean-de-Luz. Roger-Ducasse passed on news of her to Marguerite Long in a letter which demonstrates the care Emma was having to take with regard to finances and gives an insight into her life at the Villa Etchola without husband and daughter. Upon her arrival she discovered that besides the servants she was expecting, there was also the seventeen-year-old son of the gardener. Did she have to feed him as well? The lavatory was not working so she had to call the plumber and was wondering if she had to pay for the repairs. The cook was astonished at the simplicity of the menus, for in previous years ladies of the family used to have everything with champagne. The chambermaid found it more than strange that Madame Debussy got up at seven o'clock, for the ladies never used to get up before eleven o'clock, having had breakfast in bed.[3]

From here Emma wrote on 25 August to Marie Hartmann in New York in response to the reception of a photograph of Marie with her two children. Good weather and beautiful scenery did nothing to relieve her loneliness, she complained. She gave Marie the news that on her return to Paris in October she would be moving to 24 rue Vineuse in the sixteenth arrondissement, 'just beside the cemetery where my poor loves rest'.[4] This was to be her home address for the rest of her life.

In September Emma was still in Saint-Jean-de-Luz.

> Here, where everything is lovely, my radiant little girl used to be so happy. Now she is present in everything I love ... and I believe a miracle will show her to me by this adorable sea, in the sunlight, in the sweet shade of the pines, in the smell of the flowers which she loved. Then I have to return to cruel reality and carry on living without her, without Him![5]

After all her correspondence with P.-J. Toulet and her thoughtful parcels of catalogues, it is frustrating to find no mention of her reaction to his death on 6 September 1920, nor even to know when she was informed of it. He died at his home in Guéthary following a brain haemorrhage. This was possibly the result of an overdose of laudanum.[6]

Debussy's death mask in *La Revue musicale*; move to 24 rue Vineuse

In the same month Emma read an announcement in *La Revue française* of an issue soon to be published of *La Revue musicale*, being prepared by its founder, the musicologist Henry Prunières. Prunières intended this new journal to promote French

---

[3] Letter quoted in J. Depaulis, 'Roger-Ducasse et Marguerite Long, une amitié, une correspondance', *Revue Internationale de Musique francaise*, no.28, February 1989, p. 95.

[4] A. Hartmann, *Claude Debussy as I knew him*, pp. 149–50.

[5] Emma to Caplet, 15 September 1920, BnF Musique, Nla-269 (182).

[6] *Pyrénées*, organe officiel du Musée pyrénéen du Château-fort de Lourdes, p. 72, n.4.

music abroad and to inform readers at home about international music. Emma's indignation and possessive instincts were aroused by the imminent publication of the second issue, a special edition devoted entirely to Debussy, to appear in December 1920. To her horror, she read that a wood engraving by Dumser entitled 'Debussy on his deathbed', taken from an unpublished sketch by Othon Friesz, was to be included. She immediately bombarded André Caplet with letters. On 13 September she enclosed three documents, which were, according to a pencilled note down the side of her letter, a letter from Prunières and two announcements from *La Revue française*. She was furious to find that what she thought was her private property was being exploited. 'No one could have suggested the plaster cast to him – since it's my property and everyone thought that the sketch would become mine.' Caplet has added a note here: 'Everyone? Who? No one knew the sketch existed.' Emma wrote, 'Prunières doesn't even mention your collaboration!' to which Caplet has added the note, 'Ah! *C'est atroce!*'[7]

Already, Emma complained bitterly, the *Revue* was displaying a 'distinctly unfrench' flavour. She wanted nothing to do with it. The people involved were loathsome, their souls ugly.[8] Magdeleine Greslé supported her by writing to Caplet herself the same day, informing him that Emma had written to Prunières, objecting to publication of the drawing of which she had no knowledge. She feared it might be by the unknown artist Caplet had introduced at the avenue du Bois and she now begged him to forbid its publication. Emma was unable to tolerate this 'distressing theft'.[9]

Friesz wrote to Prunières acknowledging receipt of the proofs of his sketch, with which he was very satisfied, but also exclaiming that he could not understand the recriminations of Madame Debussy. It was Caplet who had asked him to make the sketch with her consent. Perhaps she was resentful because she had thought he would give it to her, he wondered.[10] Emma had to reassure Caplet that she was not blaming him for what had happened, but he had been the first person she had thought of to inform the artist directly of her opposition to publication. She had actually asked Prunières to wait until her death before publishing such material. Written down the side of this letter is a reference to another exploitation, as she saw it, of Debussy's music. 'After the crime of the *Préludes* at the Olympia nothing surprises me about Durand'.[11]

In July 1920 a Ballet-Pantomime had been performed at the Olympia music hall called *L'antre des gnomes*. It was choreographed by Georges Casella and Robert Quinault to four of Debussy's *Préludes*, 'Ondine', 'Général Lavine-eccentric', 'Danse de Puck' and 'Minstrels'. These had been orchestrated by Gabriel Grovlez, for which Durand had given his permission. Emma's had not been sought, nor did Durand need to do so. There is a long illustrated front-page review of the performance in

---

7   Emma to Caplet, 13 September 1920, BnF Musique, Nla-269 (181).
8   Emma to Caplet, 15 September 1920, BnF Musique, Nla-269 (182).
9   Magdeleine Greslé to André Caplet, September 1920, BnF Musique, Nla-269 (392).
10 C. Genovesi, 'Ventes aux enchères et dans les librairies spécialisés', *Cahiers Debussy*, 35, 2011, p. 114.
11 Emma to Caplet, 20 September 1920, BnF Musique, Nla-269 (183).

Comœdia with contributions by Louis Laloy and others, all praising every aspect of the work. The principal ballerina was Jasmine, a dancer so popular that she was even the subject of artworks by the Dadaist Francis Picabia. Emma, if she had read the review, must have been shocked to see her husband referred to by the reviewer as Claude Michel Debussy! Amongst the illustrious members of the audience were Alfred Bruneau, Lugné-Poe, Jean Cocteau and Colette.[12]

This was not her only bitter complaint to Caplet. '*Le Maître* was angry with Satie', she continued, yet now Prunières had asked Satie to contribute to his '*Monument*'. Whilst Prunières had published several articles in praise of the 'Precursor of Arceuil', Debussy had been represented as no more than a 'malfaisant impressionniste', an 'evil impressionist'. Obviously she had not forgotten Satie's letter to her of 1917, when he had referred to himself as the 'Precursor' who should stay at home far away from Debussy.[13] Any fond memories of Satie playing with Chouchou seem to have been erased. Emma ended her letter by berating Caplet for telling her he was not well, but not explaining what was wrong. He and Geneviève were expecting their first child, which would be 'something more exquisite than anything else in the world'.

On 24 October 1920 the Caplets' son, Pierre, was born and the family moved to Chaville to the southwest of Paris. On 27 November Emma wrote to him there hoping she might be able to visit them, at the same time reminding him that her adorable Chouchou would have been fifteen years old the previous month. Circumstances were accumulating to contribute to her growing depression. The letter began with a complaint of utter exhaustion from her 'miserable and interminable move' to 24 rue Vineuse. Not only had the furniture that had been kept in storage deteriorated, she was getting little help from suppliers now that she was amongst the 'nouveau pauvre', the opposite, of course, of 'nouveau riche'.[14]

When it did appear, the special Debussy issue of *La Revue musicale* contained lengthy articles by André Suarès, Alfred Cortot, Louis Laloy, Emile Vuillermoz, René Peter, D. E. Inghelbrecht, Robert Godet and J. G. Aubrey, but none by Caplet. There were six further contributions assessing Debussy's influence in other European countries, including one by Manuel de Falla on 'Spain in Debussy's music'. Emma's protestations had got nowhere, for the offending view of Debussy on his deathbed engraved after Othon Friesz's image was there for all to see. A specially commissioned musical supplement comprised thirty-two pages of compositions by Dukas, Ravel, Roussel, Satie, Schmitt, Bartok, Falla, Eugène Goossens, Malipiero and Stravinsky, illustrated with a lithograph by Raoul Dufy. Others might regard the international nature of the tribute as appropriate and gratifying. Clearly Emma found it intrusive. Also obvious was her continuing inability to find mental calm and be distracted from her two great losses, even far away from Paris.

Caplet was supportive of Emma to the extent that he did not contribute to the journal despite having been invited to do so. He wrote to Louis Aubert saying having given it some thought, this 'monument' was perfect as it was. Those who were writing

---

[12] *Comœdia*, 4 July 1920.
[13] See Chapter 17 p. 240.
[14] Emma to Caplet, 27 November 1920, BnF Musique, Nla-269 (185).

for it were better qualified than he to do so. He even stated frankly, 'Did someone say I had often met Claude Debussy? But that's a myth. I did not see a lot of him'[15] – this from a man who had known Debussy since at least 1906. Perhaps his modesty was due to his siding with Emma, a reluctance to join those she mistrusted. He did, however, keep a certain distance from her, for she complained that he never told her about his musical activities. She only heard via others what he was doing.

Hartmann's request; Trouhanova

Early in 1921 Emma was once more in touch with Arthur Hartmann on behalf of an artist friend, Hélène Dufau, who was going to New York, asking if he could introduce her to likeminded artists.[16] Dufau, like Emma, was from the Bordeaux area, having been born in 1869 in Quinsac, only about fifteen kilometres from that city. She also had a house in Guéthary, P.-J. Toulet's village. A month later Emma complained to Hartmann that she had received no reply to a letter she had written to Marie. However, she had a bigger grievance. Several months earlier she had read an article by Hartmann about Debussy.[17] Now she pointed out that in France it was not permitted to publish letters whilst family members of the deceased were alive. Hartmann must also have been asking her for more music and photographs of her husband, for Emma informed him that Debussy used to tear up everything that displeased him so she had few unfinished pages in her possession, most abandoned and unsigned. Any other manuscripts belonged to the publisher. She did, however, promise to send him some photos, signing the letter 'The very unhappy Emma Claude Debussy'.[18]

In December Caplet sent Emma a copy of his song cycle *Fables*, which would receive its first performance on 12 March 1921. Acknowledging this gift, she expressed the hope that she would soon hear his *Ballades*.[19] The first performance of Caplet's *Trois Ballades françaises*, sung by Claire Croiza, had been given on Friday 17 December 1920 in the Salle des Agriculteurs.[20] However, she needed his guidance yet again, concerning the dancer who she referred to as '*Trouhanova, Princesse Généralissime*'.[21]

At the height of her fame, in 1912 Natasha (or Natalia) Trouhanova had performed ballets choreographed by Ivan Clustine to *Istar* by Vincent d'Indy, *La tragédie de Salomé* by Florent Schmitt, *Adélaïde ou le langage des fleurs* by Ravel and *La Péri* by Dukas. During the war she had given up dancing and married Count A. A. Ignatiev, Chief of the Russian military mission at French G. H. Q., hence Emma's ironic title for her. In 1921 Trouhanova returned to dancing, appearing at

---

[15] Entry for 18 December 1920: http://www.andre-caplet.fr/biographie.htm (last accessed 14 July 2020).
[16] January 1921, A. Hartmann, *Claude Debussy as I knew him*, p. 150.
[17] She may have been referring to *Musical Courier*, 23 May 1918.
[18] February 1921, A. Hartmann, *Claude Debussy as I knew him*, pp. 151–2.
[19] Emma to Caplet between November 1920 and ca 1921, BnF Musique, Nla-269 (186).
[20] *Le Figaro*, 11 December 1920.
[21] Emma to Caplet, 20 January 1921, BnF Musique, Nla-269 (187).

the Opéra and in revues.[22] Now it appeared that Emma was making suggestions as to which works Trouhanova should choreograph, for she told Caplet she was meeting her the next day (21 January) and had thought of 'certain *Préludes* (not precisely *la Danse de Puck*!!) What do you think?' Shortly afterwards she reported to him on her interview with 'Madame TrouhaIgnatieff'.[23] Trouhanova had agreed to see 'the compulsory Durante', Jacques Durand. Emma suggested three pianists, Édouard Risler, Paul Loyonnet and Marcel Ciampi, the last of these being her preferred choice. Emma's plans had now grown to include the *Préludes* 'Danseuses de Delphes' and 'Les sons et les parfums tournent dans l'air', 'Danse' for piano, all the *Suite bergamasque* and *L'isle joyeuse*, which, as she pointed out, had been orchestrated some years ago by Bernadino Molinari.[24] She was pleased to find that Trouhanova already knew Caplet.

Her letter ended with yet another request to her patient correspondent. Could he find time to come to her house to rehearse what she called the 'Death of Isolde' with her friend Mme Gurlé, who did not know a note of it? Mme Gurlé had been invited by Fernand Lamy to sing at a concert in Valenciennes, where Lamy was Director of the Conservatoire. She had taken it upon herself to make this request as a favour to her friend without telling her she had done so. She did concede that he could refuse if he had no time, but she obviously had no conception of Caplet's condition following his wartime gassing and was making little allowance for his family commitments.

Emma's determination to give Trouhanova the opportunity to perform to Debussy's music led to a sense of panic, as arrangements did not go smoothly. Only a few days later she informed Caplet she had not been to meet her the previous day even though virtually ordered to do so ('She has married a Russian prince general after all!'). Trouhanova wanted to see all Debussy's orchestrated dance music, but Emma had now realised there was very little of this, perhaps even none at all. 'Tell me what I could show her that you yourself could orchestrate – and if you would be willing to do that.' She conceded, 'If you are not well are you at least *looking after* yourself?' but twice urged him to reply as quickly as possible.[25] Her demands were scarcely less imperious that those of the general's ballerina wife about whom she was so scathing.

Marius-François Gaillard; dedication of *Ode à la France*

Emma had an instinctive sense of possession where her husband's music was concerned. This legacy was in essence the greatest expression of his being and her feeling of 'ownership' led to bitter disputes. Her opinion was frowned upon by those with their own preconceptions. One of the earliest disputes centred on the pianist Marius-François Gaillard, born in 1900. Aged only sixteen he had won the *Prix d'Excellence* at the Conservatoire and was already making a name for himself in 1918 when

---

[22] L. Garafola, *Legacies of Twentieth-Century Dance*, Middletown, Connecticut, 2005, pp. 161–2.

[23] Emma to Caplet, ca January 1921, BnF Musique, Nla-269 (189).

[24] Not published until 1923.

[25] Emma to Caplet, undated (29 January 1921), BnF Musique, Nla-269 (188).

it was reported that despite a huge explosion that day (not a bombing but the ignition of a stockpile of munitions), there was a large audience at his piano recital on 17 March. In particular, his interpretation of twelve Debussy *Préludes* was praised.[26] The following year he received acclamation for a recital which included Debussy's *Images* and Ravel's *Gaspard de la nuit*. One reviewer placed him amongst the best interpreters of 'the new school'.[27] He was only twenty years old when he played every known piano work by Debussy by heart in a series of three evening recitals beginning on Wednesday 9 December 1920 in the Salle Gaveau. The critics were enthusiastic, one impressed with the 'beautiful boldness of youth' which enabled both composer and performer to emerge 'victorious'.[28] On 17 January 1921 he gave a two-hour recital in the Salle Gaveau, performing some Debussy *Préludes*, including 'La Cathédrale engloutie'. This was reviewed very favourably in *Le Figaro*.[29] He was certainly in the public eye this spring of 1921, giving another recital in the Salle Gaveau on 23 March.[30] Emma was so captivated by his playing that on that date she once again gave away an original manuscript of Debussy, the *Étude pour les arpèges composés*, not the version published in Debussy's lifetime (number 11 in the collection), but one he had also worked on in 1915 and marked as number 4.[31] She personally wrote a dedication in the copy, which reads, 'À Marius François Gaillard, 23 mars 1921. Emma Claude Debussy'. Even more fascinating is evidence that she dedicated a second work to him on the same date. In his catalogue of Debussy's works, François Lesure listed a dedication written on the manuscript of *Ode à la France*, which bears exactly the same words: 'À Marius François Gaillard, 23 mars 1921. Emma Claude Debussy'.[32] This was the work Debussy had begun in collaboration with Louis Laloy in 1916 but never completed, although Laloy asserted that Debussy did complete the music, which was in a pure style similar to, but even more poignant than, *Le martyre de Saint Sébastien*.[33] Laloy would return to this work in 1927–8. In fact Debussy had drafted a short score, fifteen pages for piano and voice, intended for soprano, choir and orchestra. In return for this gift, Gaillard dedicated to Emma the third of his *Mélodies chinoises*, 'Ki-Fong', also composed in 1921. This marked the beginning of an admiring friendship with Gaillard on Emma's part, which would have significant repercussions in years to come.[34]

[26] *Journal des débats politiques et littéraires*, 17 March 1918.
[27] Idem. 16 March 1919.
[28] Idem. 10 December 1920.
[29] *Le Figaro*, 19 January 1921.
[30] Advertised in *Le Ménestrel*, 18 March 1921, p. 124.
[31] This *Étude retrouvée* has been realised by Roy Howat and published in facsimile by Theodor Presser. The facsimile can be seen online at http://www.themorgan.org/sites/default/files/pdf/music/114410.pdf (last accessed 6 June 2020). See also R. Howat, 'A Thirteenth Étude of 1915: The original version of Pour les arpèges composes', *Cahiers Debussy*, no.1, 1977, pp. 16–23.
[32] F. Lesure, 'Catalogue de l'oeuvre de Claude Debussy', in Lesure, *Claude Debussy*, p. 566.
[33] L. Laloy, *La musique retrouvée*, p. 228.
[34] For a full discussion of Marius-François Gaillard see C. Rae, 'Debussyist, modernist, exoticist: Marius-François Gaillard rediscovered', *The Musical Times*, vol.152, no.1916

Demands on Caplet

Emma was still making demands of Caplet on 7 March when she repeated her desire for him to rehearse Wagner with her friend, Madame Gurlé. He had not replied, but she simply must fix these rehearsals for her friend's sake. She had heard his *Ballades* performed marvellously but had been too overcome with emotion and exhaustion to stay to thank him afterwards.[35] She had, however, been kind enough to knit Caplet's baby son Pierre a delicate blanket, for on 30 March 1921 Geneviève Caplet wrote a poetic thank you letter, saying Emma must have mingled her wool with gossamer thread from a fairy story. André Caplet added his own brief words of appreciation.[36] In view of Emma's painful hands this must have been a substantial effort.

Undated is a letter referring to a parcel of clothes. She had arranged to send it by rail, regretting that she did not have a suitable case to protect them. She was worried that illness was becoming her permanent state, but wistfully paraphrased Pelléas (with apologies to Debussy) when he asks Mélisande if he will see her again before his departure (Act IV scene 1), writing, '"Quand reverrai-je" Petit Pierre – Pardon Maître! Petit Pierre et sa douce maman'.[37] But then she had to ask for his assistance when her parcels were returned undelivered. Despite the demanding correspondence, when Emma did go to concerts of Caplet's works she always found it difficult to speak personally to him afterwards. One Sunday evening she explained in writing that she had been too moved by his music to remain behind and therefore had asked Geneviève to convey her admiration. She referred to the 'ardent piety' of the work, possibly his *Hymne à la naissance du matin*, the orchestral version of which was first performed on Sunday 27 February 1921. Since the war, Caplet's commitment to his Catholic faith had led him to concentrate on composing deeply spiritual sacred music.

Financial loan from Raoul Bardac

It was not just physical and emotional pain that Emma was suffering. Having moved to 24 rue Vineuse she was experiencing even more severe financial difficulties. This must be surmised, for according to the official document, the *Formule de Déclaration de Mutation par Décès* listing her assets and the deductions that must be made to calculate the amount of her estate to pass to her children after her death, on 21 May 1921 Raoul Bardac lent his mother 257,012.61 francs.[38] Currency fluctuations in the post-war period make it impossible to calculate this sum in today's values accurately,

---

(autumn 2011) pp. 59–80.

[35] Emma to Caplet, 7 March 1921, BnF Musique, Nla-269 (190).

[36] Geneviève Caplet to Emma, 30 March 1921, BnF Musique, Nla-32 (74–7).

[37] Two letters from Emma to Caplet between November 1920 and April 1925, BnF Musique, Nla-269 (215–6).

[38] *Formule de Déclaration de Mutation par Décès*, dated 27 June 1935. Copy of the document kindly provided by M. Vincent Laloy.

but it may well have been the equivalent of about £194,000.[39] The loan is listed as a deduction to be made from Emma's final assets so was repaid to him after she died.

This is a very specific date and amount, and there is no indication as to what such a large sum was needed for. Theoretically he was in a very strong position to lend her the money, for on 10 and 11 May the previous year, the sale by auction had taken place at the Galerie Georges Petit of Sigismond Bardac's art collection. The art collector René Gimpel wrote in his diary on 11 May 1920 under the heading 'Sigismond Bardac Sale':

> Bardac is dead. He was bitter, he was an argumentative person, but sincere as that type is. He was a good, unshakeable friend. I was very fond of him. His sale began yesterday and was very successful. The estimates were exceeded and there is nothing much of note left except his pastel by La Tour, for I bought his last very beautiful objects two years ago. The name Bardac will remain etched in the memory of the art world for a long time to come. The three brothers Joseph, Noël and Sigismond were all collectors. Only the first is still alive.[40]

The proceeds must have been huge, for the masterpieces included works by Fragonard, Boucher, Chardin, Goya, Guardi and Watteau to mention but a few, besides sculptures and antique furniture. Being part of his estate, by law much of this money must have gone to his children, Dolly, who was already living in some style with her husband, Gaston de Tinan, and Raoul Bardac, but obviously not to Emma.

From Raoul's *Curriculum Vitae* we learn that in 1919 he had resigned 'for personal reasons' from his administrative duties undertaken in London first at the *Mission Française des Transports maritimes et de la Marine marchande* then in the *Secrétariat administratif des Missions du Ministère de Commerce et du Ravitaillement (Provisions)*.[41] This sensitive personality had no doubt been shaken by three deaths, that of his father, his young step-sister and Debussy, and he had reacted badly to his wartime responsibilities. Undoubtedly, the inheritance from Sigismond Bardac was now enabling him to give up bureaucratic work. A reference to the National Probate Calendar for England and Wales indicates that in 1920 he received effects of £7,444.3s.2d from the estate of his father.[42] This sum converts in 2020 to approximately £335,000[43] (Dolly must have received the same amount). Raoul Bardac had an English solicitor acting as attorney presumably because in 1919, when his father died, he was still working in London. He put this money to practical use almost immediately.

Between 1920 and 1922 references to Raoul now appeared in such newspapers as *La Presse* and *Le Gaulois*, not for anything musical, but for horseracing. One can surmise that he had acquired enough money from his father's estate to invest in horses,

---

[39] Applying fifty-nine francs to £1 = £4,312. Then https://www.in2013dollars.com/uk/inflation/1920?amount=4312 (last accessed 3 November 2020).

[40] R. Gimpel, *Journal d'un collectionneur*, Paris, 1963, p. 161.

[41] R. Bardac, *Curriculum Vitae*, Centre de Documentation Claude Debussy, RESE-05.18.

[42] England and Wales, National Probate Calendar (Index of Wills and Administrations), 1858–1966 for Sigismond Bardac, 1920.

[43] See note 39.

for the *Écurie Raoul Bardac* (Raoul Bardac Stables) was represented at such racing venues as St. Cloud, Enghien, Dieppe and Chantilly. His face was sufficiently recognisable to be picked out in the stands by a gossip column reporter at the *Journée du Grand Prix* in Dieppe on 28 August 1921.[44] No doubt this was preferable to his administrative duties during the war years. In 1920 it was suggested to him that he become French delegate for the Merchant Navy and Maritime Transport at the *Sous-commission des réparations*, but this he declined for 'personal reasons'. His next official position would not be accepted until 1927 and that too he would soon leave for reasons of health. As for his musical compositions, an *Étude symphonique* entitled *Le printemps dans la forêt* was performed at one of the Concerts Lamoureux in the Salle Gaveau on 3 November 1919, which received very negative criticisms, citing a lack of elegant construction and proportion, no truly individual ideas,[45] and describing the work as that of a good student lacking maturity ('his spring is too green. He needs to mature').[46]

Roger-Ducasse to orchestrate *Proses lyriques*

Evidence that Emma had charged Roger-Ducasse with orchestrating a composition by Debussy comes in a July 1921 letter from this composer to Nadia Boulanger. In October 1896 Debussy himself had begun to orchestrate two of the set of four songs, *Proses lyriques*, originally composed for piano and voice in 1892–3, probably 'De soir' and 'De grève',[47] but he gave up in 1898, telling Pierre de Bréville, 'I've changed my mind. It seems to me completely useless to augment them with any old orchestral noise'.[48] Emma must have already given Roger-Ducasse Debussy's incomplete orchestral version of 'De grève',[49] for now he told Boulanger that certain manuscripts had almost met with disaster when his luggage being transported to Bordeaux caught fire in a railway carriage. His clothes and old metronome were destroyed, but 'Happily, my handwritings and Debussy's which were in my carpet-bag are saved'. These remarks have been interpreted as referring to the manuscript of *Proses lyriques*.[50] Roger-Ducasse was to struggle with the orchestration of the other two, 'De rêve' and 'De fleurs' between Emma's commission and their first performance on 9 March 1924.

During the summer of 1921 Emma returned to her familiar Saint-Jean-de Luz, where she stayed not in a villa but in the Hôtel d'Angleterre, situated on the seafront near the centre of the town. As she told Marie Hartmann, the rent for houses had doubled that year. Her unhappiness cries out. She complained of memory loss and

---

[44] *Le Gaulois*, 29 August 1921.
[45] *Le Gaulois*, 3 November 1919.
[46] *Le Figaro*, 4 November 1919.
[47] Debussy to Eugène Ysaÿe, 13 October 1896, C. p. 325.
[48] Debussy to Pierre de Bréville, 24 March 1898, C. p. 394.
[49] See Chapter 19 p. 275.
[50] July 1921 to Nadia Boulanger. Roger-Ducasse, *Lettres à Nadia Boulanger*, ed. J. Depaulis, Sprimont, 1999, p. 58.

poor eyesight in addition to her usual maladies. The hotel was miserable apart from its view of the sea but, above all, loneliness was crippling her. She took her meals alone, every evening was spent alone. Faithful 'Miss' was still there 'like a devoted ghost' but Emma was haunted by memories of her beautiful, intelligent Chouchou. She particularly remembered her sensitive way of playing the piano, 'effortlessly, in such a personal manner with a tender and intelligent sound.' Her two older children and two granddaughters, Françoise and Madeleine, were no compensation. 'I have no reason to live and I just stay here … For what? Why put up with all conceivable mental, physical and material annoyances? What's the use?'[51]

Chouchik Laloy; protective concern for Gaillard

It is clear from correspondence that Emma was still in touch with Chouchik Laloy in the 1920s. On 11 November 1921 Chouchik told her parents-in-law, Léon and Aline Laloy, that Madame Debussy had visited her, bringing two delightful presents: a milk jug from Bayonne and a piece of Moldovan embroidery.[52] On 8 July of an unspecified year, Chouchik wrote to her daughter Ninette, who was at boarding school, excusing her handwriting which was wobbly because she was returning from 'chez Mme Debussy' on the train.[53] On another occasion Emma entertained Chouchik to dinner.[54] These meetings were not frequent, however.

Little wonder, perhaps, that lonely and unhappy, Emma took such an interest in her pianist protégé, Marius-François Gaillard. On Sunday 4 December Emma wrote to Gaillard telling him he 'must not be ill'. Nor must he forget her. What is clear from this letter is that her feelings towards Gaillard were maternal and protective. She called him 'a small child who has been forgiven' (*un petit enfant pardonné*), but did not elucidate further, and invited him to lunch the following Sunday.[55] Others unkindly ascribed to Emma more inappropriate emotions. In his correspondence with Marcel Dietschy, André Schaeffner unjustly described Gaillard as 'le petit gigolo d'Emma'.[56] Her next extant letter to Gaillard was written after hearing him play a Mozart piano concerto at a Concert Pasdeloup on Saturday 18 December,[57] and this time she addressed him as 'cher enfant'. Congratulating him, she commented that he was 'exquisite – the orchestra less so, but that is between ourselves.' Noteworthy also is a glimpse of Emma carrying out familial duties, for she told Gaillard she had taken her grandchildren to the cinema.[58] This prevented her from hearing a repeat

---

[51] August 1921. A. Hartmann, *Claude Debussy as I knew him*, p. 153.
[52] Laloy archives, B13, Dossier 14, 332.100 p. 3.
[53] Laloy archives, B13, Dossier 18, 503.59.
[54] Laloy archives, B13, listed in inventory as Dossier 14, 356.124.
[55] Emma to Gaillard, 1 BnF Musique, Nla-13 (131–50).
[56] Letter from André Schaeffner to Marcel Dietschy, 12 January 1971, in N. Southon, 'Une correspondence entre André Schaeffner et Marcel Dietschy', *Cahiers Debussy*, no.34, 2010, p. 114.
[57] Listed in newspaper notices for that date – e.g. *Comœdia*, 19 December 1921.
[58] Perhaps to see *Les trois mousquetaires*, showing in several cinemas.

of the concert on Sunday 19 December. She had just met friends who had been enchanted by his interpretation of the concerto. She commanded him to telephone her to arrange a visit. She also added a little note asking 'How about Delange?', a reference to the editor of the journal *Comœdia*, which published a review of the concert.[59] She clearly wished to promote Gaillard as widely as possible, an aim which she would pursue the next year.

[59] Emma to Gaillard 2, 19 December 1921, BnF Musique, Nla-13 (131–50).

21

1922–3: Fiascos and controversies

Caplet and *Le martyre de Saint Sébastien*

January 1922 brought a flurry of correspondence between Emma and André Caplet. Her excitement had been roused by the visit of a secretary on behalf of Ida Rubinstein who informed her that Rubinstein had been engaged by Jacques Rouché, director of the Paris Opéra, to perform *Le martyre de Saint Sébastien* in June. Who would conduct this? Emma was desperate to know. Why not Caplet himself, she suggested hopefully. She obviously associated him closely with this work since he had orchestrated a large part of it and actively assisted at rehearsals. But she realised this might cause a problem with Hébertot at the Champs-Élysées.[1] The concerts of the Association des Concerts Pasdeloup were held at the latter and in February Caplet would be taking up his position as both vice-president of this Association and assistant to Rhené-Baton, principal conductor of the Concerts Pasdeloup.

Emma, as ever since her husband's death, was determined to influence the performance of his works. Three days later she was so excited she could hardly wait for Louis Laloy, who was Secretary General of the Opéra, to close the door behind him before she picked up her pen to write to Caplet. 'Laloy is just leaving'. She told him that he, Caplet, would conduct *Saint Sébastien*, if he so wished, and in addition, if he were free in the 1922–3 season, Laloy would be suggesting more concerts. 'But I'm going too fast,' she exclaimed. How pleased the *Maître*, Debussy, would be.[2] The following day she was puzzled that Laloy had not yet contacted Caplet. He should have telephoned him by now. Perhaps he received no answer, she wondered.

On 12 January Darius Milhaud conducted the first complete performance of Schoenberg's *Pierrot Lunaire* in Paris in the Salle Gaveau. Caplet must have suggested to Emma that she also should hear this work, for she made her excuses, saying she had got the date wrong, intentionally perhaps. In the same letter of apology she clung to her plan: 'I can't envisage *Saint Sébastien* without you. I must see Laloy on Tuesday. I will speak to him about it. And if I have to give in it will be with very bad grace!'[3] Whilst nothing would make her give up urging Laloy to appoint Caplet to conduct *Le martyre* at the Opéra, she was hoping Hébertot would put on the same work at the Théâtre des Champs-Élysées, telling him she was looking forward to the

---

[1] Emma to Caplet, undated (7 January 1922), BnF Musique, Nla-269 (194).
[2] Emma to Caplet, undated (10 January 1922), BnF Musique, Nla-269 (195).
[3] Emma to Caplet, fourth of four letters, undated, (May–June 1922), BnF Musique, Nla-269 (207–10).

'return of the divine *St. Sébastien* who will perhaps make Hébertot change his mind about putting on the work, and, of course, with André Caplet on the rostrum'.[4]

Raoul Bardac's troubles

Whilst Emma may not have been receiving prompt replies from Louis Laloy, unknown to her, her son Raoul was in touch with him. Before the war Laloy and Raoul had been cooperating on a 'drame lyrique', *Le songeur*.[5] The project had been abandoned when Raoul was called up, but now they were discussing its revival. However, the impression one gets from Raoul's letter of 10 January 1922 is of a man isolated and unsure of himself. His handwriting had deteriorated, he had lost the thread of his work, mentioned his 'isolement' (isolation), unimaginable things he was trying to forget. But 'if I did not have a love life [*une vie intime*], I don't know how I would survive!'[6] Laloy had suggested a composition competition in Nice, but Raoul was not enthused by the idea. He wrote to Chouchik Laloy on the same date. Clearly something serious had befallen Raoul to cause both Louis and Chouchik Laloy to contact him, but it is not clear precisely what this was. Again he emphasised to Chouchik his troubles, the urgent need to forget. 'Without her' he would be in torment, without joy, 'for joy must be found in innocent children, in our time, or in childlike beings.'[7] The reference is obscure. He was still married to Yvonne.

Perhaps a letter Raoul wrote to Louis Laloy the following year, on 27 May 1923, will help to explain matters.[8] His handwriting was stronger now. He was still considering work on *Le songeur*, but more significantly he told Laloy there was no point in explaining the whys and wherefores of his situation. It was the result of sudden events which had befallen him in the autumn of 1921 – i.e. shortly before the letters quoted above. Matters had now come to a head. What was more, he insisted his sister and mother should not suffer by being informed. Raoul's 'material existence' had become impossible. He clearly had no work, for things were so bad he had even tried to find a job where he would be posted to the Far East. The letter was written from a property he owned, 'Horizons' in Cap d'Ail, on the Mediterranean, which he would soon have to sell, when the proceeds would go to his 'beneficiaries'. This he must have bought when flush with money from his father. Desperate to stay in the south, where he felt a different person, he had cast around for ideas for employment, starting, in vain, with an administrative job at the Opera at Monte Carlo,[9] but he

---

[4] Emma to Caplet, third of four letters, undated, (May–June 1922), BnF Musique, IFN-53033848.

[5] See Chapter 13 pp. 193–4.

[6] Laloy archives, B12, Dossier 35, no.8.

[7] 'La joie doit être les enfants innocents, à notre époque, ou des êtres enfantins': Laloy archives, B12, Dossier 35, no.10.

[8] Laloy archives, B12, Dossier 35, no.10.

[9] Bardac's *Le Centaure*, a '*poème symphonique*' had premièred there. *Journal de Monaco*, 15 February 1910.

now thought he would have to return to Paris to set up a business of some sort, hoping to be able to compose in his free time.[10]

In the previous chapter, news reports of Raoul Bardac's participation in the horseracing scene were mentioned. One can only surmise that the Écurie Raoul Bardac, the horses in which he had invested after his father's death, had not brought the financial rewards he had hoped for. Reading the racing tips, one saw his horses placed high but, according to the results, they did not succeed. One must draw the conclusion that this had cost Raoul his assets. The Laloys were the only people Raoul could confide in, despite their closeness to his mother. He was relying on their silence. There is a parallel here in the unproven situation Dolly possibly found herself in, lending weight to the suspicion that Dolly and Debussy might have had recourse to Laloy's dependable confidentiality if there had been any secret correspondence between them. Little wonder Raoul did not want his mother to learn of the dire course of events when he had loaned her a large sum of money in May 1921 prior to his losses. This must also have added to his predicament.

Caplet's concerts; Gaillard to complete *Ode à la France*

Emma attended several of Caplet's recitals and concerts and was present in February when he conducted *La mer*, fully approving of his interpretation. Throughout she thought of the joy Debussy would have experienced in entrusting the work to him, for he managed to convey all the violence, the caresses, the smell of the sea.[11] On 18 and 19 March Caplet conducted Debussy's *Images* at the Concerts Pasdeloup, prior to which Emma was again in contact with him, this time about programme notes. Durand had none on this work, there had been no response from Laloy and what Charles Malherbe had previously written on 'Ibéria' and 'Rondes de printemps' was unsatisfactory; therefore they would have to use a few lines written by Daniel Chennevière.[12] Emma duly copied out some extracts from Chennevière's biography of Debussy published in 1913.[13] Her response to Caplet's performance was highly emotional, to the extent that she wrote him two letters after the concert, one expressing her joy as she had never before heard the *Images* so well conducted, the other much longer, full of gratitude at the infinite care he had taken over the interpretation. He had managed to convey intimate details which the uninitiated would not have been able to appreciate – in particular, in the 'sad gigue' he conjured up 'dancing shadows in the scented foliage, shadows of the dearest people'.[14] Her frustration with Laloy concerning *Le martyre* was growing, for in the same letter was a derogatory refer-

---

[10] Laloy archives, B12, Dossier 35, no.10.
[11] Emma to Caplet, ca February 1922, BnF Musique, Nla-269 (197).
[12] Emma to Caplet, 9 March 1922, BnF Musique, Nla-269 (199).
[13] D. Chennevière, *Claude Debussy et son œuvre*, Paris, 1913, pp. 37–8; letter from Emma to Caplet, undated (8 March 1922), BnF Musique, Nla-269 (198).
[14] Emma to Caplet, two letters, undated, 18 or 19 March 1922, BnF Musique, Nla-269 (201–2).

ence to a meeting arranged for Tuesday with *Le Chinois* (Laloy, sinologist as well as musician), to whom she had still 'said nothing'. Caplet should let her know if he wanted her 'to say or do something'.

On 1 January 1922, besides wishing him a happy New Year, Emma's maternal concern for Gaillard, who must have been either ill or exhausted, had led her to write, 'Child, give me news of you, as much as possible.' She forbade him to visit her immediately as he was better off staying in bed. But he must tell her when he could come and practise on her piano, since he liked it so much.[15] Later that month she informed him that Hébertot had been kind enough to give her a box at the Théâtre des Champs-Élysées on Friday 27 January and asked him to meet her there. She would be with 'friends'.[16] The letter, begun at 9 p.m. on 26 January, began 'Bonsoir, enfant.' Because of the late hour it was not postmarked until 7.30 the next day, so, as with her demands of Caplet, she was expecting to hear from Gaillard at very short notice. This was the final weekend of the season of the *Ballets suédois*, Jean Borlin's brilliant dance company which had been performing two works by Debussy, *La boîte à joujoux* and *Jeux*.

In March Emma attended three piano recitals given by Gaillard. Once again he performed all Debussy's piano works at the Théâtre des Champs-Élysées on 13, 20 and 27 March 1922. The critic in *Comœdia* praised Gaillard's bravery in concentrating on the works of a composer whose name appeared all too rarely in piano recitals and enjoyed the sonority, supple technique and warmth of his performance.[17] Henry Malherbe was enthusiastic about this unique project performed by a prodigious talent possessed by some mysterious fervour. His tanned face, his curly hair and beard, black eyes sparkling beneath a prominent dark brow reminded him of Claude Debussy himself, *Le Prince des Ténèbres* (The Prince of Darkness). It was certainly a memorable experience, the young pianist playing beneath alternating lights from two projectors, 'a very young man, hair aflame, seated in front of the black mass of a piano … filling the vast nave of the hall of the Opéra des Champs-Élysées.'[18] On Wednesday 15 March Emma wrote to Gaillard to apologise for not shaking his hand immediately after the first of these recitals, but she had not been feeling well ('un petit accident cardiaque'). Besides being upset that he had looked so tired out, she also complained that she had been unable to hear well from her seat. She particularly praised Gaillard's interpretation of the *Hommage à Rameau*, which 'captured the atmosphere of devout admiration under your attentive and sonorous fingers'. Even though still unwell, she was going to meet Dolly and her family in the Bois de Boulogne.[19]

In April Emma was once again concerned for the health of her 'child', worrying that his solitude was good for working and sleeping, but not for eating. Not only did she invite him for lunch and/or dinner any day, she claimed it would give her the greatest pleasure if he would come as often as possible. She would not detain him. 'I

---

[15] Emma to Gaillard 3, 1 January 1922, BnF Musique, Nla-13 (131–50).
[16] Emma to Gaillard 4, 26 January 1922, BnF Musique, Nla-13 (131–50).
[17] *Comœdia*, 27 March 1922.
[18] *Choses de Théâtre*, 1921(10)–1922(07), pp. 498–500.
[19] Emma to Gaillard 5, 16 March 1922, BnF Nla-13 (131–50).

would let you go as soon as you wanted as you have to "work". Don't let me wait in vain.'[20] Her familiarity with him also led her to ask him to book her two seats for one of Caplet's concerts rather than bothering Caplet himself. The young man, however, went straight to Caplet to ask for them, leading her to write to Caplet, 'Do excuse him. I can't hold it against him.'[21] Little wonder Emma's admiration for Gaillard led her to ask him to complete Debussy's cantata *Ode à la France*, the work Debussy had begun in collaboration with Louis Laloy in 1916, the manuscript of which she had dedicated to Gaillard on 23 March 1921.[22]

In August Gaillard travelled to Buenos Aires, where he performed his cycle of Debussy's piano works at the Teatro Opero as part of a concert tour of South America.[23] But when back in Paris it is evident that Emma constantly linked the names of Gaillard and Greslé, hoping they would perform together. Unfortunately an urgent letter addressed to the pianist written on a Sunday evening in February 1923 is now too faint to read, but one can just make out the words 'Dear Child, I am stunned [*bouleversée*] by what Madame Greslé tells me ... '[24]. We do not know what this news was. Another more legible, but undated letter also links Gaillard with Greslé. She invited Gaillard to tea on a Sunday to enjoy some *sablés* (shortbread biscuits) and to meet the (unnamed) 'Dutch poet' who was looking forward to listening to him. Greslé would also be there. She envisaged him performing a complete programme in the Hague in the summer.[25]

Le martyre, a shambles

Even into May Emma was still trying to find out from Caplet what his position was with regards to *Le martyre*. He had not mentioned it to her and she wondered if she should speak to Laloy about the matter again. On 22 and 23 April he had conducted a concert at the Théâtre des Champs-Élysées which included what was for Emma 'the sad joy ['la joie douloureuse'] of hearing *La damoiselle élue*', sung by Claire Croiza. She did not mention the performance of Arnold Schoenberg's *Cinq Pièces pour orchestre* op.16 in the same concert. Presumably she did not stay for this. She was, after all, suffering from terrible facial neuralgia whilst she was writing.[26]

Her hopes for a performance of *Le martyre* at the Concerts Pasdeloup were fulfilled when Caplet conducted his concert version with extracts of the poem on 11 and 12 May,[27] but this does not seem to have been widely advertised or reviewed,

---

[20] April 1922, BnF Nla-13 (131–50).

[21] Emma to Caplet, undated (end May/beginning June 1922), BnF IFN-53034080.

[22] See Chapter 20 p. 291.

[23] C. Rae, 'Debussyist, modernist, exoticist: Marius-François Gaillard rediscovered', *The Musical Times*, vol.152, no.1916, autumn 2011, p. 62.

[24] Emma to Gaillard 7, 18 February 1923, BnF Nla-13 (131–50).

[25] Emma to Gaillard 8, undated, BnF Nla-13 (131–50).

[26] Emma to Caplet, undated (postmarked 2 May 1922), BnF Musique, Nla-269 (202 Bis).

[27] Listed in online Biographie, http://www.andre-caplet.fr/biographie.htm (last accessed 10 July 2021). He repeated this in November 1922. *Le Ménestrel*, 4 November 1922; *Le*

probably due to the much larger production boasting the original cast which had brought Rubinstein to Emma earlier in the year and which took place at the Opéra in June 1922. Again correspondence flowed between Emma and Caplet as changes were wrought to the original work. For a start, the whole of the second act, *La chambre magique*, was to be omitted. When Emma found out about this she was shocked. Apart from the exquisite orchestral score, what would happen to the 'adorable' singing if this were suppressed? Could Caplet give it as an interlude? Presumably to discuss this, she invited him to lunch with the Laloys.[28] Writing to praise a concert of Caplet's own music the following week, she again commented on this omission. '*La chambre magique* stays and we will send Saint Sébastien for a walk whilst we listen with delight to anything you want.'[29]

Things did not go Emma's or Caplet's way. Caplet was so upset by the condition of the final dress rehearsal that he suddenly withdrew prior to the first performance on Saturday 17 June. 'My admiration and love of Debussy's music are too great for me to be able to present his work in such a state of scenic decomposition,'[30] he wrote to Rouché. Not only had the whole of Act II been cut, but the last act was a disaster. The chorus sang from the wings, which meant that 'because of its distance, the magnificent and luminous final chorus was transformed into a funeral chant.' They even let the intonation drop more than a quarter of a tone. The chorus master, Henry Defosse, now had to take over as conductor. In his account on the front page of *Comœdia*, Louis Laloy did not mention this substitution, but Charles Tenroc reviewing the performance asked, 'Was it a sudden indisposition? Or was it an excess of devotion to the memory of a great composer whose score he judged to have been sacrificed too far, drowned out by the sumptuousness of its surroundings?'[31]

On 22 June Caplet wrote a letter to the editor of *Comœdia* insisting that Laloy, whatever he might pretend, knew precisely why he had withdrawn as he had explained it to him loudly in front of witnesses. There had only been one full dress rehearsal with full cast and staging, contributing to the total lack of preparation of the technical side of the production. It should not have come as news to Laloy as he (Caplet) had already told Rubinstein and others some days previously that it was impossible to be ready by the due date. It was out of respect and love for the memory of Debussy that he had withdrawn from a performance where the poetic and musical forces were so unbalanced. He had been proved right by negative reviews.[32] These must have included that by Pierre Lalo in *Le Temps*, who emphasised that the music had been sacrificed to the poor production to the extent that it was difficult to

---

Figaro, 13 November 1922.

[28] Emma to Caplet, undated (12 May 1922), BnF Musique, Nla-269 (203).

[29] Emma to Caplet, 20 May 1922, BnF Musique, Nla-269 (204).

[30] Caplet to Jacques Rouché, undated, BnF, Bibliothèque Musée de l'Opéra, Rés Pièce-68 (5).

[31] 'Est-ce empêchement subit? Est-ce excès de dévotion à la mémoire du grand compositeur dont il jugea la partition un peu trop sacrifiée, noyée dans les somptuosités extérieures?' *Comœdia*, 19 June 1922.

[32] *Comœdia*, 22 June 1922.

comment on it at all. In particular he noted the chorus in the final act, which became a vague noise from the wings, the result of insufficient rehearsals, mediocre singing and even more mediocre playing by the orchestra.[33]

Laloy immediately refuted Caplet's claim that he had explained his reasons the night before the performance as in fact they had not talked to each other at all, one having been with the orchestra, the other in the auditorium. Only when they were leaving the Opéra did Caplet catch up with Laloy and tell him, 'Do you know what? I'm giving up. I'm giving up out of love.'[34] Laloy had simply put this down to the normal stress of final rehearsals. 'Come back tomorrow,' was his response. When Caplet did not return, Laloy telephoned him asking him to change his mind. Caplet, perhaps to cut the conversation short, told him he was ill. Laloy believed that the problems with the final tableau could have been solved the next day if they hadn't had to spend time finding a new conductor. The question he posed was: did Caplet think he was serving Debussy's work by abandoning his conducting post one day before the performance?[35]

Caplet must have warned Emma of an impending debacle prior to the Saturday performance, for she wrote a hastily scribbled letter on Wednesday night 'very late' (underlined) telling Caplet she had been ringing all morning to speak to him but had received no answer. First she reminded him she had no rights to the work. Durand (referred to disparagingly as 'Durfils') possessed them all. Caplet may have been trying to get Emma to exert influence over the production, for the Laloys, she said, had spoken to her about Caplet and Rouché, but had not been satisfied with her answers. 'Of course, I pretend that I always believed you were going to perform St. S.'[36] She desperately wanted to meet him and talk. On the back of the envelope she added that she had booked seats for Saturday so she must have been present at the first performance conducted by Defosse. Léon Vallas was also in the audience. In his first biography of Debussy, he told his readers that *Le martyre* had been performed in its entirety at the Opéra in June 1922 'but under poor conditions. It might be said that the famous work still remains an unknown quantity.'[37]

Falla's invitation to Emma

Perhaps Emma would have preferred to be in Spain in June rather than dealing with the stress of *Le martyre* in Paris. In Granada Manuel de Falla was organising a competition, a celebration of Andalusian folk song, 'El Concurso del Cante Jondo', with the collaboration of the poet Frederico Garcia Lorca, artist Ignacio Zuloaga, guitarist Andrés Segovia and others. Falla invited Emma to be present on 13 and 14 June 1922 in the Alhambra. When writing letters in French he first made rough drafts, many of which have survived, and it is from these that we read of his disappointment

---

[33] *Le Temps*, 21 June 1922.
[34] *Comœdia*, 22 June 1922.
[35] Ibid.
[36] Emma to Caplet, undated (June 1922), BnF Musique, Nla-269 (212).
[37] L. Vallas, *Debussy*, Paris, 1926, p. 164.

that she did not come, but also of the stress and sheer hard work of creating this festival.[38] Emma expressed her deep regret at being unable simply to get on a train to join him there. He should spare a thought for her when in the Alhambra, 'where the Maître would have been so happy to hear this Andalusian music which he loved so much.' She wondered if he was coming to the first performance of *Le martyre*, something she would have loved, but as the dates of his festival were so close to this, she must have realised this would be impossible. Greslé also corresponded copiously with Falla, sometimes about her projected performances of his works, often simply expressing affection, respect and concern for his health. Like Emma, she constantly hoped he would visit Paris.

Controversy over *Proses lyriques*

Meanwhile, controversy was also stirring over the performance of Roger-Ducasse's orchestration of Debussy's *Proses lyriques*. Emma, in close contact with Magdeleine Greslé, had fixed plans for her, telling Caplet, 'Regarding Croiza, tell her "la-vé-ri-té" [truth] – which is that Roger-Ducasse promised to give them [les *Proses*] to Pierné, with Madame Greslé – that's all – for I am not taking anything away from the latter to give it to the former. That is not at all to my taste.'[39]

Another letter to Caplet was just as adamant: 'I don't know if Ducasse has written to tell you. If he doesn't want or is not able to orchestrate the *Proses*, (having his own work to do), could he not pass it on to you? The *Proses* must be sung by Madame Greslé with Pierné. We must also think of both of them.'[40]

Roger-Ducasse had been working on this orchestration since the previous year, but was not finding the task straightforward by any means. He told Nadia Boulanger on 19 August 1922 that he was in the middle of it, but 'How difficult it is!' We learn that it was Gustave Samazeuilh who wanted Suzanne Balguerie or Claire Croiza to perform them, but Roger-Ducasse added, 'Madame Debussy wants the first performance to be given by Madame Greslé, which I find slightly worrying.'[41] Once again, Emma was not just encouraging performances of Debussy's works, even resurrected in unfamiliar versions, but also stipulating who should perform them. Moreover, it was not Jacques Durand who was going to be publishing these songs. It was to him that Roger-Ducasse complained once more, 'The *Proses lyriques* are wearing me out. The first one has eighteen pages of orchestration and I still have two and a half to write. I am paralysed in advance. And it is Jobert who will profit from all this. I would prefer Edgard Hamelle.'[42]

---

[38] July 1922, Archivo Manuel de Falla, 6898/2-044.

[39] First of four letters from Emma to Caplet, undated, (May–June 1922), BnF Musique, Nla-269 (207–10). '*La vérité*' is a reference to *Pelléas et Mélisande* (Golaud, Act V).

[40] Second of four letters from Emma to Caplet, undated, (May–June 1922), BnF Musique, Nla-269 (207–10).

[41] Roger-Ducasse, ed. J. Depaulis, *Lettres à Nadia Boulanger*, Sprimont, 1999, p. 66.

[42] August 1922. J. Depaulis, 'Lettres de Roger-Ducasse à son éditeur Jacques Durand', *Revue de la Société liégeoise de Musicologie*, 8, 1977, p. 72.

Jean Jobert had been an employee of Eugène Fromont, the publisher of Debussy's original version of the songs in May 1895. When Fromont died, Jobert bought the firm and opened the Éditions Jean Jobert in April 1921,[43] so it seems a logical decision that he should publish the orchestrated *Proses lyriques*, even if this was not to everyone's taste. More importantly for Emma, royalties would not disappear into Durand's coffers.

Jobert also wrote to Maurice Ravel in 1922, asking him to orchestrate two more of Debussy's compositions, his *Danse*, originally the *Tarantelle styrienne*, composed in 1890, and the 'Sarabande' from *Pour le piano* (1901). Ravel understood he could not do this without the authorisation of Madame Claude Debussy. He wrote to her on 8 June acknowledging that the two pieces were 'very orchestral'. He also regretted not having spoken to her at a recent concert in the Salle Gaveau, where Marguerite Long had told him Emma was in the lobby. He had rushed down, but she had already left. He hoped to meet her in Paris on 25 June on his way to London, where he would be recording his music for the Aeolian company. Of course, he received permission from Emma promptly and completed the transcriptions that winter. They were performed on 18 March 1923 by Paul Paray and the Lamoureux Orchestra.[44]

Return to Saint-Jean-de-Luz; further encouragement of Falla

In July 1922 Emma left once again for Saint-Jean-de-Luz, where she stayed in the Golf Hotel. From August Magdeleine Greslé rented a house nearby. Emma had already received from Falla the score of what she referred to as '*Chansons*', the *Siete canciones populares españoles* which Eschig had published that year. She expressed delight that Greslé would be singing them to his accompaniment.[45] From there each now wrote to Falla, wanting assurance that he had not been affected by a recent earthquake. Emma insisted he had 'spoiled her' with his gift of the score of *Le Tricorne*, (*The Three-Cornered Hat*) which had reached her before she left. She found it moving and splendid, but did not speak Spanish and felt too old to start learning the language, so would have to have it translated. What she wanted most of all was to meet him, perhaps halfway in San Sebastian? She was feeling ill, had not left her room and was very lonely.[46] He replied, grateful for her concern, but apologetic that he would not be coming to Paris until the winter. Nor could he spare time to travel to San Sebastian. In October he wrote again, sad not to have seen her and regretful not to have been able to show her Granada, that city evoked with such energy by the venerated *Maître* in his *Soirée dans Grenade*.[47] His correspondence with both Emma and Magdeleine Greslé was always affectionate

---

[43] https://www.jobert.fr/apropos.html (last accessed 14 July 2020).

[44] A. Orenstein, *A Ravel Reader, Correspondence, Articles, Interviews*, Dover Edition, 2003, pp. 225–6; *Maurice Ravel. L'Intégrale*, ed. M. Cornejo, p. 820.

[45] Archivo Manuel de Falla, 6898/2-002.

[46] Archivo Manuel de Falla, 6898/2-003.

[47] Archivo Manuel de Falla, 6898/2-045; 6898/2-046.

and his repeated invitations to both to come to Spain were reciprocated with vague expressions of intent to do so, but a visit from Emma never materialised. Greslé did carry out professional engagements in the country.

Emma's encouragement of Falla was heartfelt and enthusiastic. When she admired a composer or performer she would do all she could in her power to further their interests. Just as with young Gaillard, she wanted Falla to achieve all the accolades she felt he deserved – not so much in her name as in her husband's. Whenever she wrote to Falla, Debussy was guiding her train of thought. Very soon she began to address her letters and cards to him sometimes 'Mon cher Ami', but more often 'Mon cher Maître et Grand Ami'. What could be more affectionate and admiring than using the term 'Maître', usually reserved for references to her late husband? On 28 January 1923 Falla's *El Amor brujo* (*L'Amour sorcier*) was conducted by Enrique Fernández Arbós at the Concerts Colonne. Immediately Emma wrote to the composer to tell him 'Quel délicieux musicien vous êtes!' But, as ever, it was hardly for her sake that she revelled in the music. 'And how our beloved *Maître* would tell you this if he had heard your *Amour sorcier* conducted by Arbos!' She exhorted him to come to Paris rather than 'disappear', which she realised was because of his innate modesty and love of art for its own sake. She urged him to get this work performed at the Opéra. Suddenly she asked herself why she was writing so boldly to Falla. 'But I feel as if it is the *Maître* who is dictating to me.'[48]

Falla's *El Retablo de Maese Pedro*, 1923

An enthusiastic exchange of correspondence took place between Falla and Emma in the spring of 1923. Since his youth Falla had loved puppet shows and rediscovered this interest when commissioned by Winnaretta Singer, Princesse de Polignac to write a chamber opera, *El Retablo de Maese Pedro* (*Master Peter's Puppet Show*), based on an episode from Cervantes' *Don Quixote*. It received its first concert performance on 23 and 24 March in Seville, but was now to be staged for the first time with sets and costumes in Paris in the Princess's salon on Monday 25 June. Falla took great care in planning a reply to a letter from Emma, vigorously crossing out drafts until he reached the wording he wanted to express his deep emotion at her repeated desire for him to come to Paris. He addressed her as 'Bien chère Madame et Amie'. He was no longer going to delay his return to the city. How great his joy would be if the performance were honoured with her presence. This was not to forget that she and Magdeleine Greslé must still come to beautiful Andalusia.[49]

Once he was in Paris, Emma sent him an invitation to the 1923 revival of *Le martyre de Saint Sébastien*, which opened at the Opéra on Tuesday 19 June, conducted by Philippe Gaubert. He should also have lunch at her flat with Magdeleine Greslé. A message scribbled down the side of Emma's note leads one to wonder if his legendary shyness was getting the better of him: 'Yesterday at *Pepita* I waved to you, but

---

[48] Archivo Manuel de Falla, 6898/2-004.
[49] Archivo Manuel de Falla, 6898/2-060.

in vain!'[50] indicating that she had been to a performance of Albeniz's opera *Pepita Jiménez* at the Opéra-Comique. The French version performed here was translated from Spanish by Joseph de Marliave, deceased husband of pianist Marguerite Long. Falla did feel ill in Paris, but he still managed to lunch with Emma together with the critic Pierre Lalo, when 'Despite his ill health, he played them *The Puppet Show* at their request.'[51] On Sunday 24 June Emma sent him a telegram saying she was unable to go to the evening performance the next day. Instead she needed authorisation from him to attend the dress rehearsal.[52] *El Retablo de Maese Pedro* must have been a fascinating experience. Ricardo Viñes, assisted by his pupil Francis Poulenc,[53] and his nephew Hernando Viñes manipulated puppets specially carved in Spain, Vladimir Golschmann conducted a chamber orchestra and Wanda Landowska played the harpsichord. Winnaretta de Polignac was witness to the composer's painful shyness. After the public performance, she found him alone in the darkened music room behind the puppet theatre, cradling one of the hand puppets.[54] Emma received a wonderful bouquet from Falla on 3 July, a delight to her in her solitude, yet once again it was Debussy whom she put first, wishing he could enjoy the flowers. 'I am putting them next to the adored *Maître* who was so fond of you.'[55]

Whatever the state of her health, she was certainly actively promoting her husband's works. This and this alone spurred her on, as we learn from a letter to Arthur Hartmann in America in June 1923. 'The dear music of my beloved master is my sweetest refuge.' She was feeling old and lonely, overwhelmed with worries. Being so small she sometimes felt life would swallow her up, but like a little bubble, she just floated along. She complained about the cost and short supply of accommodation in Paris, including her own flat, which had been hard to find, but now she felt lost in it. She grumbled about the jumble of old sets and third-rate performers in *Pelléas et Mélisande* and Marguerite Carré's refusal to relinquish the role of Mélisande. She promised to give Hartmann one of her own copies of Debussy's '*Monsieur Croche*', as it had sold out until another edition was published.[56]

In August Emma once again communicated with Falla from the Golf Hotel, Saint-Jean-de-Luz, as ever desperate to see him. Only morphine brought some relief from terrible neuralgia, which had restricted her to her room for three weeks.[57] On 8 September Falla wrote to Magdeleine Greslé, expressing deep concern that Emma might become addicted to morphine. 'It's appalling stuff', he exclaimed.[58] On the same day he wrote a heartfelt letter to Emma, not commenting on the morphine, but demonstrating his concern, touched that she had written to him in the midst

---

[50] Archivo Manuel de Falla, 6898/2-021.
[51] J. Pahissa, *Manuel de Falla. His Life and Works*, trans. J. Wagstaff, London, 1954, p. 119.
[52] Archivo Manuel de Falla, 6898/2-005.
[53] S. Kahan, *Music's Modern Muse. A Life of Winnaretta Singer, Princesse de Polignac*, p. 236
[54] Idem. p. 237.
[55] Archivo Manuel de Falla, 6898/2-006.
[56] *Claude Debussy as I knew him*, Emma to Hartmann, 12 June and 15 June 1923, pp. 155-7.
[57] Archivo Manuel de Falla, 6898/2-007.
[58] Archivo Manuel de Falla, 7082-066.

of her misery.[59] Greslé let him know on 12 September that he could relax. The morphine injections had ceased two days earlier and now Emma was spending the day in Biarritz, meeting her daughter and friends for lunch.[60]

More cheerful was a letter from Gabriel Pierné to Emma thanking her for the best wishes she had sent on the occasion of the marriage of his daughter Simone. Emma was always welcome at the Théâtre du Châtelet when he was performing works by 'our dear Claude'.[61] But happiest of all was a letter of 3 November in which Emma expressed sheer joy at the prospect of Falla coming soon to Paris. She was feeling like 'une vieille petite fille' ('an old little girl') and had already booked tickets for a concert performance of *El Retablo de Maese Pedro* at the Concerts Wiéner. She was desperately hoping he would dine with her, to the extent that she said she would lay a place for him at her table every day, just in case.[62] Falla did indeed conduct *El Retablo* to great acclaim on 17 November, but there is no evidence of whether he accepted her invitation.

Emma named co-president of monument committee

When Henry Prunières was planning his special issue of *La Revue musicale* commemorating Debussy (December 1920), he had described it in a letter to Caplet as 'an international homage', which would be 'a veritable "monument" like those erected by Renaissance poets to artists they had loved.'[63] However, there was as yet no permanent physical monument to Debussy. Henry de Groux had failed to submit the required designs to the original monument committee so this project came to nothing.[64] Yet there was still motivation amongst Debussy's supporters to commemorate his life and on 2 July 1923 a plaque was placed on Debussy's birth house at Saint-Germain-en-Laye. Émile Vuillermoz described Emma being surrounded by 'les rares fidèles' during the ceremony. Next to this plaque was placed a second, provided by Debussy's English admirers, on behalf of whom a Mr. Johnston gave a speech. This speech was referred to in a much later article in 1927, in which the 'Englishman' was quoted as saying: 'The French do not seem to realise that they have lost a giant of musical art'.[65] Alfred Bruneau spoke of his memories of the composer and Madeleine Roch recited a poem which was reproduced on the front page of *Comœdia*.[66] Ironically, this was accompanied by a large sketch of Debussy by Sacha Guitry.[67] How many people realised that he had been married to Emma's

---

[59] Archivo Manuel de Falla, 6898/2-053.
[60] Archivo Manuel de Falla, 7082-018.
[61] Gabriel Pierné to Emma Debussy, 9 September 1923, BnF Musique, Nla-32 (82).
[62] Archivo Manuel de Falla, 6898/2-008.
[63] Letter from Henry Prunières to André Caplet, 11 June 1920, BnF Musique, Nla-269 (674).
[64] See J. M. Nectoux, 'Portrait of the artist as Roderick Usher' in *Debussy Studies*, ed. R. Langham Smith, pp. 108–38.
[65] *Comœdia*, 14 February 1927.
[66] *Le Temps*, 3 July 1923; *Le Ménestrel*, 6 July 1923.
[67] *Comœdia*, 14 July 1923.

cousin? Not only musicians had encouraged the permanent memorial to Debussy. The artist Maurice Denis, for example, who lived nearby, believed a simple statue of Mélisande crying by a fountain lamenting her lost ring would be more suitable than the large monument as suggested by a town councillor.[68]

However, a large monument was commissioned, still destined originally for Saint-Germain-en-Laye, from the sculptors who had begun their design sketches in 1919, Jan and Joël Martel and architect Jean Burkhalter. On 10 November 1923 the plans were exhibited at the Salon d'Automne. A photograph of the proposed design appeared on the front page of *Comœdia* and the following day there was an account of the visit of Alexandre Millerand, President of France, to the exhibition. He stopped in front of the maquette, beside which were standing Emma and 'several personalities from the world of music', amongst whom were Charles Widor, Louis Laloy and Marguerite Long. The Secretary General of the new monument committee, composer Georges Migot, had a speech prepared, which was reproduced in full in the paper, but unfortunately the President's official visit was so speedy that Migot had no time to present it. In the final paragraph he would have explained that they were all joining Madame Debussy in placing the monument under the President's protection, knowing that his name alone would ensure the project was realised.[69] Emma showed the design to the President, surrounded by 'musicians, virtuosi, artists, music-lovers all deeply moved by the music of the master.'[70] In 1926 Paul Sentenac remembered this occasion and the approbation the design received from art critics and other writers, including Colette, who declared that Debussy himself would have loved it. He explained that the straight lines of white marble were designed to harmonise with the '*arabesques*' of the trees providing a natural frame around it. The bas-reliefs were of figures inspired by Debussy's *Prélude à l'après-midi d'un faune, Le martyre de Saint Sébastien*. 'Mme Claude Debussy appreciates this monument as much as her husband would have done. With her, the municipality of Saint-Germain has adopted it,' he wrote.[71] Names he listed as supporters besides those mentioned above were Ravel, Inghelbrecht and Dukas. The presidents of the committee were Emma and the President of the Republic. There was also a propaganda committee, which included Gabriele d'Annunzio and Ida Rubinstein.

No doubt such a public event caused Emma much stress, even though she must have appreciated the reverence in which her husband was held. On 30 December she sent a brief letter to Arthur and Marie Hartmann, complaining once again that she was ill. This time she was covered in cupping glasses, an alternative therapy in which a suction is created on the skin. 'I wonder what I'm waiting for to die', she wrote.[72]

---

[68] *Le Bulletin de la vie artistique*, 1 July 1923.
[69] *Comœdia*, 11 November 1923.
[70] *L'Art et les artistes*, November 1923, pp. 197–9.
[71] P. Sentenac, 'Le monument pour Claude Debussy', *La Renaissance de l'art français et des industries de luxe*, 1926, July, pp. 515–21.
[72] A. Hartmann, *Claude Debussy as I knew him*, pp. 157–8.

22

1924–7: Friends and enemies

Emma helps Falla

In 1924, as a consequence of the concerts organised in Seville for the first performance of Manuel de Falla's *El Retablo de Maese Pedro*, the Orquesta Bética de Cámara was founded by Falla, the cellist Segismundo Romero and Eduardo Torres, Choirmaster of Seville Cathedral. Its conductor was Ernesto Halffter. Falla turned immediately to Emma for ideas as to what music of Debussy's would be suitable for small forces, and replying from her sickbed on 26 March, the day after the '*date cruelle*', the anniversary of Debussy's death, she suggested the *Danse sacrée et danse profane*, *Images*, *Nocturnes* and *Prélude à l'après-midi d'un faune* – 'All without trombone!' She would help to get hold of the music. In his reply Falla expressed sorrow and sympathy for her illness and the sad anniversary. He selected *L'après-midi d'un faune* and 'Nuages', the first of the three *Nocturnes*, and asked her to arrange for them to be sent to him as soon as possible.[1] The pieces were first published by Fromont, so there was no problem of royalties due to Durand. Following Emma's negotiations with Jobert, she expressed delight when he decided to lend Falla the material free of charge, a rare gesture from a publisher.[2]

Emma also encouraged Falla to come to Paris as soon as possible to give Louis Laloy the libretto of *El Retablo* to translate.[3] Despite her being a link between the two men, this was a mission doomed to failure, for a misunderstanding had already taken place concerning the project. Falla's publisher, Chester, had told Laloy in January that they were commissioning someone else to translate *El Retablo* as they had never received his letter of acceptance. They had appointed Jean-Aubry, who had already begun work on the project.[4] Laloy was surprised that he had not been informed of these developments. To Falla Emma expressed great regret at this outcome.[5]

That spring, the guitarist Andrés Segovia was in Paris giving several performances of Falla's *Homenaje*, his *Hommage à Debussy* originally published in the supplement to *La Revue musicale* of December 1920. Emma wrote to Falla eulogising this work

---

[1] Archivo Manuel de Falla, 6898/2-048.
[2] Archivo Manuel de Falla, 6898/2-023.
[3] Archivo Manuel de Falla, 6898/2-024. Laloy had translated the *Goyescas* of Granados into French some years earlier.
[4] Archivo Manuel de Falla, 7165-002 and 7165-007.
[5] Archivo Manuel de Falla, 6898/2-023.

and its interpreter, but complained that he seemed to be forgetting her, beseeching him to come to Paris.[6] Her sympathetic friend Magdeleine Greslé, however, wrote directly to Segovia asking him to give a private recital in Emma's apartment. This he agreed to in a letter of 8 March 1924, saying not only would he be pleased to pay homage to Madame Debussy and her friends, but he would also like to hear Greslé singing again, having enjoyed her performance so much the first time he heard her.[7] A postcard from Falla to Greslé indicated that this private recital had already taken place by 18 March, for he was just about to go to Madrid and was hoping to meet Segovia there and hear news of this soirée.[8] In reply, Greslé told Falla that Segovia and his guitar had also provided an unforgettable evening playing his music at her home. The guitarist was clearly generous with his time.

In May Falla was overwhelmed by work correcting proofs and preparing for a performance of *El Retablo* as well as the first concerts of his Orquesta Betica.[9] To Emma's disappointment, it was not Greslé who was chosen to sing his songs at a recital in Paris that month. She was impatient, as ever, to see him.[10] However, Falla explained that he was not only overworked, but unwell, and feared a recurrence of the dizzy spells he had suffered in Paris the previous year. Therefore he would wait until winter, when he hoped *El Amor Brujo* and *El Retablo* would be performed. He regretted the misunderstanding with Laloy, but was delighted with Jobert for giving him a free copy of the score of *L'après-midi* (he had decided to purchase the orchestral parts). As for the Paris concert without Greslé, he had had nothing to do with it. Had he known he would have been happy to ask for her collaboration.[11] Falla's revised orchestration for small forces of *Prélude à l'après-midi d'un faune* was eventually performed in Seville on 10 December.

Raoul's continued financial support

The name of Othon Friesz, who had made the wood engraving of Debussy on his deathbed, was to be found next to that of Madame Debussy in a report of the final dinner of the season of the Société des Amateurs d'Art that April. There is something incongruous in the vision of Emma, together with eminent members of society, painters, sculptors and writers all gathered in a room decorated ingeniously with balloons suspended by strings bearing tombola tickets. Following speeches, the exotic dancer Vanah-Yami, 'veiled in black', climbed onto a table to perform voluptuous oriental dances. The bohemian writer Francis Carco followed this by

---

[6] Archivo Manuel de Falla, 6898/2-009.

[7] Letter for sale at https://www.schubertiademusic.com/items/details/13905-segovia-andres-autograph-letter-to-magdeleine-gresl%C3%A9-regarding-a-recital-at-the-debussy-home (last accessed 6 June 2020).

[8] https://www.drouot.com/lot/publicShow?id=8917228 (last accessed 21 June 2020).

[9] Archivo Manuel de Falla, 6898/2-047.

[10] Archivo Manuel de Falla, 6898/2-010.

[11] Archivo Manuel de Falla, 6898/2-049. Madeleine Grey was the soloist in the concert of 27 May.

standing on a chair singing '*complaintes apaches*' ('hooligan laments'). The evening ended with dancing to a jazz band, surely not Emma's natural environment.[12]

That summer Emma returned to Saint-Jean-de-Luz to recuperate from the stresses of Paris, where once again she stayed at the Golf Hotel. A September letter to Arthur Hartmann provides a rare glimpse of her son Raoul. She complained of her disastrous troubles with housing since Debussy's death and said she had an honest business manager, but

> ... in order not to be 'on the street' I must pay a fortune, and without my son who is helping me a lot I could neither be here nor live in Paris – even with [financial] worries – and what awaits me on my return? Since 1918 the legal proceedings, overdue accounts with Durand from well before our marriage ... all – all has fallen 'on my shoulders'![13]

Evidently Raoul, rather than Dolly, had been providing support, despite his own financial worries, which Emma was not to know of. She informed Hartmann that she had been unable to find a copy of a book he wanted, nor had she yet been able to obtain *Monsieur Croche*, which was with the publisher Gallimard, but had not yet appeared. From time to time she had heard the *Préludes* played, including Hartmann's favourite, *La fille aux cheveux de lin*, which were bearable when played well, but in the cinema they could be torture when not. Clearly, Debussy's piano music was already being used to accompany films, an interesting insight in view of future discussions of the links between Debussy's music and film music.

Another society with which Emma was associated was Les Amis des Lettres françaises. In October both she and Paul Dukas chaired a musical committee which organised a 'soirée musicale' following a dinner in honour of the Spanish novelist Blasco Ibanez. The programme consisted entirely of music by Debussy, songs sung by Mme Cesbron-Viseur and *La cathédrale engloutie* played by the pianist Denyse Molié. Her fellow guests included General Mangin, who had encouraged André Caplet, Lucien Durosoir and Maurice Maréchal to continue playing during the war.[14] Emma also spent an evening at the opera at the invitation of Louis Laloy. She could drown her sorrows in company, for Laloy told his parents that the opera just about to have its première, *Nerto*,[15] was appallingly dull. He, Madame Debussy, Francis Poulenc and the abbé (Léonce Petit, former *Apache* and chaplain of the Opéra) had obviously relieved their boredom subsequently by imbibing alcohol, for he commented that they were breathing out wine-laden fumes as in a bacchanalia.[16]

Several months had passed since Emma had heard from Falla. Her loneliness and need for constant contact with her protégés, her desire to be useful to them, led to her being demanding of their time and company. On 11 November 1924 Falla

[12] *Comœdia*, 15 April 1924.
[13] September 1924. Hartmann, *Claude Debussy as I knew him*, pp. 159–60.
[14] See Chapter 16 p. 233 n.6.
[15] *Nerto* was a 'drame lyrique', music by Charles-Marie Widor, libretto by Maurice Léna based on a poem by Mistral.
[16] '... exhalant des fumes vineuses comme un bachique.' 25 October 1924, Laloy archives, B12, Dossier 17, 1924, no.180.

received a printed visiting card bearing her name upon which she had written 'How you forget me! What have I done to you?' Tellingly, on the reverse he noted, 'But how can I forget you? Quite the opposite!'[17] He wrote back the same day, saying in turn that he had not heard from her for a while. Always the hypochondriac, he complained that not just work but his dizzy spells were preoccupying him.[18]

Orchestrated *Proses lyriques* and concert version of *Khamma*

Earlier in the year, on Saturday 8 March 1924, the long-awaited first performance of Roger-Ducasse's orchestrated version of Debussy's *Proses lyriques*, originally composed in 1892–3, took place under the auspices of the Concerts Lamoureux in the Salle Gaveau, conducted by Paul Paray. They were not sung by Emma's first choice, Magdeleine Greslé, but by Suzanne Balguerie. Robert Brussel regarded Roger-Ducasse as the perfect orchestrator. Anyone not completely familiar with his works would have thought this version was by Debussy himself. It was not the music but Debussy's texts that were outdated, in his opinion.[19] Raymond Charpentier, whilst praising both orchestration and performance, wondered whether the songs gained anything from this treatment, a reminder of the ongoing debate about the value of presenting versions of the composer's works which he had not himself authorised.[20]

Towards the end of the year, on 15 and 30 November, a concert version of Debussy's ballet *Khamma* was performed, conducted by Gabriel Pierné. Less than a month later, Charles Koechlin wrote a lengthy letter to *Le Ménestrel*, responding to an accusation by André Schaeffner that the orchestration of the ballet had been carried out 'in obscure conditions'.[21] On the contrary, declared Koechlin, the orchestration had been completed by two musicians whilst Debussy was alive, before the war. The first pages were by Debussy himself, the rest by a colleague he had chosen (Koechlin). He insisted that Debussy would never have let anything pass which did not completely meet his intentions and he would have examined closely the slightest detail of the orchestration. This was not a work completed posthumously well or badly, but one carried out under Debussy's supervision, with his complete approval.[22] Raymond Charpentier questioned the authenticity of the orchestration, asking whether the manuscript had remained merely a sketch, remarking that the music was vague and disjointed.[23] Robert Brussel asked 'To what extent was this Debussy's

---

[17] 'Comme vous m'oubliez! Que vous ai-je fait?' 'Mais comment vous oublier? Tout au contraire.' Archivo Manuel de Falla, 6898/2-011.

[18] Archivo Manuel de Falla, 6898/2-050.

[19] *Le Figaro*, 10 March 1924.

[20] *Comœdia*, 10 March 1924.

[21] *Le Ménestrel*, 5 December 1924.

[22] *Le Ménestrel*, 19 December 1924. See also R. Orledge, *Debussy and the Theatre*, p. 134, where he states that Debussy orchestrated as far as bar 55 of scene 1 and Koechlin orchestrated the remaining five-sixths between 6 December 1912 and the end of January 1913.

[23] *Comœdia*, 17 November 1924.

work?' He pointed out that no one knew exactly how many manuscripts Debussy had left behind nor their state of completion.[24]

The negative reviews of the concert upset Emma. In an undated letter to Falla she exclaimed, 'I hate Paris. Concerts are two a penny. Do you know "*Khamma*" by the Maître?' She exhorted him not to feel anxious about the performance of his own works as they were too precious to deny to Parisian audiences. She remarked on the unhealthy jealousy of musicians, a vicious circle as such jealousy was indeed justifiable, she argued.[25] This letter again shows that Emma's encouragement of Falla was motherly, just as with her young protégé, Gaillard. Falla responded positively to her support, expressing constant gratitude to her in his correspondence.

On 4 November 1924 Gabriel Fauré died. Surely Emma must have attended his full state funeral at the Madeleine on 8 November? There was no mention in the press of her presence, but there were so many musicians listed that this is not surprising. It must have been a poignant occasion, especially as he was buried in the Passy cemetery not far from Debussy's grave.

Whilst, much to Emma's frustration, Jacques Durand possessed the copyright to Debussy's works, he was generous in 1924 in donating the manuscripts to libraries. On 11 June it was reported that he passed the score of *La berceuse heroïque* to the library of the Opéra,[26] and in December of the same year he gave fifty-six manuscripts to the library of the Conservatoire de Musique. Some years previously he had already given them the score of *Pelléas et Mélisande*.[27] He did not discuss these gifts with Emma.

Sacha Guitry's article on Debussy; Emma's grandchildren perform in concert

Perhaps it was Emma's disgust at the attitude of her contemporaries to Debussy's legacy that led her to copy out by hand a passage from a book published in 1925 called *L'Esprit* by Sacha Guitry, husband for eleven years to her cousin, Charlotte Lysès. It contained a lengthy passage on Debussy, which began with his acknowledgement that he had no authority to write about the composer as he did not know him. His appreciation of Debussy's significance was heartfelt. Little wonder Emma wanted to keep the passage expressing frustration that those who initially admired Debussy's music were accused of being snobs, yet in the end it was the snobs who were right. Only after his death did those who had mocked him during his lifetime lament the 'cruel loss' to French art. Why, Guitry asked repeatedly, did we have to wait until he died to render the homage due to him?[28]

---

[24] *Le Figaro*, 19 November 1924.
[25] Archivo Manuel de Falla, 6898/2-030.
[26] *Le Gaulois*, 11 June 1924.
[27] *Le Figaro*, 14 December 1924; *Le Temps*, 10 November 1924.
[28] S. Guitry, 'Claude Debussy est mort', Text copied from *L'Esprit*, pp. 239–41 as noted by Emma, Centre de Documentation Claude Debussy, RESE-06.04.

In 1920 Emma's friend and interpreter of Debussy's piano music, Marguerite Long, had succeeded Louis Diémer as professor of piano at the Paris Conservatoire. She would present her pupils in concerts to great acclaim, and sometimes gave young beginners an opportunity to perform in public. On 2 April 1925 two pupils who particularly stood out were Mesdemoiselles Madeleine and Françoise de Tinan, Emma's grandchildren, now aged twelve and thirteen. They performed two movements of Fauré's *Dolly* suite so well that they had to play an encore.[29] In a letter to Chouchik Laloy, written on 20 May 1925, Emma mentioned another concert of Marguerite Long's which she attended despite feeling unwell.[30] She was disappointed not to see Chouchik or her husband there. Life, she told her, was becoming ever more burdensome.[31] Perhaps the recent death of André Caplet on 22 April 1925 at the age of forty-six had contributed to this, although there is no extant correspondence mentioning it, no cry of lament to Laloy or other friends. He had always had weak lungs, was badly affected by his gassing during the war and died following haemoptysis. His funeral took place at the church of Saint-Pierre de Neuilly.[32]

On 22 May Falla was at the podium in Paris to conduct the première of his ballet *El amor brujo* at Le Trianon. From April to October 1925 the *Exposition internationale des arts decoratifs et industriels modernes* took place in Paris, displaying the style that would become known as Art Deco. After so many letters asking when he was going to visit her, Emma was frustrated to find that Falla and his sister had called on her whilst she was out one day. Her reason for not being at home was that she was at this Exhibition. Falla left for her what she described as 'an orgy of flowers'.[33] On 4 June (her special day when Debussy was alive) she invited him to join her for a performance of *La mer* conducted by Koussevitzky at one of the Concerts Koussevitzky at the Opéra on 6 June. He would be joining her in the box of the conductor's wife.[34] There is no indication as to whether he accepted this invitation.

Emma returned to Saint-Jean-de Luz in the summer months of 1925 and yet again tried to persuade Falla to contact her, complaining about the long months which had passed without news of him.[35] In his reply of 18 October he complained again of dizzy spells, probably due to overwork and once more asked her fruitlessly about her plans to visit him in Spain.[36]

---

[29] *Le Ménestrel*, 10 April 1925.

[30] On 19 May Long performed several pieces by Fauré in the salle Érard. Roger-Ducasse played the second piano in his reduction of the orchestral score of the *Ballade*. *Le Ménestrel*, 29 May 1925.

[31] 'La vie devient de plus en plus lourde.' Laloy archives, B12, Dossier 81, B24.

[32] *Le Figaro*, 26 April 1925.

[33] Archivo Manuel de Falla, 6898/2-026.

[34] Archivo Manuel de Falla, 6898/2-027.

[35] Archivo Manuel de Falla, 6898/2-012.

[36] Archivo Manuel de Falla, 6898/2-051.

1926: new monument committee without Emma

Despite the exhibition in 1923 displaying the design of the grand monument to Debussy designed by the Martel brothers, this had not yet come to fruition, but supporters of the project met again in 1926. Roger-Ducasse wrote to Jacques Durand in March of that year informing him that Émile Vuillermoz, Louis Laloy, Paul Dukas, Maurice Ravel and Raoul Bardac had met with him at the Opéra to form a new committee. They invited Durand to be its Secretary and also asked André Messager to join them on Friday 19 March for a meeting.[37] There is no mention of Emma despite her presence at the original unveiling of the plans three years earlier. Durand must have suggested widening the membership of the committee, for Roger-Ducasse wrote to him twice more in March, stressing that it had been decided that it should only comprise personal friends of Debussy. If he were to accept the position of Secretary this could not involve extra work. If he declined the invitation, he hoped he could still be a member.[38] The definition of 'personal friends' did not include Debussy's wife.

A campaign was also in motion to have a road in Paris named after Debussy which Gérard Bauër, writing in *Comœdia*, implored André Suarès, Paul Souday, Henry Prunières, Darius Milhaud, Arthur Honegger and Roland-Manuel to join.[39] A month later, the same paper complained that despite the city of Paris having recently decided to rename several roads, both old and new, they had remained silent on Claude Debussy, so this must now be promoted by private initiative.[40]

1926: *La revue musicale* devoted to Debussy

One great literary monument to Debussy did appear this year. The May 1926 issue of *La revue musicale* was devoted entirely to 'La jeunesse de Claude Debussy'. It contained illuminating and affectionate articles by such friends and admirers as Raymond Bonheur, Gabriel Pierné, Paul Vidal, Marguerite Vasnier (the daughter of Debussy's first great love), Henry Prunières, Maurice Emmanuel, Robert Godet, Henri de Regnier, Robert Brussel, André Messager and Charles Koechlin. There was a musical supplement of four previously unpublished songs and several illustrations. Amongst the latter was a facsimile of the first page of the manuscript of Debussy's *Nocturnes*, which caused quite a furore. The first printed edition of the *Nocturnes* had appeared in 1900, published by Fromont. Two of the movements, 'Nuages' and 'Fêtes', were performed in December of that year and in January 1901 Debussy gave his wife Lilly a copy of the manuscript of the short score, on the first page of which he wrote a dedication, 'This manuscript belongs to my little Lilly-Lilo, all rights reserved. It is also a mark of the deep and passionate joy I feel at being her

---

[37] Letter of 20 March 1926, 'Lettres de Roger-Ducasse à son éditeur Jacques Durand', J. Depaulis, *Revue de la Société liégeoise de Musicologie*, 8, 1997, pp. 5–126.

[38] Roger-Ducasse to J. Durand, 24 and 31 March 1926. Ibid.

[39] *Comœdia*, 24 April 1926.

[40] *Comœdia*, 24 May 1926.

husband. Claude Debussy, little January of 1901.'[41] When Lilly saw to her stupefaction that this first page had been reproduced in the 1926 journal she was furious, for two years previously she had thought of selling the score and had passed the page to a publisher and dealer, Monsieur Basset. Now, she claimed, she would suffer material loss for she could no longer sell the manuscript as 'previously unpublished'.[42] This information reached the press in the summer of 1927.

This was not the only controversy aroused by the journal. Emma was shocked to discover that Debussy's youthful letters to Marie Vasnier's husband were being quoted either in full or in part by Marguerite Vasnier. There ensued correspondence between Emma and the editor Henry Prunières, in which she, with Louis Laloy's support, demanded that Debussy's spelling and grammatical mistakes should be corrected before publication. Prunières insisted emphatically on reproducing the original errors, justifying his argument by saying that Marguerite Vasnier had equal rights over publication of the letters. He resolved the issue by printing Vasnier's article 'Debussy à dix-huit ans', followed by his own article 'À la Villa Médicis', which quoted the correspondence, but included a footnote explaining that the letters provided by Marguerite Vasnier were reproduced in the order established by Monsieur Vasnier.

> We felt we had to respect Debussy's clumsy and often incorrect turns of phrase. Thus we can see the progress he made, he who only a few years later went on to prove himself an accomplished writer with a lively, spirited and original style.[43]

The publication of an article by Charles Koechlin, 'Some early unpublished songs by Claude Debussy', and the appearance of four songs (*Pantomime*, *Clair de Lune*, *Pierrot* and *Apparition*) in the musical supplement to the journal also led to heated discussions between critics who disputed the value of Debussy's early works, including Léon Vallas, who would later openly disapprove of such publications in his biographies of Debussy. They were mere 'laboratory experiments ... unpublished until 1926 and should have stayed that way,' he complained.[44]

Daniel Ericourt

Emma continued to show kindness to young performers who excelled in playing Debussy's music, and in March 1926 gave a letter to the pianist Daniel Ericourt to take to New York and introduce himself to Arthur Hartmann.[45] Debussy had encouraged Ericourt as a child and at the age of thirteen he had had the privilege of turning the pages for him during the first performance of Debussy's Cello Sonata with Joseph

---

[41] 'Ce manuscrit appartient à ma petite Lilly-Lilo, tous droits réservés, il marque aussi la joie profonde et passionnée que j'ai d'être son mari Claude Debussy petite janvier de 1901.' Photograph in *La revue musicale*, 1 May 1926.

[42] *Comœdia*, 25 June 1927.

[43] H. Prunières, 'À la Villa Médicis', *La revue musicale*, 1 May 1926, p. 23.

[44] L. Vallas, *Claude Debussy et son temps*, Paris, 1932, p. 27.

[45] A. Hartmann, *Claude Debussy as I knew him*, pp. 160–1.

Salmon in March 1917.[46] In 1915 his teacher Roger-Ducasse dedicated to him the last of his *Quatre Études*.[47] He won first prize for piano at the Conservatoire in 1920. Now he had accepted the position of Professor of Music Theory at the Cincinatti Conservatory, which worried Roger-Ducasse, who did not see him as suited for a professorship, but Emma was clearly doing her best to support him. In August she thanked Hartmann for the kind welcome he had shown Ericourt and in the same letter recommended to him another young pianist who wanted to try to forge a career in America, her protégé Marius-François Gaillard.[48] She complained that in Paris Russian pianists were 'invading the place'. She was encouraging Gaillard to leave, but agreed to wait for Hartmann to approve of the move before letting him go.

Two wives of Debussy at *Pelléas et Mélisande*

Emma's financial situation did not permit her to leave Paris for the coast in the summer, which left her feeling very lonely when her friends deserted the city. 1926 was a year when the census was carried out in Paris. From this we discover that Emma's faithful companion, Chouchou's nanny Miss Louise Gibbs, was still living with her, now aged thirty-six (year of birth 1890), described as '*gouvernante.*' The only other person in the household was a servant called Emilie Ruhlmann aged twenty-five. Emma's year of birth was wrongly entered as 1864.

From Saint-Jean-de-Luz Magdeleine Greslé told Falla that Emma was spending 'a sad summer in Paris.'[49] However, that autumn the soprano Mary Garden told of an occasion which, if true, must have been extraordinary to witness. A revival of *Pelléas et Mélisande* began in May with Messager conducting and the original Mélisande, Debussy's favourite, back in the role at the age of fifty-two. On the morning of one of the performances, Garden received a huge bouquet of flowers with a note from Raoul Bardac, 'My mother, Mme Claude Debussy, is coming to the performance tonight. May I bring her up to your dressing room after the third act?' According to Garden, when the moment came she was already entertaining the Prime Minister, Aristide Briand, when the door opened. It was not Emma who entered, but Lilly, Debussy's first wife. 'We flew into each others' arms,' exclaimed Mary. 'Oh, Mary, you're back with *Pelléas*!' cried Lilly. She then declared that not only she, but Claude was there with her. She had even bought two tickets insisting, 'Claude is with me tonight, Mary, right there in the seat next to mine … his spirit is there in the house. I feel him everywhere. Don't you?' Whilst Mary was taking this in, a man entered the dressing room with 'an old lady' on his arm, dressed in black, walking with a cane (Emma was sixty-four). As she came towards Mary she began to sob with emotion. She did not see Lilly in a corner of the room. Garden was proud to tell the Prime Minister afterwards that he had been in

---

[46] See chapter 17 p. 240.

[47] C. Hopkins, 'Debussy's Solo Piano Works. Daniel Ericourt on Ivory Classics', *International Record Review*, September 2004.

[48] August 1926. A. Hartmann, *Claude Debussy as I knew him*, pp.161–3. See also chapter 17 p. 240.

[49] Archivo Manuel de Falla 7082-026.

the presence of the two wives of Claude Debussy. It is most likely that Raoul accompanied Emma to the opera and there is evidence that Emma met Mary Garden, for Mary wrote a letter to Emma on 15 October thanking her for a photograph of Debussy. She acknowledged Emma's thoughtfulness and told her she was looking forward to *Pelléas* again the following spring.[50]

Another witness of Emma's presence at a performance of the opera this season was the writer André David. He could not understand how Garden could appear to be sliding over the stage as if not touching the ground. It was Emma who explained to him that this was because of the rubber soles on her shoes, which gave the effect of floating when she walked. David noted the presence of former Prime Minister Paul Painlevé, lawyer and politician Albert Clemenceau and writer and socialite Anna de Noailles in the audience. The latter spent an interval in Emma's box, he claimed.[51]

Roger-Ducasse's completion and orchestration of *Le Roi Lear*; *Linderaja*

As Roger-Ducasse's biographer pointed out, this composer was faithful to his friends, even when a thankless task was involved.[52] He had acceded, despite reservations, to another of Emma's requests: to complete and orchestrate *Le Roi Lear*, incidental music which Debussy was supposed to have written for André Antoine's production of the play in 1904, but which did not get very far, partly due to his preoccupation at the time with Emma. By October 1926 Roger-Ducasse had completed Debussy's orchestration of what existed of the 'Fanfare' and 'Le sommeil de Lear'. He was visited by Léon Vallas, who wanted this to be given its first performance as part of his 'Conférences de la musique vivante', which he had commenced the previous year.[53] Roger-Ducasse was unable to satisfy this request, but on 26 October 1926 Marguerite Long joined him in a two-piano version in a concert given at the Salle des Agriculteurs. They also played *Lindaraja*, another two-piano work written in 1901 but never performed in Debussy's lifetime. This contained the famous *Habanera*, with the harmonic effect 'borrowed' from *Sites auriculaires* by Ravel. Both revivals had just been published by Jobert. Emma's favoured soprano, Magdeleine Greslé, sang the *Chansons de Bilitis*. Critics were present, as shown by a few newspaper reports, but commented only briefly on the works, preferring to praise the soloists' efforts. As Depaulis wrote, 'The composer from Bordeaux had to completely reinvent Debussy's thoughts, but the *Musiques pour le Roi Lear*, when given their first performance in 1926, added nothing to the glory of "Claude de France" … nor that of Roger-Ducasse.'[54]

---

[50] G. Opstad, *Debussy's Mélisande. The Lives of Georgette Leblanc, Mary Garden and Maggie Teyte*, pp. 257–8.

[51] A. David, 'Musiciens et peintres de ma jeunesse', *La nouvelle revue des deux mondes*, June 1972, pp. 576–7.

[52] J. Depaulis, *Roger-Ducasse*, Paris, 2001, p. 60.

[53] Roger-Ducasse to André Lambinet, end of October or beginning of November 1926, J. Roger-Ducasse, *Lettres à son ami André Lambinet*, Sprimont, 2001, pp. 168–9.

[54] J. Depaulis, *Roger-Ducasse*, p. 60.

In notes Dolly later wrote for her daughters, she commented on *Lindaraja* that it was not 'best Debussy' and he had actually forgotten it. When he found it again he did not have it published; it was *Nounouthe* (Granny) who did this in 1926. One day Debussy had shown the piece to Raoul, calling it '*L'Inde à Rara*' (Rara's India), but had then put it to one side.[55] Léon Vallas later described it as a 'pièce médiocre', saying that it was Madame Debussy who told him that her husband had borrowed Ravel's 'Habanera', lost it and only rediscovered it some years later, never having studied it closely.[56]

In November Emma received the present of a book *De Piano en hare componisten*, published by J. Philip Kruseman, 's-Gravenhage, bearing the dedication from its author Rient van Santen: 'For Mme Emma Claude Debussy with eternal thanks for everything she did to help realise my dream. 29 Nov. 26.'[57] She had clearly contributed to van Santen's research into her husband's piano compositions. She also continued to help Hartmann, who was asking about the '*berceuse*' from *Le Roi Lear*. She told him it did exist but had never been published and promised to ask Jean Jobert to contact him on the subject. She assured him yet again that if she found any music at all intended for him she would inform him immediately.[58]

1927: still no monument; Greslé sings Falla

On 14 February 1927 an article appeared on the front page of *Comœdia* lamenting the fact that the French had still not honoured Debussy with a monument nine years after his death. Readers were reminded that a committee had been formed in 1922 to this end and that in 1923 Madame Claude Debussy had approved the design by the Martel brothers. Momentum had to be maintained to achieve the eventual erection of this tribute to the composer. It was suggested that it should be positioned on the beautiful terrace of Saint-Germain-en-Laye, where it would be less prone to vandalism than within woodland as previously proposed.[59] However, little seemed to be happening to achieve this. There was no mention of fundraising.

In his New Year's wishes to Emma, Manuel de Falla exclaimed he had not heard from her 'for a century'![60] To her joy he returned to Paris in May 1927 for a Festival Falla at the Salle Pleyel. At the beginning of the month she expressed her delight at his imminent arrival, referring, as so often, to her terrible neuralgia.[61] On 14 May

---

[55] Hélène de Tinan, Carnet rouge, Centre de Documentation Claude Debussy, RESE 08.01.
[56] L. Vallas, *Debussy et son temps*, pp. 276–7.
[57] 'Pour Mme Emma Claude Debussy en la remerciant infiniment pour ce qu'elle a bien voulu faire pour la réalisation de mon rêve. 29 Nov. 26'. W. Niemann and Riet van Santen, *De Piano en hare componisten*, Gravenhage, 1925. Book amongst Raoul Bardac's possessions found at his house in Meyssac, kindly shown to the author by the owner in 2010.
[58] Emma to Hartmann, 13 December 1926, *Claude Debussy as I knew him*, pp. 163–4.
[59] *Comœdia*, 14 February 1927.
[60] Archivo Manuel de Falla, 6898/2-052.
[61] Archivo Manuel de Falla, 6898/2-013.

Falla played his Harpsichord Concerto, first on the piano then on the harpsichord, to great acclaim. Even more satisfying for Emma was the fact that it was Greslé accompanied by the composer who sang his *Sonéto a Córdoba*, *Psyché* and *Sept Chansons populaires*.[62] We are told that 'of all Falla's concerts in Paris, this was the one which made the most profound and lasting impression upon him.' The concert was a resounding success.[63] Falla then went on to London to play his concerto, but remembered his faithful friend, for he sent her tickets for a concert at the Théâtre des Champs-Élysées which included his ballet, *L'amour sorcier*.[64] Emma enjoyed the feeling of familiarity with Falla's family. Towards the end of the year she not only sent her best wishes to his sister, but informed him she had recently seen his cousin, the artist Pedro de Matheu, again, implying she had met him before.[65]

Le triomphe de Bacchus and Vallas's scathing views

Amongst Debussy's manuscripts in her possession, Emma came across a very early work, *Le triomphe de Bacchus*, inspired by a poem by Théodore de Banville, '*Le triomphe de Bacchos à son retour des Indes*' and composed whilst Debussy was still a student at the Conservatoire in 1882. He left only a piano duet score of an Allegro and a short Andante Cantabile, part of a work which was intended to be in four movements. Emma passed this score to Gaillard, whom she tasked with orchestrating it. This he completed in November 1927.[66] Choudens published Gaillard's piano duet version in 1928.

The publication of such works was thoroughly frowned upon by Debussy 'experts'. Léon Vallas had already published a biography of Debussy in 1926[67] followed by *Les idées de Claude Debussy, musicien français* in 1927.[68] Whilst Emma was alive Vallas would be guarded in his criticism of her influence on her husband, whom he had never met. In his biography he referred to her only obliquely, but implied that Debussy's relationship with Emma had caused him 'une sorte de retraite', (a sort of withdrawal).[69] Yet Vallas had reason to be grateful to her, for he reproduced the famous photograph taken of the composer by Pierre Louÿs, which Debussy had once ripped in half in a fit of temper. Emma had stuck it together again and allowed Vallas to use it in his book.[70] He stated that the only copy of Debussy's work on two acts of *Rodrigue et Chimène*, which the composer wanted destroyed, was stored in a

---

[62] *Le Menestrel*, 20 May 1927; *Comœdia*, 16 May 1927.

[63] J. Pahissa, *Manuel de Falla. His Life and Works*, trans. J. Wagstaff, London, 1954, p. 140.

[64] Archivo Manuel de Falla, 6898/2-014. See also *Comœdia*, 16 June 1927.

[65] November 1927. Archivo Manuel de Falla, 6898/2-015.

[66] BnF Musique, Rés Vma MS-1149.

[67] L. Vallas, *Debussy:1862–1918*, Paris, 1926.

[68] L. Vallas, *Les idées de Claude Debussy, musicien français*, Paris, 1927.

[69] L. Vallas, *Debussy*, 1926, p. 122.

[70] Idem. p. 55.

chest kept by his widow.[71] He clearly felt qualified to express himself forcefully in the newspapers. He was aware of the existence of previously unpublished works, he wrote, but these were nothing but exercises carried out by a gifted, but as yet 'very ignorant' pupil. The composer himself had forgotten them and never would have envisaged them being preserved in the archives of the Conservatoire.[72]

At least Emma's spirits must have been lifted by a letter she received in December from Falla, sending greetings for the New Year and looking forward to seeing her in a month's time. His affection for her was expressed in vivid terms. 'If thoughts could write, how frequently you would hear from me!' He was deeply touched that she had placed a photograph of him next to one of Debussy. It brought back fond memories of the first time he had knocked nervously at Debussy's door, hoping to meet the genius 'whose works had opened up a new era to music.'[73] For such a shy personality this must indeed have been a challenge.

---

[71] Idem. p. 67.
[72] Comœdia, 7 November 1927.
[73] Archivo Manuel de Falla, 6898/2-059.

23

1928–31: Litigation and invective

Lilly sues *La revue musicale*; Falla in Paris

Ten years since Debussy's death, 1928 became an *annus horribilis* for Emma. It began with more rumblings about the case Lilly Texier had brought against *La Revue musicale* following the publication in 1926 of a photograph of the manuscript of Debussy's *Nocturnes* dedicated to her.

Lilly was determined to obtain full satisfaction for what she regarded as the usurpation of her rights. In June 1927 *Comœdia* published her original complaint as it had appeared in the journal *Aux Écoutes*, together with the riposte from the editor of *La Revue musicale*, Henry Prunières.[1] Lilly believed she was being deprived financially as she could no longer claim the manuscript was previously unpublished. She had wanted to sell it as such and was therefore suing both M. Basset, to whom she had entrusted it, and *La Revue musicale* for ten thousand francs damages. Prunières pointed out that if the fact of reproducing a facsimile of an autograph reduced the value of the actual article, this would be disastrous for all dealers in autographs who reproduced them in their sales catalogues. What was more, publication of this photograph had not prevented the sale, for after its appearance Lilly Texier had managed to sell the manuscript at a higher price than her original one. It had gone to the Washington library.[2] A few days later, not having known about this transaction, *La Revue musicale* had also passed on to Lilly the offer of one of its readers to buy the manuscript for an even higher amount. Her response had been to demand ten thousand francs in damages and interest.

The case was first heard by the Civil Court (*tribunal*). The *tribunal* found no case for prejudice of Lilly's rights as she had managed to sell the item between its publication and the trial. However, upon appeal the case was passed to the Third Civil Division, the *troisième chambre*, which did find in her favour, citing a law of 1793. Whilst there is no record of Emma's reactions, obviously she was all too well aware of the case. On 14 January *Comœdia* carried a report with the headline, '*La revue musicale* perd un procès contre Mme Debussy.' ('*La revue musicale* loses its case against Mme Debussy'). The final judgement confirmed that Lilly was to receive damages of five thousand francs. Emma wrote to the paper the next day to express her astonishment at reading that *she* had won the case against Henry Prunières. In other words, she was objecting to the headline referring to 'Mme Debussy'. 'As no

---

[1] *Comœdia*, 25 June 1927.
[2] Library of Congress, Call no.ML96 D346.

one except me has the name or can carry the name of Claude Debussy with or without an adjacent name, I should be grateful if you would publish an apology in your next issue.' This letter bore the headline: 'Une lettre de Mme Claude Debussy.'[3]

In March 1928 Falla was in Paris for another Festival Manuel de Falla. He supervised a production of *L'amour sorcier* at the Opéra and on 12 March *La vida breve* and *El Retablo de Maese Pedro* were performed at the Opéra-Comique. On 19 March he conducted a concert consisting entirely of his works in the Salle Pleyel, for which Emma was delighted to receive complimentary tickets for herself and Magdeleine Greslé. As always, she emphasised the admiration and respect in which she held him: 'You know what joy it will bring me to see you and hear your adorable music'.[4] Falla himself conducted *Nuits dans les jardins d'Espagne* with Ricardo Viñes as soloist, Ninon Vallin sang the *Sept Chansons populaires* and excerpts from *Le Tricorne*. The composer also played the harpsichord in his *Concerto*. An undated card expressed Emma's delight at having been transported into a dream world, miraculously enabling her to escape her troubles. 'And now it's back to life, daytime, emptiness'.[5]

Controversial concert

On 20 March 1928 an *Hommage à Debussy* took place to mark the tenth anniversary of her husband's death, described as being given by 'La Jeunesse intellectuelle'. Alfred Bruneau represented the Ministre de l'Instruction publique et des Beaux-Arts, Léon Vallas gave a lecture on 'Claude Debussy, musicien français' and Magdeleine Greslé was amongst those interpreting Debussy's works. Poems written for the occasion by writers including Gabriel Mourey, André David and Maurice Rostand were recited.[6] A flier included with the programme reminded its readers of the prospective Martel monument destined for Saint-Germain-en-Laye which stated, 'Présidente du comité: Madame Claude Debussy',[7] thus implying that Emma was still involved in its administration, yet elsewhere there is no indication that she still held any such position. In April objections were raised to the proposed placement, as it was viewed by some as too large and too modern for Saint-Germain-en-Laye.[8]

This was only a few days before a more controversial concert. On 3 January 1928 Emma had invited Gaillard to a meeting with Louis Laloy and the publisher Choudens.[9] On 24 January she and Laloy both signed a contract with Choudens, selling the music and poem of *Ode à la France* as joint owners. Emma received twelve thousand francs, being heir to Debussy, and Laloy five hundred francs for writing the

---

[3] *Comœdia*, 17 January 1928.
[4] Archivo Manuel de Falla, 6898/2-028 and 6898/2-029.
[5] Archivo Manuel de Falla, 6898/2-043.
[6] *Le Ménestrel*, 30 March 1928.
[7] M. Wheeldon, 'The Controversy over the Ode à la France' in *Debussy's Legacy and the Construction of Reputation*, p. 147.
[8] *Le Figaro*, 14 April 1928.
[9] Emma to Gaillard, BnF Musique, Nla13 (131–50).

words.[10] At some stage in their friendship Emma had sent or presented to Falla two pages of sketches for the *Ode à la France* and as far back as 1921 she had dedicated and given a manuscript of this work to Marius-François Gaillard.[11] Yet Laloy gave a different impression when he claimed that it was only a few months prior to March 1928 that fifteen pages of music had been discovered amongst Debussy's papers which had been hastily gathered together and deposited in a safe during the bombing raids after his death. Both sides of the paper were covered with Debussy's fine writing, he said, and the score, for piano and voice, was complete. Only some words were missing and he had filled these in, using his rough notes and the melody as a guide.[12] He was writing this article as background to the first performance of the orchestrated version of *Ode à la France*, which was to take place in the Salle Pleyel on 2 April 1928, part of a concert to raise money for the monument to Debussy. To the consternation of others, Emma wanted Gaillard to carry out the orchestration. Laloy described Gaillard as 'a sensitive musician who has taken the greatest care to realise the composer's intentions, made clear in several places by markings indicating the principal instruments.'[13] But however well-intentioned the parties to this performance might have been, little can they have realised the extent of bitterness and controversy it would arouse.

The monument committee sent out a blunt communication to be published in several newspapers prior to the concert. They distanced themselves from this initiative, protesting formally against 'the abuse' being carried out in their name and informed friends and admirers of Debussy that they could not grant patronage to the undertaking when they had been deliberately excluded from its artistic and moral control. How hurtful it must have been for Emma to see her son's name listed amongst the signatories. The others were Messager, Dukas, Roger-Ducasse, Astruc, Inghelbrecht and Vuillermoz. Normally, being a member of the monument committee, Louis Laloy's name would have been included, but it was specifically pointed out that having been shown the text of the protest, he wanted to clarify his position. 'M. Laloy, whose name figures on the concert programme for one of the works being performed, wishes to state that he had nothing to do with its organisation.'[14] He was clearly in a very difficult position. Two weeks earlier he had had an article published in *Musique* explaining his relationship to the composer and Debussy's state of mind when he collaborated with him.

> The directors of the house of Choudens, which will publish the *Ode à la France*, have entrusted its orchestration to Monsieur Marius-François Gaillard, with the agreement of Madame Debussy and the author of the text, who are both acquainted with the talent, taste, feeling and dedication of this young musician.[15]

---

[10] BnF Musique, Nla-32 (Bis).

[11] See Chapter 14 p. 291.

[12] *Le Gaulois*, 26 March 1928. See also D. Priest, 'Ode à la France' in *Louis Laloy (1874–1944) on Debussy, Ravel and Stravinsky*, Aldershot U. K. and Vermont U. S., 1999, pp. 231–6.

[13] *Le Gaulois*, 26 March 1928.

[14] *Comœdia*, 29 March 1928; *Le Gaulois*, 30 March 1928.

[15] *Musique*, vol.1. no.6, 15 March 1928, pp. 245–9. Quoted in English in D. Priest, *Louis Laloy (1874–1944) on Debussy, Ravel and Stravinsky*, p. 234.

Emma's response

The invective aimed at the resurrection of Debussy's youthful works continued, particularly from Vuillermoz, who feared the damage that might be done to Debussy's reputation. What had angered the committee so much was the fact that the programme consisted of youthful works considered unworthy of the mature Debussy and of a late work, the *Ode à la France*, which in itself was controversial. Not only had Emma's choice, Marius-François Gaillard, been tasked with orchestrating three of Debussy's early works as well as the *Ode*, but he was also the star of the concert,

Emma now took to the press herself, issuing a public response on 29 March saying she was sad and astonished to see that this event, intended only to raise money for the monument, was not rallying as much support as she had envisaged. The organisers of the concert may not have taken the committee's advice, but they had consulted with her on the programme and she insisted that nothing was done without her complete approval.[16] She made Falla aware of her distress, inviting him to share her box 'if the Choudens concert with my husband's *Ode à la France* in the Salle Pleyel goes ahead … I am sad and disheartened.'[17]

On 31 March a lengthy interview was published in *L'Intransigeant* in which Emma expressed forcefully her hurt at the attitude of the monument committee. She began with an anecdote about two strangers who had approached her when she and a friend were laying flowers on Debussy's grave on the tenth anniversary of his death. They were amazed that no musicians had arrived to mark this date as would have happened in their home city of Vienna. 'Indeed,' replied Madame Debussy. 'We are in France.' No one had taken the initiative to organise such an event. A committee formed to raise funds for a monument hadn't even collected twenty-five centimes and had overlooked this anniversary. They were even disowning a concert she had authorised from which all proceeds would be donated to the Debussy monument.

Wary of legal action, Emma did not name Durand but painted a negative picture of exploitative Publisher X. He had been gathering honour and profits from *Pelléas*, endlessly publishing transcriptions of the opera. Any day now she was expecting to see the score in a jazz reduction! She was having to pay back sixty-one thousand francs in advances he had made to Debussy. He had given Debussy's manuscripts to the Conservatoire without even mentioning it to her.[18] In these circumstances, another publisher, Choudens, had taken the initiative for this concert, thus leading to the protest of the monument committee. On the choice of programme, Emma commented that everyone thought they knew Debussy's wishes better than her. She could not understand why people were so ready to deride Debussy's youthful works when the discovery of previously unpublished bars by any other Master, classic or modern, would not be greeted with such disdain.

Despite claims that the *Ode* had not been written by Debussy, Emma could confirm that the music was completed by him. If anything was missing, it was the words

---

[16] *L'Intransigeant*, 31 March 1928.
[17] Archivo Manuel de Falla, 6898/2-016.
[18] See Chapter 22 p. 315.

for the choruses. Debussy had left numerous indications and even if he had not orchestrated it himself, it could safely be said that the work was entirely as he conceived it. It was finished in 1917, a few months before his death. Proof that he had completed it was that the manuscript was entirely in his hand right to the end.[19]

Emma justified not having allowed it to be circulated amongst others by explaining that she had lost the manuscript of *Le diable dans le beffroi* after her husband had entrusted it to a 'great musician' who was now dead. The heirs of this composer had failed to return it to her and she felt forced to instigate an investigation to trace it. The 'great musician' was André Caplet, with whom Emma had had such a close relationship. To add insult to injury, Inghelbrecht had put on a ballet based on the same tale at the Opéra, making it almost unrecognisable. Debussy had also worked on *La chute de la Maison Usher*, but was so affected by the distressing plot that his nerves suffered, so the score was never completed. She owned the legal and moral rights to these unpublished works and had passed them solely to the organisers of the concert of 2 April.[20] She could not have entrusted the orchestration of *Ode à la France* to Roger-Ducasse, as he was a member of the committee so opposed to her efforts.

Besides the *Ode*, works to be performed in this concert were a setting for a choir of women's voices of a poem by Comte Anatole de Ségur, *Salut printemps, jeune saison* Debussy's submission for the Prix de Rome in 1882, *Le triomphe de Bacchus* dating from the same year, which had been completed by Gaillard at the end of 1927, and Debussy's setting for choir and orchestra of *Invocation*, text by Alphonse de Lamartine, with which he had won fourth place in the preliminary test of the Prix de Rome in 1883.

Léon Vallas not only believed the early works would do nothing to contribute to the glory of Debussy's reputation, but he pointed out that orchestral scores in Debussy's hand of *Salut printemps* and *Invocation* already existed in the library of the Conservatoire. This implied ignorance on Emma's and Gaillard's part of Debussy's early work. As for the *Ode*, it would have been better simply to publish a facsimile of the original.[21]

Gaillard's performance and reception

Emma's correspondence with Gaillard showed mounting anxiety – for example, telling him, 'I phoned you ten times yesterday morning'. She felt tyrannised.[22] Yet she was determined the concert should go ahead. The day before the concert, Louis Laloy expressed surprise at having to clarify his earlier declaration. The committee had failed to bring about any practical results in two years of existence. He had heard

---

[19] There are discrepancies between Debussy's manuscript and Laloy's and Gaillard's published score, including a chorus added at the end. See M. Wheeldon, 'The Controversy over the Ode à la France' in *Debussy's Legacy and the Construction of Reputation*, pp. 126–7.

[20] *L'Intransigeant*, 31 March 1928.

[21] *Excelsior*, 21 March 1928.

[22] Emma to Gaillard, BnF Musique, Nla13 (131–50). Letters undated and several of barely legible quality.

nothing from them for eighteen months when suddenly one of its members had come to him bearing the protest against the concert. He had not signed it, being of the view that it was better to support than oppose those who were working for the glory of Debussy.[23]

Despite this invective, the concert went ahead on 2 April 1928 in the Grande Salle Pleyel, performed by the Société des Concerts du Conservatoire and the Chœur mixte de Paris, conducted by Gaillard. Germaine Lubin sang Jeanne d'Arc in the *Ode*. Laloy harboured treasured memories of that evening, describing it in emotional terms. He felt the presence of Debussy in the music and his identification with the French people. He even had the strong feeling that Debussy had come close to God. 'Through the music of the *Ode à la France* the earthly existence of Claude Debussy reached its Christian end.'[24]

By others, it was poorly received. *Le Ménestrel* called the whole thing a 'déplorable aventure'. People thought that Debussy was being used as a pretext for 'a sort of Marius-François Gaillard festival'. The concert began at 9.15 p.m. After poorly realised Bach and interminable Rameau it was nearly 11.30 when the first note of Debussy was played. The *Triomphe de Bacchus*, *Salut printemps* and *Invocation* were such early works they only showed evidence of the student Debussy before the *Prix de Rome*. The *Ode à la France* had been completed under 'fairly obscure conditions' and 'what is more, had been orchestrated by M. M-F. Gaillard'. Whilst at certain points in the music the grandeur of *Le martyre de Saint Sébastien* was brought to mind, the orchestration was completely wrong. 'How many times did we say to ourselves, 'Debussy could not have written that'!'[25]

In his later biographies of Debussy Vallas vilified Emma and Gaillard for resuscitating the *Ode à la France*. In 1932 he dismissively described Gaillard as having had 'the impertinence to fill out the sketch and to superimpose onto it a fabricated orchestration ... The result was neither worthy nor appropriate.'[26] In 1944 he wrote that Debussy 'was only able to make a sketch of the work'. Gaillard had created a pastiche version with orchestra, he claimed. 'It cannot be classified as a work by Debussy.'[27]

Emma was furious at the reception of the concert and poor box office takings. She took the monument committee to court, blaming them for the failure. The trial would not be heard until 1931 but there it became evident that she and Choudens had envisaged raising the sum of ninety-six thousand francs.

The committee, now galvanised into action, invited more former friends and colleagues of Debussy to join. Amongst them was d'Annunzio, who responded gratefully, mentioning a '*drame indien*' on which he had hoped to cooperate with Debussy. He recalled with typical hyperbole that upon hearing from Emma of the composer's death whilst encamped at Friuli (northern Italy), 'all my pilots knew I

---

[23] *L'Intransigeant*, 1 April 1928.

[24] 'Par la musique de *l'Ode à la France* l'existence terrestre de Claude Debussy obtient sa fin chrétienne.' L. Laloy, *Debussy*, p. 126.

[25] *Le Ménestrel*, 13 April 1928.

[26] L. Vallas, *Claude Debussy et son temps*, p. 424.

[27] L. Vallas, *Achille-Claude Debussy*, Paris, 1944, pp. 53, 206.

had never sought death more ardently'.[28] In May the committee announced it had received a letter from Maurice Maeterlinck, author of the play *Pelléas et Mélisande*, who at the time of the première of Debussy's opera had distanced himself from the composer, now saying that he would consider it a great honour to serve on the committee. Thirty-eight illustrious members were listed.[29]

Lilly sues for backdated alimony

To add insult to injury, only three days before the concert, on 30 March another case had come to court brought by Rosalie Texier. When her divorce from Debussy was decreed in 1905 she had been granted alimony of four hundred francs a month, administered by Durand.[30] Now she was demanding fifteen hundred francs a month due to the rise in the cost of living since then.[31] Debussy's heirs, it was stated, were disputing her right to the alimony at all, which they believed should have ended with the liquidation of the estate. However, the court found that as the heirs still received authors' rights, the value of which was increasing steadily, the amount received by Lilly should rise to one thousand francs per month. Since 1923 royalties had not been received by Emma, but had been used to repay Debussy's outstanding debts. At this point Lilly's alimony had ceased, so now it was to be backdated by five years. In addition Emma had to pay the expenses. There was to be no end to her financial troubles.

Gaillard was thoughtful enough to commiserate with Emma on the anniversary of Chouchou's death, for he received a reply written on 16 July thanking him for having thought of her in her misery. Her sadness grew each year at the thought her little girl was no longer with her. One last extant letter to him was written following Gaillard's return from travels, when Emma was suffering from a dreadful fever. Here she complained bitterly that she never received an answer to her letters to members of the committee, 'for those good men never reply probably for fear of compromising themselves, not even a note from their secretary.' She was not going to write to them again.[32]

Support for the monument committee continued to grow as the year progressed. In September Messager invited Gabriel Astruc to join,[33] and in November the conductor Ernest Ansermet donated forty thousand francs, money raised by a concert he had given at a Debussy Festival in Buenos Aires in July.[34] Emma had little news of her own to give to Hartmann at the end of the year,[35] just regrets at her lack of

---

[28] Telegram reproduced in *Le Gaulois*, 4 April 1928.
[29] *Le Gaulois*, 13 May 1928.
[30] See Chapter 12.
[31] *Le Temps*, 31 March 1928. In *Comœdia*, 31 March 1928, the sum was quoted as thirteen hundred francs.
[32] BnF Musique Nla-13 (131–50).
[33] Astruc recalled this in *Le Temps*, 18 June 1932.
[34] *Paris-soir*, 7 November 1928, and *Journal des débats politiques et littéraires*, 7 November 1928.
[35] Hartmann, *Claude Debussy as I knew him*, pp. 164–5.

leisure time, time spent worrying, time being ill and complaints about the cost of everything. She asked if he knew Edgard Varèse, wondering if his music had any value. She described him as having a 'mysterious and Machiavellian air'.

Debussy monument campaign 1929

The first extant correspondence of Emma in 1929 is a postcard to Falla dated 6 January bearing a photograph of the emblem of Claude de France (daughter of Louis XII and Anne of Brittany), a swan pierced by an arrow, at the château of Blois. She had been listening to his music on records, perhaps the *Seven Popular Songs* with the composer at the piano accompanying Maria Barrientos (soprano), recorded in Paris in 1928 for French Columbia.[36] As ever, she would love him to come and see her. Several letters expressed her pleasure when he did write her a few lines, and she often expressed her fear of disturbing him by writing when she felt like it. 'I still think of you and your exquisite music and have listened to it devotedly. Your records are excellent!' she told him.[37]

On 23 January Gaillard performed a *Grand Gala* Debussy recital at the Théâtre des Champs-Élysées advertised as 'pour un monument au maître',[38] which included the twenty-four *Préludes*. This concert seems to have been virtually ignored by the press apart from a cryptic comment in *L'Intransigeant* that M. Gaillard brought to Debussy 'a personal vision with which one may or may not agree, but which is not indifferent.'[39]

Far more attention was paid to concerts organised by the official committee at home and abroad. *Paris-soir* listed the members of the 'Comité d'honneur' in an article published on 8 February, beginning with the presidency of Gaston Doumergue, President of the Republic, and naming such luminaries as Gustave Charpentier, Widor, Pierné, Alfred Bruneau, d'Annunzio, Maeterlinck, Toscanini, Falla and Ravel. It then listed separately the 'Comité d'action': Messager, Dukas, Gabriel Astruc, D.-E. Inghelbrecht, Louis Laloy, Émile Vuillermoz and Raoul Bardac.[40] Raoul's curriculum vitae shows that after a gap of two years he was now working for the Citroën car firm charged with reception duties for clients and organising sales.[41] This must have been out of sheer necessity, at odds with his reclusive, creative disposition.

On 24 February 1929 André Messager died. The funeral took place at the church of Saint-François de Sales, where the music played included the death scene from *Pelléas et Mélisande* and Debussy's 'Sarabande' from the suite *Pour le piano*. The whole French musical world was there, including Emma.[42] Messager was buried in Passy cemetery, near both Debussy and Fauré. His position as president of the

---

[36] Archivo Manuel de Falla, 6898/2-017. French Columbia D-11701.
[37] Archivo Manuel de Falla, 6898/2-034.
[38] *Le Figaro*, 13 January 1929; *Le Gaulois*, 15 January 1929.
[39] *L'Intransigeant*, 9 February 1929.
[40] *Paris-soir*, 8 February 1929.
[41] R. Bardac, *Curriculum vitae*, Centre de Documentation Claude Debussy, RESE-05.18.
[42] *Le Gaulois*, 2 March 1929.

Debussy Monument Committee was filled by Paul Léon, director of the Beaux-Arts. Less than a month later Emma attended another funeral, a high society event, that of Princesse Alexandre de Caraman Chimay, sister of Geneviève de Caraman Chimay, wife of Dolly's brother-in-law, Charles Pochet de Tinan.[43] Knowing Emma's financial and emotional troubles, it must have been a galling experience to be surrounded by so much wealth enjoyed by her daughter's relations by marriage.

In February Pierre Lalo published a long article explaining that there were to be two Debussy monuments. The committee had had difficulty finding a suitably large spot at Saint-Germain-en-Laye for the huge Martel monument. They had then discovered that the sculptor Antoine Bourdelle had also created a monument inspired simply by his admiration for the composer. The solution was to place the latter much smaller one in Saint-Germain-en-Laye, where it would be surrounded by trees near a fountain, and the larger one near the Bois de Boulogne in Paris.[44]

By April plans were progressing apace for Bourdelle's monument. It was announced that the necessary finances would soon be in place to prepare the terrace in Saint-Germain-en-Laye. The Tourist Board of the town had already voted in the three thousand francs necessary for first clearing it of chickens and cows.[45] Interest in the project was fostered by associating more famous names with it. A performance of *Pelléas et Mélisande* was mounted at the Opéra-Comique on 17 April with Lotte Schoene singing Mélisande, and Léon Vallas gave a series of lectures on '*Claude Debussy et son temps*' every Tuesday at the Sorbonne. Following the recent publication of his memoirs, *Le pavillon des fantômes*, Gabriel Astruc was described as being one of the most devoted of the committee, determined to provide a permanent monument in the composer's memory.[46] However, in October Bourdelle died so another sculptor had to be commissioned. Aristide Maillol was selected, who created a graceful sculpture of a crouching naked woman, even though this embodied no specific reference to Debussy.

In July the municipal council of Paris discussed the site for the larger monument in the city.[47] Then in November the journal *Comœdia* campaigned not for a monument but for a plaque to be placed on Debussy's residence, now called 80 avenue Foch. The Beaux-Arts wanted to commemorate Debussy with the simple words, 'Ici habita de 1905 à 1918 Claude Debussy, musicien français.' Whoever wrote this article knew that 'those who were closest to the composer of *Pelléas*' approved of this sober wording.[48] This was confirmed in a reply to the editor from Emma herself, published on 5 December. 'The words you are considering inscribing are definitely the only ones I could wish for, as the Maître never wanted any other title.'[49]

---

[43] *Le Gaulois*, 9 March 1929.

[44] *Comœdia*, 9 February 1929.

[45] *Comœdia*, 9 April 1929.

[46] *Paris-soir*, 21 June 1929.

[47] *L'Intransigeant*, 25 July 1929; *Paris-soir*, 25 July 1929.

[48] *Comœdia*, 22 November 1929.

[49] The plaque was discussed several times into the 1940s, but not erected. A handwritten note by Dolly (undated) expressed fear that the exterior coating of the house may not be suitable. Centre de Documentation Claude Debussy, RESE-06.05.

Emma's patronage was sought and gained for a new school of piano in Rouen. It was founded by Pierre Duvauchelle who had won first prize at the Paris Conservatoire the previous year. He was a pupil of Marguerite Long, so it was she who gathered together big names for the committee, including, besides Emma, Robert Casadesus, Louis Aubert, Roger-Ducasse, Albert Roussel and Charles Tournemire.[50]

To Saint-Jean-de-Luz; Hartmann requests violin piece

On 3 August 1929 Emma arrived in Saint-Jean-de-Luz, where she stayed at the Golf Hotel for two months. Only two days later she responded to a letter from Arthur Hartmann, who had been inquiring yet again about a composition he thought Debussy had been planning for him. Emma informed him, as she had done several times previously, that she had never heard her husband mention anything particularly intended for him, even though Debussy composed prolifically in 1915 prior to his operation. That year he had destroyed many pieces of paper and musical jottings, she reiterated.

As ever when in this part of France, Emma was nostalgic for 1917 when her husband was there and for 1918 when Chouchou was still alive, seeing them everywhere she went. The pain she suffered was cruel.[51] She must have sympathised with Hartmann's desire to possess something of Debussy's for violin, for she sent him a copy of the Violin Sonata bearing the inscription: 'To the great artist and faithful friend Arthur Hartmann, Affectionately, Emma Claude Debussy 1929'. Hartmann never performed the work in public but it is clear from markings on the score that he worked on it.[52] She cannot have realised that Hartmann was also suffering. He and Marie had separated earlier in the year and he had fallen ill immediately upon arriving in Paris in the spring. He spent three months in hospital in Neuilly, but never once got in touch with Emma. 'I was too tragically sad to see or even to want to communicate with Debussy's wife,' he later wrote.[53] He too would go on to suffer serious financial difficulties following his divorce in 1930.

On Christmas Day 1929 Emma was not alone, for she was at a party celebrating the creation of wonderful glass decorations displayed on a Christmas tree surrounded by children bearing aristocratic names and children of writers such as Francis de Croisset, Giraudoux, Rachilde. They had been made by master glass-maker André Hunebelle, the tree standing not in a salon, where they were the fashion all over Paris now, but in his studio. There was no mention of Emma's grandchildren, Françoise and Madeleine, being present, who would have been seventeen and eighteen years old. She was, however, 'surrounded by a respectful group of people'.[54]

---

[50] *Comœdia*, 2 July 1929.

[51] A. Hartmann, *Claude Debussy as I knew him*, pp. 168–9.

[52] 'Au grand artiste à l'ami fidèle Arthur Hartmann, Affectueusement, Emma Claude Debussy.' Hartmann Collection, Free Library of Philadelphia. *Claude Debussy as I knew him*, p. 320, n.9.

[53] *Claude Debussy as I knew him*, p.30, quoting Hartmann's autobiographical notes, Hartmann Collection, Free Library of Philadelphia.

[54] *Comœdia*, 25 December 1929; *Paris-soir*, 25 December 1929.

1930

1930 began with a note of sincere good wishes for the New Year from Manuel de Falla, expressing his continuing devotion, drafted on the same page as a similar message to Magdeleine Greslé.[55] He came to Paris in June 1930 to record his harpsichord concerto and some songs, but there is no record of his meeting Emma. Emma was present at a funeral on 10 June, that of Jacques Hermant, the architect of the Salle Gaveau which had hosted many recitals of Debussy's music since its opening in 1906, including those by Gaillard.[56]

Still side-lined by the monument committee, Emma received very little attention from the press this year. They continued to raise funds through concerts, and devised other promotional tactics such as a special gala concert on 30 April, which brought Debussy's *Préludes* to the audience in a novel way. The poet Jehanne d'Orliac wrote 24 poems, which were read by her and Jean Weber of the Comédie-Française in between the 24 *Préludes* played by Geneviève Dehelly. In addition, a small metal plaque reproducing the image of Debussy created by the engraver Pierre Turin and struck by the *Hôtel des Monnaies,* the Paris Mint, was sold in aid of the monument. On the back it bore the inscription 'Claude Debussy (1862–1918). Cette médaille a été frappé à l'occasion de l'érection des monuments de Claude Debussy à Paris et à Saint-Germain-en-Laye.'[57] In the same month the Paris City Council voted unanimously for the erection of the monument in the 'futur square Debussy' on the ancient fortifications at the end of the rue de Longchamp between the boulevard Flandrin and the Bois de Boulogne in the sixteenth arrondissement,[58] not its eventual situation.

1931: Emma's legal case against the monument committee

Unfortunately 1931 would once again raise unwelcome echoes of the past. The monument committee had to work hard to fuel interest in the Debussy project. Paul Le Flem contributed enthusiastic articles to *Comœdia*, rallying the public to attend concerts in homage to the composer.[59] The great pianist Paderewski sailed from America to lend his support by giving two recitals. The first took place in June and was highly praised,[60] but sadly the pianist was able neither to give the second nor to attend a reception in his honour, as he had to return home to tend to his sick wife.[61] Emma was unable to attend Paderewski's concert as she was ill.[62]

---

55 Archivo Manuel de Falla, 7082-084.
56 *Le Temps*, 10 June 1930.
57 *Le Petit Parisien*, 14 April 1930.
58 *Le Ménestrel*, 18 April 1930.
59 *Comœdia*, 16 February 1931, 31 March 1931.
60 *Comœdia*, 7 June 1931; *Le Petit Parisien*, 9 June 1931; and others.
61 *Comœdia*, 13 June 1931.
62 A. Hartmann, *Claude Debussy as I knew him*, p. 171.

Marius-François Gaillard was still giving Debussy recitals such as that on 28 January 1931 in the Salle Pleyel,[63] but this had nothing to do with fundraising. Instead, the mayhem caused by the notorious concert organised by Emma and Gaillard in April 1928 now came to a head. In February 1931 several newspapers published reports of the court case brought by Emma against the monument committee for causing the failure of this concert to raise the estimated sum of ninety-six francs deemed possible. The committee had disassociated itself from the performance of the two previously unpublished works. 'It became the source of mere tips for those who had sponsored it', wrote *Le Matin*.[64] *Le Petit Parisien* quoted the figure of 16,712 francs in receipts, whilst forty-six thousand francs had to be paid in expenses.[65] The argument of the prosecution was that this failure was caused by the negative publicity disseminated by the committee. M. Vidal-Naquet, defending the committee, declared that they had issued a press release in order to avoid confusion between the activities of their group and those of Gaillard. They had also believed that the concert as envisaged would prejudice Debussy's reputation. They claimed they had already collected subscriptions and that the Paris and Saint-Germain councils had already assigned plots for the monuments.[66] Emma's advocate chided the committee for its inertia. It had existed for twelve years yet still not erected the monuments. Its only activity had been to cause the failure of the initiative of the composer's widow.[67] Judgement was given a week later. The case was dismissed. It was deemed that the committee had committed no offence and that the note passed to the newspapers contained no words expressly intended to cause harm.[68] The outcome was that 'Mme Claude Debussy' or 'La veuve de Debussy' (Debussy's widow), was brought into the headlines to no avail. It is notable that Raoul Bardac's name was not listed amongst the members of the committee bringing the case,[69] slight compensation for the stress caused.

Despite this setback, Emma's name is to be found amongst an extraordinary list of Parisian and international guests of renown at a very elegant tea party given by Ganna Walska.[70] Royalty, politicians, socialites, personalities from industry, film, art and music were invited to this event given by this Polish opera singer, who had purchased the Théâtre des Champs-Élysées after her marriage in 1922 to the American businessman Harold F. McCormick, her fourth husband. Their divorce would be announced in October of this year, 1931.

---

[63] Advertised in *Le Figaro*, 22 January 1931.
[64] *Le Matin*, 18 February 1931.
[65] *Le Petit Parisien*, 26 February 1931.
[66] *Le Figaro*, 5 March 1931.
[67] *Le Journal*, 26 February 1931.
[68] *Le Figaro*, 5 March 1931; *Le Journal*, 5 March 1931; *Le Matin*, 5 March 1931; *Le Petit Parisien*, 5 March 1931.
[69] Listed, for example, in *Le Matin*, 5 March 1931.
[70] *Le Figaro*, 1 March 1931.

André David

The novelist André David (1899–1988) told of an incident which he dated to 1931. President Albert Lebrun was present at a Debussy Gala concert where David told him that the widow of the great musician was in the hall. Lebrun agreed to follow him to Emma's box, where she was sitting discreetly. This led to David being admonished by the head of protocol for not respecting the etiquette of the Élysée Palace. He therefore apologised to the President, who replied that if it was any consolation, he did not know the rules either.[71]

David claimed he often dined with Emma and her daughter and granddaughters on a Wednesday, and felt he knew her so well that it was as if he had been adopted by her.[72] He claimed that at Emma's home he heard both Ravel and Falla talking emotionally about what they owed Debussy. Falla, typically 'terribly shy', blushed when Emma talked admiringly of his work. 'But Madame, I would be nothing without your husband,' he replied. There is no other reference to Ravel having been entertained in Emma's apartment. David was only one year older than Gaillard so it is significant that he should have felt so nurtured as a son, following the pattern that Emma had developed of looking after and encouraging younger aspiring men. David wrote a fulsome description of Emma which chimes perfectly with those written by friends from the early years of her association with Debussy. She was the most feminine woman he knew. Everything about her exuded grace – her voice, the way she tilted her head to one side and smiled at the person talking to her, the naturally white curl which she tended carefully amongst her blond hair, her perfume, her scented bouquets of roses, violets or lilies of the valley. She had passed on her incomparable charm to her daughter and granddaughters. He stated he attended many concerts in Emma's company. With Emma and Dolly he saw and heard *Le martyre de Saint Sébastien*. He narrated an anecdote about the latter: at a rehearsal Debussy and d'Annunzio suddenly realised something was not quite right. Debussy blamed the text, d'Annunzio blamed the music. Each stood by his opinion. Meanwhile, Ida Rubinstein was rehearsing on the stage in her ordinary clothes. She suggested, 'I could perhaps do this?', whereupon she mimed the 'chemin de la Croix'. They were delighted – what they had been unable to find in words or music Rubinstein had discovered through movement.[73]

There were no long letters to the Hartmanns this year, just a short note asking Arthur about the whereabouts of his wife and children, whom he had not mentioned in the few lines he had sent her. 'I don't understand your solitude,' she wrote. Little did she know that not only had he suffered serious illness again, but had advertised his violin for sale and had sold the *Minstrels* manuscript.[74] He must have sympathised with her opinion that 'Everyone around me is poor, and life

---

[71] A. David, 'Musiciens et peintres de ma jeunesse', *La nouvelle revue des deux mondes*, June 1972, pp. 574–82.

[72] Ibid.

[73] Ibid. (Although David would only have been twelve years old in 1911).

[74] A. Hartmann, *Claude Debussy as I knew him*, p. 31.

32. Emma at her desk

becomes more and more costly.' Her last extant letter of 1931 expressed her usual desire for Falla to visit her again. She had at least met his cousin Pierre de Matheu, who had passed on good news of him.[75] Emma's 'costly' life was recorded in the 1931 census for Paris, which shows that faithful Louise Gibbs was still living with her, now aged forty-one, as well as a servant called Angèle Belleret aged twenty-seven.

[75] December 1931, Archivo Manuel de Falla, 6898/2-018.

24

1932–4: The final struggle

Inauguration of Debussy monument

On 17 June 1932 the Debussy monument was inaugurated with pomp and circumstance. In newspaper reports of the occasion there was no mention of Madame Emma Claude Debussy. There were many fulsome descriptions of the design by the Martel brothers and its position in the boulevard Lannes bordering the Bois de Boulogne. The concept was described as ingenious, particularly the significant presence of water mirroring the carvings. 'Water! Water was Debussy's best friend. He loved water, painted water, glorified it,' wrote Gabriel Astruc.[1] Emma can be seen in press photographs, seated in the third row of onlookers, watching the luminaries process.[2] These included the President of the Republic, Albert Lebrun, Jean Mistler, Under-secretary of the Beaux-Arts and the monument committee, Paul Léon, Chairman of the committee and Director-general of the Beaux-Arts, Raoul Bardac, Roger-Ducasse, Paul Dukas, D-.E. Inghelbrecht, Louis Laloy, E. Vuillermoz, Jean Messager, Robert Brussel and Gabriel Astruc. Several speeches were given in which the attempt was made to define Debussy's skill and the source of the unique attraction of his music, but his character was even more difficult to convey. How could anyone who knew the man agree with Paul Léon's dismissive statement, 'Of the life of Debussy there is little to remember and less still to conclude. No fairy-tale existence. Thoughts but no events.'?[3] Jean Mistler emphasised the beauty of what he called 'musique de jardin' (garden music) and this 'musicien de plein air' (musician of the open air) but, despite this, the occasion proved that such music is not really destined to be played outside. Only the band of the Garde Républicaine succeeded in making its fanfares resound clearly. They also lent weight to the finale of *Le martyre de Saint Sébastien*. Otherwise the voices of choirs evaporated into the air, as did the *Trois Chansons de Charles Orléans* conducted by Roger-Ducasse.[4]

The inauguration was preceded the night before by a concert of chamber music with Ninon Vallin singing the *Chansons de Bilitis*, Cortot and Thibaud performing the Violin Sonata and the Kretily Quartet playing Debussy's String Quartet. On the night of the inauguration a gala concert at the Théâtre des Champs-Élysées consisted

---

[1] *Le Temps*, 18 June 1932.
[2] Agence de presse Mondial Photo-Presse, BnF, Estampes et photographie, EI-13 (2948).
[3] 'De la vie de Debussy il y a peu à retenir et moins encore à conclure. Rien d'une existence romancée. Des pensées, point d'évènements.' *Le Temps*, 18 June 1932.
[4] *Le Ménestrel*, 24 June 1934.

of the first act of *Le martyre* conducted by Philippe Gaubert, the *Nocturnes* conducted by Gabriel Pierné, *Prélude à l'après-midi d'un faune* conducted by Weingartner, *La mer* conducted by Toscanini and the fourth act of *Pelléas et Mélisande* conducted by D.-E. Inghelbrecht with three of the original cast, Mary Garden, Hector Dufranne and Félix Vieuille. Ingeniously, Weingartner's performance was broadcast directly by radio from a concert taking place in Basel, Switzerland. Whilst this was highly commendable from a sentimental point of view, it was less so from an artistic one. The sound from the loudspeakers deprived the *Prélude* of its essential ethereal character and contrasted painfully with the live performances. It is possible that Emma expressed her gratitude to Toscanini by giving him the manuscript of a song Debussy composed for Marie Vasnier in 1881, *Les Papillons*.[5] *Comœdia* carried a report of the arrival of Mme Siegfried Wagner at Le Bourget airport in time for the concert, saying that 'Bayreuth was one of the subscribers to the monument'.[6]

Dolly later told an anecdote in line with the memories of several other people of a Parisian taxi driver. Someone, she says, took a taxi to the ceremony and upon their arrival the driver told her 'Je suis Blondin, le créateur du petit Yniold!' When Emma spoke to him he cried and explained that when not working nights he sang at the Bobino, a music-hall in Paris.[7]

One faithful friend did remember Emma on this stressful occasion. Manuel de Falla wrote to her on 11 June to tell her he would be thinking of her with all his heart. He also hoped Robert Brussel would send him a copy of the programme, for which he had written some lines.[8] It was Emma who carried out this task in September.[9]

Despite the general lack of acknowledgement by the musicians around her, Emma was still regarded by the press as a member of *Tout-Paris*, that upper-crust élite whose presence at art galleries and society events merited reporting. Only a few days before the monument ceremony she was seen at an exhibition of paintings of flowers by the writer André David, whose friendship with Emma has already been noted.[10] Not long after, she was present at a concert given by the singing pupils of Pauline Donalda, a Canadian soprano, in the Salle d'Iéna.[11] When the Opéra-Comique opened its new season that November with a gala performance of *Carmen* with Conchita Supervia in the title role, Emma was the first notable guest to be listed in *Le Petit Parisien*.[12]

---

[5] M. Rolf, 'Debussy, Gautier and Les Papillons' in *Debussy and his World*, ed. J. Fulcher, Princeton N. J., 2001, p. 114 n.1.

[6] *Comœdia*, 21 June 1932.

[7] *Causerie faite par Mme de Tinan à la discothèque de Londres Dec. 1972*, Centre de Documentation Claude Debussy RESE 08.07. Yniold is the young son of Golaud in *Pelléas et Mélisande*.

[8] Archivo Manuel de Falla, 6898-2-056. Falla had contributed to the section of the programme 'Le Florilège de Claude Debussy'.

[9] Archivo Manuel de Falla, 6898-2-057(2).

[10] *Comœdia*, 1 June 1932; *L'Intransigeant*, 9 June 1932.

[11] *Comœdia*, 5 July 1932.

[12] *Le Petit Parisien*, 11 November 1932.

In 1932 the *Archives internationales de la Danse*, an association and a magazine, were founded by Rolf de Maré, creator of the Ballets Suédois. One of the founding members of the official Friends of this association was Madame Claude Debussy. Others included Paul Valéry, Jacques Rouché, Maurice Ravel, Florent Schmitt and Gabriel Astruc.[13] Emma had therefore not been completely ostracised by organisations involving members of the monument committee.

Chanson d'un fou and *Symphonie en si mineur*

Question marks still arose over Emma's judgement when it came to allowing publication of Debussy's early works, however. Following a request from a son of Nadezhda von Meck, who had discovered some very early Debussy manuscripts amongst her papers, Emma permitted Eschig to publish *Chanson d'un fou*. She had never seen the manuscript and little did she realise that the youthful Debussy had simply copied out the work of another composer, Emile Pessard, during his days at the Conservatoire.[14] To prove the deceit, *Le Monde musical*, whose editor was Auguste Mangeot, issued a reproduction of the first page of both songs. Emma must have been acutely embarrassed. Dolly later referred to this affair in her notebook detailing for her daughters significant facts about Debussy and her mother. She called it 'L'Affaire Mangeot' asserting that it was he who had accused their grandmother of authorising publication of the song. *Nounouthe* (Granny) had acted in good faith and had been deceived, she insisted, leading to drama and rows between Mangeot and *Nounouthe* based on totally unfounded insinuations.[15]

The 'sensational discovery' of a previously unpublished symphony composed by Debussy in Moscow was heralded in both *Le Temps* and *Comœdia* in July 1932.[16] Debussy had sent this *Symphonie en si mineur* (Symphony in B minor) for four hands to Madame von Meck in 1881 and now it had been found in a Moscow market bound with a number of arrangements of symphonies for four hands.[17] Only one movement, an allegro, existed and that only for piano duet. A Debussy expert was quoted in *Le Temps* as doubting its authenticity,[18] but Madame von Meck had acknowledged receipt of Debussy's 'charmante symphonie' in a letter in February 1881, which is quoted by both Lockspeiser and Lesure. Dolly told her daughters that this *Symphonie* was published by the Soviets in 1933 and performed

---

[13] *Le Temps*, 25 May 1933.
[14] Maurice Dumesnil quoted a letter from 'Von Meck' asking for her authorisation; *Claude Debussy. Master of Dreams*, New York, 1940, p. 322. E. Lockspeiser said the song was in a collection belonging to Alexander von Meck and was sold to Schott (for whom Eschig worked in Mainz) by Georges de Meck; *Debussy: His Life and Mind*, vol.1, p. 47.
[15] Hélène de Tinan, Carnet rouge, Centre de Documentation Claude Debussy, RESE 08.01.
[16] E.g. *Comœdia*, 4 July 1932.
[17] E. Lockspeiser, *Debussy: His Life and Mind*, vol.1, p. 45.
[18] *Le Temps*, 5 July 1932. According to Lesure, the publisher N. Gilaiew said it was discovered by K. S. Bogouchevsky, a mathematician in Moscow: F. Lesure, *Catalogue de l'œuvre de Claude Debussy*, in Lesure, *Claude Debussy, Biographie critique*, p. 474.

in 1937 without the family's permission. They had not acknowledged the composer's rights and it was sold by a Russian publisher in the rue d'Anjou.[19]

To Mourillon

Emma's last extant letter to Arthur Hartmann was written on 15 August 1932.[20] After all the fanfare for the Debussy monuments, it was very sad. Here was an elderly woman, lonely and in ill health, whose doctor had advised her to spend a holiday 'somewhere dry' so she had come to Mourillon, on the eastern edge of Toulon, on the Mediterranean coast. She could not afford a good hotel and was writing from an establishment called Le Prieuré de Lamalgue, commenting on its 'lack of comfort'. Dolly and her family were staying further along the coast at Cannes, no doubt in something far grander. 'I do not have a car with which to visit them and I am waiting for her to come and see me,' she told Hartmann. When Dolly did come, she and her family took Emma out on a day trip. A photograph of Emma taken on a mountain path has the location pencilled on the back: Sainte-Maximin-la-Sainte-Baume. This small town with a famous basilica is at the foot of the Sainte-Baume mountains. Nowadays it is about an hour's drive from Toulon. Another image shows Emma with Dolly, Gaston and their daughters eating at a table on a terrace.

Hartmann had now informed Emma of his depressing state of affairs, divorce and illness, which left Emma feeling even more unhappy. Of the monument we learn that there was a fifty thousand franc surplus of money collected, which she thought should be contributed to the monument to Fauré.

Emma used her connection to the Countess Greffulhe via her daughter's marriage to further the career of the tenor David Devriès (1881–1936) when she wrote to her on 23 August 1932. Devriès wanted to sing the role of Pelléas in Vienna and Emma requested that the Countess recommend him.[21] She also kept in contact with Falla, for Magdeleine Greslé sent him a postcard of the Debussy monument on 28 October with her best wishes, saying she received news of him from Emma.[22]

Death of Lilly; Vallas's report

December 1932 brought the news that Debussy's first wife, Rosalie Texier, had died. In the papers she was described as 'the first wife of Claude Debussy, at his side during his years of hardship at the time of *Pelléas et Mélisande*'.[23] The funeral service was held at the church of Saint-François-de-Sales on 20 December. News of Lilly's death reached New York soon afterwards, for Léon Vallas, always more sympathetic towards Debussy's first wife than his second, published an affectionate article in the *New York Times* recalling her role in providing loving support to Debussy during

---

[19] Hélène de Tinan, Carnet rouge, Centre de Documentation Claude Debussy, RESE 08.01.
[20] A. Hartmann. *Claude Debussy as I knew him*, pp. 170–2
[21] M. Chimènes, *Mécènes et musiciens*, Paris, 2004, p. 656.
[22] Archivo Manuel de Falla, 7082-050.
[23] *Comœdia*, 18 December 1932; *Le Journal*, 19 December 1932.

33. Emma near Sainte-Maximin-la-Sainte-Baume, 1932

the composition of his opera: '… the inconsistent Debussy had found a woman of character – young, pretty, devoted, tender and blessed with the maternal qualities so necessary to the big child that Debussy remained to the end of his days,' he wrote. 'One day in June 1904 he left home. An imperious need of luxury, or perhaps another love affair, drew him to a rich woman belonging to the highest Paris society.' He claimed Debussy often saw Lilly and that she had been present at every one of a series of lectures he gave on Debussy over four months in 1927.

> One day I had to allude to the circumstances of her marriage, but she only smiled gently. When she came to speak to me at the end of the lectures I was greatly moved. She waited till the others had gone and then congratulated me … and said happily, 'What you say of my marriage is very interesting – and almost true!' [24]

Lilly still possessed many documents, unpublished early works, letters and a palette of paints which Debussy had used as a boy. Vallas's second book on Debussy, *Claude Debussy et son temps*, was also published this year, 1932,[25] stirring much controversy over his views on the publication of Debussy's early works and his legacy.

On the same day as Lilly's funeral, Manuel de Falla thanked Emma for a photograph of Debussy he had received. It had been awaiting him on his return from conducting in Italy. He had been delayed in writing to her by an eye problem, but was deeply touched.[26]

---

[24] L. Vallas, 'Death of "Melisande"', *The New York Times*, 8 January 1933.
[25] L Vallas, *Claude Debussy et son temps*, Paris, 1932.
[26] Archivo Manuel de Falla, 6898-2-058.

Inauguration of second Debussy monument

The second monument to Debussy, sculpted by Aristide Maillol, was inaugurated in Saint-Germain-en-Laye on Sunday 9 July 1933. Speeches were given by dignitaries and representatives of the world of the arts, music by Debussy and Rameau was performed in the open air by the *garde républicaine*, two choirs and members of the recently formed orchestra of the new Conservatoire Claude Debussy.[27] In the museum, works of another local resident, Maurice Denis, were presented. Pride of place was given to his illustration created in 1893 for *La damoiselle élue*. *Le Journal* of 10 July 1933 was the only paper to make any reference to Debussy's wife, by simply inserting a small photograph of her superimposed on an image of Emile Bollaert, Director-General of the Beaux-Arts, giving his speech.

Emile Vuillermoz, writing in *Comœdia*, pleaded for Saint-Germain-en-Laye to become the Bayreuth of France. If the composer of *Pelléas* had been born in Germany, Austria or Italy he would have been commemorated long ago with a museum, Debussy festivals or a Debussy season, he exclaimed. 'Why not found a Debussy season in the spirit of the Wagner festival in Bayreuth and the Mozart festivals in Salzburg.'[28]

Maurice Dumesnil and Debussy's *Premier Trio en sol*

In March 1933 Debussy's piano piece *Page d'album* was edited by Maurice Dumesnil and published in America in the *Etude* magazine by the Theodore Presser Company. This had been composed for the charity Le Vêtement du blessé in June 1915, but had then assumed a more personal significance when Debussy gave Emma a copy of the manuscript on her special day, 4 June, that year. Now it was to reach a wider public. Dumesnil was a concert pianist born in 1886 in France, who became an American citizen in the 1930s. He was well known for his interpretations of Debussy. He published several articles on him as well as a biography, *Claude Debussy, Master of Dreams*.[29] Writing after Emma's death, he explained that he used to visit her in her flat in the rue Vineuse several times a week. Every day she went to Debussy's graveside to collect her thoughts. In her flat he saw Debussy's Blüthner piano, rare books, watercolours and etchings, crystal glass figurines, large lampshades, deep chairs, all creating an elegant aristocratic atmosphere. Dumesnil passed on an anecdote he claimed Emma had confided in him about a watch sold by Debussy's father in order to buy items such as clothes for the grand dinner party held to celebrate his winning the Prix de Rome. Emma actually gave Dumesnil this watch with a number of other mementoes before her death, so, if true, perhaps it had been pawned rather than sold. Dumesnil died in 1974, and in 1982, amongst his papers donated to the University of Michigan School of Music, were discovered movements two to four of Debussy's *Premier Trio en sol* (First Trio in G major), written when he was employed

---

[27] This monument is now in the Musée Claude Debussy, Saint-Germain-en-Laye.
[28] *Comœdia*, 10 July 1933.
[29] M. Dumesnil, *Claude Debussy, Master of Dreams*, New York, 1940.

by Nadezhda von Meck in 1880. On the cover page of the finale Dumesnil had written a note saying it had been given to him by Emma. Accompanying this was a typed note with Emma's signature authorising publication.[30]

Auction of Emma's collection

In November 1933 the plea appeared in Comœdia, 'Will Debussy's memorabilia and manuscripts be saved from being dispersed in a sale?'[31] Emma was about to sell a large collection of Debussy's manuscripts and printed scores. Besides still paying off debts incurred by her husband, she was having to meet increasing medical expenses. A public auction was to be held in the Hôtel des Ventes, otherwise known as the Hôtel Drouot. The catalogue read: *Collections Jules Huret et Claude Debussy, G. Andrieux expert, 1 décembre 1933, Nos 174–224, p.33–41*.[32] Many questions were posed by the distressed journalist. Who would get their hands on these moving creations by the man who proudly called himself 'musicien français'? They included fragments of *Le diable dans le beffroi*, a few passages from *La légende de Tristan* and *La chute de la Maison Usher*. Notebooks contained sketches for Mallarmé's poem *Apparition*, themes for *Ibéria* and modifications to the orchestration of *Pelléas*. The composer's markings appeared on 'Sirènes' (*Nocturnes*), *La mer*, *Jeux*, *Ibéria* and *Rondes de printemps*. Important letters expressed Debussy's trenchant views on the society of his day. Surely a public library should invest in the collection? The day after the sale the newspaper exclaimed that the precious memorabilia had been scattered to the four winds. The sum total raised was forty-four thousand francs. The only purchaser mentioned was M. Vallery-Radot, who bought the unpublished manuscript of *La chute de la Maison Usher*. In fact a certain Marcel Lévy purchased the scores of *Pelléas et Mélisande*, *Prélude à l'après-midi d'un faune*, *La mer*, *Nocturnes* and *Ibéria*, probably on behalf of François Lang, a professional pianist whose passion was collecting works of art and manuscripts. Lang died in Auschwitz in 1944, but his collection of almost all Debussy's annotated manuscripts, hidden and saved by the singer Ninon Vallin, is preserved in the Bibliothèque musicale François Lang in the Abbey of Royaumont.[33] Seven pages of the manuscript of *Lindaraja*, the two-piano piece performed by Roger-Ducasse and Marguerite Long in 1926, were sold, then reappeared in the catalogue of la maison Cornuau in February 1936.[34]

---

[30] *Music at Michigan*, vol.19, no.1, fall 1985, p. 6.
[31] *Comœdia*, 27 November 1933.
[32] Centre de Documentation Claude Debussy, CATA-3.08.
[33] Le fonds Debussy in the collection François Lang: http://www.royaumont-bibliotheque-francois-lang.fr (last accessed 16 July 2021).
[34] F. Lesure, *Catalogue de l'œuvre de Claude Debussy* in Lesure, *Claude Debussy*, p. 530. The descriptions of works other than manuscripts sold but destination unknown in the catalogue are listed in 'Éléments de la bibliothèque de Debussy dans la vente de 1933', *Cahiers Debussy*, no.1, 1977, pp. 38–40.

Death of Emma and funeral

Maurice Dumesnil witnessed the decline in Emma's health towards the end of 1933. He recounted a visit to her apartment at her request of the Quatuor Pascal in the spring of 1934.[35] He may mean the Quatuor Calvet, created in 1919, of which the viola player Léon Pascal was a member in 1934. The Quatuor Pascal, comprising the violinists Jacques Dumont and Maurice Crut, viola player Léon Pascal and cellist Robert Salles, was not created officially until the 1940s. Debussy's String Quartet had figured in the repertoire of the Quatuor Calvet for ten years. They wanted to play it for Emma as a celebration of this anniversary. She therefore invited the quartet to an afternoon tea recital at which Dumesnil, his wife Evangeline Lehman and Magdeleine Greslé were also present. Dumesnil insisted that Emma had said many times that at the hour of her death she wanted to hear the slow movement of this quartet. A few days later she was taken to a clinic on the Boulevard Arago, where she was nursed by nuns. Dumesnil wrote as if he were with her on this journey to the thirteenth arrondissement, a surprising distance from the rue Vineuse in the sixteenth.[36] Her death certificate states that she died at her home, 24 rue Vineuse, on Monday 20 August at 7 a.m.

Emma's funeral was on 22 August, Debussy's birthday. They would both have been seventy-two years old. It took place at the cemetery of Passy, where Debussy's tomb awaited her. Dumesnil related that at midday two rabbis were waiting in the centre aisle wearing ceremonial garments. The presence of rabbis was confirmed by a reporter for *Comœdia*, who described Rabbi Wolff chanting prayers. Despite the noise of a phonograph blasting from a nearby window, the ceremony continued with the slow lament of the cantors in the hot sunshine. The coffin was lowered into the tomb and one by one the mourners dropped a handful of earth on top. Thus Emma joined 'Claude Debussy, Musicien de France' and her daughter Chouchou. Those present at the ceremony included M. de Fleuriau, former French Ambassador in London, M. et Mme André Citroën (Raoul's erstwhile employer), Dr Grandhomme, the Deputy Mayor of Saint-Germain-en-Laye, M. Grandchamp, Assistant Director of the Conservatoire Claude Debussy at Saint-Germain-en-Laye, Mme Jacques Lecomte de Noüy, Mlle Ullmann, Baroness Vinan, M. René Delange, Secretary General of *Excelsior*, Mme Blanche Vogt, a writer, M. André Warnod, writer and art critic, and Gustave Samazeuilh, composer and writer on music. The funeral was led by Emma's children, Raoul and Dolly, and Roger-Ducasse.[37] This list of attendees seems very impersonal, with few representatives from the arts. Dolly has not left an account of the occasion, nor referred to it publicly. Since her baptism and marriage she no longer belonged to the Jewish faith.

The day before the funeral, *Comœdia*, the paper which had always published more news of Emma than others, printed a lengthy appreciation of her efforts to support her husband and to continue to promote his music after his death. It was headed 'The admirable mission to which the wife of the great musician dedicated herself'.

---

[35] M. Dumesnil, *Claude Debussy. Master of Dreams*, pp. 323–4.
[36] Ibid.
[37] *Comœdia*, 23 August 1934 (M. de Fleuriau wrongly spelt Fleurian).

She was, wrote Jacques Claudian-Belvil, an admirable partner who never ceased to work in harmony with Debussy. No one would ever know how much the atmosphere of peace and tenderness with which she surrounded him had helped him to compose his masterpieces. She deserved recognition as his inspirational muse. He reminded his readers of her agony during Debussy's years of suffering during the war, of Debussy's determination to live to see the victory of the France he loved so passionately. His death did not bring an end to his wife's suffering, for she lost her daughter so soon afterwards. This widow and grieving mother had devoted herself entirely to the glory of her deceased husband, seeing in his work everything she loved about him and which she had to defend against short-sighted, blinkered, envious critics. She had encouraged Marguerite Long to learn and perform the *Fantaisie* for piano and orchestra and had had many previously unpublished works published and performed. She remained sweet and smiling to the end of her days, happy to witness the success of the compositions of *Claude de France*, whom she had loved so deeply and who owed her so much.[38]

Emma's life had now come full circle. Born a Jew, her origins were recognised in her burial ceremony. However, she did not join her Jewish uncle in the huge tomb in Montmartre where a plaque had awaited her arrival there ever since Osiris had the monumental statue of Moses erected.

Emma's financial legacy

The document detailing Emma's assets on her death and the deductions that had to be made in order to calculate her estate and the share of it to be passed on to her children, the *Formule de Déclaration de Mutation par Décès*,[39] was mentioned in Chapter 20, when Raoul made a loan to Emma sometime before May 1921 to be repaid to him upon her death. Her assets included furniture, jewellery and art works which had been insured for two hundred thousand francs, but sales by public auction in October and November 1934 only raised 68,283 francs. She was owed 694.20 francs from the annual sum of five thousand francs paid to her by the Osiris estate since the death of her mother, and 10,822 francs from publishing rights of Debussy's works. It also becomes clear that in June 1934, only a couple of months before she died, Emma was entitled to the revenue from government bonds in the name of her daughter, Dolly. This gave her an asset of 32,963 francs. There was another asset, which comes as a surprise: when Chouchou died, a similar form had had to be filled out declaring the child's assets, dated 16 January 1920. From this we learn that at some unspecified time, perhaps on Chouchou's birth, Emma had invested in 26,500 francs worth of *Rente Française* (French government bonds) in the name of her daughter Claude Emma Debussy. In January 1920 after tax, these were declared to be worth 31,316.80 francs. At Chouchou's death a quarter of this went to Emma and her two older children shared the remainder. At the time of Emma's death further interest had accrued on her share.

---

[38] *Comœdia*, 21 August 1934.
[39] Copy kindly provided to the author by M. Vincent Laloy.

From her assets deductions had to be made, amongst other things, for an item described as the sum of 15,616.45 francs, a pro rata payment in advance by Mesdemoiselles de Tinan (Françoise and Madeleine) to Madame Debussy relating to the sale of copyright. This was dated 16 July 1934, just over a month before her death. This would imply that her granddaughters were paying her in advance money which they would soon earn through Debussy's works. Dolly must have been working out various ways of lending money to her mother just months before she died. There was the loan from Raoul and there were arrears of rent and repairs to be paid and, of course, doctors' fees. Two thousand francs were owed for Emma's final illness. In the end, Raoul and Dolly each inherited 99,624.98 francs. It is hard to convert this sum into today's money, especially since 1935 was in the heart of the great depression and not long afterwards the war would play havoc with bank rates. One estimate results in this sum being the equivalent in 2020 of 71,990 euros for each, which converts to approximately £64,000.[40]

---

[40] https://france-inflation.com/calculateur_inflation.php to calculate anciens francs français to euros; https://www.xe.com/currencyconverter for euros to pound sterling (last accessed 8 June 2020).

25

Epilogue

The love between Emma and Claude

Emma loved Claude, staying by him even when she must have despaired of his behaviour. It was she who initially attracted Debussy towards her. She loved the company of musicians. Marguerite Long described Emma as 'a woman of genius, who had musical intuition to the most extraordinary degree and was the ideal woman for the artist he was. She had always lived around great musicians.'[1] It was Emma who first sent Debussy flowers, gave him presents. She knew his impecunious state when she fell in love with him. As Debussy wrote in December 1904, 'I am poorer than Job … I have terribly little money and Mme B [Bardac] … has no intention of giving me any, nor I of accepting any.'[2]

They both had to suffer gossip, ostracism, scathing comments. Obviously in view of their comparative circumstances Debussy would look like the one to profit materially from their association, but Emma seems to have had no qualms about giving up the certainty of the luxurious life she led with banker Sigismond Bardac. It is often said that she was demanding, unable to give up her love of luxury, frustrated by lack of financial resources and still aspiring to live in the style to which she had become accustomed with her first husband, but there is little evidence that she did not willingly and relatively speedily completely change from being a socially active society lady to a supportive wife and mother who did not hold artistic salons and 'at homes'. Their official marriage was for legal reasons rather than a desire to ensnare Debussy. He made little of this event, she did not boast of it and there seem to be no comments from those surrounding them. She was willing to sacrifice financial security for love of both the man and the music. There was never any definite promise of inheritance from Osiris. She could never have kept her divorce secret from her uncle and must have been fully aware of his fanaticism about his religion and his belief in fidelity.

Of the two, she had the harder task of maintaining the relationship, having to put up with the inevitable need for isolation and mood swings which were part and parcel of being the wife of a dedicated, often irascible composer. Judging by her attitude to younger composers and performers after his death, she had a maternal, caring instinct and it becomes clear that Debussy, despite his many crises of self-belief and sense of confinement during his marriage, realised how much he depended on her the more he travelled and the more ill he became.

---

[1] C. Dunoyer, *Marguerite Long. A Life in French Music 1874–1966*, p.60.
[2] December 1904, C. pp. 877–8.

Debussy's love of Emma was real enough to withstand accusations and scorn thrown at him by his contemporaries and sufficient to bind him to her through years of financial and physical misery. Yet he expressed publicly the opinion that a composer should probably not marry. Music was his first wife. That would always instinctively have priority. In 1903, even before eloping with Emma, he wrote,

> I love music too much to speak of it in any other way than with passion ... those who love art are hopelessly in love, and besides, no one will ever know to what extent music is a woman – which perhaps explains the frequent chastity of men of genius.[3]

In previous chapters there were several occasions when he expressed feelings of imprisonment. Even before he and Emma were officially married he felt restless (the following italics are mine):

> ... all in all, there is no peace in my soul. Is it because of the restless landscape in this corner of Paris ...? *Is it that I am definitely not made for domestic life?* So many questions for which I don't have the strength to find an answer.[4]

He had

> an insurmountable need to escape from myself and go off on adventures which seem inexplicable because *I reveal a man no one knows* ... an artist is by definition a man accustomed to dreaming ... How can anyone expect this same man to behave in his daily life according to the strict observance of its traditions, laws and other barriers erected by the hypocritical and cowardly world?[5]

How could a wife steel herself against such self-centred introversion? Emma struggled to stay positive and put up with Debussy's dark moods and brooding doubts as he tried to forge a way forward after *Pelléas* which was satisfying to him as well as to his audiences and critics. It did not help matters that she was often ill, more so the longer the marriage lasted, unable to tolerate conventional medication and dependent on homeopathic remedies. Her illnesses were no doubt aggravated by her frustration with her husband's demands. Who knows how much could be attributed to depression at the loneliness of an existence in which he shut himself away for hours on end concentrating on his music? A bitter crisis ensued when she refused to allow him to travel to America without her in 1911, possibly linked to her mistrust following the alleged discovery of his letters to Dolly, said to date from just prior to that time. This led him to complain of the difficulty of combining composing with married, or family life.

> One should ... achieve *the position of loving nothing but oneself with fierce attention to detail*! But in fact exactly the opposite happens. *First the family which gets in the way, either with too much tenderness or with blind serenity.* Then the Mistresses or the Mistress, which don't even count because one is all too happy to lose oneself in oblivion. I do without them and other temptations. One can actually do nothing about it.[6]

---

[3] *Gil Blas*, 28 June 1903.
[4] To Louis Laloy, 15 October 1907. C. p. 1036.
[5] To Jacques Durand, 8 July 1910. C. p. 1299.
[6] To André Caplet, 22 December 1911. C. p. 1472.

'Too much tenderness' or 'blind serenity.' That Emma's loving concern should be a shackle imprisoning him in a relationship which he regarded as hindering his creativity proves that she was the strong chain pinning him to an environment where at least he was able to follow his own ends. If this involved entering and re-entering the world of Edgar Allan Poe, that too was a form of self-indulgence. At the age of twenty-seven he had admitted that Poe was his favourite author, together with Flaubert.[7] In 1893, the year he saw the first production of Maeterlinck's play *Pelléas et Mélisande*, he was already grumbling about black moods, days which he described as 'fuligineuses, sombres et muettes',[8] Baudelaire's translation into French of 'dull, dark and soundless', quoting exactly the vocabulary of the first sentence of Poe's *The House of Usher*. This tale became an obsession which dominated Debussy's thoughts throughout his life whenever he was depressed and it is symptomatic that he never managed to complete the score to this work at the centre of his mind. The gothic house on the brink of crumbling around Roderick Usher became a metaphor for the stifling domination of domestic and social life, one which he lamented to others when depression was overwhelming him. 'It is possible that The Fall of the House of Usher will also be the fall of Claude Debussy', he told Dukas in 1916.[9]

The second sentence of Poe's story, as Roderick's friend approaches the melancholy house, reads, 'a sense of insufferable gloom pervaded my spirit'. The words could have been spoken by Debussy. He struggled to create his own libretto, of which there are three versions. The mental and physical description of Roderick Usher match Debussy's idea of himself: 'une âme éprise d'art, de beauté', ('a soul in love with art, with beauty'), 'ce front aux tempes trop larges' ('that forehead with over-sized temples'), Debussy's version of Poe's words 'an inordinate expansion above the regions of the temple'. He must have seen in the constant illness of Lady Madeline, Roderick's sister, an echo of Emma. 'Elle est si faible, si fragile!' ('She is so weak, so frail.') 'Ne sais-tu pas qu'elle est ma seule raison de ne point mourir?' ('Don't you know that she is the one reason for me not to die?'), Roderick cries out in Debussy's libretto.[10]

Darkness overwhelms the opera and it was this growing burden of depression to which the composer succumbed throughout his married life when frustrated by lack of inspiration or the mundane worries of daily domestic matters. Compare this with the torrent of joy expressed in *L'isle joyeuse*, or *Reflets dans l'eau*, composed during the brightest interlude in Debussy's life. When he met Emma it was as if a candle had been lit. He could not escape its rays and was drawn to her like a moth. Just as a moth is burnt in the flame, Debussy gradually felt his creativity stifled at a time when he needed to earn ever more to keep up their lifestyle, one which he made no effort to move away from.

---

[7] In answer to a questionnaire, reproduced in J. Barraqué, *Debussy*, Paris, 1962, p. 72.
[8] To Ernest Chausson, 3 September 1893. C. p. 154.
[9] Quoted by R. Orledge in *Debussy and the Theatre*, p. 102.
[10] Translation of the French text in the booklet for the CD *Claude Debussy. The Edgar Allan Poe Operas. La Chute de la Maison Usher. Le Diable dans le Beffroi*, completed and orchestrated by Robert Orledge. Panclassics PC10342.

To meet their needs Debussy constantly borrowed money, eventually taking on irksome engagements, travelling far and wide rather than staying at home in the well-appointed study so carefully tended by his wife. Everyone who visited him commented on the atmosphere of peace in the house, in particular in this room.

> A delightful house with an atmosphere of peace and work about it … In his study M. Debussy has few pictures but many books. In one corner is his piano, which at the time of my visit he had just left to sit down at his desk. Such meticulous order as his desk showed! The blue blotter almost entirely free from ink stains, a score book lying neatly on it; a couple of writing pads placed geometrically, an inkwell or two, and a rather large jar of handsome green pottery for cigarettes.

Thus wrote a journalist from the *New York Times* in 1910, a time when Emma was seriously contemplating divorce. Despite the formality of an interview, Debussy, in trying to explain his aversion to hearing his own works performed and the feeling that his compositions were a part of himself, 'almost like my own children', could not refrain from saying:

> … to me music is almost like a human being. Now, you know, if you love a person very much and you can be alone with that person, you do not ask for anything more. And the more the loved person or art is admired, the more it is taken away from you. And you only have to share with many what you previously had entirely to yourself. So that celebrity means nothing to me. I do not care for it.
>
> … there will always be an enormous breach between the soul of the man as he is and the soul he puts into his work. A man portrays himself in his work, it is true, but only part of himself. In real life I cannot live up to the ideals I have in music. I feel the difference there is in me, between Debussy the composer and Debussy the man.[11]

Emma was living with a husband and the father of her third child who was married to his music yet struggling to achieve the perfection somewhere present in his deepest consciousness, and acutely frustrated at his perceived inability to do so.

> I have forced myself to work when I felt least like it, and I have done things which did not seem so bad at the time. I would let these compositions lie for a couple of days. Then I would find they were only fit for the waste basket.[12]

Similarly he struggled with his marriage. They tried more or less living apart in the same house, sending notes to each others' rooms. Apart from occasional writing, Debussy did not take on other paid work to help with expenses, such as teaching. He had once expressed a sense of entitlement to patronage, obviating the need for such labour.[13] However this would never come about so eventually he found it essential to travel and put himself on display to bring in some much-needed money. It was then that he found out how much he depended on Emma, her meticulous ways of caring for him and her comforting presence. The other bond tying him to her was, of course, his daughter. His closeness to Chouchou was an unexpected joy; his pride

---

[11] *New York Times*, 26 June 1910.
[12] Ibid.
[13] See Chapter 8 p. 109.

in her should have been one of the most pressing reasons for clinging to life, for emerging from the depths of dark despair. Yet even this did not rescue him from the 'Factories of Nothingness', the oft-mentioned *Usines de Néant*.

Antisemitism and Vallas's biographies

Emma was strong enough in her conviction of her love and her belief in Debussy's musical genius to endure any privations. Their circle of close friends diminished but at least they could now see who was truly faithful to them. She withstood petty jibes and whisperings about their relationship. Much of this was pure antisemitism.

She was brought up and married young within a purely Jewish environment. It is unfortunately a relevant fact that throughout Debussy's and Emma's courtship and their early years together the Dreyfus Affair was running its course in France. There can be no under-estimating the intense passions it aroused. Zola's *J'accuse* appeared in 1898 but still several nationalistic antisemitic institutions were created such as *La Ligue de la Patrie francaise* in 1899 and *La Jeunesse antisémitique,* which became the *Parti national antijuif* in 1901. In 1908 the anti-Dreyfus Léon Daudet co-founded the nationalist periodical *Action française*. He had been present at the première of *Pelléas et Mélisande* in 1902 and in 1903 Debussy had addressed him as '*Cher ami*'.[14] Of Debussy's friends, Pierre Louÿs was one of the staunchest anti-Dreyfusards. No wonder he sympathised so deeply with Lilly when she attempted suicide. He emphasised to his brother Georges that it was a Jewish woman Debussy had eloped with and that Sigismond had plenty of money, which would ensure that Emma would return to him.[15]

Antisemitism did not cease with the end of the Dreyfus Affair. It is likely that Emma read a long defence of Debussy's nationalism in November 1924 which Léon Vallas concluded by saying 'He is French. No one else, except perhaps Gabriel Fauré, is of such pure French blood.'[16] In 1926 Vallas, who had never met Debussy, published his first biography of the composer. Significantly, Dolly, answering questions at the end of a talk in 1972, told her audience that 'Vallas was very good for questions about music, but not about the man!'[17] 'Or the woman', she might have added. Vallas's book was the first of his four biographies of Debussy which emphasised Debussy's modest background but increasingly accentuated the purely French stock of this '*musicien français*'.[18] As the years went by Vallas felt more at liberty to emphasise what he regarded as the negative influence of Emma upon the composer. She was not mentioned by name in the 1926 work, but 'his second marriage was characterised by a sort of withdrawal from which he only seemed to emerge with

---

[14] C. p. 814.
[15] C. p. 872.
[16] 'Il est français. Nul autre, si ce n'est celui de Gabriel Fauré, n'est de race aussi pure.' *Comœdia*, 10 November 1924.
[17] Dolly Bardac, London interview.
[18] L. Vallas, *Claude Debussy et son temps*, Paris, 1932, p. 1.

difficulty.'[19] In 1932 Emma was described as being a society lady (*cette femme du monde*), and her first husband was simply '*un financier*'.[20]

In 1944, during France's occupation, Vallas published his third biography.[21] Ten years after Emma's death he was freer to imply criticism. Here there was great stress on his preference for Lilly over Emma. He emphasised Lilly's modest background and her charm, inserting the remark that when she died in 1932 she still kept her youthful, gracious looks, implying she was more attractive than Emma.[22] She had not wanted to marry, but Debussy's threat of suicide made her consent. When he recounted Debussy's abandonment of Lilly, Vallas was at pains to stress Emma's Jewish background. 'She belonged to Jewish high society. A good musician, amateur singer, she was married to a rich Jewish banker and had a son, a composition pupil of Debussy.'[23]

There was no doubt in Vallas's mind as to who was the force behind the new relationship. With no evidence to support his assertion, he stated, 'Mme Emma Moyse had previously wanted to marry Gabriel Fauré ... She decided to marry Claude Debussy'.[24] He also alleged falsely that relations between Fauré and Debussy were damaged by the latter's relationship with Emma, repeating in a footnote the emphasis on Emma's Jewishness and quoting a specious comment, printed in *Le Figaro* in 1942, supposedly made by Fauré that he never wanted to hear the name Debussy again.[25] What was even more obviously antisemitic was Vallas's statement that

> Perhaps Mme Moyse painted an enticing picture to the musician, who was quite indifferent to these very practical views, of the advantages that a composer ... could derive for getting his work known by entering Jewish society, this being all powerful and the only dispenser of commercial profits, official backing and state subsidies for music.[26]

Vallas was at pains to express his familiarity with Lilly, claiming that Debussy saw in her '*le type de Mélisande*', and stressing her modest background, her devotion, her ability to control 'the big child he always remained' and ensure steady working conditions. He derided Laloy's version of events concerning Debussy's marriages in *La musique retrouvée*, saying he had romanticised the 'stories' and sided with the composer, 'whose behaviour had been condemned mercilessly by all his friends except Erik Satie [for whom Vallas had little respect] and Laloy himself.'[27] Scurrilously, in 1958 he also included a footnote quoting Henri Busser's book *De Pelléas aux Indes galantes*, which idealised Lilly Texier and quoted her as saying she still received visits from 'her dear Claude' until shortly before his death. Debussy confided in her his

---

[19] L. Vallas, *Debussy*, Paris, 1926, p. 122.

[20] L. Vallas, *Claude Debussy et son temps*, p. 249.

[21] L. Vallas, *Achille-Claude Debussy*, Paris, 1944.

[22] Idem. p. 38.

[23] Idem. p. 46.

[24] Ibid.

[25] *Le Figaro*, 6 June 1942. Quoted in L. Vallas, *Achille-Claude Debussy*, pp. 96–7 n.1.

[26] L. Vallas, *Achille-Claude Debussy*, p. 47.

[27] L. Vallas, *Claude Debussy et son temps*, p. 152 ; p. 249 n.1.

disappointment with the marriage to Emma, which he had entered into purely to give his name to Chouchou.[28]

Emma's family and descendants

Hélène de Tinan (Dolly)

In 1939 Dolly renewed contact with Emma's great friend, Chouchik Laloy. She wrote to her from the spa town of Plombières in the Vosges, overjoyed to have met her again when Chouchik visited her there bearing chocolates, regretting the missed years of what could have been close friendship. She felt that when she had previously been aware of Chouchik she had been but a '*larve informe*', an immature creature, since which time whole lives had gone by. Chouchik was after all only twelve years older than Dolly. Unfortunately Dolly was unable to return the visit to the Laloy home in Rahon as Chouchik soon left for Paris and Dolly went on to Switzerland.[29] This meeting probably took place before the outbreak of war.

Jewishness, according to traditional Jewish law, is passed down through the mother, which means that inevitably Emma's surviving children, Raoul and Dolly, were affected by this legacy after her death, having to live through the Second World War with the intense antisemitism that involved. Dolly's husband, Gaston de Tinan, was the great uncle of Henri Thieullent, who became the executor of Debussy's estate. Maître Thieullent, who died in 2014, remembered meeting Emma in person in 1928 or 1929 when she was sixty-six or sixty-seven. She was visiting his parents in the company of Gaston and Dolly at their large property in Gainneville near Le Havre. He recalled a woman who looked physically fit, but was wearing heavy make-up, her hair was dyed and she spoke very loudly and exuberantly.[30] He did not meet her again until 1933, the year before her death. Emma was lunching with the de Tinans and was a different woman altogether. She was ill, worn out and no longer spoke. She had aged, was very weak and did not join in any conversation during mealtimes.

Maître Thieullent described his aunt Dolly as delightful (*ravissante*) and emphasised her love of her father, Sigismond Bardac. However, he did not mention something that appears on Dolly's marriage certificate: this bears a note that she and Gaston divorced on 10 May 1938. The reason must surely have been connected to Dolly's Jewish heritage. Because both her parents were Jewish (assuming she was not the daughter of Gabriel Fauré, which was never publicly admitted or proven), she, like other Jews living in Paris, in May 1942 would be forced to wear the yellow star. This was when her possible other paternity was advantageous, for according to Maître Thieullent, Hitler's representative in the city (whose name escaped him)

---

[28] L. Vallas, *Claude Debussy et son temps*, 1958, p. 295.
[29] Letters of 12 and 23 July 1939; copies kindly provided by M. Vincent Laloy.
[30] 'Elle était encore très, assez en forme, elle était très fardée, les cheveux teints, parlant très fort et exubérante.' Author's conversation with Maître Thieullent, 26 August 2010.

34. L–R: Dolly, Françoise, Emma, Madeleine, possibly with Magdeleine Greslé and Greslé's daughter

was an ambassador with a great love of music. He said to Dolly, 'It hurts me to see you wearing the yellow star. We know you are the daughter of Gabriel Fauré. Also you have married an Arian, Monsieur de Tinan, so you need not wear the star. Sign a paper for me, declaring that you are the daughter of Gabriel Fauré.'[31] Dolly refused adamantly to do this and left Paris for Cannes.

On 31 March 1949 Dolly obtained a copy of her father Sigismond's birth certificate. This must have been to support her application for an official Certificate of French Nationality, dated 10 May 1949, for which she paid ten francs.[32] The reason for obtaining this four years after the war ended is unclear. Her nephew on her husband's side, Philippe Lagourgue, could think of none, remarking that his aunt was '*très discrète*'. From this 1949 certificate we learn that she actually married her husband Gaston twice, once on 24 January 1911 and for the second time on 18 February 1939 – only nine months after her divorce from him in 1938. This must surely have been another cautionary measure to avoid reprisal as a Jewish woman. It is stated that Gaston Pochet Lebarbier de Tinan was French by virtue of article 8 of the *ancien Code Civil*, having been born in France of a father himself born there. Dolly was officially French as her father, Sigismond Bardac, possessed French nationality, having been naturalised by decree of 18 September 1889 (as noted in Chapter 1). Gaston was made a Chevalier de la Légion d'Honneur in 1931.

It is clear on reading and listening to Dolly's memories that, unsurprisingly, she was anxious to convey an entirely positive view of her mother. She made no comments about any possible paternity of Fauré and she even claimed that the *Dolly* suite was composed when she was four years old.[33] It is strange that whilst so many of Debussy's letters sent to Emma during his travels survive, there is not one from Emma to him, some of which, it can be gleaned from Debussy's responses, clearly expressed unhappiness. This could be seen as further evidence of Dolly's desire to avoid any intimation of problems between Emma and Claude. Vincent Laloy emphasised the 'faith burning in her [Dolly] for Claude de France', of whom she was very proud.[34] All who knew Dolly recall a delightful, very intelligent woman, always pleased to talk about her step-father and to give advice on the interpretation of his piano music when asked. She herself was an accomplished pianist.

[31] 'Quand le représentant d'Hitler à Paris – le nom m'échappe – qui était un ambassadeur qui connaissait bien l'histoire de la musique, quand il a su que ma tante portait l'étoile jaune, il est venu la voir et il a dit "Ça me fait mal au cœur de vous voir porter l'étoile jaune car nous savons que vous êtes la fille de Gabriel Fauré et comme d'autre part vous avez épousé un arien, Monsieur de Tinan, vous ne devez pas porter l'étoile. Signez-moi un papier, comme quoi vous reconnaissez être la fille de Gabriel Fauré." Elle a refusé. Elle a refusé. Elle a refusé de porter l'étoile jaune …' Ibid.

[32] Copies of certificates kindly provided by M. Philippe Lagourgue, Debussy's current executor.

[33] 'Ma mère était encore Madame Bardac, et j'étais encore une toute petite fille, j'avais quatre ans à ce moment-là, Fauré a eu la gentillesse d'écrire pour moi la suite à quatre mains.' De Tinan, French interview.

[34] V. Laloy, *Souvenirs épars*, (Dolly de Tinan, née Bardac). Unpublished paper kindly provided by M. Vincent Laloy

After the war, in 1947, Dolly was upset by a new production of *Pelléas et Mélisande*, no doubt just as her mother would have been, and made every effort to have it banned, without success.[35] The symbolic sets were designed by Valentine Hugo and were deemed a shocking departure from the lyrical depictions of forests and castles of previous years. Dolly appreciated most the concert performances of the opera given once a year by Inghelbrecht, as 'unfortunate scenery' did not detract from the performances. She also mentioned a concert which took place in the Debussys' former home in the Square du Bois de Boulogne in 1952 at which Mary Garden sang. Following this, Garden visited Dolly in her own home, by which she was very touched.[36]

Dolly's husband Gaston (known to the family as *Tonton*) died in 1958. Her final address was 34 rue Scheffer, close to where her mother had lived, near the Passy cemetery. Having survived her two daughters, Dolly died on 26 February 1985. She was buried at Passy, in the tomb of her husband Gaston de Tinan and daughter Françoise, not far from Debussy's and Chouchou's grave.

Françoise and Madeleine de Tinan

Dolly's older daughter, Françoise, born in 1912, became a Personal Secretary (*secrétaire de direction*) to General Georges Philias Vanier, Minister and Head of the Canadian Legation from 1939 to 1940 and Canada's first Ambassador to France from September 1944 to 1953. She never married and a note exists claiming that she was a lesbian.[37] It is said that she was a friend of Colette de Jouvenel, known as Bel-Gazou, the daughter of the writer and actress Colette and her second husband Henri de Jouvenel.[38] Françoise died in 1959 and is buried in the de Tinan grave at Passy.

Dolly's second daughter Madeleine de Tinan, born in 1913, was briefly engaged in 1932 to a certain Lionel Hart,[39] but this relationship did not last for in 1936 Madeleine married Guy Mortier (1897–1972). A beautiful portrait of her in her elegant wedding gown designed by Molyneux appeared in at least two magazines.[40] The marriage was short-lived as she divorced in 1938, coincidentally the same year as her mother. She worked as a nurse and drove ambulances during the war and sadly was seriously injured when trapped between two military lorries, one reversing into another. She became Personal Assistant to General Chaban Delmas, who eventually became Prime Minister of France.[41] She was awarded the Croix de Guerre. In December 1966 she married Jean Bruère, seven years younger than her, the son of Ambassador

---

[35] R. Nichols and R. Langham Smith, *Claude Debussy. Pelléas et Mélisande*, p. 159.
[36] Dolly Bardac, London interview.
[37] Note in folder Dolly de Tinan, Centre de Documentation Claude Debussy, RESE 04.68.
[38] V. Laloy, *Souvenirs épars, (Dolly de Tinan, née Bardac)*.
[39] *Le Figaro*, 9 February 1932.
[40] *Les Modes: revue mensuelle illustrée des Arts décoratifs appliqués à la femme*, April 1936, and *Femina*, March 1936.
[41] Information kindly provided by M. Philippe Lagourgue.

André Bruère.[42] It was also his second marriage. She died in 1982 aged sixty-nine, three years before her mother, and is buried in the Bruère family grave, also at Passy. Neither she nor her sister Françoise had any children.

Raoul Bardac

Raoul's accounts of life with Debussy were honest and revealing. He had been working for Citroën until the time of Emma's death in 1934 (as noted, M. et Mme André Citroën were present at Emma's funeral), but he left that firm on 30 November of the same year.[43] Between then and 1940 he promoted his step-father by serving on a committee for *La Semaine Debussy* at Saint-Germaine-en-Laye in 1935,[44] publishing an article in *Terres Latines*, 'Dans l'intimité de Claude Debussy' in 1936, and in February 1940 broadcasting on Dutch radio a talk, *Causerie sur Claude Debussy*.[45]

In 1942 Raoul was arrested by the Gestapo and imprisoned in Compiègne. The horror of this was echoed in a letter written by Vincent Laloy's mother. She told of a singing lesson Dolly was taking with Marguerite (Babaïan, sister of Chouchik), presumably before Dolly left Paris for Cannes. Dolly, mad with worry, could hardly control herself. 'The household, her brother as well as numerous other artists, men of letters, doctors etc. have been in a concentration camp for ten days, where they are sleeping on the ground on straw. Her brother is over sixty years old.'[46] Dolly never mentioned these events in subsequent talks or writings.[47] Somehow Raoul was freed or escaped and managed to cross the demarcation line into Vichy France and the quiet town of Meyssac in the Corrèze, far away from Paris. This was a rural area where prior to 1940 there were few Jews, although with increasing harassment there was an influx into the region. It is unclear what Raoul did when he arrived there or how he earned his keep, but he lived in a pleasant, sizeable house in the Route de Beaulieu, owned by Doctor Couderc. This was not without problems, for there are visible signs that the house was set alight at some stage during the war. Amongst family photographs there are some in an envelope marked 'Raoul' of the picturesque Château de Curemonte in the Corrèze, only about twelve kilometres from Meyssac. This belonged to Colette's daughter Bel-Gazou, mentioned above. Colette herself took refuge there in June 1940. It is impossible to know why these

---

[42] Note in folder Dolly de Tinan, Centre de Documentation Claude Debussy, RESE 04.68; V. Laloy, *Souvenirs épars (Dolly de Tinan, née Bardac)*.

[43] R. Bardac, *Curriculum vitae*, Centre de Documentation Claude Debussy, RESE-05.18.

[44] *Le Figaro*, 3 June 1935.

[45] R. Bardac, *Causerie sur les dernières années de Claude Debussy*, 1940, Centre de Documentation Claude Debussy, RESE 05.15.

[46] 'Mme de Tinan si excitée pendant sa leçon que je plaignais de tout cœur. La maison, son frère, aussi que de nombreux autres artistes, hommes de lettres, médecins etc. depuis 10 jours sont dans un camp de c[oncentration] où ils dorment par terre, sur la paille. Son frère a plus de 60 ans.' One page of letter kindly provided by M. Vincent Laloy. The addressee is not named on this page.

[47] Maître Thieullent said that Dolly never spoke about her brother and disliked his second wife. Author's conversation with Maître Thieullent on 26 August 2010.

35. Raoul Bardac

photos were taken and whether Raoul also took refuge there at some stage, but the distant family link is interesting.

On 7 May 1944 he was arrested again by the Germans and imprisoned in Limoges, where he was tortured. Raoul left a very moving handwritten account of the moment he had to leave his house in fear. He referred to a terrible morning when danger was looming. The feeling of dread and sadness was overwhelming, the description of the house and garden loving and mournful. 'My house, my house. Do not forget me! Don't forget me and I will never forget you.'[48] He returned to Meyssac in August 1945 when France was liberated, where he was looked after by the widow of Doctor Couderc, Joanna (or Johana) Joséphine née Manévy and in that same year they married. It is not known whether he divorced his first wife, Yvonne, or if she had died. The last reference to her in correspondence appears to be in a letter he wrote to Louis Laloy in July 1931 where he included her in condolences, presumably for the death of Aline, Louis' mother, who died that year.[49]

On the thirtieth anniversary of Debussy's death Raoul gave another talk about him on the radio. He died two years later on 30 July 1950 in Meyssac, where he

---

[48] In Raoul Bardac's hand with a heading added by Hélène de Tinan dated 29–30 August. Centre de Documentation Claude Debussy, RESE 05.20.

[49] Laloy archives, B12, Dossier 35, no.11.

is buried.[50] His wife inherited Debussy's Blüthner piano, which is now housed in the Musée Labenche d'Art et d'Histoire in Brive-la-Gaillarde, some twenty-eight kilometres away. Sometimes it is played – for example, by Jean-Louis Haguenauer on a recording of all of Debussy's songs.[51] The direct lines from Emma and Claude Debussy and Emma's children have all died out, so this piano remains a rare constant physical link to those heady days of Debussy's and Emma's first love, when it was purchased in Eastbourne in 1905.

---

[50] Biographical details given in an unattributed obituary from a local paper, Centre de Documentation Claude Debussy, RESE 0.15.18.
[51] Claude Debussy, *Intégral des melodies*, Jean-Louis Hagenauer, Ligia, LIDI 0201285-14.

Select Bibliography

Archival and unpublished sources

Archivo Manuel de Falla, Granada: Correspondence between Falla and Emma Debussy, Magdeleine Greslé and Louis Laloy.
Archives Vincent Laloy: Correspondence between Louis Laloy, Chouchik Laloy, Emma Debussy and Raoul Bardac.
Bardac, Raoul, *Souvenirs de Raoul Bardac sur Claude Debussy lus à la Radio pour le 30ème anniversaire de sa mort en 1948*, Centre de Documentation Claude Debussy, RESE 05.16.
—— 'Dans l'intimité de Claude Debussy', *Terres Latines*, March 1936.
—— *Causerie sur les dernières années de Claude Debussy*, Centre de Documentation Claude Debussy, RESE 05.15.
—— *Curriculum Vitae*, Centre de Documentation Claude Debussy, RESE-08.04(1)-(3).
—— *Adieu à ma maison*, 1940, RESE-05.20.
Bibliothèque nationale de France: Correspondence between Emma Debussy, André Caplet and Marius-François Gaillard.
British Library, London: *British Institute of Recorded Sound lecture series: Dolly Bardac – Memories of Debussy and his circle*. Recorded 5 December 1972. British Library shelfmark T572. Edited version published in *Recorded Sound*, 50/51, April–July 1973, pp. 158–61, 163 (abbreviated to 'Dolly Bardac, London interview').
CD of an incomplete recording of an interview in French with Hélène de Tinan and a female interviewer, untitled, unattributed, kindly given to the author by M. Philippe Lagourgue (abbreviated to 'de Tinan, French interview').
Centre de Documentation Claude Debussy, Paris: *Causerie faite par Madame de Tinan à la Discothèque de Londres*, December 1972, Centre de Documentation Claude Debussy, RESE 08.07.(1).
Laloy, Vincent, *Souvenirs épars, (Dolly de Tinan, née Bardac)*, unpublished paper originally prepared for the *Hommage à Raoul Bardac* in Meyssac in 2006. Copy kindly given to the author by M. Laloy.

Published sources

Claude Debussy

Campos, Rémy, *Debussy à la plage*, Paris, Gallimard, 2018.
Cobb Margaret ed. *The Poetic Debussy. A Collection of his Song Texts and Selected Letters*, trans. R. Miller, Rochester N. Y. and Woodbridge U. K., University of Rochester Press, 1994.

David, André, 'Musiciens et peintres de ma jeunesse', *La Nouvelle revue des deux mondes*, June 1972, pp. 574–82.

Debussy, Claude, *Correspondance (1872–1918)*, ed. François Lesure and Denis Herlin, annotated by François Lesure, Denis Herlin, and Georges Liébert. Paris, Gallimard, 2005 (abbreviated to C.).

——*Correspondance de Claude Debussy et P.-J. Toulet*, Paris, Le Divan, 1929.

——*Lettres inédites à André Caplet (1908–1914), recueillies et présentées par Edward Lockspeiser*, Monaco, Éditions du Rocher, 1957.

Dietschy, Marcel, *La Passion de Claude Debussy*, Éditions de la Baconnière, Neuchâtel, 1962.

——*A Portrait of Claude Debussy*, ed. and trans. William Ashbrook and Margaret G. Cobb, Oxford, Clarendon Press, 1994.

Dumesnil, Maurice, *Claude Debussy, Master of Dreams*, New York, Ives Washburn, 1940.

Dunoyer, Cecilia, *Marguerite Long. A Life in French Music 1874–1966*, Bloomington and Indianapolis, Indiana University Press, 1993.

Durand, Jacques, *Quelques souvenirs d'un éditeur de musique*, 2 vols, Paris, Durand et fils, 1924, 1925.

Gauthier, André, *Debussy. Documents iconographiques*, Geneva, Pierre Cailler, 1952.

Hartmann, Arthur, *Claude Debussy as I Knew Him and Other Writings*, ed. Samuel Hsu, Sidney Grolnic and Mark Peters, Rochester N. Y. and Woodbridge U. K., University of Rochester Press, 2003.

Herlin, Denis, and Giroud, Vincent, 'An Artist High and Low, or, Debussy and Money', in E. Antokoletz and M. Wheeldon, *Rethinking Debussy*, Oxford, Oxford University Press, 2011, pp. 149–96.

Inghelbrecht, Germaine and D.-E., *Claude Debussy*, Paris, Costard, 1953.

Joly-Segalen, Annie, and Schaeffner, André, *Segalen et Debussy*, Monaco, Éditions du Rocher, 1961.

Laloy, Louis, *Claude Debussy*, Paris, Les bibliophiles fantaisistes, 1909.

——*Debussy*, Paris, Aux Armes de France, 1944.

——*La Musique retrouvée 1902–1927*, Paris, Librairie Plon, 1928.

Langham Smith, R. ed. *Debussy Studies*, Cambridge, Cambridge University Press, 1997.

Lesure, François, *Claude Debussy, Biographie critique*, Paris, Fayard, 2003. This also contains the *Catalogue de l'œuvre* compiled by F. Lesure.

——*Claude Debussy. A Critical Biography*, trans. and revised ed. by Marie Rolf, Rochester N. Y. and Woodbridge U. K., University of Rochester Press, 2019.

——*Debussy on Music*, F. Lesure, ed. and trans. R. Langham Smith, London, Secker & Warburg, 1977.

Liebich, Louise, *Claude-Achille Debussy*, London, John Lane, 1908.

Lockspeiser, Edward, *Debussy: His Life and Mind*, 2 vols, London, Cassell, 1962, 1965.

Long, Marguerite, *Au piano avec Claude Debussy*, Paris, Billaudot, 1960.

Martins, J. E., 'Les trois dernières lettres connues de Chouchou Debussy', *Cahiers Debussy*, no.31, Centre de Documentation Claude Debussy, Paris, 2007.

Nectoux, Jean-Michel, *Harmonie en bleu et or. Debussy, la musique et les arts*, Paris, Fayard, 2005.

Nichols, Roger, *Debussy Remembered*, London, Faber & Faber, 1992.

———*The Life of Debussy*, Cambridge, Cambridge University Press, 1998.
Opstad, Gillian, *Debussy's Mélisande, The Lives of Georgette Leblanc, Mary Garden and Maggie Teyte*, Woodbridge U. K., The Boydell Press, 2009.
Orledge, Robert, *Debussy and the Theatre*, Cambridge, Cambridge University Press, 1982.
———'Debussy's Musical Gifts to Emma Bardac', *Musical Quarterly*, 60, (1974) pp. 544–56.
Peter, René, *Claude Debussy*, Paris, Gallimard, 1944.
Priest, Deborah, *Louis Laloy (1874–1944) on Debussy, Ravel and Stravinsky*, Aldershot U. K. and Vermont U. S., Ashgate, 1999.
———'"Une causerie sur Claude Debussy" de Raoul Bardac', *Cahiers Debussy*, no.26, Centre de Documentation Claude Debussy, Paris, 2002, pp. 45–53.
Southon, Nicolas, 'Une correspondence entre André Schaeffner et Marcel Dietschy. Dialogue et controverses debussystes', *Cahiers Debussy*, no.34, Centre de Documentation Claude Debussy, Paris, 2010.
Strobel, Heinrich, *Claude Debussy*, Paris, Librairie Plon, 1940.
Vallas, Léon, *Debussy (1862–1918)*, Paris, Librairie Plon, 1926.
———*Claude Debussy et son temps*, Paris, Librairie Félix Alcan, 1932.
———*Achille-Claude Debussy*, Paris, Presses Universitaires de France, 1944.
———*Claude Debussy et son temps*, Paris, Éditions Albin Michel, 1958.
Vallery-Radot, Pasteur, *Lettres de Claude Debussy à sa femme Emma*, Paris, Flammarion, 1957.
———*Héros de l'esprit francais*, 'Claude Debussy', Paris, Amiot Dumont, 1952.
———*Tel était Claude Debussy*, Paris, Julliard, 1958.
Wheeldon, Marianne, *Debussy's Legacy and the Construction of Reputation*, Oxford, Oxford University Press, 2017.

Gabriele d'Annunzio

Antongini, Tom, *D'Annunzio inconnu*, Paris, Stock, 1938.
Hughes-Hallett, Lucy, *The Pike*, London, Fourth Estate, 2013.

André Caplet

Maréchal, Maurice et Durosoir, Lucien, *Deux musiciens dans la Grande Guerre*, Paris, Tallandier, 2005.
'André Caplet', *Zodiaque*, vol.26, no.107, January 1976.

Web-based sources

Durosoir, Georgie, *Le sergent André Caplet, 1916–1918*, http://www.megep.net/IMG/pdf/le_sergent_caplet.pdf (last accessed 17 July 2021).
André Caplet, 1878–1925, http://www.andre-caplet.fr (last accessed 17 July 2021).

Manuel de Falla

Manuel de Falla and his European Contemporaries: Encounters, Relationships and Influences, C. G. Collins, D.Phil thesis, University of Bangor, 19 July 2002.
Pahissa, Jaime, *Manuel de Falla. His Life and Works*, trans. Jean Wagstaff, London, Museum Press Limited, 1954.

Gabriel Fauré

Fauré-Fremiet, Philippe, *Gabriel Fauré*, Albin Michel, Paris, 1957.
Fauré, Gabriel, *A Life in Letters*, trans. and ed. J. Barrie-Jones, London, Batsford, 1989.
——*Correspondance, présentée et annotée par Jean-Michel Nectoux*, Paris, Flammarion, 1980.
——*Correspondance suivie de Lettres à Madame H., receuillies, présentées et annotées par Jean-Michel Nectoux*, Paris, Fayard, 2015.
——*Lettres intimes, présentées par Philippe Fauré-Fremiet*, Paris, Bernard Grasset, 1951.
Johnson, Graham, *Gabriel Fauré, The Songs and their Poets*, London and Farnham, Guildhall School of Music & Drama, Ashgate, 2009.
Koechlin, Charles, *Gabriel Fauré*, trans. Leslie Orry, London, Dennis Dobson Ltd., 1945.
Long, Marguerite, *Au piano avec Gabriel Fauré*, Paris, Billaudot, 1963.
Nectoux, Jean-Michel, *Gabriel Fauré. Les voix du clair-obscur*, Paris, Fayard, 2008.

Marius-François Gaillard

Rae, Caroline, 'Debussyist, modernist, exoticist: Marius-François Gaillard rediscovered', *The Musical Times*, vol.152, no.1916 (autumn 2011), pp. 59–80.
Recording of Marius-François Gaillard, *The French Piano School. Complete Debussy Recordings*, Apr, B07JJGGB1K.

Osiris

Ardoin Saint Amand, Jean-Pierre, *Osiris, l'oncle d'Arcachon*, Arcachon: Société historique et archéologique et du Pays de Buch, 1996.
Jarrassé, Dominique, *Osiris. Mécène juif, Nationaliste français*, Le Kremlin-Bicêtre, Paris, Éditions esthétique du divers, 2008.
Gab, *Monsieur Osiris*, Paris, 1911. Also online at https://gallica.bnf.fr/ark:/12148/bpt6k64714068/f12.image.texteImage (last accessed 17 July 2021).
Nahon, Gerard, *Juifs et judaïsme à Bordeaux*, Bordeaux, Mollat, 2003.

Maurice Ravel

Maurice Ravel. L'intégrale. Correspondance (1895–1937), écrits et entretiens, ed. Manuel Cornejo, Paris, Le Passeur, 2018.
Nichols, Roger, *Ravel*, Yale, Yale University Press, 2011.

Jean Roger-Ducasse

Depaulis, Jacques, *Roger-Ducasse (1873–1954)*, Paris, Séguier, 2001.
——'Lettres de Roger-Ducasse à son éditeur Jacques Durand', *Revue de la Société liégeoise de Musicologie*, 8, 1997, pp. 5–126.
——'Roger-Ducasse et Marguerite Long, une amitié, une correspondance', *Revue Internationale de Musique française*, no.28, February 1989.
Roger-Ducasse, Jean, *Lettres à son ami André Lambinet, présentées et annotées par Jacques Depaulis*, Sprimont, Mardaga, 2001.

Erik Satie

Orledge, Robert, *Satie the Composer*, Cambridge, Cambridge University Press, 1990.
——'Debussy, Satie and the Summer of 1913', *Cahiers Debussy*, no.26, Centre de Documentation Claude Debussy, Paris, 2002
Potter, Caroline, *Erik Satie. A Parisian Composer and his World*, Woodbridge U. K., The Boydell Press, 2016.
Satie, Erik, *Correspondance presque complète, réunie et présentée par Ornella Volta*, Paris, Fayard, 2000.
Volta, Ornella, *Satie seen through his letters*, London, New York, Marion Boyars, 1989.

Other sources

Chimènes, Myriam, *Mécènes et musiciens. Du salon au concert à Paris sous la IIIe République*, Paris, Fayard, 2004.
Gimpel, René, *Journal d'un collectionneur, marchand de tableaux*, Paris, Callmann-Lévy, 1963; Hermann, 2011.
Kahan, Sylvia, *Music's Modern Muse. A Life of Winnaretta Singer, Princesse de Polignac*, Rochester N. Y. and Woodbridge U. K., University of Rochester Press, 2003.
Kelly, Barbara L., *Music and Ultra-Modernism in France*, Woodbridge U. K., The Boydell Press, 2013.
Saint-Marceaux, Marguerite de, *Journal 1894–1927*, ed. Myriam Chimènes, Paris, Fayard, 2007.

Index

Page numbers in bold type refer to illustrations and their captions.

Adiny-Milliet, Ada   130
Albeniz, Isaac   129, 306–7
Aldrich, Richard   108
Allan, Maud   142, 147, 168, 174, 175, 176, 179, 194, 232, 282
Amélineau, Émile   22
Annunzio, Gabriele d'   147–9, 181, 186, **187**, 188, 191, 218–19, 230–1, 253
   affection for Chouchou   149, 155–7, 160–1, 186, 188, 208, 231, 239
   for Emma   148–9, 160, 186, 188, 208–10, 211, 239
   character   147, 161, 186, 208, 230, 239
   collaboration with Debussy   147–9, 155–6, 158–61
   dedication to Chouchou and Emma   160
   financial problems   147, 161, 208
   illness   208–9, 210, 239
   joins monument committee   309, 332
   unfinished project with Debussy   330
   wartime exploits   230, 239, 248
   Works
      La pisanelle ou la mort parfumée   186, 188
      Le martyre de Saint Sébastien   147–9, 155–7, 158–60, 210, 248, 337
      Phèdre   186
Ansermet, Ernest   242, 265, 331
Antoine, André   67–8, 320
Antongini, Tom   148
Arbos, Enrique Fernández   305, 306
Arcachon   8, 36, 55, 133, 147, 163, 233, 263
Arnoux, Comtesse d'   153, 166
Arnoux, Georges d'   151, 152, 166
Astruc, Adrien   2, 9, 10
Astruc, Gabriel   2, 71, 98, 148–9, 157, 159, 175, 184, 193, 196, 235, 327, 331, 332, 333, 339, 341
Astruc, Joseph   2
Athias, David   1, 8
Athias, Haïm   1
Aubert, Louis   44, 225, 288–9, 334
Auboyneau, Gaston   166
Aubry, Paul   152

Babaïan, Marguerite   92, 124, 359

Babaïan, Susanik *see* Laloy, Susanik (Chouchik)
Bagès, Maurice   25, 26, 30, 37
Bakst, Léon   126, 159, 184
Balakirev, Mily   176
Balguerie, Suzanne   24, 304, 314
Ballets Russes   126, 147, 176, 193, 240, 242
Banville, Théodore de   322
Bárczy, Gusztav   148
Bardac, Dolly *see* Tinan, Hélène de (Dolly)
Bardac, Édouard   10
Bardac, Emma *see* Debussy, Emma
Bardac, Germaine   153
Bardac, Joseph   10, 13, 293
Bardac, Julia   10
Bardac, Léon   10, 12
Bardac, Madeleine   153
Bardac, Noël   10, 12, 13, 152, 293
Bardac, Pauline (*aka* Paule)   10, 151, 153
Bardac, Rachel, (*aka* Régina)   10, 20
Bardac, Raoul   13, 22, 25, 42, 97, 123, 124, 153, 181, **214**, 219, 225, 235–6, 246–7, 251, 252, 254, 262, 278, 317, 319–20, 321, 327, 332, 336, 339, 346, 359–61, **360**
   career   85, 214, 218, 223, 235–6, 246–7, 278, 293–4, 298–9, 332, 346, 359
   character   32–3, 44–5, 50–1, 86, 214, 227, 236, 293, 298–9, 332
   collaboration and correspondence with Louis Laloy   193–4, 213–14, 216, 220, 246, 298–9, 360
   comments and writings on Debussy and Emma   80, 83, 84, 121, 149, 179–80, 215, 217, 236, 251, 359, 360
   death   360–1
   dedication to Chouchou   218
   dedications by Debussy   56, 57, 84, 223
   education, academic   14, 15, 32
      musical   15, 20, 32, 33, 43, 44
   financial support of Emma   292–3, 299, 313, 347
   homeopathy   194
   horses, investment in   293–4, 298–9
   illness and stress   87, 117, 193, 213–15, 216, 294

inheritance from Sigismond Bardac   274, 293
   Emma Debussy   348
   Osiris   64, 96
introduction of Debussy to Emma   42, 45, 50–1, 123–4
Jewish heritage   33, 355, 359
letter from Chouchou   252, 254
marriage to Joanna (Johanna) Couderc   360
   Yvonne Mabille   226–7, 298
military service   87, 117, 213–15, 216, 218, 223
performances of works   15, 33, 56, 85
prisoner of war   359, 360
pupil of Debussy *see* education, musical
   Fauré *see* education, musical
relationship with Debussy   43–5, 50, 56, 86, 193–4, 214–15, 235–6
   with Emma   213–14, 246, 292–3, 313
   with Sigismond Bardac   220–1
Works
   Fleurs du crepuscule   33
   Horizons   214
   Le printemps dans la forêt   294
   Le songeur   193–4, 298
   Les heures   213
   Romance for violin and piano   15
   Simone   214
   Une semaine musicale   218
Bardac, Régina Hélène (Dolly) *see* Tinan, Hélène de (Dolly)
Bardac, Sigismond   10–13, **11**, 15, 18, 20, 21, 29, 30, 31, 50, 70, 72, **152**, 153, 154, 166, 174, 183, 212, 217, 220–1, 227, 262, 274, 353, 357
   addresses   12, 18, 20, 22, 58, 151, 152, 219, 226, 274
   archaeology contribution   22
   art collection   12–13, 22, 293
      sale   293
   banker   12, 72
   character   13, 22, 30, 72, 293
   divorce   74
   executor to Osiris's will   63, 96
   inheritance from Osiris   64
   legacy   274
   legal proceedings   88
   marriage to Emma   9
   repudiation of responsibility for Chouchou   88, 106
   speculation in land (Pourville)   63
Barney, Natalie   208
Barrientos, Maria   332
Bartholoni, Jean   265

Barthou, Louis   235
Bartok, Béla   288
Basset, Monsieur   318, 325
Bathori, Jane   237
Baton, René-Emmanuel *see* Rhené-Baton
Baudelaire, Charles   282, 351
Bauer, Harold   118
Baugnies, Marguerite *see* Saint-Marceaux, Marguerite de
Beaumont, la Comtesse de   14
Beetz-Charpentier, Elisa *see* Charpentier, Elisa Beetz
Benois, Alexandre   126
Bertault, Léon (financier)   137, 168, 177, 179, 189, 196, 197, 202, 203
Bétolaud, Jacques   96
Blanche, Jacques-Emile   64, 65, 266–7
Bloch, Ernest   97–8, 232
Boëllmann, Léon   30
Boëllmann, Louise   30
Boito, Arrigo   128
Boldini, Giovanni   72
Bollaert, Emile   344
Bonheur, Raymond   56, 81, 317
Bonnat, Léon   46
Bonniot, Edmond   190
Borlin, Jean   300
Boulanger, Nadia   294, 304
Bourdelle, Antoine   333
Bréval, Lucienne   70
Bréville, Pierre de   30
Briand, Aristide   319
Brock, Gaston van   9–10, 85, 97, 106
Brooks, Romaine   147
Bruère, Jean   358–9
Bruneau, Alfred   33, 135, 247, 272, 288, 308, 326, 332
Brussel, Robert   273, 314, 317, 339, 340
Budin, Pierre   85
Burkhalter, Jean   309
Busser, Henri   101, 175, 235, 354

Caine, Hall   215
Calvet, Grégoire   273
Caplet, André   9, 108, 110, 122, 143, 144, 162, **167**, 169, 175, 178, 180, 185–6, 232, 233, 250, 252–3, 260, 263, 274, 281, 288, 297–8, 299, 301–3, 308, 329
   conducting
      Images   299
      La damoiselle élue   301
      La mer   299
      Le martyre de Saint Sébastien   157, 158, 160, 297–8, 301–3

Index

abandonment of 1922
    performance   302–3
Pelléas et Mélisande   185, 268, 276
Rapsodie for saxophone and
    orchestra   275
death   316, 329
friendship and collaboration with
    Debussy   101, 110, 127, 128–9, 133,
    134, 157, 158, 161, 163, 164, 167–8, 185,
    188, 235, 247, 252, 288
friendship and support of Emma   110,
    169, 244, 246, 250, 251, 252–3, 260–1,
    269, 271, 274–5, 276, 280, 286–90,
    292
illness   131, 133, 276, 280, 288, 290, 316
marriage   276
military service   233, 234, 235, 244, 246,
    260, 264, 313
orchestration and transcription of
    Debussy's works   128, 158, 160, 161,
    179, 195, 208, 274–5, 281
religion   292
Works
    Fables   289
    Hymne à la naissance du matin   292
    Trois ballades françaises   289, 292
Caplet, Geneviève   276, 288, 292
Caplet, Pierre   288, 292
Caraman-Chimay, Alexandre de   333
Caraman-Chimay, Geneviève de Riquet
    de   151, 152, 153, 333
Carco, Francis   312–13
Cardozo d'Urbino, Léa (Emma's maternal
    grandmother) *see* Iffla, Léa
Carlier, Léonie (wife of Daniel Osiris)   5,
    6, 8, 63
Carol-Berard, Louis   273
Carré, Albert   49, 117, 156, 273, 276
Carré, Marguerite   272–3, 276, 307
Casadesus, Robert   334
Casella, Georges   287
Cesbron-Viseur, Suzanne   313
Chabrier, Emmanuel   25, 44, 196
Chadeigne, Marcel   285
Chaigneau, Thérèse   230
Chansarel, René   280
Charpentier, Alexandre   122–3, 253
Charpentier, Elisa Beetz   253, 261, 264–5
Charpentier, Gustave   46, 56, 332
Charpentier, Raymond   314
Chausson, Ernest   17, 38, 39, 40, 136
Chennevière, Daniel   299
Chevillard, Camille   85, 101, 210, 224, 253, 273
Choisnel, Gaston   197
Chopin, Frédéric   215, 218, 223, 278

Choudens (publishing house)   280, 322,
    326–8, 330
Ciampi, Marcel   290
Citroën, Monsieur et Madame André   346,
    359
Claretie, Jules   5 n.6, 6
Claudian-Belvil, Jacques   347
Clemenceau, Paul   135, 320
Clemenceau, Sophie   135
Cocteau, Jean   88, 236, 288
Colette (Sidonie-Gabrielle Colette)   288,
    309, 358, 359
Colonna, Judas *see* Colonne, Édouard
Colonne, Édouard   2, 14, 68, 91, 95, 105, 118,
    121, 122, 135
Colonne, Madame Édouard   14, 15, 23, 33,
    56, 57, 105
Coronio, Nicolas   70, 215
Cortot, Alfred   22, 26, 40 n.15, 278, 281, 288,
    339
Couderc, Joanna (Johanna)   360
Crépel (Crespel), Doctor Victor   146, 189,
    223, 279
Crevel, Monsieur   196
Croiset, Alfred   250
Croiza, Claire   219, 272, 281, 289, 301, 304

Dalimier, Albert   212
Dalliès, Jeanne   237
Daudet, Léon   353
David, André   320, 326, 337, 340
Davidoff, Princesse   14
Debussy, Alfred (Debussy's brother)   179,
    240, 252, 253
Debussy, Chouchou (Claude Emma)   85, 88,
    92, 98–9, 101, 110, **113**, **114**, **115**, 121, 123,
    135, 138, 148, 149, 161, 163, **164**, **165**, 166,
    169, 170, 176, 177, 180, 190, 191, 194, 196,
    202, 204, 207, 211, 217, 219, 234, 236, 241,
    243, 244, **245**, 247, 252–5, 259, 262, 263,
    267, 269, 270, 278, 282, 285, 288
    appearance   113, 136, 164, 186
    Birthday Book   225
    character   112, 125, 127, 136, 142, 146, 156,
        169, 173, 178, 222, 224, 249, 252, 254–5,
        262–3, 267, 278, 295
    childhood games   116, 125, 139, 157, 161,
        173, 207, 211, 222, 239
    compositions   157, 178, 180
    d'Annunzio's affection for   149, 155–7,
        160–1, 186, 188, 208, 211, 239
    death   278–80, 285, 331, 346, 347
    dedications by d'Annunzio   160
        Raoul Bardac   218

Debussy 113
Erik Satie 195–6
diary 1919 276, 278
education 92, 107, 175
finance (bonds) and financial
 legacy 107, 347
gifts to 146, 173, 184, 208, 211, 230
guardian appointed 252
illness 89, 92, 116, 127, 156, 175, 177, 190, 196, 203, 221, 224, 232, 233, 240
legitimisation 106
notes and correspondence from Debussy 91–2, 142, 145–6, 197–8, 200–1, 205
piano lessons and practice 180–1, 218, 244, 247, 262–3, 278, 295
singing 136
upbringing 86, 92, 107, 112–14, 170, 195, 249
writings 170, 175, 184, 190
 Le petit poilu 268–9
 letter to Raoul Bardac 252, 254
Debussy, Claude 17, 25, **49, 65, 80, 82**, 106, 123, **167**, 334, 341
 See also Monuments to Debussy
advice on composing 43–4, 86–7, 101
appearance 38, 48, 65, 81, 110, 112, 161, 164, 237, 351
birth and background 1, 35, 212
character 37, 42, 44–5, 48–9, 57, 58, 60, 71, 75–7, 81, 83–4, 92, 102, 106, 108, 109, 111, 118, 122, 124, 125, 135–6, 139–40, 141, 142, 143, 144, 162, 168–9, 183, 189, 200, 202, 205, 206, 220, 225, 245, 266–7, 272, 273, 285, 349–53, 354
charity concerts 219, 237, 240, 241
commemoration concerts *see under* galas and commemoration concerts
composing process 77, 83, 137–8, 169, 205, 223, 275, 289, 352
 see also under music, attitude to problems with composing
conducting 105, 122, 134, 162, 166, 205, 206
 contracts with Durand 61, 73, 74–5, 88, 110, 111, 121, 131, 133, 137, 138, 143, 168, 173, 176, 178, 189, 194, 197, 211, 215, 222, 223, 224, 225, 230, 274
 others 111, 142, 149, 168
correspondence with Emma during travels 145–8, 197–201, 204–7
critical writings 48, 101, 195, 265, 267
 Gil Blas 59
 Monsieur Croche antidilletante 265–6, 268, 271, 307, 313

Le Mercure musical, invitation refused 74, 89
SIM journal 179, 181, 184, 195, 202
death and burial wishes 252, 261
 see also burial arrangements and commemorations of Debussy *under* Debussy, Emma
death mask 253, 261, 264–5, 286–7
death of father 143
 mother 218–19
dedications of works to Chouchou 113
 to Emma 48–9, 51, 52, 53, 54–5, 56, 61, 72, 89, 99, 103, 109–10, 117, 118, 126, 136, 137, 160, 183, 184, 185, 221, 222, 226, 234
 to Lilly Texier 317–18
 to Raoul 56, 57, 84, 223
 to others 37, 40, 49, 50, 88, 102, 136, 162, 174, 237, 280
depression 41, 49, 67, 101, 102, 121–2, 126–8, 130–1, 134, 137, 138–40, 142, 145–6, 162–3, 166, 169–70, 178, 180, 189, 191, 198, 203, 204–6, 211, 229–30, 232–3, 241, 242, 246–7, 329, 351–2
destruction of works before death 226, 332, 334
divorce from Rosalie (Lilly) Texier 56, 71, 75, 76, 232, 234
domestic life 79–84, 86, 91, 100, 101, 102, 106, 109, 116, 118, 125–6, 129, 134, 135–6, 137, 140, 141, 143, 148, 149, 157, 159, 162–3, 166, 168–9, 175, 177, 181, 198–9, 205, 229–30, 282, 350–2
duplicity 49, 58, 65–6, 124, 128, 142, 156, 185, 231
editing work 215, 218, 221, 223
employment whilst a student 35, 36, 37
factories of nothingness 89–90, 137, 163, 178, 200, 223, 230, 234, 242, 353
finances 41–2, 45, 48, 100, 106–7, 108, 109, 110, 116–17, 118, 121, 134, 137, 144, 149, 161, 168, 177, 185, 194, 196, 203–4, 210, 212, 218, 231, 349, 351
 advances from publisher, Durand 127, 163, 168, 173, 189, 193, 217, 221–2, 231, 232
 arrangements for Lilly 73, 74–5, 88, 110, 142, 194, 232, 234
 debt after death 224, 261–2, 272, 292, 331
 domestic 79–81, 111, 149, 162–3, 179, 189, 191, 292
 loans 38, 39, 71, 121, 137, 163, 174, 179, 184, 185, 189, 193, 194, 202, 207, 217, 224, 231, 261–2

friendship with Gabriel Astruc   148, 184,
    193
  Paul Dukas   98, 215, 231, 242, 243
  Manuel de Falla   129–30, 166
  Gabriel Fauré   37, 89, 123, 162, 196,
    225, 235, 241
  Mary Garden   49, 101
  Robert Godet   97–8, 169, 178, 185, 188,
    202, 211, 215, 224, 229, 230, 233–4,
    237, 247, 248
  Arthur Hartmann   119, 134, 135–6,
    141–2, 202, 203–4, 231
  Désiré-Émile Inghelbrecht   194, 196,
    201, 230, 244
  Marguerite Long   210, 242, 243
  Pierre Louÿs   40, 41, 50, 55, 59, 69, 70,
    72, 266–7, 353
  André Messager   49, 67, 70
  Jean Roger-Ducasse   32, 108–9, 234,
    237, 252, 263
  Erik Satie   87–8, 157–8, 161, 192–3, 218,
    236, 239–40, 254–5, 288
  Igor Stravinsky   139, 161, 169, 176–7,
    178, 180, 187, 196, 197, 224, 229, 230
  Pasteur Vallery-Radot   51, 143–4, 166,
    191, 217, 221, 242, 249–50, 252
  Ricardo Viñes   86, 102, 173
friendship and collaboration with
  Gabriele d'Annunzio   147–9, 155–6,
    158–60, 186, 188, 239
  André Caplet   101, 110, 127, 128–9, 133,
    134, 143, 157, 161, 163, 164, 167–8,
    185, 188, 247
  Louis Laloy   57, 68–9, 74, 83, 92, 95,
    102, 123, 125, 126, 127, 129, 133, 139,
    154, 173–4, 176, 185, 194, 235, 247–8,
    266
  Gabriel Mourey   98, 101, 107, 108, 111,
    121, 137, 162, 166, 173, 197, 326
  René Peter   38, 41, 67, 70, 171
  Gabriel Pierné   133, 135, 206, 207, 219,
    253, 308
  Victor Segalen   98, 101, 102, 105, 108,
    112, 117, 124, 191, 231
  P.-J. Toulet   90, 99, 101, 102, 107, 108,
    123, 143, 148, 166, 176, 177, 201, 242–3
friendship and rift with Maurice
  Ravel   44, 70, 95–6
friendship and support of Raoul
  Bardac   33, 43–5, 50, 84, 86–7,
    179–80, 193–4, 214–15, 218
  Jacques Durand   56, 65, 73, 74–5, 83,
    97, 100, 111, 116–17, 126, 137, 154–5,
    156, 158, 161, 162–3, 178, 180, 189,
    201, 205, 212, 213, 232, 241, 245
funeral and commemorations   253–4,
    272, 285
galas and commemoration
  concerts   188, 326, 332, 335, 337,
    339–40
  see also Monuments, inaugurations
gifts and notes from Emma   51, 53, 166
gifts to Emma   73, 109, 160, 162, 176,
    190
  see also musical gifts and messages to
    Emma
holidays see under journeys and holidays
  to
house in Avenue du Bois de
  Boulogne   79–83, 91, 102, 149, 162–3,
    179, 180, 191, 205, 211, 221, 233–4
illness   73, 101, 121–2, 125, 129, 133–4, 135,
    162, 175, 195, 196, 201, 207–8, 209, 213,
    215, 218, 225, 349
  following cancer diagnosis and
    treatment   225–6, 229–33, 236,
    240, 243, 245–7, 248–51
introduction to Emma   42, 45, 46, 51, 123
journeys and holidays to
  America (not carried out)   136,
    166–8, 350
  Amsterdam   196, 205–7
  Angers   213
  Arcachon   36, 55–6, 234–5
  Bayreuth   37
  Boston see under America
  Brussels   39, 208
  Budapest   137, 144, 146, 148
  Dieppe   37, 91, 221
  Eastbourne   76–8
  Edinburgh (cancelled)   110, 122
  Houlgate   163–6
  Jersey   61
  London   79, 100, 108, 122, 124–5, 185,
    211
  Manchester (cancelled)   118, 122
  Milan (not undertaken)   103
  Pourville   63–7, 100–1, 221–4
  Rome   37, 196, 204–5
  Russia   188, 195, 196–201
  Saint-Jean-de-Luz   241, 243–7, 264
  Turin   161–2
  Vienna   137, 144–6
Légion d'Honneur   48, 71
letters to Dolly   139, 154–5, 185, 220, 299,
    350
love of Chouchou   88, 91, 99, 112–13, 125,
    142, 145–6, 163, 169–70, 176, 177, 181,
    190, 191, 194, 198, 200–1, 205, 226, 230,
    280, 285, 352–3

marriage, attitude to   41, 42, 58–9, 71, 169, 205, 350, 351–2
  to Rosalie (Lilly) Texier   41–2, 48, 58–60, 67, 71, 87
  to Emma   10, 105–7, 145, 200, 237, 352
  see also under relationships
messages to Emma *see under* musical 'gifts' and messages to Emma
monument *see* Monuments to Debussy
music, attitude to   48, 59, 71, 76, 77, 89, 99, 101, 109, 111, 139, 144, 195, 200, 213, 235, 238, 247, 350, 352
  see also under problems with composing
musical 'gifts' and messages to Emma   54, 56, 58, 60, 75–6, 90, 91, 92, 98–9, 102–3, 128, 130, 150, 158, 168, 170, 175, 176, 177, 180, 216, 217, 219, 221, 237–8, 241, 244, 248–9
  see also under correspondence with Emma during travels
musical legacy   285, 313
  see also revival of Debussy's works *under* Debussy, Emma
'*musicien francais*'   197, 222, 238, 253, 346, 347
nature, love of   51, 76, 77, 85, 91, 101, 170, 205, 222, 224, 243, 268
newspaper articles *see under* critical writings
obsession with Poe *see under* Works, *La chute de la maison Usher*
patriotism   212, 215–16, 217, 222, 235, 238, 253
  and return to 'French' style of music   217, 224, 238, 251
pianist   37, 38, 39, 56, 183, 203, 205, 219, 241, 245
piano, Bluthner   77–8, 83, 361
problems with composing   86, 88–91, 95, 102, 111, 121, 137, 140, 169, 177, 190, 237, 240–1, 247, 352
relationships, with Emma before marriage   42, 50, 52–4, 55–6, 58–60, 61
  with Emma after marriage   90, 91–2, 102, 125, 129, 130–1, 133, 134, 135–6, 138–40, 143, 144–7, 160, 163, 166, 168–70, 176, 177, 185–6, 189–91, 195, 197–201, 248, 349
  after journeys abroad   204–7, 217, 222, 225–6, 229–30, 237
  with Gaby Dupont   38, 39–40
  with Alice Peter   40
  with Thérèse Roger   38–40, 74
  with Catherine Stevens   40
  with Lilly Texier after meeting Emma   49–50, 52, 58–60, 65, 67–9, 71, 134, 343
  with Marie Blanche Vasnier   36–7, 64, 318
  see also under letters to Dolly
religion   76, 272, 330
reluctance to have early works resurrected   95, 175
Revue musicale, la, commemorative issues   286–8, 308, 311, 317
salon attendance   37, 38–40, 74, 89, 128
sea *see under* nature, love of
vilification after leaving Lilly   68–71, 108, 109, 183, 189
  by Emma's mother Laure   220–1
war, reactions to *see under* patriotism
Works
  Apparition   318, 345
  Ariettes oubliées   37, 49, 54, 56, 99, 179
    'Il pleure dans mon cœur'   54, 119, 136, 203
  As you like it (unfinished)   90, 242–3, 248
  Cello Sonata   222, 223, 240
  Chansons de Bilitis   40, 195, 210, 237, 241, 320, 339
    'La chevelure'   40, 145
  Children's Corner   88, 111, 113–14, 118, 144, 157, 161, 195, 207, 208
    'Le petit berger'   218
    'Sérénade à la poupée'   88
  Cinq poèmes de Charles Baudelaire   43, 188
    'Le balcon'   145, 239
    'Le jet d'eau'   95
  Clair de lune   318
  Crimen amoris (unfinished)   174
  Danse sacrée et danse profane   56, 311
  D'un cahier d'esquisses   56
  En blanc et noir   222, 225, 226, 230, 237, 242, 250
  En sourdine   40
  Épigraphes antiques   210–11
  Estampes   51, 118, 144
    'Jardins sous la pluie'   192
    'La soirée dans Grenade'   50, 195, 305
  Étude retrouvée   291
  Études   222–3, 233, 236, 241, 248
    'Pour les arpèges composés'   291
    'Pour les notes répétées'   215
    'Pour les sixtes'   222
  Fantaisie for piano and orchestra   269, 280–1

Fêtes galantes (opera-ballet)
　　unfinished   175, 221
Fêtes galantes Set I   56
　　'Clair de lune'   57
　　'En sourdine'   40
Fêtes galantes Set II   56, 57–8, 61, 89
　　'Colloque sentimental'   58
　　'Le faune'   56, 57, 58
　　'Les ingénus'   58
Hommage à Haydn   131
Images for orchestra   91, 101, 118,
　　121–2, 126, 128, 192, 311
　　'Gigues'   118, 126, 177, 184
　　'Ibéria'   91, 97, 116, 118, 133, 134, 144,
　　　146, 161–2, 188, 345
　　'Rondes de printemps'   101, 118,
　　　128, 134, 158, 184, 192, 197, 205,
　　　345
Images for piano, Set I   77, 79, 84–5,
　　86, 192, 291, 299
　　'Hommage à Rameau'   218, 280,
　　　300
　　'Mouvement'   280
　　'Reflets dans l'eau'   77, 84, 351
Images for piano, Set II   102, 103, 110
　　'Et la lune descend sur le temple qui
　　　fut'   102
　　'Poissons d'or'   102, 109
Invocation   329
Isis see under *Khamma*
Jeux   178, 180, 184–5, 193, 206, 207,
　　300, 345
Khamma   142, 155, 168, 174, 175–6,
　　179, 183, 194, 232, 281–2, 314–15
L'enfant prodigue   100, 111, 181
L'isle joyeuse   56, 61, 65, 102, 210, 280,
　　290, 351
La belle au bois dormant   192
La berceuse heroïque   215, 224, 315
La boîte à joujoux   189–90, 191, 192,
　　193, 194, 195, 201–2, 207, 208, 210,
　　247, 281, 300
La chute de la Maison Usher   111, 126,
　　128, 140, 142, 163, 169, 179, 191, 203,
　　205, 229, 232–3, 329, 345, 351
La damoiselle élue   37, 38, 39, 107, 123,
　　134, 181, 344
La légende de Tristan
　　(unfinished)   98, 100, 111, 345
La mer   51, 60, 61, 72, 77, 85, 105, 107,
　　108, 118, 144, 184, 205, 275, 299, 316,
　　340, 345
La plus que lente   137, 146
Le diable dans le beffroi   73, 90, 91, 111,
　　143, 163, 169, 179, 205, 232, 329, 345

Le jet d'eau   179
Le martyre de Saint Sébastien   2,
　　147–9, 155–7, 158–60, 164, 169, 210,
　　247–8, 291, 297–8, 299, 301–3, 306,
　　337, 340
Le palais du silence (unfinished)   197,
　　203
Le promenoir des deux amants   53, 89,
　　136, 137–8, 188, 207, 210, 237
　　'Auprès de cette grotte sombre'   53,
　　　89, 137–8
　　'Crois mon conseil, chère
　　　Climène'   137–8
　　'Je tremble en voyant ton
　　　visage'   137–8
Le Roi Lear   67–8, 91, 95, 100, 320
Le triomphe de Bacchus   322, 329
Les papillons   340
Linderaja   320–1, 345
Marche écossaise   205, 206
Masques   56–7, 61
Masques et bergamasques
　　(unfinished)   127
Nocturnes   44, 122, 184, 206, 275, 285,
　　311, 317, 325, 340
　　'Fêtes'   44, 133, 317
　　'Nuages'   44, 133, 184, 317
　　'Sirènes'   44, 184, 345
*Noël des enfants qui n'ont plus de
　　maison*   225–6, 235, 237, 241
No-ja-li see under *Le palais du silence*
Ode à la France   235, 251, 291, 326–31
Oresteia (unfinished)   127
Orphée-roi (unfinished)   98, 231
Page d'album   219, 221, 240, 344
Pantomime   318
Pelléas et Mélisande   32, 38, 39, 40, 41,
　　43, 44, 45, 49, 51, 54, 56, 58, 67, 73,
　　76, 103, 108, 109–11, 117, 118, 124–5,
　　126, 140, 144, 147, 156, 160, 164, 170,
　　185–6, 192–3, 200, 210, 222, 233–4,
　　237, 263, 266, 267, 292, 309, 315,
　　328, 345
　　hundredth performance   183
　　in Boston   166
　　in Brussels   91, 92–3
　　performances after Debussy's
　　　death   268, 269, 276, 307,
　　　319–20, 333, 340
Petite suite   37, 101, 144
Pierrot   318
Pour le piano   246
　　'Sarabande'   305
Pour le vêtement du blessé see under *Page
　　d'album*

Prélude à l'après-midi d'un faune 88, 105, 106, 108, 122, 123, 144, 161, 176, 184, 205, 206, 247, 309, 311, 340, 345
Préludes, Book I 121, 133, 136, 137, 183, 185, 195, 206, 278, 291, 332, 335
    'Danseuses de Delphes' 130, 234, 290
    'Des pas sur la neige' 53, 130–1, 138
    'La cathédrale engloutie' 291, 313
    'La danse de Puck' 287, 290
    'La fille aux cheveux de lin' 136, 203, 313
    'Le vent dans la plaine' 130
    'Les collines d'Anacapri' 130
    'Les sons et les parfums tournent dans l'air du soir' 290
    'Minstrels' 203, 287
    'Voiles' 130
Préludes, Book II 173, 180, 183, 188, 195, 231, 332
    'Feux d'artifice' 216
    'Général Lavine eccentric' 287
    'Les fées sont d'exquises danseuses' 173
    'Ondine' 287
Printemps 54, 57, 111, 175, 329
Proses lyriques 39, 43, 68, 144, 188, 294, 304–5, 314
    'De fleurs' 39, 294
    'De grève' 118, 275, 294
    'De rêve' 294
    'De soir' 39, 118
Psyché (unfinished) 197
Rapsodie for clarinet and orchestra 131, 133, 163
Rapsodie for saxophone and orchestra 48, 274–5
Rodrigue et Chimène 322–3
Salut Printemps see under Printemps
Siddartha (unfinished) 98, 101, 231
Sonata for Flute, Viola and Harp 224, 233–4, 236
String Quartet 15, 37, 46, 61, 65, 68, 239, 339, 346
Suite bergamasque 290
Symphonie en si mineur 341–2
Syrinx 197
Tarantelle styrienne 305
The Fall of the House of Usher see under La chute de la Maison Usher
The little nigar 121, 195
Trio in G Major 35, 344–5
Trois ballades de François Villon 137, 138, 179, 241
    'Ballade de Villon à s'amye' 138
    'Il n'est bon bec que de Paris' 138

Trois chansons de Charles d'Orléans 110, 111, 117, 188, 339
    'Quand j'ai ouy le tabourin' 111
Trois chansons de France 52–3, 57, 89, 113, 137
    'Auprès de cette grotte sombre' 53, 130–1, 137–8
    'Le temps a laissé son manteau' 52
    'Pour ce que Plaisance est morte' 53, 229
Trois poèmes de Stéphane Mallarmé 189–91, 197, 207
Violin Sonata 230, 231, 235, 239, 240–1, 245, 247, 334, 339
Willowwood (unfinished) 100
Debussy, Claude Emma *see* Debussy, Chouchou
Debussy, Emma Claude 20, 46, **47**, 50, 57, **82**, 86, 92, 102, **114**, **116**, 118, 149, **152**, **153**, 156, **165**, 171, 208, 290, 305, 315, 319–20, 321, 332, 333, **338**, 339, **343**, 342, **356**
advice to others on performance 281, 290, 297–8, 302, 304, 311
ancestry and birth 1–3
antisemitism towards 69–70, 71–2, 353–5
auction of Debussy's works *see under* finances, sale of Debussy's works
appearance 46–7, 81, 141, 161, 337, 355
birth of Chouchou 85
    of Dolly 20
    of Raoul 13
burial arrangements for and commemorations of Debussy 268, 328
    Père-Lachaise 253–4, 261, 266, 271
    Passy 261, 263, 266, 268, 269, 271–2, 285
character 28, 46–7, 52, 53, 139, 141, 146, 154, 186, 236, 237–8, 241, 249–50, 290, 318, 337, 347, 349, 355
charity concerts and contributions 46, 219, 237, 240
Chouchou, care of 112, 146, 170, 249, 262–3
commemorations of Debussy *see under* burial arrangements for and commemorations of Debussy
concerts attended *see under* social life
correspondence from Debussy during his travels 145–7, 197–201, 204–7, 208
correspondence with Albert Carré 273, 276
André Caplet after Debussy's death 260–1, 263–5, 267, 269, 271, 274, 276, 286, 287–8, 289–90, 292, 297–8, 299, 301–3, 304

Manuel de Falla   259, 303–4, 305–8,
    311–12, 313–14, 315, 316, 321–2, 323,
    326, 328, 332, 335, 338, 340, 342, 343
Gabriel Fauré   196, 235, 259, 276
Loïe Fuller   208
Marius-François Gaillard   295, 300,
    301, 322, 326, 329, 331
Robert Godet   265–6, 267, 268, 271
Gabriel Pierné   308
Charles-Marie Widor   250, 266, 271
criticism and vilification of Emma   69,
    71, 106, 112, 139, 127, 157, 183, 191, 231,
    275, 285, 295, 327–30, 349
death   46, 346
death of mother (Laure)   219–20
dedications of works to Emma by
    d'Annunzio   160
    Debussy   48–9, 51, 52, 53, 54–5, 56, 61,
        72, 89, 103, 109–10, 117, 118, 126, 137,
        183, 234, 184, 185, 201, 221, 222, 226
    Falla   129
    Fauré   23–7
    Gaillard   291
    Ravel   32
    Roger-Ducasse   32
    Satie   192
dedications of Debussy's works to
    others   291, 327, 334
disputes and litigation with Henry
    Prunières   286–7, 318, 325–6
    with Lilly Texier   331
    with monument committee   336
    over *Chanson d'un fou*   341
         Ode à la France   291, 326–31
distribution of Debussy's works   262,
    275, 281, 291, 327, 334, 340, 345
    see also under finances, sale of
        Debussy's works
divorce from Sigismond Bardac   74
domestic life   79–84, 86, 89, 99, 100, 102,
    106, 110, 121, 123, 125–6, 128, 135–6,
    140, 141, 143, 145, 148, 156, 157, 163,
    166, 168–9, 177, 181, 184, 196, 198–9,
    205, 217, 233, 249
    after Debussy's death   261, 268–9, 286
    see also under move to, hotels
education   8
effect on composers   24, 32, 43, 77
elopement with Debussy   55, 61
'fête' (special day) see under significant
    date
family duties   65, 89, 128, 217, 237, 296
finances   74, 106, 107, 174, 212, 220–1,
    274, 299
    administration for Debussy   208

after Debussy's death   262, 274,
    281, 286, 292–3, 313, 319, 328, 331,
    337–8
Chouchou's bonds   107, 347
contract with Choudens   326, 328
death duties   292, 347–8
domestic   74, 80–1, 189, 191
legacy from Osiris   63, 81, 96–7, 221
loans received   292–3, 313, 347, 348
sale of Debussy's works   345
    Fragonard picture   262
first meeting with Debussy see under
    relationship with Debussy
friendship with Gabriele
    d'Annunzio   147–8, 160, 186, 188,
        208–10, 230–1, 239
    Édouard Colonne   95, 118, 135
    André David   320, 337, 340
    Maurice Dumesnil   46, 344–5, 346
    Arthur Hartmann   119, 135–6, 226,
        243, 245, 262, 280, 289, 307, 309,
        313, 319, 331–2, 334, 337, 342
    Marie Hartmann   119, 135–6, 141, 171,
        202, 204, 232, 280, 294–5, 309
    Chouchik Laloy   92, 107, 111, 114,
        116–18, 122–3, 128, 133, 138–9, 173,
        219–20, 265–6, 267, 269–70, 276,
        280, 285, 295, 316
    Marguerite Long   57, 209–10, 242,
        248, 280–1, 286
    Maurice Ravel   32, 305, 337
    Jean Roger-Ducasse   32, 109, 234,
        242, 252, 263, 275, 279, 286, 294,
        320, 329, 346
    Erik Satie   87, 157, 173, 192–3, 213,
        218, 236
    Catherine Stravinsky   176, 187, 196
    Igor Stravinsky   139, 166, 176, 196,
        202, 224
    Lilly Texier   52
    P.-J. Toulet   90, 102, 159, 166, 180,
        207, 236, 243, 244, 248, 249, 259,
        282–3, 286
    Pasteur Vallery-Radot   143–4, 159,
        230, 233, 238, 240, 241, 249, 252
friendship with and reliance on André
    Caplet   101, 127, 129, 131, 133, 169,
        179, 233, 244, 246, 250, 260, 274,
        276, 292, 297–8, 299–300, 301–3,
        316, 329
    Louis Laloy   102, 123, 126, 133, 173,
        176, 220, 265, 268, 271, 272, 276,
        299–300, 302, 313, 318
    Magdeleine Greslé   259, 276, 287, 301,
        304, 305, 307–8

friendship and encouragement of Daniel
  Ericourt 318–19
 Manuel de Falla 129, 259, 303–4,
  305–8, 311–12, 313–14, 315, 316,
  321–2, 323, 326, 328, 332, 335, 340,
  343
 Marius-François Gaillard 290–1,
  295–6, 300–1, 319, 322, 326–31
funeral 346–7
gifts and notes from Debussy 54, 56, 57,
 58, 60, 73, 75–6, 91, 92, 98–9, 102–3,
 128, 130, 149, 158, 160, 162, 168, 170,
 175, 177, 180, 184, 216, 217, 221, 237–8,
 241, 244, 248–9
gifts and notes to Debussy 51, 53, 166
grief after Chouchou's death 279–80,
 286, 288, 295, 331, 334
 after Debussy's death 252–5, 259–61,
  263, 264, 267, 268, 272, 278, 286,
  294–5, 300, 305, 307, 311, 313, 316, 334
holidays and journeys to Angers 213
 Arcachon 9, 55–6, 133, 234–5
 Brussels 92
 Dieppe 91, 151
 Eastbourne 76–8
 Houlgate 163–6
 Jersey 61
 London 108, 110, 125, 211
 Mourillon near Toulon 342
 Pourville 63–7, 100–1, 221–4
 Saint-Jean-de-Luz 241, **264**
  after Debussy's death 263–9, 282,
   286, 294–5, 305, 307, 313, 316, 334
  Chalet Habas 243–7
 Turin 161–2
homeopathy 100, 125, 133, 175, 193, 279, 350
illness and stress 86, 88, 89, 99–100, 101,
 114, 122, 124–5, 128, 131, 133–4, 139–40,
 142, 149, 156, 158–9, 161–2, 171, 173–4,
 175, 178, 184, 185–6, 188, 194, 196–7,
 199, 202, 204–5, 222, 223, 224, 225,
 229–30, 233, 234, 236–7, 240, 249, 253,
 263, 266–7, 288, 307–8, 309, 316, 331,
 335, 342, 350, 351
 see also grief after Debussy's death
influence on performances see under
 advice to others on performance
inheritance from Osiris 63–4, 96–7, 349
Jewish faith 48, 69, 97, 188, 220, 346–7
language skills 92, 100, 108
litigation see under disputes and litigation
loans received see under finances
marriage to Debussy 10, 105–7
 Sigismond Bardac 9–10, 13, 35, 74,
  166

maternal nature 42, 69, 83, 205, 220, 233,
 295, 300, 315, 337, 349
messages from Debussy see under gifts and
 notes from Debussy
monument committee see also under
 disputes and litigation with
 relations with 273, 309, 317
 president 309
move to 24 rue Vineuse 286, 288, 292,
 307
 hotels 269–70, 276, 278
Osiris's tomb, place in 8, 63
patronage 312, 313, 334, 341
 see also under charity concerts and
  contributions
pregnancy with Chouchou 73–4, 76,
 79, 114
publishers of Debussy's works after his
 death 274, 281, 305, 312, 322, 326–7,
 341
refusal to allow Debussy to travel to
 America 166–8, 350
relationship then friendship with
 Fauré 20, 23, 25–6, 30, 32, 63, 89, 97,
  123, 235, 241, 245, 259, 315, 342, 354
relationship with Debussy, first
 meeting 42, 45, 46, 50–1
 before marriage 43, 50, 52–4, 58–61,
  349
 marital problems with Debussy 90,
  103, 134, 139–40, 143, 155, 168–9,
  177, 185, 189, 191, 199, 204–5, 350
 marital relations after Debussy's
  journeys 206–7, 217, 226,
  229–30, 248–9
 relationship summarised 349
 with Dolly after Debussy's
  death 263, 267, 269, 278, 313, 342
 with Raoul Bardac 117, 213–14, 292–3,
  313
revival of Debussy's works 275, 280–2,
 285, 322–3
 Fantaisie for piano and
  orchestra 280–1, 347
 Khamma 314–15
 L'enfant prodigue 281
 La damoiselle élue 281
 Le martyre de Saint Sébastien 297–8,
  301–3
 Le Roi Lear 320
 Le triomphe de Bacchus 322, 329, 330
 Ode à la France 326–31
 Proses lyriques 294, 304, 305, 314
 Rapsodie for saxophone and
  orchestra 275

salon   18, 30, 31, 32
signatures   30, 107
significant date   53–4, 75, 90, 98–9, 126, 160, 176, 210, 221, 225, 344
singing, before Debussy's death   245
    given up   89, 111
    lessons and performances   14–15, 29–30, 31, 43, 105
    quality of voice   14, 28, 43, 46
    skills   23, 27
social life   29, 30, 31, 52, 56, 73–4, 90, 102, 128, 135, 140, 161, 183, 222, 333, 334, 336, 340, 349
    see also under singing, lessons and performances
storage of Debussy's works after death   263–4, 322–3, 327, 334
stress see under illness and stress
theft from house   269
villa named after Emma in Arcachon   9, 97
wartime experiences   251, 263, 268–9
    friends and relations fighting   213
        see also Bardac, Raoul; Caplet, André; Tinan, Gaston de
    stay in Angers   213
        see also under charity concerts and contributions
Debussy, Rosalie (Lilly) see Texier, Rosalie (Lilly)
Debussy, Manuel-Achille (Debussy's father)   35, 69, 71, 79, 106, 125, 140, 143, 212
Debussy, Victorine (Debussy's mother)   35, 71, 79, 106, 125, 142, 143, 163, 191, 193, 196, 210, 218–19
Defosse, Henry   302, 303
Dehelly, Geneviève   335
Delange, René   296, 346
Delmet, Paul   53
Demellier, Hélène   95
Denis, Maurice   309, 344
Desjardins, Abel   60, 68
Dettelbach, Madame Charles   71
Devriès, David   342
Diaghilev, Sergei   98, 126, 127, 139, 176, 178, 184, 193, 200, 240, 242
Diémer, Louis   31, 316
Dietschy, Marcel   21, 42, 48, 106, 130, 139, 154, 295
Donalda, Pauline   340
Dorbon, Louis   134, 265, 266, 268
Doumergue, Gaston   332
Dreyfus Affair   72, 353
Dreyfus, Jacob Hanoch   97
Drumont, Edouard Adolphe   10

Dubois, Théodore   272
Dufau, Hélène   289
Dufranne, Hector   340
Dufy, Raoul   288
Dujardin-Beaumetz, Monsieur   97
Dukas, Paul   17, 70, 98, 135, 147, 215, 219, 226, 231, 233, 234, 242, 243, 253, 259, 272, 288, 289, 309, 313, 317, 327, 332, 339
Dumesnil, Maurice   46, 271, 344–5, 346
Dumser, Lucien   253, 287
Duparc, Henri   136
Dupin, Étienne   37
Dupont, Gabrielle (Gaby)   38, 39, 41
Durand, Jacques   37, 56, 57, 61, 63, 65, 77, 90–1, 103, 110, 111, 118, 125, 126, 129, 131, 133, 135, 158, 160, 162, 177, 178, 180, 183, 191, 201, 205, 212, 213, 221, 225, 226, 245, 253–4, 263, 272, 287, 290, 304, 311, 317
    contracts with Debussy   61, 73, 74, 88, 110, 111, 121, 131, 133, 137, 138, 143, 168, 173, 176, 178, 189, 194, 195, 197, 211, 215, 222, 223, 224, 225, 230
    donation of Debussy's manuscripts to Conservatoire   315
    financial arrangements with Debussy   73, 74–5, 88, 121, 127, 131, 142, 168, 173, 176, 179, 184, 189, 194, 221–2, 232, 261, 331
    friendship and support of Debussy   73, 75, 83, 100, 116–17, 121, 131, 139, 154–5, 162–3, 225, 231, 241, 251
    negotiations with Emma after Debussy's death   274, 282, 287, 313, 328, 329
Durosoir, Lucien   233, 313
Duse, Eleonore   147
Duvauchelle, Pierre   334

Edwards, Misia see Sert, Misia
Emmanuel, Maurice   317
Enesco, George   22, 52
Engel, Pierre-Émile   123
Ericourt, Daniel   240, 318–19
Escudier, Madame   38

Falla, Manuel de   **260**, 262, 303–4, 311–12, 327, 332
    admiration of Debussy   129–30, 259, 311, 337, 343
    character   129, 259, 307, 337
    contribution to La Revue musicale   288
    correspondence with Emma   259, 303–4, 305–8, 311–12, 313–14, 315, 316, 321–2, 323, 326, 328, 332, 335, 338, 340, 342, 343
    dedication to Emma   129

friendship with Emma   129–30, 166, 259,
      262, 303–4, 305–8, 311–12, 313–14, 315,
      316, 321, 323, 326, 327, 328, 332, 335,
      337, 338, 340, 342, 343
   illness   259, 307, 312, 314, 316
   meets Debussy   129
   monument committee honorary
      member   332
   Works
      Deux danses pour harpe   129
      El amor brujo (L'amour sorcier)   306,
         312, 316, 322, 326
      El retablo de Maese Pedro (Master
         Peter's Puppet Show)   306–7, 308,
         311, 312, 326
      El sombrero de tres picos (Le
         tricorne)   305, 326
      Harpsichord Concerto   322, 326, 335
      Homenaje pour le tombeau de Claude
         Debussy   311
      La vida breve   166, 326
      Nuits dans les jardins d'Espagne   326
      Pièces espagnoles   129
      Psyché   322
      Siete canciones populares españoles
         (Sept chansons populaires)   305,
         322, 326, 332
      Sonéto a Córdoba   322
      Trois melodies   129
      'Séguidille'   129
Fauré, Gabriel   17, **19**, 27, 30, 33, 52, 71, 135,
      162, 273, 342
   appearance   20
   attitude to Debussy   123, 196, 241, 259, 354
   correspondence with Emma   196, 235,
      259, 276
   death   315
   dedications to Dolly Bardac   25, 30
      to Emma Bardac   23–6, 27, 29
      to Sigismond Bardac   29
   director of Conservatoire   89, 196
   education   17
   engagement to Marianne Viardot   17
   friendship with Debussy   37, 89, 123, 162,
      225, 235, 241, 259, 354
   marriage   18
   monument committee member   273
   paternity of Dolly (alleged)   20–2, 24,
      355–7, 358
   relationship then friendship with Emma
      Bardac   20–9, 30, 32, 63, 123, 183,
      235, 241, 245, 259, 276, 342, 357
   relationships with other women   17,
      21–2, 30–1
   teacher of Raoul Bardac   15, 20, 32, 33
   Works
      Après un rêve   17
      Arpège   29–30
      Au cimetière   37
      Ballade   210
      Barcarolle no. 5   29
      Cinq mélodies, op. 58   21, 23, 24
      Dolly   25, 26–7, 30, 196, 316
         'Le pas espagnol'   25, 196
      La bonne chanson   23–6, 30, 32, 52, 57,
         77, 245
         'Donc, ce sera par un clair jour
            d'été'   23
         'La lune blanche'   23
         'N'est-ce pas?'   24
      La naissance de Vénus   29, 31
      Les roses d'Ispahan   136
      Nocturne no. 1   17
      Nocturne no. 6   29–30
      Nocturne no. 7   31
      Pelléas et Mélisande   25, 183
      Pleurs d'or   29
      Prison   27
      Prométhée   33, 44
      Salve Regina   27, 29
      Soir   27–8, 30
      Tantum ergo   29
Fauré-Fremiet, Emmanuel   18, 27
Fauré-Fremiet, Marie see Fremiet, Marie
Fauré-Fremiet, Philippe   18, 21, 24, 235
Féart, Rose   135, 144, 210, 241, 250, 265
Ferguson, Madame Thomas   8
   Elisabeth   8, 9, 97
   Elisa   8, 97
Ferrand, Stanislas   9
Féval, Paul   233
Février, Henry   147
Flem, Paul le   335
Fleuriau, Aimé Joseph de   346
Fontaine, Arthur   213
Fontaine, Lucien   41, 60
Fremiet, Emmanuel   18, 25, 63
Fremiet, Marie   18, 21, 26, 27, 31, 33
Friesz, Othon   253, 287–8, 312
Fromont, Eugène   45, 305, 311, 317
Fuchs, Henrietta   37
Fuller, Loïe   184, 208

Gab see Henry, Gabrielle
Gaillard, Marius-François   290–1, 300–1, 331
   Buenos Aires concerts   301
   correspondence from Emma   295, 300,
      301, 322, 326, 329, 331
   criticism of   291, 295, 330, 332

dedication to Emma   291
dedications and gifts from Emma   291, 327
encouragement and promotion by Emma   295–6, 300–1, 319, 326–7
interpretation of Debussy   291, 300
Le triomphe de Bacchus
   orchestration   322, 329
Mélodies chinoises   291
Ode à la France, dedication, orchestration and performance   291, 301, 326–31, 336
performances   290–1, 300–1, 328, 330, 332, 335, 336
recording   366
Gallimard, Gaston   265, 267, 268, 271, 313
Garban, Lucien   44
Gard, Roger Martin du   32, 43
Garden, Helen   70
Garden, Mary   42, 49, 69, 70, 92, 108, 319–20, 340
Gasco, Albert   205
Gatti-Casazza, Giulio   111
Gaubert, Philippe   306, 340
Gauthier-Villars, Henri (Willy)   31, 105, 135
Gédalge, André   33
Gémier, Firmin   177, 242
Gheusi, Pierre-Barthélemy   225, 268, 281, 282
Gibbs, Louise   263, 280, 295, 319, 338
Gide, André   267
Gieseking, Walter   278
Gimpel, René   13, 261, 262, 293
Godet, Robert   42, 52, 56, 83, 97–8, 169, 173, 178, 180–1, 185, 188, 202, 211, 215, 224, 229, 230, 234, 237, 241, 248, 271, 288, 317
   correspondence with Emma after Debussy's death   265–6, 267, 268, 271
   proposed biography of Debussy   265–6, 267
Golschmann, Vladimir   307
Goossens, Eugene   288
Gounod, Charles   17, 192
Grandchamp, Monsieur   346
Grandhomme, Docteur   346
Greffulhe, Comtesse Élisabeth   74, 89, 128, 152, 342
Greslé, Magdeleine   278, 301, 304, 314, 346, **356**
   friendship with Manuel de Falla   304, 305, 306, 307–8, 312, 319, 335, 342
   performances   276, 306, 320, 322, 326
   support of Emma   259, 263, 271, 278, 287, 305, 307–8, 312
Grévy, Jules   35
Groux, Henry de   169, 273, 308
Grovlez, Gabriel   287

Gui, Vittorio   161–2
Guiard, Madame Georges   237
Guitry, Lucien   64
Guitry, Sacha   64, 308, 315
Gurlé, Madame   290, 292

Haguenauer, Jean-Louis   361
Hahn, Reynaldo   17, 71, 128, 153 n.5, 183
Haïm, Charlotte (Emma's paternal grandmother)   1
Hallfter, Ernesto   311
Hall, Elise   48, 274
Hamelle, Edgard   304
Haraucourt, Edmond   234
Hartmann, Arthur   119, 134, 135–6, 141–2, 146, 169, 202, 203–4, 226, 231, 240, 243, 245, 262, 280, 289, 309, 313, 318–19, 321, 331–2, 334, 337, 342
Hartmann, Georges   41
Hartmann, Marie   119, 135–6, 141, 171, 202, 204, 232, 280, 309, 334
Hébertot, Jacques   297, 300
Heilbronn, Lob Bule   10
Hellé, André   189–90, 191, 281
Henry, Gabrielle *aka* Gab   5 n.5, 15
Hérédia, Louise de   41
Hermant, Jacques   335
Honegger, Arthur   317
Howat, Roy   226, 291 n.31
Hubay, Jenö   137
Hugo, Valentine   358
Hunebelle, André   334
Huvelin, Paul   238

Ibanez, Blasco   313
Iffla, Aimée (Emma's maternal aunt)   8, 64
   Daniel *see* Osiris, Daniel Iffla
   Daniel (Osiris's grandfather)   8
   Désir Isaac (Emma's maternal grandfather)   1, 2
   Laure *see* Moyse, Laure
   Léa   1, 2
   Rachel *see* Moyse, Laure
   William   3, 9
Indy, Vincent d'   30, 210, 273, 289
Inghelbrecht, Désiré-Émile   68, 157, 184, 194, 196, 201, 206, 230, 234, 244, 276, 281, 288, 309, 327, 332, 339, 340, 358

Jasmine (ballerina)   288
Jean-Aubry, Georges   28, 101, 211, 231, 275, 288, 311
Jenoc, Roger   265, 267
Jobert, Jean   281, 304–5, 311, 312, 320, 321

Johnson, Graham 25
Jouvenel, Colette de (Bel-Gazou) 358
Jouvenel, Henri de 358
Jullien, Adolphe 33

Killick, Ada 247, 262–3
Klingsor, Tristan 32
Koechlin, Charles 20, 22, 23–4, 43, 183, 314, 317, 318
Koussevitzky, Sergei 188, 191, 197, 201, 316

Lacerda, Francisco de 101
Lafferre, Louis 254
Laforgue, Jules 55, 90
Lagourgue, Philippe 357
Lalo, Pierre 85, 128, 302, 307, 333
Laloy, Aline 359, 360
Laloy, Chouchik (Susanik) 92, 102, 107, 110, 111, 114, 116–18, 122–3, 128, 138–9, 154–5, 163, 194, 211, 219–21, 265–6, 267, 269–70, 271, 272, 276, 280, 285, 295, 298, 316, 355
Laloy, Jean 154
Laloy, Louis 57, 58, 68, 74, 83, 89, 91, 92, 93, 95, 101, 102, 110, 114, 118, 123, 125, 126, 127, 139, 154, 160, 174, 177, 194, 219–21, 253, 264, 265–6, 285, 288, 299, 309, 311, 317, 332, 339, 354
  biography of Debussy 114, 123–4, 129, 264, 268, 271
  collaboration and correspondence with Raoul Bardac 193–4, 213–14, 216, 220, 246, 298–9, 360
  Le martyre de Saint Sébastien revival 247–8, 301–3
  Ode à la France involvement 235, 251, 291, 301, 326–31
  support of Emma after Debussy's death 266, 268, 271, 272, 276, 313, 318
Laloy, Nicole (Nicolette) 116, 123, 211, 280
Laloy, Ninette 154–5, 280, 295
Laloy, Susanik *see* Laloy, Chouchik (Susanik)
Laloy, Vincent 154, 358
Lambinet, André 109, 147, 149, 275
Lambinet, Charles 20
Lamy, Fernand 290
Landowska, Wanda 307
Lang, François 345
Larronde, Carlos 273
Leblanc, Georgette 166
Lebrun, Albert 337
Lecomte de Noüy, Mme Jacques 346
Leer, Jacques Von *see* Lier, Jacques Van
Lehman, Evangeline 346
Lejeune, Charlotte *see* Lysès, Charlotte

Lelarge, Monsieur 217
Léon, Paul 333, 339
Lerolle, Henry 39, 40
Lévy, Marcel 345
Lhermite, Tristan 52, 137
Liebich, Louise 100, 109
Lier, Jacques Van 76
Linder, Max 217
Long, Marguerite 25, 29, 57, **209**, 209–10, 218, 242, 243, 244, 248, 279, 280–1, 286, 305, 307, 309, 316, 320, 334, 345, 347, 349
Loubet, Émile 96
Lorca, Frederico Garcia 303
Louÿs, Georges 69, 353
Louÿs, Pierre 40, 41, 50, 55, 58, 59, 69, 70, 72, 266–7, 322, 353
Löwe, Ferdinand 146
Loyonnet, Paul 290
Lubin, Germaine 330
Lysès, Charlotte 8, 64, 96, 315

Mabille, Yvonne 226–7, 360
Maddison, Adela 30–1, 33, 52
Maddison, Frederick Brunning 30
Maeterlinck, Maurice 43, 73, 92, 166, 195, 331, 332, 351
Mahler, Alma 135
Mahler, Gustav 135
Maillol, Aristide 333, 344
Malherbe, Charles 300
Malipiero, Gian Francesco 288
Mallarmé, Stéphane 36, 190–1
Mangeot, Auguste 341
Mangin, General Charles 313
Manouvrier, Albert 236
Maré, Rolf de 341
Maréchal, Maurice 313
Marliave, Joseph de 210, 242, 307
Marmontel, Antoine 35
Marot, Blanche 285
Martel brothers, Jan and Joël 309, 317, 321, 339
Matheu, Pedro de 322, 338
Martin, Maurice 207, 210
Marty, Georges 89
Massenet, Jules 31, 33, 164
Mauclair, Camille 51, 273
Maupeou, Comtesse de 31
Mauté, Mathilde 23
Mayeur, Pierre 275
Meck, Nadezhda von 35, 234, 341, 345
Mélicourt-Lefebvre, Armand-Constant 64
Mendès, Rabbi Lodoïs 9
Mercié, Antonin 6, 8
Mérode, Cléo de 72

Messager, André   17, 37, 42, 49, 67, 70, 134, 137, 140, 268, 276, 281, 317, 319, 327, 331, 332
Messager, Jean   339
Metchnikoff, Elie   97
Michel, Alexandre   20
Migot, Georges   18, 309
Milhaud, Darius   237, 297, 317
Milhaud, Madeleine   218
Millerand, Alexandre   309
Mirès, Jules   4
Miss (Chouchou's governess) see Gibbs, Louise
Missa, Edmond   68
Mistler, Jean   339
Mitraud, Monsieur   10
Molié, Denyse   313
Molinari, Bernadino   217, 249, 290
Monchicourt, Paul Milliet   64
Monod, Lucien   73 n.40
Montesquiou, Robert de   30, 147, 148
Monument committees   186, 273, 317, 329, 331, 332–3, 335
  Ode à la France dispute   327–31, 336
Monuments to Debussy   273, 285, 308–9, 317, 321, 333, 335, 342
  inaugurations   308, 339–40, 344
Moreau-Sainti, Madame   36
Morice, Charles   174–5, 221
Mortier, Guy   358
Mourey, Gabriel   98, 101, 107, 108, 111, 121, 137, 162, 166, 173, 197, 326
Mussorgsky, Modest   110, 114
Moyse, Aaron Charles (Emma's brother)   3, 8
  Emma Léa see Debussy, Emma Claude
  Isaac Jacob (Emma's paternal grandfather)   1
  Isaac Jules (Emma's father)   2, 3, 8, 10, 13
  Laure (Emma's mother)   2, 3, 8, 9, 10, 13, 63, 64, 65, **66**, 84, 96–7, 116, 156, 175, 181, 196
    attitude to Debussy   220–1
    death   219–21
  Nelly (Emma's sister)   3, 8, 10, 13, 117
  Raoul (Emma's brother)   8, 9, 13

Natanson, Misia see Sert, Misia
Nectoux, Jean-Michel   20
Nichols, Roger   218
Nicoll, Colonel   243
Nijinsky, Vaslav   176, 178, 184–5
Nin, Joachim   244
Noailles, Anna de   320

Ochsé, Fernand   184
Orléans, Charles d'   52
Orledge, Robert   28, 88, 190, 203
Orliac, Jehanne d'   335
Osiris, Daniel Iffla   3–8, **4, 7**, 15, 18, 347
  admiration of Napoleon   5, 6
  death   6, 96–7
  education   4
  executors   8, 64, 96, 97
  financial success   4–5, 10, 12, 72
  honours   6
  marriage   5
  name change   5
  patriotism   6
  philanthropy   5–6, 9, 96–7
  railways, finance of   12
  speculation in land (Pourville)   63
  synagogues, construction   8, 9
  tomb (statue of Moses)   6, 8, 9, 63, 219, 347
  villas in Arcachon   8, 9, 36, 55, 63, 96, 97
  wills   6, 8, 63–4, 96–7, 153, 219, 221

Padarewski, Ignacy Jan   335
Paray, Paul   305, 314
Pascal, Léon   346
Pelouze, Eugène   35
Pereire brothers   4
  Émile   8, 9
Perruchon, Geneviève see Caplet, Geneviève
Pessard, Emile   341
Peter, Alice   40
Peter, Michel   40
Peter, René   38, 40, 41, 67, 70, 171, 288
Petit, Abbé Léonce   313
Péquin, Monsieur   210
Philipott, Monsieur   96
Picabia, Francis   288
Pierné, Gabriel   71, 133, 135, 206, 207, 219, 253, 273, 280 n.5, 304, 308, 314, 317, 332, 340
Pitt, Percy   125
Planté, Francis   246, 249
Poe, Edgar Allan   73, 111, 126, 157, 169, 179, 191, 205, 232, 351
  see also under Works, *le diable dans le beffroi; la chute de la maison Usher*
Polignac, Prince Edmond de   22, 31, 33
Polignac, Princesse Edmond de   21–2, 24, 25, 27–8, 38, 133, 230, 306–7
Poulenc, Francis   307, 313
Poulet, Gaston   241, 245, 247
Proust, Marcel   25, 152, 153, 183
Prunières, Henry   52, 240, 254, 286–8, 308, 317, 318, 325

Quinault, Robert   287

Rabaud, Henri   26, 250
Rackham, Arthur   173
Radisc, Bela   146, 148
Rameau, Jean-Philippe   217, 251
Ravel, Maurice   17, 22, 23, 33, 44, 70, 92, 95,
    114, 123 n.16, 128, 129, 158, 191, 227, 244,
    259, 273, 288, 289, 291, 305, 309, 317, 332,
    337, 341
  dedication to Emma   32
  Histoires naturelles   95
  Sites auriculaires   320
Rees, Richard Van   206
Régnier, Henri de   254, 317
Remacle, Jeanne   26
Renoir, Pierre-Auguste   18
Reyer, Ernest   123
Rhené-Baton, Emmanuel   273, 297
Rimsky-Korsakov, Nikolai   126
Risler, Édouard   26, 290
Rist, Edward   73 n.40
Robert, Julia   37
Robert, Paul   71
Roch, Madeleine   308
Roger, Pauline   39
Roger, Thérèse   37, 38–40, 134
Roger-Ducasse, Jean   22, 23, 24, 108–9, 110,
    147, 149, 237, 242, 252, 254, 263, 272,
    286, 294, 317, 319, 327, 329, 334, 339,
    345, 346
  dedication to Emma   32, 109
  Dolly's piano teacher   84
  friendship with Debussy   32, 108, 234,
    237, 252, 272
  with Emma   32, 234, 252, 263, 279,
    286, 294, 329, 346
  orchestration of Debussy's works
    Le Roi Lear   320
    Rapsodie for saxophone and
      orchestra   275
    Proses lyriques   275, 294, 304, 314
Roland-Manuel, Alexis   191, 317
Romero, Segismundo   311
Romilly, Madame Gérard de   41, 112
Rostand, Maurice   326
Rouché, Jacques   248, 297, 302, 303, 341
Roussel, Albert   273, 288, 334
Roux, Émile   97
Rubinstein, Ida   147–9, 157, 158, 159, 160, 161,
    186, 210, 297, 302, 309, 337
Ruhlmann, Emilie   319
Rummel, Walter   202, 230, 236
Russell, Henry   166–8, 179, 185, 189, 194

Sainbris, Antoine Guillot de   29
Saint-Marceaux, Marguerite de   17–18, 22, 31,
    37, 38–40, 52, 71, 74, 159–60
Saint-Marceaux, René de   17
Saint-Saëns, Camille   17, 25, 31, 33, 250
Salmon, Joseph   240, 318–19
Samain, Albert   27–30
Samazeuilh, Gustave   254, 272, 304, 346
Santen, Riet van   321
Sargent, John Singer   20, 26
Satie, Conrad   157
Satie, Erik   88, 129, 161, 169, 212, 213, 218, 230,
    254–5, 259, 288, 354
  character   87–8, 157–8, 192
  contribution to *La Revue musicale*
    1920   288
  dedication to Chouchou   195–6
  dedication to Emma   192–3
  friendship with Emma   87, 173, 192–3,
    213, 218, 236, 239–40
  friendship and rift with Debussy   41,
    87–8, 157–8, 161, 169, 173, 192–3,
    239–40, 254–5, 288
  love of children   88, 157, 192, 195–6, 288
  Works
    Chapitres tournés en tous sens   192–3
      'Celle qui parle trop'   192
      'Le porteur de grosses pierres'   192
      'Regrets des enfermés'   192–3
    *Croquis et agaceries d'un gros
      bonhomme en bois*   192
    'Españaña'   195–6
    Enfantillages pittoresques   192
    Gymnopédies   87, 157
    Morceaux en forme de poire   158
    Parade   240, 242
Saussine, Comtesse de   25
Scey-Montbéliard, Prince Louis de   21
Schaeffner, André   112, 139, 295, 314
Schlumberger, Gustave   72
Schmitt, Florent   22, 273, 288, 289, 341
Schneider, Louis   214
Schoenberg, Arnold   215, 297, 301
Schoene, Lotte   333
Schumann, Robert   114
Scott, Sir Walter   180
Segalen, Victor   98, 101, 102, 105, 108, 112, 117,
    124, 191, 231
Segovia, Andrés   303, 311–12
Seligman, Germain   13
Sentenac, Paul   309
Sert, Misia   41, 70, 176, 209, 254
Singer, Otto   20
Singer, Winnaretta *see* Polignac, Princesse
    Edmond de

Index

Sisley, Alfred 20
Souday, Paul 317
Southey, Robert 170
Speyer, Sir Edgar 100, 105, 185, 211
Stendhal 282, 283
Stevens, Alfred 40
Strauss, Richard 98, 108, 215
Stravinsky, Catherine 40, 176, 187, 196
Stravinsky, Igor 113, 129, 139, 161, 166, 169, 175, 176–7, 178, 180, 187, 196, 197, 202, 224, 229, 230, 259, 288
   Petrouchka 139, 161, 175, 180, 242
   The Firebird 139, 229, 242
   The Rite of Spring 2, 176–7, 180, 185, 187
Strobel, Heinrich 69, 72, 110
Suarès, André 288, 317
Supervia, Conchita 340
Szanto, Theodore 137

Taconnet, Maurice 152
Tchaikovsky, Piotr Il'yich 35
Tenroc, Charles 302
Teyte, Maggie 110, 118, 123, 201
Texier, Rosalie (Lilly) 1, 41, 44, 48, **49**, 50, 51, 52, 57, 58, 63, 73, 87, 92, 112, 171, 183, 189, 232, 317–18, 319–20, 343, 353–4
   abortion 42
   appearance 41, 48, 67
   character 41, 42, 52, 60, 71, 112, 343, 354
   death 342
   divorce 74–5
   financial arrangements 67, 74–5, 88, 110, 121, 142, 194, 232, 234, 331
   marriage to Debussy 41–2, 87
      breakdown of marriage 48, 50, 52, 58–61, 65, 67–71, 75, 124, 134, 354
   litigation against Emma Debussy 331
      La Revue musicale 317–18, 325
   suicide attempt 68, 73, 97, 353
   support of others towards 69–70, 353–4
Thibaud, Jacques 340
Thieullent, Henri 20, 355
Tinan, Charles Pochet le Barbier de 152
Tinan, Françoise de (Dolly's daughter) 174, 225, 246, 263, 295, 316, 334, 348, **356**, 358
Tinan, Gaston de 151–2, **152**, 154, 219, **223**, 223, 342, 355, 357
Tinan, Hélène de (Dolly) 23, **26**, 29, 45, 46, 51, **66**, 74, 76, 87, 90, 99, 102, 109, 110, **115, 116**, 117, 123, **152, 153**, 181, 212, 219, 246, 250, 252, 254, 262, 269, **277**, 278, 295, 321, 333 n.49, 340, 342, 346, 355, **356**, 357–8, 355–8
   baptism into Catholic church 151, 346
   birth 20

   births of children 174, 184
   contact with Chouchik Laloy 107, 355
   control of information about Emma 21, 106, 155, 358
   death 358
   dedication of Fauré's *Dolly* suite 25, 196, 358
   divorce 355, 357
   engagement 151
   illness 237, 263, 266
   inheritance from Sigismond Bardac 274, 293
      Emma Debussy 348
      Osiris 64, 96, 153
   Jewish heritage 151, 355–7
   letters to Debussy 139, 154–5, 220, 299, 350
   life with Debussy and Emma 65, 79, 83–4, 101, 102, 109, 116, 133
   love of Chouchou 85–6
   love of father 355
   marriage 151–2, 154, 168
      see also under remarriage
   notebook 51, 77–8, 321, 341–2
   paternity question 20–1, 24, 355–7, 358
   piano lessons 84, 108
   pregnancy 162, 171
   relationship with Debussy (alleged) *see under* letters to Debussy
   remarriage 357
   singing lessons 359
   support of Emma after Debussy's death 263, 267, 268
   wartime experiences 355, 357
Tinan, Jean de 152
Tinan, Madeleine de (Dolly's daughter) 184, 225, 246, 263, 278, 295, 316, 334, 348, **356**, 358–9
Torres, Eduardo 311
Toscanini, Arturo 103, 108, 332, 340
Toulet, Marie 246, 249, 282, 286
Toulet, Paul-Jean 90, 99, 101, 107, 123, 143, 148, 159, 174, 176, 177, 180, 201, 202, 207, 236, 246
   collaboration with Debussy 90, 242–3
   death 286
   friendship with Emma 159, 166, 180, 207, 236, 242–4, 248, 249, 253, 259, 282–3, 286
   requests for mementos of Debussy 248, 282–3
Tournemire, Charles 334
Tronquin, Monsieur 239, 240, 241
Trouhanova, Natasha (Natalia) 289–90
Turin, Pierre 335
Twain, Mark 233

Urbino, Léa Cardozo d' (Emma's maternal grandmother) *see* Iffla, Léa
Ullmann, Madame   346

Vallas, Léon   41, 241, 303, 318, 320, 326
  antisemitism   353–4
  criticism of Emma   241, 275, 321, 322–3, 329, 343, 353–4
  lectures   333
  publications   318, 322, 353–4
  scepticism about revival of Debussy's early works   275, 281–2, 318, 321, 322–3, 329
  support of Lilly   342–3, 354
Vallery-Radot, Pasteur   46, 51, 71, 74, 96, 143–4, 159, 176, 191, 217, 221, 230, 233, 237, 238, 240, 241, 242, 249–50, 252–3, 261, 345
Vallin, Ninon   188, 207, 208, 285, 339, 345
Vana-Yami   312
Vannier, Doctor   125
Varèse, Edgard   128, 143, 281, 332
Vasnier, Marguerite   317, 318
Vasnier, Marie Blanche   **36**, 36, 49, 64, 318
Verdi, Giuseppe   209
Vergin, Eugénie Élise *see* Colonne, Madame Édouard
Verlaine, Paul   21, 23, 25, 27, 36, 56, 57, 174
Verne, Jules   230
Viardot, Marianne   17
Viardot, Pauline   14, 15, 17
Vidal, Paul   317
Vidal-Naquet, Monsieur   336
Vieuille, Félix   340
Viñes, Hernando   307

Viñes, Ricardo   52, 86, 102, 109, 174, 183, 188, 244, 259, 307, 326
Vinon, Baroness   346
Vizentini, Paul   164
Vogt, Blanche   346
Vuillermoz, Émile   95, 159, 179, 188, 195, 202, 213–14, 285, 288, 308, 317, 327, 332, 339, 344

Wagner, Richard   38, 175, 210, 215
Wagner, Madame Siegfried   340
Walska, Ganna   336
Warnod, André   346
Weber, Carl Maria von   126
Weber, Jean   335
Weil, Elie   10
Weil, Marcelle Henriette Léa   14, 219, 225
Weil, Nelly *see* Moyse, Nelly
Weil, Maude   240
Weil, Raoul   14
Weil, Yvonne   240
Weingartner, Felix   33, 340
Widor, Charles-Marie   17, 33, 250, 266, 271, 309, 313 n.15, 332
Willy *see* Gauthier-Villars, Henri
Wilson, Daniel   35
Wilson-Pelouze, Marguerite   35
Wittouck, Monsieur et Madame   208
Wood, Sir Henry   100, 108, 110, 122

Ysaÿe, Eugène   15, 37, 88

Zamoïska, Countess   38
Ziloti, Alexandre   188, 191
Zola, Emile   353
Zuloaga, Ignacio   303